NIGHT OF POWER

ALSO BY ROBERT FISK

Night of Power

THE BETRAYAL OF THE MIDDLE EAST

ROBERT FISK

4th ESTATE • *London*

4th Estate
An imprint of HarperCollins*Publishers*
1 London Bridge Street
London SE1 9GF

www.4thEstate.co.uk

HarperCollins*Publishers*
Macken House, 39/40 Mayor Street Upper
Dublin 1, D01 C9W8

First published in Great Britain in 2024 by 4th Estate

1

Set in Dante MT Std
Printed and bound in the UK using 100%
renewable electricity at CPI Group (UK) Ltd

For Nelofer

We sent it down in the Night of Power!
But how can you know what is the Night of Power?
The Night of Power is better than a thousand months.
In it, the angels and the Spirit are sent swarming down,
By their Lord's leave, attending to every command.

Peace is that Night, till the break of dawn.

The Qur'an: A New Translation by Tarif Khalidi, sura 97:1–5

CONTENTS

MAPS

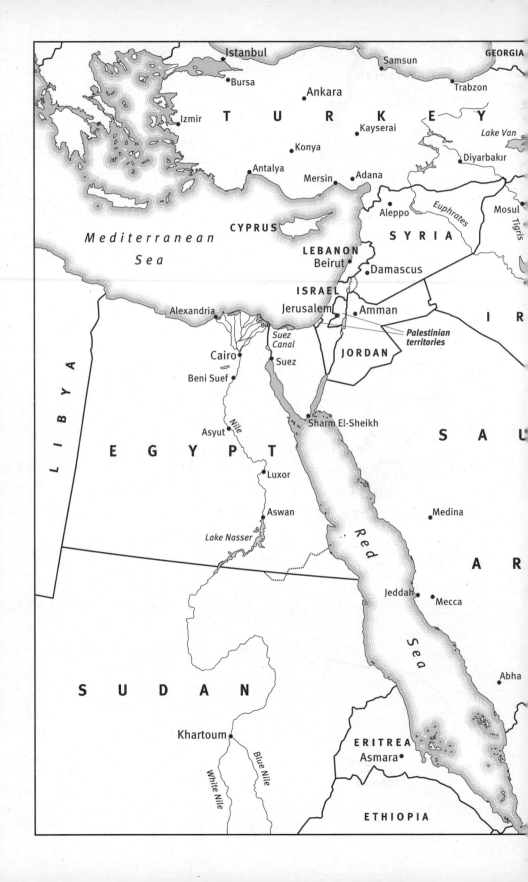

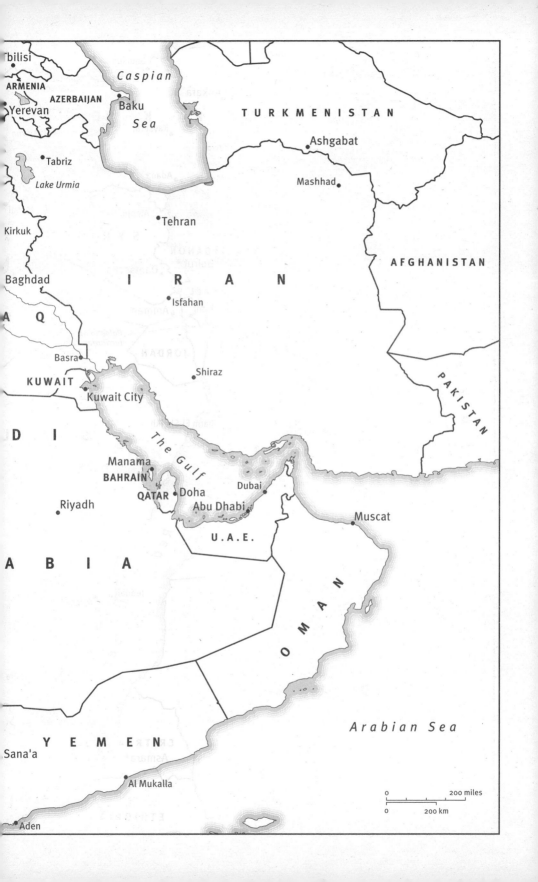

0   40 miles
0   40 km

LEBANON

SYRIA

Tyre

Golan Heights

Acre

Occupied by Israel since 1967

Haifa

Sea of Galilee

Nazareth

Mediterranean Sea

Jenin

Netanya

Nablus

Jordan

WEST

Tel Aviv

Lod

BANK

Ramallah

JORDAN

Jericho

Jerusalem

Bethlehem

Ashdod

Ashkelon

Dead Sea

Erez

Gaza City

Hebron

GAZA

Rahat

Khan Younis

Rafah

Beersheba

ISRAEL

Negev Desert

EGYPT

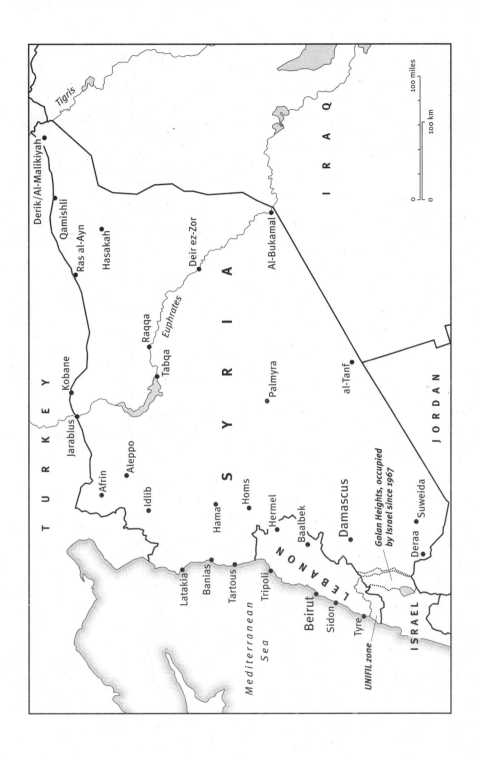

100 miles

100 km

Tigris

TURKEY

Derik/Al-Malikiyah

Qamishli

Ras al-Ayn

Hasakah

Deir ez-Zor

Al-Bukamal

IRAQ

Raqqa

Euphrates

Tabqa

Palmyra

al-Tanf

Kobane

Jarablus

Afrin

Aleppo

Idlib

S Y R I A

JORDAN

Hama

Homs

Hermel

Baalbek

Damascus

*Golan Heights, occupied
by Israel since 1967*

Deraa

Suweida

Latakia

Banias

Tartous

Tripoli

L E B A N O N

Beirut

Sidon

Tyre

UNIFIL zone

ISRAEL

*Mediterranean
Sea*

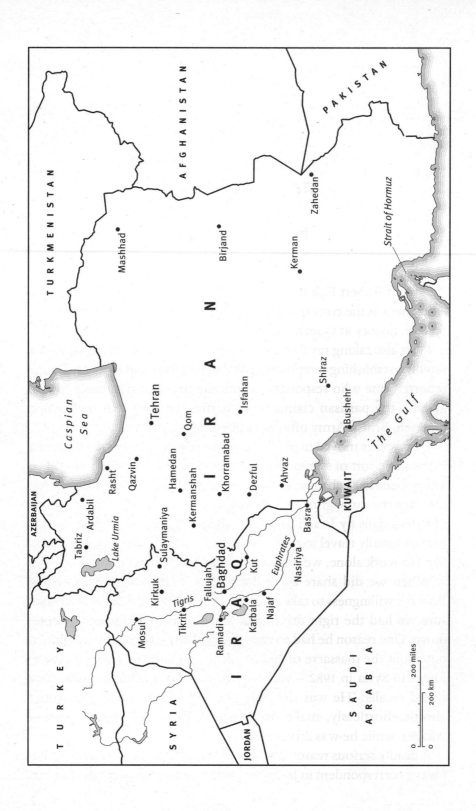

TURKMENISTAN

AFGHANISTAN

PAKISTAN

Strait of Hormuz

AZERBAIJAN

TURKEY

SYRIA

JORDAN

Caspian Sea

Lake Urmia

I R A N

Mashhad

Birjand

Zahedan

Kerman

Shiraz

Bushehr

The Gulf

Tehran

Qom

Isfahan

Tabriz

Ardabil

Rasht

Qazvin

Hamedan

Khorramabad

Dezful

Ahvaz

Kermanshah

Sulaymaniya

Kirkuk

Mosul

Tikrit

Baghdad

Fallujah

Ramadi

Karbala

Najaf

Kut

Nasiriya

Basra

KUWAIT

SAUDI ARABIA

I R A Q

Tigris

Euphrates

0   200 miles

0   200 km

FOREWORD

by Patrick Cockburn

I first met Robert Fisk in Belfast in 1972 at the height of the Troubles when he was the correspondent for *The Times* and I was writing a PhD on Irish history at Queen's University.

I was also taking my first tentative steps as a journalist, while he was rapidly establishing a reputation as a meticulous and highly informed reporter, one who responded sceptically to – and rigorously investigated – the partisan claims of all parties, be they IRA or Unionist gunmen, British Army officers or government officials.

Our careers moved in parallel directions because we were interested in the same sort of stories. We both went to Beirut in the mid-1970s to write about the Lebanese Civil War and the Israeli invasions. We often reported the same grim events, such as the Sabra and Shatila massacre of Palestinians by Israeli-backed Christian militiamen in 1982, but we did not usually travel together because, aside from the fact that Robert liked to work alone, we wrote for competing newspapers.

When we did share a car during the wars, I was impressed by Robert's willingness to take risks, yet to do so without bravado, making sure we had the right driver and petrol that had not been watered down. One reason he had so many journalistic scoops – such as finding out about the massacre of 20,000 people in Hama by Hafez al-Assad's forces in Syria in 1982 – was that he was an untiring traveller. One friend recalls: 'He was the only person I'll ever know who could, almost effortlessly, make up limericks about the south Lebanese villages, while he was driving through them.'

A deadly serious reason lay behind his visits to these villages. When I was a correspondent in Jerusalem in the 1990s, they were the target of repeated Israeli airstrikes, which the Israeli military would declare were solely directed at 'terrorists', and, if there were any dead or wounded, they were invariably described as gunmen not civilians. Almost nobody checked if this was true – except Robert, who would drive again and again to these same shattered villages and report in graphic detail about the dead bodies of men, women and children, and interview survivors. When Israel stuck with its denial of responsibility, he would unearth further evidence in the shape of videos and travel to America to show arms manufacturers fragments of their missiles that had torn apart some Lebanese community.

Robert was suited to Beirut with its free and somewhat anarchic atmosphere, a place always on edge, and its people – Lebanese, Palestinian, exiles of all sorts – born survivors, though sometimes the odds against them proved too great. He had a natural sympathy for their sufferings and a rage against those who inflicted them. His sympathy was not confined to present-day victims: for decades he wrote about the Armenian genocide, carried out by the Ottoman Turks during the First World War. He would publicise long-lost diaries and documents about the mass slaughter of an estimated 1.5 million Armenians, stories other correspondents felt were far from the conventional news agenda and better left to historians.

But Robert was more than a journalist cataloguing present-day developments and woes. He was a historian as well as a reporter, who wrote, among many other books, *The Great War for Civilisation: The Conquest of the Middle East* and now *The Night of Power: The Betrayal of the Middle East*. I never finished my PhD in Belfast because the violence became too intense for academic work, but Robert did get his doctorate from Trinity College Dublin for his thesis on Irish neutrality in the Second World War. He was more than a person who covered 'the news', since his journalism – for all his scoops and revelations – had such depth. He was, in the truest sense, 'a historian of the present'.

Robert combined a journalist's skills as an eyewitness recording and interpreting events with a historian's ability to place them in a broader context and longer time frame. His books avoid the failing of many of even the best academic histories, which is that the author largely knows what happened second-hand. The weakness of journalism is the precise opposite: the reporter focuses exclusively on what he or she witnesses in front of them, ignoring or minimising the significance of what they do not see, but which is of equal or greater significance. By its very nature, journalism dilutes the truth not just through proprietorial or editorial bias, though that is important, but because shortage of space and the need to appeal to a wide audience necessitate oversimplification. Yet the real life of peoples and countries is complicated – all the arrows never point conveniently in the same direction – and what appears in the media will, at best, be a well-informed synopsis of events. Only through books such as this can the complex but invariably fascinating reality be accessed. The great American journalist Seymour Hersh once told me: 'When people ask me how to begin an investigation, I always say to them: "Read, read, read."'

Robert was a magnificent reporter who bubbled with nervous energy, often shifting his weight from one foot to the other, notebook in hand, as he questioned eyewitnesses relentlessly and probed into what had really occurred. He took nothing for granted and was openly contemptuous of those who did. He did not invent the old journalistic saying 'Never believe anything until it is officially denied', but he fully agreed with its sceptical message. He was suspicious of reporters who cultivated diplomats and 'official sources' that could not be named, and whose likely partisan bias was unmentioned but whose veracity we were invited to take on trust.

Some journalists responded to Robert's criticism with baffled resentment: during the US-led counter-invasion of Kuwait in 1991, one embedded American journalist complained that Robert was unfairly reporting on events about which information should have been confined to an officially sanctioned 'pool' of correspondents. Another US journalist based in London in the early 1980s told me that he considered Robert to be a brilliant writer and the best reporter he had ever known, but he had been struck by the number of his colleagues who grimaced at Robert's name. 'I have thought about this,' he said, 'and I think that 80 per cent of the reason for this is pure envy on their part.' Truly, hell hath no fury like a reporter 'scooped', let alone one who has been regularly 'scooped'. Robert did this again and again over half a century, so it was scarcely surprising that rival journalists often nurtured bitter and resentful feelings towards him.

He probably won more important journalistic awards in the course of his career than any other British or American reporter, but denunciations of what he wrote by hostile critics are perhaps a more distinguished mark of integrity. Who now remembers the long forgotten British government minister who responded to Robert's sceptical but even-handed coverage of the US-led invasion of Iraq in 2003 by describing Robert as 'a dupe of Saddam Hussein's regime'?

Inevitably, anybody reporting honestly on war and conflict will make enemies – and there is probably something wrong with their work if they do not. Governments whose armies are trying to kill each other are unlikely to hesitate when telling lies about each other. They detest the journalist who exposes these falsehoods and commonly demonise him as unpatriotic or an enemy pawn, since all wars are, and have always been, propaganda wars. Nothing much can be done to stop this, which has been an inevitable feature of armed conflict since Egyptian pharaohs were inscribing mendacious hieroglyphs about their non-existent victories on monuments 4,000 years ago. But it should be possible to alert the public to the falsity of this propaganda by describing, in a convincing manner, what is really going on and why it is happening. Robert was well aware of this, writing that 'armies at war – like their governments – are best observed with a mighty degree of scepticism, even cynicism. So far as armies and militias are concerned there are no good guys.' It is not that Robert thought good people did not exist, but he generally found them among the victims rather than the perpetrators of violence.

We saw more of each other after we both joined the *Independent*, Robert in 1989 and myself in 1990. He had decided to leave *The Times* after the paper jibbed at publishing his story, supported by copious evidence, about how a US cruiser, *USS Vincennes*, in the Gulf had shot down an Iranian civilian airliner flying between Bandar Abbas and Dubai in 1988, killing all 290 people on board. I was mostly in Iraq during the First Gulf War and Robert was in Kuwait. After the overthrow of Saddam Hussein in 2003, we drove out together from Baghdad across the desert to Jordan. I recall that we were stopped for a long time on the Jordanian side of the border because Robert had secured, from the wreckage of some police headquarters in Basra in southern Iraq, a file of laudatory poems written to Saddam's ferocious police chief in the city by his underlings on the occasion of his birthday. Some of the Jordanian officials thought these craven poetic offerings were hilarious, but others found the documents mysterious and kept us waiting for hours at the bleak border post while they obtained official permission from Amman to let us cross.

As we grew older, we grew closer. We both had doubts about the beneficial outcome of the so-called Arab Spring in 2011, having seen similar optimism over the invasion of Iraq produce a paroxysm of violence. Neither of us believed that Bashar al-Assad and his regime was going to fall, at a time when this was conventional wisdom among politicians and in the media. To suggest anything to the contrary got one immediately pilloried as a supporter of Assad. The sensible course was to ignore these diatribes and Robert and I used to counsel each other not to overreact and thereby give legs to some crude distortion of one's views.

Over the last 15 years of his life, we talked almost once a week about everything from the state of the world to the state of ourselves, supplementing phone calls with periodic emails. A life spent describing crises and wars made Robert more philosophical about the coronavirus pandemic than those with less direct experience of calamities. In one of the last emails I received from him shortly before he died in Dublin on 30 October 2020, he wrote that 'Covid-19, unless it suddenly turns into a tiger, will be seen as just another risk to human life – like car crashes, cancer, war, etc. Humans don't necessarily fight disease, injustice and sorrow. They just survive and bash on regardless.'

He was correct in recognising that war, plague and violent death will always be with us, along with official lies about them, as will, hopefully, those who try to explain what is really happening. The British First World War prime minister David Lloyd George once said of that conflict that 'if people really knew [the truth], the war would be stopped tomorrow. But, of course, they don't know and can't know.' Robert was keenly interested in the 1914–18 war because his father, who had fought in it, took him on visits to the Somme and other battlefields from an early age. In describing the conflicts and wars of his own era, Robert sought in his journalism and books to tell people – contrary to what Lloyd George believed could and should be revealed to the public – about the terrible things that happen and to identify those responsible for these horrors.

Canterbury, September 2023

PREFACE

He who writes a book should write it only if he keeps
constantly in view that everyone is his enemy, that
everyone is an expert in his field, that everyone has nothing
on his mind but his subject, and that everyone is ready and
willing to challenge him. Nor must an author be satisfied
with this. He should lay his book aside, and not be content
with half-baked views, for a book, once composed, is
wonderfully seductive …

Jahiz (died 868), al-Hayawan (1:88) (translated by Tarif Khalidi)

A few days after I arrived in the Middle East as a correspondent in 1976,
I fell ferociously ill with a form of dysentery. I lay sick in my Cairo
hotel bed, reflecting on the wisdom of my new assignment. One
midday, I forced myself to climb out of bed, wash, dress and walk into
the vast square behind my hotel. It was a pit of traffic, the people cling-
ing to the sides of old red and cream buses, a mass of Egyptians pushing
their way across narrow overpasses and through a fetid bus station of
broken concrete seats amid clouds of dust and fumes.

I collapsed onto one of these seats, semi-conscious, having vomited
all over the road, as people passed by with indifference. I loathed this
place, this square, this city. I knew – beyond any shadow of doubt –
that I must resign this new posting for *The Times of London*. The job of
Middle East Correspondent was not for me. This very *midan*, this third
circle of cement hell, surrounded by fading apartment blocks that
mocked the elegance of French boulevards, overwhelmed by a giant

Stalinist office block, was a place of utter hopelessness. Its very name, for me, was a dictator's joke, synonymous with a closed society which could never emerge from the grey dictatorship in which it was wrapped. It was called Freedom Square. Tahrir Square.

Just under thirty-five years later, I stood in that same square and thanked God that I had, through danger and fear and loneliness and excitement and adventure and fury and incendiary anger, stayed in the Middle East. The old concrete bus station seats had gone and the hotel was a shell, but the monstrosity of the Mugamma building, the fading French-style apartment blocks and the pink-stone Egyptian museum were still there. It was the same place. But now a million Egyptians fought for it, conquered it and altered the course of Arab history.

Thank God, I'd always said to myself, that I worked for a paper which printed every word of my reports, that I was for much of the time working for an editor who treated the Middle East's dictators and Israel's and America's lobbyists with the contempt they deserved. Our own cowardice, the manufacture of deceit, the safe, formulaic expressions used to mask the reality of this tragic place, have turned us journalists into blood-soaked brothers of the politicians who go to war. In Iraq. In Afghanistan. In Pakistan. In Yemen. By proxy in Lebanon. In Libya and Syria. And of course, in 'Palestine'.

When Barack Obama was elected US president, it was not easy to point out that governments are not about 'good' and 'bad guys', but about power; and that Israeli power in Washington was far too embedded to allow a young and idealistic leader to break the dangerous, uncritical support of America for its closest Middle East ally. In 2009, I went to Cairo to hear Obama deliver his reach-out speech to the Muslim world. I liked him, but I was worried about the self-confidence of his speech, its headmaster's morality, its careful history lessons, harsh on Israel and sympathetic to the Muslim world when it came to precedent, but low on detail. The West loved it and the Arab elites liked it, but the people of the Middle East remained suspicious. Obama's address was duly eviscerated by Israel's determination to continue its colonisation of Jerusalem and the West Bank.

Obama's December 2009 acceptance of the Nobel Peace Prize proved that he had become an apologist for war, a cauterising but appropriate successor to George W. Bush. Obama could not follow the non-violent example of Mahatma Gandhi and Martin Luther King, he said, because 'I face the world as it is.' And so he sent 30,000 more troops to Afghanistan, moving deeper into the corruption and decay of both Pakistan and Afghanistan while staging a withdrawal from Iraq on a scale more illusory than real. In Iran, in 'Palestine', in Lebanon, in Egypt and in the Arabian peninsula, fires were burning whose chemical attributes could never be acknowledged by Western leaders. Even in the Balkans, only a false peace prevents us from discerning the furies that still bubble away beneath the wolf-skin of history.

I reported all this from Pakistan, from Afghanistan and Iran and Iraq and Syria and Egypt and the Gulf and from 'Palestine' and Israel and from Lebanon, but nothing I wrote seemed to have any effect. In 2006, I reported on the second Israeli massacre of civilians at Qana in southern Lebanon; the Lebanese soldiers who carried the victims' bodies in plastic bags found them so light to carry that they could take two corpses in their arms. My own report on those slaughtered children had not the slightest effect. No one, as I have often said, could claim later that they hadn't been warned.

One early autumn evening, I sat on my balcony overlooking the Mediterranean and wondered whether I should have remained so many decades in the Middle East. Amid sands and cities where the heat slashed at you, I had witnessed such bloodbaths and massacres, seen so many mass graves, described so many tortures and executions, written so many times of the West's oppression of the Muslim world. Had it really been wise – or sane – to have spent so long here?

Our wars in Iraq, in Bosnia and in Kosovo contained a sinister pattern, a 'normalisation' of war. If our outrageous assaults on our enemies were too much for the audience, we either apologised – accidents happen in war, do they not? – or we blamed the victims. If we bombed a bunker packed with civilians in Baghdad, it was only because Saddam had used identical bunkers for command and control operations. So when we bombed Afghanistan in 2001 and destroyed entire villages, it was because al-Qaeda or the Taliban had been hiding there or – if they hadn't – their tactic of hiding in other villages was to blame. And in 2003, we created a pageant of identical ruthlessness against the Iraqis.

Our 'allies' in the Middle East followed our example. In Lebanon in 2006, the Israelis attacked bridges and motorways and power stations and entire civilian villages and mobile phone transmitters and Red

Cross offices and ambulances, just as they later attacked roads and medical centres and UN facilities in Gaza. Once the precedent had been set, this new atrocity became a start-line for the next killings.

The fact that the Geneva Conventions specifically forbid the kind of attacks which the Americans and British and Israelis launched meant nothing. Were we not all engaged in a new form of conflict against 'world terror'? And if the Americans could bomb a hospital in Serbia or a civilian housing estate in Baghdad, who were the hypocritical West to object when the Israeli army slaughtered the innocents of Lebanon and Gaza in identical ways?

This, then, is another theme of this book; the 'normalisation' of this latest warfare, which deletes the protection of civilians enshrined in international law in favour of a new and cruel morality: 11 September 2001 really did change the world forever, and the new world that emerged made the traditional laws of war as outdated as they were irrelevant. Is it any wonder that Muammar Gaddafi of Libya and then Bashar al-Assad of Syria were outraged at our hypocrisy when we condemned them for committing war crimes on the same scale as we had already done ourselves?

My pessimism is even greater now. I did not come upon the title of this volume by chance. The 'night of power' falls on the twenty-seventh day of the Muslim fasting month of Ramadan and marks the moment at which Muslims believe the Qur'an was first revealed to the Prophet Mohamed. 'Whoever prays during this night in true faith and hope,' he said, 'will be pardoned his previous errors.' Muslims cannot understand how they, the believers, find themselves under our military and political and economic and cultural control, and their frustration and fury are therefore turned against us. The crack of shellfire and the misery of countless thousands of innocents are recorded here, in fear and horror and in the faint hope that learning about history may help us comprehend the terrible nature of this tragedy.

When I began this book, in the spring of 2012, my parents Bill and Peggy Fisk were long dead. They have no part in this story, but I am still pondering the choice I made to live most of my life in the terrible aftermath of their wars of 1914–18 and 1939–45. Sitting on my Beirut balcony, I remembered the letter I received from *The Times* foreign editor in 1976, offering me the post of Middle East Correspondent. If I had known then what I know now, would I have agreed to spend so much of my life in the heart of such darkness? I came to the conclusion that I would have done so. Not because I have been able to chronicle history – I have long grown out of such romanticism – but the answer lies somewhere in the pages of this book. For watching history at such close range – even at the risk of one's own life – is like reading a great and tragic novel, its drama and violence so powerful that you cannot put it down. I want to know what happens next. So I read on, promising myself to finish just one more chapter. And then another. Until I look up, overwhelmed by the devastation and breadth of history, and discover light between the curtains. I have been reading until dawn.

Beirut, May 2014

1

Legacy

Little Lamb, who made thee?
Dost thou know who made thee?

William Blake, 'The Lamb', *Songs of Innocence* (1789–94)

For little Sayef, there will be no future, no awakening, no 'Arab Spring'. Fourteen months old, his head twice the size it should be, blind and paralysed, he lies on a small, soft red blanket cushioned by a cheap mattress, occasionally crying. Sayeffedin Abdulaziz Mohamed – his full name – has a kind face on his outsize head and they say he smiles when other children visit. But he will never know the history of the world around him, never enjoy the freedoms of a new Middle East. He can move only his hands and take only bottled milk because he cannot swallow. He lives in a prison whose doors will remain forever closed.

Many of the Fallujah families who have children with what doctors call 'congenital birth anomalies' prefer to keep their doors closed to strangers, regarding their children as a mark of personal shame rather than proof that something terrible took place here between 2004 and 2007 when the Americans fought battles against insurgents in the city.*

---

* The first Battle of Fallujah, 'Operation Vigilant Resolve' (April–May 2004), and the second Battle of Fallujah, 'Operation al-Fajr' – 'The Dawn' – and 'Operation Phantom Fury' (November–December 2004); after four years of bitter fighting, American forces retreated from Fallujah in the autumn of 2007, handing the city over to the Iraqi army as part of a larger operation known as 'the Great Sunni Awakening'. In 2014, al-Qaeda-linked Sunni insurgents, Islamic State in Iraq and the Levant (ISIS), took control of Fallujah and after a long siege, the Iraqi army eventually recaptured the city in June 2016.

After at first denying the use of phosphorus shells during the second Battle of Fallujah, US forces later admitted that they had fired the munitions against buildings in the city. Independent reports have spoken of a birth defect rate far higher than other areas of Iraq, let alone other Arab countries, but no one can produce cast-iron evidence that American munitions have caused the tragedy of Fallujah's children.

Sayef lives in the al-Shuhada district of Fallujah, in one of the more dangerous streets in the city. Cops stand with automatic weapons at the door of Sayef's home when we visit, but two of these armed, uniformed men come inside with us and are visibly moved by the helpless baby on the floor.

'My son cannot support himself,' Mohamed says, fondling his son's enlarged head. 'He can move only his hands. Sometimes he can't take even the milk, so we have to take him to hospital to be given fluids. He was blind when he was born. In addition, my poor little man's kidney has shut down. His legs don't move. His blindness is due to hydrocephalus.' Mohamed holds Sayef's useless legs and moves them gently as we watch the baby on his blanket. His small chest rises and falls slowly. His head is shaven, like a marine's, his arms crushed underneath him.

Both Mohamed and his wife are in their mid-thirties. Unlike many tribal families in the area, they are not related and their two daughters, born before the battles of Fallujah, are in perfect health. Sayef was born on 27 January 2011. Mohamed works for an irrigation mechanics company but admits that, with a salary of only $100 a month, he receives financial help from relatives. He was outside Fallujah during the 2004 conflict but returned two months after the second battle, only to find his house mined; he received government funding to rebuild his home.

I ask whom he blames for Sayef's suffering, expecting a tirade of abuse against the Americans, the Iraqi government, the health ministry – the people of Fallujah have long been portrayed as 'pro-terrorist' and 'anti-west' in the world's press. But Mohamed is silent for a few moments. 'I am only asking for help from God,' he says. Which proves, I guess, that Fallujah – far from being a city of 'terror' – includes some very brave men.

The cops escort us to Fallujah General Hospital, a bright, sparkling Qatar-funded institution that puts most Baghdad hospitals to shame. It smells clean, with that special antiseptic hospital odour that exudes health safety, but in 2012, this is a hospital of stories almost too terrible to tell.

The pictures flash up on a screen on an upper floor of the hospital. A baby with a hugely deformed mouth. A child with a defect of the spinal cord, material from the spine outside the body. A baby with a vast Cyclopean eye. Another baby with only half a head, still-born like the rest, date of birth 17 June 2009. Yet another picture flicks onto the screen. Date of birth 6 July 2009, it shows a tiny child with half a right arm, no left leg, no genitalia. These babies never lived.

'We see this all the time now,' says a female doctor who has delivered some of these still-born children. 'I've never seen anything as bad as this in all my service,' she says. The photographs are too awful to contemplate. They cannot be published in anything but a medical journal.

There is a no-nonsense attitude from the doctors, who know that we know about this tragedy. But what is so shameful is that these deformities continue unmonitored. One Fallujah doctor, an obstetrician trained in Britain who has purchased a £79,000 scanning machine for prenatal detection of congenital abnormalities, asks why the Ministry of Health in Baghdad will not hold a full official investigation. 'I have been to see the ministry,' she says. 'They said they would have a committee. I went to the committee. And they have done nothing.'

If the number of stillborn children of Fallujah is a disgrace, the medical staff at the hospital prove their honesty by repeatedly warning of the danger of reaching conclusions too soon. 'I delivered that baby,' the obstetrician says as another picture flashes on the screen. 'I don't think this has anything to do with American weapons. The parents were close relatives. Tribal marriages here involve a lot of families who are close by blood.'

Dr Samira Alaani has documented a research paper into the 'increased prevalence of birth defects' in Fallujah. Congenital heart defects, the paper says, reached 'unprecedented numbers' in 2010, and these numbers continue to rise. Even while we are speaking, a nurse brings a message to Dr Alaani. We go at once to an incubator next to the hospital delivery room. Zeid Mohamed is just twenty-four days old. He lies sleeping, his mother watching through the glass. His father is a security guard and the couple married three years ago. There is no

family record of birth defects. But Zeid has only four fingers on each of
his little hands.

Dr Alaani's computer files contain a hundred Zeids. 'These parents
want to know what happened to their children,' she says. 'They
deserve an answer.' She is right. But neither the Iraqi authorities, nor
the Americans, nor the British, nor any major NGO appears willing or
able to help.

Dr Chris Busby, a visiting professor at the University of Ulster who
has surveyed almost 5,000 people in Fallujah, originally agreed that it
was impossible to be specific about the cause of birth defects as well as
cancers. In 2010, he claimed in a report that infant mortality in Fallujah
was found in eighty out of every 1,000 births, compared to nineteen in
Egypt, seventeen in Jordan and only 9.7 in Kuwait. However, in a
further report the following year, Busby and other colleagues stated
categorically that 'a uranium-based weapon of some type was
employed in the Battle of Fallujah, and is the main cause of the high
levels of cancer and congenital disease'.*

In the doctor's office at Fallujah General Hospital, there are photographs that defy words. How can you begin to describe a dead baby
with one leg and a head four times the size of its body? It's the same old
story. When children died in a plague of cancers in southern Iraq after
the 1991 Gulf War, the Americans and the British did not want to know.
Nor, of course, did Saddam Hussein. Now the same was happening in
Fallujah. But there has been no 'peer-reviewed epidemiological data',
so the brave people of Fallujah have no chance of finding out the truth.

It was the same when I met each child all those years ago. Thirteen-
year-old Dhamia Qassem suffered heart failure during treatment for
acute leukaemia. Ahmed Walid, a baby during the 1991 bombings of
Iraq, developed chronic myeloid leukaemia in 1995. Many of the
parents were present with their children during the air raids and some

---

* 'Uranium and other contaminants in hair from the parents of children with congenital
anomalies in Fallujah, Iraq', 30 August 2011. The report was compiled by Busby, Samira
Alaani, Mohamed Tafash, Malak Hamdan and Eleonore Blaurock-Busch. On the release of
this document, Busby remarked that 'what we have found makes it perfectly clear that a
new generation of Uranium-based weapons exists … and leads to shocking increases in
cancer and congenital illness in innocent civilians and soldiers alike'. He told me later that
he believed 'there is no evidence that phosphorus causes birth anomalies'. Which did not
correlate with the suspicions of Fallujah's doctors.

spoke of strange smells, of insecticide and flowers. Western diplomats – who otherwise chose to remain silent – wondered whether any of the children might have been stricken by the smoke from Saddam's bombed chemical warfare factories. In Basra, I found Dr Jawad Khadim al-Ali who had drawn maps of the clusters of the new child and adult cancer cases across southern Iraq, some from the very battlefields in which US tanks fired DU (depleted uranium) munitions at Saddam's armoured forces. What was astonishing, however, was the British government's pitiful response.

Lord Gilbert at the Ministry of Defence said that my account of a possible link between DU ammunition and children's cancer was 'a wilful perversion of reality'. Particles from DU warheads became diffi-cult to detect, he wrote, 'even with the most sophisticated monitoring equipment'. Yet when an Atomic Energy Agency official wrote to the Royal Ordnance in London in 1998, he said that the spread of radioac-tivity and toxic contamination would be 'a risk to both the military and the civilian population' if not dealt with in peacetime.

Outside the home of each deformed child in Fallujah stands my police escort, a squad of toughs from the local constabulary, all Sunnis, for this city was the heart of the Sunni insurgency against the new and 'democratic' Shia-controlled al-Maliki government which the United States left behind when it finally scuttled out of Iraq in 2011. But the cops are targets, too, of that other institution which Washington intro-duced like a bacillus into the country and which it left behind eight years later.

'Al-Qaeda killed two of our men here two days ago,' one of my escorts said. 'Then they called us up to tell us the name of their opera-tion – on a police radio!' We were standing outside Sayef Mohamed's home. We had six policemen with us, one wearing a ski mask. As a police colonel said later, standing in the old US Marine base that is now his shabby headquarters, 'Al-Qaeda are still here. They are a nuisance, to me personally when I have to move around the city, but they are not what they were.' This would change.

Opposite was the newly rebuilt railway station and the pale stencil of 'USMC' was still on the barrack wall. But the word 'security' was as much a façade as 'democracy'. Many of the army checkpoints looked eerily like their American predecessors. But the soldiers are Iraqis, smoking cigarettes, grinning to friends, waving anti-bomb 'wands' at our car, munching on sandwiches. Their regimental sleeve patches carry an assortment of swords and shields and animal insignia, a shadow of the logos of the long-departed 82nd Airborne and the 3rd Armored Cavalry. There was a feeling of empire departed.

Not that Iraq didn't have problems. Its vice president, Tariq al-Hashemi, had just fled Baghdad for Iraqi Kurdistan, then flown to Qatar and then to Saudi Arabia. He claimed that three of his men had been tortured to death in a Baghdad prison – the al-Maliki administration said only one had died, and for medical reasons. The central government even wanted to discipline the authorities at the airport at Erbil, the Kurdish capital, for allowing al-Hashemi to fly to Qatar. 'Iraqi law is one and it applies to all, including Kurdistan,' an Iraqi government spokesman announced. But it doesn't. Iraqi Kurdistan is almost a separate state, with its own flag, its own language. On the highway to Erbil, there's a forty-mile stretch which is generally regarded as unsafe – al-Qaeda territory – and then you're into Kurdistan.

I am on the highway with an Iraqi journalist, Sadd Tahr Hussein, and Dr Lubna Naji, a twenty-five-year-old medical practitioner. What of her country? I ask. She shakes her head. 'There is no real country anymore. I talk to my friends, mostly doctors – and all talk of moving out of Iraq. They all dream of going outside. Because home is where you *belong* – where you are wanted. We've lost our sense of something that belongs to us, our homeland.' You hear this a lot. The government, they tell you in Baghdad, is unashamedly sectarian. And corrupt. 'For me, I prefer to die here, like a tree standing up, not to melt away,' says Hussein. 'That's the difference between the older and the younger generations.' We drive past so many checkpoints together that I'm almost giddy. By the time I reach Erbil, I've counted thirteen different camouflage uniforms. Those in black around Baghdad are Nouri al-Maliki's Shiite Dawa party. All the cops are militiamen, I'm told. Wages are £300 for policemen, £500 for army officers. In Iraq, that's worth risking your life for.

But what happened to Iraq back in the days when the sectarian war first began, the legacy of George W. Bush's 2003 invasion and regime change and the discovery of 'weapons of mass destruction'? Dr Naji shudders. 'I was a fourth year medical student at the forensic medicine institute next to the mortuary and you wouldn't believe what we saw. I remember a body coming in once. It had been decapitated and someone had sewn a dog's head on it. Can you imagine who would do such a thing?'

I know Dr Naji's mortuary well. The offices were in a modern two-storey concrete block beside a square of trees. The corpses were housed in a dirty brick building behind. I used to visit the city morgue every other day after the 2003 Anglo-US invasion, to meet its director, Faik Amin Bakr, and count corpses. I would visit these places with a kind of dead humour – the kind you use when you are looking at massacre victims in the midday heat. I remember one day there was a dead man on a trolley in the sun. Noticing his right sock had a hole in it, I said to a colleague: 'If you're going to get murdered in Baghdad, remember to wear a new pair of socks.' That's how pitiless we could be. You go on a story in a war and you're there to report on the atrocity, to speak for the dead, but not to cry.

My colleague and friend Haider Al Safi and I were almost inseparable over these months, along with our driver Mohamed al Khazraji. Haider was a Shia, Mohamed a Sunni, lifelong friends. There was a massacre every night in Baghdad, the most vicious carnage in post-invasion Iraq. June, July, August 2003 were the worst months. Each morning the corpses arrived, blasted by gunfire, knifed, shot in the head or stomach; victims of the 'liberation' of Iraq and of the anarchy which we introduced, along with the 'freedom' we were so keen to give its people.

At the Yarmouk camp they had so many bodies that I found them lying in the yard because the fridge was already filled. On stretchers with blankets thrown over them, on the hot concrete beneath the sun, the flies swarming around them in the forty-five-degree heat. At the city morgue, the morticians appear at the fridge doors in dirty green overalls, scarcely glancing at the wailing relatives by the gate. The Anglo-American occupation authorities never mentioned, until years later, the innocent dead. Many of them were shot down by US soldiers at checkpoints or after ambushes on occupation troops or hit by American bullets at wedding parties. Others were cut down by insurgents or for family revenge or by the plague of thieves that our invasion of Iraq let loose.

After a while, after days at the mortuaries, we got to know the victims. Their fathers and wives and cousins would tell us how they dressed, how they worked, how many children they had left behind. The families wept and said no one cared about them and, after

expressing our sorrow over and over again, I came to the conclusion
that they were right.

How many were killed in Iraq in the first five months of American
occupation? Or between the American entry into Baghdad in 2003 and
2005? Of course, there is no total figure. For months, US military officials followed a rule invented by General Tommy Franks, the
CENTCOM commander in 2003: 'We don't do body counts.' But the
Pentagon did 'do' body counts of civilians, albeit in a highly misleading
way. The *New York Times* revealed in 2005 that the US military had kept
figures for civilian deaths – but only of civilians killed by insurgents.
The total came to 25,902. However, civilians killed by US or British
troops or other members of the occupation forces were not included in
this figure.*

For the record, here is a little of the cull in human life in Baghdad in
the week of 14–20 September 2003. Hassan Ahmed was twenty-six. At
the Baghdad morgue, his cousin Sadeq produced a photograph of the
young man for me. Hassan has a thin, slightly bearded face and is wearing a bright purple shirt. His father, a soldier, was killed in the Iran–Iraq
war in 1982, when Hassan was just five years old. At 3 p.m. on 17
September, Hassan was walking in the street in his home neighbourhood of Al-Biyaa when someone shot him twice in the head.

Old Sarhan Daoud, almost toothless and bespectacled, was standing
outside the Baghdad city morgue in a long white dishdash robe. A few
hours earlier, his only sons, nineteen-year-old Ahmed and twenty-
seven-year-old Ali, were shot down outside their Baghdad home. There
was talk of a revenge killing, but the father wasn't certain. After half an
hour, Ahmed and Ali were brought out in their plywood caskets and
roped to the top of a minivan into which cousins and uncles and the old
father climbed for the funeral journey to the family's home village.

On the walls of the city mortuary, families have for weeks been leaving photographs of those who disappeared since the 'liberation'. 'We
lost Mr Abdul-emir al-Noor al-Moussawi last Wednesday, 11 June 2003,
in Baghdad,' it said beneath the photograph of a dignified man in suit

---

* See the *New York Times*, 30 October 2005, 'US quietly issues estimate of Iraqi civilian
casualties' by Sabrina Tavernise. The American statistics, which Tavernise makes clear are
flawed, suggest that twenty-six civilians were being killed per day in 2004, rising to forty
later in the year. By August 2005, the daily figure was sixty-three – but this does not
include Iraqis killed by American firepower.

and tie. 'He is seventy-one years old. Hair white. Wearing a grey dish-dash. A reward will be paid to anyone with information.' Another poster. 'Sami Saleh Mohamed Tamur from Ninevah governorate. Taxi driver, disappeared in a car, a Caprice registration number 75760.' Then there is sixteen-year-old Beida Jaffer Sadr, a schoolgirl apparently kidnapped in Baghdad whose father's telephone number is printed below her picture. 'Blond hair, brown eyes, wearing a black skirt.'

Why should we list these names today? We know about American torture and rape of Iraqi prisoners at Abu Ghraib. We know about the massacres by US troops – in Afghanistan as well as in Iraq – and we know about the British torture of prisoners in Basra. But the British and then the Americans left. The Arab awakening arrived. Wasn't Syrian president Bashar al-Assad now responsible for killing more inno-cents in three years than George W. Bush or Tony Blair in Iraq in the same period of time? But these Iraqi names, in their tens of thousands, are part of our legacy. We ignore them at our peril.

Of course, the 'Coalition Provisional Authority' tried to put another gloss on all this. Saddam Hussein ruled through terror. Tens of thou-sands of his victims were found in the mass graves of Iraq, men and women who had no death certificates, no funerals, no justice. At the Abu Ghraib prison, Saddam's head doctor – reappointed by the jail's new American guards when they took over – told me that when 'secu-rity prisoners' were hanged at night, he was ordered not to issue death certificates. It might be argued that in the previous regime, the govern-ment committed the crimes. Now, the Iraqi people were committing them, but it is the duty of an occupying power to protect the people under its control. The mandate of the 'Coalition Provisional Authority' required it to care for the people of Iraq. It didn't.*

---

* By 1 January 2013, the so-called 'Syrian Observatory for Human Rights' – upon which journalists placed far too much reliance – claimed 45,000 as the statistic for the dead in almost two years of Syria's civil conflict, although the UN Human Rights Commission – apparently anxious to put pressure on the Security Council – topped this up with another 15,000 on 3 January 2013. Yet even this 60,000 (later raised to 70,000) appeared to include 12,000 of the government's own soldiers and supporters killed by the armed opposition. In an unhappy parallel to the Pentagon's own twisted figures on Iraq, the SOHR admitted that rebel fighters among the Syrian dead were counted among civilian fatalities if they had only taken up arms after the conflict began in early 2011. By mid-2013, fatalities were said to have reached 100,000. A year later, we would be talking of 200,000. Statistics in the Middle East are like death: treated with doubtful respect and best avoided.

In Baghdad, the smell of the dead poured into the street through the mortuary's air-conditioning ducts. There was a wail of grief from the yard behind us where fifty people waited in the shade of the mortuary wall. There were wooden coffins in the street, stacked against the wall, lying on the pavement. When the bodies were released, they were taken to the mosque in coffins and then buried in shrouds.

In the blazing heat of an Iraqi summer, some families buried their dead without notifying the authorities. Some bodies remained unidentified, and there are no autopsies. The morticians would not say why, but one of the mortuary officials had a bleak story to tell. 'The Ministry of Health has instructed the doctors that there should be no autopsies in cases where the Americans bring in the bodies – because they will already have performed the operation.' But this cannot be true, I said. US forces would never perform autopsies unless, perhaps, they themselves were involved in the deaths. Not long ago, six corpses arrived at the Baghdad mortuary after being brought in by US forces. Three were unidentified. Three had names but their families could not be found. All had suffered 'traumatic wounds to the head', the normal phrase for gunshot wounds. There were no autopsies.

Death was now so routine that even the most tragic became a footnote. One man was shot dead by a US soldier as he overtook their convoy on the way to his Baghdad wedding. We only found out because his marriage was to have been celebrated in a hotel occupied by journalists. A US tank collided with a bus north of Baghdad. Seven civilians were killed. The Americans agreed to open an investigation, but it made scarcely a paragraph in the local press. An American tank crossing the motorway at Abu Ghraib sideswiped a car carrying two girls and their mother, all of whom were crushed to death. It didn't even make the news in Baghdad.

Our driver Mohamed al-Khazraji's brother-in-law was killed by thieves a few weeks ago and now both Mohamed and Haider were anxious before the New Year of 2004. Worried for my safety, for their own lives, for their families' security. We would avoid all cars with tinted windows, all US convoys and, when possible, all checkpoints. 'I think, Robert,' Haider would begin, and I would already be hunching my shoulders below the back of the rear seat of the car, 'that this might be the moment for you to bury your head.' Yet still we travelled around the city.

Ali Salman Ali was the first victim of Saddam's capture, but he died on Christmas Day, two weeks after Iraq's caliph had been seized.* As his seventy-one-year-old father Salman Ghazi told it, Ali must have been among the first of Iraq's Shia Muslims to scream his delight in the street after the ex-dictator emerged from his hole beside the Tigris river. 'He shouted that the Americans had come to save us and liberated us from that terrible regime,' Salman Ghazi said, his dark eyes staring at my notebook. Behind me, the dead man's twelve cousins were heaving his coffin from the Baghdad mortuary onto the back of a rusting white pick-up.

There was a kind of weariness among the men in their damp tribal robes standing in the mud at the morgue. 'That same afternoon he was celebrating, they came for him,' his father said. 'He had gone out shopping to Qaddamiya in his car and they were in another car that caught up with him and overtook him and opened fire on him with rifles.' Who were 'they'? I asked. The father looked at another of his sons and then at a cousin who had muttered the word 'Wahhabis'.

This was the first time I heard the Wahhabis blamed for a murder by a member of his family. In the last year of his rule, Saddam had craftily allowed the existence of 'the committees of the faith' to represent the purist, ascetic, often Saudi-funded and inspired Sunni Muslims who were now in the vanguard of the anti-American insurgency. As a Shia, Ali Salman Ali had been the victim of a sectarian killing – which is why his family was so uneasy about blaming 'Sunnis' for his killing. They lived alongside Sunnis. And, as I was always being told, Sunnis intermarried with Shia. Calling the murderers 'Wahhabis' let the Sunnis off the hook. Then the father pointed at my notebook. 'We shall call his killers "terrorists",' he said.

As usual, there was no mention of Ali Salman's death by the occupation authorities. He was not a Westerner. Ali's father said I could take pictures of the coffin as it was placed on the back of the pick-up and one of the cousins broke down in tears and kissed the wooden box. 'Today, this place, Iraq, is filled with such carelessness,' his father said. 'There is no path to follow, no authority and no one to take care of the people.'

The suburb of Al-Adil was as good a place as any in Baghdad to understand what kind of information the occupation armies wanted. It

---

* Saddam was captured on 13 December 2003.

was middle class in a downmarket Iraqi way, educated families living in villas shadowed by palm trees in their dusty gardens. When I arrived, the 82nd Airborne were paying a social call with two Abrams tanks, six Humvees and a company of soldiers and a group of armed and hooded men. I wandered up to them and the first masked man waved me forward with two fingers. 'Iraqi?' I asked. He nodded.

Just behind him, the Americans from Charlie Company were handing out leaflets. An Iraqi interpreter showed me a photocopy of a bearded man dancing at what must have been his wedding, his hands held aloft, grinning at the camera. 'We are looking for him,' he said. Several middle-aged men beside me looked at the picture and shrugged their shoulders. The Americans were weighed down with flak jackets and helmets and rifles and they were trying to be friendly. They had learned some basic Arabic and were saying 'shukran' – thank you – each time they finished speaking.

At the gateway of a single-storey villa, I found a man in a long grey galabiya gown. 'They are polite,' he said of the Americans. 'They are looking for men who have attacked them. But they have also been asking about the sewage system here and asking if we have enough electricity. They have caused no problems.' At this point, a group of young men joined us beneath the trees and the man in the gown suddenly transmogrified into someone else. 'The Americans dragged a sick man from his home here and they threw him in a truck and one of the Americans put his foot on the man's back – such humiliation! – and then they drove him away. The Americans behave like barbarians.'

I could see what was happening. The Iraqi to whom I was talking was being watched by the hooded gunmen, but he was also being listened to by men who if they weren't members of the resistance were certainly sympathetic to them. So he was to be friendly to the Americans and also to hate them. He spoke of American politeness and talked of American cruelty, all in the space of thirty seconds. In Al-Adil, it wasn't difficult for an Iraqi to adopt a split personality. It was a national psychotic disorder.

Captain Joseph Eskindo was a bright, articulate man. 'We've had some attacks here on the Iraqi police,' he said. 'One was killed close to here and we want to find the people who did it.' The masked men, some of whom had dark-blue helmets and jungle fatigues, stood behind us. 'They're the Iraqi Civil Defense Corps, they're locals and they don't want to be recognised. We take them with us to areas they don't live in, but there's always a chance someone will know them, which is why they hide their faces.'

All the while, leaflets were being handed to every householder in Al-Adil, another of which caught my eye. There were pictures of a heavy machine gun, a rocket-propelled grenade, an anti-tank rocket and a line of cowed Iraqi men standing in front of a wall with their hands tied behind their backs, watched by an American soldier. And underneath, in Arabic, were printed the words: 'The Coalition Authorities have announced a new policy.' Anyone found with one of these weapons 'will be sentenced by the courts to between fifteen years and life imprisonment'. Who, I wondered, could have produced this humiliating, threatening leaflet? What it represented was occupation. It was also rubbish. No court was sentencing anyone to fifteen years in prison, let alone life. And no such sentence would stand once an Iraqi government took over from the Americans.

I asked about the arrest of the sick man and suddenly a plausible story emerged. 'He's a schizophrenic who's been attacking children,' the captain said. 'The neighbours complained to us because he'd just taken a little boy and thrown him on his head onto the road. We medi-vacked the child to hospital and we've taken the man to a police station.' So much for American barbarism.

But not far away, I came across a message spray-painted on a wall. 'American soldiers,' it said. 'Run away to your home before you will be a body in black bag, then be dropped in a river or valley.' I asked the young captain whether he didn't ever wonder if he might end up in that bag. 'Yes, sure,' he said.

Then an old man approached us in a blue gown, holding a stick. He told the interpreter that a former leading Baathist lived down the same road and kept two guards in his house. 'Ask him for the address and we'll come back and check it out later,' Captain Eskindo said. I watched the old man shuffling away and realised that he had at that very moment done what would have been expected of him under Saddam's regime. He had betrayed his neighbour.

On the last day of March 2004, an old Iraqi friend of mine arrived in Baghdad from Fallujah. 'The bodies were hanging upside down on the side of the bridge,' he said. 'They had no hands, no feet, one had no head.' He was shaking as he told me what he saw. 'The people of Fallujah were just driving over the bridge as if nothing was happening. When we left,' my friend continued, 'there were no helicopters, no police, no soldiers, all seemed quite normal – except for the bodies. They were burned brown. I couldn't tell if they were men or women.'

The four Western men, mercenaries – or 'contractors' as we were enjoined to call them – had been dragged from their cars in the centre of Fallujah, mutilated, stoned, burned, beaten with iron pipes. One of them was decapitated, then dragged through the streets behind a car. What the Anglo-American occupation power later called a 'particularly brutal' crime was all too real on the videotapes that were taken by Iraqi camera crews in Fallujah.

The crowds – and they were local civilians, not insurgents – jumped up and down and laughed and trussed up one of the bodies with yellow tape, tied it to the rear bumper of a car and dragged it down the main street of Fallujah. The drivers of cars and trucks hooted with impatience to overtake this obscene cortege, as if such horrors were an everyday occurrence. One of the dead men was wearing military identification dog tags. A US passport lay next to another corpse. A local civilian said that the mujahidin had thrown two grenades at each car before dragging the occupants onto the road. Word later spread that the mercenaries' police escort had deliberately blocked their route through Fallujah to enable the attackers to throw the grenades. 'We will pacify that city,' hollered Brigadier General Mark Kimmitt, the US deputy chief of operations, who had been boasting only the previous day that US Marines in Fallujah were encountering fewer security problems. And so began the first Battle of Fallujah.

But the 'pacification' of Fallujah had begun within a month of the 2003 invasion, when American paratroopers opened fire on crowds protesting their occupation of a local school, killing sixteen men and wounding at least seventy others. The Americans claimed that gunmen in the crowd had fired at them. One eyewitness said two shots came from a car. But reporters found no bullet holes in the school from which the US forces had fired.

Scarcely three months after the 2003 invasion, an American soldier died five miles from Fallujah at a scruffy village called Khan Dhari. All the Iraqis who saw him lifted from the wreckage of his Humvee said he was still wearing his helmet but had a dark-red wound on his right side. The soldiers, they said, were shouting after the bomb went off, the first half of their convoy speeding forward, the last two vehicles coming to a standstill behind the smoking wreckage.

The Iraqis didn't mourn the American soldier they saw die. 'It is a letter for Bush,' a fat man in a long white galabiya announced as a squad of US military police in anti-bomb visors searched for more explosives along the highway.

Khan Dhari was a Sunni, Wahhabi town whose inhabitants admired the guerrillas now assaulting the American occupiers. They were aware – as the Americans were not – that their town had a deep significance in the story of Iraq's war against foreigners. In 1920, during the insurgency against the post-war British occupation, the son of a local tribal leader, Sheikh Dhari, killed a British officer here, an imperial adventurer called Lieutenant Colonel Gerard Evelyn Leachman who had arrived to renegotiate payments made to the sheikh for his loyalty to the Baghdad administration. The British promptly advanced towards Fallujah and inflicted 'heavy punishment' on the area around the city. The very location of the murder of the most senior British officer on 12 August 1920 was now the scene of the first killing of a US soldier by a roadside bomb in 2003. Nor did the story end there. Harith al-Dhari, a descendant of the 1920s tribal leader, would in 2006 be sought by the American-supported Iraqi government for 'inciting sectarian strife'. This al-Dhari, leader of the Association of Muslim Scholars, complained that Shiite ministers in the government had been angered by his recent visit to Saudi Arabia, whose Sunni rulers were increasingly fearful of Shiite rule in Iraq. Harith al-Dhari was also rumoured to be a leader of an insurgent group calling itself the '1920 Revolution Brigades'.

Supporters of the latest Iraqi insurgency now gathered around me to watch the Americans dig up part of the road with picks and axes, their heavy machine guns pointed at the car. 'After the bomb, they were shouting at each other and screaming,' a carpenter called Rafed remarked. 'This is only fifty metres from the scene of another ambush last month when they burned out an American jeep.' But it was another man who approached me. 'This is the way we deal with occupiers,' he said. 'They came and said they were liberators but when we realised they were occupiers, we had to fight. We are people of steel. The Americans and all the other occupiers will burn.' Then he said something chilling. 'I have a one-year-old daughter,' he said. 'And I would happily put a bomb in her clothes and send her to the Americans to kill them.'

It must have taken hours to put a heavy bomb beneath the central reservation at Khan Dhari, I realised. It must have been at night. And these drinks sellers and old shopkeepers must have seen the men at work, knowing that a command-detonated bomb would be triggered by a man behind or among them.

Fallujah, the city of a hundred minarets, was conservative and loyal – up to a point – in the days of Saddam's rule. But it was liberating itself from the Baathist regime before the Americans even reached the city. In April 2004, it was to be blasted again in 'Operation Vigilant Resolve' that became known as the first Battle of Fallujah. Having reportedly forced a third of the population to flee, the US Marines surrounded the city. Failing to prevent many of its men returning by truck before the battle, the Americans staged a half-hearted attempt to take Fallujah, called up four air strikes on individual houses and then meekly handed over control to a former Baathist brigadier general who promptly gave the place its freedom once again.

Those of us reporting from Baghdad were already aware of the extraordinary disparity between the claims of gritted-teeth optimism uttered by the Western occupying powers and the terrible drama being enacted among Iraqis, the mixture of banal banter from American spokesmen and the heartbreaking tragedy which we were visiting upon the people of this immensely wealthy, deeply wounded, brave and dangerous nation. The schism between the West's version of Iraq and Iraq's view of itself was one of the most destructive elements of the 2003 invasion and its aftermath.

The stories of mistreatment and abuse were becoming a familiar pattern. One of the men in the old intelligence compound complained that an American soldier had stolen money from him. Such claims were routinely dismissed, but too many reports were coming in of identical theft during American raids for them all to be dismissed as exaggeration.*

---

* Not that we could be romantic about the behaviour of all Iraqi civilians. If the Americans were dismissive of their own mass killing at Amiriyah in February 1991 when they visited the underground bunker, now a memorial site, Iraqi looters had stormed into the Baathist-inspired shrine after the 'liberation' of Baghdad and stolen the gold rings of the victims, which had been stored in glass cases in the neighbouring exhibition hall.

The stories we reported became ever more outrageous. Outside Fallujah in mid-September 2003, I discovered a human brain beside the main highway to Baghdad, blasted from its owner's head when the Americans ambushed their own Iraqi policemen the previous night. A few inches away were a policeman's teeth, the clean dentures of a young man. 'I don't know if they are the teeth of my brother – I don't even know if my brother is alive or dead,' Ahmed Mohamed shouted at me. 'The Americans took the dead and the wounded away – they won't tell us anything.'

Ahmed was an Iraqi policeman working for the Americans. US officials formally stated that they had 'no information' about the killing of the nine cops and the wounding of five others in the early hours of 12 September, but they were not telling the truth. Soldiers of the 3rd Infantry Division had fired thousands of bullets in the ambush, hundreds of them hitting the wall of a building in the neighbouring Jordanian hospital compound. And if they had really needed 'information', they had only to look at the 40 mm grenade cartridges scattered in the sand near the brains and teeth. On each was printed the coding 'AMM LOT MA-92A170-024', a US code for grenades belt-fired from an American M-19.

Back in Fallujah, it wasn't difficult to put the story together. The local American-trained and American-paid police chief, Qahtan Adnan Hamad, described how, not long after midnight, gunmen in a BMW had opened fire on the mayor's office in Fallujah. Two squads of policemen – again, American-trained and American-paid – set off in pursuit. Since the Americans would not reveal the truth, it was left to Ahmed Mohamed, whose twenty-eight-year-old brother Walid was one of the policemen who gave chase, to describe what happened. 'The police chased them in two vehicles, a Nissan pick-up and a Honda car, and they set off down the old Kandar road towards Baghdad. But the Americans were there, outside the Jordanian hospital, to ambush cars on the road.' According to one of the policemen who was wounded in the second vehicle, the Americans suddenly appeared on the darkened road. 'When they shouted at us, we stopped immediately,' he said. 'We tried to tell them we were police. They just kept on shooting.'

This was true. I found thousands of brass cartridge cases at the scene, along with the dark-green grenade cartridges. At least 150 rounds had impacted on the breezeblock wall of the Jordanian hospital and two rooms had been burned out, flames blackening the outside of the building. Several Iraqis said that a Jordanian doctor in the hospital had been killed and five nurses wounded.

So what happened? Did the Americans shoot down their own Iraqi policemen under the mistaken impression that they were 'subversives' and then, once their bullets had smashed into the hospital, had they come under attack from the Jordanian guards on the roof? All they would speak of were their own casualties: two US soldiers had been killed and seven others wounded in a raid in the neighbouring town of Ramadi. This gave the impression yet again that American lives were infinitely more valuable than Iraqi lives.

There were other things beside the Fallujah highway; a torn, bloodstained fragment of a policeman's blue shirt, a primitive tourniquet, medical gauze and lots of blackened blood. The 3rd Infantry Division was tired, the story went. They invaded Iraq in March, hadn't been home since and morale was low. But rumour was beginning to turn this massacre into something far more dangerous.

Here are the words of the brother of another policeman caught in the ambush: 'The Americans were forced to leave Fallujah after much fighting following their killing of sixteen demonstrators in April 2003. They were forced to hire a Fallujah police force. But they wanted to return to Fallujah so they arranged the ambush. The BMW "gunmen" were Americans, who were supposed to show there was no security in Fallujah … Our police kept crying out, "We're the police." And the Americans went on shooting.'

So the April killings by the 82nd Airborne and the subsequent withdrawal of US forces from the city were connected by the Iraqis to the shooting of the nine policemen; just over six months later, the people of Fallujah would desecrate the bodies of those American mercenaries, which would lead to the first American battle for Fallujah in 2004.

Killings were now like heartbeats in Iraq. After the country's 'liberation', the Baath party's enemies were given open season to hunt down hundreds of the former regime's officials without the slightest attempt by the Anglo-American armies or their newly installed police force to end the cleansing.

Many of the executions were carried out with the same cruelty that Saddam's henchmen once used against the regime's opponents. In

Najaf, Baathists were shot down by men on motorcycles or riding in taxis. Sunni Muslims suspected the Badr Brigades were responsible, the militia for the Supreme Council for Islamic Revolution in Iraq (SCIRI) whose representatives sit on the governing council. Among the most savage of recent attacks was that on Dhamia Abbas, a teacher walking her two four-year-old sons to school when they were sprayed with bullets from an AK-47 rifle. 'I left the Baath party five years ago,' she said from her hospital bed. 'But they have been threatening me and following me. I was wearing a full veil when they shot me. I want to take my sons and leave Iraq.' She was unaware that her two boys had already died from their wounds.

It was as if this wanton ruthlessness communicated itself to the new occupiers of Iraq. In May 2004, television stations around the world received terrifying footage from a camera mounted beside the 30 mm cannon of a US Apache helicopter on patrol over central Iraq on 1 December the previous year. The pictures recorded the last moments of men who might – or might not – have been insurgents planning an ambush on a country road close to an American checkpoint. A lorry and a pick-up come into view as well as a man, apparently unaware of the hovering helicopter.

One of two helicopter pilots is heard to say: 'Big truck over here. He's having a little pow-wow.' The driver of the pick-up takes out a tube-shaped object that may be a rocket-propelled grenade launcher from the vehicle and runs into a field to the left of the screen. He drops the object in the field and returns to the truck. The pilot then radios: 'I got a guy running, throwing a weapon.' Another voice then instructs him: 'Engage – smoke him.' At this point, a tractor arrives close to where the man dropped the object and one of the Iraqis approaches the driver. The camera registers the bullets hitting the first man. The pilot then opens fire on the truck, before waiting to see if he's hit the last of the three men. The third man is then seen crawling from his cover beneath the blazing truck, obviously wounded. The pilot reports back: 'Wait. Someone wounded by the truck.' An officer responds: 'Hit him – hit the truck and him. Go forward.' The pilot fires and the man is vaporised within a second. Deliberately shooting a wounded man is a war crime under the Geneva Conventions.

The occupation authorities in Baghdad had chosen to keep this incident secret; watching the video footage, it was easy to see why.

American and British personnel disenchanted by the now disastrous Blair–Bush adventure in Iraq tried for weeks to persuade Western television stations to broadcast the video, which they regarded as shameful and illegal. Yet despite the efforts of reporters in both Baghdad and New York, most television editors chose to censor the tape on the grounds that the pictures were too terrible to show.*

Each time I returned to Iraq, it was like finding a razor blade in a bar of chocolate. Outside Iraq, you were told that things were getting better and you started to believe that maybe 'New Iraq' was going to work after all. But each time I returned, I realised the truth; it was the same old Iraq, just a little bit worse than when I left.

How to account for this bloodlust? The Americans assigned culpability to the Iraqis, to their 'native' cruelty and 'age-old' antagonisms. I tried to understand this reality by watching the videos taken by the killers to record their own grisly handiwork, a new form of routine that would be enthusiastically followed by Syrian rebels ten years later. I flew to Doha where Ayman Gaballah, the deputy chief editor of Qatar's Al Jazeera satellite channel, showed me those tapes which even his television station could not bring itself to broadcast.

There is no proof to the claims that Al Jazeera's reporters were ever tipped off about anti-American attacks before they happened, but there is plenty of proof that some things were too awful to see. I was given a seat in the newsroom. On the screen in front of me was a half-naked man, held to the floor while a man in a hood produces a small butcher's knife and slowly carves through the victim's throat, the poor man's shriek of pain dying in froths of blood until his head is eventually torn from his body.

Another tape shows eighteen Iraqi policemen held captive against a demand for the release of Iraqi women prisoners. They stare at the camera hopelessly. The deadline has passed. Al Jazeera aired the initial pictures and the written demands but cut the next scene, which shows the eighteen men trussed up and blindfolded in front of a ditch. A hooded man then fires a pistol into the back of one of their heads and – along with other men off-camera – goes from one body to the next, firing again and again. Some of the victims are still alive, and the

---

* Only Canal Plus in France, ABC in America and the Canadian Broadcasting Corporation had the courage to air the shocking footage.

hooded man goes to each one and fires into their heads. Then, in the background, a bearded youth approaches the camera, holding an Islamic flag. He is singing. I asked the Al Jazeera reporters how humans could commit such atrocities. One suggested that eleven years of UN-imposed sanctions had changed the mentality of Iraqis.

By mid-2008, the refugee statistics had become so stunning that they were almost mundane. Four million of Iraq's 23 million people had fled their homes – more than 1.2 million to Syria, 50,000 to Jordan, 20,000 to the Gulf, 70,000 to Egypt, 57,000 to Iran, up to 40,000 to Lebanon, 10,000 to Turkey. Sweden accepted 9,000, Germany fewer – where an outrageous political debate suggested that Christian Iraqi refugees should have preference over Muslim Iraqis. With its usual magnanimity, George Bush's America had accepted just over 500.

The American commentariat's decision that the Iraqis no longer deserved our Western sacrifices may have started in 2004 when David Brooks announced in the *New York Times* that Shiite extremism was America's principal enemy in Iraq. The US, he wrote, was fighting a battle 'against people who vehemently oppose a democratic Iraq' and America's task was 'to crush those enemies without making life impossible for those who fundamentally want what we want'. In this context, Muqtada al-Sadr was a 'hotheaded murderer who terrorises people wherever he goes'. 'The terrorists are enemies of civilisation,' Brooks concluded. 'They must be defeated.'

This chimed with the US occupation line that Sadr was a 'firebrand' who must be 'arrested or killed'. That this nationalist, whose 70,000-strong Mahdi Army would soon control half of Baghdad, could be pronounced an enemy of the United States showed just how frustrated Washington's policies had become. But when Thomas Friedman announced in the *New York Times* that America's real threat in Iraq was not the mythical WMD but PMD, 'people of mass destruction', he found a new enemy: not the Shias, but the Sunnis.

According to Friedman, UN sanctions had 'pulverised' and 'chewed up' Iraqis. This and 'Saddamism' had driven Iraqi youth to Wahhabism. If Friedman had correctly identified the effect of UN sanctions as an invisible wound in Iraq's population, he naturally made no reference to America's primary role in their imposition.

On 3 November articles appeared in the *New York Times* and *USA Today*, the first by David Brooks, the second by Ralph Peters, a post-war US military intelligence officer in Germany. Brooks wrote of 'a complete social disintegration' in Iraq. American blunders accepted, this break-up had been 'exacerbated by the same old Iraqi demons: greed, blood lust and a mind-boggling unwillingness to compromise for the common good, even in the face of self-immolation'.

Peters was more to the point. He had supported Saddam's removal, he wrote, because, 'based on firsthand experience I was convinced that the Middle East was so politically, socially, morally and intellectually stagnant that we had to risk intervention'. Only a military coup, he declared, 'could hold the artificial country together'. America 'did give the Iraqis a unique chance to build a rule-of-law democracy. They preferred to indulge in old hatreds, confessional violence, ethnic bigotry and a culture of corruption ... Arab societies can't support democracy as we know it.' The violence on Baghdad's streets was a symptom 'of the comprehensive inability of the Arab world to progress in any sphere of organised human endeavour'.*

This was the vital political traction that American tanks needed to thrash their way out of the desert sands of Iraq. America had done its best for a benighted people, but they were not grateful. The phrase 'democracy as we know it' gave the game away. Iraq had to become a Western country to qualify for US support.

Five years after the first Battle of Fallujah, a remarkable account of civilian bloodshed there was published by Ahmed Mansour, an Al Jazeera journalist who – unlike his 'embedded' Western colleagues – endured the conflict among the people of the city. Mansour helped a frightened old woman and her grandchildren onto a truck that was leaving Fallujah. Within two hours, the vehicle was hit by an American airstrike. To Mansour's horror, the refugees he had just seen were brought to the hospital in pieces. 'It was impossible to tell which torn limb belonged to which dead body, and the bodies were piled atop each other in a sickening mass of blood and flesh,' he wrote. 'Even now, as I sit typing this paragraph, it is impossible to remember these fallen children without weeping.'

---

* Another of Peters' conclusions was that 'if the Arab world and Iran embark on an orgy of bloodshed, the harsh truth is that we may be the beneficiaries'. Since the last such 'orgy' – the 1980–88 war between the Gulf-backed Baathist regime in Iraq and post-revolutionary Iran – secured Saddam's role as the all-powerful leader of the Arab world, this was a pretty dodgy thesis.

2

The Age of the Dictator

Evil, if rightly understood,
Is but the Skeleton of Good
Divested of its Flesh and Blood.

John Byrom (1692–1763) from *On the Origin of Evil*

Squinting against the scornful sun of the Egyptian Western Desert, Lieutenant General Robert Charles Kingston looked like a soldier in an old war movie. He had a thick face, a square jaw and slightly hooded eyes and he punched out his words like a prizefighter. 'If the Russians or any other enemy or potential enemy want to take on the United States,' he told us, 'I'm going to give them that opportunity.' He spoke in a monotone, breaking up his sentences into three-word segments as if he was dictating messages over a field radio. He had commanded two brigades in Vietnam and looked like a man who had lost little sleep over the final result of America's far eastern adventure.

Now the Americans were losing again. Two years before Kingston's appearance in Egypt, America's 'policeman of the Gulf', the Shah of Iran, had been dethroned in a bloody revolution led by Iranian Islamists and their secular allies. Only a few months later, Soviet president Leonid Brezhnev, fearful that his country's communist satrapy in Kabul might be overthrown by Muslim mujahidin, sent the Soviet army into Afghanistan; President Jimmy Carter's response was a pathetic refusal to participate in the Moscow Olympic Games. Saddam Hussein, with America's encouragement, had invaded Iran scarcely a year before General Kingston's proclamation, but his legions had floundered in the deserts east of the Tigris.

Even more devastating for the US, Egyptian president Anwar Sadat – America's new friend in the Middle East – had just been assassinated by Islamists from within the same Egyptian army that was now staging manoeuvres alongside General Kingston's Rapid Deployment Joint Task Force, which was supposed to spread confidence among the pro-Western nations of the Middle East that America would defend both its interests and its friends. The RDF showed that America was ready to fight, but its specific tasks were less clear. Was it there to defend Arab states from Soviet aggression or, as some Arab leaders feared, to involve them in a conflict with the Soviets if American interests were attacked?

Great armies were training in the Western Desert and there were many remarks of approval from President Ronald Reagan's men, until the Egyptian soldiers charged in a tide across the desert floor. *Allahu akbar*, they were screaming. God is greater. Kingston and his colleagues fell silent. For all the sophistication of their communications, the brilliance of their practice bombing runs and their helicopter attacks, they had not witnessed anything like this before.

Caspar Weinberger, Reagan's defense secretary, did not hide US intentions. Although he talked of the Soviet threat to the Gulf, he referred specifically to the need to 'defend the access routes' that the Soviets might use in a further invasion of the Muslim world. And a glance at the map suggested, despite the Soviet hardware stored in Libya, that a Soviet attack was unlikely to arrive by way of Egypt.

A more intriguing clue came in a few seconds of film that were included in a documentary about the RDF shown to us in Cairo. Produced by the US government, it contained a graphic illustrating the invasion routes which the Soviets might take to reach the Gulf. Three bright-red arrows moved south from the headquarters of the twenty-two Soviet divisions which the Americans believed were stationed along the western Iranian border, sweeping into Iran from newly occupied Afghanistan and south from the Soviet–Iranian frontier east of the Caspian. One arrow then cut through Iranian Kurdistan and plunged southwards through Iraq towards the Iraqi port of Basra.

Nor was there much doubt that the US was preparing for the possibility of fighting its enemies north of the Gulf. This was why Arab nations had been so slow to express their enthusiasm for the presence of American troops or to offer them bases. The Americans said they would only come to the aid of countries which sought their assistance, but was Iran likely to ask for help from Washington? Those Arab leaders who believed in the Plot were also well aware that in the worst conflict scenario, the Americans would form a front line against the Soviets down the Iraq–Iranian frontier, along the very line now formed by the battlefronts of the Iraq–Iran war. In these circumstances, Iraq might well be asked to fight on the American side.

On 27 February 1982, less than three months after the US was demonstrating its military determination to support its Arab 'friends' in the Egyptian desert, Washington removed Iraq from its list of 'terrorist states'. By November 1983, the White House was being briefed by the State Department about Iraq's 'almost daily use' of chemical weapons, but even this would not put Iraq back on the hateful 'terrorism' list. Howard Teicher, a staff member of the US National Security Council responsible for the Middle East and political-military affairs, accompanied Reagan's special envoy Donald Rumsfeld to Baghdad to meet Saddam in 1983, three years after the start of Iraq's war with Iran. 'CIA director William [Casey] personally spearheaded the effort to ensure that Iraq had sufficient military weapons, ammunition and vehicles to avoid losing the Iran–Iraq war,' Teicher would testify in 1995.

Similar strategic military advice, Teicher said, was passed to Saddam 'through various meetings with European and Middle Eastern heads of state'. Teicher was present at many of these meetings, including between George Bush Senior and the Egyptian president, Hosni Mubarak. However, in case the war continued, Washington's assistance was to become even more lethal for Iran's front-line soldiers. A 1994 US Senate report by Donald Riegle was to reveal that the US licensed batches of anthrax bacilli and other biological agents for export to Saddam 'in the 1980s'. Years afterwards, the British Foreign Office was to claim that no such export occurred, later stating that such exports were 'consistent with the requirements of legitimate scientific research'.

This was also a lie. The destinations for the anthrax bacilli listed in the Riegle report included the Iraq Atomic Energy Agency and the Iraq Atomic Energy Commission – Iraq's nuclear weapons research facility.* These were the biological 'weapons of mass destruction' that Bush and Blair would use as part-excuse for the 2003 invasion of Iraq. A year before, in a speech speedily forgotten at the time, Bush had also blamed Saddam for the attempted assassination of his father.

An earlier invasion – Israel's 1982 assault on Lebanon – had itself been prompted by an attempt on the life of the Israeli ambassador to the United Kingdom. Shlomo Argov was shot and seriously wounded outside the Dorchester Hotel, and Israel immediately blamed Yasser Arafat's PLO. Arafat condemned the attack, since he knew – as Israel itself was well aware – that the PLO, whose destruction was Israel's primary aim in Lebanon, had nothing to do with the attempt on Argov's life. For it was Sabri Khalil al-Banna, the Palestinian renegade who worked as a mercenary in the Middle East under his patronymic of Abu Nidal, who ordered the ambassador's murder – on the instructions of Saddam Hussein. Saddam wanted to crush his Syrian Baathist rivals by destroying Syria's protectorate in Lebanon† and involving Syrian troops in an all-out war with Israel. For Syria was the only Arab ally of Iran, the Islamic Republic with which Saddam was now in a life-or-death struggle.

In Baghdad, Saddam had nothing to fear. His new American ally was supporting him, and Reagan's decision to 'de-list' Iraq from America's inventory of 'terrorist states' on 27 February 1982 ensured that Saddam could rely on Washington's acquiescence in his immoral war with Iran

---

* Quite apart from the mendacity of its 'dossiers' on Iraq's 'weapons of mass destruction' prior to the 2003 invasion, the British government was to achieve an extraordinary reputation for dishonesty over weapons exported to – or used against – Iraq. In 2011, UK armed forces minister Nick Harvey admitted he misled MPs about a Ministry of Defence review which concluded that DU weapons used by the UK in Iraq were permissible under the Geneva Conventions. The 'review', he later agreed, never took place, but he claimed he had made his statement 'in good faith'. In the 2003 invasion, US and UK forces used at least 142,000 kg of DU, 1,900 kg of it by British Challenger tanks which fired 420 DU rounds.

† Since the 1920s' French mandate for Syria and Lebanon – granted by the League of Nations after the collapse of the Ottoman Empire – Syria had extended its sisterly love to Lebanon, which was administered from Damascus until its recognition as a state, albeit sectarian, during the Second World War. After civil war broke out in 1976, Syrian troops entered Lebanon under the guise of the Palestine Liberation Army (PLA) to suppress the rise of the Palestine Liberation Organization (PLO) and to prevent the disintegration of Lebanon. In 2005, after the assassination of prime minister Rafiq Hariri, the Syrian army was forced to withdraw all its occupying forces from Lebanon.

– and in his equally dirty war against Iraq's majority Shia Muslim community who wanted to kill him. An assassination attempt on Saddam's life by villagers from Dujail, south of Baghdad, had taken place – on 8 July 1982. Saddam had just left Dujail when his convoy was attacked by ten men armed with Kalashnikov rifles. All were killed, whether at the time or later.

Rumsfeld's visit to Baghdad on 19 December 1983, to ensure Saddam of Washington's continued support, gave the Iraqi dictator a free hand to deal as ferociously as he wished with Iraqi fifth columnists without fear of American complaints. The system of patriarchal lineage enabled the secret police to trace the male line of entire families and then liqui-date them. Their womenfolk were tortured and often raped. By the time of Rumsfeld's second visit to Iraq in 1984 – to assure foreign minis-ter Tariq Aziz that official US criticism of Saddam's use of gas against Iranians would not interrupt America's military support – the Dujail detainees were already dying under torture.* In 1985, with at least forty Shiites having died in detention or during interrogation, another nine-ty-six rebels were sentenced to death and executed. Washington uttered not a whimper.

In 2008, I would be invited to a Gulf state to meet an analyst who had helped to translate the incriminating court documents which sealed the fate of Saddam at his 2005 trial. Yet eighteen months after Saddam's execution, this man asked me not to reveal his identity because he feared for his life in the 'new' Iraq. We met in a restaurant, where he produced a black folder containing the 1982 secret police documents compiled for Saddam himself; it was frightening, fearful testament to the earnestness and cruelty of the mukhabarat security services in their hunt for the men who had plotted to assassinate Saddam outside Dujail.

A sheaf of papers from Saddam's 'Regime Crimes Liaison Office' listed the accused and their menfolk. It was an object lesson in how to destroy an Iraqi tribal family. Of the al-Tayyar sub-tribe of the Abu Haider tribe of Dujail, for example, there was a great-grandfather called Abdullah with three children – Asad,

---

* Readers who can stomach the details of these interrogations and executions should read the judgment of the Dujail trial at the Iraqi High Tribunal – albeit in an imperfect English translation – in Case No 1/C1/2005 of the tribunal's archives.

Mohammed and Suheil – who themselves had nine children. Only one male issue of Abdullah's entire family would escape Saddam's executioners.

But these were just the male children of one family. In 1982, Saddam's murderers were after many more, as the following document made clear:

The Arab Socialist Baath Party
One Arab Nation
With an Everlasting message

Salutations:

The families opposing the party and the revolution are the families of the criminals who are dead, or sentenced, or those who have escaped justice because they are members of the al-Dawa party. Detailed reports have been sent previously to the head of the [Baath] party through the party command chain, and are as follows: the family of the dead criminal Latif Abbas Mohammed and his brother are affected. Also the criminal Raid Said Juwad and his sisters and brothers. His father and mother are originally from the al-Najaf governorate. Also the dead criminal Abbas Habib Jaafar. Also the family of the dead criminal Khalil Jamil Ayoub whose brother Hassan Mohammed Abdallah is presently a deserter [who is] a [military] warrant officer, and his family are opposed to the [Baath] party and revolution. His son killed the student Imad Kamil, the head of the Student National Union in al-Dujail Secondary [School].

May you persist with the struggle for the everlasting message of our nation.

[Signed] Comrade Mohammed Ibrahim Darwish
8 July 1982

At the end of one letter from the Baath party's higher command was the note: 'Deal with them in the usual way.' It was in the handwriting of Barzan al-Tikriti, Saddam's half-brother and a leader of the Iraqi mukhabarat.

After the fall of Saddam's regime, it was easy to say that the Iraqi dictator had lived in an illusory world. But until the war with Iran began to suck away the treasure of the one land in the Arab world with both oil and water, he had used Iraq's wealth wisely. The country had the highest educational standards of the Arab world, the finest health-care, the most liberal laws on women, among the best transport communications in the Middle East.

If America could ignore Saddam's terrifying human rights abuses and his use of chemical warfare after his unprovoked invasion of Iran, why should they care if the dictator's dispute over Kuwait's 'theft' of Iraqi oil led to the annexation of the tiny emirate? In this context, the conversation between Saddam and US ambassador to Iraq April Glaspie prior to the 1990 invasion of Kuwait looks quite different. For years, the world was led to believe that Glaspie told Saddam on 25 July 1990 that the US government 'doesn't interfere in border disputes' between Arab states. According to one semi-official transcript published by the *New York Times*, Glaspie told Saddam that the US had 'no opinion on your Arab-Arab conflicts, like your border disagreement with Kuwait', a remark which Saddam supposedly regarded as an expression of America's indif-ference. Iraqi troops crossed the border on 2 August that year.

Diplomats who feel they have been misquoted should speak out at once to set the record straight, but Glaspie remained silent for eighteen years. Long retired and now living in South Africa, her interview with the Saudi-owned daily *Al-Hayat* was as detailed as it was revealing, but it was largely ignored.

According to Glaspie, her Baghdad meeting with Saddam on 25 July 1990 provided an opportunity to repeat her instructions from the State Department, 'the essence of which was: "Do not occupy Kuwait, keep your hands off that country."' Iraqi foreign minister Tariq Aziz and two aides were in the room 'to note down the minutes of the meeting'. Saddam, Glaspie recalled, 'started by informing me about the petulant behaviour of the Kuwaitis'. She feared he was about to claim Kuwait as a province of Iraq, but she denied telling him that America did 'not interfere in border disputes between Arab states'. This, she said, was 'a fabrication concocted by Tariq Aziz ... What I did say was that "He was not to interfere in Kuwait or anywhere else."'

If Glaspie's version of the meeting is taken at face value, it appears that she did her best to convince an increasingly delusional dictator that he should not invade Kuwait, and that America would go to war if he did. But placed in its recent historical context, a quite different story emerges. On her own evidence, Glaspie warns Saddam not to invade Kuwait – but she does not tell him that America would go to war to liberate the emirate. She says that she 'never gave Saddam the impression we would not intervene in a border dispute', but this double negative – assuming Glaspie's words were correctly reported – was unlikely to have a brutal dictator shaking in his shoes.

Her contention that she 'was unable to convince Saddam that we would carry through what we warned we would' is ridiculous; Washington had made no such specific threat. The US had privately tolerated – indeed, encouraged – Saddam's use of gas against Iran, helped him to develop biological weapons and shown not the slightest interest in the vicious suppression of his internal enemies. Why on earth would America 'intervene' now?

Saddam's invasion and occupation of Kuwait, the arrival of US troops in Saudi Arabia and the Saudi monarchy's refusal to allow Osama bin Laden to liberate Kuwait with Arab fighters would profoundly change the history of the Middle East and the world. America's subsequent betrayal of the Iraqi Shiite uprising against Saddam would be followed by a purgatory of sanctions which smothered the Iraqi population in a cloak of poverty, disease and death on an even more unprecedented scale.*

For Iraq's retreat from Kuwait was not to bring UN sanctions to an end. These were now to be continued until Saddam himself was deposed or forced into exile. Robert Gates, later Barack Obama's defense secretary, announced that Saddam was 'discredited and cannot be redeemed ... All possible sanctions will be maintained until he is gone.' Thus Saddam Hussein, whose survival had been all-important

---

* The American official asked to calculate the Iraqi death toll of the Kuwait invasion and Saddam's defeat was Beth Osborne Daponte, a demographer at the US Census Bureau. She estimated that 158,000 Iraqis – half of them women and children – died in the war for Kuwait and its aftermath. Daponte was dismissed when she decided to publish her research and was smeared by her supervisor for using 'false information' and exhibiting 'untrustworthiness and unreliability'. Daponte's sin may have been her inclusion of deaths during the Shia and Kurdish rebellions which occurred after Washington had declared the war over. She was reinstated only after the American Civil Liberties Union threatened legal action.

to Washington only four years earlier, must be destroyed. No longer feted by the US, which had fed him the biological seeds for his new weapons. He was 'discredited' not for his unprovoked aggression against Iran, nor for his use of chemicals against Iran or its Kurdish Iraqi allies in Halabja, nor indeed for his barbarous treatment of the Shiites of Dujail, but because, for the Americans, he had invaded the wrong country.

So appalled were they by this civilian torment, successive UN humanitarian coordinators in Iraq, Denis Halliday and Hans von Sponeck, resigned within two years of each other. Halliday was later to refer to the post-1991 sanctions as a 'genocide'. Meanwhile, Arab nations that had relied upon Saddam to defend them from Shiite Iran in the 1980s were told by the Americans that they now faced threats from Saddam himself.

Saddam had overcome his domestic enemies when the Americans and British allowed him to suppress the uprisings that followed his retreat from Kuwait. Neither the Saudis nor the newly liberated Kuwaitis were prepared to tolerate a Shiite Iraqi state on their northern border; this awful prospect would be postponed until after the US invasion of Iraq in 2003. But the atrocities which Saddam's army were permitted by the West to commit against the Shiites enraged a population that would be expected twelve years later to welcome the Anglo-American invaders. During the massacre of Shiites, 'Allied' troops were still on Iraqi soil, one exile Iraqi students group was to complain, 'and they did nothing to prevent it. The Allies betrayed the Iraqi people, a betrayal that will be forever engraved on the minds of Iraqi civilians.' The Americans ignored such sentiments.

As the years passed, US and RAF aircraft, supposedly protecting Iraqis living beneath 'no-fly' zones but in reality using this tactic to bite away at Iraq's remaining military facilities, bombed the country almost daily. Any memory of our military pact with Saddam in the 1980s had now been wiped out. 'Allied' officials now talked of the need to 'degrade' Saddam, his weapons of mass destruction and the infrastructure we had promised not to hit. In a six-week period in April to May 1999, Amnesty International was to report the death in air strikes of twenty Iraqi civilians, including women and children. In August of that year, Amnesty recorded another fifty civilian dead and scores more injured in US and UK raids. In a house in Jassan in southern Iraq, fifteen members of the same family were reported killed when a missile struck their home on 17 August. Iraqi civilians living near the protective 'no-fly' zones were being killed by the same American and British aircraft that were supposed to protect them.

As his enemies starved and de-medicated Iraqis to death, Saddam displayed the familiar paranoia of every autocrat: suspicion and love. And in the summer of 2002, there was in Baghdad a man of such ruthlessness that details of his interrogation were sent directly to Saddam. As mentioned earlier, Abu Nidal had served Saddam most loyally by organising an attack on the Israeli ambassador to London in 1982. As a result – and as Saddam hoped – Israel invaded Lebanon, and struck at the 40,000-strong army which Syrian president Hafez al-Assad maintained in his vassal state.

He chose the right man to start a war. Abu Nidal was a gun for hire, a mercenary who had ordered the killing of Jews in an Istanbul synagogue, of Palestinians close to Yasser Arafat and of passengers at Rome and Vienna airports, along with hundreds of members of his own assassination teams accused of betrayal. Abu Nidal's men staged attacks in twenty countries over more than three decades. His victims included Salah Khalaf (Abu Iyad), Arafat's deputy and head of intelligence, who had opposed Saddam's invasion of Kuwait and argued with the Iraqi dictator. According to the writer Patrick Seale, the internal revolutions within Abu Nidal's 'Fatah Revolutionary Council' ended in mass graves in Lebanon and Libya.

If Abu Nidal could start a war, however, he could not avoid his master's fury a year later. After his 'Revolutionary Council' had criticised Jordan and the United Arab Emirates in 1983 – both major supporters of Saddam's war against Iran – Abu Nidal was summarily expelled from Iraq by Tariq Aziz. A Palestinian present at that meeting later described how Aziz told Abu Nidal that 'President Saddam has come to the conclusion that you have become a dangerous burden to us ... you are to leave Iraq the moment you step out of this door.' But in 2002, as America promised to dethrone him, Saddam learned that Abu Nidal had returned to Baghdad. The first Washington learned of this was on 21 August that year, when Iraq released photographs of the killer's body, shot in the head, lying in a hospital bed with blood soaking through the pillow, even a copy of a forged Yemeni passport. Suicide, they said. Tahir Haboush, the head of Iraqi intelligence, stated that Abu Nidal had used the document to enter Iraq illegally via Iran in 1999. But it all seemed far too neat. How could anyone enter a police state like Iraq and not be discovered for three years? And the suggestion that Iraqi secret police had been taking Abu Nidal to court when he asked to go home and change, shooting himself while the cops were waiting patiently downstairs, was surely incredible.

George Bush was to use Saddam's reported – but non-existent – relationship with al-Qaeda as one of the many specious reasons for his 2003 invasion, along with Iraq's equally mythical possession of WMD. Now Western reports suggested that Iraqi security police had themselves shot Abu Nidal because his presence had become an embarrassment. The White House was quick to see an opportunity. Abu Nidal, its spokesman announced, had been given 'safe haven' in Iraq, a fact which demonstrated Saddam's links to 'global terror'.

But Iraqi security police files show clearly that Iraq's intelligence operatives genuinely believed that the Palestinian assassin had been working for the Americans as well as Egypt and Kuwait on the eve of the Bush–Blair invasion; he had been trying to find evidence linking Saddam to al-Qaeda.* The Iraqi papers suggest that Abu Nidal did indeed kill himself after confessing to the 'treacherous crime of spying against this righteous country'.

Did Abu Nidal really shoot himself? Or was he 'suicided' on the instructions of Saddam? We shall never know, but it is possible that he decided to die by his own hand rather than endure the sadistic executioners of Abu Ghraib.

After punishment came that moment for deep affection which Saddam craved. On 16 October 2002, the Iraqi government announced that the nation had re-elected him for another seven-year term – with 100 per cent of the vote. The White House's po-faced reaction that this was 'not a serious vote' missed the point. Izzat Ibrahim, the vice-chairman of the party's Revolutionary Command Council, acknowledged that 'someone who does not know the Iraqi people, he will not believe this percentage, but it is real … We don't have opposition in Iraq.' The result was certainly better than the 96.3 per cent of the vote that

---

* The *Washington Post* had already reported in 1999 that CIA agents had infiltrated the UN's arms inspectors to spy on Saddam's intelligence services – at least two years before Abu Nidal's 1999 return to Baghdad.

Saddam's fellow dictator in Egypt gained for his third six-year term in 1993 – for which Hosni Mubarak was congratulated by the White House.

Nor did the people's trust in Saddam go unrewarded. In return for a 100 per cent vote, they would receive a 100 per cent liberation of all prisoners in Iraq's hell-hole prisons. Every inmate would be amnestied – save for those who had spied for America, Saddam decreed.

In the aftermath of the invasion a few months later, we journalists got our hands on videos of some of the most pornographic violence in Saddam's Iraq any of us could stomach. One tape showed his security police whipping and beating near-naked Shiite prisoners in the court-yard of their headquarters. The men are covered in blood and excrement, screaming and whimpering. They are kicked and their testicles are crushed and pieces of wood forced between their teeth as they are pushed into sewers and clubbed around the face.

These videos showed that there were spectators, uniformed Baathists, present during the torture of these poor men. I showed a few seconds of these films at lectures I gave in Britain, Ireland and the United States in 2003 and some members of the audience left, nause-ated. Who were these videos made for? For Saddam? For the victims' families? Or for humiliation, so that these men would know forever – if they survived – that their suffering had been recorded. Within two years, of course, we would be viewing photographs and videos of sadism and humiliation from perhaps the very same penitentiary; the victims would again be Iraqis, but the torturers would be American.

By the time George W. Bush decided to invade Iraq, Washington's alliance with Saddam had been erased from institutional memory. While European leaders bamboozled their people and parliaments into war, the would-be invaders set off to hoodwink the Arabs as well. They were out of luck. Perhaps Arabs have a longer historical memory, or maybe their leaders spent so much time hoaxing their own populations that they could identify the same tactic.

Arabs possessed a shrewd and unsettling idea of what the future held, both for the Americans in their forthcoming occupation of Iraq and for the rest of the Middle East. More than 70 per cent of Arabs in Egypt, Jordan and Lebanon believed that an American invasion would increase 'terrorist operations' and more than 15 per cent said that there would be an attack on American forces within days.

In Lebanon, where 241 American servicemen had been killed in the suicide bombing of the US Marine headquarters on 23 October 1983, a staggering 81.5 per cent of respondents stated that an Iraq war would increase 'terrorist operations'. In Egypt, respondents were asked to assume that America had succeeded in overthrowing Saddam's regime and established a new pro-American Iraqi government. When asked, 34.9 per cent said there would be attacks on American troops 'within days', 17 per cent 'within weeks' and 10.9 per cent 'within months'. Reflecting the exact opposite of Bush's stated objective, Arabs believed an Iraqi invasion would have little effect on stemming 'terrorism'. For the most part, their opinions were spot on.

The Beirut poll company's director, Jawad Adra, said the figures clearly showed the degree of Arab opposition and the disappointment with US policy in the Middle East. 'They cannot isolate any issue from the bias which is detected in US policy on the Palestinians,' he told me. Vice President Dick Cheney would be told precisely the same when he sought Arab support for an attack on Iraq in the week before the invasion – not that he paid any attention. In every Arab capital he visited, Cheney was told to turn his attention to the bloody Palestinian–Israeli war and to forget the 'axis of evil' until Bush brought his Israeli allies into line. All Cheney's efforts to pretend that the conflict in the West Bank, Gaza and Israel was separate from Iraq failed. One Saudi newspaper carried a front-page article condemning US policy in the region – almost unheard of in the Kingdom – while foreign minister Prince Saud al-Faisal told the Americans they could not use the vast Prince Sultan Air Base in the Kingdom for any war against Baghdad.

Cheney's press handlers repeatedly claimed that Arab leaders privately gave their support to an American strike on Iraq. Gulf Arab officials called Western journalists to insist that this was untrue; what Arab kings and princes said in private was exactly what they said in public: an invasion of Iraq would prove a disaster. Several times, Cheney was told that if Saddam was overthrown, Iraq could break apart, with incalculable effects on its neighbours.

Repeatedly, Cheney was asked for evidence that Saddam was involved in 9/11, so he invented a new dogma for the Arabs: 'The United States will not permit the forces of terror to gain the tools of genocide,' he promised. The Arabs asked themselves what this new

'genocide' was supposed to be. Were UN sanctions not already inflicting a 'genocide' on Iraqis?

Cheney's 'dark side' of the war on terror, the institutionalised US
torture and murder of its enemies, shamed his country even before
Saddam was captured in Iraq. But there were weird parallels between
the Bush administration and Saddam. Both believed that they were
loved – Cheney by his allies, Saddam by his people. And both intimidated their populations: Bush by panicking Americans about the terror
to come and Saddam with his equally terrifying secret police.

Post invasion, the American military in Iraq covered their retreats and
defeats in verbal trash. It was a 'slight uptick', Brigadier General Mark
Kimmitt assured us. Not a sudden wave of violence, not even a 'spike'
– another of the general's favourite expressions. Later, we would be
introduced to the 'surge', which became an entire military strategy. A
'surge' was a positive word; it represented an unstoppable tide. In reality, a 'surge' meant reinforcements – extra troops that are only sent
when an army is in trouble.

Our hands grew numb recording all this – the Five o'Clock Follies.
From the hot, dangerous streets of Baghdad with their twelve-hour
electricity cuts and two-mile petrol queues and their gunfire we made
our way each week through palisades of concrete drums, US army
checkpoints and searches, into a vast air-conditioned conference centre,
a cavernous Saddamite structure once used for presidential summits,
where General Kimmitt proved that things were not as bad as we
might think.

This macabre weekly ritual was enacted in the 'Green Zone', in
which imperial life was endured amid rose gardens, swimming pools
and bars – all dominated by Saddam's massive presidential palace with
its domes and marble columns. Even the triumphal entrance arch,
guarded by concrete walls thirty feet high and squads of American
soldiers, spoke more of Lutyens and New Delhi than the 'New Iraq'.
Inside the echoing banqueting halls, Bush's vision of a perfect Middle
East future was made manifest. The new US embassy would be here in
this vast compound, the largest on earth, constructed in cosy proximity
to the offices of the soon-to-be 'sovereign' Iraqi government.

Next to Kimmitt on that lacklustre day in 2004 stood the spectral
figure of Dan Senor, spokesman for the 'Coalition Provisional

Authority' who with his unsmiling demeanour resembled the kind of doctor who quietly advises his patients to settle their affairs.

But this was Good News Week. US proconsul Paul Bremer – head of the CPA – had been discussing the Iraqi Ministry of Education's 2005 budget and attended a 'town hall' meeting of Iraqi schoolchildren. The same Iraqi ministry had been holding a symposium of 200 Iraqi civil and religious leaders on the development of the educational system, and fifty-six kilometres of rail track was being upgraded between Basra and Umm Qasr. American troops were 'continuing to conduct precision operations against anti-Coalition elements and enemies of the Iraqi people'. This sounded positively Soviet.

There is a whole school of literature on the military excuses for this war and its awful cost in human lives. The American preparation for the 2003 invasion and the early days of the occupation were, in Berkeley journalism professor Mark Danner's expression, 'a war of imagination'. Americans illegally seized Iraq and slaughtered thousands, and then declared it liberated and set up an occupation authority – whose arrogance emboldened a resistance movement which began even before US forces reached Baghdad. In Danner's words, the Americans 'put their faith in ideology and hope – in the dream of a welcoming landscape, magically transformed'. Right-wing American intellectuals concluded that 'Baathism was an Arab form of fascism transplanted to Iraq'.

In the minds of Bremer and his army of bureaucrats and military acolytes, the search for Saddam and his two sons, Uday and Qusay, assumed an importance totally out of proportion to any results their capture or killing might bring. They were the Frankensteins of Iraq; no crime was too terrible for them, yet to compare Saddam with Hitler was to misunderstand Saddam's role in Arab history. Baathism existed long before Saddam, and the autocracy he ruled was the product rather than the cause of Iraq's dysfunctional politics.

Yet the Americans set after Saddam and his sons with a vengeance which had something in common with Saddam's own frenzy to cut down the patrilineal inheritance of the Shiites of Dujail. Not long before Kimmitt let loose his definition of 'terrorism', Lieutenant Colonel Steve Russell of the US 4th Infantry Division claimed he had found enough weapons in the northern Iraqi city of Tikrit, the tribal home of Saddam, to launch fifty guerrilla attacks. 'They are not moving weapons here,' Russell said. 'This is the head of the snake.' A week later, they captured the snake itself.

The destruction of Saddam's family had begun almost five months earlier, when Uday and Qusay were given away by friends while hiding in a villa in Mosul. Uday, the debauched playboy, and his brother, Special Republican Guard supervisor Qusay, were betrayed on the evening of 20 July, and 200 US troops, including Special Forces and CIA agents from the so-called 'Task Force 20', stormed the house next morning. The brothers fired back with automatic rifles, as did Qusay's fourteen-year-old son Mustafa. The Americans aimed two TOW anti-armour missiles into the house and called up an OH-58 Kiowa helicopter to shoot a rocket into the building. 'Task Force 20' was the unit that blasted to death the occupants of a convoy heading for the Syrian border the same month, a convoy whose occupants were meant to include Saddam and his two sons; the victims turned out to be smugglers. American intelligence was also responsible for the air raid on the Saddam villa in the Mansour district of Baghdad at the end of April which was supposed to kill Saddam, Uday and Qusay, but only slaughtered sixteen civilians.

But the 'lion cubs of Iraq' – Saddam's own description of his sons – were indeed killed in the July raid, along with fourteen-year-old Mustafa and a bodyguard. Shiite areas of Baghdad exploded in celebratory automatic rifle fire at the news of the deaths. But how to convince Iraqis that the 'Two Evils' – as *Time* magazine had called them – were really dead? In the mystical world of Saddam the bodies could be those of 'doubles', actors paid to imitate the real caliphs of Iraq.

In the West, the deaths of Uday and Qusay were regarded as proof that America's invasion was to be successful. The dead 'bodyguard' would remain anonymous and the killing of Qusay's son was airbrushed from the story, so all attention was directed at Saddam's sons. But why, I asked General Ricardo Sanchez at his boastful press conference in the Green Zone, could his men not have put the brothers on trial, if only to emphasise the ghastliness of Saddam's rule? Sanchez replied that an officer with a bullhorn had ordered the brothers to give themselves up before military action began. Twice the Americans attempted to storm the upper floor of the villa, receiving four wounded when the occupants fired at them. Yet the Americans were experts in siege techniques. No Iraqi would doubt the truth if

Uday and Qusay emerged with their hands up. But Sanchez agreed that the military preparations for the attack had been intended to 'neutralise the target'.

Arabs have never been squeamish about death. It is we Westerners who agonise over our moral sensitivities at the sight of a mortuary mugshot. I cannot think of an Iraqi who hasn't seen the decapitated victims of air raids and massacres, military corpses torn to pieces by dogs in the deserts of Iraq or the mass graves of Kurdistan. Uday's head, with its bullet wound, might be a little hard to ameliorate, although many Iraqis would like to have fired the fatal shot themselves.

Victors have a habit of showing that their enemies are vanquished. On 25 July, therefore, the Americans followed a Baath party tradition of showing executed enemies on television. Back in 1963, when Abdul Karim Qassem's corpse had been shown on Iraqi screens, the ex-prime minister appeared in black and white, propped up in a chair but very dead. In 2003, it was all in colour. The faces of Uday and Qusay had been carefully reconstructed – their bodies on trolleys, stitched up and with colour injected into their faces – but also very dead. The Americans showed them off for the same reason the Baathists displayed Qassem's riddled body: to persuade the Iraqi people that the old regime was gone.

Only an occupation army could have produced the photographs of the corpses just in time for the one day – Friday, the Muslim sabbath – when there were no Iraqi newspapers to publish them. But after the first day's visit to the morgue by the world's press, the corpses were, so to speak, re-heated for Iraqi consumption. However, a growing number of Iraqi young men were to see in these pictures not the death throes of a corrupt regime but the opportunity to revenge themselves upon the foreigners in Iraq. These men may have hated the sons of Saddam, but every Iraqi understood what these photographs represented: the Saddam-like tradition of destroying a family's male line. This tribal elimination meant that those who had hitherto hesitated to join the resistance to occupation could now commit themselves to a guerrilla war.

Nor did the 'respect' visited upon the cadavers of Saddam's sons apply to other victims of the Americans. Just four days after the deaths of Uday and Qusay, Mohamed Eadem put his key in the padlock of the

Kindi hospital mortuary, placed a tissue over his nose and heaved open the great freezer door to show us two sets of human remains. There on the floor lay a pile of blackened bones and flesh on plastic sheets, the latest victims of the Iraq war. Both men had been shot to death in the Baghdad slums of Hay al-Gailani. Their crime had been to drive into a barbed-wire entanglement on a road where US troops had erected a chicane. 'Failed to stop at a checkpoint' was the official reason given for the deaths, though few could imagine the horror behind those words. The Americans peppered the men's car with bullets. The vehicle burst into flames and the Americans left. For half an hour, the car blazed out of control. Whether the Iraqi occupants had died of their wounds or were burned alive, no one knew.

The people of Hay al-Gailani had to wait for the smouldering car to cool before they could remove the terrible remains from what was left of the front seats. 'There were just bones and flesh,' Eadem said. And of course, there were no identity papers and the number plate had been turned into molten metal, so they hadn't the slightest idea who the dead men were. Four locals from Hay al-Gailani had turned up at the hospital at 10.30 with plastic bags containing the remains. No American troops contacted the mortuary about the identity of the men they had just killed, although somewhere in Baghdad that night there were relatives wondering why these men had not come home.

Onto all this was grafted the illusion of global-led stability. The Polish and Japanese armies would soon be here. Ruud Lubbers of the UN High Commission for Refugees turned up in Baghdad to announce that tens of thousands of Iraqi refugees would return within a year.* Was it safe to come back to Iraq? someone asked. 'Well, we're here,' Lubbers replied, smiling. But even as he left his press conference, the UN radios were crackling with static. A convoy had been attacked on the Hilla road, with one UN Iraqi employee killed. On 16 August, within a month of Lubbers' tepid assurance, the UN headquarters in Baghdad was destroyed by a suicide bomber with its head of mission, Sérgio Vieira de Mello, killed.

---

* At the time, according to Lubbers, there were 204,000 Iraqis in Iran, 300,000 in Jordan, 22,250 in Saudi Arabia, up to 72,000 in Syria, 50,900 in Germany (not to mention 20,000 asylum seekers) and 38,500 in the Netherlands. But millions more Iraqis would be fleeing their country after the invasion.

Saddam's capture in mid-December 2003 – he was discovered in a hole beside the Tigris not far from Ouja, where his sons were buried – instantly transformed the former tyrant into a scraggy, on-the-run bagman. Our television screens showed an unkempt, wild and haunted creature who announced himself to his captors as the 'president of Iraq' but who had chosen to surrender without a fight. No martyrdom on the battlefield would end this man's life. We journalists reported his discovery and climbed into his hiding place, examined his tiny library and his paltry larder. Paul Bremer was beside himself with joy. He did not understand that this was not another 'tipping point', but final confirmation to the resistance that they could fight without fear of Saddam's return.

We all knew how his trial would end. Capital punishment may have offended the sensibilities of the occupiers, but Saddam could not escape death. Yet at the same time, we could not escape Saddam. So powerful was his persona that his capture did not erase his presence.

A few days later, I was covering yet another bombing in the grey winter grime of Baghdad. An office belonging to the Shiite Supreme Council for Islamic Revolution in Iraq had been blown up, with one man killed. The SCIRI was hated by many Sunni Muslims. During the 1980–88 Iran–Iraq war, many Baath party members of the Iraqi army captured by Iranian forces were interrogated and tortured inside Iran by Shiite Iraqi exiles from the SCIRI. There were scores to settle. A gaggle of clerics were standing amid the pile of concrete and yellow bricks. It had been a religious school until one day someone decided to hang up a notice declaring it to be an office of the Badr Brigades, SCIRI's militia. The Iran–Iraq war, arguably the greatest of Saddam's follies, thus continued to exact death.

Saddam's formal interrogation by the FBI began on 7 February 2004. Records of these interrogations were not completely divulged; one background paper was heavily edited and the last interview on 28 June was partially censored. We do not know if these deletions referred to the dictator's close personal alliance with the US in the 1980s.

By June 2004, however, it was time for bread and circuses. The Iraqis, amid mass killings and kidnappings which the Americans appeared unable to suppress, had to be distracted. The trial of the century was about to begin, and the message was simple. Show

Saddam to the Iraqis. Remind them how it used to be. Make them grateful. Make him pay. Charge him before the full majesty of Iraq's new 'democratic' laws. And may George Bush win the next American election in four months' time.

Journalists were expected to turn this into a success story and, sure enough, on 29 June, BBC World Service television told viewers that Saddam's court appearance was 'exactly what Iraqis have been waiting for'. Unfortunately, what Iraqis were 'waiting for' was electricity, security, freedom from crime and genuine elections, rather than the trial of the miserable old murderer.

The first day of Saddam's trial was to be a political rather than a judicial act, a photo op as symbolically important as the pulling down of his statue. More symbolic, however, was the ominous event that occurred at the Iraqi ministry of interior a few hours earlier. The ministry was now under the new and 'sovereign' Iraqi government set up by the Americans. But after dark on 29 June, the US army turned up to raid the ministry. Human rights abuses, they claimed, had been committed in the building. US troops grabbed 146 prisoners and handcuffed a large number of American-paid security staff, including a colonel. Hours later, the cops were released, the prisoners handed back and the police demanded a formal apology, adding that they would go on strike if they didn't get one. 'New Iraq', it seemed, might have characteristics reminiscent of the old one.

Saddam asked if he would have the right to a lawyer before facing what journalists now called 'Iraqi justice'. Salem Chalabi, a close relative of the convicted fraudster and former friend of the Pentagon Ahmed Chalabi, was originally to lead the Iraqi tribunal's work. No surprise, therefore, that Saddam asked for counsel. There was also the little problem of the Iraqi tribunal's judges, all of whom turned out to be lawyers without, apparently, any judicial skills. Many had spent years in exile – the kind with whom a growing number of Iraqis who stayed and endured Saddam's rule were increasingly disenchanted.

Iraqis watched as much of the trial that their occupiers permitted them to see. And there he was. Bags beneath his eyes, beard greying, finger-jabbing with anger, Saddam was alert, cynical, defiant, abusive, proud. Yet history must record that America's new 'independent' government in Baghdad gave him an initial hearing worthy of the brutal old dictator himself. He was brought to court in chains and handcuffs. The judge insisted his own name should be kept secret, as were the names of the other judges and the location of the court. There was no defence counsel. For hours, the Iraqi judges managed to censor Saddam's evidence from the soundtrack of the videotaped proceedings – so that the world should not hear the wretched man's defence.

This was the first example of 'new' Iraq's justice system at work – yet the court tapes appeared with the logo 'Cleared by US Military'. So what did the Iraqis and their American mentors want to hide? The voice of the Beast of Baghdad as he turned on the court itself, pointing out that the investigating lawyer had no right to speak 'on behalf of the so-called Coalition'? Saddam's arrogant refusal to take personal responsibility for the 1990 invasion of Kuwait? Or his dismissive response to the mass gassings of Halabja?

Perhaps the Americans, and the Iraqis they had appointed to run the country, were taken by surprise. Saddam, we had been told over previous days, was 'disoriented', 'downcast' and a 'shadow of his former self'. But the moment the mute videotape began to air, the old combative Saddam was evidently still alive. He insisted the Americans were promoting his trial, not the Iraqis.

Watching that face, we asked ourselves how much Saddam had reflected on the crimes with which he was charged. One looked into those big, tired eyes and wondered if he understood pain and grief and sin in the same way as us. And then he talked and the question slid away. He demanded to be introduced to the judge. 'I am an investigative judge,' the young lawyer told him without giving his name. In fact, he was Raid Juhi, a thirty-three-year-old Shia Muslim who had been a judge for ten years under Saddam's own regime, a point he conceded to Saddam later in the hearing. He was also the same judge who had accused the Shia prelate Muqtada al-Sadr of murder the previous April. To no one's surprise, he had been appointed by the former US proconsul in Iraq, Paul Bremer.

Already, one suspected, Saddam had sniffed out what this court represented for him: the United States. 'I am Saddam Hussein, the President of Iraq,' he announced – exactly what he said when American troops dragged him from his hole on the Tigris riverbank. 'Would you identify yourself?' the defendant asked the judge. When Juhi said he represented the coalition, Saddam admonished him. Iraqis should judge Iraqis, but not on behalf of foreign powers, he snapped.

'Remember, you're a judge – don't talk for the occupiers.' Then he turned lawyer himself. 'Were these laws of which I am accused written under Saddam Hussein?' Juhi agreed that they were. 'So what entitles you to use them against the president who signed them?' Here was the old, familiar arrogance, the president who believed that he was above the law.

But then, watching that face with its expressive mouth and bright white crooked teeth, a dreadful thought occurred. Could it be that this awful man knew less than we thought? Could it be that his apparat-chiks and satraps and grovelling generals, even his own sons, kept from him the iniquities of his regime? Might it be possible that the price of power was ignorance, the cost of guilt a mere suggestion that the laws of Iraq were not adhered to as fairly as they might have been?

I think not. I remember how, a decade and a half ago, Saddam asked a group of Kurds whether he should hang 'the spy' Farzad Bazoft and how, once the crowd had obligingly told him to execute the young freelance reporter from the *Observer*, he straightaway ordered his hang-ing. No, I think Saddam knew. I think he regarded brutality as strength, cruelty as justice, death as something to be endured by other people. Of course, there was that smart black jacket, the crisply cleaned shirt, the cheap biro and the piece of folded, slightly torn yellow exercise paper that he withdrew from his inside pocket when he wanted to take notes. 'I respect the will of the people,' he said at one stage. 'This is not a court. It is an investigation.'

The key moment came at this point. Saddam said that the court was illegal because the Anglo-American war which brought it into being was also illegal – it had no backing from the UN Security Council. Then he crouched slightly in his seat and asked with irony: 'Am I not supposed to meet with lawyers? Just for ten minutes?' How many of Saddam's victims must have begged, in the same way, for ten minutes more.

If the secrecies of the court were disturbing, the blatant censorship of the hearings bore an uncanny resemblance to the kind of 'justice' of which Saddam himself once approved. A team of US military officers censored all coverage of the trial's opening day, destroying videotape of Saddam in chains and deleting the recorded legal submissions of eleven senior members of his former regime. An American network cameraman who demanded the return of his tapes said he was told by a US officer: 'They belong to us now. And anyway, we don't trust you guys.'

According to American journalists present at the thirty-minute hearing of Saddam and eleven of his former ministers at Baghdad airport, an American admiral in civilian clothes told camera crews that the judge had demanded there should be no sound recording of the hearing. He ordered crews to unplug their sound wires. Several of the six crews present pretended to obey the US admiral's instruction. 'We learned later,' one of them told me, 'that the judge didn't order us to turn off our sound. The Americans lied – it was they who wanted no sound.'

Initially, crews were told that a US Department of Defense camera crew would provide the sound for their silent tapes. But when CNN and CBS crews went to the former occupation authority headquarters – now officially the US embassy – they found that three US officers ordered the censorship of tape showing Saddam being led into the courtroom with a chain round his waist which was connected to handcuffs around his wrists. The Americans gave no reason for this censorship.

Television stations throughout the world were astonished when the first tapes of Saddam's trial arrived without sound; nor were they told that the Americans censored the material. Judge Raid Juhi wanted the world to hear Saddam's voice. Nevertheless, the Americans also erased the entire audiotape of the hearings of the eleven former Saddam ministers, including that of Tariq Aziz, the former deputy prime minister, and Saddam's cousin, 'Chemical' Ali Hassan al-Majid, accused of gassing the Kurds at Halabja. The US Department of Defense tape of their hearings was taken by the US authorities, so there was now no available audio record of the words of these eleven men, save for the notebooks of 'pool' reporters who were present. Juhi said when he was appointed that he had 'no secrets – a judge must not be ashamed of the decisions he takes'. The Americans thought otherwise.

But they could not decide how to confront the idea of Saddam. They had demonised him, invaded his country, hunted for him, seized him; yet now, the dictator was playing a more important – and more dangerous – role in Iraq than he had before his capture. Saddam's trial was not so much a travesty of justice as a travesty of the accusations which should have been brought against the defendant. In a fair trial, wrote

Gwynne Dyer, the writer who first exposed the enormity of Saddam's use of gas against the Kurds, if Saddam had been charged with the chemical massacre committed at Halabja, it would have been impossible to prevent defence lawyers from pointing out that every US administration from 1980 until 1992 was complicit in his crimes. Yet Saddam's 1980 invasion of Iran and his suppression of the Shiite and Kurdish revolts in 1991 were deemed unworthy of the court's attention. Saddam was instead to be tried for the judicial murder of 148 of his would-be assassins and their family members from Dujail – a heinous offence, but trifling in comparison with his other crimes. This was extraordinary. Saddam would not have to defend himself from any crime if it involved Washington. And so he would not be able to disclose the details of that special relationship in public. The United States could avoid being called to account by tutoring the judges and lawyers involved to concentrate upon a crime committed almost a quarter of a century ago.

There were many other flaws in the trial process: death threats against the jury, hearings disrupted by defence lawyers, witnesses who refused to appear. Rejecting the idea of an international court, the Americans decided that only Iraqis should judge the ex-dictator. More serious was American financial and technical support for the trial, which cost the US more than $100 million for the supply of advisers, lawyers and forensic investigators as well as courtroom construction.* Could such a trial be fair? Yet the shock of Saddam's appearance was for Iraqis swiftly obscured by their own post-invasion agony.

The moment Saddam was sentenced in 2006 – by which time Iraq had turned into hell on earth – the dictator could not be tried for any other crimes. Amnesty International, describing the hearings as 'a fundamentally flawed process', said that Saddam's execution was a foregone conclusion since the Iraqi Appeals Court provided only 'a veneer of legitimacy'. Although hearings into the genocide of the

---

* Eighteen translators had worked on Saddam's trial and they were not all happy at the outcome. 'He was cross-examined on a document that I found,' one of them told me after Saddam's execution. 'It was a four-page paper that summarised the original Iraqi investigations into Dujail. But I had mixed feelings about the trial. We were cross-departmental. There was the FBI, the DEA, US marshals ... The idea was not that it was about bringing justice to the former regime – it was to show Iraqis how justice works, how to set up justice.'

Kurds had begun, their sudden suspension – when Saddam was sentenced for the Dujail killings – was a serious legal setback. Even when three of Saddam's closest aides were sentenced to death in June 2007 for their part in the mass murder of 182,000 Kurds in 1988, a Kurdish parliamentarian, Mahmoud Othman, complained that this trial had also been incomplete, 'since at no moment was it stated who helped Saddam to make chemical weapons, which countries and which companies helped him and used them against us'. Most damning of all was the conclusion of Nehal Bhuta of the University of Toronto who had witnessed the Saddam court proceedings for Human Rights Watch. For him, the trial indicated that 'for the Iraqi government, it was a means of providing revenge rather than real concern about legality or due process'.

Saddam clearly thought the same. When Judge Rauf Abdul Rahman read out the death sentence, he shouted 'Allahu Akbar! Long live Iraq! Long live the Iraqi people! Down with the traitors!' The 'traitors' were the court, the judge and the American occupiers. Sitting only a few feet away, BBC World Affairs Editor John Simpson spotted 'the small smile of triumph' on Saddam's face.

Saddam asked to be executed by firing squad, but the Iraqi judge insisted that he would be hanged. In Washington, George Bush announced that this was 'a good day for the Iraqi people'. Nouri al-Maliki, the Shia Muslim prime minister of a Shia-controlled Iraqi government, foolishly believed that this would mark the end of the Sunni Muslim rebellion.

In the early hours of 30 December 2006, Saddam ate his last meal – chicken and rice with a cup of hot water and honey. He read, so they said, some verses from the Qur'an. Not long before the end, his first wife Sajida spoke to a friend of mine. She had given up hope of any reprieve, she said. 'Whatever could be done has been done – we can only wait for time to take its course.' Shortly before 6 a.m., his American captors handed Saddam to his Iraqi executioners at 'Camp Justice' in the Baghdad suburb of Qazimein. It was a holy day for all Muslims, the beginning of the Eid al-Adha. Was this execution day chosen by chance?

Officially, Saddam was 'submissive'. But a mobile-phone video taken secretly by one of the men who crowded into the execution chamber shows that he did not die like a coward. He shouts: 'Palestine is Arab!'

His hands are already tied and the noose is placed around his neck. He appears to bend forward to help the hooded young man who holds the rope. Saddam is then taunted by his Shiite executioners with the name of the young Shiite prelate Muqtada al-Sadr, whose family the condemned man had once tried to liquidate. Saddam turns on his tormentors. 'Muqtada!' he replies. 'Is this what you call being a man?' A Shiite slogan can be heard – another insult to Saddam – and a man cries: 'Go to hell!' Saddam, well aware of the anarchy across the country, replies: 'The hell that is Iraq?' A voice, identified as that of trial prosecutor Munqith al-Faroun, says: 'Please, stop. The man is facing execution.' As Saddam recites for a second time the shahada – the profession of faith – the trap door fails. Then it springs open and he falls. A loud cracking is the sound of his neck breaking. It becomes Iraq's most popular video. Who could be more deserving of so ignominious an end?

But history will continue to pose another question: what about the other guilty men? No, George Bush is not Saddam. Nor is Tony Blair. But hundreds of thousands were now dead, along with thousands of Western troops, because Bush and Blair – and let us not forget the prime ministers of Spain, Italy and Australia – went to war in 2003 on a potage of lies and with great brutality. We encouraged Saddam's invasion of Iran, we sold him the components of his chemical weapons. But what about the mass killings we perpetrated in 1991 and 2003 with our depleted uranium shells and our 'bunker buster' bombs and our phosphorus, in the murderous post-invasion sieges of Fallujah, and in the disaster of anarchy we unleashed on the Iraqi population in the aftermath of our 'victory'? Who will be found guilty of these crimes?

It is only proper that we should reflect upon the near-unimaginable toll of death by the time of Saddam's hanging. The World Health Organisation and the Iraqi Ministry of Health produced a survey in mid-2006 which suggested that 151,000 died from violence in the fifteen months up to June 2006, but that the real figure might be as high as 223,000. In early 2008, the British-based Opinion Research Business estimated that more than a million Iraqis had been killed since the 2003 invasion, and that a fifth of Iraqi homes had lost at least one member of their family.

Whichever statistics were closer to the truth, the 2003 invasion gave Iraqis neither a 'new' Iraq, nor freedom from fear, nor security;

what it offered was a nominal change of their country's ownership, from Baathist dictatorship to American hegemony, to be imposed as ruthlessly and carelessly and as unfairly as that of their previous dictator.

Saddam's own hegemony had not ended; it was extended. America's war of imagination was blessed with the foundational idea that Saddam represented evil, which must be destroyed as a precursor to a shining new Middle East. But when Iraqis in their millions reflected on their personal tragedies, there wasn't much difference between the violence of the 'evil' age of Saddam and the violence of the age of America. It might be argued that after their sufferings under Saddam, Iraqis could better endure their post-liberation vale of sorrows, but that didn't make the nature of their adversity any more bearable.

A day after his execution, the Americans flew Saddam's body in a US military helicopter to his home town of Ouja, where he was buried in a bleak reception hall close to the cemetery containing his sons Uday and Qusay and his grandson Mustafa.

But in a very literal sense, Saddam now haunted Iraq. Ten days after his execution, the genocide trial of his fellow criminals resumed in Baghdad with Saddam's high-backed black vinyl seat still present. And in a series of scratchy audio recordings played by the prosecutor, Saddam's voice was heard urging his associates to use chemical weapons on the Kurds of northern Iraq, assuring his officials that chemical attacks could kill 'thousands'. Later, Saddam tells Izzat Ibrahim al-Douri, his vice president: 'I don't know if you know this, Comrade Izzat, but chemical weapons are not used unless I personally give the orders.'

Had Saddam been tried for the Halabja gassings, such evidence would have been damning – but it would also have permitted the defendant to discuss America's role in providing military assistance to his regime. The evidence in court was certainly sufficient to hang Ali Hassan al-Majid, Saddam's cousin who had earned the sobriquet 'Chemical Ali'. He would go to the gallows on 25 January 2010.

The menace of the noose cast its shadow across the 'new' Iraq in response to 'terrorism' – not the 'terrorism' that Saddam identified among his enemies, but the 'terrorism' that the Americans and their new Iraqi government faced in their war against insurgents. Brutality and the execution chamber were as much a part of post-Saddam Iraq as they were before. While respecting 'the decision of the Iraqi people' in condemning Saddam, European leaders and other abolitionists went through the emotions of deploring the use of capital punishment. But when others went to the gallows in Baghdad, they were silent. For in the few months before Saddam's hanging, fifty condemned men had been executed in Iraq, one of them hanged twice over because the hangman's cord broke at the first attempt.

By the time US oversight officially vanished with the ascension of the Shia-led 'sovereign' government of Iraq in 2006, the cruel habits of the Saddam era were once more entrenched. One ex-prisoner testified that he had seen fellow inmates who had lost limbs and organs under interrogation. Amnesty announced that more than a thousand Iraqis faced execution on the basis of confessions extracted under torture. Saddam had used the death penalty on a promiscuous scale and the new Iraqi government was desperate to suppress the anarchy that had started in the immediate aftermath of the invasion. The Iraqi Penal Code of 1969 remained in force but additional capital crimes were created under two anti-terrorism laws in 2005, including 'support' for armed groups.

By returning to the state savagery of the past, however, the Iraqi government showed its powerlessness. An insurgency prepared to confront the most powerful nation on earth was not going to be inhibited by a return to Baathist-style repression. Besides, suicide bombers were not to be deterred by the death penalty. Nor was Nouri al-Maliki's government above condemning its own party enemies, however murderous they may have been.

Sickened by the evidence they had amassed and by the frequency of the hangings, several Westerners who visited the execution chambers of the 'new' Iraq spoke to me in the months after Saddam's death. The executions were carried out in secret in a small, cramped cell in the old military intelligence headquarters at Kadhimiya in which Saddam was himself hanged. There is no public record of these killings, but most of the victims were 'suspected' insurgents. The few brave souls who spoke of the prison horror were good men trying to right wrongs amid brutality. These investigators provided only a glimpse into the new Iraqi incubus. Those who told this story of the dark Saddamite side of the post-Saddam world were as depressed as they were filled with hopelessness. They were also fearful; one told me that he might be murdered if his identity was known.

The condemned men in Qazimein were said to include rapists and murderers as well as insurgents. In many cases, it seemed that the Iraqis had no idea of the true identity of their captives. And for years, even the Americans in charge of Abu Ghraib did not know all of their prisoners. Here is the personal testimony to me of a Western official to the Anglo-US Iraq Survey Group seeking the celebrated weapons of mass destruction:

> We used to go to the interrogation rooms at Abu Ghraib and ask for a particular prisoner. After about forty minutes, the Americans brought in this hooded guy, shuffling along, shackled hand and foot. He had a big beard. We asked where he received his education. He repeatedly said: 'Mosul'. Then he said he'd left school at fourteen – remember, this guy is supposed to be a missile scientist. We said:'We know you've got a PhD and went to the Sorbonne – we'd like you to help us with information about Saddam's missile project.' But I said to myself: 'This guy doesn't know anything about fucking missiles.' Then it turned out he had a different name from the man we'd asked for – he'd been picked up on the road four months earlier – he didn't know why … It was a complete farce. The incompetence of the US military was astounding, criminal.

The executions never ended. In just one day in February 2012, Iraq hanged fourteen men, bringing to sixty-five the number sent to the gallows in less than two months. Pleas from the UN human rights office were ignored.

In the summer of 2013, the Iraqi minister of justice admitted that 1,200 people were on death row, seventeen of them women. One of these was Samar Sa'ad Abdullah, a twenty-three-year-old found guilty in 2005 of the murder of her uncle, his wife and one of their children. She claimed her fiancé was guilty but had confessed, she said, because police had beaten her and given her electric shocks. She would still be awaiting the hangman's noose in 2014. Could Saddam have bettered this?

Newspapers now covered mass executions in one or two paragraphs beneath the headline 'News in brief'. On 20 August 2013, for example, an Egyptian newspaper reported the hanging of seventeen men, one of them an unnamed Egyptian citizen, all but one for 'terrorist' convictions, bringing to sixty-seven the number of executed prisoners so far that year. In mid-January 2014, another twenty-six 'terrorists' were executed.*

But if Saddamism survived in Iraq in even more perverted form after its namesake's death, the United States had not. Back in 1981, General Robert C. Kingston had stood in the Egyptian desert and been prepared to go into combat against the Soviet Union. Twenty-six years later, his forces and his beloved 82nd Airborne were losing a war against ill-armed Iraqi insurgents and a plague of Islamist fighters.

In February 2007, one of Iraq's principal insurgent groups – the Sunni Iraqi Islamic Resistance Movement – set out its terms for a ceasefire with its American military enemies. In a statement passed to me in Beirut, Abu Salih Al-Jeelani, one of its military leaders, demanded the cancellation of the new Iraqi constitution – presumably because the document awarded oil-bearing areas of Iraq to Shia and Kurds, but not to the minority Sunni community. Al-Jeelani suggested the UN, the Arab League or the Islamic Conference might lead negotiations with the Americans, adding further demands for the release of 5,000 detainees in Iraqi prisons.

The Americans, of course, would never countenance such demands. But the fact that they could be made demonstrated all the fall from grace of the US as a strategic world power. On 10 February 2007, Bush appointed General David Howell Petraeus as his new commander in Iraq. Petraeus would later become head of CENTCOM, but in the press he was dubbed 'the last chance general'. Robert Kingston, the

---

* Since 2009, international interest in Iraq's human rights record had declined in almost exact proportion to the imminence of US military withdrawal. In early 2010, the *Los Angeles Times* quoted Iraqi officials as saying that more than 100 prisoners were tortured with electric shocks, suffocated with plastic bags or beaten. Five months later, an Amnesty report said that 30,000 prisoners were being held in Iraq without charge or trial, tortured, killed and disappeared. By late January 2012, Human Rights Watch stated that the US government was leaving behind it in Iraq 'a budding police state' which was 'slipping back into authoritarianism'. In fact, the transition from Saddamite barbarity to post-invasion cruelty was almost imperceptible.

general who had been ready to take on the Soviet Union, would die aged seventy-eight in a Virginia hospital barely two weeks after Petraeus' promotion. He was buried at Arlington, unaware that the Middle East was destroying his army's authority in ways he could never have imagined.

3

Walking on Windows

By the North Gate, the wind blows full of sand,
Lonely from the beginning of time until now!
Trees fall, the grass goes yellow with autumn.
I climb the towers and towers to watch out the barbarous
    land:
Desolate castle, the sky, the wide desert …
Bones white with a thousand frosts,
High heaps, covered with trees and grass;
Who brought this to pass?
Who has brought the flaming imperial anger?

'Lament of the Frontier Guard' from *Cathay*
(from the Chinese of Rihaku) by Ezra Pound (1915)

I sit in a dive bar on 44th Street, uncertain how to approach Sue Niederer and Celeste Zappala. They'd been put at the back of the 2005 Veterans' Day parade in New York, with their little crowd of anti-war veterans and their memories of boys who left for Iraq and came back in coffins. Later, I sit between the two women and remember the blood splashed across the road at Khan Dhari and the 82nd Airborne washing away the brains from the highway in central Fallujah. I've seen the corpses. Now here are the mothers.

On 3 February 2004, Sue's son Seth was looking for 'improvised explosive devices' when a booby trap blew up next to him. Sue's voice rises in indignation, angry and brave. 'I remember very clearly my son's last words before he went back after his two weeks' vacation. "I don't know who my enemy is," he said. "It's a worthless, senseless war, a war of religion. We'll never win it." He wasn't killed. He was murdered. He was murdered by the US administration. He was out looking for IEDs. He found one, stopped his convoy and was blown up.' Iskandariya, where Seth died, is a Sunni Muslim town south of Baghdad, throat-cutting country where insurgents man their own checkpoints.

Celeste's son Sherwood was killed on 26 April 2004, his end as tragic as it was unnecessary. He was protecting a group of military inspectors from the Iraq Survey Group who were looking for President Bush's mythical weapons of mass destruction when a perfume factory they were searching in Baghdad exploded. 'He was getting out of the cab of his truck to help the wounded when some debris came crashing out of the sky and hit him,' Celeste says. 'I will always remember that my son died just a month after George W. Bush made that videotape in front of the press – the one where he made a joke about looking for weapons of mass destruction and pretended to search under his desk for the weapons. He was making fun of the fact he hadn't found them – but my son died looking for them and they didn't exist.'

Sherwood and his wife Deborah had a young son. 'We always tell him that his father was a hero,' Celeste says. Sherwood had joined the National Guard in 1997, believing that he could use the money to pay off his college loan. 'He'd told us he would go and do the job and that he would bring all his men home safely. There were fifteen of them, all from Pennsylvania, and he kept his word. They all came home safely – except for Sherwood.'

Is it so surprising that this little group of mothers and ex-soldiers should have trailed along behind the Veterans' Parade in New York? I say goodbye to them and head off into the November cold and noise of Times Square. Up on a giant television screen, Vice President Cheney is solemnly bowing his head in the Arlington cemetery, honouring the fallen. And I wonder if he will ever understand his betrayal of the men and women back on 44th Street.

For Iraqis, the American dead are just numbers – just as dead Iraqis are for most Americans. But you have to go to America to understand. In a little town in Madison, Wisconsin, I picked up the local paper, the *Capital Times*. Sergeant Warren Hansen, Specialist Eugene Uhl and Second Lieutenant Jeremy Wolfe of the 101st Airborne Division were all on their way home for the last time.

Two of the three men were killed in a Black Hawk helicopter crash over Tikrit just over a week earlier, but of course President Bush wouldn't be attending their funerals. The man who declined to serve in Vietnam but sent 146,000 young Americans into the biggest rats' nest in the Middle East didn't do funerals. Furthermore, the American television networks feebly accepted the new Pentagon ruling that they couldn't show the coffins of America's young men returning from Iraq. The dead who come home did so in virtual secrecy.

Things were changing. At a lecture I gave in Madison, a young man in the audience stood up to say that his brother had written home from Iraq to say that the war was a mess, that Americans shouldn't be dying in Iraq. After the lecture, he showed me his brother's picture and passed on a message that the soldier wanted to meet me in Baghdad the following month. Or take the case of Drew Plummer from North Carolina, who enlisted during his last year in high school, just three months before 11 September 2001. Home on leave, he joined his father Lou, a former member of the US 2nd Armored Division, at a 'bring our troops home' vigil. Asked for his opinion on Iraq, Drew replied, 'I just don't agree with what we're doing right now. I don't think our guys should be dying in Iraq. But I'm not a pacifist. I'll do my part.'

But free speech now carried a price for the military. The US Navy charged Drew with violating Article 134 of the Uniform Code of Military Justice: Disloyal Statements. At his official hearing, he was asked if he 'sympathised' with the enemy or was considering 'acts of sabotage'. He denied this, but was convicted and demoted.

Yet still the US press turned their backs on all this. How revealing, for example, to find that the number of seriously wounded soldiers brought home to America from Iraq was already – in November 2003 – approaching 2,200. In all, there had been nearly 7,000 medical evacuations of soldiers from Iraq, many with psychological problems. This was disclosed by the Pentagon to a group of French diplomats in Washington. The French press carried the story, unlike the papers of small-town America.

And while the Pentagon was now planning to have 100,000 GIs in Iraq until 2006, the journalistic heavyweights were stoking the fires of patriotism with an even more chilling propaganda line. Claiming that Saddam's torturers were attacking American troops, David Brooks wrote in the *New York Times* that 'history shows that Americans are willing to make sacrifices. The real doubts come when we see ourselves inflicting them. What will happen to the national mood when the news programs start broadcasting images of the brutal measures our own troops will have to adopt?'

Why was the *New York Times* providing space for the advocacy of war crimes by US soldiers? I doubted if the US channels would broadcast any images of 'brutal measures' – they'd already had the chance to do so and declined. But was the groundwork being laid for just such atrocities in Iraq, for the 'normalisation' of torture?

As a foreign correspondent, I long ago developed a fascination for reporting from the 'bad' side in an international conflict. In Iraq in 2003, I chose to report from Baghdad as the Americans invaded, telling the story of suffering Iraqis, just as – in the terrifying Syrian civil war almost a decade later – I covered the Assad government's ruthless battle against its peaceful and then increasingly murderous armed enemies.

Of course, I was not the only writer who chose this role. With my colleagues, I was routinely condemned as 'anti-Semitic' or 'pro-terrorist' or 'pro-Saddam' or 'pro-Assad' or simply as 'fascist'. I was accused of working for both the Israeli Mossad and the Syrian secret service and had to adopt the old maxim that a reporter covering the Middle East has to grow used to the sticks and stones. Western governments and their journalist cronies would attack us regularly, but I always believed that those who suffered on the 'other' side deserved to have their story told, that Western powers should not have the press corps as their foot-soldiers.

Besides, certain patterns emerged when you were bombed by the 'good guys'. Precedents became 'normalised' and could be used again in other wars by other armed forces. War crimes were thus transformed into military tactics in much the same way as politicians like Tony Blair turned war into a political option.

There was a curtain between the Americans and those of us who were reporting the suffering of Iraqis, a lapse of knowledge which the Americans were content to live with. The more dangerous it became for reporters to travel out of Baghdad, the easier it was for US generals to claim that Iraq was safe. The worse it got, the better it became. I travelled out to Khalidiya one evening to report an ambush on the

Americans. I found a Humvee burned out, a troop transporter smashed by rockets and an Iraqi lorry, riddled by American bullets in the aftermath of the attack, smouldering on the central reservation. 'I saw the Americans flying through the air, blasted upwards,' an Iraqi mechanic told me, standing with an oil lamp in his garage. 'The wounded Americans were on the road, shouting and screaming.' The mechanic's friends described seeing arms and legs and pieces of uniform scattered across the highway.

One of the first to tear the curtain aside was the much-decorated veteran of the Korean and Vietnam wars, retired colonel David Hackworth, who published scores of accounts by junior officers proving the US military was lying about the war. 'Hack', a brave, bombastic, caustic but honourable man, also wrote for *Newsweek* magazine and spoke a soldier's truth to power, cheerfully enduring the spite and malice of the Pentagon and its assorted 'expert' journalists. As early as December 2003, he reprinted the account of a young American soldier in the US 4th Infantry Division who had participated in a battle in the Iraqi city of Samarra after which the Pentagon announced that its men had killed fifty-four of the 'enemy'.

The anonymous soldier's story was devastating. His convoy, he wrote, was carrying new Iraqi currency to stock local banks in Samarra, escorted by Abrams tanks and Bradley fighting vehicles. 'The reports of fifty-four enemy killed will sound great on the home front,' the officer wrote:

> but the greater story is much more disturbing ... When we
> received the first incoming rounds, all I could think of was how
> the hell did the Iraqis ... find out about this shipment? This was
> not broadcast on the local news, but Iraqi police knew about it
> ... Hack, most of the insurgents were civilians, not insurgents or
> criminals ... I am very concerned in the coming days we will
> find we killed many civilians as well as Iraqi regular fighters ...
> We are probably turning many Iraqis against us and I am afraid
> instead of climbing out of the hole, we are digging ourselves in
> deeper.

Two weeks later, an Associated Press report supported the anonymous soldier's account of US brutality in Samarra, describing how US soldiers used sledgehammers, crowbars, explosives and armoured vehicles to attack the 'resistance' in the city. 'Samarra has been a little bit of a thorn in our side,' the AP man quoted Colonel Nate Sassaman as saying. 'It hasn't come along as quickly as other cities in the rebuilding of Iraq.' 'They've made a mistake to attack US forces,' Sassaman went on. 'We're gonna clean this place.'

Three months after the Samarra battle, Marine Major General James 'Mad Dog' Mattis was giving a bleak and chilling warning to Iraqis in Fallujah and Ramadi. 'We expect to be the best of friends to Iraqis who are trying to put their country back together,' he told his men as they took over from the 82nd Airborne almost exactly a year after the invasion. 'And for those who want to fight, to the foreign fighters and former regime people, they'll regret it. We're going to handle them very roughly.' Quite apart from Mattis' sloppy identification of his enemies – the marines' antagonists were primarily Iraqi Sunnis who had opposed Saddam as well as the US – what did 'very roughly' mean?

Hackworth had been dead two years when *Newsweek* raised a banner above the doldrums of American mainstream reporting, which had largely distinguished itself by critical support for the war. In April 2007, however, when US fatalities in Iraq had reached 3,230, *Newsweek* brought the American dead back to life. Bush would not look at the coffins of the dead – nor let the press see them. But *Newsweek* gathered dozens of letters home from soldiers who were soon to die in the war, and their ghosts spoke directly to its readers of the folly of a totally avoidable conflict.

Some of the letters expressed outrage at the Iraqis who burned and paraded the corpses of the American mercenaries whose murders had provoked the first US siege of Fallujah. 'I wanted so badly to shoot those bastards parading around the streets,' Marine Captain Michael D. Martino wrote home in March 2004. 'I have no respect for these people who claim Islam is the only true religion and don't even follow the rules of the Koran.' Army Second Lieutenant Brian Smith was amazed that 'dragging a corpse could horrify or engage a population'. After a report that a Bradley vehicle captain had been killed in Khalidiya, Smith and his men entered the town, 'killing anything that moved'. He was an eloquent observer of the high-tech war in which he and his men were now involved: 'Hosing down person-shaped, gritty green blobs scampering around in the gunner's sight does not really allow for full appreciation of the impact of the act of ending the life of another human being ... In the end, I felt and feel nothing.'

After Smith and his men ended the first siege of Fallujah by handing over the city to ex-Baathists and, ultimately, to insurgents, he reflected on the humiliation of the marines and of the dreadful revelation that prisoners had been tortured at Abu Ghraib. 'What did Hajji learn that week?' he asked in a letter home on 11 May 2004. 'First, the US can be defeated. Second, if he surrenders he will be stripped naked, have electrodes attached to his testicles and [be] made to stand in a tub of water. F–ing brilliant.'

By January 2005, Marine Lance Corporal Richard Chad Clifton realised 'we're in Iraq because it doesn't matter about freeing Iraqis. They will piss away their freedoms ... it's in their culture. But at least all these foreign fighters and extremists now have a battlefield, a place to stick it to us Americans. I'd rather fight them here than have my family killed in a bombing or [have] snipers gun down an innocent in the street [in America].'*

By 2006, as the sectarian war in Iraq grew more profound, and as Bush agreed to a 'surge' of troops around the country, Army Staff Sergeant Ronald Lee Paulsen reflected a cynicism that could be found in other soldiers' letters:

> Remember what I told ya that as the forces swept through
> Baghdad the bad guys would move to the surrounding areas?
> Well, guess what? They're here. For the last two weeks, the
> camp has been mortared daily. We lost one of our CA [civil
> affairs] teams to a roadside bomb. I'm really getting pissed off ...
> You have to hand it to the US Army, though. We're training the
> best terrorists in the world.

---

* Under the Obama administration, two Chechen brothers did set off a pressure cooker bomb which killed three civilians participating in the Boston Marathon on 15 April 2013. The surviving brother said the two had been partly motivated by the Iraq war; and the authorities, perhaps picking up on the relevant country, promptly charged him with setting off a 'weapon of mass destruction'.

Twenty-six pages in *Newsweek* allowed us to hear the voices of those who in some cases knew all too well why they were about to die. Martino was thirty-two when he was killed in his helicopter, brought down by enemy fire in November 2005. Smith, two years younger, was shot dead in July 2004. Clifton was only nineteen when he was killed in Anbar province in 2005. Paulsen was fifty-three when he died from IED injuries forty miles from Baghdad in October 2006.

But not only the dead talked. In 2007, the *New York Times* published a letter from seven enlisted men from the 82nd Airborne – two of whom would die in Iraq just three weeks later – in which they challenged the US government narrative of the war. A 'vast majority' of Iraqis, they wrote, 'feel increasingly insecure and view us as an occupation force that has failed to produce normalcy after four years and is increasingly unlikely to do as we continue to arm each warring faction'. The seven men recognised that the Iraqi government was now run by a Shiite-dominated alliance – the very system that would propel the country into a civil war after the Americans retreated – and in the most revealing section of their letter, they described how:

> Political reconciliation in Iraq will occur, but not at our
> insistence or in ways that meet our benchmarks ... Four years
> into our occupation, we have failed on every promise, while we
> have substituted Baath party tyranny with a tyranny of Islamist,
> militia and criminal violence.

Until the publication of this letter, the journalists covering the war had focused not on the failure of US military policy but the victories of American soldiers and the cunning of their adversaries. In the years that followed the 2003 invasion, I collected files of articles which foisted all kinds of dramatic scenarios upon readers, most of them based upon those 'official sources' so beloved of the Washington press corps.

It would be remiss to ignore the compassion with which American soldiers and marines could speak of their experience in Iraq. Take Benjamin Busch, a Marine Corps reserve infantry officer in the 4th Light Armored Reconnaissance Battalion who served two tours of combat duty in Iraq and whose letters home in the summer of 2005 are a model of literacy, political and human comprehension.

Based in Ramadi, Busch understands with clinical humour the dilemma of Iraqis confronted by a freedom they had never experienced before. On 25 May 2005 he wrote:

> So what news about the new government you may ask. Well the Provisional Military Governor was replaced by the Transitional Governor who resigned under threat and was replaced with another Transitional Governor. He was then replaced by the Emergency Appointed Governor who was just replaced by the Selected Governor chosen by the elected Provincial Council. He never made a speech or publicised his views, never debated the other candidates and was not present during the selection, never making an acceptance speech. He was promptly kidnapped by a rival tribe … The recently displaced Emergency Appointed Governor returned in hopes of regaining the position; however, the Deputy Governor is now serving as the Acting Governor while the actual Selected Governor is in captivity. But there was an election so democracy is in full bloom, I am to understand.*

Busch's enthusiasm to create a democracy in Iraq nudged uneasily with an occupier's impatience. This profound if uneasy observation raised an obvious question: why could we not read journalism of this quality in papers like the *Los Angeles Times*? More importantly, it emphasised an almost unique phenomenon of the Iraq war: that whereas in most conflicts, a soldier's private thoughts often reflected the real policies that lay behind wars, in Iraq it was the public statements that all too often betrayed the brutality with which America continued its military campaign.

Major General Mattis was building up a ferocious reputation for threats and video-game jocularity while enjoying the reputation of an 'intense intellectual'. He repeatedly talked about the need to respect

---

* Busch would have been amused to know that a British history of the Mamluk period (1750–1831) suggests that local government was much the same in Iraq a quarter of a millennium before the US Marines reached Ramadi. In words spookily similar to Busch's much later account, Zaki Saleh, an Iraqi teacher and academic, published a volume in 1957 on British foreign policy in Mesopotamia – some of it based on Brigadier Stephen Longrigg's earlier history of Iraq.

Iraqis and to act with disciplined behaviour. Many officers did. But reporting the American war, we found that some commanders gave almost manic speeches to their soldiers. Lieutenant Colonel Gareth F. Brandl of the 22nd Marine Expeditionary Unit, for example, spoke thus to his men before the second Battle of Fallujah:

> The marines that I have had wounded over the past five months have been attacked by a faceless enemy. But the enemy has got a face. He's called Satan. He lives in Fallujah. And we're going to destroy him.

Shortly after the invasion of Iraq, the Americans had set up a special unit, Task Force 121, to conduct a covert and ruthless offensive against the growing number of insurgents in Iraq. One of its principle planners was Lieutenant General William G. Boykin, military assistant to the US undersecretary of defense for intelligence and an odd character, to put it mildly. An evangelical Christian, he told an Oregon religious group that violent Islamists hated the US 'because we're a Christian nation, because our foundation and our roots are Judeo-Christian'. He even claimed that George W. Bush was 'in the White House because God put him there'.

These weren't the crackpot ravings of some junior officer. These were the bigoted reflections of one of the top American military men charged with winning the war against guerrilla fighters in a Muslim nation. And if Bush's initial post-9/11 remark that the West must embark on a 'crusade' against 'terrorists' was immediately disowned by his staff, here was proof positive for the Iraqis that the US military intended to fight a religious war in their country. Bush later remarked that Boykin's words did not 'reflect' his 'point of view', but neither the president nor defense secretary Donald Rumsfeld uttered a word of criticism.

If not exhorting soldiers to fight with Old Testament enthusiasm, far more dangerous semantics were getting loose in the colonialist language of the American occupiers. 'You have to understand the Arab mind,' Captain Todd Brown, a company commander with the 4th Infantry Division, remarked. 'The only thing they understand is force – force, pride and saving face.'

The *New York Times* reporter Dexter Filkins recorded how US troops were encasing villages in razor-wire fences after repeated attacks on American soldiers, how civilians were forced to carry English-language identification cards, how buildings belonging to insurgents were demolished and how relatives of suspected rebels were imprisoned. All this was at the cost of the goodwill of the people. And the American response, Filkins noted shrewdly, was 'beginning to echo the Israeli counter-insurgency campaign in the occupied territories' of Gaza and the West Bank, where Israeli forces had 'for decades' been demolishing buildings where insurgents had supposedly planned attacks.

A few months earlier, Brigadier General Michael A. Vane – the deputy chief of staff of 'Doctrine, Concepts and Strategy, Training and Doctrine Command' – in an otherwise mundane letter to *Army Magazine* – had revealed US and Israeli military intelligence contacts. 'Experience continues to teach us many lessons,' he wrote, 'and we continue to evaluate and address those lessons, embedding and incorporating them appropriately into our concepts, doctrine and training. For example, we recently travelled to Israel to glean lessons learned from their counterterrorist operations in urban areas.'

Thus were new precedents set. Just as the Israeli army employed brutal and disproportionate violence and assassination against their Arab guerrilla enemies, US forces themselves were encouraged by the Israelis to adopt these same bloody and often internationally illegal practices. If Israeli forces could enjoy a reputation of 'purity of arms',* then American officers could boast of the restraint and discipline of their own soldiers, however cruel their tactics.

Many dispatches at this time recorded the close cooperation of American and Israeli military officers. Seymour Hersh wrote that the Pentagon sought

> active and secret help in the war against the Iraqi insurgency in Israel, America's closest ally in the Middle East. According to American and Israeli military and intelligence officials, Israeli commandos and intelligence units have been working closely with their American counterparts at the Special Forces training

---

* Israel Defense Forces' official code that a 'soldier shall not employ his weaponry and power … to harm non-combatants' – a code that is repeated in political and military speeches, but scarcely upheld in action.

centre at Fort Bragg, North Carolina, and in Israel to help them
prepare for operations in Iraq.

William Boykin's boss Stephen Cambone was an enthusiastic supporter
of American-Israeli cooperation. 'Those who have to deal with like
problems tend to share information as best they can,' he told 'defence
writers' in Washington. The two nations were 'working together' even
if there was no 'formal dialogue'. The *Los Angeles Times* recounted that
'a senior US Army official said on condition of anonymity' that the
Israelis 'certainly have a wealth of experience from a military standpoint in dealing with domestic terror, urban terror, military operations
in urban terrain, and there is a great deal of knowledge sharing going
on right now'.

Israel was also cheerleading the war on Iraq, providing 'evidence' of
Saddam's weapons of mass destruction every bit as fraudulent as that
of Bush and Blair while at the same time enthusiastically endorsing the
post-war humiliation of Tehran, Damascus and the Palestinian leadership in Ramallah. Shoal Mofaz, the Israeli defence minister, told
members of the Conference of Presidents of Major American Jewish
Organizations in February 2003 that after Iraq, the US should generate
'political, economic, diplomatic pressure' on Iran.

Journalists of Jewish origin, both Israeli and American, had warned
much earlier that Israel's friends in the US were demanding that Bush
and his administration go to war in Iraq. Joe Klein wrote cynically in
Time magazine that:

> A stronger Israel is very much embedded in the rationale for war
> with Iraq. It is a part of the argument that dare not speak its
> name, a fantasy quietly cherished by the neo-conservative
> faction in the Bush administration and by many leaders of the
> American Jewish community.

Evidence of close cooperation between US and Israeli security apparatus had emerged piecemeal after the invasion. Reporters who covered
both the Israeli occupation of Palestinian land and the American occupation of Iraq could see at first hand the similarities between the
strategies of the two armies when confronted by unarmed and armed
rebellion.

I had travelled to Samarra after an ambush on US troops in the city, just two weeks after the battle described so vividly by David Hackworth's anonymous 4th Infantry Division soldier. Now, the Americans had just killed another eighteen Iraqis during demonstrations by Sunni Muslims protesting the seizure of Saddam, eleven of them in Samarra. In Ramadi, videotape showed unarmed supporters of Saddam being shot in semi-darkness as they fled from American troops. The disproportionate use of live fire had long been a tactic of Israeli troops confronting demonstrators in Palestinian lands.

Again, the proliferation of concrete walls across Baghdad could only remind journalists of the massive Israeli wall constructed by Ariel Sharon's government. Just as the Western denizens of the Green Zone and its Emerald Palace sealed themselves off from Iraq by steel and concrete, so the Israelis had shut the Palestinians out of their lives. Scarcely a year after US Marines in Haditha murdered twenty-four Iraqi men, women and children, the Americans had built a twelve-foot-high wall around the Iraqi town to prevent attacks on their forces.

When Israeli soldiers killed civilians in the Palestinian territories or in occupied Lebanon after their first invasion of 1976, the guilty went largely unpunished.* In the Haditha massacre on 19 November 2005, children and elderly civilians were among the twenty-four dead who were shot many times at close range. The marines initially claimed that fifteen civilians had been killed by a bomb targeting an American convoy. Journalists played a leading role in uncovering what was by any definition a war crime but by mid-June 2008, six marine defendants had had their cases dropped and a seventh, a staff sergeant, was convicted only of 'negligent dereliction of duty'.

One precedent begat another. Unsurprisingly, it turned out that the Americans, having sought guidance over Iraq from the Israelis, received Israel's 'rules of engagement' for the suppression of the Palestinians. This could hardly have been avoided when Washington's

---

* In 1978, Lieutenant Daniel Pinto, the acting commander of an Israeli infantry company, strangled four Lebanese peasants whose bodies, tied hand and foot, were later found in a well. Pinto was court-martialled for his atrocity but General Rafael Eitan, the Israeli chief of staff, reduced his sentence from twelve to two years and then ordered his release. Israeli troops who killed seven Palestinians in a temporary Israeli prison in Sidon in 1982 went unpunished after the Israeli army stated it 'could not ascertain who was responsible for the killings' and that soldiers had no 'connection' with the deaths.

first proconsul in Iraq was such an enthusiastic supporter of the Israeli military. Having travelled to Israel courtesy of the Jewish Institute for National Security Affairs, former General Jay Garner co-signed a letter in 2000 expressing the view that 'during the current upheavals in Israel, the Israel Defense Forces have exercised remarkable restraint in the face of lethal violence orchestrated by the leadership of [the] Palestinian Authority'.

America's use of mercenaries was another major tactical – and moral – error. Israel, too, had used local militias to fearful effect in Lebanon, to crush its enemies, reduce its own casualties and avoid responsibility for the more criminal acts perpetrated during its eighteen-year occupation.* Initially, the US introduced thousands of hired fighters from around the world to guard American and Iraqi government locations, military camps, industrial facilities and diplomats in Baghdad. Former American and British soldiers were hired by the occupation authorities and by foreign companies, at extortionate rates. A year after the invasion, heavily armed Britons working at over three hundred security firms far outnumbered Britain's own 8,000-strong regular force in southern Iraq. Although major US and British security companies began operating in Iraq early in the war, dozens of small firms set up shop with little vetting of their employees and no real rules of engagement.

The degree to which these mercenaries were substitutes for the occupation army became quickly apparent. Security firms were escorting convoys while armed plain-clothes men from a US company guarded American military forces at night inside the former presidential palace. When a US helicopter crashed near Fallujah in 2003, it was an American security company that took control of the area and began rescue operations. Mercenary casualties were not included in the

---

* Israel invaded Lebanon in 1976, and again in 1982, occupying southern Lebanon. Israel armed and uniformed the Lebanese Christian Phalangists – whose pathological hatred of the Palestinians reached its height at the Sabra and Chatila massacre in September 1982 – and it also created the 'South Lebanon Army' (SLA) militia, led successively by two cashiered Lebanese army officers, to suppress the growing and largely Shia Muslim insurrection against its rule. The Phalange contaminated the entire Israeli occupation, while the SLA murdered and intimidated Lebanese opposed to the occupation, before itself being infiltrated by Hizbollah and fleeing across the border along with Israeli troops during a chaotic retreat in May 2000.

military fatality or injury lists put out by the occupation authorities –
which might have accounted for the persistent suspicion among Iraqis
that the United States was underestimating its figures for military dead
and wounded.*

I first noticed the huge number of hired gunmen from Britain and
other European countries arriving in Baghdad when they poured into
the Al-Hamra Hotel on 25 March 2004, some of them wearing cowboy
hats, strutting around the car park draped in belts of machine-gun
ammunition and swigging beer. When I suggested to two of them that
their outrageous costumes positively invited an armed attack on the
hotel, one of them bawled at me: 'You should be pleased to see us,
mate – if we weren't here, you'd be fucking dead.' Within days, these
men were sitting by the hotel pool, rifles at their feet. In other hotels,
guests and staff complained that security men had held drunken parties
while heavily armed. A manager's plea to conceal their weapons in
holdalls was ignored. Three days later, the world saw the terrible
images of the four mercenaries, slaughtered and strung up in Fallujah,
two of them from an old railway bridge. These were the 'contractors'
whose dismemberment led to the first Battle of Fallujah. All of them
worked for Blackwater.

The research of Jeremy Scahill into the events of 16 September 2007,
when Blackwater's mercenaries killed seventeen Iraqi civilians and
wounded another twenty-four in Nissour Square while escorting US
State Department officials through Baghdad, had far-reaching effects.
Despite a State Department claim that the armed Blackwater men
were attacked by 'insurgents', eyewitness accounts and later investigations told a tale of murderous gunfire from the US escorts who cut
down civilians, enraging Iraqis who were used to the shooting sprees
of gunmen employed by the occupation forces.

None of us had any excuse to be surprised. Over three years earlier,
I was reporting that:

Blackwater's thugs with guns now push and punch Iraqis who
get in their way: Kurdish journalists twice walked out of a
Bremer press conference because of their mistreatment by these

---

* In mid-2007, Reuters reported that 933 'contractors' had died in Iraq since the start of
the war, well over 200 of them Americans.

men. Baghdad is alive with mysterious Westerners draped with
hardware, shouting and abusing Iraqis in the street, drinking
heavily in the city's poorly defended hotels. They have become,
for ordinary Iraqis, the image of everything that is wrong with
the West ... there is a disturbing increase in reports that
mercenaries are shooting down innocent Iraqis with total
impunity.

Months before the Nissour killings, Scahill grasped what Blackwater
really represented for a right-wing, aggressive American administration. Such a government did not need to send soldiers in vast numbers
to unpopular wars or plead for a coalition of other nations to share
their fate, or even seek the support of popular opinion, if 'the mercenary firms offer a privatised alternative'.

Well, at a price. British company director David Claridge of the
security firm Janusian estimated in early 2004 that British companies
alone had earned up to $1,200 million from contracts in Iraq. A British
firm, Erinys, was employing 14,000 Iraqis as watchmen and security
guards to protect the country's oil fields and pipelines. A South African-
owned group, Meteoric Tactical Solutions, had a £270,000 contract
with the UK government's Department for International Development
to protect senior British staff in Baghdad. Many companies operated
from small, anonymous villas in middle-class areas of Baghdad.
Payments of $120,000 a year soon far exceeded the most avaricious
dreams of any hired gunmen. Security personnel in Fallujah originally
picked up $1,000 a day. Within two years, a French company was
charging diplomats $2,000 an hour for a trip outside Baghdad's Green
Zone.

Like all wars, Iraq turned brutal. Its reasons fraudulent, its occupation ferocious, its 'victors' ever more cruel in responding to the
insurgency which overwhelmed them, the conflict was from the start
also tangled up in a web of political naivety and Christian muscular-
ity. Denying the pressures from Israel's lobby while placing a naive
reliance on the non-existent effectiveness of Israeli 'anti-terrorist'
operations, tolerating the inhuman behaviour of American soldiers,
employing a proxy force of greedy mercenary adventurers, mixing
Christian religious extremism with the absurd political goal of

're-making' the Middle East, the West's adventure in Iraq was bound
to turn into a catastrophe.

As American casualties continued to rise and US troops found themselves unable to control a sectarian Shia–Sunni civil war, Washington
took the step of creating its own local 'South Lebanon Army'-style
militia. Henceforth, Washington would pay Iraqi Sunni tribes to fight
their own Sunni al-Qaeda allies in the resistance – even if their newly
recruited friends continued the 'national' struggle against US occupation.

Men who had fought in Saddam's army, ex-intelligence operatives
and brutal security men from the Baath, and militiamen from Anbar
province and Iraqi Sunni Salafists more faithful to their tribe than the
al-Qaeda fighters all now took the American president's dollar. So did
Shia Muslims in the deeply compromised Iraqi police force and the
Shia gunmen who had joined the personal government protection
squads of newly installed Iraqi ministers. Exactly when the Iraqi
resistance war became a civil war is impossible to determine, since
the two overlapped. The guerrilla battle against the Americans would
be temporarily suppressed in favour of sectarian conflict, before
firing up again as resistance units tried to break the effects of the
'surge'.

Historians will no doubt focus on 22 February 2006 as the day the
sectarian war took on epic proportions. The al-Askari Mosque at
Samarra is one of the most sacred Shia shrines, tomb of the tenth and
eleventh imams, and thus scarcely less important than the great shrines
of the Imams Ali and Hussein – grandson and son-in-law of the Prophet
Mohamed – at Najaf and Karbala. The remains of Ali al-Hadi and his
son Hasan al-Askari at Samarra are not only a still-living part of Shia
history but are also foundational figures of the great Sunni–Shia division.

Whether or not the Americans realised this, they had invaded the
physical centre of the tragic theological struggle between Shia and
Sunni Muslims. When Dan Senor and other US spokesmen began to
talk of 'civil war' as early as 2003, Iraqis were puzzled and deeply
disturbed. And as the anti-American resistance forces grew in number,
so did the warnings of civil war from the foreign occupation authorities
in Baghdad. It was as if the Americans knew what the people of Iraq
were still unaware of.

Iraqi government officials would later insist that the 2006 Samarra bombing, which destroyed the massive golden dome of the al-Askari mosque, was carried out by a largely Saudi unit of al-Qaeda. That Sunni militants were to blame was self-evident to the Shia of Iraq, who had valiantly restrained their anger after constant provocation by car-bombers in previous months. Within twenty-four hours of the Samarra destruction, however, the Shia Muslims unleashed a pogrom against their fellow Sunnis, killing at least 1,300 within days. The Americans expressed themselves powerless to prevent this carnage, although Articles 47–78 of the 1949 Geneva Conventions oblige an occupying power to protect civilians within its territory. The sadistic nightly murders across Iraq spread like a disease from Baghdad across the west and north of the country.

Syria was one of the first sanctuaries available to Iraqis fleeing their homes, a dictatorship which opened its borders to refugees by the thousand, most of them Shia Muslims but many Sunnis. Washington regularly condemned Syria for allowing resistance cadres from other Arab countries to transit Syrian territory on their way to fight in the Iraqi war, a claim that was not without merit. But the Syrian military intelligence service suspected that Washington was not above encouraging the very violence which fuelled the sectarian conflict.

In the third week of April 2006, I went to the gleaming steel office block on the western side of Damascus, where one of the most trusted men in the Syrian intelligence services waited to see me. I first met General Mohamed Mansour when he commanded Syrian military intelligence in the border city of Qamishli, just south of the Turkish frontier. Back in 1991, I was expelled from Turkey and lost my only legal entry point into Kurdish-run and US-protected northern Iraq. After a phone call from Damascus to General Mansour in Qamishli, I was speeding up the international highway to Homs and Aleppo. General Mansour, one of Assad's experts on the Saddam regime, arranged for my transport across the Tigris and – after my foray in northern Iraq was finished – back to Syria.

Now General Mansour sat with even more confidence, in his office scarcely a hundred metres from one of Syria's most fearsome prisons. Coffee and French biscuits were served, and a plain-clothes man entered from time to time to whisper in the general's ear. Just six months earlier, Brigadier General Ghazi Kanaan, the Alawite* minister of defence – and formerly Mansour's opposite number as head of military intelligence in Lebanon – had committed suicide in his Damascus office. Cynics claimed he had been murdered by the regime, which suspected him of plotting – along with former vice president Abdul Halim Khaddam – to overthrow Bashar al-Assad. It seemed wise to ask General Mansour about Iraq before touching on the demise of his former comrade-in-arms.

His was a ferocious narrative of disaster in Iraq, a fearful portrait of America desperately trying to provoke a civil war around Baghdad in order to reduce its own military casualties. It was a scenario in which Saddam, although in American custody for well over two years, remained Washington's best friend, in which Syria had struck at the Iraqi insurgents with a ruthlessness that the US largely ignored. And in which General Kanaan had committed suicide because of his own mental instability.

The Americans, General Mansour suspected, were trying to provoke an Iraqi civil war so that Sunni insurgents spent their energies killing their Shia co-religionists rather than soldiers of the Western occupation forces. 'I swear to you that we have good information,' the general said, finger stabbing the air. 'One young Iraqi man told us that he was trained by the Americans as a policeman in Baghdad and spent 70 per cent of his time learning to drive and 30 per cent in weapons training. They said to him: "Come back in a week." When he went back, they gave him a mobile phone and told him to drive into a crowded area near a mosque and phone them. He waited in the car, but couldn't get the right mobile signal. So he got out of the car to where he received a better signal. Then his own car blew up.'

It seemed impossible, but I remembered how many times Iraqis in Baghdad told me similar stories. And I knew where much of the Syrian information was gleaned: from the tens of thousands of Shia Muslim pilgrims who came to pray at the Sayeda Zainab mosque in southern

---

* A Shia sect in all but name, a remnant of the Shiite Muslim upsurge that swept Islam a thousand years ago. Like the Shiites, the Alawites believe that the Prophet's cousin and son-in-law Ali – hence Alawite – was robbed of his inheritance by the three caliphs. Most Alawites belong to four tribes: the Matawira, the Haddadin, the Khaiyatin and the Kalbiya. Hafez al-Assad's grandfather Sulieman belonged to the Kalbiya; the majority of Syria's ruling elite belongs to this minority sect.

Damascus. Mansour spoke to these people personally, men and women from the slums of Baghdad, Hilla and Iskandariya, as well as Najaf and Basra. Sunnis from Fallujah and Ramadi also visited Damascus to see friends and relatives, and talked freely of American tactics in Iraq.

In the anarchic world of Iraq, many US groups operated outside any laws or rules. No one could account for the murder – by 2006 – of 191 university teachers and professors – nor for the assassination in Iraq of more than fifty former Iraqi fighter-bomber pilots who had attacked Iran in the 1980–88 war. Amid this chaos, General Mansour asked me, how could Syria be expected to lessen the number of attacks on Americans inside Iraq? 'It was never safe, our border,' he said, before telling me that the rampart running for hundreds of miles along Syria's border with Iraq had been heightened. 'I have had barbed wire put on top,' he insisted. 'And up to now we have caught 1,500 non-Syrian and non-Iraqi Arabs trying to cross and we have stopped 2,700 Syrians from crossing … Our army is there – but the Iraqi army and the Americans are not there on the other side.'

How much credibility should a reporter give to Bashar al-Assad's number-two army intelligence officer? None, the Americans would say. Yet Mansour was every bit as senior as the supposedly reliable US intelligence officers quoted so obsequiously by American correspondents. Of some things, my Syrian 'sources' were certain. General Mansour was watching the court appearances of Saddam Hussein with an obsession born of his intelligence days in Qamishli. What would happen to the Iraqi dictator who was the truly mortal enemy of the late Hafez al-Assad? I asked. 'He will be killed,' the general replied with a smile.

Ardent for some desperate glory amid the chaos, Washington now sought out the 'last chance general', David Petraeus, to pacify Iraq and end the humiliation of the army. The 'surge' did not just involve the injection of thousands of extra American troops into Iraq. It included a high-risk counter-insurgency operation that would seal off whole areas of Baghdad, enclosing neighbourhoods with walls and barricades, and allowing only Iraqis with newly issued identity cards to enter.

After 'gating' off streets with wire and concrete, instituting 'visitor' registration and ensuring that civilians lived inside a 'controlled population', US forces would be able to concentrate on the reconstruction which the American authorities had so failed to provide. But the 'secure environment' this was intended to create took no account of the reality of occupation. Insurgents were not all foreigners, despite the presence of al-Qaeda in Iraq. They came from the population centres that would be 'gated' and would, if undiscovered, hold identity cards issued by the Americans. And the Iraqi security forces were so infiltrated by insurgents that weapons and intelligence information would make their way into the 'communities'.

A former US officer of the Vietnam era whose son was due to return to Iraq in February 2007 prepared two assessments of the region. He was highly sceptical:

> Any Sunni who's in the Iraqi Army, his first loyalty is to the insurgency. Any Shia's first loyalty is to the head of his particular political party and its militia. Any Kurd in the Iraqi Army, his first loyalty is to either [Kurdish leaders] Barzani or Talabani. There is no independent Iraqi Army. These people really have no choice. They are trying to save their families from starvation and reprisal.

This was common sense that was fully understood by junior officers. 'These tactics would have had a chance of working three years ago when the US governed Iraq, but [they] now play to the strengths of the insurrectionists,' the ex-soldier told his son. And in an eloquent postscript which few would now dispute, he set out the historical truth of the whole Bush adventure into Iraq.

> The United States has become part of a set of ancient feuds and blood debts. It has created more of its own. It is far out of its depth. To become a power in the area, it must create an entirely new strategy. If the US simply wants to dominate, which appears to be the case, then a combination of providing the protection and guarantees of US citizenship to all those who agree to obey our edicts, with utter brutality to those who will not agree, is the most efficacious model available.

Here was the tragedy made simple. Having embarked on the folly of post-9/11 revenge in Afghanistan, America set out in Iraq upon a war which had nothing to do with the ancient land they decided to conquer.

As for Baghdad's 'gated communities', they caught on better in America than they did in Iraq. The image of Sun Belt suburbia on the Tigris encouraged one congressman interviewed on CNN to refer to the armed Sunni thugs in the militia as a form of 'Neighbourhood Watch'. It was as if the very walls which now divided Baghdad were a sign of progress rather than sectarian division; which is why Nouri al-Maliki, with rare political nuance, ordered a halt to their construction.

Sunni groups did not want to cooperate with Maliki's Shia-led government, which they regarded as illegitimate; Shia Muslim leaders feared that the militiamen would try to re-impose Saddamite Sunni rule on Iraq, or that they merely constituted al-Qaeda in a new form. Some Sunni units had been given arms, ammunition, cash, fuel and other supplies from the Americans, but via the Iraqi army – upon which the US had already spent £15 billion and whose manpower was primarily Shia. No wonder American officers feared 'it could amount to the Americans arming both sides in a future civil war'.

Everyone knew that the 'surge' was only an attempt to secure an American withdrawal with 'honour' and that the White House was prepared to contemplate a war that it didn't win – providing that it didn't lose. If the 'surge' was another word for 'reinforcements', the subsequent retreat of the extra US soldiers would have to be covered by another imaginative verbal substitute. The Pentagon used 'drawdown', a word newspapers happily adopted.

Small voices warned of the future. In June 2007, an Iraqi doctor, Abdul Kareem al-Obeidi, the head of the Iraqi Child Mental Health Association, wrote to the UN Secretary-General, Ban Ki-moon, about the 'unbearable traumas and heart-wrenching experiences' of Iraqi children. In a world grown tired of Iraq and which followed only the results of the 'surge', his words received little coverage, but they should be enshrined in any history of the following years. Iraqi children and adolescents, al-Obeidi wrote, formed more than 55 per cent of its population. Iraqi children were

suffering from continuous exposure to violence; many are killed and mutilated every day. They suffer from neglect and abuse, including deprivation, oppression, loss of parents through death or imprisonment ... This is a crisis that needs urgent attention.

Our children carry the future of Iraq and that future is being
corrupted. The risk is great, not just for our country but for the
region and for the world.

The propaganda war became as ingenious as it was bloody. Tapes of
executions were now replaced by resistance footage of US soldiers
dying in the cities and towns of Iraq. The videotape and the mobile-
phone camera became as incendiary as the gun. 'Juba, the Baghdad
Sniper' became a real-life character in a series of videos released by the
Islamic Army that showed real-time attacks on American forces. The
ice-cold sniper-killer of past wars had found his place in Baghdad's
gruesome stardom.*

As technology became the handmaiden of the humblest soldier, any
war crime could be filmed. Janina Struk, a freelance documentary
photographer, produced a work in 2011 that included a section on the
photographs and videos produced by US combat troops in Iraq. If
Vietnam veterans could return home with photos of their own atrocities, Struk discovered that American soldiers in Iraq had gone several
steps further. On one website, she found a photograph 'that showed
five American marines smiling and fooling around for the camera
beside a charred corpse', with the remark 'Cooked Iraqi!' A rotting
cadaver lying in a street carried the comment: 'Bad day for this dude'.
A picture of a dead man with entrails and brains hanging from his body
carried the testament 'What every Iraqi should look like'.

Another video, thought to have been made by British mercenaries,
showed 'someone with an automatic weapon randomly shooting from
the back of a fast-moving vehicle at approaching civilian cars'. Among
many other amateur productions, Struk came across one captioned
'The Enemy', which included

images of an Iraqi man being shot in the street, an aerial view of
more than two dozen people being blown up, images of
blindfolded men with their hands tied, people with their heads

---

* America's own 'most lethal sniper' in Iraq was Christopher Scott Kyle, killing an officially
confirmed total of 160 Muslim fighters. He won a host of awards for military valour, a
'Grateful Nation Award' from the Jewish Institute for National Security Affairs (JINSA), and
was murdered along with a companion by Eddie Ray Routh, a fellow marine whom Kyle
had taken to a shooting range in the US to help him with post-traumatic stress disorder.

blown off, destroyed buildings and scenes of gruesome body parts. Awesome helmet-cam footage from some soldier in Iraq ... features a close-up of a severed head lying in a street, then footage shot from a moving vehicle as soldiers fire rounds of ammunition on a deserted, bombed-out street.

Weirdly, US Central Command was to note that while it was forbidden to photograph detainees or casualties, these videos did not appear to 'violate policy'. But if Struk could find these obscenities on footage, what had she not found? Already the horrors of Abu Ghraib were being shrugged away. And then up popped a junior officer in the United States charged with killing an Iraqi army general by stuffing him upside down in a sleeping bag and sitting on his chest because he was 'uncooperative'.

General Abed Hamed Mowhoush had given himself up to the Americans in 2003 to secure the release of his sons. Already severely beaten with fists, a club and a rubber hose by Iraqi interrogators working for the CIA, he was thrust upside down into the sleeping bag by US Chief Warrant Officer Lewis Welshofer Jnr, an action which caused the general to expire. Once Welshofer was brought to court for sentencing more than two years later, a kind of institutionalised racism took over. The military jury convicted Welshofer of 'negligent homicide'; he forfeited $6,000 of his salary and was confined to barracks for sixty days. But what caught my eye was the sympathetic detail. Welshofer's wife Barbara, the AP reported, 'testified that she was worried about providing for their three children if her husband was sent to prison. "I love him more for fighting this," she said, tears welling up in her eyes. "He's always said that you need to do the right thing, and sometimes the right thing is the hardest thing to do."'

The real scandal in these reports is that we were not told anything about the general's family. General Mowhoush came across as an object, a dehumanised creature who wouldn't let the Americans 'break the back' of the insurgency. But the case received few headlines. Who cared if another Iraqi had bitten the dust?

For who could be held to account when we regarded ourselves as the most honourable of creatures, doing endless battle with the killers of 11 September out of love for our country or our people. We told those countries we intended to invade that we were going to bring them 'democracy'. I couldn't help wondering how many of the innocents slaughtered at Haditha took the opportunity to vote in the Iraqi elections – before their 'liberators' murdered them.

We were pulling at the threads of this society with no sense of responsibility as occupiers, just as we had no serious plans for state reconstruction. Washington never wanted Iraq's land, of course – the country's resources were a different matter – but its tactics did fit neatly into the prairies of the old West. The tribes could be divided and the occupiers would pay less in blood, as long as they chose to stay. One set of tribes could be bought off with guns and firewater, the other with guns and dollar bills. Serious resistance, however, would invoke the 'flaming imperial anger' of all occupation armies.

The Afghan war started as a war of revenge, of punishment for 9/11, but Iraq was an ideological war. Its tactics involved political greed, faith, ignorance, institutional racism and a mythical view of the Middle East in which Israel was held up as an example of virtue and efficiency and in which Arabs reverted to their historical role of untutored barbarians to be offered the fruits of Western freedom. The American military knew that this war could not be won. From 'liberation' to democracy-building to guerrilla war and then civil war, US ambitions crumbled away until withdrawal became the only strategic core of American policy in Iraq.

The last letter of a young soldier who served in Iraq provides an eloquent epiphany to the occupation. Daniel Somers was twenty-one when he was sent to Baghdad, where he ran more than 400 combat missions from the turret of a Humvee. He returned in 2006 to further intelligence work in Mosul but he was suffering from traumatic brain injury, enduring hallucinations caused by the horrors he had experienced.

On 10 June 2013, Somers took his life, leaving a devastating letter to his parents and to his young wife. It is as moving a testament of loss as any written by or about soldiers who died in combat. 'I am sorry it has come to this,' he wrote, but 'to sleep forever seems to be the most merciful thing'.

Somers blamed the veterans' affairs system for his lack of care after 'the physical illnesses which have struck me down again and again, for which they also offer no help'. Was it any wonder, he asked, that 'the

latest figures show twenty-two veterans killing themselves each day?'
In the months that followed his suicide, the American media covered
in great detail the questions he raised about the lack of adequate medical treatment for combat veterans. But there were two terrible
paragraphs in Daniel Somers' letter which the press paid little attention
to:

> You must not blame yourself. The simple truth is this: During
> my first deployment, I was made to participate in things, the
> enormity of which is hard to describe. War crimes, crimes
> against humanity. Though I did not participate willingly, and
> made what I thought was my best effort to stop these events,
> there are some things that a person simply cannot come back
> from. I take some pride in that, actually, as to move on in life
> after being part of such a thing would be the mark of a sociopath
> in my mind. These things go far beyond what most are even
> aware of.
>
> To force me to do these things and then participate in the
> ensuing cover-up is more than any government has the right to
> demand. Then, the same government has turned around and
> abandoned me.

We still do not know what these 'war crimes' were. Journalists
contented themselves with the observation that Somers had provided
no details about these 'crimes against humanity', although the dead
soldier stated clearly that they occurred during his first tour in Iraq – a
period in which dozens of war crimes were later revealed to have taken
place. Presumably, these 'crimes' were committed during interrogations and were followed by the usual set of official lies to obscure the
truth. We have, perhaps, still only learned of a fraction of the wicked
deeds committed in our name in Iraq. Many thousands of US service-
men and women must have been contaminated in this way.

We should conclude this particular story of folly and crime with the
courageous words which Daniel Somers used to end his last letter to
his family. The world was better, he wrote, without him in it:

That is what brought me to my actual final mission. Not suicide, but a mercy killing. I know how to kill, and I know how to do it so that there is no pain whatsoever. It was quick, and I did not suffer. And above all, now I am free.

4

Painting
Othello Black

'There's only one thing more to be done,' continued the
gratified Badger. 'Toad, I want you solemnly to repeat,
before your friends here, what you fully admitted to me in
the smoking-room just now. First, you are sorry for what
you've done, and you see the folly of it all?'

There was a long, long pause. Toad looked desperately this
way and that, while the other animals waited in grave
silence. At last he spoke.

'No!' he said, a little sullenly, but stoutly; 'I'm *not* sorry.
And it wasn't folly at all! It was simply glorious!'

Kenneth Grahame, *The Wind in the Willows*

On 28 October 2008, Tom Geddes, a sixty-four-year-old retired
librarian, wrote to the British defence secretary, John Hutton. He
wanted to know why British troops were in Iraq. In the initial stages
of the war, Geddes wrote, 'we knew that claims that Iraq was
threatening us with weapons of mass destruction were untrue …
Subsequent revelations have confirmed that Tony Blair and his
government were falsifying whatever the real reasons were for those
attacks and indeed seem guilty of war crimes for unprovoked large-
scale murder.' Unless Hutton or the government could justify Britain's
war activities, he continued, 'you cannot expect to have the country
on your side'.

The letter was polite in its directness, but Geddes was angered by the reply he received. 'We acknowledge,' the letter said:

> that violence has claimed the lives of many thousands of Iraqi civilians over the last five years, either through terrorism or sectarian violence. Any loss of innocent lives is tragic and the Government is committed to ensuring that civilian casualties are avoided. Insurgents and terrorists are not, I regret to say, so scrupulous.

The reply came from an unnamed member of the Ministry of Defence's 'Iraq Operations Team, Directorate of Operations'. Its anonymity was no surprise; what was astonishing was that this outrageous letter could have been written almost six years after the invasion.

Its sleight of hand was evident, as it advised Geddes that 'it is important to remember that our decision to take action in Iraq was driven by Saddam Hussein's refusal to cooperate with the UN-sponsored weapons inspections ... The former Prime Minister [Blair] has expressed his regret for any information, given in good faith, concerning weapons of mass destruction in Iraq, which has subsequently proven to be incorrect.' This was amazing. Saddam did not 'refuse to cooperate' with the UN weapons inspectors. The problem was that he did cooperate with them, and the UN weapons team under Hans Blix was about to prove that these 'weapons of mass destruction' were non-existent. Indeed, Blix himself was reporting ever speedier cooperation from Iraq, when the Americans forced his team to leave Baghdad so that Bush and Blair could begin their illegal invasion. Any reader of this letter could note the weasel words. Blair did not give his information 'in good faith'. He – and the Ministry of Defence – knew they were untrue.

There was more in this extraordinary letter for Geddes to wonder at. 'We can assure you,' it continued, 'that the Government would not have engaged in military action if it were not satisfied that such a decision was justified and lawful. The former Attorney General, Lord Goldsmith, confirmed on 17 March 2003 that authority to use force against Iraq existed from the combined effect of UN Security Council Resolutions 678, 687 and 1441.' As a stunned Geddes pointed out in his reply, 'you must be aware that the decision to wage war on Iraq was neither justified nor lawful. The Attorney General's advice has been widely described as "flawed". Given that his previous advice was that an attack would be unlawful, we all know what "flawed" means. I suspect the MoD also knows.'

No doubt the letter was a standard reply, sent to all dissenting British men and women. The claim that 'millions of Iraqis now live free of Saddam's oppression and have control of their own destiny' was pure public relations – not least because it failed to mention that up to a million Iraqis happened to be dead as a result of the invasion. The letter praised improvements in the Iraqi economy, something Geddes could not reconcile 'with all the contracts granted so corruptly to American firms'. There was another imperishable paragraph at the end of the anonymous correspondent's letter which noted that 'our brave service-men and women … are … preparing Basra airport for transfer to Iraqi control'. This was perfectly true – since their retreat from the city, Basra airport was the only square mile of Iraq in which the British were still in occupation. The letter ended with the hope that it had gone 'some way to addressing your concerns', a declaration that caused Tom Geddes to reply: 'I am grateful for the length of your response, but shocked by its contents.'

Shock was perhaps a mild reaction when the Chilcot Inquiry into the Iraq war would later reveal that Lord Goldsmith had initially expressed grave doubts about the legality of the impending invasion, telling Blair that 'in the absence of a fresh resolution by the Security Council which would at least involve a new determination of a flagrant breach [by Iraq], military action would be unlawful'. Did the civil serv-ant who wrote to Geddes not know of this, or of Goldsmith's contention that 'on the basis of the material which I have been shown … there would not be any grounds for regarding an Iraqi use of WMD as imminent'?

The Chilcot Inquiry would hear of two further letters from Goldsmith to Blair, both advising that UN Security Council resolution 1441 did not expressly authorise the use of force. The second of the two, on 12 February 2003, explicitly stated that 'if action were to be taken without a further Security Council decision … I would expect the government to be accused of acting unlawfully.' But by 17 March, Goldsmith had caved to Blair's pressure and decided that a new resolu-tion was not needed after all.

The lies and omissions in the letter to Tom Geddes reflect the falsehoods upon which the Iraqi war was launched. But they also demonstrate that this dishonesty was maintained for years. Blair's own appearance before Chilcot in January 2010 emphasised the degree to which the 'story' of the entire tragedy had remained unchanged.

To have witnessed the bloodletting in Iraq produced an unusual effect on those who grasped the depth of the Bush–Blair deceit first hand. I think journalists were especially provoked by his refusal to admit, ever, that the war was wrong. His assertion to Chilcot that he was still 'proud' of the war created a profound anger that infected our writing.

I was on assignment in Jerusalem when Blair gave his evidence to the inquiry in January 2010. The *Independent* asked me to respond to his appearance, and I spent the day sitting before the television and furiously scribbling his words onto my notepad. That evening, my fingers pounded the keyboard in exasperation as I tried to explain what he'd called a 'binary distinction' between regime change and weapons of mass destruction. This 'binary distinction', I wrote, divided the blood that had flowed over my shoes in the emergency room of a Baghdad hospital in March 2003 from the sight of Blair in the London conference centre in his business suit and clean conscience.

Blair, it transpired from his evidence, went to war because of al-Qaeda, but thought they would let him win in Iraq. So it was all al-Qaeda's fault. We didn't kill '100,000' Iraqis (I noticed Blair used the lowest figure available). No, it was the terrorists, al-Qaeda, insurgents, Iranians. It was the fault of 'sectarians' – a seventeenth-century term, though hitherto unknown in a Middle Eastern context.

Blair's evidence went on for six hours. From time to time, there was a slip. Trying to explain that no decisions were taken at the infamous meeting with George Bush at his Texas ranch in 2002, Blair suddenly blurted out that he thought there had been 'conversations with the Israelis'. What did this mean? Were Israelis at the critical Texas meeting? Israel, as we have seen, was the only nation – apart from the US and Britain – that totally supported the war. An Israeli foreign ministry 'source' had at the time said that an Iraqi invasion 'will certainly take people away from the Israel–Palestine file'. The inquiry never picked up on this intriguing clue.

Blair stuck obstinately to his story, even though he knew no one believed it. By the end of the day in London, the tragedy of Iraq seemed to seep into that conference centre. Of course we could never have an apology from him. Blair was talking about judgement, about being 'frank' and 'absolutely and completely' honest.

We'd had to 'stick in there and see it out,' Blair said. So that's what the dead, the wounded, the bombs, the rape and Abu Ghraib was all about. Members of the audience, who included the families of dead UK servicemen and women, were led from the hall, some shouting 'murderer' and 'liar' at Blair, who was not only unrepentant but also suggested that we may have to invade Iran.*

You only had to listen to Blair's language in a September 2010 interview with Andrew Marr to understand how words had replaced accountability. 'I definitely ...', 'I believed absolutely clearly ...', 'Let me state clearly and unequivocally', 'The intelligence picture was clear', 'legal justification was quite clear', 'We said completely accurately ...', 'Because I believed strongly, then and now ...', 'My definitive view in the end is ...' On and on, Blair went. You would have thought we had won the war in Iraq, that we were winning the war in Afghanistan, that we were going to win the next war in Iran. 'I am saying that it is wholly unacceptable for Iran to have nuclear weapons capability.' The Iranians had 'to get that message loud and clear'.

Yes, Blair agreed, 'people' disagreed about the war. 'People always look for a conspiracy.' And – this was my favourite – 'This debate will go on.' Iraq had been a disaster. And why? 'People are driving car bombs into crowded suburbs,' Blair said at one point, as if this was an odd tribal habit that had nothing to do with the 2003 invasion.

These early interviews with Blair are interesting not for the dishonesty of his words but for the seamlessness with which he streamed them. By September 2003, he was able to say of Saddam's WMD that 'we know perfectly well that he had these weapons, he had these programmes', but this was obfuscation. Blair was referring to the weapons Saddam had possessed more than a decade earlier and which

* Among the sourest and most Dickensian political commentators of this period was Simon Carr of the *Independent*, whose daily reports were as much a joy to read as they were a torment for their victims. 'He can contradict himself with such solidity it's hard to see the sleight involved,' Carr wrote when Blair finally, in 2011, expressed regret.

had not existed for years. The 'programmes' were what Blair was hoping the Iraq Survey Group would come up with when they admitted a few days later that there weren't any weapons of mass destruction.

The AP ran a blunt story on New Year's Day 2004. 'In nine months,' it read, 'not a single item has been found in Iraq from a long and classified intelligence list of weapons of mass destruction which guided the work of dozens of elite teams from Special Forces, the military, the CIA and the Pentagon during the most secretive, expensive and fruitless weapons hunt in history.' The truth at last, but the story concentrated not on the lies of the US president, but on the difficulties that the non-discovery of Iraqi WMD presented 'for the United States in its efforts to curb Iran, North Korea and others'. The fraudulent reasons given for the war, in other words, were less important than their effect upon Washington's efforts to threaten other states.

Walking up the staircase at 10 Downing Street, every British prime minister can observe the portraits of their predecessors – Churchill among them. Blair may not have thought he was Churchill, but he certainly made speeches that were intended to be 'historic'. On 10 November 2003, he spoke of Iraq at the Lord Mayor's Banquet in the Guildhall in apocalyptic terms. 'Let us be clear what is happening in Iraq,' he said. 'It is the battle of seminal importance for the early twenty-first century. It will define relations between the Muslim world and the West.'

Though these words have been largely forgotten, they contained some truth – albeit not the one that Blair intended. The sectarian divisions which the Americans sowed in Iraq, the volcano of sectarian war and the induction of outside regional powers in support of their co-religionists, were to spread to Syria and thus to Lebanon. Bush supporters liked to suggest that the Iraq invasion had brought about the Arab revolutions of 2011 by creating freedom and democracy in Iraq. But what their aggression actually achieved was the introduction of a new front in al-Qaeda's war against both the West and the Shia Muslims of the region, a battle that could – and did – spread far beyond Iraq. Just as Syrians had fought alongside the resistance in Iraq, so Iraqi Sunnis later flocked to the Islamist colours in Syria. Instead of winning the battle of which he talked at the Guildhall, Blair and his American allies lost it. Within ten years, it would indeed 'define relations between the

Muslim world and the West', and many of the elements of Blair's speech could be found in the speeches of Bashar al-Assad as he fought a war against remarkably similar opponents.

Once the war in Iraq began to contaminate the Bush administration, we were asked to forget the neo-conservative, pro-Israeli proselytisers who helped to propel Bush and defense secretary Rumsfeld into it, with grotesquely inaccurate prophecies of a new Middle East of democratic, pro-Israeli Arab states. The neo-cons got it wrong, but to criticise them was to identify yourself as a racist or an anti-Semite.

But it was the neo-cons who were, along with Israel itself, among the most fervent advocates of the Iraqi invasion. They had seized upon an all-too-true fact of life in most of the Middle East: that Arabs states were mostly squalid, corrupt, brutal dictatorships. No surprise there. We Westerners created most of their dictators, drew the borders of most of the Arab nations and propped up their obedient leaders – bombing them, of course, if they nationalised the Suez Canal, helped the IRA, set off bombs in Berlin that killed US personnel or invaded Kuwait. But the artificial countries that we brought into existence could not produce democracy. Living in nations which in many cases they did not believe in, the Arab peoples had confidence only in their tribes, while their ruthless leaders held patriarchal power through networks of tribal and sectarian alliances.

Though it never occurred to the illusionists – the Blairs and the Bushes and the neo-cons and the journalists who nursed their dreams and nightmares – they might have found their opposite numbers in the crazed government of Saddam Hussein. Just as Bush and Blair claimed they did not wish to invade Iraq when in fact they intended to do just that, Saddam warned of an impending American invasion while apparently believing that the US and Britain were bluffing. And just as his threat of a 'mother of all battles' for Kuwait turned into a headlong military retreat in 1991, so his promise to destroy the American invaders in 2003 proved utterly worthless.

Even if the disciples of Bush and Blair had not bothered to read the British history of native insurrection in Iraq sixty-three years before their own invasion, there was ample evidence that their invasion would follow a remarkably similar path to the nineteenth-century British invasion of Egypt and its subsequent occupation.

In 1879, William Gladstone excoriated the Conservative government for its 'most wanton invasion of Afghanistan'. But he believed in the British Empire and fully supported British invasion of Egypt. The Khedive Ismail, ostensibly obedient to the Ottoman Empire, had gambled on Egypt's economy by accepting vast loans from European bankers at extortionate rates of interest. Egypt was bankrupted, its administration effectively taken over by British and French civil servants working for their own bondholders, and two European ministers were imposed on Ismail's government. When Ismail resisted, the British and French prevailed upon Constantinople to replace him with his son Tewfik. Egyptian opposition to the country's sudden impoverishment – similar to that endured by Iraqis under American-supported UN sanctions after 1990 – took on an Islamic rhetoric.

The 'classic' mistake that the British and French made in their economic takeover of Egypt was in alienating the native army of Egyptians. Anti-European sentiment and attacks on consuls in Alexandria persuaded the British that the native people of that magnificent city should be taught a lesson; Egyptian political opposition would be curbed at the same time.

Egyptian improvements to their coastal forts at Alexandria, the historian John Newsinger noted, became 'a suitable pretext for military action' since 'they were presented as a threat to British warships' even though the Royal Navy 'did not entertain the slightest apprehension with regard to them'. Here was an eerie foretaste of the weapons of mass destruction that did not exist in 2003. When the Egyptians responded by suspending work on their forts, they were told to surrender them; their refusal to do so was met by a ten-hour British bombardment. Five men were killed on the British side, with twenty-eight wounded; on the Egyptian side, 2,000 people – many of them civilians – were killed and wounded.

Far from being appalled by the casualties, Gladstone felt that 'in being party to this work I have been a labourer in the cause of peace'. The nineteenth-century poet Wilfrid Scawen Blunt made the following assessment of his character:

> The insincerities of debate were ingrained in him … if he had a
> new distasteful policy to pursue his first objective was to
> persuade himself into a belief that it was really congenial to him

… Thus he was always saved the too close consciousness of his insincerities, for like the tragedian in Dickens, when he had to act Othello he began by painting himself black all over.

This assessment of Gladstone is a picture-perfect impression of Blair, who said in his own memoirs that while he could not bring the dead back to life, he hoped 'to redeem something from the tragedy of death, in the actions of a life, my life, that continues still'.

Yet the parallels with Iraq do not end there. The autocratic Khedive Tewfik defected to the British, who then invaded Egypt to crush the surviving nationalist government and its army. On 13 September 1882, the British overwhelmed Egyptian defences at the Battle of Tel el-Kebir. Estimates of the Egyptian dead ranged from 2,000 to 8,000; the British lost fifty-seven men. They would consolidate their control over Egypt using methods familiar to us: in the words of a later historian, 'military raids, secret police, informants, massive imprisonment … and the systematic use of torture'.

Just over seventy years after Gladstone's folly, a Tory government under Anthony Eden decided to invade Egypt yet again, following Colonel Nasser's nationalisation of the Suez Canal. Historians will also notice a persistent theme of the Iraqi and Suez narratives: in both, most British government ministers insisted on maintaining their 'official' version of the invasions to the end.

Anthony Eden and most of his cabinet colleagues did everything they could to conceal the shameful story of Britain's plan – drawn up in secret with France and Israel – to invade Egypt and topple Nasser, even to the point of destroying the secret documents of the agreement at Sèvres, where the three powers concocted their bloody expedition. Put simply, they agreed that Israel would invade Egypt and that Britain and France would then 'intervene' on the ground to 'safeguard' the Suez Canal. The real purpose of this 'intervention' would be the overthrow of Nasser.

Major General Tim Cross, sent to Washington to monitor American plans for Iraq, told Blair that post-war planning was 'woefully thin' and pleaded with the prime minister to postpone his invasion. Even two months after the invasion, Cross told the Chilcot Inquiry, no clear policy and strategy for British reconstruction efforts had emerged. The

Americans, according to Edward Chaplin, then head of the Foreign Office's Middle East section and later UK ambassador to Iraq, had a 'blind spot' over post-war planning.

When the first US tanks rumbled onto the Tigris river bridge in Baghdad, not a single officer had been instructed to preserve the city. British soldiers did nothing when they witnessed mass looting in Basra, while in Baghdad the US military failed to respond to the sacking of the Iraq Museum and the burning of the Islamic library.

Eight years later, the now-retired Rumsfeld expressed sorrow for Iraqis who had died under torture during Saddam's rule and for the families of dead Americans, although he showed his irritation when his interviewer, Gideon Rachman of the *Financial Times*, wondered what fellow diners might think about 'the elderly former defence secretary eating a comfortable Sunday lunch in a Washington hotel when the killing continues in Iraq and Afghanistan'.

But how could anyone preparing for an illusory war design plans for what would follow? Especially if – the moment Iraq was conquered – their plans involved the next Middle East war. General Wesley K. Clark, the newly retired hero of the 1998 Kosovo war, recalled visiting the Pentagon about ten days after the 9/11 attacks on New York and Washington. After meeting Rumsfeld and his deputy Paul Wolfowitz:

> I went downstairs just to say hello to some of the people on the
> Joint Staff who used to work for me and one of the generals
> called me in … He says, 'We have made the decision to go to war
> with Iraq.' This was on or about 20 September [2001]. I said,
> 'We're going to war with Iraq? Why? … did they find some
> information connecting Saddam to al-Qaeda?' He said, 'No, No
> … I guess it's like, we don't know what to do about terrorists but
> we've got a good military and we can take down governments.' I
> came back to see him a few weeks later and by that time we were
> bombing in Afghanistan. I said, 'Are we still going to war with
> Iraq?' He said, 'Oh, it's worse than that'… He reached over on his
> desk and picked up a piece of paper. He said, 'I just got this …
> from the Secretary of Defense's office today. This is a memo that
> describes how we are going to take out seven countries in five
> years. Starting with Iraq, and then Syria and Lebanon. Then
> Libya, Somalia and Sudan. Then finishing off [with] Iran.'

This goes beyond black comedy, yet it was unstoppable. Like the lies that accompanied every facet of this dreadful adventure, the war in Iraq took on a ghastly life of its own, its dishonesty infecting every element of the conflict: the sham 'liberation', the casual and embedded corruption of every international trade and rebuilding project in the occupied nation, the sadism and torture in its prisons, the mass bloodletting unleashed upon the land in which civilisation supposedly began.

Almost daily, we would hear evidence of political, economic and military fraud. News stories which in other circumstances would have called an entire conflict into question were so frequent that they became banal. As the US Defense Department released further evidence that there had been no contact between Saddam and Osama bin Laden, US vice president Dick Cheney was still claiming that there was. Blair was revealed to have had three telephone conversations – within ten days of the invasion – with the immensely powerful and equally disreputable media warlord Rupert Murdoch, who proceeded to support Blair's act of aggression.

When bombs were detonated on the London Underground and a bus in July 2005, killing fifty-two people, Blair denied that there was any connection with British involvement in the Iraq war, yet one of the killers appeared on a pre-suicide videotape saying that Iraq was the reason for his action. The director general of MI5 at the time, Eliza Manningham-Buller, later gave evidence to Chilcot that there was such an increase in the warnings of internal 'terrorist threats' after the invasion of Iraq that MI5 received a 100 per cent increase in its budget.

My colleague Patrick Cockburn and I had railed against the lies for years, but it was Blair's 2009 BBC interview that revealed the final truth – or lie. Asked whether if he had known there were no weapons of mass destruction in Iraq, he would still have gone to war against Saddam, Blair blandly replied:

I would still have thought it right to remove him. I mean, obviously you would have had to use and deploy different arguments about the nature of the threat.

And there we had it: Blair's 'Toad of Toad Hall' moment. Linguistics was scarcely necessary to strip the bark off this rotten tree. What did 'right' mean? And the word 'obviously' betrayed how Blair's mind worked; if one set of arguments didn't work, it was natural to try another. He might have said one thing in the House of Commons but he wasn't sorry, because he still wanted to invade Iraq. And thus Blair spoke of the 'different arguments' which he would have to 'use' or 'deploy' if the WMD didn't exist. To go to war depended not on the truth, but on words as weapons.

As the years passed, this set of lies and variations became so normal that even our outrage at their lies became – and remains today – diminished.* The dishonesty helped not only to contaminate, but to 'normalise' war. Our moral defences simply crumbled away in the face of their constant, monstrous fantasy.

There is almost always a visionary element to imperial expansion. Nineteenth-century Western fascination with the lands of the Christian Bible provided added justification to European and American ambitions in the Middle East. The arrival of Western nations was portrayed not as colonial land-grabbing but as an almost missionary attempt to return the peoples of the region to the prosperity which they supposedly enjoyed in ancient times. As Lieutenant General Sir Stanley Maude told the people of Baghdad just over a week after his capture of the city in March 1917, it was the wish of the Western Allies 'that you should prosper even as in the past when your lands were fertile, when your ancestors gave to the world Literature, Science and Art, and when Baghdad City was one of the wonders of the world'.

The new occupiers spotted the need to avoid any suspicion of their own commercial interests in Mesopotamia. While the 'commercial prosperity' of its people remained 'of the closest concern to the British Government,' declared the commander of British forces in Iraq, it had no wish 'to impose upon you alien institutions'. Maude made no mention of the still-secret 1916 agreement between Britain and France to divide up the Middle East Arab lands between them. And despite an appropriate clause about the British desire that 'the Arab race may rise

---

* My own newspaper files are packed with articles denouncing the war by generals and columnists. In 2006, a growing circle of US ex-generals called for Donald Rumsfeld's resignation. But they did so from the safety of pensioned retirement, and condemned the defense secretary not for his dissembling and wilful distortion of events, but for his 'absolute failures in managing the war against Saddam'.

once more to greatness and renown', no reference was made to British support for Zionist aspirations.

Those more interested in the divine could also predict future abundance. The Scottish chaplain Dr William Ewing, who lectured British troops on the Bible lands in the Great War, ends his dramatic account of Gallipoli and Mesopotamia with the following encomium for the future of British-ruled Iraq:

> It may be hoped that the weary centuries of misrule are over at last. The people trust the integrity and high purpose of the Power now established astride the Tigris in the ancient seat of religious and political authority in Mesopotamia. The breath of freedom will quicken the spirit of hope and enterprise. Beauty and fertility will return to the vast plains where untold wealth waits the hand of the husbandman.*

But the Mesopotamia about which these men enthused was fertile in water rather than oil. There was no mention of Iraq's known oil deposits – nor of Iraq's importance in safeguarding from Britain's enemies the known oil supplies already coming from the wells of neighbouring Persia.

Next to Ewing's book on my library shelf is a beautiful volume of paintings by Donald Maxwell, an official British war artist in Mesopotamia. He writes enthusiastically of the 'adventurous iron pipes' that carry crude oil from the fields of the Anglo-Persian Oil Company to Abadan. And while acknowledging the city's 'choking dustiness and its depressing isolation', its 'roaring furnaces and its all-pervading smell of hot oil', the painter is seduced by the landscape.

---

* In a tent hospital at Amara, Ewing lectured on the biblical land, only to discover that while soldiers shared his interest in ancient history, they did so with somewhat less accuracy. 'One referred to the country with more reverence than knowledge as "partly the Holy Land where Jesus used to walk". A keen-faced boy questioned me closely as to whether there were now any remains of "the pillar of salt" ... he explained, "the pillar of salt Lot's wife turned into". He meant to have a chip of that pillar to take home to his mother. A "hefty chap" with a New Testament in his hand wanted to know how far up the river Sodom and Gomorrah were.' But Ewing was cross-questioned by other soldiers about the birthplace of Abraham, the Tower of Babel, Babylon, Nineveh and, of course, the Garden of Eden. The more knowledgeable soldiers, Ewing could not resist telling his readers, came from Scotland.

Oil was romantic, an offshoot of the Victorian industrial revolution rather than a source of political and military power. As he journeys up the Tigris, Maxwell is overwhelmed by the biblical land through which he passes. His last chapter describes Mesopotamia's 'enormous productive potentialities' and, while he talks of the waters of its two great rivers, he condemns those in 1922 – when the insurrection against British rule was already underway – who would have Britain leave Mesopotamia for financial reasons. 'On the other hand,' Maxwell writes:

> wise men have told us that the Mesopotamian oilfields near
> Mosul are to be of great importance, like the Persian wells that
> have their pipe-line outfall at Abadan, and that a firm and
> fatherly hand is necessary to keep the country in a state of trade
> development.

If Britain was to abandon the land, Maxwell predicts, it will 'revert to chaos'. His conclusion begins to read like narratives of later Iraqi history:

> We read daily in our newspapers of rumours of war with restless
> tribes around Mosul, and of raids and skirmishes. The land …
> where Abraham dwelt, with its silent traces of the great
> civilisations which it fostered, Babylonian and Assyrian, Persian,
> Greek and Arabian, is once more, by the chances of war, an open
> book, and time alone will show what is to be written therein.

Maxwell's text has none of the certainties with which the West embarked upon its vast and lamentable occupation in 2003. But the 'firm and fatherly hand' of which he spoke was ready to be clamped upon Mesopotamia even before the Great War ended. In July 1918, the Admiralty's oil expert, Rear Admiral Sir Edmond Slade, urged his masters to 'assist British companies to obtain control of as many oil lands in foreign countries as possible', the production to be sold only to or through British companies. Sir Maurice Hankey, Secretary of the War Cabinet in London, had been approached by 'people with knowledge of oil production' who had warned him of a likely decrease in US and Mexican imports after the war. The retention of the oil-bearing regions in Mesopotamia and Persia in British hands, Hankey wrote to Arthur Balfour, would be 'a first-class British War Aim'.

The key word here was 'retention'. For the difference between 1918 and 2003 was that Britain, France and later America were bound to control Iraqi oil and its profits from the start. The French originally wanted to incorporate Mosul into their own post-1914–18 League of Nations mandate territory, because of its known oil-producing capacity. At this time, no one knew that Iraq would have the fifth largest proven oil reserves in the world. By drafting in an 'alien' Sunni Muslim from Arabia – King Faisal – to rule over the Iraqi Shiite majority, and with two Anglo–Iraqi treaties that effectively gave the UK control over its frontiers for decades, Iraq became an oil 'vassal' state.

But since Saddam's invasion of Kuwait and the emirate's liberation in 1991, the US had targeted Iraq for destabilisation. In 1995, for example, the CIA asked Congress for $15 million to continue covert operations against Iraq – and a measly $4 million to pursue what the Clinton administration called 'dual containment' in Iran. This was not intended to dethrone Saddam – rather to 'weaken' him – although the Iraqi regime's decision in November 2000 to convert its dollar reserves into euros may have profoundly changed US decision-making. Oil had always been sold for dollars, thus allowing the US to have a substantial control over the market. Once the euro entered the oil market, the dollar's power could be threatened. When Iran threatened to switch to euros, it was added to the 'axis of evil'. 'Regime change' might be the only solution.

In the years following the 2003 invasion of Iraq, I gave many lectures on the Middle East across the world, and I was endlessly asked whether the occupation of Iraq was really all about oil. My reply was always the same: if the major export of Iraq had been beetroot, did anyone believe the American 82nd Airborne would really have gone to Fallujah and Mosul?

The US and British governments repeatedly denied that oil provided a motive for the invasion. White House spokesman Ari Fleischer refused to countenance such an idea when he was questioned by journalists on 6 February 2003. 'This is not about that,' he said. 'This is about saving lives, about protecting the American people.' Blair played the same game, more verbosely and using one of his favourite put-downs: the conspiracy theory of history.

> Let me just deal with the oil thing because … the oil conspiracy
> theory is honestly one of the most absurd when you analyse it.
> The fact is that, if the oil that Iraq has was our concern, I mean
> we could probably cut a deal with Saddam tomorrow in relation
> to the oil. It's not the oil that is the issue, it is the weapons.

A dishonesty may be denied at the time but – uncovered eight years
later – it is an inconvenience, a momentary irritation. In 2011, however,
secret memoranda revealed by the *Independent* showed that the Foreign
Office was talking to major British oil companies in 2002 about the
financial benefits they stood to gain from the forthcoming invasion of
Iraq.

Five months before the March 2003 attack on Iraq, the then UK
trade minister Baroness Symons was telling BP that the government
believed British energy firms should be given a share of Iraq's oil and
gas reserves as a reward for Blair's commitment to US plans for regime
change. BP feared it was being 'locked out' of deals that Washington
was making with foreign companies. 'Baroness Symons agreed,'
according to a 31 October 2002 memo, 'that it would be difficult to
justify British companies losing out in Iraq … if the UK had itself been
a conspicuous supporter of the US government throughout the crisis.'
The following month, the Foreign Office invited BP to discuss opportunities in Iraq 'post-regime change', its minutes recording that 'Iraq is
the big oil prospect. BP is desperate to get in there and anxious that
political deals should not deny them the opportunity.'

A thousand documents obtained under Britain's Freedom of
Information act – legislation which Blair introduced and then, understandably, regretted – showed that five meetings were held between
British ministers, civil servants and executives of BP and Shell in late
2002, scarcely five months before the invasion. Yet on 12 March 2003,
Lord Browne, then BP's chief executive, said, 'It is not, in my or BP's
opinion, a war about oil.' A BP company statement the same day said
that it had 'no strategic interest in Iraq'. And – the same day yet again
– Shell claimed it had 'neither sought nor attended meetings with officials in the UK Government on the subject of Iraq'. But, it added with
Blair-like deviousness, 'the subject has only come up during conversations during normal meetings we attend from time to time with
officials'. As Greg Muttitt remarked in the *Independent*, 'oil was one of

the government's most important strategic considerations, and it secretly colluded with oil companies to give them access to that huge prize'.

The divvying up of Iraq's oil wealth was to become an enduring scandal of the occupation, along with the massive corruption in which US companies, contractors and Iraqi officials became involved. The costs were inevitably as dishonest as the lies that created the war. Within weeks, I was chatting to a young oil exploration analyst who had just arrived in Baghdad. 'I can't believe it,' he told me. 'Everyone I meet asks for bribes. I'm told I have to pay the Iraqi authorities even for meetings with them. Then when I complained to the Americans at the Green Zone just now, their officials asked for cash to sort it out!' I knew corruption was the cancer of the Arab world, but I did not conceive of how an occupying power supposedly delivering Iraqis their long-sought freedom could turn into a mafia, and at such breathtaking speed.

Oil is slippery stuff, but not as slippery as the figures that were now being peddled by Iraq's occupiers. Up around Kirkuk, the authorities were even keeping the sabotage figures secret – they could not prevent their pipelines to Turkey from being blown up. And down in Baghdad, the statistics were being faked. In Kirkuk, for example, the occupation powers reported sabotage only when television cameras captured a blown pipe. US infantry and helicopters were patrolling the pipeline but, in the ravines and tribal areas through which it passed, long sections were indefensible.

Thus the only substantial oil revenues the Americans could boast were from the south of Iraq. In the middle of that first August of the occupation, US proconsul Paul Bremer gave the impression that production stood at around 1.5 million barrels a day, but the real figure at that time was 780,000 barrels. In the words of an oil man with whom I became friends, this was 'an inexcusable catastrophe' – when the Americans attacked Iraq the previous March, the country had been producing 2.7 million barrels a day.

Anarchy sucked up money. Bremer's administrators secretly decided that well over half the $20 billion earmarked for Iraq would go towards security for its oil production infrastructure. Even after the war began, a detailed analysis by Yahya Sadowski of the American University of Beirut suggested that repairing existing wells and pipes in post-war Iraq would cost more than $1 billion, that raising production to 3.5 million barrels a day would take three years and cost $8 billion investment and another £20 billion for repairs to the electrical grid which powered the pumps and refineries. Some said that bringing production up to six million barrels a day would cost up to $100 billion. In other words, the September 2003 Bush budget request of $87 billion that had horrified Congress was likely to rise towards $200 billion.

Since the 1920s, only around 2,300 wells had been drilled in Iraq – and those were in the valleys of the Tigris and Euphrates. Its deserts were – and still are – almost totally unexplored. Officially, Iraq contained 12 per cent of the world's oil reserves, but it could contain as much as 25 per cent. This was the irony of America's new power in Iraq. US oil deposits were increasingly depleted and by 2025 oil imports might account for 70 per cent of domestic demand. The US might now have up to 25 per cent of the world's reserves under its military control; the cost of making it flow could produce an American economic crisis and it was this – rather than the daily killing of young American service-men and women – that lay behind a growing sense of panic in the Bush administration. Washington had got its hands on the biggest treasure chest in the world, but it couldn't open the lid. No wonder they were cooking the books in Baghdad.

It was not long before major Bush election campaign donors were awarded $8 billion worth of contracts to rebuild both Iraq and Afghanistan. According to a Washington research group that investi-gated government ethics, more than seventy companies and individual contractors gave over $500,000 in donations to Bush's 2000 election campaign. Major contracts were awarded without competi-tion; the main recipient was KBR, a subsidiary of Halliburton – which Cheney headed before he resigned to run with Bush in 2000, and which was given $2.3 billion to support the military and restore Iraq's oil industry.

More worrying in the long term was the disappearance of billions of dollars from Iraq's own treasury. Only seven months after the inva-sion, the charity Christian Aid was demanding to know why $4 billion of Iraq's oil revenues and other funds were unaccounted for. Less than a year later, the same group was accusing Iraq's occupiers of handing power to the new Iraqi government without explaining what it had done with approximately $20 billion of Iraq's own money.

A month later, Paul Krugman asked in the *New York Times* why only $400 million out of congressionally approved funds of $18.4 billion had been spent on reconstruction, concluding that almost all the money spent by the Coalition Provisional Authority came from Iraqi sources, mostly from those oil revenues. Auditors were unable to find out what Halliburton did with $1.4 billion. Christian Aid perceptively asked what precedent these billion-dollar black holes set for the new Iraqi government. Helen Collinson, one of the charity's officials, noted that 'too many oil-rich countries go down the road of unaccountable government, riches for the few and poverty for the many'. What had the occupying power got to hide? But the precedent which Krugman feared had already been learned. US auditors were aware that the new set of wealthy Iraqis preened by the Bush administration for future political power were themselves involved in diverting their own country's funds. An Iraqi investigating the pre-war oil-for-food scandal was assassinated. Other Iraqi civil servants spoke privately of the physical dangers they faced when asked to audit their own ministries.

On 14 July 2004 – the very same day that Lord Butler declared that Tony Blair's decisions for invading Iraq were made in 'good faith' – I came face to face with the results. Just a few hours before Butler's pronouncement, Sabr Karim paid the price for working for the new Iraq. The father of seven was a senior auditor in Iraq's new Industry Ministry whose job was to scrutinise the lucrative contracts given to local businessmen to rebuild his country. He had arrived home in a suburb of Baghdad with his family's breakfast when two men in a pick-up fired two bullets into his stomach and two into his head. His children found him lying on the pavement, one leg still in his car.

In Iraq, the funeral tent is traditionally pitched in the street outside the victim's home, but when I went to pay my respects it was blocked in by cars to prevent suicide bombers from driving a vehicle into the tent. For when Sabr Karim's brother and son-in-law had gone to the family's local mosque to collect a coffin, someone had left a bomb in it. This was the bloody, perverse reality which we reporters could witness with our own eyes in the 'new' Iraq. It was venal enough under Saddam, of course, but now the West was supposed to be in charge, its awesome financial power protecting the future of the newly liberated land. This, however, was another day in the life – and death – of 'new' Iraq.

Sabr Karim had worked for the Industry Ministry for thirty years. 'He was a very honest guy,' his brother Yahyia told me. 'He took care of the government's money and in the last few months, as you know, there were millions of dollars in contracts going through the ministry. His job was to check this. Yes, he had received threats. He never talked about them.'

The details of Sabr Karim's murder were as horrifying as they were routine, and – in the 'new' Iraq – familiar. He had gone out for the family breakfast for three consecutive days – routine was a fatal mistake for anyone in danger – and when he returned he had not seen the car parked on the corner of his street in which three men were watching him, one talking on a mobile phone. Neighbours later recalled that when one of the men closed his phone, a Nissan pick-up suddenly appeared. 'They obviously didn't know Sabr or the area, but they were told he had arrived,' Yahyia said. 'They arrived immediately and they were very professional killers. Two bullets in the stomach and two in the head. Then they climbed back straight away ... and drove away at such high speed that no one had a chance even to shoot at them.' Sabr Karim's eldest son, twenty-year-old Akram, came and sat beside us. 'For thirty-five years, we have lived in a closed society,' he said. 'And now we are told we can have democracy – but this is freedom and liberty for killers.'

There was chicken and beef for the funeral lunch outside Sabr Karim's home, and yogurt and fresh vegetables and strong, hot tea. Some of the visitors suggested that there was so much corruption in the new Industry Ministry that the police would not follow up on the murder. There were a few careful allusions to Sabr Karim's work – could this have been an inside job, a contractor who did not want his theft of state funds to be discovered? Or was it just another attack on a civil servant working for the new American-backed government?

The Karim family were Shiites, living in a largely Sunni area of Baghdad, and Sunni-led insurgents had denounced as collaborators all who were now employed by Ayad Allawi, the new US-appointed Iraqi prime minister. That same day, Allawi, once a CIA asset, an MI6 agent and a Baathist, had announced the creation of a new 'Directorate for National Security' to enforce law and order. It was a title with which all Iraqis were familiar. Saddam Hussein operated a 'Directorate for General Security'; and when Allawi was asked if ex-Baathists would be employed in his new institution, he replied that his security men would be 'professionals'. All Iraqis knew what that meant.

To ensure that his raft of reconstruction contracts to US companies remained secure after his departure as head of the CPA, Bremer instituted a set of laws which the 'new' and 'sovereign' government of Iraq could not change – thus ensuring that American companies would continue to cream off Iraq's money after he left. One of the most insidious was the re-introduction of Saddam's 1984 law banning strikes. A strong trade union movement could provide a vital base of democratic power in a new nation, but Bremer preferred to protect big business.

The twin saga of the West's attempts to hijack Iraq's oil and the Iraqi government's determination to crush its own country's trade union movement is a story of international immorality and Iraqi government turpitude. The heroes of the story are Hassan Jumaa, one of the most resilient and courageous trade union leaders in the Middle East, and Greg Muttitt, the English researcher who doggedly, over ten years, investigated the disgraceful 'resource war' which the Americans and British fought in Iraq.

Naomi Klein was the first writer to recognise the coincidence of US torture in Iraq and the 'shock therapy' of forcing Iraqi 'authorities' to auction off, illegally, the country's oil reserves. So stunned would Iraqis be by US firepower that they would emerge from the smoke and rubble to find themselves living in an Arabic Singapore, a 'Tiger on the Tigris'. The problem was that the Iraqis had not been shocked enough. As Paul Bremer droned on about the need for democracy, Iraqis decided they did not want their oil reserves to be sold off to foreign companies. Trade unionists, tribesmen, religious leaders; all were against the frantic deals to which they were supposed to give their support. So Bremer suddenly lost his enthusiasm for democracy. Relinquishing the power of the occupiers to the occupied would mean, as Klein pointed out, 'abandoning the dream of turning Iraq into a model privatised economy'. Bremer blocked the holding of local elections and blacklisted the trade unions.

Now we come to Hassan Jumaa, who almost singlehandedly set up a new oil union in the southern port of Basra, both to protect the rights of oil workers and the industry from foreign control. He had noticed that US and British troops surrounded the oil fields with armour as soon as they crossed the Iraqi border – and that KBR, US vice president

Dick Cheney's former company, followed Western troops into the oil
facilities. 'It was our duty as oil workers to protect the oil installations
since they are the property of the Iraqi people,' Jumaa told Muttitt.
Jumaa had worked in the Iraqi oil industry for more than thirty years
and although he was an 'activist' against Saddam, he was, until 2003 at
least, no trade unionist. From that date, he exhibited all the characteristics which the West claimed they expected of newly liberated Iraqis
– patriotism, selflessness and a demand for freedom of expression – and
incurred the opposition of both the Western multinationals and the
authorities in Baghdad. Jumaa 'mobilised' the oil workers against the
Iraqi government's determination to sell the country's greatest wealth
to Big Oil, ten years of struggle that at one point had the authorities in
Baghdad threatening to move oil activists from the south of Iraq – a
largely Shia area – to suburbs of Baghdad where they would almost
certainly be murdered in the city's sectarian war.

Jumaa and his colleagues had to learn about the complex produc-
tion-sharing agreements (PSAs) which the oil giants tried to foist on the
Iraqis – with the help of the newly appointed ministers and civil servants in the oil ministry. As one NGO investigation pointed out, their
purpose was largely political; PSAs are immune to public scrutiny and
lock countries into economic agreements with companies that cannot
be altered for decades, while also usually exempting oil companies
from new laws that might affect their profits.

But there was a political problem, as Muttitt cynically worked out:

> The USA was liberator not coloniser, so its politicians said, and
> its goal was to bring democracy. Forcing the Iraqis to hand
> control of their oil to multinational companies didn't really fit
> this narrative. The solution, as ever, was to deny that oil
> privatisation was a policy decision at all; instead it was portrayed
> as a self-evident necessity.

The Americans, as occupiers, could not take control of Iraq's natural
resources; but they did have 'a legal and moral duty' to provide security. Hence the pressure on the Iraqi government to agree on contracts
in which foreign oil companies would be paid fixed fees on each barrel
produced and have their costs reimbursed. This bullying of Baghdad
began in earnest alongside General Petraeus' military 'surge' in 2007.

The army's 'stabilisation' of the Iraq war would take place as Iraq's own economy was 'stabilised' – in favour of the multinationals. Muttitt traced the original US plans back to neo-con Douglas Feith's Pentagon pre-invasion Energy Infrastructure Planning Group, which suggested that repairing war damage to the country's oil infrastructure would 'discourage private sector involvement'. KBR would carry out initial repairs; long-term contracts with multinational companies would follow.

As the first permanent Iraqi government was formed under Nouri al-Maliki in May 2006, its priority was supposed to be a law legalising the return of Western multinationals to run the oil sector. The 'surge' would guarantee the survival of the new government, provided it delivered on a series of 'benchmarks'. Congress even passed a bill that would cut off US reconstruction funding if the oil law was not passed by parliament. The new constitution of Iraq insisted that such a law must indeed be passed by MPs, but the parliament declined to do so. As a result, al-Maliki's government began awarding contracts to oil companies without it.

Klein believes that James Baker's Iraq Study Group played a dramatic role in 'the boldest attempt at crisis exploration' when it called in December 2006 for the US to 'assist Iraqi leaders to reorganise the national oil industry as a commercial enterprise' and to 'encourage investment in Iraq's oil sector by the international community and by international energy companies'. The Bush administration even helped to draft the oil law by which companies like Shell and BP could sign thirty-year contracts in which they would keep a large share of Iraq's oil profits. The increasing bloodbath overwhelming Iraq provided an opportune moment to push through the oil law, which many MPs had never heard of.

Muttitt took the view that the new contracts were illegal, and 'will last only as long as there's a government in Baghdad that supports them'. Now the government's repression of trade unions increased, along with a growing authoritarianism that looked suspiciously like Saddamism. Muttitt was explaining the need to understand 'the nature of a resource war in the twenty-first century' so that Iraqi people could comprehend the degree to which they were being robbed of their natural wealth. In any event, he wrote, the Iraqi government 'went ahead and auctioned off 60 per cent of the country's proven reserves, under contracts of dubious legality to companies such as BP, Shell and Exxon'. It was the biggest sell-off in the history of oil.

While many of his colleagues were concentrating on the Petraeus 'surge', Muttitt was sitting through the Ruritanian oil auctions and thus able to give us a darkly comic account of the illegal sell-off. Hussain al-Shahristani, the oil minister who had been cruelly tortured under Saddam, was now anxious to go ahead with the sale of Iraq's birthright to international consortia. The second auction was held at the Iraqi oil ministry in Baghdad in December 2009; Iraq disposed of the 12.6 billion barrel Majnoon oil field near Basra and the Halfaya field in Maysan. Muttitt wrote:

> the rapidity of the process was quite shocking. These fields, accounting for the vast majority of Iraq's future economy, were going under the hammer at fifteen-minute intervals. This was not development: it was a revolution. What was going through Shahristani's mind? Did he have any doubts? If he did, he didn't show them.

On the second day went West Qurna Phase II, Gharraf, Badra, Najma; almost 60 per cent of Iraq's reserves had been accounted for in two rounds of auctioning.

One MP, Shatha al-Musawi, tried to bring a legal case against the first contract – a BP deal with the China National Petroleum Company for the Rumaila field – but it would have cost her $250,000. 'Most of the governing institutions are working without law and violating the constitution every day,' she told Muttitt, 'because they decided not to have an effective parliament. We really have a dictatorship.' She was right. Trade union offices were raided, computers purloined, equipment smashed, union leaders arrested. Most Iraqis, as Muttitt said, 'didn't want an oil law to put multinationals in charge of their oil ... Iraqis believe and believed very passionately that the oil belongs in Iraqi hands.'

What is also obvious to anyone investigating this scandalous behaviour was that the corruption which undermined 'new' Iraq had been endemic long before the 2003 Anglo-American invasion. Bribery on a grand scale had been an essential part of the West's dealings with Iraq under Saddam, and was now continuing, in much the same way as the brutality of Saddamism was seamlessly perpetuated long after the dictator's execution.

As Ed Harriman, a researcher into US and UK malfeasance in the Middle East, was to point out in 2007, the US official charged with overseeing Iraq's reconstruction

> found that almost all the American money set aside to rebuild Iraq – more than $21 billion appropriated by Congress four years ago – has been spent. So too has some $20 billion of the Iraqis' own money handed out by Paul Bremer … during the first year of the occupation. Much of the money was used to pay for American goods and services and never reached Iraq. Much of the rest disappeared and has never been properly accounted for.

Harriman concluded that

> for well over a year Iraq has had the reputation of being the most corrupt regime in the Middle East. It's getting worse. Judge Radhi al-Radhi, who heads Iraq's Commission on Public Integrity, says his staff are currently investigating $11 billion in questionable payments. But Iraqi officials and ministers are unlikely to go to prison, or even face trial. The prime minister, Nouri al-Maliki, is entitled to – and does – exempt their officials … Aside from looting their ministry budgets, Iraq's officials and politicians, with criminal help, siphon their country's oil direct from the pipelines.*

In an earlier investigation, Harriman examined six US government committee, accountability and audit reports, which revealed the mentality of the American occupation authorities:

> handing out truckloads of dollars for which neither they nor the recipients felt any need to be accountable. The audits have so far

---

* The trail of 'lost' money was to achieve *Gone-with-the-Wind* proportions. By 2010, the US Defense Department was unable to account for almost $9 billion taken from Iraqi oil revenues for use in reconstruction; a report by the US Special Investigator for Iraq Reconstruction said that $8.7 billion out of $9.1 billion withdrawn between 2004 and 2007 from an account set up by the UN Security Council could not be found.

referred more than a hundred contracts, involving billions of
dollars paid to American personnel and corporations, for
investigation and possible criminal prosecution. They have also
discovered that $8.8 billion that passed through the new Iraqi
government ministries in Baghdad while Bremer was in charge
is unaccounted for, with little prospect of finding out where it
went. A further $3.4 billion earmarked by Congress for Iraqi
development has since been siphoned off to finance 'security'.

The word 'security' was beginning to have a malign effect on all fiscal
matters involving Iraq. By 2006, foreign and local mercenaries
accounted for almost half the 'Western' security forces in Iraq and
were sucking money from the country.* 'America,' columnist Frank
Rich wrote the following year, 'has routinely betrayed the very values
of democratic governance that it hopes to export to Iraq.'

Rich condemned Blackwater's owner, Erik Prince, for 'salivating
over the next payday' as he expanded his company into a 'full spec-
trum' defence contractor which offered everything from remotely
piloted blimps to armoured trucks. The Pentagon's Bush-appointed
inspector general, who delivered a corruption report to Congress in
2005 that was full of redactions, insisted that Rumsfeld and Wolfowitz
knew nothing of these financial crimes; the same inspector general,
Joseph Schmitz, soon afterwards became chief operating officer for
Blackwater's parent company, the Prince Group. An army scholar of
military ethics, Colonel Ted Westhusing, a witness to corruption, died
of a gunshot wound to the head while training Iraqi security forces for
General Petraeus. The colonel left behind a letter, which Rich quoted
in the New York Times. 'I cannot support,' Westhusing wrote, 'a mission
that leads to corruption, human rights abuse and liars.' Though desig-
nated a suicide, a Los Angeles Times reporter wrote that some believed
Westhusing was murdered by contractors fearing he might turn whis-
tleblower.

A year later, the New York Times described Blackwater as 'the non-
pareil war profiteer' which 'keeps outdoing its own mercenary record.

---

* By March 2010, 207,553 mercenaries would be working in Iraq and Afghanistan, a ratio
of 1.18 mercenaries per soldier. Between 2003 and 2007, $85 billion of contracts had been
placed with private suppliers in Iraq by US agencies.

Blackwater executives,' it continued, 'have used inside influence as administration fund-raisers to multiply their no-bid war contracts [in Iraq] a thousandfold to more than $1 billion.'

Within the frontiers of Iraq, old sectarian divisions were re-opened by Western oil companies that chose to sign production contracts with the regional Kurdish administration in the north – in defiance of the federal government in Baghdad. In October 2011, Exxon Mobil signed an exploration deal that included three areas in dispute between Kurds and Arab Iraqis. A company with close ties to George W. Bush, Hunt Oil of Dallas, signed a deal with the Kurdish Regional Government, welcomed in advance by a State Department official in an email that said: 'getting an American company to sign a deal with the KRG will make big news back home. Please keep us posted.'

The rape of Iraq had no end. Within the Xanadu palace on the banks of the Tigris, journalists were handed leaflets by the Americans, advising them that persistent questions on unhelpful topics would not be tolerated. It was not difficult to see why. There was virtually no coverage in the international media, for example, of the extraordinary steps the US took to control the food production of Iraq's ancient lands in favour of American companies – forbidding farmers, whose ancestors had over ten thousand years produced the seed for almost every variety of wheat in the modern world, from re-using their own seeds. Only a few environmentalists and activist magazines investigated Paul Bremer's infamous Order 81, which forbad farmers to save their own seeds; henceforth, they could only plant seeds from licensed, authorised US distributors. Every year, Iraqis were expected to destroy any seed and repurchase seeds from 'an authorised supplier' or face fines or imprisonment. The new seeds would be genetically modified. 'Iraq,' as a Swiss magazine pointed out, 'was to become a giant live laboratory for testing GMO wheat, and the Iraqis were the human guinea pigs of the experiment.'

And so it went on. In 2007, the Americans were forced to admit that 190,000 rifles and pistols supplied over two years to Iraqi 'security' forces had gone missing, 110,000 of them Soviet AK-47 assault rifles. Amnesty International had previously reported that 350,000 AK-47s and other weapons were removed from Bosnia and Serbia by private contractors working for the Pentagon – and sent to Iraq. In addition, 135,000 items of body armour and 115,000 helmets had also vanished.

Had they been sold to insurgents? The original arms distribution –
embarrassingly for the Pentagon – was led by Petraeus, now lauding
his mighty military 'surge' in Iraq.*

Nation-creation, it seemed, took no account of the people living
inside this 'creation'. Iraqis thus came to understand that the pressure
to hand the nation's oil wealth over to Western companies was inti-
mately bound up with the occupation itself; protests against the
occupation therefore merged with anger against the oil sell-off. After
supporters of Muqtada al-Sadr protested at the US occupation in their
hundreds of thousands, the Iraqi government introduced legislation
stating that demonstrations could only take place on football fields.
Al-Sadr's people had campaigned ever since the invasion against any
deals with oil companies belonging to countries involved in the occupation. This is surely one reason why Bremer himself spoke so harshly
against al-Sadr as early as 2004, issuing an arrest warrant for him and
even closing his newspaper, *Al-Hawza Nateqa* – another lesson in the
kind of 'freedom' that the Americans claimed to have brought to Iraq.

Al-Hawza Nateqa's sin, among many, was to criticise Paul Bremer
and 'to provoke violence against the Coalition Forces'. On 6 August
2003 – so said Bremer's letter – the paper had accused the US of invading Iraq 'not only to remove Saddam and steal Iraq's oil but to destroy
the cultural structures and the character and civilisation of the Iraqi
people'. On 21 August, it had claimed that the Americans in the
Baghdad Shia slum of Sadr City were 'fighting Islam and its symbols'.
This represented, according to Bremer, 'a serious threat of violence
against the Coalition Forces and against the Iraqi people who are cooperating with the CPA in the reconstruction of Iraq'. Bremer did not
mention that a US helicopter crew had removed an Islamic flag from
an electricity pole in Sadr City in the incident.

'Suppression of the press,' shouted journalists outside the paper's
offices. *Al-Hawza Nateqa* was merely 'letting our people know what is
going on in secret'. From the Balfour Declaration of 1917 to the new
'criminal constitution in Iraq', the people had been lied to, a printed

---

* No one seemed untouched by money scandals, even if they involved abuse of power
rather than corruption. How were Iraqis supposed to react, for example, when they
learned that each member of parliament – weaned on America's unregulated finances –
received $30,000 a month, including $9,000 salary for himself and thirty bodyguards, and a
pension of $7,200 a month for ten years after retirement?

sheet on the gate announced. The 'honest voices' of journalists could not be silenced.

Inevitably, a war that was fought on a bedrock of lies and dissimulation, of brutality and coercion, underscored by a pseudo-Christian 'ethic', infected the Middle East. The millions of American soldiers and other Western troops who passed through Iraq brought a plague with them. From Afghanistan, they were to bring the infection of al-Qaeda. They smothered Iraq with injustice and fed the cult of the suicide bomber. They brought the disease of civil war. They injected Iraq with corruption on a far grander scale than that which had existed under Saddam. They stamped the seal of torture on Abu Ghraib just as they had refined it in Afghanistan. They sectarianised a country that, for all its Saddamite cruelty and venality, had hitherto held its Sunnis and Shiites together. And because the Shiites would inevitably rule in this new 'democracy', the American soldiers gave Iran the victory it had sought so vainly in the 1980–88 war against Saddam. Indeed, men who had attacked the US embassy in Kuwait in the bad old days of the 1980s would now help to run Iraq. The 'Dawa' party were 'terrorists' then; now they were 'democrats'.

But the sickness continued. America's disaster in Iraq infected Jordan and then Lebanon with al-Qaeda. The arrival of gunmen from Fatah al-Islam in the Nahr al-Bared Palestinian camp in the north of Lebanon in 2007, and the scores of civilian dead, were a direct result of the Sunni uprising in Iraq. Al-Qaeda had arrived in Lebanon courtesy of Bashar al-Assad's Syrian regime, it is true; but within four years, al-Qaeda and its affiliates were arriving in Syria to fight Assad himself, and then cross-fertilising with the Sunni Islamist militias in Iraq. And Iraq under the Americans even re-infected Afghanistan with the suicide bomber. When the great Western armies took their armour and weapons home, there was an almost primordial quality to their decay after years of baking in the alien soil of the Middle East. By 2007, the financial toll of America's wars in Iraq and Afghanistan had reached $1.6 trillion, and within three years President Barack Obama was asking Congress for a further $33 billion to continue the struggle in both countries. In 2011 he wanted another $708 billion for the US Defense Department.

Long before the end of America's Iraqi adventure, the usual 'experts' were calling the very existence of Iraq into question. Why should a sandpit created by Winston Churchill out of three separate communities any longer be called a nation? Iraq, the columnist David Brooks wrote, had the same 'warlord structure' that had caused mass murder in Rwanda, Bosnia and Sierra Leone – 'stupid men who would be the dregs of society under normal conditions ... become revered leaders'. This process came about, so Brooks announced, because of 'trauma, chaos and stress'. Then came the usual racist slurs against the crushed but still courageous people of Iraq, represented by these same 'stupid men', who 'kill for fun, faith and profit – because they find it more rewarding to massacre and loot than to farm and labour'.

This slanderous verbal assault against an entire people had surely been brought about by the 'trauma, chaos and stress' of invasion and occupation. The sectarianism that Saddam had practised was rekindled and exacerbated, according to Brooks, not by the West's predilection for sectarian politics under the guise of 'democracy', but by mental 'turmoil'. The legitimacy of the invasion was no more questioned that it was by the British Ministry of Defence in its letter to Tom Geddes almost two years later.

Brooks' prescription? 'Soft partition'. He favoured 'a country divided into separate sectarian areas to reduce contact and conflict'. Without daring to use the old 'divide and conquer' mantra, he recommended just that: a central government 'to handle oil revenues and manage the currency, etc' and sectarian statelets that would recognise that 'Iraq is broken'.

But surely partition can only be preceded by the abandonment of all that the land of Iraq meant for its people? The assault on the Iraq Museum of Archaeology in 2003, the mass theft of its artefacts, the burning of the Qur'anic library in Baghdad, partly performed this task. But the real assault started within weeks of the Western invasion.

When I saw with my own eyes this historical lobotomy, it was with a parallel level of horror to the fury I felt when I saw the corpses in the Baghdad mortuary – and the mass graves, too, of Saddam's regime. Within three months of the Anglo-American invasion, I travelled south from Baghdad, across the overheated deserts, to report on the work of those whom my newspaper would call the 'Raiders of the Lost Iraq'. It was one of those dispatches that called for the present tense:

It looks as though a B-52 has carpet-bombed the city called Mother of Scorpions. I clamber around twenty-foot craters and try to recognise one of the greatest cities of civilisation. But the thieves have done their work. They have broken or stolen everything. For ten square miles, they have dug up and smashed and gouged into the ancient earth, and destroyed the priceless heritage of Mesopotamia. The Sumerian palaces, the temple walls, the great pillars, oil lamps and giant pots and delicately patterned plates and dishes, all have been smashed to bits.

The thief had been looking for early Sumerian antiquities, and so everything above the earliest layers of civilisation had to be thrown away. The robber probably took no more than sixty seconds to hurl away these pots and plates made 2,000 years before Christ, his only concession to history the empty packet of cheap Iraqi cigarettes that lay beside the wreckage. Printed on it was a harp and the name of the manufacturer: Sumer.

The Mother of Scorpions – 'Um Alkarab' – lies in an area called Jokhr, the name of the nearest modern-day village some forty miles north-west of Nasiriyah. The clay houses are almost identical to those of the Sumerians who learned, perhaps 7,000 years ago, to irrigate this land with the canals and ditches that brought the waters of the Tigris to the desert. In the neighbouring city of Umma, the thieves were still at work when I arrived. I walked right up to them as they sat outside their tents, strung out between amateur piles of excavations. They were joking, I wrote in the *Independent*:

> with the armed guards who are supposed to protect the sites – and whom I increasingly suspect of sharing in the theft – and laugh when one of the local tribesmen, holding a Kalashnikov rifle, shouts across the wreckage: 'We do not come to harm you.' The harm has already been done, not to them or us, but to that which belongs to us all under the soil.

Joanne Farchakh, a Lebanese archaeologist who was conducting a study of the post-war mass theft of Iraq's cultural history, believes that no archaeological destruction on this scale has occurred for at least a thousand years. 'These cities are among the most important in

Sumerian civilisation, and Um Alkarab and Umma are now effectively gone,' she says. 'They have been destroyed.'

The Bush administration's reaction was beneath contempt. After the White House spokesman Ari Fleischer tried to shirk responsibility for widespread looting by claiming it was 'a reaction to oppression' and Donald Rumsfeld's shameful response, 'Stuff happens!', the most meretricious remark came from Brigadier General Vincent Brooks, the spokesman for the US Central Command in Qatar. 'I don't think that anyone anticipated that the riches of Iraq would be looted by the Iraqi people,' he said. This was preposterous. The idea that 'the Iraqi people' were alone responsible for the theft of their country's treasures was almost racist. Weren't the foreign buyers implicated in this cultural genocide?

Trucks, cars, planes and boats took Iraq's historical plunder to Europe, the US, the Emirates, Jordan and Japan. Websites began to offer Mesopotamian artifacts up to 7,000 years old. An invasion whose purpose was corrupted before it began led to an extinction of history and left its people with neither a past nor a future. When we retreated from what we had created from the ruins of Saddam's domain, we had destroyed the truth as surely as we had taken Iraq's oil. And we allowed its prehistory to be taken from the people of Iraq; we 'suicided' them; as surely as they would 'suicide' us.

5

'You Have Your Mission – And I Have Mine'

Now the house was full of men and women; and all the lords of the Philistines were there; and there were upon the roof about three thousand men and women …

And Samson called unto the LORD, and said, O Lord GOD, I pray thee … that I may be at once avenged upon the Philistines for my two eyes.

And Samson took hold of the two middle pillars upon which the house stood …

And Samson said, Let me die with the Philistines. And he bowed himself with all his might; and the house fell upon the lords, and upon all the people that were therein. So the dead which he slew at his death were more than they which he slew in his life.

Judges 16: 27–30

'The last time I saw Hassan, he was standing in the gateway you've just walked through.' His mother Labiba Oweydah points at the garden gate behind me with its shroud of bougainvillea. 'I thought he was going to go and that I might not see him again and I said "Come back". But he said to me: "Leaving is not like returning. It is not important for me to return."' With those words, Hassan Jamal Sulieman Oweydah left the Mieh Mieh refugee camp in Lebanon to become a suicide bomber. In December 2004, he rammed his explosives-laden car into an American military convoy at Tel Afar, the first Palestinian 'martyr' in the war against the United States' occupation of Iraq.

Never before had anyone in the West seen the face of a suicide bomber in Iraq; snapshots showed him to be a slim, bearded man. It took me weeks to persuade Palestinian friends in Beirut to arrange for me to meet his family. I was given an address in the Palestinian camp of Ein el-Helweh, the largest and most uncontrolled in Lebanon, a midden of concrete huts amid a web of power lines and bakeries, 'martyrs' portraits and rusted Mercedes; from there an old acquaintance directed me to the smaller camp of Mieh Mieh, which had started life as an Allied prison camp for Nazi suspects after the liberation of Lebanon from Vichy France in 1941. There, guarded by young, armed men, was the gateway of flowers under which Hassan Oweydah had stood eighteen months earlier, before he left for 'martyrdom' in Iraq.

The Oweydah family originally came from Acre in what is now northern Israel. They fled to Lebanon in 1948, part of the great Nakba 'disaster' that drove about 750,000 Palestinians into exile. Hassan's father married four times and the boy had two brothers by Labiba. Two of his uncles were killed in the 1982 Israeli invasion of Lebanon. Another relative had been killed by the Israelis in 1989.

Hassan was only seventeen when he left for Iraq during the 2003 Anglo-American invasion. 'He was devout, a single man, always thinking of his family – but he talked of "martyrdom" to his father and sisters,' his uncle, Maher Oweydah, said. 'He arrived in Baghdad two days after the Americans reached the city and he called us on the phone from there. He had wanted to "martyr" himself in Palestine but he could not cross the [Lebanese] border – that is why he chose Iraq.' His mother remembered another call from her son, just before his suicide attack. 'He telephoned to say he was getting married in heaven. I said to him: "Come back to Lebanon and you can get a wife here and go to 'martyr' yourself in Palestine later." He said: "No, I will find a bride in the 'higher heaven'."'

Labiba leads me into the living room of the family home. There is a television and a DVD player and within a few seconds an audience of young men and aunts and little boys and girls, have arranged themselves on the metal chairs and on the floor. On the screen is Hassan Oweydah, saying goodbye to his mother and talking of his forthcoming death. The family sit in silence to watch him. Hassan and comrades crawling through barbed wire. Hassan swimming in the pale blue Tigris river. Hassan undergoing weapons training in an orchard beside the water. At one point, Hassan is laughing at the wheel of a battered Iraqi car. He waves at the camera. Was this the suicide vehicle?

The tape cuts here. Labiba tells me that 'they' have recovered his body, that it was buried in the sand close to the town but will one day be returned to her. What was left of Hassan Oweydah was probably sprayed across the wreckage of the US convoy and I don't think his mother believes the story of his body returning to her. None of the other twenty-five Palestinians from Ein el-Helweh and Mieh Mieh who 'suicided' themselves in Iraq, nor others from Sabra and Chatila were ever brought back to the camps. Already, by June 2006 – just over three years after the US invasion – 1,000 suicide bombers from across the Arab world had blown themselves up in Iraq.

While all the Palestinians who arrived from Lebanon intended to die in Iraq, not all were car bombers. Faraj Mohamed Abdullah Zeidan, a friend of Hassan Oweydah, was killed in a gun battle with US troops in April 2006. Ahmed Ali Ahwad, a member of the al-Ansar religious movement, was in charge of a local anti-aircraft ammunition store in Iraq and was killed by an American missile. But Ahmed al-Faran from Mieh Mieh appears to have been a suicide bomber. He was killed in a 'martyrdom operation', his friends say, in Fallujah. Funerals there may not be, but details of each death are carefully preserved in the camps. Another man attacked a US base but while he was withdrawing – according to his colleagues – he was shot dead by a wounded American soldier. Two more Palestinians who died in combat in Iraq were cousins.

Conversations with the Oweydah family suggested that Palestinians who sought 'martyrdom' would let others in the camp know of their desire before being 'called' to leave their homes on specific days – perhaps when the supply of suicide bombers in Iraq was running short. 'We all waited to be called,' a middle-aged man confided to me. They would cross the Lebanese–Syrian border north of Masnaa, be taken to an area east of Aleppo and then transit into Iraq just south of the Kurdish town of Dohuk.

Of course, I had to ask about Osama bin Laden. He was still alive, his coloured photograph adorning the walls of Sunni Muslim areas of

Lebanon, including Ein el-Helweh. There was even an al-Qaeda office in the camp, a single concrete room, although when I called one hot afternoon, the two denizens appeared bored, claiming to have met Bin Laden himself until they were told that I personally knew their presumptive leader. Hassan Oweydah's family – like those of other Palestinian 'martyrs' in Iraq – said they had no direct connection with Bin Laden's al-Qaeda.

'Every Muslim wishes he had met Bin Laden,' Maher Oweydah tells me, 'but to us he was not an organisation or an intellectual ... Bin Laden represents an ideology.' Hassan Oweydah was apparently as outraged as Bin Laden at the US invasion of Iraq. 'He thought this was a crusade against all Arab and Muslim centres. He felt we should resist.'

Maher has clearly been a political and religious influence on the family. 'The Americans have fallen into a trap in Iraq. They had no idea what they were walking into. Who would have thought, two days after the fall of Baghdad, when Hassan arrived there, that there would be such a resistance?' So why – it was a question which had to be asked – did the Palestinians defend Saddam Hussein?

'He supported the Palestinians and every Palestinian "martyr's" family received $25,000 from him. But that is not a defence of Saddam as such. For us, Saddam was a dictator oppressing his people. But if we are to talk of this so-called "democracy of the Americans" – well, of course, Iraqis were victims [of Saddam], but that period was definitely better than the American occupation.' As for Saddam's oppression of Iraq's Shia Muslims, Maher Oweydah – like thousands of Iraqi Sunnis – had little sympathy. 'The truth is that Saddam was a Sunni and his struggle was with the Shia. Then after the invasion of Iraq, the Shia clerics and intellectuals and politicians entered the country on the American tanks.' The family nod their approval at this narrative.

So there we have it, an admission that Hassan had died not just in a war of liberation but amid a sectarian conflict in which he had taken sides. For when he travelled to Baghdad, Saddam was still in power. And after the 2003 American invasion, Tel Afar fell into the hands of Sunni Muslim insurgents who dispossessed the 150,000 Shia Muslims of the town from their homes. Abu Musab al-Zarqawi, the head of al-Qaeda in Iraq, was based there, close to Syria where some of his men had trained. The fighters of Tel Afar would return to their old training grounds on the Syrian side of the border a decade later and – in the late spring of 2014 – they would retake the Iraqi town in which Hassan Oweydah had died and declare it part of an 'Islamic Caliphate', destroying in just minutes the Iraqi–Syrian frontier posts and the ninety-eight-year-old Sykes–Picot agreement that secretly divided the Middle East between British and French colonial powers.

I turn to Labiba again. What was her reaction when she heard of her son's death? 'I did not imagine it, not in a million years. It shocked me completely. I know he wanted to go to Palestine – but … I could not imagine him being martyred in Iraq. But I am a proud mother. I will meet him in heaven. I am happy he will be married in the spring of heaven.'

I watch as they pull corpses from the rubble of the Zeir family home while hundreds of angry men scream at American troops to let them rescue the wounded. The children's bodies are more or less intact; the adults come out in parts. The Zeirs – a Christian family, for this street of the city is a small Christian enclave – were all watching a football match on television, but they were also receiving visitors to one of their female relatives who was ill. Officers of the new Iraqi police force, fire brigade personnel and even some of the wounded are clawing with their hands at the bricks and muck in an effort to find survivors. The suicide bombing will be claimed later, by al-Qaeda. The target was the Jebel al-Lubnan Hotel in Baghdad. The staff of the Motorola phone company moved out a day earlier. The bomb arrived in a car and detonated in a narrow street in the Karada district of the city, scarcely 500 metres from the plinth from which the Americans had pulled down the statue of Saddam just under a year earlier.

The US authorities announced that American citizens had been wounded in the bombing, a statement that only further enraged the men trying to reach their loved ones. 'We are suffering and they don't care,' a woman in a black abaya gown screams at me. 'Why is it only you people who are so precious? It is us who are dying.' Everyone we see brought from the smashed buildings is dead, their last journey to the ambulances wreathed in smoke. In the darkness, US helicopters are circling. No one blames the suicide bomber.

When she uttered those extraordinary words about 'the spring of heaven', Hassan Oweydah's mother Labiba presented me with the great ocean of incomprehension that we Westerners must struggle, earnestly but hopelessly, to understand. The cult of the suicide bomber has become the most powerful weapon the Muslim world has produced in our time. I have grown so used to this phenomenon that I often take it for granted, a troubling habit for a journalist. When I first heard that a Lebanese Shia Muslim had deliberately blown himself up attacking the US embassy in Beirut in 1983, I did not believe the story. But the constant suicide attacks on Israel's occupation army in Lebanon, and on the American and French military bases in Beirut, meant that an aberration became routine.

This trauma of the mind spread in an almost natural fashion to the Sunni Palestinians in their war against Israel, to the Afghans in their war against the Americans, to the Sunni and Shia Iraqis in their war against US occupation, and in what was to become a monstrous Sunni protest against us in New York and Washington and London and Bali and across the world. And then, perhaps most tragically of all, between Muslims themselves. So that eventually Osama bin Laden found himself appalled by the sectarian nature of the very organisation he had created.

Many times I have interviewed the families of those who have taken their own lives – Lebanese Hizbollah, Palestinians, Iraqis of both Muslim sects, Jordanians – and have learned of that fatal call; a code word uttered by a carefully instructed imam at prayers, a visit to the family by an earnest young man, a fixation with injustice, with the absolute impossibility of finding dignity on earth. I long ago reached the conclusion that the men and women who suicide themselves to kill their enemies have already killed their own souls – that they are dead before they strap on the explosives belt or turn the ignition of the car bomb.

In both fear and dark fascination, we try to rationalise this histori-cally, to seek precedents: Tsarist anarchists, Kamikaze pilots, even perhaps our own 1914–18 war dead, who supposedly 'gave their lives' – but for 'King and Country', rather than for God. But the sectarian suicide war in which Hassan Oweydah was participating surely invoked as much hatred, perhaps even self-hatred, as it did self-sacrifice.

There are many theses in the West about the 'psyche' of the suicide bomber, most of them as lacking in serious analysis as the suicider is bereft of humour. The West's intelligence services have spent much time fruitlessly searching for a 'profile' of the suicide killer. Many of the

Palestinian men and women who have blown themselves up among Israelis have lacked both adult religious teaching and the kind of education that only moderate wealth might have given them. And the killers of 11 September 2001 included graduates and middle-class men.

The problem for Western 'experts', of course, was that in order to work within the political architecture of Bush's 'war on terror', they had to construct a suicide bomber who was essentially wicked, 'mindless' and who was possessed of a perverted sense of supremacy. To search the wretched foundations of the unjust world in which Arab Muslims lived and died would mean exploring historical events for which the West might well be to blame. And since the narrative laid down by the US and European governments – and of course by CNN, Fox News and, far too often, by the BBC – was that suicide killers hated our 'way of life', any research into what politicians like to call 'root causes' had to be bland enough for us to revert quickly to psychology – rather than the West's political and physical cruelty – as an explanation for violent events.

Hassan Oweydah lived amid great poverty. But when in 2001 I first met Samir Jarrah, the father of the Lebanese student who hijacked United Airlines Flight 93 on 11 September 2001, he went to great lengths to tell me about his son's education. Samir was a social security inspector, Ziad's mother a French teacher, his uncle a banker. This was no deprived slum-dweller aching to strike at an alien society that had impoverished him. At home, he drank alcohol, went to nightclubs, had girlfriends. Yet still he boarded the Newark–San Francisco flight with box cutters and flew it into the ground.

When I went to see Samir again two years later, in the family's three-storey home in the Bekaa Valley, he told a slightly different story. In 1982, when Israeli troops surrounded the Lebanese capital in an invasion that cost up to 17,500 lives, Ziad was seven years old and lived in Beirut, 'an alert boy' who moved with his sisters to the safety of a new school in the Christian town of Zahle.

Ziad Jarrah would ask his father to buy books for him at Librarie Antoine in Hamra Street in West Beirut; in a disturbing moment, Samir told me that 'Ziad always wanted books about aircraft – when he was young, he always wanted to fly. In toyshops, he'd always pick out model airplanes. He was in the Scouts and the "Youth Against Drugs" group. He always wanted to help people. He always prayed and kept Ramadan. But one day he asked me to pray during Ramadan. I didn't usually pray. His mother did occasionally. She used to tell him: "Forget praying – go and be a boy – you're not a teenager twice." Ziad gave me a smile then. He said to me: "I hope God opens your eyes … I hope that you'll be praying one day."'

It was in Germany that Ziad Jarrah met and lived alongside Mohamed Atta, the Egyptian leader of the 9/11 killers and pilot of the American Airlines plane that crashed into the World Trade Center. Ziad visited Afghanistan and family members apparently travelled to Pakistan to seek his return. It was as if a screen had been drawn between the young man and his Lebanese family.

Perhaps the equation made by the suicider is mathematical rather than spiritual; that the mass physical effect of their death assumes an importance that the individual could never aspire to in life. This would require a strong element of self-regard, even self-righteousness, a characteristic shared by Bin Laden. The suicide bomber has the freedom not only to contemplate the suffering he will cause to others. He sees his victims. But if the murderer is already – in spirit, if not in body – dead, then he is merely confronting a scene that has already, in one sense, taken place. He is no longer responsible for those he kills. They, too, have already died.

The Israelis and the Americans tried to erase the word 'suicide' from their lexicon. If suicide was acknowledged as a chosen form of death, there was a danger that the suicidal event could be seen as an act of courage rather than nihilism. Thus Israeli and US government spokesmen vainly tried to use the phrase 'homicide bomber' when referring to a man or woman who had killed themselves.* But disguising the culprit's self-destructive impulse would not persuade a fearful public from thinking about the act of violence to which it referred. Having robbed the suicide killer of his or her motive, it left no explanation for the crime.

But within the Middle East, it was not, perhaps surprisingly, the religion of the suicide bomber that was most admired, although it was

---

* This was implausible as well as naive; by logical extension, a killer was always 'homicidal' – he was trying to kill another human being. But Fox News and, unfortunately, the AP went along with this deliberate misnomer, which was invented by the White House, for several years.

expected that he would be a Muslim.* Nor was he respected because he was a mass killer, but because something hitherto invincible now proved vulnerable. It was the same when the first suicide bombers struck in Lebanon. The Lebanese could scarcely believe that Israeli soldiers could die in such numbers; they were even more amazed that the Israeli army had been brought low by so simple a technique. Nurtured in whatever misery or privilege, the suicide bomber had come of age.

By 2006, over the mosques of Sidon and Tripoli, they were trumpeting their 'martyrs', Palestinians and Lebanese who travelled from the slums and refugee camps of Lebanon to the wastes of the Iraq war. One of the most recent fighters had been killed in the US air attack on the Baquba hideout of Abu Musab al-Zarqawi. The death of Saleh Qilawi was hailed through mosque loudspeakers in the Ein el-Helweh camp in Sidon.

Qilawi left Sidon for Iraq in the summer of 2005. As his parents 'celebrated' his death, they received greetings from members of the Isbar al-Ansar movement that was behind an 'Islamist' uprising in the mountains of northern Lebanon in 2000. In the Sidon camp, Darwish Hitti 'celebrated' the death of his son Mohamed, who had been killed with his friend Mohamed Yorshali in June 2006. That summer in Lebanon, we heard many stories of the young men who had travelled through Syria to Iraq; one man apparently returned to Tripoli, having been badly wounded – but not killed – by his 'suicide' bomb and tore down the local posters of his own 'martyrdom'. But there were wider concerns in Lebanon at this time, reflected in my own report from Beirut in July 2006. I little realised how terrifyingly relevant these paragraphs would become eight years later, as Syria and then Iraq were engulfed in inter-Muslim warfare and in the creation of an 'Islamic Caliphate':

For Lebanon, these are tense times. The largest community in the country, the Shias, feel many common bonds with their fellow Shias in Iraq and are bitterly distressed at the destruction

---

* Where anti-Israeli suicide bombers in Lebanon turned out to be pro-Syrian leftists rather than Islamists, their role in the story was largely ignored by both Israelis and Muslims, for different reasons of course.

of mosques and other holy places for which the Americans place the blame on Sunni insurgents.

The second largest Muslim community in Lebanon are Sunnis, who increasingly express their support for their Iraqi coreligionists … Since the Alawite community which dominates political power in Syria is in effect Shia and the majority of Syrians are Sunni it is not difficult to understand the darker nightmares which afflict the people of this region. If the civil conflict in Iraq were to move west, it could open up religious fault lines from Baghdad to Lebanon, a distance of only 500 miles but an awesome prospect for the entire Arab world.

Suicide as a weapon of war remains most frightening to us not because of its awesome negation of our human desire to live, but because of its inversion of life. We may accept that paradise lies through jihad – as soldiers of the 1914–18 war might have accepted that their country demanded their sacrifice – but that a martyr might be married in the spring of heaven seems to mock us. How can we take the joys of human existence and procreation into the afterlife?

Almost two years after I first met Labiba Oweydah – and more than three years after her son Hassan killed himself at Tel Afar – I returned to see the family in their miserable home outside the Lebanese city of Sidon. I travelled there with filmmaker and actress Nelofer Pazira, who was later to become my wife. But a sinister surprise awaited us: Hassan's brother Khaled, dressed in a black Armani T-shirt, a carefully crafted conquistador's beard, gelled hair; handsome, young – just eighteen – and adored by his sisters. He was their hero, their teacher, their representative and their soon-to-be martyred brother.

The moment he walked onto the porch of the house, Nelofer and I both realised that he would be next to die. Khaled was quite frank about his intentions. Behind him was the sitting room in which photographs of his brother Hassan still adorned the walls. Khaled clearly thought he was destined for the same paradise.

It was easy to understand the psychological trauma of these families. Labiba, for example, constantly expressed her pride in her son Hassan and looked with almost equal love at his still living brother. But when Nelofer urged Khaled to remain alive for his mother's sake, the woman was close to tears. She was torn apart by her love as a mother and her duty as the woman who had brought another would-be 'martyr' into the world. When I told him that he should abandon all thoughts of being a suicide bomber – that he could influence more people in the world by being a journalist – he put his head back and shot me a world-weary grin. 'You have your mission,' he said. 'And I have mine.' Yes, he was ready to immolate himself.

Not even a disparaging remark about those who would send him on his mission – that they were prepared to live in this world while sending others to their death – could discourage him. 'I am not going to become a martyr for people,' he replied. 'I am doing it for God.' It was the same old argument. We could produce a hundred peaceful ways for him to resolve the injustices of this world, but the moment Khaled invoked the name of God, our suggestions became irrelevant. If a Western president could invoke a war of 'good against evil', his antagonists could do the same.

Khaled's Uncle Maher – who at our last meeting had referred to Osama bin Laden as 'an ideology' and spoken of the Iraqi Shia with such cynicism – sat with the family. We talked of the Palestinian desire to fight in Iraq. 'It's difficult to reach Palestine these days,' he told me. 'Iraq is easier.' Too true. The passage of suicide bombers from the Mediterranean coast to the deserts of Iraq was a planned if not particularly sophisticated affair. But what was astonishing was the sheer scale of the suicide campaign, the vast numbers of young men and occasionally women who wilfully destroyed themselves amid the American convoys, outside the Iraqi police stations, in markets and around mosques and in shopping streets and on lonely roads beside remote checkpoints.

The ferocity of our enemies made disturbing reading for millions of people who had been encouraged to believe in the moral worth of invasion or occupation. Reporters are used to compiling the casualties of war; scarcely a newsroom wall in the Middle East was without its list of hostages or US military or British army fatalities or individual attacks on Western personnel. Yet oddly, editors had never tried to count the frequency of suicide killings – surely one of the most potent lists of all. Never had the true figures for this historically unprecedented campaign of self-liquidation been calculated.

I spent a month trowelling through official statistics, Arabic-language newspapers and Western media reports; my enquiry showed that 1,121

Muslim suicide bombers had blown themselves up in Iraq in five years, between the Anglo-US invasion and March 2008. This was a conservative figure and the true estimate may have been double this number. If life was cheap in Iraq, death was cheaper.

This was perhaps the most ghoulish legacy of George W. Bush's invasion of Iraq. Suicide bombers in Iraq had killed at least 13,000 men, women and children and wounded at least 16,112 people. Again, these were the very minimum statistics. For 529 of the suicide bombings in Iraq, I could find no figures for wounded available, and the number of critically injured who later died remains unknown. Compared to the hundreds of thousands of Iraqis who had been killed since the invasion, the victims of suicide bombers might appear insignificant; but the killers' ability to terrorise was incalculable.

As the cult of suicide bombing leached across frontiers, they would sometimes arrive on target in groups of eight or even ten. During the Second World War, the Japanese government encouraged its pilots to think of themselves as a collective suicide unit whose insignia of imminent death – white Rising Sun headbands and white scarves – prefigured the yellow headbands imprinted with Qur'anic script worn by Hizbollah guerrillas when they set out to attack Israeli soldiers in the occupied zone of southern Lebanon.* In Iraq, however, those who directed the army of suiciders needed to invent an ever more ambitious series of disguises for their protégés. The bombers thus turned up at the scene of their self-destruction dressed as car mechanics, soldiers, police officers, middle-aged housewives, sweet-sellers, worshippers and – on at least one occasion – a 'harmless' shepherd. They carried their bombs in fuel trucks and garbage trucks, on donkeys and bicycles, motorbikes and mopeds. There appeared, at this stage, to be no central 'brain' behind these attacks; although groups of bombers obviously existed, inspiration, imitation and the

---

* While there is evidence that Japanese suicide pilots were sometimes coerced and intimidated into their final flights against US warships in the Pacific, many believed that they were dying for their emperor. For them, the fall of cherry blossom and the divine wind – the kamikaze – blessed their souls as they aimed their dive-bombers at US aircraft carriers. But they were dying to avoid defeat rather than achieve victory. Even an industrialised dictatorship like Japan, facing the imminent collapse of its entire society at the hands of a superpower, could only mobilise 4,615 kamikaze pilots. Of these 3,860 died; Iraqi suicide bombers alone may have reached half that figure in five years.

globalised influence of the internet appeared sufficient to empower the bombers of Iraq.*

American soldiers and Iraqi cops were the principal targets in the early months of the suiciders. In July 2004, a bomber drove a Renault car into a mass of unemployed young men looking for jobs in the police force as they lined up in a recruiting queue in a boulevard in Baquba. When he blew himself up, he slaughtered at least a hundred would-be policemen. There were already clues about the thoroughness of the suicide network. At the mayor's office in Karbala, a senior police officer emerged; the bomber, he told me, had followed a military convoy into the street outside, 'tailing' the rear vehicle past a checkpoint of Iraqi police and US 101st Airborne troops until he reached the gate where he immolated himself.

The most politically powerful attacks had occurred inside Western bases and offices, including the Green Zone in Baghdad – two in one day in 2004 – and against the UN headquarters and the International Red Cross headquarters in Baghdad. By December of that year, British officials were warning that there were more 'spectacular' suicides to come; the first suicide assault on a mosque took place the following month, when a bomber on a bicycle blew himself up in a Shia mosque in Baquba, killing four men and wounding another thirty-nine.

Bombers attacked the funerals of Shia Muslims their own comrades had killed, even wedding parties. Schools, university campuses and shopping precincts were now included on the target lists, most of the victims once again being Shia.

We knew from their families that Palestinians, Saudis, Syrians and Algerians had been among the bombers. In a few cases, we had names. But in most cases, the 'authorities' had no idea to whom the bloodied limbs and headless torsos belonged. Although neither the Iraqi govern-

---

* Throughout the first five years of war, suiciders attacked twenty-four US bases at a cost of one hundred American dead and fifteen Iraqis, and forty-three US patrols and checkpoints which took the lives of 116 American personnel and at least fifty-six civilians, fifteen of whom appear to have been shot by American soldiers in response to the attacks and another twenty-six of whom were children standing next to a US patrol. At least 365 attacks were staged against Iraqi police or paramilitary forces. Their targets included a minimum of 147 police stations (1,577 deaths), forty-three army and police recruitment centres (939 dead), ninety-one checkpoints (at least 564 fatalities), ninety-two security patrols (465 dead) and other police targets (escorts, convoys accompanying government ministers, etc).

ment nor its American mentors would admit this, scarcely ten out of more than a thousand suicide bombers had been identified by early 2008. One of them, who attacked an Iraqi police unit in June 2005, turned out to be a former police commando called Abu Mohamed al-Dulaimi, but the US and Iraqi authorities had little intelligence on the provenance of these killers. On at least twenty-seven occasions, Iraqi officials claimed to have recovered passports and identity pictures that proved their 'foreign' origin, but they never produced these documents for public inspection. There was even doubt that the two suicide bombers who blew themselves up in a bird market in 2008 were mentally retarded young women, as the Iraqi government was to allege.

But there were women suicide bombers. US military figures showed that female suicide attacks had risen from eight in 2007 to sixteen in less than six months of 2008. A Sunni woman who killed fifteen people in Diyala province in December 2007 was a former Baath party member whose two sons joined al-Qaeda and had been killed by the Iraqi military. On 17 May the same year, a double female suicide bombing unit attacked a pro-American militia and a police patrol. An American officer claimed that two women suicide bombers were the wives of an al-Qaeda leader who was killed by US forces. One of the most fearful female suicide bombings occurred in 2010, when a woman dressed in a black abaya gown set off explosives as she joined a queue of Shia pilgrims outside a rest tent in Baghdad, killing fifty-four people – including eighteen women and twelve children.

The terror of the unknown became almost as critical as the fear of death. The US military briefed reporters that the suicide killers were high on drugs, had been 'professionally' brainwashed, were former mental patients, blackmailed criminals or obsessed by after-life sex – anything rather than humans readily prepared to throw away their lives for a cause. That families could feel proud of those who killed themselves – like the Oweydah family in Lebanon – was unworthy of discussion.

In Iraq, military ignorance was even more dangerous. Nothing could better illustrate the lack of knowledge of those supposedly controlling the country than the two contradictory statements made by Americans and their Iraqi protégés in March 2007. For just as David Satterfield, US secretary of state Condoleezza Rice's adviser on Iraq, was claiming that 90 per cent of suicide bombers were crossing the Iraqi border from Syria, Iraq's prime minister, Nouri al-Maliki, was announcing that 'most' of the suiciders came from Saudi Arabia.* Many in Baghdad, including some government ministers, believed that the bombers came from much closer to home – that they were, in fact, Iraqis.

It will be many years before we have a clear idea of the origin and number of men and women who killed themselves in the Iraq war, since the conflict grew even more terrifying after the American departure.† Long before I reached the figure of 500 during my own research, al-Qaeda's Abu Musab al-Zarqawi was boasting of there being '800 martyrs' among his supporters. His killing brought not the slightest reduction in suicide bombings, nor in the number of 'manipulators' in charge of Iraq's suicide squads, and the record of such killings increased to epic proportions.

One of George W. Bush's most insidious legacies in Iraq thus remains its most mysterious: the marriage of nationalism and religious ferocity, the birth of an unprecedentedly huge army of Muslims inspired by the idea of death. Those without modern arms sought solace in religion and countenanced the end of life with something approaching nonchalance. All the science of the West could not defend us from this unique weapon. We could, like the Crusaders in the days of the Assassins, build walls. We could surround ourselves with fields of fire and trenches and concrete fortresses bristling with machine guns. But just as British prime minister Stanley Baldwin believed in 1932 that 'the bomber will always get through', so the suicider, having abandoned life, no longer feared the military machines of his opponents. Those who sent the suiciders on their way used a cheap formula to advertise their unique weapon, cruelly imitating the mantra of the Western arms salesman who wishes to publicise the unique selling point of his product. You love life. We love death. It was a falsification of Islam, but it was calculated to place the onus of fear upon the enemies of Islam. And in the Middle East during those terrible years, I

---

* In 2008, the US military estimated that 40 per cent of jihadis in Iraq were Saudis.

† The US military, upbeat to the desolate end, characterised their 2010 withdrawal from Iraq as a 'reposturing' of forces, a word faintly familiar to those of us who remembered the American Marine 'redeployment' from Lebanon in 1984.

would repeatedly ask myself the same question, with the interest of a guilty witness: technology versus God – who will win?

One evening in Afghanistan in late 1996, outside a hut in the light of a paraffin lamp, I asked Osama bin Laden if he realised that he was a hunted man. He snapped back at me, quite angrily: 'Danger is a part of our life. Do you realise we spent ten years fighting against the Russians and the KGB?' He didn't care about his life. He didn't want to die, but he was prepared for a 'martyrdom' which was, he often said, a long cherished ambition. And when this consummation was finally realised, I muttered the first words that came into my head, the tired old maxim, derived from the Bible, that those who live by the sword, die by the sword.* Bin Laden was a has-been, I cynically told a radio interviewer later that day. In the Arab revolutions of 2011, not one among the millions of protesters had shouted his name. History had passed him by.

I should have felt some emotion when a man of such power and such public infamy – a man with whom I had spent hours in conversation – was suddenly, inevitably, done to death. Like many journalists, I sometimes regarded those about whom I wrote as characters in a play, and few could fulfil such a role as colourfully as Bin Laden. While his fortitude was obvious – he showed nothing else in his battle with the Soviet army and with the Americans when they surrounded him in the Tora Bora mountains – his self-righteousness was awesome. I was infuriated by his self-regard, the way in which his white dishdash and plastic sandals gave way in his dull post-9/11 videotapes to a gold-fringed robe and more sonorous voice, as if living in a cave conferred upon him the status of the Prophet himself. If the Americans had provided Bin Laden with the justification for his war against the 'Crusaders', I suspected that by the end of his life he was providing them with the same excuse for their own savagery and sense of eternal moral purpose.

I met Osama bin Laden three times, once in Sudan and twice in Afghanistan, and he became a kind of albatross for me. No conversation with any Arab, with any journalist – no introduction to any

---

* 'For all they that take the sword shall perish with the sword' is attributed to Jesus in Matthew 26:52 (the King James Bible).

audience at any lecture – could be complete without a reference to my meeting the man who planned the international crimes against humanity of 11 September 2001, who created al-Qaeda, the most ferocious, disciplined, cruelly inspirational, dangerous guerrilla army in modern history. Was I not the reporter to whom Bin Laden – sitting in his Afghan mountain camp – promised in 1997 that 'from this mountain upon which you are sitting, we broke the Russian army and we destroyed the Soviet Union. And I pray to God that he will permit us to turn the United States into a shadow of itself'? In my notebook at the time, next to these words, I scribbled the word 'rhetoric'. I was wrong.

But there was, oddly, a frailty about this man. Physically, he was as lean as a mountain goat. While he carried a stick when he trudged through Afghanistan's boulder-strewn mountains, I never believed in the constant reports of kidney ailments or secret medical operations to save his life. Yet when in 1996, at the end of our first meeting in Afghanistan, I asked after his family, he insisted that I should see the tents in which they would live among the refugees of Peshawar. By the light of the paraffin lamp, I took his photograph, a smile on his face, and he called two of his sons, fifteen-year-old Omar and seventeen-year-old Saad, to sit beside him. Suddenly Osama bin Laden was a proud Arab father, the warrior at home, a family man. He smiled again, a mixture of self-conviction, vanity and a slight sense of humility.

Omar posed very self-consciously beside his father, the obedient, honoured son. I was moved to ask the boy something that he clearly did not expect. My question was genuine enough, but I wanted to see if Bin Laden's son would tell the truth. Was he happy? I asked him. The boy thought about this for a moment. 'Yes,' he replied sheepishly, 'I am happy.' His father looked at his son, the concerned expression diluted into a nod of self-confidence.

But Omar, I now know, was not happy. He did not want to follow his father's dreams of struggle on the path to heaven. Thirteen years later, as an adult with a son of his own, Omar recounted his memory of our meeting:

> I was stunned by his [Fisk's] question. During my entire life, few people had ever really cared about my feelings, and certainly no one had ever asked whether or not I was happy. For a split second I wondered if Fisk was merely being polite, but he

seemed so sincere that I wanted to please him with my response.
I finally replied: 'Yes, I am happy.'

   Fisk didn't question me further, but my tongue ached to take
back those words – to confide the truth, that I was the most
miserable boy alive, and that I hated the hatred and violence my
father was promoting. I wanted to pull Fisk to the side and tell
him that one day I would find the courage to speak out against
my father and work for the cause of peace. I was bursting, but
too cowardly to speak out yet.

I asked Bin Laden if I could take his photograph with Omar and Saad.
He could scarcely refuse. 'I was excited when my father agreed,' Omar
was to recall all those years later:

> because he was not a fan of photography, and his approval to be
> in a picture with me meant more than the photo itself. After Fisk
> left us I had the nerve to ask, 'Father, are you nervous about
> what this reporter might say?' My father shrugged and said, 'No.
> He will be fair.'*

Bin Laden asked to see me for a fourth meeting just after America's
post-9/11 invasion of Afghanistan, but I received his message too late.
And the Taliban unit I met inside Afghanistan refused to continue our
journey towards Kandahar when the village in front of us exploded in
fire during an American air raid. I would never see Bin Laden again.
Once, months after his flight from Afghanistan, I received a message
that he wanted to read my book *The Great War for Civilisation*. I agreed
that I would bring a copy of the Arabic edition to Islamabad and that
someone from al-Qaeda would come to the bed-and-breakfast villa in
which I always stayed in the Pakistani capital. I scarcely had time to

---

* His father's faith in my reporting must have been somewhat damaged by the front-page
headline which a sub-editor on the *Independent* placed over my interview, to the effect that
I had 'tracked' Bin Laden down to his 'lair' in Afghanistan. It was Bin Laden who asked to
see me; I did not seek him out, and it was his own armed men who brought me to his
camps. I was never blindfolded, and no one tried to conceal the route we took across the
plains and mountains of Afghanistan to meet Bin Laden – but I could scarcely 'track him
down to his lair' any more than could his American enemies, who at that time didn't have
the slightest idea of Bin Laden's location.

check in before a small, thin, stooped man with a white beard arrived. He was frightened, whispering that he feared the Pakistani security services would arrest him if he stayed more than a minute. So with an Arab friend, we took this elderly messenger on a night-time tour of Islamabad, the old man sitting in the back of the car, clutching the book.

Could I see Bin Laden? I asked. No. Bin Laden was sorry, he said. This would not be possible. 'You know the problems we have now,' he said to me. 'You know he would see you – but it is impossible.' And for the first time, I realised that America's dead-or-alive target really was in hiding for his life. If he was too frightened to see me, then it would be a long time before I heard from him again. I felt sure he must be in Pakistan. I surmised that he was probably in Karachi, where he had friends among the Sunni clergy. The old man in the back of the car suddenly spoke again. 'Write down questions for him – I will take them to him. He will reply to you.' The next morning, I wrote down twelve questions for Osama bin Laden on two sheets of A4 paper, demanding to know what victory al-Qaeda could claim when it had drawn the United States and its allies into the Muslim country of Afghanistan – and when America was likely, in a matter of months, to invade Iraq as well? How could such a war end?

I was in America when I heard Bin Laden's audiotape in which, one by one, he answered my questions, even in the right order – although he made no reference to me. Bin Laden gave his support to the people of Iraq. He talked about 'Iraq's children' and 'the sons of Iraq'. His message to Western countries was unequivocal. 'What business do your governments have in allying yourselves with the gang of criminals in the White House against Muslims?' He was ready to fight the West inside the Islamic world. The Middle East, in other words, was a trap. When I met him in 1997, he had lost interest in attacking Britain or France, America's European allies in the Middle East. Now Britain was back at the top of his hit list, along with Canada, Italy, Germany and Australia.

But within the Middle East, those who regarded themselves as followers of al-Qaeda came to regard not just the West but all those outside their own narrow Salafist convictions as being equally deserving of God's contempt. In Iraq, al-Qaeda became an essential part of the sectarian killing machine, its suicide bombers tearing apart Shia

Muslims at prayer or Christians leaving their churches. Bin Laden may have been Wahhabist, but an inter-Muslim conflict was never part of his ideology. He had never been a 'controller' of al-Qaeda's operations.

As we now know, absolutist arguments raged continually between local al-Qaeda sponsors and those who believed they could interpret the words of their absent master. US intelligence intercepted correspondence between these groups and drip-fed them to the media with the appropriate message: that Abu Musab al-Zarqawi in Iraq saw himself as a rival to Bin Laden. This was an interpretation which allowed the Americans to exaggerate their victory when they killed the Jordanian-born guerrilla leader in June 2006, but which distracted attention from the far more important ideological shift contained in al-Zarqawi's letters to Bin Laden: that not only infidels – Christians, Jews, 'Crusader' states and the West in general – but 'apostates', those who had abandoned 'true' Islam, were also al-Qaeda's enemies. Thus Muslims of the Shia faith became as treacherous and hateful as Bin Laden's more traditional antagonists.

When Bin Laden created his most intransigent of guerrilla institutions, however, his principal enemies were as much the Gulf rulers and Arab dictators – all of them Sunni Muslims – as their masters in Washington or Tel Aviv. Indeed, when he spoke to me in 1996, his fury was directed at the Saudi royal family, since they had become a tool of the Americans. The Saudi regime, he said, had 'lost its legitimacy' after it jailed many Saudi religious ulema in 1995. The Kingdom had in 1990 invited the Americans into the land of Mecca and Medina to protect the royal family from Saddam after his invasion of Kuwait. Bin Laden himself could have led his loyal fighters against Saddam – without any American help. And it was clear to me at the time that he could conceive of himself as a future ruler of Arabia.

But as the years of solitude imprisoned him with his family in the Abbottabad compound, Bin Laden's leadership of al-Qaeda – already notional – was perverted by others. Those who craved his approval had integrated Saudi Arabia's sectarian hatred of the Shia into their own struggle for Islam, and al-Qaeda inevitably became associated not with a struggle for purity but a cruel battle against the men, women and children of the minority Shia sect whose only national majority in the Arab world existed in Iraq. Thus as the floodlights were turned on in Iraq, they revealed a theatre of sectarian horror on a scale which Bin

Laden could never have imagined. True, the 2003 Anglo-American invasion provoked this terrible carnage, but al-Qaeda's association with the Sunni side in the civil war meant that the armies of suicide bombers would be turned against other people of the Muslim faith. Only in his last days on earth did Bin Laden fully appreciate the extent of his betrayal, and the need to re-shape, reform – even rename – al-Qaeda. Too late.

On the night of 1 May 2011, Osama bin Laden chose his youngest wife Amal to take to bed while his two elder wives, Khairiya and Sharifa, slept on the first floor of their home. The couple would be together only a few hours, until almost exactly 00.50 on 2 May, when they were awakened by the noise of what at first sounded like a storm. Their three-year-old son Husain was still asleep. In the dry but compelling words of Pakistan's official commission of inquiry, the couple went to the balcony to see what was happening:

> it was a moonless night and pitch dark. Amal reached to turn on the light but the Shaikh [Osama] said 'No!' He went to the door to call for his son Khalid, who lived on the first floor with his mother Sharifa. Amal went to see her children. She had five children. When she returned the Shaikh's two daughters Maryam and Sumaiya had come up from their rooms on the first floor. They recited the kalima [the declaration of faith] and verses from the Holy Quran. The Shaikh said American helicopters had arrived and they should all leave his room immediately. They were unwilling to do so. Maryam and her children went to the balcony. The Shaikh reached for his weapon.

Only one account of Bin Laden's six-year life in hiding and of his death comes near to the truth. It was contained in the concise prose of a commission of honourable men in that most corrupt of Asian Muslim states, Pakistan – the country in which Bin Laden was assassinated – whose government immediately and characteristically suppressed the report. We owe it to Qatar's Al Jazeera television channel that we can read this secret Pakistani account that surely provides the most accurate narrative of the murder of Osama bin Laden.

Paragraph by paragraph, the Pakistani commission, led by a Supreme Court judge and three other officials, provided accounts from each of Bin Laden's female relatives so that, in the report, the drama is re-enacted over and over again through the eyes of each witness, the reader observing the American raid from a constantly different but ultimately always fatal perspective. Sumaiya, one of Bin Laden's daughters, for example, grappled with a US soldier and ran to her father's room:

> Although she did not see her father fall, she saw him on the floor. He had been hit in the forehead and she knew he was dead. His face was 'clear' and recognisable. According to her, blood flowed 'backwards over his head' … The American soldiers asked her to identify the body. She said, 'my father'.

Sumaiya's sister Maryam also identified her father. 'When they were later led out of the room, Sumaiya looked back and saw her father's body was gone. According to her, it was less than ten minutes from the time they were first awoken by the noise of the helicopters and the killing of her father.' Sharifa, one of the older wives, described how their son Khalid bin Laden twice went to see his father and 'shortly afterwards, an American entered her room and took out the hard disc of a computer in the room. Then another American came into the room and told them they had killed Osama bin Laden.'

As the Pakistani commission members observed, 'the wives, children and grandchildren of OBL, the children of Abrar, and the wife and children of Ibrahim survived. OBL, his son Khalid, his couriers i.e. the brothers Abrar and Ibrahim, and Abrar's wife Bushra were killed.' Maryam was taken to hospital. 'The rest were taken away for detailed interrogation by the ISI.'

This is the first mention in the Pakistani document of the Pakistani Inter-Services Intelligence, one of the most sinister organisations in the Middle East or south-west Asia. The ISI is Pakistan's top security agency and has been friends with the United States, Saudi Arabia, the Taliban, Bin Laden and al-Qaeda, as well as sundry Afghan militia groups, an eclectic bunch of security 'assets'. Is it surprising, then, that in their report, the commission reveal that by the time they met with the wives, the women had already been in the custody of the ISI for five months?

According to the family, the raiding Americans took away a jewellery box, two gold lockets with emeralds and a purse that contained Bin Laden's will. The four commission members hoovered up a treasure trove of personal details about Bin Laden, his family and retainers; the two older wives were said respectively to have postgraduate degrees in Arabic literature and Islamic studies; the Bin Laden families and those of his couriers did not mix, and the children did not play together. Something of the grey nature of family life was contained in a bleak sentence from the report. 'OBL personally saw to the religious education of his grandchildren,' it says, 'and supervised their play time, which included cultivating vegetable plots with simple prizes for best performances.'

Maryam told the commission interrogators that Bin Laden never visited a doctor. It was Amal who had to visit hospital, to give birth to two of his children when the family lived near Haripur. Some items in the report were already known – Bin Laden's near-capture, for example, when stopped for a speeding offence prior to his refuge in Abbottabad – while others merely added evidence of the gloomy existence of his family; in the compound, Khalid bin Laden looked after a cow to which Abrar would bring fodder, while the daughter of one of the couriers recognised on Al Jazeera television the man she knew as 'poor uncle' who lived upstairs. The television set was swiftly removed.

The Pakistani report records how the Americans may have benefited from aerial reconnaissance during their flood relief operations in the period between August and October 2010. During this same period, the commission noted, 'the Americans had also identified the OBL compound … as his likely residence by tracking the movements of Ibrahim and Abrar'.* After the raid, which may have been assisted by 'ground operators' and in which US Special Forces fired around thirty bullets, OBL's corpse was put aboard a Black Hawk helicopter and was taken to Afghanistan where he had spent so many years as a mujahid, fighting the Soviet army and then planning his war against the West.

---

* The Pakistani commission also noted 'suspicious activities' by CIA ground personnel around the Bin Laden compound prior to the raid, including the cutting down of trees – to clear the approach for the helicopters – the hiring of a house in the vicinity by 'supposed USAID employees' and the movement of four to five Prado/Land Cruisers from the US embassy in Islamabad en route towards Abbottabad on 1 May, which contained personnel who 'may have been CIA agents to assist the helicopters'.

Yet the report's account of Bin Laden's death is almost dwarfed by the commission's unprecedented, excoriating condemnation of the country's authorities, from the ISI, the Pakistani army, air force and police, to individual ministers who had either overlooked, permitted, did not care about or even assisted this remarkable breach of sovereignty. Understandably, perhaps, the West paid little or no attention to this highly detailed and revealing part of the text. We may set aside the emotional reaction of the four members of the Pakistani commission towards the Bin Laden killing but there can be no doubting their sense of anger and shame at the culpable negligence of their own security agencies.

The ISI, according to the commission, 'apparently knew nothing' about a fake hepatitis B immunisation programme carried out under CIA auspices that may have helped to track Ibrahim as Bin Laden's courier. Under the fake cover of USAID and fraudulently using the charity Save the Children, Dr Shakeel Afridi, chief medical officer of the Khyber Agency, tried to find Bin Laden's secret refuge for the Americans. US defense secretary Leon Panetta later blew Afridi's cover and sought his release from ISI custody. Save the Children condemned the scandalous use of charities by American intelligence agents and the danger in which this placed their innocent doctors and other employees, while vaccinations for tens of thousands of children were held in customs and rendered useless as a result of the CIA's actions. 'The CIA needs to answer for this,' Save the Children's Pakistan manager David Wright said more than a year later. Of course, the CIA did nothing of the kind.

The US attack and Bin Laden's killing could not be seen in isolation from the political background or Pakistan's history. 'The whole episode ... appears ... to be a story of complacency, ignorance, negligence, incompetence, irresponsibility and possibly worse at various levels inside and outside the government.' The ISI's own director general told the commission that the reality for Pakistan was not defined by the might of the US. It was defined by the fact that 'we are a very weak state. It all boils down to corrupt and low grade governance ...' A US intelligence officer had the gall to say: 'You're so cheap ... we can buy you with a visa, with a visit to the US, even with a dinner.'

Could there be a more accurate description not only of Pakistan, but of almost any Arab or Middle East Muslim nation in thrall to

Washington? Is this not also a description of Egypt, Jordan, Syria, the Gulf states, of Libya or Tunisia under their dictators and kings – even after their real or prospective revolutions? Is this not a fair reflection of a future Turkey, once its usefulness to the United States and the Gulf as an arms and finance trans-shipment point to civil war in Syria has been exhausted? For Turkey has been performing the very same role in Syria and with the Islamists of Iraq that Pakistan played after the Soviet invasion of 1979. There was a weird symmetry in the decision of Bin Laden, a man who believed in a frontier-less caliphate, to seek refuge in a country which represented exactly the kind of corrupt pro-Western dictatorship that al-Qaeda – and Bin Laden himself – had sworn to overthrow.

The United States went to great lengths to explain that a form of Muslim prayer was recited over Bin Laden's remains before they were dropped into the sea. In the words of the commission, the Americans 'took his body and dumped it into the Indian Ocean with the storyline that it was buried in accordance with Islamic rituals. According to some religious authorities, Islam does not permit the burial at sea of persons who die on land.' Just over two weeks after this strange cere-mony, I went to see one of Lebanon's most forceful Sunni Salafist preachers, Sheikh Da'i al-Islam al-Shahal, in the northern city of Tripoli, a fierce opponent of the Bashar al-Assad regime in Syria.

A big man in a white robe, a massive white beard and representing the 'Institution of the Salafist Party', he said. 'Bin Laden's killing helped America, but US losses will be greater. Maybe the new head of al-Qaeda will be much more brutal. And throwing his body in the sea, this is something the Arab and Muslim world cannot accept. Throwing him to the whales and the fishes shows a bitterness that does not befit human nature. We have a saying that "an excuse is worse than guilt". What is wrong with people saying where he is buried? Maybe they could have buried him on a far mountain where people would not go ...'*

---

* I doubted very much if the distance of a mountain would have prevented pilgrims from visiting Bin Laden's grave – just as they still travel to the al-Qaeda fighters' cemetery in Kandahar – which is presumably why the Americans chose to throw his corpse into the Indian Ocean.

I was far more interested in the mountain of hard drives, discs and documents that the Americans had seized at Bin Laden's compound. I wanted to know what he was thinking in the last weeks of his life, cut off for five years with his vegetable gardens and flickering television. Did he realise the monumental, ferocious changes that he had unleashed upon the Islamists of the Middle East, a society increasingly unstable and sectarian, its Muslim unity against the West abandoned in favour of Salafist purity, loyal to sect rather than religion?

I knew that in his last weeks he must have watched the Tunisian and Egyptian revolutions on his television set, and I wrote that he must have regarded himself as a failure. But precisely a week before his assassination, we now know, Bin Laden was writing a long letter to Sheikh Mahmoud Atiyya abdul Rahman, one of his senior al-Qaeda advisers, in which he proclaimed that the revolutions were 'a great and glorious event' which would probably encompass 'the majority of the Islamic world' and take Muslims out of America's control. Bin Laden appeared delighted that Washington was anxious about these events and regarded the Arab revolts as 'the beginning of a new era for the whole [Muslim] nation ... the most important events that the nation has witnessed for centuries'.

But did this reflect Bin Laden's considered view, or was he seeking solace in an imagined al-Qaeda victory, a fantasy world in which his life's struggle for Islam fitted neatly into a pattern of historical uprisings which in reality had little to do with the violent campaign that al-Qaeda had been fighting for the past eighteen years? The documents that the Americans released depict a Bin Laden who has become a solitary, lonely man, unsure if his messages to al-Qaeda operatives are reaching their destination, fearful of security leaks, suspicious of new leaders within the organisation and aware that his commands no longer carry the respect they had when he was free.

For several years, there had been arguments within al-Qaeda about Abu Musab al-Zarqawi's Islamist group in Iraq and its successors.* As

---

* Originally called 'al-Qaeda in Iraq' and then – in the truly eccentric world of 'terrorist' nomenclature, which must have confused even the militants themselves – the 'Islamic State in Iraq', then the 'Islamic State in Iraq and the Levant' (ISIS, the final 's' representing Shams, which can mean both Damascus or 'the Levant'), and then finally just plain 'Islamic State' or Caliphate. The White House, EU and journalists eventually settled on ISIS, perhaps because this was an Egyptian goddess as well as the name of a dog in a popular television series.

long ago as 2007, we find al-Qaeda operatives arguing about ISIS. One letter expressed fear that 'political mistakes' in a speech by Abdullah al-Rashid al-Baghdadi – al-Zarqawi's successor and soon to share his fate as victim of an American air raid – revealed that ISIS were 'extremists'. By mid-2010, as al-Qaeda-affiliated groups like ISIS were conducting a ferocious and sectarian campaign of suicide bombing against Shia Muslims in Iraq and cutting down many Sunnis in their attacks, Bin Laden realised that his original cause had been perverted.

A message Bin Laden wrote to Atiyya abdul Rahman between June and 21 October 2010, while praising the mujahidin who were 'the vanguard and standard-bearers of the Islamic community in fighting the Crusader-Zionist alliance', lamented how 'some of the brothers became totally absorbed in fighting our local enemies' and how 'miscalculations by the brothers planning the operations … resulted in the killing of Muslims'. No innocent Muslims should fall victim to such operations 'except when it is absolutely essential', Bin Laden added with chilling pragmatism.

Bin Laden had exhorted his followers in his 2010 letter not to 'carry out several attacks [at a time] without exercising caution' because this would cause innocent casualties and reduce the people's support for the mujahidin. But al-Qaeda–ISIS attacks in Iraq were not delivered 'without caution' for civilians – they were deliberate assaults on civilians of the Shia faith. When Sheikh al-Shahal, the Sunni prelate in Lebanon, had warned me that a new head of al-Qaeda might be 'much more brutal', he had grasped only half the problem. The newly dead Bin Laden had in life been unable to control vast numbers of al-Qaeda operatives who were already following a sectarian path that was beyond the imagination of the al-Qaeda fighters I met at Bin Laden's camp in Afghanistan fifteen years earlier. As long ago as 2008, Khalil-al-Anani, an Egyptian writer, noted that new fringe groups were demanding an Islamic Caliphate 'over the dead bodies of their coreligionists'. These men had 'little use for the doctrinaire proclivities of al-Qaeda'. Al-Anani ominously predicted that 'a new fundamentalist organisation even more morbid than al-Qaeda may emerge in an attempt to fill the void left by the demise of conventional jihadist groups'. The day may come, he warned, 'when the likes of Bin Laden and al-Zawahri seem moderate in comparison'.

Who would have dreamed that Bin Laden would ever be called 'moderate'? But there he was in 2010, still urging his followers to avoid 'targeting the apostates in mosques', criticising the 'unnecessary civilian casualties' when 'infidel Imams' were attacked at public locations.

There were times when Bin Laden remembered his original military ambition, which he had explained to me in Afghanistan in 1996: the overthrow of the Saudi dynasty. Fourteen years on, he was writing that in the view of the Saudi rulers, 'we are their worst enemies and our presence in Yemen threatens their royalty's existence in addition to their abiding by the American wishes to fight us, so they will pump huge funds into recruiting the Yemeni tribes to kill us. They will win over the swords of the majority, which will put the Mujahidin forces in Yemen under enemy fire and in a very serious situation.'*

But in the messages and letters which passed between Abbottabad and the hunted al-Qaeda men still loyal to Bin Laden, there is an almost indifferent attitude towards the suicide killers who now moved like armies across the Middle East. Several times, Bin Laden mentions al-Qaeda attacks without even recognising that these were suicide operations. It is as if the suicide bomber has become so normal – so natural a part of the Islamist armoury – that the unique nature of his self-sacrifice has become irrelevant. Was the bomber, too, also supposed to see his death as routine, even natural? There is, in the 2010 letter, a remarkable passage about the psychology of the lone suicider in which Bin Laden gives some deeply disturbing advice to Atiyya abdul Rahman:

> You should send [a message] to the brothers in all the regions
> saying that a minimum of two brothers should be sent for
> suicide operations ... We have experienced this in many

---

* Bin Laden's tribal roots were in Yemen and he saw the country as a source of supplies and recruits for al-Qaeda, but he constantly – though vainly – warned his followers not to embark on a revolution there. 'Yemen represents an important centre of gravity in supporting fronts with men, and if war broke out there, then the supply lines to other fronts would be disrupted ...' The country, Bin Laden said, was suffering from a food and health crisis and was in no position to enter a war, but – and this was clearly a pivotal idea in his mind – Yemen formed 'the launching point towards all other oil nations'. In other words, al-Qaeda's future attacks on Saudi Arabia, Qatar and other Arab Gulf states would come from Yemen.

operations where the percentage of success was very low, due to
the psychological effects that overcome the brother in such
cases.

Bin Laden was advising Rahman more in the manner of a scientist
trying to prevent a mechanical fault than a man sympathetic to the
imminent self-annihilation of a human being. The 'psychological
effects' are a common technical problem, it seems, overcome by the
availability of a second human bomb whose presence will ensure the
necessary detonation. All this, of course, comes from a man whose
courage is beyond question, but who preferred six years of self-hiber-
nation to the millisecond of extinction.

Yet when he advises his comrades on the need for another suicide
aviation operation, he talks of selecting a maximum of ten men who
will 'have to be picked with the utmost care and with very accurate
specifications, one of which is that they are willing to conduct suicide
actions and are prepared to do daring, important and precise missions
that we may ask of them in the future … It would be nice if you would
ask the brothers in all regions if they have a brother distinguished by
his good manners, integrity, courage and secretiveness, who can operate in the US.'

By 2010, Bin Laden had been in isolation for five years and was in no
position to organise a repeat performance of 9/11. But his words were
again those of a scientist choosing a weapon rather than an ideologue
searching for the material of martyrdom. Bin Laden's conviction that
'good manners' was a characteristic likely to help a suicider conceal
himself in America says a lot about his understanding of the United
States. But equally revealing is the way in which he lists the qualities of
such a man – before he wants to know if he will actually conduct a
suicide operation. This is the voice of an armourer rather than a political leader. Or was Bin Laden still unable to fully comprehend the mind
of the suicide bomber whose operations he had so enthusiastically
encouraged?

Here is revealed the dichotomy within Bin Laden's own mind.
While he would never question the text of the Qur'an or dream of
reinterpreting its holy words, he accepted that he had gone beyond the
experience of the early Islamic fighters. From their story and example,
he had helped to fashion a new Islamist force uniquely equipped to

struggle against a non-Islamic power which feared casualties more than defeat. The suicide bomber – or the suicide pilot – had no counterpart in the West. His 'martyrdom' became his weapon; no wonder Bin Laden spent so much time assessing his performance. In war, the sword had been superseded by the suicide bomber, whose life – and death – reflected the absolutes in which Muslims could now fight their oppressors.

But in the macabre fairyland in which he lived in Abbottabad, Bin Laden was still reliving life as the great plotter, planning the assassination of both Barack Obama and General David Petraeus with the enthusiasm with which he had endorsed the 2001 attacks in America almost a decade earlier. His instructions were not without unintended humour. The vice president was not to be targeted, for instance, because when Obama – 'the head of infidelity' – was killed, Joe Biden would take over the presidency and 'is totally unprepared for that post, which will lead the US into a crisis'.

Yet Bin Laden was dismayed by the deviant path his version of Islamism had taken, especially in Iraq. He wrote that 'swords conquer and knowledge enlightens; and capturing the hearts comes before controlling nations'. Although he was killed more than three years before Abu Bakr al-Baghdadi declared his Islamic State, the fifty-three-year-old al-Qaeda leader had by 2010 clearly fathomed the dangers inherent in the Iraqi guerrilla regime. The vicious sectarian campaigns already carried out in al-Qaeda's name were well known to him.

Faced with this growing Iraqi Islamic State threat to al-Qaeda's reputation in the Muslim world, Bin Laden – with a patience born of self-incarceration – exhorted his followers to 'put forward your maximum efforts to achieve unity and resolve any conflicts between all of the Jihadi entities in Iraq'.

Bin Laden wanted an al-Qaeda letter circulated for his 'brothers' in Iraq and elsewhere, 'in the form of questions and answers', but it was, of course, far too late for such inter-al-Qaeda correspondence. What he did appreciate, however, was the means of transmitting such messages, the power of the internet. While he had long reflected upon the power of traditional newspapers and television and the way in which 'the destructive media bombardment against Arab culture ... serves the interests of the west', Bin Laden's understanding of the internet was undoubtedly fostered by Adam Yahiye Gadahn, one of al-Qaeda's more intriguing of advisers who had the ear of Bin Laden at the end of his life. An Oregon-born Muslim convert of partially Jewish origin, Gadahn – originally Adam Pearlman – gave long, occasionally violent and sometimes immensely boring video sermons in which he praised 'the slitting of the throats of the infidels' while inviting George W. Bush to abandon his 'unbelief' and become 'our brothers in Islam'. Bin Laden clearly appreciated his grasp of the Western media and American politics.

In a long letter to Bin Laden in the last weeks of the latter's life,* Gadahn corrected Bin Laden's historical mistakes, dissected the American media and repeatedly attacked al-Baghdadi's 'Islamic State in Iraq' in terms much more critical than those used by Bin Laden himself. On Gadahn's mind, however, was the tenth anniversary of the crimes of September 2001 and 'how it will be marketed in the Media, and How to Exploit the Media in General'.

Of far greater matter, however, were Gadahn's growing fears of al-Baghdadi's now truly ferocious 'Islamic State in Iraq'. Aware of the dangers that al-Zarqawi had represented before his death in the US air raid, Gadahn told Bin Laden that jihadi internet forums were 'repulsive to most of the Muslims ... It also distorts the face of al-Qaeda, due to what you know of bigotry.' While he was 'at ease' with the declaration of an Islamic State in Iraq, Gadahn wrote, 'I was not at ease with al-Zarqawi's ... moves, which he took in the name of al-Qaeda.'

Gadahn may have been longwinded, but he accurately identified the 'Islamic State's' visceral hatred of Christians, which would reach its apogee almost exactly three years later in al-Baghdadi's bloody assault on Iraq's Christians in Mosul and other towns.

Gadahn, whose own father had become a Christian as an alternative to atheism, wrote emotionally about the savagery of al-Qaeda's Iraqi allies. Was not the policy of the 'Islamic State', he asked:

exactly [the same as] the Bush policy that rebuffed Europe and the wise men of the world? Bush said 'either with us or with the terrorists' and did not leave a space for neutrality. Here this

---

* Gadahn's letter was believed by the Americans who furnished it to West Point to have been written 'post-January 2011'.

group in Iraq is telling the Christians – either [you are] with us or [you are with the Shia] al-Maliki government and no space for neutrality. Either you pay the Jizya [tax imposed on non-Muslims] to our fictitious state that cannot defend itself, and has no chance of defending you, or we will destroy your goods. Is this the justice that we are talking about, and that the Sheikh [Bin Laden] talks about in his statements and messages?

The 2010 church attack in Baghdad shocked millions of Muslims – Sunnis as well as Shia – across the Middle East. Even the Lebanese, whose 1975–90 civil war was fought largely between Maronite Christians and Muslims, managed to cloak their conflict in political rather than religious clothes – of 'socialist' and 'populist' forces against 'isolationists' – and most Arabs realised at once that Bin Laden's outrageous 'Islamic State' offspring in Iraq had torn up the discreet linguistic covering with which they normally concealed religious tension. I was aware from friends in Pakistan that Bin Laden knew of the contents of my reports in the *Independent*, even if he didn't always receive copies of them. But when the paper published an article I wrote five days after the church slaughter in Baghdad, Gadahn sent a well-translated text to Bin Laden. 'I have read a new article by Robert Fisk expressing his reaction – and other people's reaction – to the attack on the church in Baghdad, and allow me to translate to you the most important parts,' Gadahn told his boss – and then sent almost the entire text. The speed with which the church massacre by al-Qaeda had frightened the peoples of the Middle East, I had written, was

a sign of just how fragile is the earth's crust beneath their feet. Unlike our Western television news, al-Jazeera and al-Arabiya [television] show the full horror of such carnage. Arms, legs, beheaded torsos leave no doubt of what they mean. Every Christian in the region understood what this attack meant. Indeed, given the sectarian nature of the assaults on Shia Iraqis, I'm beginning to wonder whether al-Qaeda itself – far from being the centre/kernel/font of 'world terror' as we imagine – might be one of the most sectarian organisations ever invented. Nor, I suspect, is there just one al-Qaeda but several, feeding off the injustices of the region, a blood transfusion which the West (and I'm including the Israelis here) feeds into its body.

Gadahn's influence on Bin Laden cannot be fully assessed unless we see the documents from Abbottabad that the Americans kept secret. But he was the most forthright in al-Qaeda in condemning the murderous new jihadi movements and the threat that they represented to al-Qaeda itself. Gadahn recalled a conversation he had with an Arab living in Pakistan who claimed that 'all mosques now are mosques of evil informers, spies and government employees and they have no mercy on them'. Instead of appearing to compromise, al-Qaeda should renounce these 'horrible acts' in the public statement Bin Laden wished to make, Gadahn proposed.

The declaration that Gadahn believed Bin Laden should make was littered with references to 'horrible acts', 'distorted jurisprudence', 'blind revenge' and 'pre-Islamic intolerance', and it ended with a truly divine verdict: 'We warn those responsible for those crimes, of disgrace in this lifetime and painful torture in the other. The consequences of injustice are grave, and injustice is the darkness of the Day of Judgement.' This was strong stuff with which to confront Bin Laden. But the publicist in Gadahn could not resist two clichéd propaganda lines: 'No to detonating mosques and markets' and 'Aggression causes God's anger and delays victory'. This was unlikely to temper the activities of the Taliban, and certainly not the 'Islamic State'.

How was Bin Laden to respond to this candid analysis of al-Qaeda's disastrous alliance with the butchers of Pakistan and Iraq? Did he understand the need to dissociate al-Qaeda from the Iraqi sectarians? All we have is the letter he wrote to Attiya abdul Rahman a week before his assassination. If the Americans found a reply to Gadahn, they have chosen to keep its contents secret. In that last known letter, dated 25 April 2011, he had, as we know, expressed his admiration for the Arab revolutions in Egypt and Tunisia.

Much of his 'final' letter involves the security of his lieutenants and that of his own family. He gives advice on 'controlling children' in their families – teaching them a local language, forbidding them to leave the house without an adult 'who will control the volume of their voices'. His son Hamza would be travelling secretly from Iran and would need to change cars in a tunnel in Pakistan to prevent his being followed or tracked by satellite.* There was no mention of the grotesque sectarian bloodbaths that had stained al-Qaeda's name nor any talk of a declaration to end such atrocities.

There was an intriguing paragraph in this last letter which suggests that Bin Laden was thinking of negotiating with his enemies, or at least his British adversaries. This should not be taken out of context, and it would certainly never have met with the approval of Abu Bakr al-Baghdadi's future hordes. It certainly did not mean that Bin Laden feared those who wished to destroy al-Qaeda. But he certainly knew of secret talks between British intelligence agents and the Taliban in the summer of 2007 and he had now heard that the UK was offering a withdrawal from Afghanistan in return for what in effect would be an al-Qaeda ceasefire with the British.

However, we still have to remember that the Bin Laden correspondence is not only a partial collection but a heavily censored one. West Point's 'Combating Terrorism Center' conceded that it been handed one letter – about a possible change in the moniker 'al-Qaeda' – with the author, recipient and even the date marked as 'unknown', and was 'part of a longer letter not released to the CTC'. What was contained in the redacted section of this message that was too politically dangerous or too sensitive that it could not be revealed? And why would any West Point institute accept such compromised material?

More important, however, is how much evidence of Bin Laden's interest in a political agreement – at the very least a military truce, however closely defined – has been kept from us, and why. Could Bin Laden have ever agreed to such contact with the infidel Crusaders against whom he had declared war fourteen years before his death? The American SEAL attack on Bin Laden's Abbottabad compound ensured that no such future could be envisaged. Al-Zawahiri finally excommunicated the 'Islamic State' from al-Qaeda when al-Baghdadi extended his 'Caliphate' across the newly destroyed frontier of Syria in 2013. But al-Qaeda became as humiliated by the refusal of the 'Islamic State' to abide by its rules as it lost influence by breaking its affiliation

---

* Gadahn had been worried that the movement of journalists seeking to interview members of al-Qaeda could be 'involuntarily monitored' by satellite and mentioned Ahmed Zeidan, one of Al Jazeera Arabic's best-informed reporters in Islamabad. Zeidan's interviews had never led to attacks on Taliban leaders. It would, Gadahn warned, 'be prudent and a defeat to the enemy to avoid any meetings with journalists'.

with al-Baghdadi's ferocious 'statelet'. And when the US came to confronting this new threat, Washington described it in clichés it had never employed against al-Qaeda. Thus the 'Islamic State' became 'apocalyptic' with an 'end-of-time' ideology that would have to be pursued – as Obama's secretary of state John Kerry was reduced to saying in September 2014 – 'to the gates of hell'.

It is a bright cool morning in west Beirut, 19 November 2013. I am walking to my grocers when a long, low growl of an explosion touches the air pressure. Suicide bomb. It must be. All bombers are suiciders in Lebanon now, just as they are in Syria, in Iraq ... My mobile purrs. Samira, my landlord's niece, is listening to the family television and even before she speaks I hear a presenter speaking of the *safara Iraniya* – the Iranian embassy. Abed, my driver, has been retired and I look around desperately for a taxi, see an old man driving a clapped-out Mercedes, and chase after him. Before I can speak, he asks me if I am a *sahafa*, a journalist, and assumes I'm heading for the embassy.

His car radio speaks of many dead, and we drive off with the old engine of his taxi roaring. By the time we get within a mile of the Iranian compound, the roads are clogged with shouting soldiers and, after I run half a mile up the hill towards the embassy, dozens of Hizbollah gunmen, big bright new silver pistols in their hands, are screaming at the crowds, some gawping at the smoke and fire, others holding hands to their faces with blood dribbling between their fingers. On the roadway is a huge pool of blood through which the fire brigade are running their hoses and civil defence men, slopping through the gore, are shrieking into two-way radios. My Lebanese television colleagues are barking into their microphones. A double suicide bombing, the Iranian cultural attaché killed, at least twenty-six dead, 150 wounded. All the vile detritus of the event lies around me; the leg under the broken balcony, the bits of teeth, the jaw with beard still attached, the blood swamping the pavements as well as the road.

We could not forget amid the burning cars and shoes and remnants of flesh that sixty-six Lebanese were killed in the bombing of Shiite and Sunni targets here in recent weeks. Now that figure stands at ninety-two. There was no government in Lebanon and the Lebanese army remained the only state institution functioning in the country – apart from the central bank – and after the bombings here, Lebanese troops were outnumbered by the scores of Hizbollah men. Were the Hizbollah now the army of Lebanon in this suburb of Jnah? For Jnah is a Shia area of Beirut and the bombers were most assuredly working for some Sunni gang undoubtedly loyal in some way to al-Baghdadi's 'Islamic State'.

It wasn't difficult to find the sectarianism that al-Qaeda was now heir to. In the north Lebanese city of Tripoli, Sunnis had been blaming the Shiite Hizbollah and the Syrian (Shia) Alawites for bombs that killed forty-seven worshippers at two mosques. Now it was the Shiites' turn.

As usual, the movie of the carnage plays in reverse as we learn what happened in the minutes and then the hours before the bombs exploded. CCTV cameras show two men arriving outside the embassy seconds before the explosion in a stolen Chevrolet TrailBlazer 4×4. One of them, wearing an explosive belt, moves towards the huge iron embassy gate and detonates himself. The gate is torn down, but the second bomber waiting in the car – with, it turned out, another fifty kilograms of explosives – cannot drive through the gate towards the embassy complex inside; he suddenly finds himself blocked by a lorry carrying bottled water.

The man in charge of the embassy's security, Radwan Fares, runs into the street with his colleagues, most of them Hizbollah guards, and sees the water truck and, immediately behind it, the black Chevrolet, which starts to move. Fares opens fire at the man in the Chevrolet. At the same time, so we learn later from the Internal Security Forces, the Lebanese government's paramilitary police, a young ISF corporal called Haitham Ayoub chases the vehicle on foot and even tries to yank open the driver's door. A brave and fatal act. The bomber blows up his Chevrolet, instantly killing Fares, four of his colleagues and the coura-geous Corporal Ayoub.

On the night before the bombings, the two men checked into the luxurious Sheraton Four Points Hotel in central Beirut, just as the hijackers in America spent a quiet night in good hotels before they set off to massacre the innocent on 11 September 2001. And just as the 9/11 killers went for symbolic targets, so the Beirut bombers went to the fulcrum of Iranian-Syrian-Hizbollah-Shiite power in Lebanon, the Embassy of the Islamic Republic.

There was a claim, almost at once. The 'Abdullah Azzam Brigades', an outfit claiming to protect Sunnis and allied to al-Qaeda, was led by a Saudi called Saleh al-Qarawi. He reportedly fought against US forces in the second Battle of Fallujah in Iraq and was closely associated with al-Zarqawi whose 'al-Qaeda in Iraq' had, of course, almost single-handedly turned Bin Laden's army of fighters into the most sectarian organisation in the world. The 'Abdullah Azzam Brigades' had previously taken responsibility for missile attacks on two ships in the Middle East, an oil tanker and a US naval craft moored at Aqaba in Jordan.*

And finally, the suiciders themselves; the 'minimum of two brothers', as Bin Laden had laid down, the bomber on foot and the 'companion' in the Chevrolet who would 'support and bolster him'. But technically this bombing needed two suiciders: one to tear down the protective iron gate, the other to drive through it and incinerate the embassy. A mere water truck defeated the plan. Explosives usually pulverise the remains of the bombers, but the ISF discovered enough bits to use their DNA, and within five days identified the sectarian al-Qaeda killers.

Mouin Abu Dahr was born into a mixed Sunni–Shia family, but had become preoccupied with the sermons of a white-bearded and eloquent Sunni Salafist preacher called Sheikh Ahmad Assir, an anti-Assad, anti-Hizbollah imam from Sidon, where Abu Dahr lived. I had interviewed Assir earlier that year. His anti-Assad message never seemed very eloquent to me, but his 'faithful' subsequently fought bloody street battles with the Lebanese army, and he was now on the run. Abu Dahr had himself visited Syria to fight alongside the Sunni militias trying to overthrow Assad. On his Facebook page, the bomber-to-be was wearing a black beard and expressed his admiration for Assir. A neighbour recounted how Abu Dahr also travelled to Sweden where he 'was taken under the wing of an imam'. He rushed back to Lebanon to attend the funeral of the Assir men shot by the army. Since then, a friend said, 'he talked to me about martyrdom and thought his family was not religious enough'. When Assir accused the army of not

---

* The commander of the 'Abdullah Azzam Brigades' turned out to be a Saudi national called Majid bin Mohamed al-Majid, who was arrested in December 2013 after apparently entering Lebanon to receive medical treatment for a kidney ailment. A week later, the government announced that he had died in a military hospital – of kidney failure.

bothering about the Shia Hizbollah's presence in Syria to help the Assad regime, Abu Dahr's fury increased, 'concluding that the Sunnis of Lebanon were unjustly treated'.

Like Abu Dahr, Adnan Moussa Mohamed had fought with the Sunni fighters in Syria – but unlike his Lebanese comrade, he was a Palestinian. His mother recalled that Mohamed, a twenty-one-year-old car mechanic from the village of Bassouriyeh, 'was pious and went regularly to the mosque. I cannot believe that my son committed this appalling crime.' Mohamed's family also denounced the 'heinous crime' in which their son had participated. According to an uncle, neighbours had warned Mohamed's father that his son was attending Assir's rallies in Sidon. 'He tried several times to change his [son's] views but he refused and left the family home,' the man said. Mohamed had disappeared six months before he killed himself in the Iranian embassy attack. An acquaintance of Mohamed's family told journalists he 'should have blown himself up in Israel, not among Muslims'. Bin Laden might have agreed.

About a hundred metres from the Iranian embassy that day, walking away from the fire and smoke, I was chatting to a reporter from Lebanese television when she suddenly grabbed my arm and pulled me from the pavement. 'Look where you are stepping,' she said. And close to my foot was a tiny strip of bloody, transparent skin. There were dark splashes on the wall behind, but my attention was caught by this fragile piece of humanity beside me. The woman shrugged, and I knew what she meant. That's it, she was saying. That's what it's worth.

Where was it Hassan Oweydah's mother told me her son was going? To the 'higher heaven'? To be married in the 'spring of heaven'? So this unmentionable thing on the pavement was part of the banal routine through which these two young men must pass, a tearing-apart as easily consummated as the last words of Hassan Oweydah as he spoke to his mother beneath the gateway shrouded in bougainvillea. 'It is not important for me to return.'

6

'The Gloves Are Coming Off, Gentlemen ...'

Through me, you enter into the city of woes,
Through me you enter into eternal pain,
Through me you enter the population of loss.
... Abandon all hope, you who enter here.

Dante's *The Divine Comedy*, Canto III, 1–7
(translation by Robert Pinsky)

First, our enemies created the suicide bomber. Then we invented our own digital suicide bomber: the camera. Look at the way US army reservist Lynndie England held the leash of the naked, bearded Iraqi in Abu Ghraib prison. No sadistic movie could outdo the damage of this image.

The Muslim suicide bomber cries out that God is Greatest, while Lynndie England's partner-in-crime boyfriend's home garden is plastered with a legend from the Book of Hosea about sexual sin and righteousness. Could neo-conservative Christianity have collided so violently, so revoltingly, so obscenely with Islam? And who were the innocent supposed to be in these vile photographs? The American torturers and humiliators? Or the Iraqi victims?*

For a year, Iraqis had been trying to tell journalists of the brutal treatment they were receiving at the hands of their occupiers. Now

---

* England received a three-and-a-half year sentence for her part in the abuse, her then lover Charles Graner ten years. Thousands of others who committed far worse crimes in later years went, of course, unpunished.

General Richard Myers, chairman of the US Joint Chiefs, was warning that the release of these pictures and tapes would allow al-Qaeda to 'seize upon these images and videos as grist for their propaganda mill'. But when we discovered that not one but several Iraqis identified themselves as the man smeared with excrement, the prisoner with wires attached to his hands, we knew at once that there was nothing unusual about the treatment of prisoners at Abu Ghraib. The Americans insisted – however terrible they admitted the photos to be – that these were only symbolic wires, that the man in the snapshot had never been electrocuted. How then to explain the testimony of Haj Ali, a former district mayor, who said that he had also been hooded, made to stand on a box with electrical wires attached to his body parts? He said that in his case, the wires were live, that 'it felt like my eyeballs were coming out of their sockets'.

What we saw in those photographs, of course, was not a single 'bad apple' moment in America's attempt to break its enemies in Iraq, but a normal procedure visited upon tens of thousands of innocents in Iraq and Afghanistan, indeed around the world.

Naomi Klein, that irrepressible chronicler of American malfeasance in Iraq, concluded that torture was part of the Bush administration's policy of 'Shock and Awe', that the massive bombardment and invasion of the country was followed by the economic shock tactics of privatising Iraq's resources, which was followed almost seamlessly by 'the shock of the torture chamber'. Rarely has the road to perdition been so neatly catalogued. The violence of invasion was eagerly photographed. The economic pulverisation could be acknowledged in a series of ad-hoc laws, press conferences and complex energy deals. But the shock of 'torture' was not supposed to be revealed so flagrantly, certainly not with privately owned digital cameras. The camera was indeed a suicide bomber, but one that destroyed our power and prestige, demonstrating that we ourselves were our own worst enemies, while portraying our militant antagonists as victims with a cause infinitely worth fighting for.

And I remembered that terrifying videotape I watched in 2003 of the whipping of Iraqi prisoners by Saddam's security police, of the pain and excrement and blood. As I continued to show clips from that tape in lectures, I was trying to illustrate not only the ferocity of the regime which America had overthrown but the way in which abuse and atrocity had been adopted, refined and enthusiastically committed by those who wanted to bring 'democracy' to Iraq.

I became convinced that the American pictures of the Iraqis so cruelly treated were taken for precisely the same reason as the Saddam videos. Let us remember the Abu Ghraib pictures we did not see but which the journalist who broke the story of Abu Ghraib, Seymour Hersh, talked about in 2004. We didn't know, Hersh told a lecture audience, some of the worst things that happened at Abu Ghraib:

> Videos. OK? There are women there ... they were passing letters out, communications out to their men ... those women who were arrested with young boys, children, in cases that have been recorded, the boys were sodomised, with the cameras rolling, and the worst above all of them is the soundtrack of the boys shrieking.

So in Abu Ghraib, the Americans had decided that the photos would be the breaking point, the moment of capitulation for these young men. Who taught these young Americans that it was a good idea to encourage a female soldier to point at an Arab who was being forced to masturbate, to humiliate an Iraqi by hooding him with female lingerie? We weren't just talking 'sick' here; we were talking professionals.

Al Jazeera tried to discover if abuse was, in fact, US policy. They studied a Pentagon press conference of November 2005 in which General Peter Pace, chairman of the Joint Chiefs, is telling journalists how soldiers should react to the cruel treatment of prisoners. He points out proudly that it is an American soldier's duty to intervene if he sees evidence of torture. Then the camera moves to defense secretary Donald Rumsfeld, who suddenly interrupts – to Pace's consternation – 'I don't think you mean they have an obligation to physically stop it. It's to report it.'

But of course, in the case of Abu Ghraib, it was American soldiers who were themselves performing the acts of torture. Years later, we would learn that this abuse had already been 'road-tested' at Guantanamo. A Pentagon investigation revealed that at Guantanamo, Mohamed al-Qahtani, accused of being the 'twentieth hijacker' of 9/11, was forced to stand naked in front of women, to wear a bra, was told he was homosexual and threatened with leashed dogs. American

insistence that Abu Ghraib was an isolated affair, a former US
intelligence officer was to write later, 'stands in sharp contrast to my
own experiences as an interrogator in Iraq'.

In the Middle East today, the Abu Ghraib pictures have acquired the
status of those infamous snapshots of the Vietnam war: the Saigon
police chief executing his Vietcong prisoner, the naked girl burned by
napalm. But they represented something more: they stood in for all the
tortures and humiliations and rapes that were successfully kept secret,
that would never enter the history books. In every war, the same
phenomenon has occurred. Evidence emerges of an atrocity – and the
authorities expect us to believe that this is the only abuse or murder of
its kind to have occurred; that we have, in other words, just learned of
the one and only act of indiscipline to have taken place in the entire
conflict.

It was the same story with Haditha in November 2005, when US
Marines massacred twenty-four men, women and children in revenge
for the killing of a fellow marine. US personnel had shot the civilians,
including the elderly and infants, many times at close range. Not one
US Marine was imprisoned, a trial result described by a lawyer for the
victims as 'an assault on humanity'. When the American massacre was
revealed, I asked in the *Independent* whether Haditha might be just 'the
tip of the mass grave'. The corpses we glimpsed, the grainy footage of
the cadavers and the dead children; might these be just a few of many?
'Did the handiwork of America's slums go further?'

Of course they did. In 2011, new evidence emerged that in March
2006 – six months after the Haditha atrocity – US troops killed at least
ten Iraqi civilians in cold blood, including five children, one only five
months old, and a seventy-six-year-old blind man in a wheelchair in a
house in the town of Ishaki – before ordering an air strike that
destroyed the building. The murders only came to light in 2011, when
WikiLeaks published a letter from Philip Alston, the UN's rapporteur
on extrajudicial killings. Although the Americans claimed an al-Qaeda
suspect had been seized from a room in the house after fierce fighting,
Alston reported that a Tikrit autopsy showed the victims had been
handcuffed and shot in the head. An original report by the Iraqi military, which was paid and armed by the US, stated that 'the Americans
gathered the family members in a room and executed eleven persons,
including five children, four women and two men. Then they bombed

the house, burned three vehicles and killed the animals.' The US military, which declined to respond to Alston's letter, announced an investigation which was not followed by any action.* The US Marine Jason Washburn, who completed three tours of duty in Iraq and was a member of the same unit which killed the twenty-four civilians in Haditha, was to agree that Haditha itself was no isolated incident. 'It's the one that just happened to be uncovered,' he said.†

Early in the Iraq conflict, we discovered that only a narrow line separated indiscipline and fear from brutality and murder. I found the evidence of this when in July 2003, US soldiers in armoured vehicles accompanied by military police and US plain-clothes agents arrived in the Mansour district of Baghdad after a tip-off that Saddam was hiding there. But they turned their house raid into a bloodbath, opening fire on scores of Iraqi civilians and killing up to eleven of them. A car caught fire, cremating its occupants.

These incidents, which became routine, showed how panic and slovenly, ill-trained soldiers – along, sadly, with what must have been indifference towards a native population – could lead within seconds to a heedless mass killing of innocents. There was no official inquiry. No one was charged with these unlawful killings nor could the Iraqi authorities intervene; the US has refused to sign up to the International Criminal Court for fear its soldiers serving overseas may be forced to appear before it. But this was us. These young soldiers were our representatives in Iraq. And they had innocent blood on their hands.

Our failure to care about Iraqis was not only symbolised by our

---

* Within ten years of the invasion, the world had become so accustomed to US war crimes in Iraq that they rarely merited prominent media attention. Soldiers from the 101st Airborne broke into the home of fourteen-year-old Abeer Qassim al-Janabi in Mahmoudiyah, south of Baghdad, in March 2006 – the same month as the Ishaki outrage – shot her father, mother and six-year-old sister and then raped the girl before covering her face with a pillow and shooting her too. Then they burned her body. The mass murder was turned into an award-winning movie, *Redacted* – which was then predictably attacked by right-wing columnists for putting US lives in danger in Iraq.

† Among many incidents Washburn was to recall in 2008 was of a woman who was approaching his men – and who paid a terrifying price for their suspicions. 'She was carting a huge bag and she looked like she was heading toward us,' Washburn later testified, 'so we lit her up with the Mark 19, which is an automatic grenade launcher, and when the dust settled, we realised that the bag was full of groceries. She had been trying to bring us food and we blew her to pieces.'

refusal to count their dead while enumerating the suffering of every wounded man and woman among our Western armies. We had no sympathy or attachment towards these people – despite our desire to bestow 'democracy' upon them – and no comprehension that they were our equals. It was this that lay behind the torture and the killings, in Afghanistan as well as Iraq.

While they were obedient to our wishes and our plans for their nations, we tolerated their shortcomings; their strange language, their alien religion and outdated tribal customs. But once the Iraqis turned upon our army of occupation with their roadside explosives and suicide bombers, they became Arab 'hajis' or 'cloth-heads'. Remind yourself that these people are Muslims, and they will all become little Mohamed Attas, progeny of the senior 9/11 pilot. Killing a roomful of civilians in Haditha is only a step further along the road from all those promiscuous air strikes which we are told kill 'terrorists', but which sometimes – in Afghanistan – turned out to be wedding parties.

In a way, reporters – 'holed up in hotels, hemmed in by drivers and translators and official security and military escorts', as the journalist Chris Hedges was to put it – were also to blame, as we meekly catalogued the number of 'terrorist' dead supposedly scored in remote corners of Mesopotamia. For fear of the insurgents' knife, we could no longer investigate. And the Americans liked it that way. Who knows what horrors were being committed far away in the sands?

In the years after 2003, our wickedness trickled out like contaminated water. But our inhumanity started much earlier, within weeks of our 'liberation' of Afghanistan in 2001. And when we met our victims, we could only admire their courage and agree that what had been done to them was a crime against human rights and humanity itself. They did not ask for this acknowledgement. Nor, thankfully, did they ask for our remorse. We had tried to take their hope away – and they had kept their faith without any help from us.

In the *Independent*, I would keep a record of the persecution that often moved through a malevolent web of competing intelligence services, from the Pakistani security matrix so eloquently condemned in the official Pakistani government report on Bin Laden's assassination, to the British and American collaboration in torture. Our reports, I have to say, rarely elicited a response – let alone an apology – from the clearly unstable and pitiful men who abused these people on our behalf. As a journalist, I naturally sought after my own breed among the ex-prisoners.

Sami al-Haj walks with pain on his steel crutch; almost six years in the nightmare of Guantanamo have taken their toll on the Al Jazeera journalist and now, in the safety of a hotel in the small Norwegian town of Lillehammer, he is a figure of both dignity and shame. The Americans told him they were sorry when they eventually freed him – after the beatings he suffered, the force-feeding, the humiliations and interrogations by British, American and Canadian intelligence officers – and he hopes one day he'll be able to walk without his stick.

The grotesque saga began for al-Haj on 15 December 2001, when he was travelling from Islamabad to Kandahar in south-western Afghanistan with Sadah al-Haq, a fellow correspondent from the Arab satellite channel, to cover the new regional government. At least seventy other journalists were crossing the Pakistani border at Chaman, but an officer stopped al-Haj. 'He told me there was a paper from the Pakistani intelligence service for my arrest. My name was misspelled, my passport number was incorrect, it said I was born in 1964 – the right date is 1969. I said I had renewed my visa in Islamabad and asked why, if I was wanted, they had not arrested me there?' The Pakistani Inter-Services Intelligence packed al-Haj off to the former British military cantonment at Quetta, where he was thrown into a cell with a group of Saudi prisoners. 'At 11 p.m., we were taken to Quetta airport and handed over to the Americans.' A US soldier searched him and confiscated his belongings, before putting them on a propeller aircraft with no seats, tying them to the floor with ropes. 'One man said he was in pain and wanted to go to a bathroom. They told him to shut up but he went on talking so they hit him and when he refused to stop talking, they tied a rope in his mouth.'

Sami al-Haj speaks carefully, each detail of his – and others' – suffering of equal importance to him. He still cannot believe he is free, able to live once more with his Azeri wife Asma and their eight-year-old son Mohamed; the boy was only fourteen months old when he disappeared down the black hole of America's secret prisons.

Al-Haj's story had a familiar ring to anyone investigating the rendition of prisoners from Pakistan to US bases in Afghanistan and Guantanamo. His aircraft flew for an hour and a half before landing to

collect more captives and flying on to the giant American base at
Bagram:

> We arrived in the early hours of the morning and they took the
> shackles off our feet and pushed us out of the plane. They hit me
> and pushed me down on the asphalt. We heard screams and
> dogs barking. I collapsed with my right leg under me, and I felt
> the ligaments tearing. When I fell, the soldiers started treading
> on me. First, they walked on my back, then – when they saw me
> looking at my leg – they started kicking my leg. I had folded my
> leg to protect it but they kicked it to straighten it out. The bags
> were taken off. One soldier shouted at me: 'Why did you come
> to fight Americans?' … They tied us all together, a soldier
> pulling at each end. There were six to eight of us on each rope.

Al-Haj recalls being dragged with his fellow captives into a hangar
where another soldier threatened to shoot him. 'There were twenty or
thirty soldiers with US flag patches on their sleeves, five or six of them
women, and I was told to take my clothes off. I refused and they started
to jab me in the back with sticks and threatened to set the dogs on me
if I did not take off my underclothes.' Ordered to dress in a uniform, he
was taken to a room where two Americans were waiting for him.

> I had a number – I was No 35 and this is how they addressed me,
> as a number – and the first American shouted at me: 'You filmed
> Bin Laden.' I said I did not film Bin Laden but that I was a
> journalist. I again gave my name, my age, my nationality.

Ten days later, he was again accused of filming Bin Laden; this time
al-Haj pointed out that his passport entry and exit visas showed that
when Bin Laden appeared on Al Jazeera, he was in the Qatari capital,
Doha. After sixteen days at Bagram, another aircraft took al-Haj to the
US base at Kandahar, where on arrival the prisoners were again made
to lie on the ground.

The same dreary round of interrogations recommenced – al-Haj was
now 'Prisoner No 448' – and he was told he was being held by mistake:

An American soldier said: 'Co-operate with us, and you will be
released.' They meant I had to work for them. There was
another man who spoke perfect English. I thought he was
British ... He brought me chocolate – it was Kit Kat – and I was
so hungry I could have eaten the wrapping paper.

There were few other acts of kindness during al-Haj's five months at
Kandahar. He says the prisoners were not allowed to wash and had lice
'crawling all over us'. The Red Cross brought the captives copies of the
Qur'an – ten for each tent and two Bibles – 'but the Americans tore
pages out of the Qur'ans and threw them in the toilets. They wanted
us to see this and they kept saying they were on a crusade.'

On 13 June, al-Haj was taken from his tent, once more his head was
covered with a black bag and he was put on board a jet aircraft. He was
forced to take two tablets before he was gagged and the bag was
replaced by goggles with the eye-pieces painted black. The tablets
made him tired but he was still awake when he was forced to change
aircraft at an airbase which, he later learned, was in Turkey. The flight
to Guantanamo took twelve to fourteen hours, after which an hour-
long boat journey took them to the prison. Al-Haj was escorted to a
medical clinic and then to another interrogation with three intelligence
officers, whereupon he was forced to account for his movements in
Afghanistan all over again.

The next day there was another interrogation and it was the
same old story. They said, 'You are here by mistake. You will be
released.' They gave me a picture of my son, which had been
taken from my wallet ... Then after two months, two more
British men came to see me. They said they were from UK
intelligence. They wanted to know whom I knew, whom I'd
met. I said I couldn't help them.

Al-Haj's senior interrogator at Guantanamo, Stephen Rodriguez,
wanted again to seek al-Haj's help:

He said to me: 'Our job is to prevent "things" happening. I'll
give you a chance to think about this. You can have US
citizenship, your family will be looked after, you'll have a villa in

the US, we'll look after your son's education, you'll have a bank
account.' He had brought with him some Arabic magazines and
told me I could read them. In those ten minutes, I felt I had gone
back to being a human being again. Then soldiers came to take
me back to my cell – and the magazines were taken away.

By the summer of 2003, al-Haj was receiving other strange visitors.
'Two Canadian intelligence officers came and they showed me lots of
photos of people and wanted to know if I recognised them. I knew
none of them.' 'They asked me: "Did you see any Canadians with Bin
Laden?"' In over 200 interrogations, al-Haj was asked about his employers, Al Jazeera. In one session, he says another American said to him:
'After you get out of here, al-Qaeda will recruit you and we want to
know who you meet. We want to know what it's like on the inside.
After your training and work with us, you could become an analyst, to
analyse their speech, we can train you to store information, to sketch
people. There is a link between Al Jazeera and al-Qaeda.'

'I said: "I will not do this – first of all because I'm a journalist and this
is not my job. Also because I fear for my life and my family." Then they
tried threats. They said: "You'll stay here all your life – you'll never see
your son again," hinting they had proof I was a "terrorist". They said:
"You interviewed Abul-Hafez al-Mauretania, the third man in al-
Qaeda." And I said: "Yes, we made an interview with him in Kandahar
for Al Jazeera."' Many beatings followed from the guards.

In January 2007, Sami al-Haj began a hunger strike and completed
480 days of hunger strike, by which time his medical condition had
deteriorated and he was bleeding from his anus. This was the moment
his interrogators decided to release him. Neither the British nor the
Canadian authorities have ever admitted talking to Sami al-Haj, and he
never received an official apology from the Americans.

The treatment of innocent men like al-Haj told us a lot about the illegal
world in which George Bush believed we should live. 11 September
2001 had become a piece of legislation that allowed us to arrest whom
we wanted, question whom we wanted, abuse whom we wanted, lock
up whom we wanted, invade whatever countries we wanted. This was
the Bush administration's memorial to the dead of the World Trade
Center, the Pentagon and Pennsylvania.

Invention was an essential part of torture. After an infamous email from US intelligence operative Captain Ponce to fellow officers in August 2003, relaying a request that 'the gloves are coming off gentlemen regarding these detainees ... we want these individuals broken', General Ricardo Sanchez, the American commander whom we last met trying to explain why Saddam's sons were killed rather than taken prisoner, authorised new interrogation methods. They included 'pride and ego down', 'exploit[ing] Arab fear of dogs', 'light control' and 'stress positions'.

For the most part, American and British torturers and their mercenary assistants were to get away with the atrocities they committed in Iraq, Afghanistan and Guantanamo. Any suggestion that they should pay for their crimes was invariably smothered in a lather of patriotism; that without the vigilance of the CIA and other intelligence authorities, the US, Britain and the rest of what we once called the 'free world' would lie unprotected against the evil of 'terrorism'.

This veil covered a vast tableau of human rights violations, ill treatment, extrajudicial killings, torture and massacres, often dressed up in the language of heroism rather than barbarism. The infinitely thin line between indiscipline, ill treatment and slaughter could just fade away. And this system of cruelty was cemented in place by both the impunity offered to the torturers and the sense of normality with which their actions were graced. Ultimately, it was not just the perpetrators but we ourselves who had become 'socialised to atrocity'.

The detailed profanities of torture need not occupy too much of this chapter. I am more interested in the *spirit* of torture; not just in the excuses of those who inflict pain, but in the prescriptive way in which power presents us with an excusable, even admirable portrayal of barbarity.

As Christendom embarked upon a Renaissance of humanism, its liberal values reaching their apogee in nineteenth-century Europe, the Western world began to worship more tangible gods. After the ferocity of oppression by church and state, every human was to be regarded as an individual, which may be why the dead of the 1914–18 war were the first to be given identified graves. Modern philosophy could not prevent war, but it would encourage the moral precept, inscribed in the Hague Convention of 1907 and the 1949 Geneva Convention, that there must be laws of war, outlawing depravities beyond which no nation's soldiers or bureaucrats should march.

That these new rules have been largely disregarded does not deprive them of their worth or their message: that each individual man, woman or child has what we now acknowledge to be human rights. The Armenian genocide of the First World War and the Jewish genocide of the Second World War prompted the post-1945 world to reflect more seriously about these rights, which were, in the 1948 UN Universal Declaration of Human Rights, called 'inalienable'. In the years since, some human beings have found these rights more 'inalienable' than others, but the idea persisted. Even the most odious of dictators abided by the slogan – if not the deed.

The Roman Empire lacked any notion of 'human rights', its law and justice taking no account of pain. Samuel Dill, among the most eloquent of classical scholars, wrote of a vein of 'coarse insensibility to suffering in the Roman character', which became 'more and more indurated under the influence of licensed cruelty'.

It is the word 'licensed' that contains the clue to our modern hardness of heart, our lack of mercy towards those we are told to suppress or destroy. Power gives both licence and impunity. And since impunity implies trust – that 'gentlemen' will obey orders without question, however revolted they may find such instructions – then they may later be permitted to embrace the glory of victory. This is well illustrated by the behaviour of US troops in the Philippines in 1906, a year before the second Hague Convention, when America brutally crushed an uprising by the ethnic Muslim Moro people, a final and hopeless battle in the Philippine war of independence. It is a tale not without significance in our study of America's occupation of Afghanistan and Iraq.

Mark Twain wrote a deeply sarcastic essay about the 'battle' a few days later:

> we lost fifteen men killed outright, and we had thirty-two
> wounded … The enemy numbered six hundred – including
> women and children – and we abolished them utterly, leaving
> not even a baby alive to cry for its dead mother. This is
> incomparably the greatest victory that was ever achieved by the
> Christian soldiers of the United States.

Twain recorded the headlines over the following days – 'Women Slain in Moro Massacre', 'With Children They Mixed in Mob in Crater, and All Died Together', 'Death List is Now 900', 'Impossible to Tell Sexes Apart in Fierce Battle on Top of Mount Dajo' – and remarked that 'the naked savages were so far away, down in the bottom of that trap, that our soldiers could not tell the breasts of a woman from the rudimentary paps of a man – so far away that they couldn't tell a toddling child from a black six-footer'.

The Moro massacre was initially – as Twain predicted – a public relations disaster. It could not be regarded as a 'brilliant feat of arms', even 'if Christian America represented by its salaried soldiers, had shot them down with Bibles ... instead of bullets'. But subsequent accounts of the mass killings claimed that the Moro women had been used as human shields by their men-folk and were thus what we would today call 'collateral damage'. US troops wrote home about other atrocities in the Philippines, including the torching of villages and the killing of their occupants. A form of water torture was also used to extract information during the eight-year anti-independence campaign.* There was, therefore, nothing new about America's cruelty in Iraq. The Philippines was the first imperial war fought by the United States, and the pattern of 'shock and awe' inflicted on the Moro people was to be repeated in the Middle East.

But there are two elements to the institution of torture that we largely ignore. Torture as a form of coercion – like rape – is too often separated from war itself. The deliberate infliction of death on a large scale can be moderated in history writing and reporting by the assurance that 'rules of war' exist; torture and violence against women supposedly lie outside of them. But torture and rape are as much 'common methods of war' as tanks, guns, drones and the wholesale massacre of soldiers or civilians. All these institutions of suffering and death were also interchangeable among nations, one precedent commending itself to others. The army that will kill the innocent

---

* The US did not grant the Philippines independence for another forty years, but a policy of real self-government and economic development – unlike the sale of Iraq's assets to foreign buyers under Paul Bremer's stewardship – largely deprived the resistance of its native support. Insurgents also murdered Philippine civilians who collaborated with the Americans. The Moro Muslims were a minority among the country's more than 80 per cent Christian Catholic population.

through ill-discipline, fear or race hatred, will have no compunction in submitting men and women to the obscenity of the torture chamber. By the same token, guerrilla forces will also apply these methods of war to their own struggle. The Philippine independence fighters were reported to have killed American prisoners – cutting off their genitals before suffocating them or burning them alive – with as much enthusiasm as the ISIS killers of 2014 were to cut the throats of their enemies.

Torture is also regarded as more acceptable, or at least less reprehensible, when it is perpetrated by non-Western nations, even if their torturers are working for governments that we in Europe and the US support, finance and arm. When I first arrived in the Middle East in 1976, for instance, I found that editors, while prepared to condemn Arab regimes that tortured their nationals, regarded this wickedness as somehow 'normal', presumably because these methods of oppression were a constant practice.

In the late 1970s Arab regime torture was something all too familiar in the Middle East, and not something that would end 'overnight'. For the Arab dictators and generals and kings and princes who dominated the region were themselves also at war with their people.

The Israelis, of course, were always a unique case – never practising torture against their own people, but routinely subjecting their captive and occupied people, the Palestinians, to torture and human rights abuses on a scale that would never be tolerated by any other Western nation. In theory, the question here was whether we regarded Israel as a Western nation or in some way 'special', neither 'us' nor Middle Eastern, in which case journalists would impose special rules of reporting. In reality, European guilt for the Jewish Holocaust, America's uncritical and total support for Israel and the fear of being accused of anti-Semitism effectively suppressed most editorial condemnation of Israel's atrocities, whether committed in 'peace' or war.

Of all the Arab states, Egypt provided us with the most detailed accounts of state torture, because the Mubarak dictatorship gave visas to visiting correspondents as routinely as it abused and executed its prisoners. Reporting was more difficult for journalists and Western news agency staff who maintained regional headquarters in the Egyptian capital since any serious investigation of regime torture would invariably bring a government threat to close their offices.

Those of us based in Beirut rather than Cairo were under no such pressure, and my own archives contain dozens of dispatches on Egyptian government suppression and torture. In just one five-year period from 1993 to 1997, for example, I was regularly filing reports from cities far from Cairo as Mubarak's security apparatus fought a merciless war with Gama'a Islamiya insurgents, using both police torture and then military courts to liquidate the Islamist uprising. My reports would prove to be painfully similar to those I had written for *The Times* about British army abuses in Northern Ireland in the 1970s – and almost identical to those I was to send to the *Independent* during the American 'war on terror' in post-2003 Iraq and the subsequent sectarian conflict.

As usual, there were many victims and few heroes. The brave and outstanding work by the Egyptian lawyers and human rights groups who compiled thousands of detailed testimonies of torture and sent them to the Egyptian as well as Western governments never received a single reply. Their evidence was supported by years of reporting from Amnesty International and dozens of torture files published by Human Rights Watch. 'The Americans read our reports, they know what's going on,' Mohamed Moneib told me in 1996, adding that even as a secretary general of his human rights group he could not persuade any Western embassy to make a statement about human rights violations.

Lawyers, who would no longer allow me to publish their names for fear of arrest, told me that there was a campaign in Wadi al-Jadid prison to eliminate suspects before they were brought to trial. Another lawyer stated that prisoners were 'stripped and kicked' and each given 'a woman's name' to shame and dehumanise them. 'They can wear only their underclothes for a week and then they are given a yellow prison uniform.' Male rape in Egyptian prisons, of course, was similar to the shame and sexual degradation suffered by male and female inmates at American hands in Abu Ghraib less than a decade later. Indeed, the false death certificates were identical to those issued for dead bodies by Algeria's police torturers at the very same time – during the savage conflict between the pouvoir and the Islamists in the former French possession.

Magdi Hussein, one of Egypt's most courageous newspaper editors, was to highlight the extraordinary cooperation between Arab governments which practised torture; which meant all of them. 'This moves laterally across the Arab world,' he told me in 1997, when the Gama'a was about to crack under Mubarak's security regime. 'Algeria and Tunisia are using the same techniques. The experience of investigating and interrogating suspects is being shared by the Egyptians. They are exchanging experiences between themselves – exchanging information about people, about those who fought in Afghanistan. They are filling in spaces in each other's information.' The 'Afghani' Arabs were widely defined by Egypt, Algeria and other Maghreb countries as the 'font' of the Islamist revolution. Faced with their own GIA insurrection, the Algerians sent a military delegation to Syria to learn how the Assad regime crushed the Muslim Brotherhood revolt in Hama in 1982. When Hafez al-Assad's son Bashar was facing insurrection after 2011, the Syrians in turn asked the Algerians how they had suppressed the GIA.

And American intelligence operatives were kept up to date. Hassan Alfi, the Egyptian interior minister, welcomed the FBI's director, Louis Freeh, to Cairo in February 1997 'to exchange information and to coop-erate with the Egyptian authorities in all aspects of security'. According to Alfi, 'some crimes require more action, cooperation and exchange of information between international security services'. Freeh opened an FBI 'investigative' office in downtown Cairo which was identical to a bureau in Tel Aviv, part of an expansion, according to the US embassy, 'in US anti-terror … responsibilities'.

Egyptian state television publicised military trials, showing the pris-oners demanding an Islamic state but censoring out their claims of torture. These ritualised court appearances were mesmeric and I found myself drawn to the spartan military halls in which the conflict between secular nationalism and Islamist absolutism was played out in theatri-cal form. Looking back, I can see now how these stage performances were dress rehearsals for a far more frightening Middle Eastern conflict two decades later – when it was the Islamists themselves who would be sentencing secular nationalist army officers to death – and cutting their throats on videotape so that we could witness their 'justice'.

Pain and death were a permanent backdrop to dictatorship which, by the time I arrived in the region in 1976, had long been regarded as almost 'traditional'; state-imposed physical pain on a population was part of everyday life, an essential element of this painful theatre of the absurd which Arab men and women were expected to endure, along with fake elections, corruption and one-party – even one-family – rule.

Saddam's Iraq committed semi-genocidal crimes against its majority Shia community and the minority Kurds as well as other regime opponents; Syria's Assad clan imposed a cloak of refined torture, mass imprisonment and slaughter – all to maintain their cancerous rule. Western governments who maintained warm political, trade and military relations with these police states possessed intimate details of the instruments of repression they used. How could the UK be ignorant, for example, of Bahrain's state torture system when the country's intelligence headquarters was controlled by Colonel Ian Henderson, a former British Special Branch officer who had cut his teeth on the Mau Mau insurrection in Kenya?*

I do not use the word 'cancer' lightly. For the blanket of oppression that lay for so many years across the Middle East created an exclusive, near-fatal societal sickness from which its peoples would eventually recover in a courageous, joyful, often horribly violent and almost universally tragic awakening. But those world leaders, journalists and 'experts' who reacted to this pitifully named 'Arab Spring' with televised, real-time banalities, wilfully forgot what went before. The dungeons of the East German-built security headquarters in Damascus and the mukhabarat basements in Baghdad – and then our own adoption of mass torture in the Islamic world – produced the frightening, cult-like institutions that would turn so savagely against us and their own people before the first decade of the twenty-first century had ended.

In accepting this vile pantheon of physical torment, we sought solace from its effectiveness. In Syria, for example, Hafez al-Assad's ruthless crushing of the Muslim Brotherhood uprising in Hama in 1982 was regarded in the West more as a distressing event – necessary to maintain 'stability' in one of Israel's hostile neighbours – than an act of barbarity. In Egypt, the crushing of violent Islamism in 1997 provided sinister justification for the appalling suffering that the regime's oppo-

---

* Bahrain's senior torturer was a Jordanian army colonel who was also Henderson's official interpreter. Henderson – in charge of what was officially called the 'General Directorate of State Security Investigations' – died in 2013, the proud holder of Bahrain's Order of Sheikh Isa bin Salman bin al-Khalifa, the Order of Bahrain, and the emirate's Medal of Military Merit (1st Class). The UK must also have admired Henderson's contribution to Bahrain's 'security', since the Queen awarded him a CBE in 1984. When I wrote about Henderson, I was myself rewarded with a cartoon in the Bahraini newspaper *Akhbar Al Khaleej*, in which I was depicted as a rabid dog.

nents were forced to undergo. The gloves would never be 'coming off' in Egypt, Syria or Iraq – because the sadists who ran the torture chambers never wore gloves in the first place. And when Western military powers returned to the Middle East in 2001, the very idea that we would contemplate treating the people of the Middle East with the cumbersome legal constraints that we applied to ourselves swiftly became ridiculous.

By the time journalists understood the extent of these crimes in the Muslim world, torture had already acquired that fateful 'normality' which accompanies all such perversity. After years in Northern Ireland, I was used to hearing the excuses, conceits and lies of the British army, of the deliberate 'ill treatment' that began with the 'Five Techniques' (starvation, sleep deprivation, hooding, 'white noise' and wall-standing) and then of the inevitable brutality towards civilians and extrajudicial killings that stained the British army in the province between 1971 and 1990.

But I could never have guessed, more than three decades later, that I would be confronted in southern Iraq by the very same insouciance and arrogance from the British army that had been so familiar to me in Northern Ireland. I arrived at the UK military press office at Basra airport on a bleak Friday afternoon in January 2004. I showed the officers documents in my possession – one of them signed by a British sergeant – that an Iraqi hotel receptionist called Baha Mousa had died in British custody, and a statement from Baha Mousa's father that the British army waited three days before admitting to the family that he was dead. But the British military spokesman couldn't help – Tony Blair was about to arrive. One of the officers laughed. 'Call the Ministry of Defence,' he said dismissively. Not a word of compassion about the dead man, whose own wife had just died of cancer, nor for his small and now orphaned sons.

Over the coming years, photographs of Baha Mousa's dead face were to appear in newspapers and on television around the world. In the pictures, his eyes are closed, his eyelids puffy and swollen, blood on his broken nose, a dark purple weal running from his left forehead to his jaw, surgical tapes and a white syringe protruding from his crooked mouth. Dead men, so the cliché goes, tell no tales. But dead bodies do.

★   ★   ★

The Mousa family home was a breezeblock and concrete affair down a sad alley, with lakes of sewage fringing the road junctions. It was unusually hot for a January day and there were few people on the streets of Basra, but everyone knew where we wanted to go. We had long developed an instinct for hunting down stories in the cities of Iraq; half of our attention was on finding the address, the other half on the guys who might be hunting for us.

Lieutenant Colonel Daoud Mousa of the Iraqi police was a plump fifty-eight-year-old in a smart blue uniform. Half grieving father, half suspicious cop, he was aware that the crime he most wanted to solve was also his own tragedy. The last time he saw his son Baha Mousa alive was on 14 September 2003, as British soldiers raided the Basra hotel where the twenty-six-year-old worked as a receptionist. 'He was lying with the other seven staff on the marble floor with his hands over his head. I said to him: "The British officer says you'll be freed in a couple of hours."' The officer, a second lieutenant, even gave the Iraqi colonel a piece of paper and wrote '2Lt. Mike' on it, alongside an indecipherable signature and a Basra telephone number. But the promise was not kept. The 1st Battalion The Queen's Regiment saw to that.

'Three days later, I was looking at my son's body,' the colonel said. 'The British came to say he had "died in custody". His nose was broken and there was blood above his mouth and I could see the bruising of his ribs and thighs. The skin was ripped off his wrists where the handcuffs had been.' Baha Mousa's body was proof of what he had endured. I scribbled the father's words into my notebook; Nelofer took pictures. He talked slowly, sitting on the cement floor of his slum cabin.

No one hid the fact that the men picked up at the Haitham Hotel – where British troops had earlier found four weapons in a safe – were brutally treated while in the custody of the Royal Military Police. One of Baha's colleagues, Kifah Taha, gave a chilling account of the treatment the eight men received once they arrived at a British interrogation centre in Basra. By terrible coincidence, the building had formerly been the secret service headquarters of Ali al-Majid, known as 'Chemical Ali' for his gassing of the Kurds in northern Iraq. Our witness told a story of British brutality that could not have been far different from the events that occurred in this same grim compound under Ali al-Majid's rule:

We were put in a big room with our hands tied and with bags
over our heads. But I could see through some holes in my hood.
Soldiers would come in and they would kick us, picking on one
after the other. They set on Baha especially, and he kept crying
that he couldn't breathe in the hood ... But they laughed at him
and [...] Then they increased the kicking on him and he
collapsed on the floor. None of us could stand or sit because it
was too painful.

None of the prisoners said he was questioned about the discovery of
the weapons at the hotel. Indeed, the man who had hidden two rifles
and two pistols in the hotel safe – one of the partners in the hotel – fled
after the British arrived and was still on the run.

As so often in the Middle East, it was an investigator from Amnesty
International who had tipped us off about Baha Mousa's killing. While
we journalists followed the daily 'story' of Iraq, Amnesty amassed fold-
ers of information, persistently demanding to speak to authorities who
were more than happy to display evidence of Saddam's crimes but
unwilling to be confronted with their own. Without publicity, Amnesty
had already demanded an independent inquiry into Baha Mousa's
death and the abuse of the other prisoners, but the UK Ministry of
Defence was attempting to keep its investigation within the army.
Two soldiers arrested in connection with the young man's killing had
since been released. Baha Mousa's family were outraged. What should
they do? they asked us, seeking help from a British journalist whose
fellow citizens had committed this crime. Ask Amnesty to find a lawyer
to act for Baha Mousa, I said. Call Human Rights Watch. Go for the
Brits in the London courts. Let me write about it.

Baha Mousa's brother Alaa said, 'They gave us $3,000 in compensa-
tion, then said we could have another $5,000 – but they wouldn't
accept responsibility for his murder.* We reject this money. We want

---

* In December 2003, the Mousa family did receive a letter from a British claims officer
called Perkins that offered the further $5,000 as a 'final settlement' of the 'incident' which
would be made 'without admission of liability on behalf of the British Contingent of the
Coalition Forces in Iraq'. It took the British defence ministry another five years before they
agreed to pay almost £3 million to Baha Mousa's family and to the other Iraqis assaulted
with him. By the end of 2012, the UK had paid out £14 million to 205 Iraqis unlawfully
detained and abused during Britain's occupation and was negotiating 196 more payments.

justice.' The Mousa family had been given an international death certif-
icate by the British army at the Shaiba military medical centre outside
Basra. It was dated 21 September 2003, but again carried an indecipherable signature. It stated that Baha Mousa's death had been caused by
'cardiorespiratory arrest: asphyxia'. But the anonymous British officer
who had signed the document mysteriously failed to fill in the columns
marked 'due to/as a consequence of' and 'approximate interval
between onset (of asphyxia) and death'. More seriously still, the British
army failed to complete the form's request for 'Regt. Corps/RAF
Command' and 'Ship/Unit/RAF Station'.

Kifah Taha was still in his Basra hospital room when I went to see
him. He said that all the prisoners were given a nickname by the British
soldiers who beat them. 'They called us by the names of footballers,'
Taha said. 'I remember one – it was "Van Boston". They kept giving us
these names and kept telling us to repeat them so we would remember
who we were. Beckham was another name.' Marco van Basten, to
whom Taha was referring, was the Dutch footballer famous for destroying English footballing hopes some years before. Punching the prisoners
to make them shriek with pain, a British military court would hear
years later, was an assault that the soldiers had nicknamed 'the choir'.

It was the contention of Baha Mousa's father that his son was deliberately kicked to death by the soldiers because they had discovered that
his father had persuaded the British officer – 'Second Lieutenant Mike'
– to arrest several British soldiers who had stolen money from the
hotel during the raid. 'The officer made one of the men open his shirt
and he found the money and the soldier was disarmed. But the military
inquiry didn't want to hear about this – they weren't interested in the
theft or why the soldiers who were stealing the money would want to
mistreat my son as a result of what I did.'

Sitting in the family's home in Basra listening to this mendacious
tale, I felt nothing but shame.*

---

* British lawyers felt the same. They fought for the Mousa family in the British courts,
and Public Interest Lawyers supported the cases of many other victims of British cruelty in
Iraq. Phil Shiner, the human rights lawyer who took the Mousa case to the House of Lords
in 2007, wrote to me two years later to say – 'as I know that you are the journalist who
first exposed the Baha Mousa case' – that he was anxious that the world should know
'what is happening regarding the UK's use of torture and forbidden interrogation
techniques in Iraq'.

After an eight-year campaign for justice led by the *Independent*, a British army inquiry stated that Baha Mousa had suffered ninety-three injuries and described his killing as 'an appalling episode of serious gratuitous violence'. The 1,400-page report also said that a 'large number' of soldiers assaulted Baha Mousa. But of the seven British soldiers who were charged, six were found not guilty; the seventh, Corporal Donald Payne, was imprisoned for just a year and dismissed from the army after pleading guilty to 'inhumane treatment' of a prisoner. A 2007 court martial had showed accused soldiers 'not remembering' details more than 600 times.

By the time the public inquiry described Baha Mousa's injuries, the old nonsense about 'hearts and minds' was as dry as the sand on the desert floor. Two years after they staged their humiliating retreat from Basra in 2009, the British withdrew their last contingent from Iraq. They suffered 179 fatalities, large enough for army relatives to accuse Blair of murdering their children but infinitesimal in comparison to the Iraqi body count. We abandoned the country and it was left to the Iraqis themselves – men like Daoud Mousa, carrying the grief of his son's death with him forever – to endure the pain and sorrow to come.

Yet because I reported the tragedy of Baha Mousa at first hand, I returned again and again to the question of our capacity, wilfully, cruelly, to cause immense suffering to the innocent. Are human beings at war by definition bound to commit atrocities? The International Committee of the Red Cross and the Red Crescent Movement tried to answer this question in 2004. Were combatants unaware of international humanitarian law? Unlikely, I would think. They didn't care. For their report, the ICRC and RCM interviewed hundreds of fighters in Colombia, Bosnia, Georgia and the Congo, and suggested that those who commit reprehensible acts see themselves as victims, which then gives them the 'right' to act savagely against their opponents. Corporal Donald Payne, imprisoned for a year for 'inhumane treatment', was to tell the court martial that Baha Mousa's killers had acted out of revenge for the killing of four soldiers in mid-2003.

The Red Cross–Red Crescent document, however, also suggested that 'the moral disengagement of a fighter is the product of his or her membership of a group and within a hierarchy, where submission to authority and conformism play an essential role'. Here it is possible to understand the usefulness of this 'role'; the fighters are 'gentlemen' who, when 'the gloves are coming off', know that they are obeying their hierarchy. Such cruelty was then abetted with a bodyguard of clichés – 'police operations', 'clean up', 'surgical strikes' – while 'modern methods of warfare, whereby you can kill by remote-control, facilitate such justifications, especially when the media are not present to show the realities of a conflict'. To the physical distance, the report concluded, was added psychological distance. During the UK military inquiry into Baha Mousa's killing, a video was shown in which a clearly identified British soldier could be seen in the same room as Mousa, shouting at one detainee: 'Get up, you fucking ape.'

A glance at the childish but poisonous epithets used by Messrs Bush and Blair at their London news conference in November 2003 – in which the two men conflated 9/11, violence in Turkey, the chaos in post-invasion Iraq, Kashmir, Palestine and Chechnya – demonstrates just how potent this demonisation could be. Blair's language was laced with banalities – 'the evil these terrorists pose to innocent people', 'no holding back, no compromise, no hesitation in confronting this menace', 'fanatics of terror', 'callous, brutal murderers', 'fanaticism and extremism', 'they're prepared to kill anyone, they're prepared to shed any amount of bloodshed' – while Bush chorused the same mediocrities. The 'mission' of the West, however, was 'noble' and 'necessary' in 'the defence of freedom and the advance of democracy' – this was Blair again, who concluded that 'in virtually every place there is trouble and difficulty, these terrorists and fanatics are making it worse'.

Blair naturally could not refer to the division of Kashmir, the occupation of Palestine, nor Russian war crimes in Chechnya; for this would have necessitated a discussion of injustice or the seizing of foreign lands or martial law, the very reasons why these lands were afflicted by such bloodshed. Deprived of this context, 'terrorists' could be despised or – as the Red Cross–Red Crescent report put it – denied their 'humanity'. Thus 'terrorists' or anyone associated with them, speaking like them or looking like them became a 'terrorist' and thus doomed to suffer beating or torture or murder.

And so when Dick Cheney talked of working on the 'dark side', his expression expressed a rationale that would embrace extrajudicial killing, 'enhanced interrogation techniques' or mere racist cruelty. In this sense, Baha Mousa was as much a victim of our crimes as those al-Qaeda suspects undergoing waterboarding torture at Guantanamo. It is pertinent to note, however, that while Blair and Bush could produce all manner of infantile expressions to express their hatred of 'terror', Cheney produced a single phrase which far more disturbingly captured his own intentions. The 'dark side' is synonymous with terror, and this was intended to intimidate our enemies; the CIA's global torture centres were understandably referred to as 'black sites'. US officers in Baghdad ran an interrogation cell that they called the 'Black Room'.*

'One reason why the Americans introduced "extraordinary rendition",' said my colleague Justin Huggler is that 'the military and the CIA have rules – even if they don't obey them – but by renditioning people to other countries where they know they're going to be tortured, there's no law or military process. The purpose of rendition is to torture.'

The only law that applied to rendition – the freighting of young men to Arab and other countries for the most cruel tortures – turned out to be the acceptance by Western courts of that very information gleaned by the torturers from their victims, however contaminated it may be. In August 2004, the use of torture to obtain evidence against suspected 'terrorists' was endorsed by the British Court of Appeal, when two judges allowed the country's home secretary to hold 'terror' suspects on the basis of intelligence from prisoners who had been tortured at Guantanamo and other US camps. Lord Justice Laws was 'quite unable' to see why the British minister could not rely on evidence 'coming into his hands which has or may have been obtained through torture by agencies of other states over which he has no power of direction'. Why, he asked, should the law impose 'a duty of solemn enquiry as to the interrogation methods used by agencies of other sovereign states'?

Nor was there any solemnity about the methods of rendition. Dana Priest of the *Washington Post* won a series of press awards for her exposure of this villainous practice. Members of the US 'Rendition Group' belonging to the CIA's 'Counterterrorist Center' (CTC), she wrote:

---

* With just such a purpose did the Gestapo hope to terrorise those who resisted Nazi rule by adopting a policy they called *nacht und nebel*, 'night and fog', which invariably meant liquidation. The US did not, of course, seek to emulate the German Sicherheitsdienst, although the individual suffering endured in some of America's 'terror' prisons might have been worthy of SS depravity.

follow a simple but standard procedure: dressed head to toe in black, including masks, they blindfold and cut the clothes off their new captives, then administer an enema and sleeping drugs. They outfit detainees in a diaper and jumpsuit for what can be a day-long trip. Their destinations: either a detention facility operated by cooperative countries in the Middle East and Central Asia, including Afghanistan, or one of the CIA's own covert prisons – referred to in classified documents as 'black sites', which at various times have been operated in eight countries, including several in Eastern Europe.

The key phrase in Priest's dispatch was the reference to 'cooperative countries' in the Middle East. This did not mean 'moderate allies', for it included Syria, a supposedly 'terrorist'-supporting regime, alongside the obedient Egyptian dictatorship and other Arab autocracies. And we all knew about the abhorrent treatment of prisoners in these countries' jails. Our detailed journalistic investigation of torture and human rights abuses and executions in Egypt, our newspaper reports on these iniquities – along with our detailed examination of Syrian state torture and executions – left no doubt about the fate of anyone sent to these Middle East nations, trussed up, blindfolded, drugged and tagged 'terrorist'.

Over the coming years, Muslim men would be air-freighted across the world, often via Europe, to torture chambers in Damascus, Cairo, Rabat and Tripoli – even back in Afghanistan, at Bagram – for near-unimaginable suffering. The Americans were, in effect, asking the Muslim regimes to do the torturing for them. And if the CTC learned later that their suspect had died, how could they be blamed? If American officers could torture their victims with waterboarding, beatings with rifle butts during naked interrogation or by hurling men against walls, Arab sadists were on hand to ramp up the suffering with their plugs and electrodes on the genitals of the men whom the Americans handed over. The nightmarish stories of knives, clubs and wires made no difference to the pilots and crews who flew these prisoners to perdition, nor to the European nations that allowed these flights to refuel on their sovereign territory. They eagerly accepted Washington's assurances that US aircraft in transit were not carrying prisoners for interrogation, shrugging their shoulders when it was later revealed that the Americans had lied.

A similar casuistry was used by the UK to deport Arab aliens to their home countries when their governments were known to sanction torture. Discovering that several dictatorships were unwilling to sign declarations that deportees would not be tortured, Tony Blair condoned UK deportations on the grounds that the British were satisfied, without any promises at all, that they would not be harmed.

The history of sending Arabs back to 'justice' in their own lands goes back almost half a century. In 1972, Colonel Mohamed Amekrane of the Moroccan air force fled to Gibraltar after participating in an attempt to assassinate King Hassan. He and a fellow officer landed on the British overseas territory in an air force helicopter and sought political asylum from the UK government. The king, a close ally of Britain but himself responsible for thousands of prisoner 'disappearances', demanded Amekrane's return. British foreign secretary Alec Douglas-Home was on holiday in Scotland, but he must have known the fate awaiting Amekrane if he was sent back to Morocco.

A little judicial sleight of hand was thus enacted. For while the European Convention on Human Rights gave anyone the right to leave their country, no treaty obliged a country to give that person asylum. Amekrane could not be officially extradited, so the British decided that he and a colleague must be deported from Gibraltar as undesirable aliens to Morocco – 'because this was the place from which they came'. There were 3,000 loyal Moroccans in Gibraltar who would be angry if they stayed, a Foreign Office minister explained, and the presence of the two men would, according to a government statement, 'not have been conducive to the public good'. Douglas-Home was later said to have received assurances that Amekrane would not be put to death. So the British sent him back to Morocco – where he was executed by firing squad.

There was an instructive moment some months later when Amekrane's widow demanded compensation from the British government for its failure to give her husband a right of appeal after denying him asylum. She received £37,500 – ex gratia, of course, without guilt. It was a variation of the blood money that would be offered to Iraqis like Daoud Mousa more than thirty years later.

The word 'rendition' became part of that subtle vocabulary that officials used to hide their brutal intentions, but the expression had a

century-old pedigree. Researching the life of his grandfather Henry
Cockburn – a senior British diplomat in Korea during Japan's early
twentieth-century occupation of the peninsula – my colleague Patrick
Cockburn found that his forbear had tried to prevent a Korean journalist being handed over to Japanese military officers. Yang ki-Tak had
been tortured in a Japanese prison for his critical articles on the occupation and sought refuge in his Seoul newspaper office, a British-owned
property that the Japanese could not enter under treaty terms – unless
the UK consul agreed. Henry Cockburn wrote a memorandum in
August 1908 to the British ambassador in Tokyo entitled 'Rendition of
a Corean [sic]', the first known recorded use of the word in modern
politics. So fiercely did Cockburn fight for Yang's protection that when
he was eventually forced to hand him over, the Japanese had agreed to
keep him in hospital and give him a fair trial, after which they were
forced to release him.

In 2007, George W. Bush openly told the world that in addition to
the prisoners in Guantanamo, 'a small number of suspected terrorist
leaders and operatives captured during the war have been held and
questioned outside the United States, in a separate program operated
by the Central Intelligence Agency ... [who] used an alternative set of
procedures. These procedures were designed to be safe, to comply
with our laws, our constitution and our treaty obligations.' Again, the
linguistics revealed the cruelty. The Orwellian use of the word
'program', coupled with Cheney's reference to the 'dark side' six years
earlier, was clear enough and was only emphasised by the sinister
'alternative set of procedures'. It was as if the 'suspected terrorist leaders' were to be treated to some form of 'safe' aggressive therapy whose
rules were, of course, state-sanctioned through law, even 'compliant'
with the US constitution.

But Bush unwittingly delivered these acts of barbarism into the
public domain when he also announced that fourteen 'high-value
detainees' would be transferred to Guantanamo, where they would be
interviewed by the Red Cross. Their confidential report of these meetings was revealed in early 2009, and thus we received the first officially
recorded account of Abu Zubaydah's torture, much of it apparently
perpetrated in the CIA 'black site' in Poland used by the Nazis in the
Second World War. Zein Abu Zubaydah was a senior al-Qaeda official
originally captured in Pakistan.

He survived 'waterboarding' eighty-three times. Yemeni-Saudi Walid bin Attash, and Pakistani Khalid Sheikh Mohamed, both senior al-Qaeda men allegedly involved in the 9/11 attacks, were among dozens of prisoners to discover the meaning of Bush's 'alternative set of procedures', with Mohamed being 'waterboarded' 183 times. Their interviews, recorded in isolation, were in many ways identical – thus adding to the authenticity of their accounts, the sheer repetition only emphasising the banality of their treatment.

If this was what detainees suffered under the Americans, however, they could expect far worse when they were outsourced to America's Arab allies. Take the case of Mohamed al-Zery and Ahmed Agiza, who were renditioned on a CIA aircraft from Sweden to Egypt in 2001. The Swedish government had obtained assurances that the two would not be tortured, a promise that was broken. According to al-Zery's Swedish asylum lawyer, Kjell Jonsson, 'he was kept in a very cold, very small cell and he was beaten; the most painful torture was … where electrodes were put to all sensitive parts of his body many times, under surveillance by a medical doctor'. Agiza's mother would describe how her son was interrogated in an underground prison. 'As soon as he was asked a question and he replied, "I don't know", they would apply electric shocks to his body and beat him … During the first month of interrogation, he was naked and not given any clothes. He almost froze to death.'*

In his investigation of these cases, the journalist Stephen Grey spoke to Michael Scheuer, who in the late 1990s headed the CIA unit ordered to find Bin Laden. While admitting that 'mistakes' were sometimes made, Scheuer believed it a 'worthwhile' activity to get anyone 'off the street' who might be trying to kill Americans, even if torture might be used in the countries to which prisoners were sent.

---

* The legal infection of evidence-through-torture only grew worse. Three years after the UK Court of Appeal had ruled such testimony admissible if it was gained through torture perpetrated by foreign governments, the European parliament condemned the legal opinion of UK Foreign Office adviser Michael Wood, 'according to which "receiving or possessing" information extracted under torture, is not … prohibited' by the UN Convention against Torture. The EU parliament also noted that 170 stopovers were made by CIA-operated aircraft at UK airports and 147 at Irish airports, and that 1,245 flights operated by the CIA flew into European airspace or landed at European airports in the four years ending December 2005, although not all these aircraft were carrying 'renditioned' prisoners.

But as lawyers and journalists continued to investigate 'rendition', its Arab connections became clearer. In 2002, for instance, it turned out that thirteen Egyptians had been seized by the CIA in the Balkans in 1998, of whom five were alleged to be planning to blow up the US embassy in Tirana. The five were seized with the help of Albanian police and flown to Cairo on a CIA-chartered jet, with two of them executed after their arrival. The Egyptians may have thought they were owed a favour – since 1993, Cairo had reportedly assisted in transferring detainees from Nigeria, the Philippines, Kenya and South Africa to the United States.

The policy of threatening and blackmailing client nations who dared to expose US torture continued under Obama's presidency. In 2009, it emerged in a British court that Washington had threatened to withdraw cooperation in 'terrorist' cases if a UK court ordered the disclosure of secret torture evidence. Secret CIA documents held by the British Foreign Office, it emerged, included details of the interrogation of Binyam Mohamed, the British resident who was flown to Morocco by CIA agents before being sent to Afghanistan and held for four years at Guantanamo. Mohamed alleged that British agents knew he was being ill-treated in US custody. UK judges were shocked by the American threat, adding:

> we did not consider that a democracy governed by the rule of
> law would expect a court in another democracy to suppress a
> summary of the evidence contained in reports by its own
> officials ... relevant to allegations of torture and cruel,
> inhumane, or degrading treatment, politically embarrassing
> though it might be ... We had no reason ... to anticipate there
> would be made a threat of the gravity of the kind made by the
> United States government that it would reconsider its
> intelligence-sharing relationship, when all the considerations in
> relation to open justice pointed to us providing a limited but
> important summary of results.

But had not the UK Court of Appeal, only five years earlier, ruled that evidence acquired under torture in other countries could be used in British courts – providing Britain had been in no position to prevent such cruelty? Why should Washington expect its UK ally to demand details of

American torture when Britain was content to share the benefits of information provided by those same torture sessions? The British foreign secretary David Miliband had earlier insisted the interrogation details be kept secret – until the UK High Court ruled that he had not properly considered the 'medieval' tortures alleged by Binyam Mohamed. Miliband would later suffer a humiliating rebuff when court papers revealed the extent of Mohamed's suffering – and when it became known that the British security services knew all along that he had been shackled, threatened and deprived of sleep for long periods by the CIA.

As more detainees were able to tell their story, the evidence only grew worse. Scotland Yard were soon investigating claims that an MI5 intelligence officer had been present when CIA interrogators had brutalised British resident Shaker Aamer in the Bagram prison in Afghanistan, his head repeatedly 'banged so hard against a wall that it bounced'.*

For decades, Syria's intelligence services had competed in terrorising a largely Sunni Muslim population. Their favoured torture implements included a chair, originally designed by the East German regime, to slowly break the backs of suspects held in the mukhabarat headquarters in central Damascus. Human rights groups had for many years sent out appeals for prisoners facing execution or life imprisonment, to no effect. Amnesty International reported in 1995 that after it had submitted the names of 1,000 victims of human rights violations to the Syrian authorities, not a single response had been received.

After 500 Islamist prisoners were massacred at Tadmor military prison in 1980, rights groups took a special interest in the bleak, grey concrete complex close to the Roman ruins of Palmyra. In 1996, Human Rights Watch recorded the account of a former prisoner who had witnessed executions:

---

* Aamer was to testify that two MI5 or MI6 officers, a man and a woman, personally interrogated him in a prison in Kandahar in 2002 after he had been subjected to beatings and sleep deprivation by the Americans. The British woman was called 'Sally'. During his beating in Bagram, Aamer said the UK agent introduced himself as 'John'. The same – or another – 'John' advised Binyam Mohamed before his transfer to Morocco and the obscene torture he endured there, that 'he had an opportunity to help us and help himself. The US authorities will be deciding what to do with him and this will depend to a very large degree on his degree of cooperation.' Britain's involvement in torture – albeit at one fist removed – was by 2010 estimated to have cost the country more than £30 million in compensation.

They used incredible methods to kill people. Courtyard Four had a raised basin ... They were hit with the sharp edge of an axe, and then cut up into pieces. Prisoners were also roped and dragged until they died. This would be done randomly, to those who were found innocent by the court as well as those who were sentenced to death.

In the surreal atmosphere of a hotel in Boston, Massachusetts, I listened to a former Tadmor prisoner, now a US citizen, recalling how inmates knew that a firing squad was about to execute a prisoner when they smelled a particular aftershave wafting from the courtyard. It belonged to Brigadier General Ghazi Kanaan, the former Syrian intelligence commander in Lebanon, who only visited Tadmor to witness executions.

No one could claim ignorance of the barbaric nature of the Syrian regime's prisons. The US State Department would regularly excoriate Syria's human rights record. But after George W. Bush declared his 'war on terror', Washington adopted an attitude of near-complacency towards Syria's annihilation of its Islamist enemies and their torture and execution. And anxious to demonstrate his 'anti-terrorist' credentials, President Bashar al-Assad allowed his intelligence services to cooperate with the CIA and even permitted the US to send 'terror suspects' to Damascus for local interrogation. The United States knew exactly what would happen to anyone it 'rendered' unto Bashar.*

In November 2003, Amnesty International produced two urgent reports on prisoners in Syria whom it feared were destined for 'torture and ill treatment'. One was for Hasan Mustafa, a thirty-two-year-old Kurdish silversmith from Ain al-Arab [Kobani] in northern Syria, arrested two months after his brother Khalil had been reportedly tortured to death in detention on 10 August. His family found 'severe injuries and bruises visible on his corpse, including a leg broken in two places, a missing eye and a head wound', according to Amnesty. Scores of Syrian Kurds had been detained over the years for the peaceful expression of grievances – including the regime's refusal to grant them

---

* To add the ironic touch necessary for any drama of Middle East brutality, this same state repression of which Washington now wished to take advantage, was to be one of the reasons advanced by the Americans – just eight years later and months after the start of the Arab revolutions – for the overthrow of the Assad regime.

full citizenship. Twelve years later, Ain al-Arab would acquire a new
and bloody reputation when it was contested between Kurdish militias
supported by US air strikes and hundreds of armed men from the
'Islamic Caliphate'.

The other Syrian life appealed by Amnesty in November 2003 was
that of Abdullah Almalki, a Canadian citizen. He was arrested when he
arrived at Damascus airport in May 2002, detained at the Sednaya
prison and initially denied access to diplomats from the Canadian
consulate. Almalki, Amnesty said, had been 'subjected to a form of
torture known as the dullab, which involves hanging the victim from a
suspended tyre and beating him ... with sticks and cables. He has
apparently also been given electric shocks and has been beaten around
his body with cables as well as kicked in the head.'

Thirty-one-year-old Almalki was born in Syria but became a Canadian
citizen in 1991, working in Afghan refugee camps and for a UN reconstruction agency before returning to start an electronics company in
Ottawa. The Canadian Security Intelligence Service (CSIS) took an
interest in him partly because of his friendship with Maher Arar, another
software engineer. He had travelled to Damascus to see his sick grandmother, but once he was put under torture, it quickly became apparent
that his arrest was based on information sent to the Syrians by Canada.
The Canadian authorities had shared intelligence information with the
Syrian mukhabarat, supplying his torturers with questions about his
supposed – though non-existent – association with al-Qaeda.

Almalki was released after twenty-two months of mistreatment,
although when I met him in Canada five years later, he was still a nervous, frightened man. He told me about the four CSIS interrogations
that preceded his departure from Canada in 2002. CSIS wanted to
know if he was sending funds or electronic components to 'terrorists'.
For months, he said, he had been held in the Damascus 'Palestine'
prison in a 'tiny hole' and whipped with steel, while the Syrians acted
upon a letter to them that stated that the Royal Canadian Mounted
Police believed him to be linked to al-Qaeda and engaged in activities
that posed an 'imminent threat' to Canada. The RCMP sent similarly
outrageous letters to Canadian government liaison officers in
Islamabad, Rome, Delhi, Washington, London, Berlin and Paris.

Those who find this tale incredible may peruse the official Canadian
inquiry by former Supreme Court justice Frank Iacobucci into the

imprisonment and torture of Almalki and other Canadian citizens in Syria and Egypt. Almalki also benefited from the investigations of the Canadian journalist Kerry Pither. The Syrians were to complain bitterly when they learned that Washington had recommenced its campaign against human rights abuses in Syria. First the West allowed its citizens to be tortured in Damascus, the Syrians said – and then it condemned the regime for doing to its prisoners exactly what it had done to Westerners when their governments had sent questions to their state torturers.

But why could those complicit in Almalki's torture not be held accountable for their involvement? They were at least accomplices, even if the Iacobucci report claimed they had not sought the men's imprisonment or torture. The RCMP were not the Syrian mukhabarat – but they acted together. Almalki drove me to Ottawa airport in the snow after our breakfast in 2009, admitting that he was still too mentally broken by his months of Syrian torture to find employment. CSIS didn't follow him anymore, but no one would say he was innocent. And how could they when the RCMP liaison officer had written a damning and highly incriminating letter in January 2003 to General Hassan Khalil of Syrian military intelligence in the following terms:

> Depending on his [Almalki's] willingness to answer truthfully and depending on the answers he provides to you, a second series of questions has been prepared for him ... I would like to propose that during my next visit to Damascus ... I meet with personnel in your agency in order to further discuss this matter ... Also be aware that we are in possession of large volumes of highly sensitive documents and information, seized during investigative efforts or obtained from confidential informants associated to terrorist cells operating in Canada. Our Service is readily willing to share this information with your Service.*

---

* The 'quality' and 'accuracy' of Almalki's answers – his 'willingness to answer truthfully' – depended, of course, on the skill of the victim's torturers in coaxing from him the answers the RCMP wished to peruse. The Iacobucci report makes it clear that the RCMP were well aware of the possibility that their citizen was being brutally interrogated. That a senior Canadian police officer would go on to outline for Syria's intelligence regime the internal composition of its own security services, let alone offer 'large volumes of highly sensitive documents' seems almost beyond belief. Which is how the Syrians must have regarded the offer, though they were no doubt obliged.

Even when he was eventually freed from his Syrian prison, Canadian officials in Damascus would not allow Almalki to stay in the consulate. One of them, he said, later told him that Canada regularly gave passports to the families of leading Syrian officials.

Almalki's friend Maher Arar had an even more disgraceful experience; US agents seized him at Kennedy Airport on his way home to Canada from a holiday in Tunisia and then 'renditioned' him directly to Syria, even though he was travelling on his Canadian passport. Despite Maher's ten-month torment – he suffered the usual Syrian beatings and whippings with electric cable and was imprisoned in a tiny, rat-infested cell – the US never apologised for its crime, nor made any reparations to a man against whom no charges were ever laid. Even the Syrians, who routinely tortured false confessions from Arar, were forced into the hitherto unheard of admission that their victim was 'totally innocent'.

This time, the RCMP were revealed to have told the US authorities that Arar was an al-Qaeda suspect, thus prompting the Americans to send him to Syria. His plane travelled via Portland, Maine and Rome before landing in Amman, where the Jordanians obligingly drove the trussed-up Arar to Damascus. Not only were the RCMP again accomplices to a serious crime committed against a Canadian citizen; so fearful were they that their intelligence arrangements with Syria's intelligence thugs would be revealed that they raided the home and office of Juliet O'Neill, the *Ottawa Star* reporter who had obtained secret documents about this connivance.*

Arar's horrific story created a scandal in Canada when Iacobucci's official investigation, set up to examine the conduct of Canadian officials, cleared him of any links to terrorism. The Canadian government settled out of court with him for $10.5 million and the country's prime minister Stephen Harper personally apologised to him for his 'terrible ordeal'. It would be comforting to record that Washington also admit-

* O'Neill was arrested under one of those bits of legislation that so many parliaments passed in panic after 11 September 2001, this time Section 4 of the Canadian Security of Information Act. 'I cannot remember a blacker day for freedom of the press in this country,' O'Neill's editor, Scott Anderson, said. 'This sort of star-chamber, police-state attitude that has crept into government and law enforcement post 9/11 is jeopardising some of the basic rights we take for granted.' The *Toronto Star* remarked that it was starting to look 'as if the RCMP is out of control'.

ted its guilt. Far from it. While individual congressmen expressed their personal sense of shame, Arar remained on the US 'terrorist watch list', a decision that US Homeland Security Secretary Michael Chertoff said was 'supported by information developed by US law enforcement agencies'.

Alas, the evidence of the outrageous behaviour of Canada's intelligence services continued to accumulate. Yet it seemed that the Canadian intelligence service had still not understood the moral implications of its agents' actions. Years after Arar, and Almalki had been freed, Geoffrey O'Brian, the CSIS adviser on operations and legislation, blandly told a stunned Canadian parliamentary public safety committee that CSIS still used information that may have been obtained through torture. There were situations – 'unusual' and 'once-in-a-life-time' – where information acquired through torture 'can be of value to the national security of the country'. The 'simple truth', O'Brian said 'is, if we get information which can prevent something like the Air India bombing, the Twin Towers – whatever, frankly – this is the time when we will use it despite the provenance of that information.'

The truth, however, was that no such 'unusual' or 'once-in-a-life-time' situations have ever occurred. In fact, a year before the 1985 Air India bombing by Sikh militants that killed 329 passengers off the Irish coast, CSIS agents received two warnings of the bombing – not through torture but from willing informers – but dismissed both as 'unreliable'. US intelligence had multiple warnings of aircraft attacks in 2001, and ignored them all.*

Canada's conservative press claimed that the authorities would be right to make use of any information obtained through torture if it seemed credible and involved a terrorist act against Canada, but this missed the point. Evidence from torture victims was inherently unreliable because most victims, like Arar, agreed to any fabricated confession in order to end their suffering. The real problem was that in

---

* The inquiries and parliamentary evidence piling up in Ottawa contained many revelations that were largely forgotten in the drama of the torture stories. O'Brian told the parliamentary committee, for example, that CSIS shared information with agencies in 147 countries and the 'vast majority of those countries have human rights records that are not as glowing as ours'. Iacobucci discovered the name of one of the principal Syrian torturers with whom O'Brian's men liaised: George Salloum. The Syrian mukhabarat, it seems, used a Christian agent to torture its largely Muslim clientele.

accepting evidence acquired through such criminal action, CSIS morally contaminated themselves. By accepting information derived from torture in Arab dictatorships, the West had, in effect, given credence to the racist belief that Arabs or Muslims were somehow inured to suffering – even when the victims inconveniently turned out to be citizens of Western nations. The moment we supped from the torturers' trough, 'we' became 'them'.

Bob Herbert, an old op-ed stalwart of the *New York Times*, caught the greater hypocrisy in all this in a piece of journalism that should have earned him a Pulitzer. The United States had long purported to be outraged over Syria's bad behaviour, he wrote:

> From the US perspective, Syria is led by a gangster regime that has, among other things, sponsored terrorism, aided the insurgency in Iraq and engaged in torture. So here's the question: If Syria is such a bad actor – and it is – why would the Bush administration seize a Canadian citizen at Kennedy airport in New York, put him on an executive jet, fly him in shackles to the Middle East, and then hand him over to the Syrians, who promptly tortured him?

Bush's administration, Herbert wrote, was trying to 'have it both ways' in its 'war on terror':

> It claims to be fighting for freedom, democracy and the rule of law, and it condemns barbaric behavior whenever it is committed by someone else. At the same time, it is engaged in its own barbaric behavior, while going out of its way to keep that behavior concealed from the American public and the world at large.

New York Times columnist Nicholas Kristof, like Herbert, understood the nature of America's national disgrace – more than one hundred inmates had died in US prisons, he wrote. Yet there were heroes, Kristoff insisted, and:

among those I admire most are the military lawyers who risked
their careers, defied the Pentagon and antagonized their
drinking buddies – all for the sake of Muslim terror suspects
where the evidence was often ambiguous. At a time when we as
a nation took the expedient path, these military officers took the
honorable one, and they deserve medals for their courage.

Of course, they received none. And despite all the evidence of cruelty,
sadism and murder in America's torture prisons, the debate continued
long after the world learned of its widespread use. Five years after
'waterboarding' had become routine, Michael Mukasey, George W.
Bush's nominee for attorney general, said that while he found it 'repug-
nant', he could not describe it as 'illegal'. He would not want his words,
he said, to threaten 'professional interrogators in the field, who must
perform their duty under the most stressful conditions'.

It is true that some of those who abused their prisoners were
haunted by the experience. Eric Fair, a 'contract' interrogator in early
2004, attached to the 82nd Airborne Division, wrote of how prisoners
were punched and kicked, and of his nightmares three years after he
had stripped a prisoner and forced him to stand sleepless in his cell.
Despite his best efforts, Fair wrote:

> I cannot ignore the mistakes I made at the interrogation facility
> in Fallujah. I failed to disobey a meritless order, I failed to
> protect a prisoner in my custody and I failed to uphold the
> standards of human decency. Instead, I intimidated, degraded
> and humiliated a man who could not defend himself. I
> compromised my values. I will never forgive myself.

Mukasey's concern for America's own torturers was one thing,
however; actively helping the criminals of other regimes another.
Tony Blair's blessing upon the unstable Muammar Gaddafi in March
2004 allowed Libya's intelligence services, hitherto regarded as a security threat to all Western nations, to move among the agents of Europe
and the United States. Libyan intelligence officers, for example, were
allowed to visit Guantanamo to interrogate Omar Deghayes, a Libyan
citizen who was also a British resident. Deghayes had been arrested in
Lahore by Pakistani security agents in 2002 and handed over to the

Americans who classed him an 'enemy combatant', although his lawyers later said they could prove his was a case of mistaken identity.* Deghayes was released from detention in 2007, an innocent man.

The depth of Blair's outrageous relationship with Gaddafi was only revealed after the Libyan leader had been killed in the 2011 revolution. As so often, it was a human rights group rather than a journalist who played the key role in exposing the immoral role that UK intelligence had played in 'renditioning' Gaddafi's opponents to Libya for torture. A Human Rights Watch investigator identified the mukhabarat office in Tripoli, where he found a trove of correspondence that proved MI6 had tricked a leading member of the 'Libyan Islamic Fighting Group', Abu Munthir al-Saadi, to travel to Hong Kong to meet diplomats in order to arrange a visit to the UK. He was arrested on arrival. Blair was by then en route to Libya to meet a leader whose arrogance, fantasies and ambitions had much in common with Benito Mussolini.

No sooner had Blair and Gaddafi declared their determination to make 'common cause' in 'counterterrorism' – followed by the announcement of a £110 million gas exploration project between Libya and Anglo-Dutch Shell – than al-Saadi and his family were put aboard an aircraft in Hong Kong and flown to Tripoli, where they were thrown into jail. Al-Saadi was to endure six years in prison, beaten, tortured with electrodes and threatened with execution.

Amid such abuse of legality as well as torture of the 'law's' victims, it is important to remember that Guantanamo did contain some of al-Qaeda's senior figures; it was the illegality of their detention – and then of their torture – that turned America's prisoners into innocents. Some freed Guantanamo detainees returned to al-Qaeda in the Middle East. Abu al-Hareth Mohamed al-Oufi, freed in 2007, underwent a Saudi government 'rehabilitation' programme, only to emerge as an al-Qaeda field commander in Yemen and denounce the programme. Then he surrendered and asked to attend the Saudi course all over again.

---

* Evidence of Deghayes' militant behaviour relied on a videotape of an armed fighter who resembled him in Chechnya. But his attorney said that the man on the tape was probably not Deghayes – and had anyway already been killed. Thomas White, the former US Army Secretary, was to admit in 2008 that one third of the Guantanamo inmates did not belong there.

Torture and 'rendition' was a gamble by the Bush administration – to be played in the dark, of course – that would leave its practitioners open to legal accusations of war crimes while leaving its creators untouched. Hence the torturers and their assistants desperately tried to hide the evidence. This became obvious when in November 2005 the CIA destroyed ninety-two videotapes depicting the brutal interrogation and torture – in most cases, 'waterboarding' – of prisoners, especially Abu Zubaydah and Abd al-Rahim al-Nashiri. A woman who would later become the CIA station chief in London was ordered to destroy the tapes by Jose A. Rodriguez Jr, the then head of the CIA's clandestine branch. Four years later, an eighteen-month investigation revealed that the tapes had been held in Thailand where the torture had taken place, thus adding another south-east Asian nation to the list of CIA 'black sites'.

Nothing could have more painfully symbolised the moral depths to which the American nation had been taken than the revelations in 2011 that US doctors at Guantanamo had deliberately concealed or ignored evidence that their patients were being tortured. Dr Vincent Iacopino and Stephen Xenakis examined the medical records and interrogations of nine prisoners in a report for *PLoS Medicine* and concluded that 'medical doctors and mental health personnel assigned to the US Department of Defense neglected and/or concealed medical evidence of intentional harm'. The doctors 'had an ethical duty not to do any harm', Iacopino told journalists. 'They could have and should have had the courage to document the abuse, but unfortunately that wasn't done.'

Instead, medical personnel took notes as detainees were body-slammed into doors – intervening only when this brutality might prevent the next round of interrogations. 'Longest time with the cloth over his face so far has been seventeen seconds,' one medical professional noted clinically. 'This is sure to increase shortly. NO useful information so far.'

When those who have pledged to alleviate suffering help to perpetuate it, we enter an especially dark planet. The medical staff at Guantanamo were not seeking scientific or medical knowledge by their complicity. Presumably – and there is no other conclusion – they had ideologically abandoned the Hippocratic Oath to patients, in which a doctor promises that he 'will take care that they suffer no hurt or damage'.

Yet still there were those – politicians, commentators, journalists – who gave their support to torture. Always, it was the 'ticking bomb scenario' that they used for justification. The most obtuse of these writers, Bruce Anderson, wrote an opinion article in the *Independent* as late as 2010 that was a terrifying exhortation to human atrocity, delivered on the premise that a nuclear bomb might be about to explode in the centre of London.

Just over two years later, however, a Democrat Senate Intelligence Committee report on CIA torture dispelled all doubts about the 'ticking bomb'. It never existed. The 528-page document was as blunt as it was gruesome, demonstrating that the CIA's 'enhanced interrogation techniques' were largely ineffective and may have provided false leads and bogus intelligence.* Abu Zubaydah, it transpired, was assaulted almost non-stop for seventeen days in August 2002, slammed against walls, stuffed in a coffin-shaped box and waterboarded until he coughed, vomited.

At least five CIA detainees had food forced into their rectums in a procedure that had no medical value. The horror, as one newspaper observed, was in the detail. US resident Majid Khan, for example, who spent time in the CIA's infamous Salt Pit 'black site' in Afghanistan, was tied face down with his head higher than his feet and then, to quote from the agency cable, a 'lunch tray, consisting of hummus, pasta with sauce, nuts and raisins was pureed and rectally infused'.† Doctors performed this obscene task. CIA bosses did not want to hear questions about 'legality' from their torturers in Thailand. 'Such

---

* At one point, it appeared the CIA did not have an accurate figure for prisoners interrogated at 'black' sites, a CIA director telling the Senate committee in 2007 that ninety-seven detainees were being held when in fact the number was 119, thirty-nine of whom had been tortured. The turnover of US prisoners throughout the world in four years – detained or, in some cases, tortured – had by the end of 2005 reached more than 83,000, of whom 14,500 remained in custody, largely in Iraq.

† In 2002, at a dungeon known as COBALT (another code for the 'Salt Pit' in which Majid Khan was tortured), suspected militant and father of four Gul Rahman was subjected to sleep deprivation, 'auditory overload', total darkness, a cold shower and 'rough treatment'. Naked from the waist down, he was chained to the concrete floor and apparently froze to death. Shortly after this incident, the COBALT manager was recommended a bonus of $2,500 for 'consistently superior work'. A company that sent psychiatrists to help run the torture system received $81 million from the US government when its contract ended in 2009.

language is not helpful,' Jose Rodriguez – the CIA counter-terrorism boss who ordered the videotapes of torture destroyed for fear of leaks – cautioned his subordinates. Another twenty-one-hour section of recordings of Abu Zubaydah's 'waterboarding' had gone missing years earlier.*

The report originally ran to around 6,000 pages, but the CIA and its Republican supporters, with the honourable exception of Vietnam veteran John McCain, scorned the revelations. The interrogations had yielded vital information, they insisted, even though the report specifically proved that such claims had been fabricated. Dick Cheney called the document 'full of crap'. 'What happened here,' Cheney told Fox News, 'was that we asked the agency to go take steps and put in place programs that were designed to catch the bastards who killed 3,000 of us on 9/11 and make sure that it never happened again, and that's exactly what they did.'

Barack Obama's response was conciliatory but oddly unemotional. Such torture and 'brutal activity' violated 'who we are as a people,' he said. 'Terrible mistakes' were made. Anyone who repeated them under his watch would be acting illegally. But why did the president use the word 'mistakes' when the CIA torture was a standing policy of the CIA and those in charge of it? At least seven years earlier, the US military had adopted similarly anodyne descriptions of their misbehaviour and of its results. When prisoners tried to commit suicide, they were guilty of 'manipulative self-injurious behaviour'; if they succeeded, they had committed an 'asymmetrical act of war'. Force-feeding at Guantanamo was 'intensified assisted feeding'. A doctor at the prison wrote of a 'feeding process'. When he left Guantanamo, the same doctor was awarded a Legion of Merit medal for his 'inspiring leadership and exemplary performance', which 'significantly improved the quality of healthcare for residents of Guantanamo Bay'.

There were times, indeed, when torture seemed to be more about linguistics than pain. How, for instance, did torture turn into 'enhanced

---

* The tapes would presumably have shown what the Senate committee discovered from the CIA: that Abu Zubaydah was so broken by torture that his interrogator had merely to raise his eyebrows for the prisoner to walk to the 'water table'. Two snaps of the CIA man's fingers, and Zubaydah would obediently lie down and wait to be 'waterboarded', at times so distressed 'that he was unable effectively to communicate' – a state in which he was presumably not able to reveal much information.

interrogation techniques'? 'Enhanced' suggests something better, more learned, even less costly. 'Interrogators' have special skills; which implies training, application, learned work perhaps. And that is, in a manner of speaking, what torture is all about. It's not the way I would describe the process of slamming people into walls, half drowning them and ramming hummus up their rectums. But to avoid such graphic descriptions, the American media happily resorted to using those words 'enhanced interrogation techniques' by their acronym. Suffering was transmogrified into 'EIT'.

And all this, let us remember, is part of a 'program', something carefully planned, a performance. Strap the victim down, cloth over his face, pour on the water and then another bout of wall-slamming. And we only know the half of it; 5,000 or more pages were censored from the Senate report.

The CIA's director John Brennan, perhaps feeling the heat of human rights lawyers breathing down his neck, did admit that some of the 'techniques' were unauthorised and 'abhorrent'. As Cheney said, torture 'was something that we very carefully avoided', the words 'very carefully' producing a shudder. Brennan announced that 'we fell short when it came to holding some officers accountable', but it was perfectly clear that the officers were not going to be held accountable. Nor was John Brennan. Nor was Dick Cheney. And nor were the Arab regimes to whom the CIA 'rendered' those victims deemed worthy of even viler treatment than could be meted out in America's own secret prisons. Of the fifty-four countries involved in the CIA's 'program' of 'rendition' twelve can be identified as Algeria, Egypt, Iran, Iraq, Jordan, Morocco, Saudi Arabia, Syria, Turkey, the United Arab Emirates, Yemen and Libya.

There would be no accountability for Arab torturers any more than there would be for the American 'renditioners'. There would, on the contrary, be a new and closer intelligence alliance between the two sides that continued long after the US had expressed its mea culpas for torture. American and Egyptian security services re-engaged following Field Marshal al-Sisi's coup against the elected Muslim Brotherhood president in 2013. Three years after the US and EU had expressed their determination to dethrone Bashar al-Assad in Syria in 2011 for his brutality towards his people, the West's local security operatives were re-taking the road to Damascus to refurbish their old relationships with the Syrian regime's practitioners of 'enhanced interrogation techniques'. The men they met, long hardened by their ruthlessness in defending the Baathist state, were now fighting America's own ISIS enemies.

Without implying sympathy for any of the sadists who inflicted such pain on their fellow human beings, it is necessary to ask what effect their own experiences have had upon them. If we could later claim that European-born Muslims had been 'radicalised' to join violent Islamist groups by preachers, the internet or the injustices inflicted upon Muslims by their countries of adoption, what about those who were 'radicalised' by the duty or desire to inflict suffering in the torture chambers of the state? Some of them, like their Arab allies-in-torture, were obviously psychopaths who basked in the knowledge that they performed their wicked deeds with official permission. If the release of the Senate report on CIA torture was 'ideologically motivated' – the Republican response to the work of the all-Democrat committee – what was the motivation of those who tortured their victims? Were they 'ideologically motivated' too? Or had some darker spirit been let loose?

This question is not new, and its answer involves our own moral response to the dirty business of war. Is crime a natural part of the 'art of war' – and thus torture and war are one and the same? Henry Cockburn, his grandson tells us, 'thought the torture chamber might be an essential foundation of military occupation and not one of its excesses'. We might say that conflict itself is a form of torture.

In this sense, the Al Jazeera journalist Sami al-Haj, the hotel receptionist Baha Mousa and Canadian software engineer Maher Arar are all victims of war. So were the prisoners of the Mubarak regime and of the United States in Iraq and Afghanistan. If the Egyptian dictatorship was not at war with another nation, it regarded itself as at war with the state's enemies – or the enemies of Mubarak – just as Hafez al-Assad did in the 1980s and as his son did after 2011. We may choose which war is 'just' or 'unjust', but once war ceases to be 'evil' in itself, the crimes of war become part of the phenomenon of war. The US Marines are not the SS, but once Hitler's legions become the moral compass of our actions, we have lost the 'justice' behind our war, whatever its motives.

And when nations themselves, and their institutions, are complicit in crimes of war, we are all guilty of torture. However much we may deny it, this means that we wish to inflict suffering on our fellow humans, even if our victims turn out to be innocent. Only personal responsibility can relieve us of this burden. In an age when military crimes are committed less 'under orders' and more through encouragement, secret understandings, coded words and viciously skewed semantics, there is no chance of our saying 'not guilty' – unless, of course, that personal responsibility extends to our leaders. It is a cliché to ask why a British soldier or an American marine or a CIA torturer should be arraigned for war crimes, if their commanders-in-chief or their dictators do not suffer the same fate. I have long wearied of the demands for Bush and Blair to stand before an international court for their illegal wars – there is no point in demanding something that will never happen. But for our own sakes, we should still demand that our leaders stand before a court.

The Nuremberg Tribunal still holds out a challenge to us today. The words of the court's chief American prosecutor, Robert H. Jackson, are as relevant now as when they were first written down amid the ruins of Europe:

> War is essentially an evil thing; its consequences are not
> confined to the belligerent states alone, but affect the whole
> world. To initiate a war of aggression … is the supreme
> international crime, differing only from other war crimes in that
> it contains within itself the accumulated evil of the whole …
> Crimes against international law are committed by men, not by
> abstract entities, and only by punishing individuals who commit
> such crimes can the provisions of international law be enforced.

7

The Dog in the Manger

The plain of Galilee was a veritable garden. Here flourished, in the greatest abundance, the vine and the fig; while the low hills were covered with olive groves, and the corn waved thickly on the rich, fat land ... None could then have dreamed of the dangers that were then to come, or believed that this rich cultivation and teeming populations would disappear.

Jewish Palestine in AD 70, according to G. A. Henty's
For the Temple: A Tale of the Fall of Jerusalem

Two years before the young and fiercely Zionist Mark Sykes died, he gave his total support to one of the supreme refugee documents of history. It is, of course, that mendacious, deceitful, hypocritical Declaration of Arthur Balfour, the British foreign secretary. The date is 2 November 1917. His Majesty's Government, the declaration states:

view with favour the establishment in Palestine of a national home for the Jewish people, and will use their best endeavours to facilitate the achievement of this object, it being clearly understood that nothing shall be done which may prejudice the civil and religious rights of existing non-Jewish communities in Palestine.

This critical paragraph has been dissected, misquoted, cursed and adored for more than a century, but it is perfectly clear to even the most careless reader what mischief it portends. Note how the British plan is to facilitate for the Jewish people the 'achievement of a national home'; whereas the government only gently insists that nothing should be done to 'prejudice the civil and religious rights' of 'existing' non-Jews. These non-Jews are undefined and thus cannot be awarded a 'national home'. And if their 'civil and religious rights' must not be 'prejudiced', there is no mention of their political rights. Besides, they are merely 'communities', tribes. And tribes emigrate, do they not?

These 'non-Jewish communities' are the Muslim and Christian Arabs of Palestine. And – while you would never guess as much from the declaration – they constitute the vast majority of the population of Palestine. Yet these 'non-Jewish communities' are apparently not entitled to a 'home' whose 'establishment' can be 'viewed with favour' by the British. For this document is a one-sentence handbook for dispossession, for flight and terror and refugees.*

It left not the slightest doubt whom the British government favoured. Balfour had addressed his note to Lord Rothschild, among the most prominent Zionists and Jewish citizens of Britain, and the foreign secretary's four-line introduction to the hand-delivered note stated that it was 'a declaration of sympathy with Jewish Zionist aspirations'.† Should anyone question this, we should note that only two years later, Balfour himself would write in an oft-quoted memorandum to his successor that 'Zionism ... is ... of far profounder import than the desires and prejudices of the 700,000 Arabs who now inhabit

---

* The last words of the Balfour Declaration expressed the British government's 'understanding' that it should not prejudice 'the civil and political status enjoyed by Jews in any other country'. This near-addendum reflected the concern of Edwin Montagu, the Jewish Liberal but anti-Zionist cabinet minister who feared that Jews might no longer be regarded as citizens of their countries of birth if they had now been given a 'national home' in a Palestine ghetto. The declaration itself ran to exactly sixty-eight words, the most profoundly brief and dangerous promise of British imperial history.

† Readers anxious to discover the full context of this torment must study the memoirs and papers of Balfour himself, of David Lloyd George, Lord Curzon, Chaim Weizmann, Theodor Herzl and the writings of both Jewish and Arab historians. The terrible story of Europe's anti-Semitism and its pogroms against the Jews are an essential part of this narrative.

that ancient land.' Observe the cynicism. The 'non-Jewish communities' are at last identified as 'Arabs', although their majority status cannot be mentioned. Their 'desires' are unexplained, although certainly of less profound 'import' than Zionism – which has now replaced the 'Jewish people' of the original declaration. The Arabs still have no 'national home'. They merely 'inhabit' the 'ancient land'. And those who simply 'inhabit' land can always be persuaded or driven to 'exist' somewhere else. And so it was to be.

A Briton in the Middle East would hear the word 'Balfour' used almost every day, spat out with fury and anger, snarled by old men and women who, learning that the visitor to their home was from England, would nod conspiratorially, muttering the word 'Balfour' repeatedly, like a mantra or a punctuation mark. When I first arrived in Beirut in the mid-1970s, most of the middle-aged Palestinians I met were the original Arab refugees from 1948 Palestine, still holding the keys to homes from which they had been forbidden to return a quarter of a century earlier.

As the years went by, I would interview their children and then their grandchildren, the family's hope of return steadily shifting to despair and then to anger. It was a credit to the courage of these godforsaken people that they would follow the recitation of Balfour's name with an almost mischievous grin, a smile of forgiveness, an acknowledgement that the British reporter listening to them could not be held personally responsible for a sentence typed up in London during the First World War. I would routinely smile back, shamelessly raise my hands and, in a bland, cocky way, I would say: 'Sorry'. And that would be it: Balfour acknowledged. How could we not hang our heads in shame?

The words of the Balfour Declaration were an obvious, undeniable betrayal of a people. I quickly learned to recite them with great accuracy, but I would put more and more stress on the words 'non-Jewish communities'. And I realised, each time I entered an exiled Palestinian's home, that these people shared a kind of conspiracy with me. We both knew that the Balfour Declaration, the fate of the Arab Palestinians, the massacres and dispossession and then the occupation of their land, was a gross injustice. In a later age, we could go to war to return a Muslim population to their homes in Kosovo. But the refugee Arabs of Palestine would never return to their homes of 1948. So how could one make amends? It was impossible.

Historians have long debated the real reasons behind Britain's unprecedented decision to support a Jewish 'homeland' in Palestine.* True, the government in London was anxious to win the support of Russian and American Jews for the Allied cause against the Kaiser's Germany in the First World War, but why risk enraging the Arab populations of the Middle East? For details of this, we must turn to the disreputable correspondence between Hussein bin Ali, the Sharif of Mecca, and the British high commissioner to Egypt, Sir Henry McMahon. In these papers of 1915 – more than two years before Balfour's letter to Rothschild – Britain agreed to recognise Arab independence after the war within boundaries proposed by the sharif – with the exception of 'portions of Syria' west of Damascus, Homs, Hama and Aleppo. If the names of these cities today have a far darker and more violent contemporary shadow, the sharif paid too little attention to them more than a century ago, at least until Balfour's public declaration. It then created mass protests across the Middle East at the denial of Arab independence and political freedom in Palestine.

The British dispatched the director of its Arab Bureau in Cairo to tell Hussein that 'Jewish settlement in Palestine would only be allowed in so far as would be consistent with the political and economic freedom of the Arab population'. This was certainly more than Balfour had vouchsafed to the Arabs. Hussein accepted this duplicitous message at face value and told his followers that the settlement of Jews would not conflict with Arab independence in Palestine. But the Arab inhabitants of that sad old Ottoman possession, proud majority though they were, realised that they would ultimately lose much of their land and their homes.

Historians who write soon after the events they are studying often come closer to the truth than their successors. Thus George Antonius, in his devastating 1938 *The Arab Awakening*, dismissed claims that the

---

* It wasn't even original. Scholars have responded with varying degrees of credulity to the notion that Napoleon sought to restore the Jews to the land of their forefathers. It was during his ultimately hopeless battle for Acre that Napoleon apparently issued a proclamation to the Jews 'of Asia and Africa' to 're-establish the ancient Jerusalem', adding that he had already given weapons to Jewish 'battalions' outside Aleppo. The sadistic ruler of Acre, Ahmad Pasha al-Jazzar (*jazzar* means 'butcher' in Arabic), was principally assisted in military as well as banking advice by Haim Farhi, whose prominent Jewish family came from Damascus. Was Napoleon's generous proclamation intended to persuade Farhi to change sides and support the French army? Farhi did not do so although, since he was later blinded by his ruler, it might have been a good idea.

British cabinet wished to reward world Jewry for using its influence to bring the United States into the war or to reward Chaim Weizmann for the invention of a new explosive.* The dominant motive for the declaration, in Antonius' view, was 'securing Palestine … as a bulwark to the British position in Egypt and an overland link with the West'.†

What is quite remarkable about the whole disgraceful affair is the way in which Britain continued to pretend that Zionism could create a homeland in a country whose majority population was overwhelmingly against such a project, feared its effects and violently opposed its implementation. After serious inter-Jewish rioting and then Arab attacks in Jaffa in the summer of 1921, for example, we find Churchill, now colonial secretary, telling the Commons that there were in Palestine '500,000 Moslems, 65,000 Christians, and about 63,000 Jews' and that about 7,000 Jews had been brought into Palestine 'under the Zionist scheme of immigration'. The Arabs, he said:

> believe that in the next few years they are going to be swamped
> by scores of thousands of immigrants from Central Europe, who
> will push them off the land, eat up the scanty substance of the
> country and eventually gain absolute control of its institutions
> and destinies. As a matter of fact these fears are illusory.

The Zionists, Churchill went on, had made 'ardent declarations' of their hope to make Palestine 'a predominantly Jewish country', but they did so only to obtain outside support. Herbert Samuel, the British high commissioner in Palestine, had himself declared that new Jewish immigrants would be able to 'develop the country to the advantage of all its inhabitants'. And Churchill repeated that 'there really is nothing for the Arabs to be frightened about'.

Yet only a few moments later, the colonial secretary was lyrically describing how he had visited 'a fertile and thriving estate [in Rishon le

---

* Weizmann, the first president of Israel, was a biochemist known for his scientific work on acetone, a chemical essential in the making of cordite, which contributed to the British war effort.

† These explanations, however, fail to take account of British anti-Semitism – even inside the British cabinet – and new evidence that Lloyd George's government might have tried to detach Turkey from its alliance to the Central Powers and in return allow Palestine to remain 'in the area over which the Allies might be willing to allow the Turkish flag to fly'.

Zion], where the scanty soil gave place to good crops and good cultivation, and then to vineyards and finally to the most beautiful, luxurious orange groves ... I defy anybody, after seeing work of this kind, achieved by so much labour, effort and skill, to say that the British government ... could cast it all aside and leave it to be rudely and brutally overturned by the incursion of a fanatical attack by the Arab population from outside.'

The 'non-Jewish communities' had become capable of 'a fanatical attack', their brutality in stark contrast to the hard-working, skilful Jewish population. Churchill's repeated promises that Jewish immigration would be measured by 'the expanding wealth and development' of Palestine – which was 'greatly under-populated' – would take on a quite different meaning sixteen years later when he appeared before the Peel Commission after the outbreak of the Arab Revolt. He expressed the view that if the 'absorptive capacity' and the 'breeding over a number of years' of the 'Jewish National Home' produced 'an increasing Jewish population', then 'that population should not in any way be restricted from reaching a majority position ... I think in the main that would be the spirit of the Balfour Declaration.'

This was not at all how the document was interpreted by those who produced it. Churchill, championing the Jewish homeland from the start, stated now, in 1937, that 'certainly we committed ourselves to the idea that someday, somehow, far off in the future, subject to justice and economic convenience, there might well be a great Jewish State there, numbered by millions, far exceeding the present inhabitants of the country and to cut them off from that would be a wrong'. In such circumstances, he said, there would have to be 'justice' and 'fair consideration to those displaced'. And then came the ultimate racist bias – for the Jews and against the Arabs – upon which he would expand in his further testimony. If more Jews came to Palestine, he said, then the Jewish 'homeland'

> will become all Palestine eventually, provided that at each stage there is no harsh injustice done to the other residents. Why is there harsh injustice done if people come in and make a livelihood for more and make the desert into palm groves and olive groves? ... The injustice is when those who live in the country leave it to be a desert for thousands of years.

Churchill thought the Jewish state would be created 'someday ... far off' – 'a century or more', as he later remarked. It would, in fact, come into existence just over eleven years later, but Churchill had set out the ground rules for a new version of the Balfour Declaration. There should, he announced, be no 'harsh injustice' of 'other residents' if 'people' arrived to make the desert flourish. In other words, the right-ful possessors of a land were not those who owned it, but those who could make the best use of its resources. And Churchill went on to pour his scorn upon the Arabs, who were

> a poor people, conquered, living under the Turks fairly well ...
> [and] lived fairly easily in a flat squalor typical of pre-war
> Turkish empire provinces and then when the war came they
> became our enemies and they filled the armies against us and
> fired their rifles and shot our men ... They were beaten then and
> at our disposition. Mercy may impose many restraints. The
> question is how you give back to them in accordance with the
> new facts ... some of the positions which they held.

This was astounding. The Palestinian Arabs, Muslim and Christian, were no longer merely 'existing non-Jewish communities' whose civil and religious rights could not be prejudiced. They were a conquered people living amid 'flat squalor' who had taken up arms against Britain 'and shot our men' and who must submit to 'new facts'.

Churchill's anti-Arab sentiments were now clear. 'I have a great regard for Arabs,' he said, 'but at the same time you find where the Arab goes it is often desert.' Asked whether the Arabs had not created a civilisation in Spain, Churchill retorted: 'I am glad they were thrown out ... It is a lower manifestation, the Arab.' It was for 'the good of the world' that Palestine should be cultivated 'and it will never be culti-vated by the Arabs'.

This was not the worst of it. For in his final testimony to the 1937 Peel Commission, Churchill gave a highly intemperate, racially charged and deeply offensive reason for the dispossession of the Arabs of Palestine, a glossary of the real psychological foundations of the Balfour Declaration that might have found favour among the European dictators of the time:

I do not admit that the dog in the manger has the final right to
the manger, even though he may have lain there for a very long
time. I do not admit that right. I do not admit, for instance, that
a great wrong has been done to the Red Indians of America, or
the black people of Australia. I do not admit that a wrong has
been done to those people by the fact that a stronger race, a
higher grade race, or, at any rate, a more worldly wise race, to
put it that way, has come in and taken their place.

And there you have it. The Arabs of Palestine were no longer 'non-Jewish communities' but the 'dog in the manger', the idle animal whose
rights were no longer sustained by its presence. This was the logical
underpinning of colonialism, the seizure of other people's land on the
grounds that those who have 'come in and taken their place' would
make better use of it. The strong must rule over the weak who believed
that the land 'belonged' to them, however many years they had lived
there.

Lord Peel's Commission recommended the partition of Palestine, a
cruel harbinger of so many late twentieth- and early twenty-first-cen-
tury 'solutions' to the Arab–Israeli struggle. The Arabs would turn it
down. Churchill's testimony did not appear in the final report but he
wrote directly to Peel, asking him to keep at least some of his evidence
secret. 'You assured me that our conversation was confidential and
private,' he pleaded. 'There are a few references to nationalities which
would not be suited to appear in a permanent record.'

Much though God would be worshipped, revered and fought for, his
presence – Qur'anic, biblical, Judaic – would come together in
spiritual, political and colonial agony in the land called, with varying
geographical boundaries and end dates, Palestine. The majority
Muslims claimed their right to the territory because they lived in it,
owned most of it and because the Prophet Mohamed had, they
believed, travelled to heaven from the very centre of Jerusalem.
Christian claims were based on the Bible, the birthplace of Jesus,
which lay just twelve miles from the city, and a largely unexpressed
belief that the Crusades should have been successful. Jewish adher-
ence to Palestine had almost always been religious; the heritage of
the Jewish empire, the expulsion from Jerusalem, the Bible, the

prayers of every Jew for centuries, and the small population of Jews who still lived in that most holy of cities.

But the late nineteenth-century origin of the Jewish demand for a state in Palestine was primarily political, intended to resolve the generations of anti-Semitism that afflicted the Jews of Europe. Theodor Herzl's *Der Judenstaat* (The Jewish State) was a prescient and eloquent proposal to end the generations of persecution. In 1896, Herzl was imagining 'the restoration of the Jewish state' and, in essence, the founding declaration of a future Israel: 'Let the sovereignty be granted us over a portion of the globe large enough to satisfy the rightful requirements of a nation; the rest we shall manage for ourselves.'

The problem, as Herzl saw for himself, was that another people, the largely Muslim Arabs of Ottoman Palestine, already lived in this 'portion of the globe'. 'An infiltration [of Jews] is bound to end badly,' he wrote. 'It continues till the inevitable moment when the native population feels itself threatened, and forces the government to stop a further influx of Jews. Immigration is consequently futile unless we have the sovereign right to continue such immigration.' Herzl thought that a portion of Argentina as much as Palestine might become the Jewish homeland, yet within a year, the First Zionist Congress, chaired by Herzl himself, declared that 'the aim of Zionism is to create for the Jewish people a home in Palestine secured by public law'. But who would 'grant' the 'sovereignty' and 'public law' of which Herzl wrote?

It certainly wouldn't be the Palestinian Arab population – who at this stage had no sovereign national identity and, in Herzl's words, would 'feel itself threatened'. The sultan would permit only limited Jewish immigration to other parts of his empire. Ruhi Khalidi, another member of the great Khalidi clan, the nephew of Jerusalem's then mayor and a newly elected member of the Ottoman parliament, sought vainly in Constantinople to halt Jewish immigration, telling members that Zionists were forming a militia in Palestine. But Herzl, an Israeli historian would later write, 'viewed the [Arab] natives as primitive and backward, and ... did not consider them a society with collective political rights over the land in which they formed the overwhelming majority.' He 'hoped that economic benefits would reconcile the Arab population to the Zionist enterprise in Palestine'.

The casual way in which this civilisation would shove aside the fears and aspirations of the Arabs in the First World War would prove only that the superpowers of the time cared exclusively for their national interests. In retrospect, the infamous Hussein-McMahon correspondence can be seen as the deceitful and disingenuous promise that it represented. Far from offering Hussein a caliphate across the Middle East in return for an Arab uprising against the Turks, it 'cabin'd cribb'd, confin'd' Hussein's state, setting aside lands which 'cannot be said to be purely Arab' or which required 'special administrative arrangements'. The equally mendacious Sykes–Picot agreement that carved up the Middle East into British and French zones merely formalised European ambitions. From the early days of the British mandate, therefore, the Arabs and Jews of Palestine were holders of two conflicting promises, one of which might be honoured, the other of which must be proved false.

Today, the Palestinians commemorate their lost land with poetry and art, but it is a place of lost orange groves and olive trees and snug village houses. Paintings, photographs and postcards of those years between 1914 and 1948 reveal ghosts of the future as well as of the past. In a gallery in Beirut's Clemenceau Street hangs a majestic series of landscapes and portraits taken between those two critical dates. One photograph depicts a Palestinian Arab porter carrying a grand piano, another in Jerusalem lugging a wardrobe on his back. Jerusalem lies there in 1933, the slopes below al-Aqsa empty of roads, the view across the Mount of Olives containing only four houses; British troops search an Arab in the Old City.

Khalil Raad, the first prominent Palestinian photographer, took all these pictures. Born in Lebanon in 1854, his family moved to Jerusalem after the death of his father, and in the First World War he became a photographer for the Turkish army. There is Raad himself on horseback – in Ottoman uniform.

Violence is never far from these pictures. One startling photograph shows nine young men wearing the tarbush hat, gathered in a narrow old Jerusalem street with what appears to be a bearded Muslim cleric. 'Strike Day, 2 November 1929, in protest of the Balfour declaration,' it says on the caption. The men are holding donation boxes for the 'Emergency Relief Committee', set up to assist victims of Arab riots over Jewish access to the Wailing Wall. During the 'Buraq Uprising' – named after the horse that supposedly carried the Prophet from Mecca to Jerusalem and back – Arabs attacked Jewish homes, murdering 133

Jews. More than a hundred Arabs were subsequently killed, mostly by British police gunfire.

When did the modern Jewish–Arab conflict begin? The Balfour Declaration contradicted the earlier Sykes–Picot agreement, which had itself left the Palestine question unresolved. 'The Sykes–Picot accords represent the start of history!' a British historian was to proclaim a century later. Or maybe the Bible, the Torah, the Qur'an, the Crusades, the Moorish expulsions from Spain (in which the Muslims and Jews were fellow victims), or the Ottoman Empire? Or the evangelical passions of Victorian clergymen and novelists, and the ambitions of European empires? In retrospect, however, we can see that Balfour's 1917 declaration ensured the creation of a future Israel on Palestinian land and an expanded Israeli power and occupation over the territory of mandate Palestine* after the 1967 Arab–Israeli war.

The context of these events counted against the Palestinian Arabs. When Balfour wrote his declaration, refugees were pouring out of Russia after the Bolshevik Revolution. Hundreds of thousands of Christian refugees were also scattered across the Middle East, survivors of the first industrial holocaust of the twentieth century: the 1915 Armenian genocide.

The American Middle East Relief set up food posts and shelter, hospitals and orphanages, for these destitute refugees who, according to the victorious allies, would go back to their homes in Asia Minor. But they did not. They were betrayed as surely as the Palestinian Arabs in 1948. The League of Nations failed the Armenians, just as the United Nations would later fail to honour its promises to the Palestinians.

We can in this way plot 'refugeedom' through the Middle East in two stages. The first occurred during and immediately after the First World War, when hundreds of thousands of hungry, terrified people sought refuge from slaughter and genocide in Europe and the Levant, and the second stage was made manifest in the aftermath of the Second World War, when millions of displaced people crisscrossed a broken Europe in search of homes that no longer existed.

---

* A League of Nations mandate for British administration of the territories of Palestine and Transjordan at the end of the First World War.

But this second stage of 'refugeedom' must include the earlier shameful pre-Second World War years when the West closed its doors to its Jewish brethren and sent tens of thousands of them back to Nazi Germany, Nazi Austria and what would soon be Nazi-occupied Europe. Shiploads of Jews seeking sanctuary from Hitler's barbarism were returned by the US and Canada to their tormentors. This refusal would profoundly influence support for the future Israel by Europe and America, a propitiation for their own moral guilt as much as a demonstration of love for world Jewry and its history of persecution.

Thus the immediate significance of the Balfour Declaration for the Arabs and the 'refugeedom' it foreshadowed was ignored. Then the growing Palestinian fear of organised mass Jewish migration in the 1930s, which led to an armed rebellion by the Arabs, was largely outweighed by the world's fear of Hitler and war.* And the actual dispossession of the 750,000 Arabs of Palestine was accomplished immediately after the Second World War, when Europe was again experiencing mass 'refugeedom' and when a proportion of those same European refugees sought to follow Balfour's promise and travel to Palestine itself. At such a crisis, the plight of a few hundred thousand Arabs counted for nothing. These were, of course, the same generation of Arabs whom Churchill had dismissed only eleven years earlier as Britain's First World War 'enemies'.

It is instructive to observe how faithfully the British press followed Churchill's contempt for the Palestinian Arabs' supposedly age-old indolence, just as the American and to some extent the British media have largely gone along today with the American–Israeli version of the Middle East tragedy. When the 1936–39 Arab Rebellion against Jewish immigration neared its end, *Picture Post* told its readers how 'cynics' suggested the British were in Palestine to protect Iraq's Mosul oil pipe-line terminal on the Mediterranean, to command the Suez Canal or to guard the air route to India. It described Britain's 'heartbreaking attempt to keep incompatible promises' but then launched into famil-iar territory. 'The fact is that a modern ... and cooperative state such as

---

* The need to maintain good relations with the Arabs on the eve of the Second World War – and after the Arab Revolt – prompted Neville Chamberlain in 1939 to place further restrictions on Jews travelling to or buying land in Palestine, and to reject partition. Churchill was rightly enraged by Chamberlain's pusillanimity and these regulations lapsed after he became prime minister in 1940.

the Zionists are creating is incompatible with the feudal and nomadic tradition of the Arabs. They see farms ... growing up and flourishing beside their own backward medieval fields.' A caption even identified rebels as 'Arab terrorists'.

For those 'medieval fields', remember the 'flat squalor' of Arab Palestine described by Churchill.* *Picture Post* also 'balanced' a single picture of an unidentified Muslim Palestinian above the caption 'An Arab Speaks' with nine photographs of Jews, who spoke of Nazi persecution in their original homelands and the 'earthly paradise' of living in Palestine.

The civil war in Palestine after the Second World War and the collapse of the British mandate was as immoral as it was bloody. The story of the UN's own partition plan, its acceptance by the Jews and rejection by the Arabs, Israel's declaration of statehood in 1948, the subsequent and first Arab–Israeli war and the dispossession of the Arabs, has been told in libraries of books. I have many times written about these days of triumph (for the Jews) and disaster (for the Arabs), recording the memories of those on both sides who fought and suffered. Henceforth, only the Arabs would be called Palestinians. The Palestinian Jews have become Israelis.

Anyone who tries to tell what he or she believes is the 'truth' in the Middle East will be the target of lies and campaigns of slander, but you must continue to 'tell the story'. No one is going to admit later that they got it wrong, that maybe your reports were closer to reality than they wished to believe. The only reward a journalist can enjoy is to carry on. If you stop, then you lose. So today, when I try to learn more about the story of Palestine, I search for new ways to understand what happened; not by reciting a chronology, but by 'dipping in' to the events, by concentrating on a letter, a book, an individual memory, by visiting the homes of those who made history and those who suffered from it.

*   *   *

---

* In 1937, Churchill was also imagining an 'all-powerful' Jewish army 'equipped with the most deadly weapons of war' which in the future 'would plunge out into the new undeveloped lands that lie around them'. Although east Jerusalem and the West Bank and Gaza were scarcely 'undeveloped', this was a remarkably prophetic account of the capture of Palestinian territories in the six-day 1967 Arab–Israeli war.

There are no armed guards on the gate of Number 17 Ben Gurion Boulevard in Tel Aviv, just a tired, two-storey villa set back from the street on this cold February day and an open door that leads to a dark kitchen and a little room with a cot on the floor. Upstairs is the bejewelled centre of this little home, David Ben Gurion's library of 20,000 books. I pad through this den, scribbling in my notebook any clues to the mind of Israel's first and most emotional of prime ministers.

It was the set of Ben Gurion's quotations that caught my eye, statements on the eternal morality of the State of Israel, messages from the great man in time of war. Here he is, for example, during Israel's War of Independence – the Palestinian Arab Nakba – when he feared that Jewish forces would destroy Muslim holy places in Jerusalem: 'Further to my previous order relating to the Old City – you should see to it that the special force to be appointed for guarding the Old City uses mercilessly machine guns against any Jew, and especially any Jewish soldier, who will try to pillage or to desecrate any Christian or Moslim [sic] holy place.' In 1967, he boasted of how, during the establishment of the State of Israel, 'we did not damage any single mosque'.

Yet he was already creating myths. The undamaged mosques, he wrote in the same statement, were found in villages 'without a single Moslem, as all of them had already fled during the [British] Mandatory rule and before the declaration of the State'. Amid the detritus of Ben Gurion's life, there are musings on the morality and supposed purity of Israel's nascent army. The truth is that Israel destroyed many mosques, that the original Palestinian Arab victims of the 1947–48 war did not all flee, as Ben Gurion suggested; many were murdered in their villages.

Israeli and Arab historians have catalogued many other massacres by Israel's forces in this period. The Israeli academic Ilan Pappe's ground-breaking work on the Palestinian dispossession makes it clear that the Haganah militia's Plan Dalet, theoretically a defensive operation to protect the new Israeli state, was in fact 'a blueprint for ethnic cleansing'. Avi Shlaim, a distinguished Israeli scholar, called David Ben Gurion 'the great expeller of the Palestinians in 1948'. Both Pappe and the Palestinian historian Walid Khalidi agreed that 'Plan D' was not only a plan to cope with the anticipated invasion by Arab nations 'but, in many ways, a master plan for the expulsion of as many Palestinians as could be expelled'.

Britain's own 1948 departure from Palestine was as ignominious as it was pitiful. Jewish attacks on British troops had now acquired the same sobriquet of 'terrorism' that the Arabs had earned a decade earlier for daring to resist occupation. This cancerous word would migrate across the world over the next seventy years, its generic use allowing vengeful superpowers and Middle Eastern states to unleash atrocities on a mass scale.

Young Major Derek Cooper, an officer in the 17/21 Lancers, was one of the few British officers who tried to protect the Arabs of Jaffa in 1948, winning a Military Cross under Israeli mortar fire. He was furious at the treatment of the Palestinians driven from their homes by the Israelis after the Arabs turned down the UN partition plan for Palestine. His memory of the Palestinian refugees crowding around his retreating armoured vehicle was to mark the rest of his life. I came across him, seventy years old, in an abandoned building close to the Beirut front line during the Israeli army's cruel 1982 siege of the city, while he was working for Oxfam, delivering food to refugees in the camps under bombardment.

The remains of some of those Palestinian Arab casualties were only rediscovered sixty-five years later, when workers began renovating the old Muslim cemetery in Jaffa. Agence France-Presse (AFP) found an eighty-year-old fisherman called Atar Zeinab, a teenager in 1948, who described how he 'carried to the cemetery sixty bodies during a period of three or four months'. Because of the bullets and flying grenade fragments, Zeinab said, the bodies were dumped on top of each other in existing family crypts, contrary to Muslim custom. 'We carried them early in the morning or in the night,' he said. 'We put women, children and men in the same place ... nobody prayed for these people.'

Could it have worked, the world of Palestine that existed before the end of empire, before the declaration of the State of Israel, before the Nakba, before the Arab armies invaded the land in a vain attempt to destroy what would become Israel? I don't think it was ever intended to exist, the pseudo bi-national state which the British thought they ruled but which they had bequeathed to the Jews, offering only 'rights' to the 'non-Jewish communities', but there are some who still remember Palestine of the 1930s with nostalgia.

Which brought me to the Tel Aviv seafront one mild November day in 2012 and to a block of anonymous modern apartments, home to a remarkable lady. On the wall of her apartment is a large photograph of a ravishingly beautiful young woman with long, dark hair, sitting on a lawn with a handsome young man in British army uniform. I am sitting opposite this lady of ninety-five, her memories of the old Palestine and the new Israel as sharp as a teenager's.

The man is Moshe Dayan, the former Israeli chief of staff who conquered east Jerusalem, the West Bank, Gaza and Golan in 1967, Israel's golden boy whose values – so Ruth Dayan believed – had been distorted by the country's present leadership. Benjamin Netanyahu is prime minister, Avigdor Lieberman his foreign minister. Many times, Ruth Dayan has spoken out, eloquently and painfully, to tell the world that the country's right-wing, extremist governments are ruining Israel, that Zionism has 'run its course'.

Now she sits in her tartan skirt, eyes sharp as an eagle's, surveying her journalist visitor. 'Modern science is amazing,' she says. 'I could look you up on the internet in two minutes. I read that you are pro-Arab. You shouldn't be. You should be pro-world.' I told Ruth Dayan that she should not believe all she reads on the internet, that a recent website sent to me on hard copy denounced me as a Mossad agent because I had 'revealed' in the *Independent* that my mother's maiden name was Rose. Ruth Dayan bursts into laughter.

'When Israelis tell me there is "no one to talk to" [among the Palestinians], it gets on my nerves,' she says. 'Most people who deal in politics, they don't see Arabs. I go to the territories – but I have to have a [Israeli] permit to get into Ramallah.' I notice that she uses the single word 'territories' for the Israeli-occupied Arab lands. Ruth Dayan's accent in English is poised, slightly upper crust and she obviously admires the country which ruled mandate Palestine until 1948. 'I am an Anglophile,' she says proudly, a woman born in Ottoman Palestine in 1917, moving to London with her parents where the London School of Economics was 'the nursery of socialism'.

Ruth Dayan has an acute memory, some corners of which I choose not to disturb. Moshe Dayan was a war hero with socialist ideals – publicly, at least – but he was a notorious womaniser and he and Ruth divorced in 1971 after thirty-six years of marriage. So I ask about the early Dayan, the man in the photograph in British uniform. They were deeply in love, she says, and she was eight months pregnant when he was arrested by the British, one of thirty-four Jewish militants, in 1939.

He was later released to serve in the 1941 Allied invasion of Lebanon, where a Vichy French sniper shot him in the face.

Ruth Dayan is nostalgic for the values that she believes existed in the original Palestine, where Arab and Jew lived together. Her home was near the American Colony Hotel in Jerusalem, a four-storey house in which there were Arabs and Polish Jewish families. 'My older son was born in an Arab house in 1942.'

When Ruth returned to Palestine at the age of twelve in 1929, 'I didn't know I was Jewish – I didn't know what Palestine was. My mother taught at an Arabic kindergarten, just inside the old city of Jerusalem. We went to a playground on Mount Zion, provided by a Jew provided it was for the Arabs as well as the Jews. I was taught Arabic at home ... The things we did up to 1948 didn't hurt anyone. If only the Arabs had accepted the UN resolution. I'm not for a Jewish state. But I am an Israeli. I thought this should be one country and everyone should live happily ever after. I was born here and I have a right to live here – the same goes for the Arab population ... Now when I see what's happening around us, this frightens me more.'

Ruth is an aristocratic lady. Her sister Reuma married Ezer Weizman, Israeli defence minister and later president. Feminist, patriot, pining for the old Israel, fearful of global warming. 'I don't believe in religion,' she tells me. But what did her husband, Moshe Dayan, believe in?

Shlomo Sand is a caltrop amid the Israeli people, a child of Polish Holocaust survivors – leftist, anti-Zionist, academic – who does not consider that religion gives a people the right to a land. He condemns what he calls Moshe Dayan's (and Ben Gurion's) 'biblical mythology', in which the Exodus and the Jewish people's march through Sinai are interwoven with the 1956 Suez war, the conquest of Canaan with Israel's creation in 1948 and the 1967 occupation of the West Bank. Dayan's *Living with the Bible* describes how Israel's geography and history 'helped our imagination to vault over the past and return to antiquity'. Was this, I wonder later, the real parting of the ways for Moshe and Ruth, rather than what she was to call Moshe's 'such bad taste in women'?

Dayan, of all Israelis, is the most important figure in the subsequent occupation of all of Palestine, for it was he who led the attack and capture of east Jerusalem in 1967. Uri Avnery, that most steadfast, begrudging and brave of Israel's old liberals, was to write more than three and a half decades after the capture of Jerusalem that 'Israel has invented something unprecedented: eternal occupation. In 1967, because no pressure was brought to bear on Israel to return the occupied territories, Moshe Dayan came up with a brilliant idea – to continue the occupation forever.'

Dayan's belief or conjecture that biblical 'history' justifies Israel's existence lies at the heart of the more than half century of occupation of east Jerusalem and the West Bank and Golan and, today, the ever growing and internationally illegal seizure of Arab land. For those who want to expand Israel's frontiers, the continued existence of a Jewish community in these territories counts for much less than the integrity of biblical history.

Yet if their theological and biblical roots are their land deeds from God, these are remarkably dodgy documents, not least because of the chorus of Jewish voices that dispute the biblical legends upon which so much faith rests. Sand contends that in the 1970s, when Israel was caught up in the momentum of territorial expansion, 'without the Old Testament in its hand and the "exile" of the Jewish people in its memory, it would have had no justification for annexing Arab Jerusalem and establishing settlements in the West Bank'. But the veracity of biblical 'history' raises far more serious doubts. Avnery wrote that 'there can no longer be the slightest doubt that the Exodus never happened ... in a hundred years of frantic archaeological searching by devout Christian and Zionist zealots, not a shred of concrete evidence for a conquest of Canaan has been found.' Contemporary Egyptian records made no mention of these events. Avnery said that the Haggadah, which tells the story of the Exodus from Egypt, influences 'our collective behaviour and Israeli national policy' yet remains 'a cry from the heart of a defenceless, persecuted people who had no means to take revenge on their torturers'. Out of context, Avnery believed, this text can set Israelis 'on an evil course ... They are out to kill us, so we must – according to another Jewish injunction – kill them first.'

Miko Peled, whose father Mattityahu was an Israeli general in the 1967 war – but later condemned his country's seizure of the West Bank, Gaza, Golan and Sinai as a 'cynical campaign of territorial expansion' – condemned Israel's intention to expel 50,000 Palestinian residents

from the Jerusalem suburb of Silwan so that it can build an archaeological park that glorifies its Jewish past. His mother remembered the
Palestinians forced to leave west Jerusalem in 1948. She was offered
one of their 'beautiful, spacious homes', her son recalled, but refused.
'She could not bear the thought of living in the home of a family that
was forced out and now lives in a refugee camp. She said the coffee
was still warm on the tables as the [Israeli] soldiers came in and began
the looting.'

The fate of hundreds of thousands of Palestinian Arabs, let alone the
decades of misery they would endure in the aftermath of Israel's creation, scarcely occurred to those Americans who, with growing horror,
watched not only pre-war Nazi Germany's anti-Jewish laws and
violence but the West's grotesque refusal to assist the millions of Jews
already pleading for sanctuary.

Dorothy Thompson, the influential American reporter and columnist, was among the first to appreciate the terrifying fate that awaited
the Jews of Europe; she was deported from Nazi Germany on Hitler's
orders years after writing a ferocious account of an interview with the
Führer. In 1932, she had described Hitler as 'a man whose countenance
is a caricature, a man whose framework seems … without bones. He is
inconsequent and voluble, ill-poised, insecure.'

Thompson was to become perhaps the loudest warning bell in the
US for European Jewry and addressed American Jewish groups with
rousing speeches on the plight of their co-religionists, denouncing the
1938 Munich agreement and defending the motives of Herschel
Grynszpan, the German Jew who assassinated a Nazi diplomat in Paris
– an action that allowed Hitler to launch the Kristallnacht terror against
the Jews.

Thompson endured anti-Semitic abuse for her articles. She berated
Churchill in 1941 for not arming the Palestinian Jews to defend their
land from Hitler's armies for 'they must not be allowed to perish like
rats'. At the international conference held in New York in 1942 to
agitate for unrestricted Jewish immigration to Palestine, she was, in the
words of her biographer, 'wholeheartedly sympathetic to the Zionist
movement'.

But on her first visit to Palestine in 1945, Thompson realised that
Zionism was not the 'liberal crusade' she thought it to be. By the
following year, she found the situation in Palestine was 'not the way it

has been presented by many of the Zionists'. The Arabs should not be dispossessed. Thompson was appalled by the violence of Menachem Begin's Irgun and his bombing of the King David Hotel.* She condemned Jewish 'terrorism'. And she was henceforth vilified by those whom she had so long defended.

Now she herself was 'anti-Semitic' and the 'apostle of the Hitlerian technique'. In 1947, the *New York Post* dropped her regular column, effectively silencing her voice in the city where she had so often espoused the Jewish cause. She was not alone. On the eve of Begin's fund-raising visit to the United States in 1948, a letter signed by some of the most prominent Jewish notables appeared in the *New York Times*, calling the future Israeli prime minister a fascist, and condemned him for the mass killing of civilians in Deir Yassin. Begin's 'Freedom Party' had 'preached an admixture of ultra-nationalism, religious mysticism and racial superiority'.† This unprecedented letter was signed, among twenty-six others, by Albert Einstein and Hannah Arendt.

Thompson's treatment by Israel's supposed 'friends' in America was a sign of things to come for any American journalist who dared to

---

* The Zionist militia's attack on the hotel – the British headquarters in Jerusalem at the time – took place in July 1946, killing ninety-one and wounding forty-six, mostly British employees, civilian and military. Begin founded the right-wing Likud party in 1973, and became Israel's prime minister (1977–83), during which he authorised the bombing of the Osirak nuclear plant in Iraq and the 1982 invasion of Lebanon.

† There was nothing new in the idea that immigration to Palestine had dangerous political implications for the Jewish people. In his diary for 9 July 1933, the Jewish academic Victor Klemperer, whose account of survival in Dresden before and during the Second World War is a classic personal history of courage and resilience under Nazi persecution, wrote that 'We hear a lot about Palestine now; it does not appeal to us. Anyone who goes there exchanges nationalism and narrowness for nationalism and narrowness. Also it is a country for capitalists. It is about the size of the province of East Prussia; inhabitants: 200,000 Jews and 800,000 Arabs.' If he grasped the demographics, Klemperer was to write far more bitterly a year later that 'to me the Zionists, who want to go back to the Jewish state of AD 70 (destruction of Jerusalem by Titus), are just as offensive as the Nazis. With their nosing after blood, their ancient "cultural roots", their partly canting, partly obtuse winding back of the world they are altogether a match for the National Socialists ...' Only the Allied fire-bombing of Dresden in February 1945 – and the burning of his and his wife's papers in the Gestapo headquarters – saved the Klemperers from deportation; survive though he did, Klemperer might have done better to seek salvation in Palestine before the war. A liberal German in the best sense of the word, he quoted in 1942 a family friend who said that if he had to choose a nationalism, 'then I'll choose Jewish nationalism, which doesn't persecute me'.

question Israel's behaviour towards the Arabs, to condemn its brutality or to question the country's integrity or those who so slavishly supported it. She was, her biographer wrote, 'the first and most prominent journalist to be smeared with the label of "anti-Semite"', despite what he called her 'ardent and absolutely sincere hope that Israel will flourish and give expression to the deepest moral instincts of the Jewish religion'.

For Thompson, the establishment of the State of Israel was 'a recipe for perpetual war'. It should be 'a secular, political' entity 'with no prior claim on virtue' and must expect 'to live in the same atmosphere of free criticism which every other state in the world must endure'. Yet how could this be when its founders not only created their state on the land of others but did so violently, ruthlessly, and with dispossession aforethought? It was not so much the tenets of Zionism itself – the 're-establishment' of a Jewish homeland after centuries of persecution – but the wilful negation of the suffering of hundreds of thousands of innocents, who had nothing to do with Hitler's crimes but were deliberately deprived of their homes amid the West's desire for atonement. It is important at this point to return to the work of Ilan Pappe and his predecessor among the 'new historians' of Israel, Benny Morris.

It was 2006 before Pappe felt able to write of the 'ethnic cleansing' of Palestine, of 'the Zionist ideological impulse to have an exclusively Jewish presence in Palestine' and of how 'the Zionist policy was first based on retaliation against Palestinian attacks in February 1947, and it transformed into an initiative to ethnically cleanse the country as a whole in March 1948'. On the evening of 10 March that year, military orders were dispatched to Jewish military units 'to prepare for the systematic expulsion of the Palestinians from vast areas of the country'. It took six months to complete the project, wrote Pappe, and when it was over:

> More than half of Palestine's native population, close to 800,000 people, had been uprooted, 531 villages had been destroyed, and eleven urban neighbourhoods emptied of their inhabitants. The plan … and above all its systematic implementation in the following months, was a clear-cut case of an ethnic-cleansing operation, regarded under international law today as a crime against humanity.

Using primarily Israeli military archives, the revisionist Israeli historians 'were able to confirm many cases of massive expulsions from
villages and towns and revealed that the Jewish forces had committed
a considerable number of atrocities, including massacres'. Pappe found
himself condemned with the same abuse that Thompson and so many
others have suffered. He was an Israel-hater, his translations from
Hebrew distorted and perverted. He was, according to Morris himself,
'one of the world's sloppiest historians'.

But Morris, who had first revealed many of the atrocities that
accompanied Israel's birth, was to formulate the extraordinary argument that he would have felt 'no pangs of conscience' if he had been
among Jewish commanders and watched the 50,000 Arabs expelled
from Lod. As he told Israeli journalist Ari Shavit in 2004:

> in certain conditions, expulsion is not a war crime. I don't think
> that the expulsions of 1948 were war crimes. You can't make an
> omelette without breaking eggs. You have to dirty your hands
> ... A society that aims to kill you forces you to destroy it. When
> the choice is between destroying or being destroyed, it's better
> to destroy ... when the choice is between ethnic cleansing and
> genocide – the annihilation of your people – I prefer ethnic
> cleansing ... That is what Zionism faced. A Jewish state would
> not have come into being without the uprooting of 700,000
> Palestinians. Therefore it was necessary to uproot them. There
> was no choice but to expel that population.

Morris' words deeply shocked his colleagues. Compared to the 'ethnic
cleansing' of Bosnia and the Second World War, he said, Israel's acts
were 'small' war crimes:

> But my feeling is that this place would be quieter and know less
> suffering if the matter had been resolved once and for all. If Ben
> Gurion had carried out a large expulsion and cleansed the whole
> country – the whole Land of Israel, as far as the Jordan River ...
> If he had carried out a full expulsion – rather than a partial one –
> he would have stabilised the State of Israel for generations.

The 'non-completion of the transfer was a mistake,' Morris concluded. In other words, Ben Gurion, far from planning the removal of an entire people from their homes and possessions in what was to become Israel, had not gone far enough. He should have dispossessed and expelled the Palestinians of the West Bank as well – a feat that later right-wing Israeli governments were to partially achieve with their own mass land-thefts in the occupied territories.

To grasp the enormity of what Morris describes, the reader must appreciate that he found evidence of twenty-four cases of massacre in the Israeli archives:

> In some cases, four or five people were executed, in others the numbers were seventy, eighty, one hundred. There was also a great deal of arbitrary killing. Two old men are spotted walking in a field – they are shot. A woman is found in an abandoned village – she is shot. There are cases such as the village of Dawayima, in which a column entered the village with all guns blazing and killed anything that moved. The worst cases were Saliha (seventy to eighty killed), Dayr Yassin (100–110), Lod (250), Dawayima (hundreds) … At Jaffa there was a massacre about which nothing had been known until now … In Operation Hiram [in the north, in October 1948] there was an unusually high concentration of executions of people against a wall or next to a well in an orderly fashion. That can't be chance. It's a pattern. Apparently, various officers who took part in the operation understood that the expulsion order they received permitted them to do these deeds in order to encourage the population to take to the roads … Ben Gurion silenced the matter. He covered up for the officers who did the massacres.

As Morris says, these may be 'small war crimes' in comparison to those committed in the Second World War or in Bosnia in the 1990s. But they lay bare the reality of the 'purity of arms' upon which the Israeli army's morality was supposed to be based in the coming decades. Later war crimes committed by Israeli forces cannot be explained without a transparent understanding of the pitiless behaviour of Israel's soldiers during the foundation of their state.

Over the next two decades, the story of Israel's 1947–48 struggle would be retold in fiction and film, most of which reflected the now familiar David and Goliath story of little Israel's battle for survival against Arabs who were neither dispossessed nor driven from their homes but merely fled on the orders of Arab invaders. Ben Gurion called Leon Uris' *Exodus*, a Zionist epic published in 1958 in which Bedouin Arabs are described as 'the dregs of humanity', 'the best thing ever written about Israel'. Uris, denigrated by critics and scholars, admitted that he was 'definitely biased', but his book was a bestseller among Jewish-Americans.

Large Palestinian libraries were looted from Arab homes by the Israelis in 1948 – during the Nakba – when 100,000 fled into Lebanon from Galilee. But in 1982, I watched as Israeli troops loaded tons of archive documents from the Institute of Palestine Studies in the Hamra district of the Lebanese capital onto military trucks. The Palestinian story, it seemed, was too dangerous for the archive proof of Palestinian suffering to survive. Even today, the Palestinian Oral History Archive at the American University of Beirut is still completing its record of oral testimonies of 1948 Nakba survivors, although many of those who were originally recorded in the 1990s were now already dead.

The Palestinians were not the only ones to start their lives in another land. Many of the Jews who immigrated to what became Israel arrived from a Europe that had destroyed their lives. Amos Oz, one of Israel's most prominent novelists, spoke of the 'unrequited love' that European Jews felt for the culture they left behind. 'It is ironic and painful for me today,' he wrote in 2005, 'to reflect on the fact that seventy or eighty years ago the only Europeans in the whole of Europe were my father and my mother, and my grandparents and other secular Jews like them:

Everyone was a Bulgarian patriot, a Swedish patriot, an Irish patriot. They were Europeans. They never regarded themselves as Russians, or Polish, or Lithuanian or whatever. They were Europeans.

Oz was right to refer to the Jewish love of Iraq, Yemen, Morocco and Tunisia that the Jews of these countries felt before they were, in Oz's words, 'kicked out'. But he made a critical error when he added that

Israel is a refugee camp. Palestine is a refugee camp. It is a tragic and painful conflict between two refugee camps, two former victims of Europe in two different ways: the Arabs through colonialism, imperialism, exploitation, humiliation; the Jews through persecution, rejection, and ultimately an unprecedented mass murder.

Jews would object, quite rightly, to any parallel between their own suffering more than half a century before – extermination – and the present occupation endured by Palestinians. But the balance between the 'refugee camp' of Israel – now a nuclear power with a boundless economy and permanent American financial and military support – and an Israeli-occupied, oppressed, truncated 22 per cent of 'Palestine' is utterly fraudulent. Most of the world accepts Israel's right to exist within defined internationally accepted borders – but not its permanent exploitation and armed domination of territory which does not belong to it. How is one to explain that one wealthy and secure and militarily all-powerful 'refugee camp' (Israel) owns or occupies a smaller and poverty-stricken and fearful 'refugee camp' of Palestinians?

The birth of the Israeli state and its subsequent existence on lands that only half a century before had been owned and farmed by a majority Arab population were supported by Hollywood movies and novels that extolled the image of a plucky nation of Jewish victims of Nazism rising, phoenix-like, from the ashes of the Second World War. Yet the Arab enemies whom these victims were to fight in their new land were neither Germans nor Nazis. There was a strange discordance, as the years went by, between the desire to associate Palestinian history with the German murderers of European Jews, and the modern, indestructible Israeli state that was supposedly a part of the new post-war world.

Putting aside the divisions between the original pre-war Jewish immigrants and the post-war Jewish refugees, there continues to be a dichotomy between the memory of a well-educated, resourceful, honourable and cultured European Jewish people who allowed themselves to be eliminated so meekly in the gas chambers, and an Israel in the Middle East which, as the last defence of the Jewish people, can destroy all its enemies. That Israel's victories have grown steadily less convincing over time does not change its claim to be the final bastion against the destruction of the Jewish people.

This has led to an unnatural combination of fear and confidence, in which a bombastic prime minister like Benjamin Netanyahu could claim in the twenty-first century that Iran's crackpot President Ahmadinejad was more dangerous than Hitler. For Netanyahu and his supporters, as *Haaretz* explained in 2013, Israel was supposed to be Czechoslovakia before Hitler's conquest; the Geneva nuclear accord with Iran in the same year was the 1938 Munich agreement; the UN Security Council's five permanent members were Chamberlain's heirs, and American Jews should now atone for their silence during the Holocaust.

The path to Hitler's war must therefore be forever invoked to protect an Israeli state which proved that Hitler failed in his mission to eliminate the Jewish people. Whoever expressed doubt about the reality of these parallels was, obviously, also anti-Semitic. The Americans must always support an Israel whose suffering people it had ignored before their state existed, and Europe must always support an Israel whose missing six million souls had been destroyed by Europe itself. Surely this is the predicament which Dorothy Thompson wrote of when she said that Israel must expect 'to live in the same atmosphere of free criticism which every other state in the world must endure'. It did not.

But when Hitler's victims reached the shores of Palestine before, during and after the war, they were able to imagine a new world in which their very identities could be united in a future dissociated from their past existence. The founders of the state of Israel, the new Jewish citizens of this nation, changed their names. They adopted Hebrew names in place of the Yiddish, German or Russian identities they had inherited from the past. The diaspora Jew became the Israeli Jew. Thus David Gryn became David Ben Gurion, Moisey Kitaigorodsky became Moshe Dayan and Isaak Rabitchiov was Yitzhak Rabin. Golda Meir emerged from Golda Mabovitch, Shimon Peres from Szymon Perski, and the violent nationalist Menachem Begin from Mieczyslaw Biegun. Ariel Sheineman would be Ariel Sharon, Benjamin Mileikowsky would be known as Benjamin Netanyahu.

Yet was Israel to be the Prophet Isaiah's 'light unto the nations', a beacon of spiritual and moral guidance as well as a sovereign home for the Jewish people? Or was it to become, more prosaically, a colonial project with good public relations, a company with an expanding and

aggressive real estate market whose Jewish shareholders would grudgingly accept those Arabs who remained within its original 1948 borders
but would steadily narrow the title of their corporation down to the
'Nation State of the Jewish People'. Those 'existing non-Jewish
communities' of Palestinians outside its notional borders would live in
the occupied 'territories' of what Israel called 'Judea and Samaria' or, if
they were well behaved, in east Jerusalem, or in the squalor of unoccu-
pied Gaza. If they 'existed' in Jerusalem, then their homes and property
could be taken from them; if the Arabs lived in the West Bank, they
could lose the lands of their forefathers whenever the Israeli government chose to expand its colonies.

The idea that the colonisation of Palestine began only with Israel's
crushing military victory over the rest of the former mandate in 1967,
however, is historically untrue. For Shlomo Sand, it started in the nineteenth century and never stopped. 'Even between 1949 and 1967,' he
would say. 'It was an internal colonisation. Both the right-wingers and
the leftists, except for the communists, accepted the slogan of
"Judaising the Galilee". That's why no Israeli politician will ever make
a serious effort to compromise with the Palestinians.'

The destruction of Arab villages continued for years after the war
was over, some of them demolished as late as 1953. Typical of these
was Kafr Birim and Iqrit in the north of Israel, Christian villages whose
residents were 'temporarily' expelled by the Israeli army in November
1948, reportedly because military operations continued in the area.
Some crossed into Lebanon, others remained in caves above their
homes and then settled close to their former property. But they were
never to return. Iqrit was razed in 1951, Kafr Birim two years later, only
its church and bell-tower surviving.

When I talked over many years to the Palestinian refugees in
Lebanon, they would often describe their homes in detail. These were
for the most part peasants or farming people from villages which were,
in the words of Walid Khalidi, 'literally ... wiped off the face of the
earth'. Sometimes I travelled to modern-day Israel to find their homes;
often I would discover only a long-abandoned graveyard or a
bricked-up mosque, Jewish Israeli homes long ago built on the site and
now bearing a new name, in Hebrew. Occasionally, I took back the
front-door keys of Palestinian refugees and tried out these wretched
things in the doors of their ancient houses – for in the cities of western

Palestine, many properties had survived. However true, it is a cliché to report that the locks had been changed.

The 'rebirth' of ancient Israel in its biblical landscape and the acquisition of land and property inside the state – and then in the newly captured territories of the West Bank and Golan, Gaza and Sinai after the 1967 war – was all part of the Zionist project. If the 1947–48 conflict of statehood provided Israel with land, the results of the 1967 Six-Day War would allow Israeli political parties to seek electoral favour in the decades to come by promising ever greater expansion into occupied Arab territory and over the whole of old British-mandate Palestine – the very scenario which Churchill had so cunningly surmised thirty years earlier.

It is important to remember that while the lands conquered by Israel in 1967 included the rest of mandate Palestine, state authority in the West Bank and Gaza was previously administered by, respectively, Jordan and Egypt. King Hussein's soldiers were positioned along the walls of the Old City of Jerusalem because the non-Israeli part of Palestine had been annexed by the Hashemite monarchy in 1950. The division between Arab east and Israeli west Jerusalem ran along what was called the 'Green Line' – because this was supposedly the colour of the crayon in which the UN drew the armistice frontier in 1949.* In Jerusalem, the 'Green Line' disappeared after the Six-Day War, to be replaced by the 'Seam Line', which might, I suppose, persuade visitors that Jerusalem is forever stitched together, as the Israelis would have the world believe.

They wear their wounds well, the buildings of the old 'Green Line'. Forget the new hotels across the road, the state-of-the-art tramway that glistens down the highway; just take a look at the bullet holes on the walls to the left, the shell gashes in the preserved façade of what was once an Israeli army bunker and is now, thirty-four years later,

---

* Reporters and historians should be aware of such stories. The provenance of the 'Green Line' separating Greek and Turkish Cypriots after the Greek coup and Turkish invasion of the island of Cyprus in 1974 was allegedly the work of a British officer who also used a green pencil to mark the buffer zone. No sooner had yet another frontier emerged between east and west Beirut at the start of the 1975–90 Lebanese civil war, than this, too, became a 'Green Line' – named, we were told by journalists at the time, after the Cypriot version. Why green, the colour of life and fertility, should have been used to mark these infernal places – rather than the more appropriate red of blood and fire – remains a mystery.

Raphie Etgar's little art gallery. A hundred metres away was the Arab Legion. Just three hundred feet from here was the Jordanian frontier. Yes, this really is the 1967 'border' to which Palestinian 'president' Mahmoud Abbas insists the Israelis must retreat, the 'frontier' which Benjamin Netanyahu regards as too 'vulnerable' to return in any future Palestinian–Israeli peace treaty. Allow an Arab army back to the land over the road and Jerusalem is again divided, no longer the 'eternal and indivisible' Jewish capital of Jerusalem. Allow the Israelis to maintain their illegal annexation of this same land, and east Jerusalem can never be the 'capital' of Arab Palestine – whatever 'Palestine' might turn out to be. The quotation marks are essential in existential territory.

The art inside Raphie Etgar's Museum of the Seam is about war and peace, about Baghdad and 9/11, about suicide bombers, and a Charlie Chaplin factory of cogwheels of Islamic calligraphy. Raphie Etgar was a former tank commander, fought in two wars – in 1967 in Sinai, a year later in the bloody battle of Karameh of which, perhaps, the less said the better, and on Golan in 1973 – and 'saw death very close to my eyes and lost quite a few of my friends'.*

But hark to his thoughts on war and peace:

> The fact that our museum is located on the 'green line seam' is significant, no doubt – but it's more a conceptual 'seam' … In the exhibition, we deal with the 'clash of civilisations' – I would expect visitors to see this in the context of East and West.

The ex-tank commander is speaking to me in the autumn of 2011. He certainly bears no love for his prime minister, Benjamin Netanyahu, nor for the Palestinian president, Mahmoud Abbas.

'I was sitting in front of the television … Netanyahu was the best actor,' Etgar continued. 'He knows how to give his show and unless you know that he is always playing this game, you would be tempted to believe what he says. He is the best acrobat in the Middle East. Then

---

* Planning to avenge itself on Yasser Arafat's Fatah movement after more than thirty PLO raids into the newly occupied West Bank, the Israeli army attacked the Karameh Palestinian camp inside Jordan in 1968. But they found themselves fighting determined resistance not only from the guerrillas but the Jordanian army as well, losing thirty-three Israeli soldiers. The PLO lost 150 men and the Jordanians at least forty, but the fifteen-hour battle was a moral and propaganda victory for the Palestinians.

came the Palestinian president who didn't leave me an inch of hope that he would open the door and not repeat his accusations. Here we were with a chance, where people could sit together and try to find something new. But it was just a repetition of the same old game, Netanyahu with his gimmicks and his playful voice. I could believe in a Shakespeare play more than I could believe in these lectures.'

Outside the room, the traffic hums down the old 'Green Line'. Would Raphie Etgar allow the Palestinians to have a capital in east Jerusalem, just across the road? There is no hesitation:

> If I was in charge, I would not share Jerusalem. I think the
> Palestinians are touching a very, very sensitive point here. They
> should get 'Palestine' as a country, as a place for living. Give
> them the West Bank ... I don't think they would do less well if
> they ran the whole business from Ramallah.

Paris and London were international cities for the West, Etgar says. 'Jerusalem should be as international as all these cities in the world.' But it should not be the capital of Palestine. And suddenly I'm aware that we've slipped over a precipice, Etgar and I. After all, the Palestinians are only asking for the Arab east of Jerusalem. Etgar talks about sharing 'a sense of human rights' but Jerusalem has too many 'bleeding stones'. The Palestinians and Arabs might have to accept a Muslim-Arab 'quarter' in east Jerusalem.

I climb to the watchtower on the roof from where I can see Mount Scopus and the Mount of Olives. It might once have been a good idea to go back to the 'Green Line', Raphie Etgar said before I left him. 'But things were changed by time.' There it was: history, always lying like a rug over Jerusalem. I tried to close the old iron shutters on the stairwell. But they, too, had been rusted and congealed into the wall in the years since 1967.

So have UN Security Council resolutions. Between 1970 and the summer of 2018, the US protected its Israeli ally by vetoing forty-four UN Security Council resolutions critical of Israel.* But the most

---

* Russia used its UN Security Council veto eleven times in the first seven years of the Syrian war to protect its ally Bashar al-Assad, especially against proposed resolutions on the alleged use of chemical weapons by the regime in Damascus.

contentious of all UN agreements on the Middle East was Security
Council Resolution 242, which was passed on 22 November 1967, just
over five months after the end of the 5–10 June Six-Day War in which
Israel captured east Jerusalem, the West Bank, Gaza, Golan and the
Sinai and was supposed to provide the path to a permanent peace in
the Middle East.

It was based on two fundamental objectives: the 'withdrawal of
Israel [*sic*] armed forces from territories occupied in the recent conflict'
and respect for 'the sovereignty, territorial integrity and political independence of every state in the area and the right to live in peace within
secure and recognised boundaries'. 'Palestine', of course, was not a
state in 1967 – nor is it now – and Israeli withdrawal from the West
Bank meant at the time a retreat from Jordanian sovereign territory.
These objectives were to be founded on the principle of 'the inadmissibility of the acquisition of territory by war and the need to work for a
just and lasting peace in which every state in the area can live in security'. All well and good, you might say. The Israelis would not keep the
land they conquered because it did not belong to them, but everyone
could be secure and sovereign and independent behind their 'recognised' boundaries.

But like the devious Balfour Declaration half a century earlier, UN
Security Council Resolution 242 contained a grave and dangerous
grammatical problem. In Balfour, it was the absence of the word 'political' in reference to the 'civil and religious rights' of the 'non-Jewish
communities' (Arabs) in Palestine – and to their status of 'existing'
rather than inhabiting the land. In Security Council Resolution 242, it
was the absence of the definite article 'the' before the phrase 'territories occupied' in the war, that supplied the detonation for this later
time-bomb. This egregious omission allowed the rust to rot the locks
off this 'peace' initiative.

Did Israel have to withdraw from all the Arab land it had seized in
the 1967 conflict, or just from those parts which, perhaps, it wished to
leave for strategic or political reasons? There was no talk in the Security
Council of Jewish colonisation in these lands; which could not, we
must remember, be 'acquired' by war. There was not a word of Zionist
expansion, of Greater Israel. Surely, the resolution's defenders would
say, the principle of the 'inadmissibility of the acquisition of territory
by war' prevented any such misreading. But the absence of the word

'the' – as well as the inclusion of the word 'states' and, perhaps more seriously, the phrase 'recognised boundaries' – was to turn the UN resolution into another handbook for refugeedom; in this case, not only for the quarter of a million Palestinians who fled the West Bank during the 1967 war but for the entire population of the 22 per cent of Palestine that was left to the Arabs, in which they would henceforth endure decades of Israeli occupation.

In reality, Israel would give up Sinai in 1982 in accordance with 242, but kept east Jerusalem, which it would annex, and the West Bank indefinitely. It evacuated its colonies from Gaza in 2005, although Resolution 242 said nothing about imprisoning almost two million Palestinians civilians, which the Israelis did a year later after Palestinians voted for Hamas in fair elections. In 1967, no one dreamed that the Israeli–Arab conflict would still be in ferocious progress fifty years later. And as an *Independent* reader wrote to me in 2006, the Security Council clearly never intended the absence of a definite article to give Israel an excuse to colonise the West Bank and east Jerusalem.

Unfortunately, our reader was wrong. My own file on the ignominious results of 242 contains an elucidating paper by international lawyer John McHugo. He researched through the original UN discussions and sets out what pro-Israeli lawyers would claim for years to come: that the resolution unanimously called for withdrawal from Arab territories but that this did not mean 'all' Arab territories.* The story of Resolution 242 is made even more confusing by the French translation, which refers to an Israeli retreat 'des territoires occupés'; this can only mean 'from the'. The Spanish text also used the definite article.

But the British, apparently following some strong-arm tactics from the Americans, did not use 'the'. Lord Caradon, the UK's ambassador at the UN, insisted on putting in the phrase about the 'inadmissibility of the acquisition of territory by war' in order to stop the Israelis claiming that they could cherry-pick which lands to return. Britain accepted Jordan's rule over the West Bank – since the PLO were at the time still

---

* McHugo was a Visiting Fellow at the Scottish Centre for International Law at Edinburgh University in 2002 when he wrote 'Resolution 242: A legal reappraisal of the right-wing Israeli interpretation of the withdrawal phrase with reference to the conflict between Israel and the Palestinians', later published in the *International and Comparative Law Quarterly*, Vol. 51, Oct. 2002, pp. 851–881.

shunned as super-terrorists – but it did no good. Abba Eban, Israel's man on the East river, did his best to persuade Caradon to delete both 'the' and the bit about the 'inadmissibility of the acquisition of territory by war'. He won the first battle, but not the second. McHugo correctly states that 242 'was to be construed as a single, integral whole, that no part of the Resolution is to be considered in isolation from the others' and that 'a partial withdrawal would surely only be partial compliance with the principle'. This was a good argument for lawyers, but much less reassuring for Palestinians.

US diplomat George Ball was to recount how, when the Arabs negotiated over 242 in early November 1967, the US ambassador to the UN, Arthur Goldberg, told King Hussein of Jordan that America 'could guarantee that everything would be returned by Israel'. The Arabs distrusted Goldberg because he was known to be pro-Zionist, but the king was much comforted when US secretary of state Dean Rusk assured him that the US 'did not approve of Israeli retention of the West Bank'. King Hussein was further encouraged when he met President Johnson, who told him that Israeli withdrawal might take place in 'six months'. Goldberg further boosted his confidence. 'Don't worry. They're on board,' he said of the Israelis.

It's intriguing to note that several other nations at the UN were deeply troubled by the absence of 'the'. The Indian delegate, for example, pointed out that the resolution referred to 'all the territories – I repeat all the territories – occupied by Israel', while the Soviet Union stated that 'we understand the decision to mean the withdrawal of Israeli forces from all, and we repeat, all territories belonging to Arab states and seized by Israel'. Brazil expressed reservations about 'the clarity of the wording'. The Argentinians 'would have preferred a clearer text'.

In other words, the future tragedy was spotted at the time, but we did nothing. The Americans and the Israelis had stitched it up. They had not, after all, made any objection to the reference to security for 'every state in the area' – they did not suggest the wording should have read merely 'states in the area' which might not have included Israel. The Arabs were not happy, but foolishly relied on Caradon's assurance that 'all the' territories was what 242 really meant, even if it didn't say so. Israel still fought hard to avoid the 'inadmissibility' section, even when it had got rid of 'the'.

The reference to 'every state in the area' in paragraph 1(ii) of the resolution contained its own trap for the future. For once Jordan renounced all claims on the West Bank in 1988 and acknowledged the PLO as representatives of the 'State of Palestine', Resolution 242 held out no 'sovereignty, territorial integrity and political independence' for 'Palestine'. How could a non-existent state have 'security'? After the Oslo Accords, Western demands for Israel's security would be matched only by the requirement that the Palestinians should have a 'viable' state, never a secure one. It was therefore perhaps inevitable that Israel would later refer to the Arab lands which its army ruled not as 'occupied' but as 'disputed'.

Then there emerges the problem of the 'recognised boundaries' which, according to 242's para 1(ii) 'every state in the area' has the right to live behind. But Israel's boundaries did not represent the borders marked out in the original UN partition plan for Palestine of November 1947, which was anyway rejected at the time by the Arabs. This was General Assembly (and thus unbinding) Resolution 181, which Yasser Arafat would later claim provided Palestinians with sovereignty and national independence. And if the Arabs did not recognise this non-UN 'boundary', what if they were to demand that Israel's retreat continued not just under the terms of withdrawal from 'territories occupied' in the 1967 war but to the original borders of Israel proposed by the UN? Of course, the Arabs would not do so. But the question of 'recognised boundaries' opened the door to a dark room which no Western nation wished to enter, for Israel does not actually possess an eastern frontier.

Does Israel's border therefore lie between east and west Jerusalem? Certainly not for the Israelis after they illegally annexed all of Jerusalem; even less so after President Donald Trump acknowledged it as Israel's capital in 2018. So does Israel's eastern frontier lie along the old 'Green Line' or the 'seam' line or whatever notional name is given to the old 'boundary' between Israel and the Jordanian-controlled West Bank? Does it lie along the line of Israel's 'security barrier' that either follows the old 'Green Line' or moves far forward of it and eastwards into occupied Palestinian land? Or does it lie along the whole length of the Jordan river still further to the east, between 'Palestine' and present-day Jordan?

Amid such obfuscation was the opportunity born for Israel to consolidate its military advance into Arab territory with a land grab for the most prominent hilltops and the most fertile property in the West Bank for Jews, constructed on land legally owned for generations by Arabs, destroying any chance that Palestinian Arabs could have a 'viable' state, let alone a secure one. These 'settlements' would become the focus of the world's last colonial war, and their fate will determine the future of Israel. Will the Jews of what was Palestine annex the West Bank and turn its inhabitants into vote-less 'guest workers' and all of mandate Palestine into an Apartheid Israel?

There is a mantra that all sides will repeat: that the only other way to 'resolve' Israeli rule over the West Bank would be a 'transfer' of the Palestinians across the Jordan into the Hashemite kingdom on the other side of the river. In other words, expulsion. Ethnic cleansing. But this could not happen, we are told. The world would never permit such a crime against humanity to be repeated today. Really?

Keys must always be the symbol of the Palestinian Nakba, that terrible last turning of the lock of those front doors. Goodbye – only for a few days. Then the refugees would return – after a month at the most – and walk back into the houses many had owned for generations. Almost seventy years to the day since it was last used, I held one in my hand. Since mid-May 1948 until mid-June 2018, it had been secreted in a hovel in the slums of Sabra and Chatila in Beirut. The farmer who owned this key lived in the Palestine border village of Al-Khalisa in Galilee and locked up his home for the last time on 11 May 1948, when the Jewish Haganah militia refused the villagers' request to stay on their land.

In 2018, the village is the Israeli frontier town of Kiryat Shmona in the Galilee, and the few Al-Khalisa refugees in the squalid camps of Lebanon can still see their lands if they travel to the far south of their country and look across the border fence. Few camps could be more vile than Chatila, where Dr Mohamed Issa Khatib runs his shabby 'Museum of Memory' in a concrete shack adorned with ancient Palestinian farm scythes, photocopies of British and Ottoman land deeds, old 1940s radio sets and brass coffee pots – and keys.

Khatib was born in Lebanon just after his parents fled Al-Khalisa. The 'right of return' was forbidden to them and Israel's Absentee Property Law of 1950 meant they had no lands to which to return.

Mohamed Khatib worked until his retirement in 2008 as a doctor for the United Nations Relief and Works Agency, set up in 1949 to look after Palestinian refugees from the Nakba. It now cares for around five million Palestinians, many of them grandchildren of the 1947–48 refugees.

In Khatib's museum of wretchedness there is a faint odour of rust and old paper. The documents and brown passports are familiar to me. Over the years, I have read through so many similar land deeds and identity cards. Khatib blames the British for the Palestinian disaster and points to the keys. 'You did this,' he says. So what, I ask, did the Palestinians do wrong in all these years?

> Their mistake was to leave, to go out of Palestine. They should have stayed [in 1947 and 1948]. Our fathers and grandfathers should have stayed, even if they felt themselves in danger, they should have stayed on their land, even if they died.

How bitter a conclusion, I thought. Many Palestinians died because they did not leave; think Deir Yassin.

I leave him, with the feeling that history stretches out into the future as well as the past, and with the belief that he will never return and that his little museum is a symbol of regret rather than hope. I put the useless key back into its wooden box and close the lid. So much for Balfour.

8

The Israeli Empire

The Catholic Gaelic Irish, while actually occupying a good deal more land than had originally been allotted to them, lost none of their resentment because they regarded it all as theirs in the first place. And the Protestants, less numerous … felt insecure and more like a beleaguered garrison surrounded by enemies than masters in their own homes. Living daily among the Irish whose rights to land they had usurped, they fortified their farms and made security their watchword; security against whatever trouble might be brewing for them in the woods and bogs outside their windows.

Historian Robert Kee describes the seventeenth-century
English settlement of Ireland

When Israelis commemorated the Second Holocaust of the twentieth century in January 2010, I was in the Gulbenkian Library in Jerusalem, holding the records of the victims of the century's First Holocaust. It was a strange sensation. The Armenians were not participating in the official ceremonies to remember six million Jews murdered by the Nazis, perhaps because Israel refuses to acknowledge that Armenia's million and a half dead of 1915–23 were victims of a Turkish holocaust.

George Hintlian, historian and prominent member of the 2,000-strong Armenian community in Jerusalem, pointed to the posters advertising Armenia's 24 April commemorations. All but one had been defaced, torn from the ancient walls or spray-painted with graffiti in Hebrew. 'Maybe they don't like it that there was another genocide,' Hintlian says. 'These are things we can't explain.' More than seventy members of Hintlian's family were murdered in 1915, when German diplomats and army officers also witnessed the system of executions, rail-car deportations to cholera camps, and asphyxiation by smoke in caves – the world's first 'gas' chambers. One witness, the German vice-consul in Erzerum, Max von Scheubner-Richter, became one of Hitler's closest friends and advisers.

Hintlian and I walked together in the cold afternoon through the darkened interior of the St James monastery of Jerusalem. He opened a cabinet to reveal a hidden staircase up which priests would creep when local invaders passed through Jerusalem. In this dank, pious place, Ronald Henry Amherst Storrs, 'the first military governor of Jerusalem since Pontius Pilate' in his own inaccurate description, would often sit to ponder what he called 'the glory and the misery of a people'.

Up to 15,000 Armenians lived in Palestine until 1948, many of them survivors of the First Holocaust. But 10,000 of them shared the same fate as the Palestinian Arabs, fleeing or driven from their homes by the soldiers of the new Israeli state. Most Armenians lost their businesses in Haifa and Jaffa, many of them seeking refuge in Jerusalem. A few set out for Cyprus where they were dispossessed for a third time by the 1974 Turkish invasion. As a seventeen-year-old, Garbis Hintlian, George's father, survived the death march from his home in Talas in Cappadocia. 'We lost my uncle – my grandfather was axed to death in front of him.' After the 1918 Armistice, Garbis worked for the British, carrying files of evidence to the initial Constantinople trials of Turkish war criminals. 'Today', as Hintlian remarked hopelessly, 'six thousand Armenians are residents of Jerusalem and the West Bank – they cannot travel and they are counted as Palestinian Armenians. For Israeli bureaucracy, they are Palestinians.'

When the first Turkish pogrom of Armenians occurred between 1894 and 1896, European Christians responded with outrage; Theodor Herzl, the father of modern Zionism, however, offered to help the Ottoman sultan in return for Palestine and the establishment there of a Jewish state.* Herzl met the sultan in 1901 and tried to persuade the Armenians to end their rebellion. They did not trust him; nor did other European Jews. The historian Rachel Elboim-Dror described Herzl as 'a leader who subordinated humanitarian considerations and served the Turkish authorities for the sake of the ideal of the Jewish state'. This drama, she said, 'is just one illustration of the frequent clash between political goals and moral principles' in Israel, including the country's 'long-standing position of not recognising the Armenian genocide'. She calls these episodes 'tragic dilemmas'. But they are surely not 'dilemmas' at all. Historical, proven facts must take precedence over 'political goals'. Arab deniers of the Jewish Holocaust may have political reasons for their dishonesty, but their falsehoods are hardly 'tragic'. They are deeply immoral.

Hintlian and his compatriots were forgotten until after the 2008 Gaza war. 'For three decades, no documentary on the Armenian genocide could be shown on Israeli television because it would offend the Turks,' Hintlian said. But when the Turkish prime minister, Recep Tayyip Erdogan, denounced the war in Gaza, 'suddenly ... important Israelis demanded that a documentary be shown'. So the newspapers *Maariv* and *Yedioth Ahronoth* began to mention the Armenian genocide and George Hintlian turned up in person on Israeli television along-side Netanyahu's deputy foreign minister Danny Ayalon and then Knesset speaker Reuven Rivlin, who said that Israel should commemorate the Armenian genocide 'every year'. The Israeli press began to call the Armenian genocide a Shoah, the same word Israelis use for the Jewish Holocaust. As Hintlian put it with withering accuracy: 'We have been upgraded!' With the improvement of relations between Turkey and Israel in 2014, the Armenians were forgotten again. The Israeli president – the same Reuven Rivlin who four years earlier demanded that the anniversary of the Armenian genocide be observed every year – refused to use the term 'genocide' in any official statements.

---

* The Hamidian massacres, perpetrated under Sultan Abdul Hamid II, took the lives of up to 200,000 Armenians, 25,000 Assyrians and perhaps 100,000 Albanians in an orgy of mass murders, rapes and church-burning. These crimes against humanity, as we would describe them today, were intended to crush all Armenian political – and later military – resistance to the collapsing Ottoman Empire. In retrospect, they were also a dry-run for the Armenian genocide of 1915.

If a nation cannot acknowledge, for reasons of state, the history of a Middle Eastern people whose terrible historical experience was so close to their own, how can Israel admit the full truth of another Middle Eastern people's suffering and dispossession and despair brought about by the creation and continued existence of Israel itself? Censorship, propaganda, calumny and lies not only allowed Israel to bury the 1948–49 Palestinian Arab story, but portrayed its hundreds of thousands of victims as terrorists, murderers, neo-Nazis, anti-Semites and existential threats to the Israeli state itself.

And here we approach the nuclear centre of the Zionist project for Israel. A Jewish people who aspire to be 'a light among the nations' built their nation largely upon the land of another people. And they did so as liberal socialists, as a risen people whose history of persecution at least gave them a unique insight into the results of human suffering. And even if the war of independence that Israel fought was cruel but necessary, the country, as it matured, would surely blossom into the 'beacon of democracy' amid the wilderness of Arab dictatorships which its supporters still claim it to be.

Israelis themselves can sum up the degrading failure of their country to live up to these lofty principles in just a few paragraphs. Here is the response of Israeli-Irish writer and academic Ronit Lentin to the shocking 2018 Israeli Nationality Bill that caused uproar across the Arab world and Europe. The legislation, she wrote, was a victory for Benjamin Netanyahu's right-wing and religious coalition which now enshrined in law 'what Zionist colonialism has always been about:

> It was socialist liberal Zionism that colonised Palestine,
> discriminated against the Palestinian owners of the land,
> occupied Palestinian lands in 1948 and 1967, stole their lands
> and properties and declared them 'present absentees', enacted
> laws that grant racially based automatic citizenship to people
> with a Jewish mother but not to the Palestine-born owners of
> the land, conducted a permanent war against the Palestinians,
> enforced a military regime on the Palestinians [in Israel]*

---

* 'Present absentees', another of those word games to which the Middle East regularly gives birth, is the spectral expression adopted by Israeli officials for those Palestinians who remained within Israel during and after 1948.

between 1948 and 1966, started the settlement project in the West Bank, and illegally annexed Jerusalem and the [Syrian] Golan Heights.

Since the advent of the alt-right Israeli regime, the Gaza Strip has been under bombardment and siege, its people starved and deprived of livelihood, electricity and drinkable water; villages of Bedouin citizens have been repeatedly demolished; and extrajudicial executions of Palestinians by Israeli soldiers go mostly unpunished. And the list goes on: night raids, administrative detention, the detention and torture of children, etc. Meanwhile Israeli Jews hark back to an imaginary past 'democracy', live in a consumers' bubble and tell themselves they are the real victims, and that Israel has the right to defend its never-declared 'borders'.

Netanyahu's government, Lentin added, should be thanked 'for dropping the democratic pretence and finally admitting that Israel is a racial colony and an apartheid state'.*

You don't have to salute every sentence of Lentin's angry letter in order to understand her impatience.† Such fury is often generated when a seemingly endless and provable injustice is perpetrated over many years against an innocent people yet continues to be justified with ever more political success to a gullible Western audience. 'Palestine,' as Edward Said wrote:

> is a thankless cause, one in which if you truly serve you get nothing back but opprobrium, abuse and ostracism … Palestine is the cruellest, most difficult cause to uphold, not because it is unjust, but because it is just and yet dangerous to speak … How many friends avoid the subject? How many colleagues want none of Palestine's controversy? How many bien pensant

---

* Israel's defenders can point out that America, Canada and Australia were founded by racist European colonisers who dispossessed and confiscated land from the natives or reduced them to penury and violence. The problem is that Israel's colonisation of native Arab land continues apace today in the occupied West Bank.

† Despite internal prejudices towards its own immigrants, Israel cannot be described as a racial colony or an apartheid state for its Jewish citizens – only for Arabs.

liberals have time for Bosnia and Chechnya and Somalia and
Rwanda, South Africa, Nicaragua and Vietnam and human
rights everywhere on earth, but not for Palestine?

Writers, academics, journalists who have constantly argued the need
to support a crushed and occupied people have paid for their insolence
with their careers or reputations. Norman Finkelstein, the son of
Holocaust survivors, was famously refused entry to Israel – and infa-
mously refused tenure at DePaul University in Chicago – because of
his condemnation of Israel's assault on the Palestinians and his clinical
dissection of the work of one of Israel's persistent lobbyists. But the
threats and filth uttered against Amira Hass and Gideon Levy, two of
Israel's finest journalists who both work for *Haaretz* – not to forget Ilan
Pappe and the Israeli filmmaker Ram Loevy – prove that Israeli nationality no more protects those who dare to confront the state's
occupation of Arab land than their religion or their integrity.

To condemn Israel for its systematic, constant and deliberate abuse
of human rights was to be anti-Semitic, racist, pro-terrorist, Nazi, evil
and beyond conscience. The hatred for Australian Jewish journalist
Antony Loewenstein after his ground-breaking 2006 investigation of
Israel's overseas supporters, *My Israel Question*, was a carbon copy of
the scurrilous and defamatory remarks typed up by Dorothy
Thompson's detractors sixty years earlier.

But perhaps the most sinister element of the ever-growing extent of
the post-1967 Israeli land theft and colonisation was the state of
'normalcy' with which it came to be regarded in the West by those
who might otherwise have identified such grand larceny as an international crime. Perhaps this is because the pervasive use of the word
'settlement' gave colonisation a spurious legitimacy. There was also a
natural confusion after the 1967 war between the fact of Israeli 'occupation' and the concomitant act of colonisation. And if the creation of
Israel could be regarded as a civilisational event, why should its
people's continued expansion eastwards not be greeted with the same
exhilaration? The word 'settlement' – rather than 'colony' – became
part of the journalistic lexicon, and thus deformed the political reality
of what was taking place.

Within five years, Israel was laying firm claim to the West Bank,
prime minister Golda Meir's senior adviser insisting that the Jordan

river should become 'Israel's agreed border'; seven months later, Moshe Dayan was calling for the annexation of occupied Arab land and talking of the 'new horizons' that had opened for Israel since the war. Four days after proclaiming his respect for all holy places in Jerusalem in 1967, Israeli bulldozers demolished 700 years of Muslim history, ancient houses and Islamic shrines and the Sheikh Eid mosque that dated from the time of Saladin. So much for Ben Gurion's 1967 assertion, which I found on the wall of his Tel Aviv home, that 'we did not damage any single mosque'.

And then there was the vast eleventh-century Mamilla cemetery wherein were buried companions of the Prophet Mohamed only a few hundred metres to the west of Jerusalem's city walls, but in Israeli hands since 1948. Both before and after the 1967 war, the cemetery was swept away by Israeli bulldozers, leaving only an eighth of the site intact. It became a garden, a public lavatory and a car park. In years to come, it would be a prime parcel of Jerusalem real estate and was given to the Simon Wiesenthal Center for a 'Museum of Tolerance'.

I met Wiesenthal, one of the world's most renowned Jewish Holocaust survivors, in Vienna in the late 1980s, when he was campaigning for a memorial to the Roma people who were murdered in the same Nazi mass liquidations. He died in 2005; the Jerusalem centre that was founded in his name decided to build its $150 million museum of 'tolerance' on top of the historic Mamilla graveyard. It would be difficult to find a more inappropriate site for an institution supposedly promoting 'respect among Jews and people of all faiths'. But the Center advertised the project in 'Jerusalem's rejuvenated city centre' and added that the cemetery had been regarded as deconsecrated by Muslim religious authorities, a view not shared by the Al Aqsa association, the Sharia court and several relatives of the dead. And so a little more of the Palestinian Arab presence in the city was, quite literally, erased – in the name of 'tolerance'. Another 'created fact'.

The deletion of Palestinian history went hand in hand with Palestinian house demolition, annexation and Jewish colony construction and it continued, almost incredibly, with little resistance outside the Middle East. The David-and-Goliath framework in which the 1967 war was cast made it difficult for any Western nation to point the finger at an aggressive, expansionist Israel. It is instructive to note that when Dayan was objecting to the very existence of a Palestinian state in June 1973, the idea of such an entity was referred to in the *Guardian* as merely a 'sandwich state' since it would lie between the old Israeli 'Green Line' and the Jordan river. Two decades later, under the terms of the Oslo Accords, which envisaged the very Palestinian state which Dayan opposed, all discussion of Jewish 'settlements' was to be delayed until 'final status' talks, by which time a schedule of Israeli military withdrawals from the occupied Palestinian territories should have been completed. But Oslo, which was based on UN Security Council Resolution 242, was contaminated from the start when the withdrawals themselves were predictably delayed. And, most crucial of all, there was no mention in the interim agreement of an end to the expansion of Jewish colonisation, merely a prohibition of 'unilateral steps'.

Charting the vast spread of settlers' red roofs across the hilltops of the West Bank, all encircled by acres of barbed wire and walls, became not so much a 'story' for the hundreds of journalists based in the region, but a tired routine, a tale to be updated with each new 'settlement' announcement and subsequent protest – from the Palestinians whose land was taken from them and from the Palestinian Authority. And from the small Israeli activist and leftist groups who, long after Yitzhak Rabin's murder* and the death of Oslo, bravely fought to tell the truth of this unique form of aggression.

But the colonies grew exponentially and the feeble international complaints had no effect on the Israeli government; the larger the number of new settlers, the lower the story on the pages of the international press. The number of Jewish colonists living on Palestinian land rose from 80,000 at the time of the Oslo agreement to 220,000 ten years later. Article 49 of the International Committee of the Red Cross 1949 Geneva Conventions is quite specific: 'The Occupying Power shall not deport or transfer parts of its own civilian population into the territory it occupies.' Both the UN Security Council and General Assembly, the ICRC and the International Court of Justice agreed that Article 49 applied to Israeli-occupied territories. This, too, mattered not. In any case, the very word 'occupied' would soon come with a question mark attached. How, after all, could any territories be

---

* Rabin was assassinated in November 1995 by Yigal Amir, a right-wing extremist who opposed the 1993 signing of the peace accord.

regarded as 'occupied' if they had not previously belonged to a sovereign state? Moshe Dayan asked this question at the UN General Assembly in 1977. And so the epic story of the colonisation of the West Bank was to continue for the next four decades, its legality contingent upon definition.

The clichés were adopted almost as speedily as the Israelis had decided to build an immense fortress wall, firstly around Jerusalem, but then north and south of the city and as far as twelve miles deep into Palestinian territory, cutting and escarping its way over the landscape to embrace most of the Jewish colonies. The stated reason for this unprecedented act, begun in 2002, was the need to prevent further Palestinian suicide bombings during the second intifada uprising; and for years, journalists were to refer to this monstrous construction as a 'separation barrier'.

This was the BBC's favourite weasel expression, although correspondents preferred 'security barrier', 'separation fence', 'separation wall' and 'security fence'. It did deter suicide bombers, but it also gobbled up more Arab land. In places, it soared up to twenty-six feet, more than twice the height of the Berlin Wall. Ditches, barbed wire, patrol roads and reinforced concrete watchtowers completed this grim travesty of 'peace'. But as the wall grew to 440 miles in length, journalists clung to the language of 'normalcy'. A 'barrier', after all, is surely just a pole across a road, at most a police checkpoint, while a 'fence' is something we might find between gardens or neighbouring fields. So why should we be surprised when Italian prime minister Silvio Berlusconi, travelling through the massive obstruction outside Bethlehem in February 2010, said that he did not 'notice' it. But visitors to Jerusalem were awestruck by the wall's surpassing grey ugliness. Its immensity dwarfed the landscape of low hills and Palestinian villages and crudely humiliated the beauty of the original Ottoman walls, churches, mosques and synagogues.

Ultimately, the wall was found to have put nearly 15 per cent of West Bank land on the Israeli side and disrupted the lives of a third of the Palestinian population. It would, the UN discovered, entrap 274,000 Palestinians in tiny enclaves and cut off another 400,000 from their fields, jobs, schools and hospitals. Only 11 per cent of the structure would follow the old 'Green Line'. The Israeli response was to produce one figure only: 'the 6.5 million Israelis who will be better protected when the fence is finished'. But the UN believed that Palestinians caught by the wall 'will choose to move out'. So was that the real reason for the wall? Or did it have several purposes?

When in 2004 the Palestinians attempted to stop further construction of the wall by appealing to the International Court of Justice in the Hague, the Israelis simply rejected the court's decision: that they should cease all construction and dismantle those sections already built. The Palestinians, initially elated at its findings, thought that 'international opinion' would bring them victory, but it would not. Prime minister Ariel Sharon's spokesman said that the court's decision belonged to 'the garbage can of history'.

Israelis had long talked of creating 'facts on the ground' and George W. Bush seems to have mimicked this expression in a letter to Sharon by referring to 'new realities on the ground' – as if they had occurred by accident or by some freak geological event. The political and geographical freedom which this gave the Israelis could and would apply to all future land expropriations and the steady Judaisation of Jerusalem. Donald Trump's decision fourteen years later to recognise Jerusalem as the capital of Israel can therefore be seen as a logical outcome to the blessing which Bush gave to the colonisation of the West Bank.

Sharon's 2005 closure of Israel's nine illegal 'settlements' in Gaza was the first colonial withdrawal since it abandoned Sinai in 1982. His own friend and adviser, Dov Weisglass, famously described this as 'formaldehyde', a disturbing plan to withdraw from Gaza in order to consolidate its grip on the occupied territories of the West Bank. Sharon had pulled Israel's colonists out without any prior negotiation with the Palestinian Authority – and thus felt free to continue 'settlement' building elsewhere, again without any contact with the Palestinian leadership.

Sharon's announcement of 'disengagement' came at a significant moment, only two weeks after the unofficial Gaza Accord that had been warmly welcomed by US secretary of state Colin Powell. Far more dramatically, twenty-seven Israeli pilots had earlier published a letter to their commander, refusing to bomb any more civilian targets in the occupied territories. The *Independent*'s Jerusalem correspondent Donald Macintyre drew attention to a potential scandal over election funding that had threatened to touch Sharon's son Omri: did Israel's prime minister want to keep this at bay with a dramatic gesture? More likely, as columnist Jonathan Freedland wrote, Sharon knew Israel 'would have to uproot settlements and give up on Gaza, but in return it would be able to keep choice cuts of the West Bank and do so with the blessing of the United States ... Sharon saw what the Likud [party] rebels could not see: that by giving up Greatest Israel, they could win Greater Israel forever.'

'Area C' doesn't sound very ominous. A land of stone-sprinkled grey hills and soft green valleys, it was, by 2010, part of the wreckage of the equally wrecked Oslo Accords, accounting for 60 per cent of the Israeli-occupied West Bank that was eventually supposed to be handed over to its Palestinian inhabitants. But glance at the statistics and leaf through the pile of demolition orders lying on the table in front of Abed Kasab, head of the local council in the miserable village of Jiftlik, and it looked like ethnic cleansing via bureaucracy.

Perverse might be the word for the paperwork involved. Palestinian houses that cannot be permitted to stand, roofs that must be taken down, wells closed, sewage systems demolished; in one village I even saw a primitive electricity system in which Palestinians must sink their electrical poles cemented into concrete blocks standing on the surface of the dirt road. There are times, I realised, when madness must be regarded as deliberate.

I was driving around the West Bank's 'Area C' with the Israeli journalist Amira Hass, whose chronicle of Israel's colonial shame must one day become a textbook of modern journalism. Imagine her constant and suppressed indignation as you read the following words, for there were times when the evidence placed before us made us shake our heads in disbelief.

Let's start with the bureaucracy. 'Ro'i' signed a batch of demolition papers for Jiftlik in December 2009, all duly delivered, in Arabic and Hebrew, to Abed Kasab. There were twenty-one of them, all from 'The High Planning Council Monitoring [sic] Sub-Committee of the Civil Administration of the Area of Judea and Samaria', the occupied West Bank. And as Abed Kasab put it to us, that was the least of his problems. Palestinian requests to build houses were either delayed for years or refused, while houses built without permission were ruthlessly torn down.

The winter sun blazed through the door of Kasab's office and cigarette smoke drifted through the room as the angry men of Jiftlik
shouted their grievances. 'Buildings, new roads, reservoirs, we have
been waiting three years to get permits. We cannot get a permit for a
new health clinic. We are short of water for both human and agricultural use. Getting permission to rehabilitate the water system costs
70,000 Israeli shekels [about $20,000] – it costs more than the rehabili-
tation system itself.'

A drive along the wild roads of 'Area C', from the outskirts of
Jerusalem to the semi-humid basin of the Jordan valley, runs through
dark hills and stony valleys lined with ancient caves, until, further east,
lie the fields of the Palestinians and the Jewish colonists' palm groves
and the huts of Palestinian sheep farmers. This paradise is a double
illusion. One group of inhabitants, the Israelis, may remember their
history and live in paradise. The smaller group, the Palestinian Arabs,
are able to look across these wonderful lands and remember their past
– but they are in limbo.

Hass and I came across an even more outrageous example of this
apartheid-by-permit in the village of Zbeidat, where the European
Union's humanitarian aid division installed eighteen waste water
systems to prevent the hamlet's vile-smelling sewage running through
the gardens and across the main road into the fields. The system was
installed because the location lay inside 'Area B' – jointly administered
by the Palestinian Authority as well as the Israelis – where no planning
permission was required. Yet now the aid workers were told by the
Israelis that work 'must stop' on six of the eighteen shafts – a prelude
to their demolition – because part of the village stands in 'Area C'; even
though no one, neither Israelis nor Palestinians, knew the exact border-
line between 'B' and 'C'.

But in one way, this storm of paperwork is intended to obscure the
terrible reality of 'Area C'. Many Israeli activists as well as Western
NGOs suspect Israel intends to force the Palestinians here to leave their
homes. 'Area C' is the richest of the occupied Palestinian lands, with
cheese production and animal farms.

Jewish scholars in both Israel and America continued to tell the truth
about the history and the purpose of the occupation of Arab land.
Scholar Henry Siegman believes that the post-1967 Jewish colonies
were designed to make a return to the old border impossible. He

concludes that 'the issue dividing Israeli governments has not been the presence of settlements in the West Bank. Shimon Peres of the Labour Party played a key role in launching the settlement enterprise. Their differences have been over what to do with the Palestinians whose lands were being confiscated.'

Subsequent academic studies, Siegman wrote, 'reveal the massive scale of Israel's theft of Palestinian lands and the involvement of every part of Israeli society in advancing the settlement enterprise in clear and deliberate violation not only of international law but of Israel's own laws.'* Reviewing a book on the 'architecture of occupation',† Yonatan Mendel writes that 'the Israeli political leadership, settlers, judges, army officers, security men – even architects – have a part in the shaping of houses, roads, windows, cladding and angles, to facilitate the complex mission of occupying the Palestinian territories'. Mendel's explanation is breathtaking in both its simplicity and its honesty:

A single settlement only marked the beginning of a 'securing' project: it was not enough in itself. Logic required that more settlements be built around it. Then, in order to secure the newly established blocks of settlements, a secure network of roads was needed to run between them, but in order to secure the roads, more settlements needed to be constructed along them ... This evolving master-plan, which begins with placing civilians in the front line and ends with layer upon layer of security to secure security, ignores the crucial fact that the settlers and settlements were the central cause of security threats and a major incitement to Palestinians. In other words, the security imperative is one of the greatest threats to Israel's security.

And so each Palestinian attempt to end the colonisation of Arab land was met by Israeli contempt. When the Palestinian 'prime minister'

---

* Security, according to Siegman, was the reason offered by Israel to justify the founding of the settlements. 'But the overwhelming majority of them actually created new security problems, if only because vast military and intelligence resources had to be diverted to their defence. The settlements have also enraged the Palestinians, whose land has been stolen to make room for them – this too has done nothing to increase Israel's security.'

† Eyal Weizman's *Hollow Land: Israel's Architecture of Occupation* (London: Verso, 2007).

Salam Fayyad appealed to the EU not to upgrade its liaison with Israel until it ended its settlement construction, Israel accused him of trying to undermine the country's relations with the EU – and withheld part of the Palestinian Authority's $75 million monthly tax revenue. When veterans of the anti-apartheid struggle in South Africa visited the West Bank in 2008 and stated that the segregation endured by Palestinians was in some way worse than the experience of the black majority under white rule, they were accused of trying to 'delegitimise' Israel.

In east Jerusalem, there stood for more than seventy years an architecturally uninspiring edifice known as Shepherd Hotel. Constructed in the 1930s by the former grand mufti of Jerusalem, Haj Amin al-Husseini, it later passed into the hands of the Jordanian government after the British withdrawal. But following the 1967 war and Israel's annexation of east Jerusalem, the hotel fell under the definition of 'absentee property' and in the 1980s was bought by casino billionaire and Zionist Irving Moskowitz, a devotee of Jewish colonial settlement. He decided to bulldoze the site for twenty Jewish apartments in this most Muslim district of east Jerusalem and the approval of his plans in 2009 brought forth much apoplexy from the Obama administration.

For the Americans, Benjamin Netanyahu's enthusiasm for the project showed his contempt for Obama's demands that he 'freeze' settlements. For Zionists, however, the hotel's original owner evoked far more powerful emotions. Haj Amin al-Husseini was initially promoted by the British mandate authorities in Palestine but later sought sanctuary in Nazi Berlin and broadcast anti-Jewish tirades over German state radio. He was an ambitious nationalist whose wicked attempts to persuade Hitler to send Jews to the 'East' were to blight his people for a generation. But he neither instigated the Jewish Holocaust nor even provoked it, and his attempts to raise an Arab 'legion' to fight for Hitler had by May 1942 collected a meagre 130 volunteers.*

---

* In total – and Haj Amin was not involved in their recruitment – an estimated 6,300 Arabs joined German military organisations during the war, 1,300 of them from Palestine, Syria and Iraq. However, 9,000 Palestinian Arabs fought for the British army and hundreds of thousands of their fellow Arabs from north Africa served in the French army, both in 1939–40 and after 1942; by 1944, almost a quarter of a million Muslims from the Maghreb were in the Free French forces and up to 110,000 were killed, wounded or listed as missing in the Second World War.

No matter. The moment Obama's newly installed secretary of state Hillary Clinton objected to this latest decision to place more Jewish settlers inside the east Jerusalem suburb of Sheikh Jarrar, Netanyahu's controversial foreign minister Avigdor Lieberman told Israeli embassies to circulate an infamous photograph of the 1941 meeting between Haj Amin and Hitler. The picture showed Haj Amin sitting in an armchair in the German chancellery and looking at an animated Hitler, who is gesticulating with his hands and in mid-speech. There are several versions of the scene, but there is no doubt about the meeting. Haj Amin was seeking German assistance for 'the suppression of the Jewish homeland' in Palestine.

For Israel, the picture is of more than historical importance. It has used Haj Amin's self-exile in wartime Germany to contaminate the Palestinian Arabs today as an anti-Semitic and pro-Nazi people, a totally unjustified accusation that would be repeated again by Lieberman, Netanyahu and other imaginative extremists of the Israeli right. The Israeli foreign ministry stated that Lieberman wanted the photograph disseminated 'so that the facts are known' – as if the grand mufti's frolicking with Nazi leaders had hitherto been kept secret. The grand mufti's relationship with the Nazis more than seventy years earlier had become a marketing card for Jewish colonial expansion on Arab land. When the Shepherd Hotel was finally bulldozed in 2011, Jewish settlers compared it to the destruction of the homes of Hitler and Himmler.

That Palestinians were themselves Nazis was a theme that occurred regularly in the Israeli narrative of the Middle East conflict. When the Israeli army was approaching Beirut in 1982, prime minister Menachem Begin wrote a letter to President Ronald Reagan in which he fantasised that he was marching on 'Berlin' to liquidate 'Hitler'. And if all Palestinians were Nazis – and if Arafat was Hitler – what were their lives worth? It was Lieberman who said after thirty Palestinian protesters had been shot dead in April 2018 that 'there are no innocent people in the Gaza Strip'.

And if the Palestinians were all guilty, if they had been led by 'Hitler', then what was their property worth, their land, their heritage, their legal entitlement as a people? The legacy of Hitler's Germany and the grand mufti's support for the persecution of the Jews of Europe had become not just a reason for disinheriting the Palestinians but of making them collectively 'guilty' of Haj Amin's turpitude – in the same way that Israel regarded the two million inhabitants of the Gaza Strip as sharing the same guilt as Hamas.

In this interpretation of Jewish suffering, historians on the fringe of Holocaust research embroidered a new tale in which Haj Amin and the Palestinians became more culpable of the greatest war crime of the twentieth century than Hitler himself. A book by Barry Rubin and Wolfgang Schwanitz published in 2014 claimed that without the Jew-hating grand mufti the greatest crime against humanity in generations would not have taken place. How could the Palestinians therefore be trusted with a state when they and their fellow Arabs, to use the words of Rubin and Schwanitz, 'demonstrated how the same radical vision that had once found the Nazis to be congenial, right-thinking allies, had such a powerful, long-lived effect in shaping the contemporary Middle East'? This, the authors asserted, was 'the terrible secret of modern Middle East history'.

It is not difficult to dredge up racist drivel by the bucket-load from Palestinian and other Arab leaders, which anyone living in the Arab world must always fight. And Arabs point out, correctly, that Israeli politicians have variously called Palestinians 'cockroaches in a glass jar', 'ants', 'serpents' and 'crocodiles'. But the Rubin–Schwanitz thesis went much further. Much of the material to support their theory came from Fritz Grobba, a Muslim-Arab affairs officer in the Nazi foreign ministry who was a former German envoy to Kabul, Baghdad and Riyadh, and from the observation that Haj Amin and his colleagues were the only Nazi allies (excluding fascist movements) who gave their support to the 'genocide plan'.*

---

* The authors recorded some fatuous conversations between the Palestinian leader and Nazi officers, the former favourably comparing Islam to Nazism and the latter explaining their admiration for the religion, even though both sides knew this was ridiculous. Having established that these two views had little in common, the authors then made an astonishing leap of faith by recording Hitler's suicide – and adding that 'the Third Reich's Arab and Islamist allies were just getting started in conducting what would become the longest war of all'. This idea lies at the centre of the whole 'Islamofascist' narrative – see the later work of Christopher Hitchens, Norman Podhoretz and the speeches of George W. Bush – in which Nazism still exists in Arab anti-Semitism, and in which the mufti was, in the words of American historian Sean McMeekin, 'a pioneer in race murder' for inciting Arab mobs to lynch Jews in Jerusalem in the 1920s. McMeekin quoted Hitler as telling Haj Amin that he would annihilate 'the Jews living under British protection in Arab lands', a sentiment which the Palestinian heard 'with an air of gratification'. But the source, again, is Grobba. And the

The grand mufti was amoral and racist, but dumping the Holocaust on this wretched figure is an insult to history as well as to the six million victims of a devilish regime. But it provided the means to denigrate the entire Palestinian people when the real criminals were neither Muslim nor Arab but Europeans.

Outside Israel's contempt for the Palestinians, this grubby story might have consumed little more than academic research. But Netanyahu gave Israel's own imprimatur to the claim that Haj Amin had planted the idea of Jewish extermination in Hitler's mind. In a speech to the World Zionist Congress in Jerusalem in 2015, he described the meeting between the grand mufti and Hitler thus:

> Hitler didn't want to exterminate the Jews at the time, he
> wanted to expel the Jews. And Haj-Amin al-Husseini went to
> Hitler and said, 'If you expel them, they'll all come here [to
> Palestine]'. 'So what should I do with them?' he [Hitler] asked.
> He [Haj Amin] said: 'Burn them'.

But there is no evidence that such a dialogue ever took place. Netanyahu was condemned by Israeli scholars for both his 'fake' history and his shocking absolution of Hitler, an argument given added force when Chancellor Angela Merkel's spokesman replied that 'responsibility for this crime against humanity is German and very much our own'.

But the connection between Palestinian 'responsibility' for the Holocaust and the colonisation of Arab land had been established. After the grand mufti's behaviour in the Second World War, the act of Jewish 'settlement' could be regarded as an appropriate punishment for those who tried to destroy their race. And the Palestinians, whose own land had been lost, erased or occupied by the Israelis in 1948 and 1967, were to be cast as the potential destroyers of the Jewish people. Whether it was the bias of columnists syndicated to small town American newspapers or the hateful expressions of Western journalists who vilified the Palestinians and their leadership, my own files contain

---

problem is obvious. If we believe this account, how much more of the Nazi version of history are we supposed to trust? And if they lied so much – which the Nazis did – how come we must assume their honesty in recording Haj Amin's actions and words?

hundreds of articles that – had the victims of their attacks been Jews rather than largely Muslim Arabs – would have swiftly provoked accusations of anti-Semitism.*

It is as depressing as it is wearying to thumb through the newspaper clippings of the deliberate, unstoppable expansion and permanence of Israeli colonisation of the Palestinian West Bank. Each new housing project built on 'disputed' Arab land and then acclaimed by Israel's colonists and political leaders as an 'indisputable' part of Israel. 'Disputed' land became undisputed once the Israelis seized it.

Palestinian anger was mocked by the fact, evident to any of us visiting the settlements, that the bulldozers clearing the land, the trucks bringing the cement and the drills digging the foundations of these colonies were usually themselves Palestinians. More than 25,000 Palestinians were in 2010 engaged in building houses for Israelis on the lands of their own Arab people. For salaries of up to $1,300 a month, this army of Palestinian builders was helping to create the very Jewish colonies which would prevent the creation of their own 'viable' state. It was a sign of desperation when Palestinian lawyer Diana Buttu, confronted by the end of a settlement 'freeze' that never really existed, suggested that the US should fund Israeli settlers to leave their colonies. Blanket US support for Israel could be 'used for more productive purposes,' Buttu advised, coining yet another word in the tragic history of 'Palestine': 'de-occupation'. But there is a vital difference between 'de-occupation' and a mere delay in colonial expansion in return for direct talks between Mahmoud Abbas and Benjamin Netanyahu. In fact, in October 2010 the latter proposed yet another 'freeze' on settlements in return for Palestinian recognition of Israel as 'the nation state of the Jewish people'.

But the Palestinians had already recognised 'the State of Israel' when they originally embarked on talks for a 'two-state solution', and Arafat

---

* An article by columnist and Fox News commentator Cal Thomas in the *Des Moines Register*, claims in 2002 that the Israeli military had discovered documents from Arafat's compound in Ramallah which proved 'the Palestinian leader's direct involvement in the murder of Israeli civilians'. Thomas says these included the cost of 'martyr' posters and a requisition order for bullets. 'Arafat's "bookkeeping",' he wrote, 'is reminiscent of the way the Nazis kept meticulous records while they systematically murdered Jews ... His is the nest of snakes that the Israeli military is trying to destroy.'

had once spoken of Israel as 'a Jewish state'. This Israeli demand was temporarily forgotten when Obama agreed to what could only be described as a bribe. In return for yet another 'freeze', he approved the transfer of twenty F-35 Lightning fighter jets to Israel at a cost of $3 billion to the US taxpayer. This was not the American-funded 'de-colonisation' which Buttu had imagined, but a far greater US financial contribution to Israel's military power as collateral for a mere gesture – a temporary lull in stealing Arab land – which might induce Abbas and his Palestinian Authority officials to resume talks with the Israelis. But for these negotiations, Abbas insisted, there must be a total halt to the Jewish colonisation of the West Bank. Now it was his turn to seek statehood for 'Palestine' at the UN General Assembly.

In September 2011, Abbas submitted an application for the admission of Palestine to full membership of the UN. But Obama, as expected, had already turned it down. His own melancholic response was to say that 'peace will not come through statements and resolutions at the United Nations … it is the Israelis and the Palestinians – not us – who must reach agreement … on borders, on security, on refugees and Jerusalem.' Obama only spoke of Israeli suffering. And by treating Israelis and Palestinians as equals, you would think, as Hanan Ashrawi stingingly observed in *Haaretz*, 'it was the Palestinians who occupy Israel'.

The Arab awakening in Tunisia, Egypt and Libya was added to the list of reasons why land could not be given back to its Palestinian owners. 'We can't know who will end up with any piece of territory we give up,' Netanyahu said. 'This is such a delicate moment,' preached Tom Friedman in the *New York Times*, agreeing with Netanyahu's analysis.

But not 'delicate' enough to stop the unstoppable: another 300 houses for the West Bank Jewish settlement of Shilo in February 2012, along with retroactive permission for 200 already built 'illegally'; and in June, 851 more on Palestinian land, a plan which, as the US State Department said, 'contradicts Israeli commitments and obligations'.

Jewish settlers were now regularly attacking Palestinians, their homes, property and mosques. Palestinian attacks, including the murder of Jewish settlers, would now be 'balanced' with mob violence by armed men from West Bank colonies. Arab property was attacked by settlers angry at Abbas' demand for statehood and often left the words 'price tag' in Hebrew on the walls of homes and damaged mosques; it was another euphemistic phrase to add to the vocabulary of occupation. These attacks were carried out against Palestinians inside Israel as well as the West Bank, against Christian Arabs as well as Muslims. 'Jesus is the son of a whore', 'Death to Christianity' and 'Mohamed is a pig' were scarcely original, but they certainly constituted hate crime. Olive trees were destroyed by the hundred. Israeli and UN human rights groups calculated that there were 167 violent attacks in 2009, 312 in 2010 and 411 in 2011.

Netanyahu, who had done so much to encourage the settler movement, realised that the creature he had nurtured could bite back. The burning of a mosque in the Israeli Galilee village of Touba Zangaria in October 2011 was, according to the prime minister, 'unworthy of the state of Israel'. When Jewish settlers, hearing that several 'outposts' were to be demolished, stormed an Israeli army base near the West Bank town of Qalqilya, Netanyahu found their behaviour 'intolerable', but described those responsible not as 'terrorists' but as 'anarchists'. The destruction of another 'outpost' by Israeli troops in December was followed by the burning of another mosque near Ramallah. The 'anarchists' need not have worried. In October 2012, the Washington-based Foundation for Middle East Peace was reporting that more Jewish settlements had been built in the nineteen years since the 1993 Oslo Accords than were constructed since 1967. A year later, Netanyahu would authorise another 1,700 Jewish homes in the West Bank and east Jerusalem. Already, Obama was using another phrase: 'Israeli settlement activity'.

The record of Israeli property theft and national dishonour was to continue unabated. And the colonisation of another people's lands was treated with the same fear, obfuscation and subterfuge by presidents, prime ministers, ambassadors and, most cringingly of all, by journalists. If reasons of state could dominate the language of diplomacy, if lobby groups and elections could emasculate the language of American presidents, was it necessary for journalists and 'commentators' to acquiesce in this illegal undertaking by subverting their language and using the most infantile of clichés to obscure the truth of the crime?

This chapter on the subjugation of the Palestinians has been littered with the language of circumlocution. Many of the actual words or expressions have been positive rather than negative, even uplifting.

Settlements, new horizons, facts on the ground, new realities, enterprise, neighbourhoods, residents, words intended to fit comfortably into a world that would otherwise be disconcerting to our moral sensitivities. Then we have the neutrality of non-violent language, which must protect us from the reality of dispossession. Security, barrier, fence, outposts, disengagement, freeze, moratorium, time out. Yet all this can be portrayed as part of a continuum of hope rather than distress. Our journey through this vernacular is guarded by the most familiar terms of the Israeli–Palestinian conflict. Peace process. Road map.

The moment we stray from this linguistic highway, we have to negotiate a more troubled path. Disputed territory, unauthorised outposts, unilateral action, problematic, negative signals, price tags, anarchists, displacement, dislocation. And here we run into even more serious problems. Occupation, demolition, thinning out, terrorists. Or the word we must repeat more frequently than any other in order to justify its defeat, by any means: terror.

Euphemism has a more ominous effect when it is intended to obscure the disinclination of one group of people to have their land taken from them by another group of people. Emotionally, we are distanced from events by this dictionary of understatement and belittlement and avoidance. This is not fake news. It is a fake response to news, a method of ignoring the subjugation of a people which anywhere else in the world would produce an international outcry. It can be encapsulated in a single question. Why use all this circumlocution unless there is something to hide?

There were times, in the post-Oslo years, when I would search for hope amid the wreckage of Israel's liberals. Like Yeshayahu Leibowitz and Israel Shahak, Uri Avnery was always one of my Middle East heroes. It was somehow fitting that first news of his plight – a massive heart attack in late August 2018 – should reach me via one of Israel's staunchest enemies, the Lebanese Druze leader Walid Jumblatt expressing his sympathy. Avnery, ninety-four, was an Israeli political philosopher and in Jumblatt's words, 'an indispensable mind to understand the history of fascism, a major destructive element of the twentieth century'. Avnery, he added, also understood 'the history of Zionism, another despicable apartheid theory that is an offshoot of fascism'.

In fact, Avnery was himself a Zionist, or at least a believer in a left-wing, courageous but humble 'light among the nations' Israel, the kind many of us would like to believe in. 'The misfortune of being an incorrigible optimist,' is how he described his predicament to me. After he played chess with Arafat in Beirut in 1982, Israeli ministers said he should be tried for treason.

I think Avnery was proud of that. His curmudgeonly, brave personality could embrace the occasional political martyrdom, something which modern socialists are now almost all too frightened to do. He had staked his reputation on the integrity and persistence of Palestinian demands. 'When I met Arafat in 1982, the terms were all there,' he told me in 2012. 'The Palestinian minimum and maximum terms are the same: a Palestinian state next to Israel, comprising the West Bank, Gaza and East Jerusalem as a capital, small exchanges of land and a symbolic solution to the refugee problem. But this lies on the table like a wilted flower.'

Avnery lived in a book-crammed room close to the sea in a modest, quiet street. He often pondered the demise of the Israeli 'Left' – they were 'hibernating', he said after Ehud Barak, the Labour prime minister, had come back from the Camp David talks in 2000 as the self-proclaimed leader of the 'peace camp' 'and told us we have no partner for peace. This was a death blow. It was not Netanyahu who said this, but the leader of the Labour party.'

Badly wounded as a soldier in the 1948 war, Avnery feared nationalism. Wherein lies its power? he asked less than five years before his death. 'It seems that the human being needs a sense of belonging, belonging to a certain culture, tradition, historic memories (real or invented), homeland, language.' But he foresaw a future in which 'Israel, the nation-state of the Israeli people, closely aligned with the nation-state of the Palestinian people, will be a member of a regional Union that will include the Arab states and hopefully Turkey and Iran, as a proud member of the United States of the World.'

But less than six months before his death, Avnery asked how Israel would 'survive in the next decades as a colonial power, surrounded by Arab and Muslim states which may one day unite against it? How is Israel to remain master of the West Bank and the Gaza Strip, populated by the Palestinian people, not to mention East Jerusalem and the shrines holy to a billion and a half Muslims throughout the world?' In a note to my editor just after I heard from Jumblatt of Avnery's heart attack, I wrote that 'his is a light which may be about to go out at a dangerous moment in Israeli history'. He died on 20 August 2018.

And not without reason. For in Avnery's last years, the Jewish colonisation project in the Palestinian West Bank no longer represented merely an economic enterprise or the fulfilment of a messianic promise. It was now to become a form of collective punishment. When 'Palestine' was finally given non-member observer status by the United Nations General Assembly in December 2012, the Israeli government said that 3,000 more Jewish homes would be constructed in the West Bank – and stated quite specifically that this was in response to the UN vote.

John Kerry had warned Israel not to destroy the prospect of a Palestinian state, a prospect that even the meekest of diplomats had already abandoned. 'If the choice is one state, Israel can either be Jewish or democratic,' Kerry pontificated. 'It cannot be both, and it won't ever really be at peace.' But why should Netanyahu care, when Donald Trump was ominously tweeting that 'we cannot let Israel be treated with such total disdain and disrespect. Stay strong Israel, 20 January is fast approaching!' The Israeli prime minister fawningly thanked the US president-elect for his 'clear-cut support for Israel'.

After prevaricating for years over these acts of colonisation, Obama crowned his final days in office by at last declining to use a UN veto that would have spared Israel international condemnation after yet further settlement construction. Israel's latest act of colonisation was described in the UN resolution as a 'flagrant violation of international law'. But Obama's refusal to stand by Israel after Trump's electoral triumph looked more like an act of presidential petulance.

If only Obama and his secretary of state had stood up to Israel earlier in his presidency and in harsher language, they might have had some effect. Journalists like Alexandra Schwartzbrod, from the French daily *Libération*, spotted the reason why Obama delayed. 'The colonisation of the West Bank is a poison which is slowly but surely killing all hope of peace between Israelis and Palestinians,' she wrote in the autumn of 2016. But if Obama withheld his UN veto, he would delay until after the November elections to avoid damaging Hillary Clinton's presidential chances. Which is exactly what he did.

There was some evidence that Israelis were themselves ready to confront the dangers. When the Israeli director Shimon Dotan showed his new film on Jewish settlers, *Les Colons*, at the international Tel Aviv film festival in May 2016, he was politely interviewed by the right-wing press; his aim, he said, 'was to tell the story in the clearest possible manner of how we came to the hopeless situation that we are in today'. The film proved that colonisation was not the act of a minority of Jews preparing for the return of the Messiah; it was created by the Israeli state itself. According to recent studies, Israel had invested a 'Pharaonic budget' of at least 44 billion euros in colonial development in the half-century that followed the 1967 Six-Day War. Trump's arrival in the White House deleted such historical memory.

What characterised this extraordinary and largely meaningless debate between the Israeli and US governments was the singular lack of compassion towards the principal victims of Jewish colonisation. While Israel, save for a very occasional high court order to desist, could ignore the Palestinians whose lands were being stolen, the Americans never expressed their own sorrow for the heartbreak of those Arabs whose property was being 'confiscated'. The continuation of Israeli colony construction was repeatedly criticised or condemned by Washington as 'unhelpful' to the 'peace process' or sometimes 'illegal', but even Kerry could only express his abhorrence at these international acts of larceny by emphasising the danger they posed to the 'democracy' of Israel. In the eyes of the US administration, Israel's moral self-injury took precedence over the real wounds caused to the Arabs by America's supposedly 'democratic' ally.

In adopting this attitude, the US was abiding by the contention of Israel's own right-wing governments: that the Palestinians were unworthy of the equality which human rights laws should bestow upon them and should come to heel quickly if they did not wish their Israeli occupiers to take even more of their land. Palestinians alone were responsible for 'terror'. Any suggestion that Palestinian pain might be as devastating as Israel's suffering would bring forth wholesale condemnation of the occupied people.

The individual personal anguish of Palestinians could thus not be compared to the purgatory that the Jewish people had endured. And if numbers alone could cancel the Armenians' right to regard themselves as victims of genocide – since a million and a half dead in 1915 does not come close to six million between 1939 and 1945 – what chance did the Palestinians have of claiming the world's sympathy?

It's like a silver wedding. Let's dig up that old tale of a quarter century ago, when I watched Israel take the Palestinian Khatib family's land. We filmed the bulldozers closing in on the garden wall of the house of Mohamed and Saida Khatib and their son Sulieman amid their little orchard of olives, grapes, figs, apricots and almonds, beside Saida's old chicken coop. 'It's mine – it was my father's and my father's father's,' old Mohamed told me then. His thirty-five-year-old schoolteacher son was going to the Israeli court to prevent this act of theft, he said. The family had refused compensation. The land belonged to them.

As the years passed and the expanding Jewish colony of Psgat Zeev moved down the valley below the Arab village of Hizme, I preferred not to return to the building site that surrounded the Palestinian family's home and garden.

We had done our best. Journalism is a transitory profession. I had wars to cover, and the Khatibs were not the only Palestinians to lose their property to Israel's colonisation. A good excuse, that; the more normal a crime, the less you need to report it. Besides, other wars turned the spotlight away from the Palestinian tragedy.

But on the twenty-fifth anniversary of Oslo, and that old film we made, I was back in Jerusalem and I could no longer ignore the track down to the house. So in September 2018, I took the old road to Hizme village once again, a broader highway now, a big Israeli checkpoint on the corner and cut off from the Jewish settlement of Psgat Zeev by that ghastly old colossus, the Wall. Hizme was the Khatib family village, where I suspected the family must have gone after their home was taken from them. And there I found Sulieman's brother Ahmed and he phoned Sulieman who had not, as I feared, emigrated to Europe or America, but who now lived in a crowded apartment with his wife and five children scarcely two miles away. Sixty now and a trifle broader but with the same ponderous accent in English, Sulieman was a sadder man today. Though not without a vain hope that the family's legal case against the Israelis might be reopened. Had his family not expressed their willingness to stay within the Jewish settlement? Had they not been told that the land was needed for roads rather than settlers' homes? The family lawyers had failed them, Sulieman said. But the Khatibs had never accepted compensation. 'Compensation means you sold your land to them – and (then) you give them the right to have it.'

Mohamed and Saida were now dead, buried in Hizme village. Mohamed died two years ago, Saida in 2002. 'They didn't forget the land,' Sulieman says.

On a bright, hot, sparkling morning, Sulieman and I travelled back to the site of his home. We stopped on the old track to the house where now some large boulders were placed across the earth. Sulieman gingerly walked between them and down a smart, paved road between villas with lawns and trees and red roofs and parking places for residents. No one noticed Sulieman and he walked with increasing confidence between the settlers' houses. 'This is the first time I've come here since this was built,' Sulieman says, looking over a low wall, down towards what was his family's property. 'It's a strange feeling. I can't imagine what was here and what is here now.'

I used to think that dispossession and courage are twins in the mind of a refugee. They are not. Dispossession is the end; courage can be as pathetic as it is irrelevant. 'Now the settlers are living luxuriously on the ruins of other people,' Sulieman says. 'They don't know [our story] and they don't know ... what it was before. It's a bad history. And when the Israelis demolished our house ... they should have taken into account our feelings, our humanity.'

I ask Sulieman to identify the country he is looking at now when he stares at the site of his family house. 'It's Palestine – but with Israeli buildings,' he replies. 'It's the land of Hizme and Beit Hanina village, all these houses you see. I consider myself living abroad, but in the same district ... Sometimes, I think I can do nothing – because ... Israel was established on the land of others, not just on our individual land. And it's not easy to get it back from a state or a government like this. They are still expanding on other lands.'

Oslo hangs over us like a shadow. As long as there is occupation, there will be no peace. No, Sulieman will not leave 'Palestine' because it is his 'homeland'. But could Sulieman have believed, when I met him and his parents twenty-five years ago, what would happen? 'I didn't imagine it. And after this long time, after the wall and the settlements, you can't even notice that this was once your land.'

But it is Chaim Silberstein's land. He insists on showing me Jacob's stone. It lies in Beit El – the 'House of God' – which is the name of the colony of almost 7,000 Jews just outside Ramallah. Right here was where the ancient Jewish patriarch lay down on his stone, so it is written, and dreamed of the ladder to heaven upon which angels ascended and descended. The twenty-fifth anniversary of Oslo was a strange anniversary upon which to remember all those winged creatures plodding up and down. But I have to admit that God's message to Jacob all those thousands of years ago was a bit less prosaic and certainly more long term.

So much for Oslo, then, and all those withdrawal agreements and the Palestinian state-that-isn't, although, not far from a thousand-year-old wormwood tree, Chaim becomes lyrical about the modern-day descendants of Jacob and the Americans who are trying to make God's dream come true. It's odd to hear the name of Trump up here, within the walls of Beit El and guarded by the guns of Israel's settlers.

It is exactly four months since the American president honoured his promise to move the US embassy from Tel Aviv to Jerusalem, a diplomatic inauguration splashed with the blood of fifty-eight unarmed Palestinian protesters killed by Israeli soldiers on the Gaza border on 14 May.*

Silberstein is a fifty-eight-year-old Beit El councillor, having moved here from South Africa in 1985 'to live in the land of Israel' and 'according to the precepts of the Torah'. He's also a canny public speaker who talks in complete sentences with scarcely a pause or grammatical slip.

'I think that the composition of the Trump team today is fantastic – I'm talking about Greenblatt, Kushner, Friedman, [Trump's national security advisor] John Bolton, [US ambassador to the UN Nikki] Haley, Trump. I mean, my gosh, it's a dream for Israel. I didn't think we could even wish for anything better. I can't imagine finding greater supporters for Israel.'

And there was far less sympathy in Chaim Silberstein's exegesis on the Palestinians of the West Bank.

---

* Oslo had envisaged that both Israel and Palestine would refrain from taking 'any unilateral steps that would prejudice the outcome of the negotiations'. No one dreamed in 1993 that it would be the United States itself that would perpetrate the 'unilateral act' – which would not only 'prejudice' the agreement but effectively destroy it a quarter of a century later.

There never was a Palestinian people. There never was a
Palestinian history. This land never belonged to them, ever …
They never had a state, they never had any rights to their
country.

Beit El is a place apart for Silberstein. 'I moved here for ideological
reasons. I am a Zionist and I believe in Zion … Beit El goes back 3,000
years and this is a way to express the return of the native Jews to the
homeland. So for me, that's a real expression of my identity and my
nationality.' If he talks faith, he also talks war, and says that if Beit El
falls to its enemies, Tel Aviv will fall. 'We are the flak jacket of the
[Israeli] coastal plain.'

I pray for peace every day … And I believe that we will find a
solution, ultimately, where Israel will have a state from the
Jordan to the [Mediterranean] sea, where the Arabs that are
living in the [new] State of Israel either have Israeli citizenship or
Jordanian citizenship – or Jordan is actually the Palestinian state
… I think the Palestinians are passé – they're so twentieth
century! The Arab countries are not interested any more in the
Palestinians. I read often that they despise them.

The idea that Jordan might emerge, once again, as a 'mother state' for
the Palestinians, is a truly colonial concept. Israeli columnist and
researcher Shmuel Rosner was even more startlingly explicit when he
told *New York Times* readers that

Israel doesn't really believe that a tiny Palestinian enclave
trapped between Israel and Jordan could be economically viable.
And so it has always hoped that Israel's eventual separation from
the Palestinians will include a guarantee of – to put it bluntly –
adult supervision.

Here was colonialism made clear. Rosner gives us no hint that this lack
of 'viability' is caused by Israel's refusal to withdraw from the very
territories that would make the 'enclave' viable. And thus he enjoins
us, with a certain embarrassment, that the Palestinians need 'adult
supervision'. This was the racist reason all imperial nations advanced

when they explained why independence could not be given to the people of the lands they controlled.

I am no longer shocked. America is acquiescent. The world has no more sense of shock over the fate of the Palestinians than the Palestinians themselves. What was it Sulieman Khatib told me when we returned to his place of dispossession? 'After this long time, after the wall and the settlements, you can't even notice that this was once your land.'

So I make a demand of Amira Hass – the only Israeli journalist to live in the Palestinian West Bank, a tower of both strength and despair – and ask her to show me something that will shock me. And she takes me down a road outside Ramallah that I remember, years ago, was a highway that led to Jerusalem. But now, just over a hill, it deteriorates into a half-tarmac road, a set of closed, rusting shop doors and garbage. The same old late summer smell of raw sewage creeps up the road. It lies, green and gentle, in a pool at the bottom of the wall.

The Wall. Towering twenty-six feet above us, stern, monstrous in its determination, coiling and snaking between apartment blocks, and skulking in wadis and turning back on itself until you have two walls, one after the other. You shake your head for a moment when – suddenly, through some miscalculation, surely – there is no wall at all but a shopping street or a bare hillside of scrub and rock. And then the splash of red, sloping roofs and pools and trees of the colonies and, yes, more walls and barbed-wire fences and yet bigger walls. And then once more the beast itself, guardian of Israel's colonies: The Wall.

But the section of The Wall to which Amira takes me is a truly miserable place. It's the old road from Ramallah to Jerusalem, lined with lost wealth and once-loved homes which now ends at The Wall. 'Now if this is not shocking, I don't know what "shocking" is,' Amira says. 'It's a destruction of people's life – it's the end of the world. See here? We go straight to Jerusalem. Not now. This was a busy road and you can see here how people invested in homes with a little bit of grace, the strength of the houses, the stone. Look at the Hebrew signs – because these Palestinians used to have so many Israeli customers. Even the name "carpenter" is in Hebrew.'

But almost all the shops are closed, the houses shuttered, weeds and dry sticks along the broken kerb. The graffiti are pitiful, the sun merciless, the sky so caked with heat that the grey of The Wall sometimes merges into the grey stone of the sky. 'It is pathetic,' Amira Hass says, without emotion. 'This place – I've always been showing it to people; always, you know, probably a hundred times – and it never stops shocking me.'

The sewage, once you get used to it, is somehow appropriate. It's like a place where imagination has dried up, leaving only a grim little pool behind. The silence is not oppressive, but it demands an answer. What does The Wall say to us? I ask Amira. 'I think what it tells me,' she begins. 'Because it cannot drive the Palestinians away, it has to hide them. It has to conceal them from our eyes. Some might go out to work over there for Jews. And this is seen as "doing [Palestinians] a favour". Israelis do not enter, because for Israelis, "we don't need these areas – we don't need it – it is garbage – this is sewage". The wall is about how strong is the need to be pure. And how many people partic-ipated in this act of violence? They say it's because of the suicide attacks, but the legal and bureaucratic infrastructure for this separation existed before the wall. So the wall is a kind of graphic or plastic or tangible expression of laws of separation that existed before.'

And this is an Israeli who is speaking to me, whose socialism, I think, has given her a hard, Marxist courage. She guesses she has only between a hundred and five hundred readers left – thank God, say many of us, that her newspaper *Haaretz*, still exists. She has grown used to the hate and abuse from her own people.

But she is a realist. 'Look, we cannot ignore that for a certain period, [the wall] did serve the immediate role of security,' she says. And she is right. The Palestinian campaign of suicide bombing was cut short. But The Wall was also a machine for expansion: it crept forward onto Arab land which was no more a part of the State of Israel than the vast colo-nies now holding around 450,000 Jews across the West Bank. Not yet, at any rate.*

Amira drives on, past a military base where she points out the words – in English – spray-painted on a wall. 'Jews did 9/11'. With such words,

---

* Jewish academics were among the first to point out the dark significance of the wall and its equally sinister purpose. The late Tony Judt raged against the wall's existence as early as 2003 – 'It will destroy villages, livelihoods and whatever remains of Arab-Jewish community. It costs approximately $1 million per mile and will bring nothing but humiliation and discomfort to both sides.'

could the Palestinians incriminate their society more utterly in the eyes of the West? But there is other graffiti. In a tiny Palestinian village perhaps two hundred metres from the nearest Jewish settlement, she points to the words spray-painted onto the wall of a Palestinian home after Jews from the settlement raided the village. 'Judea and Samaria,' it says in Hebrew. 'Blood will be shed.'

Aisha Farah shows us the roof of her home, where her solar panels have been shattered by tiny stones – fired from a slingshot by religious students, she says – and despite her seventy-four years, she doesn't mince her words. I work out silently that she was born in the original mandate Palestine in 1944, the same year Amira Hass' mother was sent to Bergen-Belsen. The Jewish colony above Aisha Fara's home is Beit El, the settlement in which Chaim Silberstein lives, his place of 3,000-year-old biblical history, his 'moral and ideological community'. Like Beit El, Aisha Fara's home is in 'Area C', the 60 per cent of the West Bank which Silberstein wishes to see annexed by Israel.

'The thieves came before sunset,' Farah says of the stone-throwers. 'They burned our trees three times. But thieves do not remain forever. And the people scattered all over will return to their homes, God willing ... You ask me who they are? You sent them. You have it all in your cameras.' Amira listens carefully. 'For her,' she says, 'history is like a long, long chain of expulsion. These are things you stop writing about. Normalcy again.'

This, I think, has affected Amira Hass, the way in which a media report falls away once it has become a daily event. Nobody holds page one for this anymore. And the privileges of being an Israeli citizen in Ramallah are ever present:

In a way, when we were bombed [by the Israelis], it was easier because I was with everyone. This is something I can feel – the fear of bombs, of course, I share it. But closure, for example, this is something I cannot understand. I cannot really grasp it. For me a wall is just something ugly on the way [to Jerusalem]. But for Palestinians, it is the end of the world.

9

'Going Wild'

You who live secure
In your warm houses,
Who return at evening to find
Hot food and friendly faces:

Consider whether this is a man,
Who labours in the mud
Who knows no peace
Who fights for a crust of bread
Who dies at a yes or a no.
Consider whether this is a woman,
Without hair or name
With no more strength to remember
Eyes empty and womb cold
As a frog in winter.

'Shema' ('Listen') by Primo Levi, 10 January 1946
(translated by Ruth Feldman and Brian Swann)

One Saturday afternoon in 2012, I found the location of a village called Huj. The road sign said 'Sderot', the Israeli city where the Hamas missiles fall. But by my calculations, Huj lay, long destroyed, across the fields from a scruffy recreation centre near the entrance to Sderot, a series of shabby villas on a little ring road where Israeli children were playing.

Huj's day of destiny came on 31 May 1948, when the Israeli Negev Brigade's 7th Battalion, facing an advancing Egyptian army, arrived in the village. In Israeli historian Benny Morris' words, 'the brigade expelled the villagers of Huj ... to the Gaza Strip. Huj had traditionally been friendly; in 1946, its inhabitants had hidden Haganah men from a British dragnet. In mid-December 1947, while on a visit to Gaza, the mukhtar [mayor] and his brother were shot dead by a mob that accused them of "collaboration". But at the end of May, given the proximity of the advancing Egyptian column, the Negev Brigade decided to expel the inhabitants – and then looted and blew up their houses.'

The next month, they pleaded to go back. The Israeli 'Department of Minority Affairs' noted that they deserved special treatment since they had been 'loyal', but the Israeli army decided they should not go back. So the Palestinians of Huj festered on in the Gaza Strip where their descendants lived as refugees. In 1948, Huj lay inside the district of Dorot where there lived, according to the 1931 British census, an Arab majority. But the present-day Sderot, writes the Palestinian historian Walid Khalidi, was built on farmland belonging to another Palestinian Arab village called Najd; its inhabitants shared the same fate as the people of Huj. On 12 and 13 May 1948, the Negev Brigade of the Israeli army – again, according to Morris – drove them out. They, too, were sent into exile in Gaza.

You can see Huj and Najd on Munther Khaled Abu Khader's much-reproduced map of mandate Palestine and its modern-day Israeli towns, lying south-east and north in what is now Sderot. Sderot was founded in 1951 but Asraf Simi, who arrived there in 1962 and later worked in the local library, knew nothing of this. She shrugged her shoulders when I asked about them. 'We didn't hear anything about Arabs around here,' she said. 'My uncle came near the beginning, around 1955, and was living in a tent here – and we all thought this would be one of the most modern cities in Israel! I'm not frightened – but I'm not happy about the ceasefire. I think we should have gone in there to finish it all forever.'

Another irony. Asraf Simi was born in Morocco and learned Moroccan-accented Arabic before she left for Israel at the age of seventeen. And she does not know that today, in the squalor of Gaza, live well over 6,000 descendants of the people of Huj. Thus does the tragedy of the Palestinian Nakba connect directly with the Israelis of

Sderot. The thousands of rockets that have fallen around them over the years come from the very place where now live the families who lived on this land.

Gaza is the sliver on the map, the unlovely hiatus between present-day Israel and the Egyptian Arab desert. No longer, thanks to Ariel Sharon, embellished with the necessary dignity of occupation, this corner of mandate Palestine is now the rubbish pit of the Palestinian conflict, the place where the civilians whom nobody wants and the armed group whom everyone would like to destroy exist in mutual disharmony. The Jewish colonies on the coast of Gaza are now as much a historical memory as Gaza's role in the equally temporary Oslo 'peace'. It is as much a place of suffering and shame as it is a place of filth and disease and slaughter. We turn away from the criminalisation of a whole people – in this case two million Palestinians, most of them refugees or the children or grandchildren of refugees from what is now Israel and from present-day towns like Beersheba, Ashdod, Ashkelon and Sderot.

Unlike the West Bank, however, Palestinian Gaza endures something worse than occupation: a permanent state of siege. Sometimes it is of the medieval variety: massive bombardment by Israel. Sometimes it takes on a more diplomatic cruelty: sanctions levied against a people who did not vote in the way Israel and the West and most Arab nations wished them to vote, in what everyone acknowledged at the time to be a democratic election. And like all sieges, it has engendered a special kind of corruption and arrogance among the victims.

There is a unique precedent here, however. If the 2,173 square miles of the West Bank are being successfully consumed by another nation, Gaza's 146 square miles are being crushed by that same nation but are un-destroyable. For its inhabitants cannot flee to neighbouring Egypt, which participates in the siege; and they cannot flee to their original family homes in Palestine because they exist today in Israel. They cannot be trucked overland to the West Bank because Israel is stealing this land for its own people.

Thus what I called this 'unlovely hiatus' is even more doomed than its less stricken Palestinian pseudo-statelet to the north-east. Gaza is a dwarf, only just over 2 per cent of mandate Palestine, but with a far more fatal inheritance than its Palestinian neighbour. The West Bank is where Palestinians lose their lands; Gaza is where they lose their lives.

Although Oslo's creators fantasised that it would become part of the 'Palestine' state, Gaza's destiny was isolation. It has been a junkyard of history, variously ruled by Christians and Muslims, ruined and rebuilt under the Ottomans and fought over by the British and Turks in the First World War. One of the most verdant and peaceful locations amid the slums of Gaza remains the Commonwealth War Graves Commission cemetery with its 3,217 graves from 1917. Its keeper, Ibrahim Jaradeh MBE, himself became a refugee in 1948 when Israeli troops captured his home town of Beersheba.

The Israelis captured Gaza from the Egyptians in the 1967 Six-Day War and thereafter it remained under Israeli occupation for thirty-eight years. Clusters of Jewish colonies were installed on the Gaza coastline on the usual biblical pretexts, until Sharon closed them down in 2005 to concentrate his colonial expansion in the West Bank.

The 1993 Oslo agreement flourished and died in Gaza amid false hopes, Palestinian corruption and the legitimate, credible but – for Israel and America and the EU – infuriating victory of Hamas at the 2006 Palestinian parliamentary elections.

The ideological history of this stubborn but otherwise uninspiring and politically remote movement has been told many times; from its inception as the charitable Islamic Society in Gaza with origins in the old 1935 Egyptian Muslim Brotherhood, it was to transform itself through the Israeli–Palestinian conflict, first as a social movement with no militant ambitions, then as a putative Israeli ally and subsequently with a virulently anti-Semitic charter that called for the destruction of Israel. After its victory in the 2006 elections, it was to become for the West the officially hated and ostracised 'resistance/terrorist' authority of Gaza. In reality, the largely conservative Gaza Palestinians had voted for Hamas more out of disgust at Palestinian Authority corruption than any new-found love for a holy struggle against Israel and the West.

So certain were they of an Abbas victory, however, that the Western powers declared the election free and fair, which made their reaction to the real result even more inexcusable. Just as the Americans had failed to construct a 'day-after' plan for post-invasion Iraq, so the US had no policy in place to confront a Hamas success at the polls. Hamas's immediate call for a joint Fatah-Hamas government was ignored; how could Israel negotiate for peace with a Palestinian Authority dominated by 'terrorists' who had so often called for its destruction and who had 'rained' Qassam rockets onto Sderot?

So the Americans effectively demanded the abandonment by Hamas of its own charter and cut off aid to the now Hamas-dominated PA. Its new prime minister Ismail Haniyeh praised Abbas and promised to use 'all avenues' 'to put an end to the state of conflict in the region and bring peace to the region'. He was wasting his time. Hamas would be boycotted and the results ignored by the Western democracies which had praised the legitimacy of the election. The Palestinians had voted for the wrong people.

Israel wanted Abbas to crush Hamas. He had failed to do so electorally, so he must do so militarily. Violent disputes broke out between the security apparatus of Hamas and Fatah. In the West Bank, Fatah could arrest and torture Hamas supporters. Hamas, with the arrogance of all newly successful 'resistance' groups, now ruled over Gaza.

There remain deep suspicions that the Western powers conspired to overthrow the results of the Hamas victory in 2007 by supporting a clumsily organised coup – to be staged by Abbas and his electorally defeated Fatah movement. If a coup was being planned, Hamas forestalled it. The wholesale massacre and dispossession of Abbas supporters – and innocent civilians – that began on 10 June 2007 was a frightful moment in Palestinian history; men who had fought together in Beirut against Israel's 1982 siege now killed each other with equal venom. Abbas' fighters were gunned down outside their homes, thrown from rooftops or executed in the streets. At least 350 Palestinians were killed.

Henceforth, there would be two 'Palestines'; a Hamas 'Palestine', steadily gathering financial and military support from the Egyptian Muslim Brotherhood, Qatar and later Iran; and a Fatah 'Palestine', governed by Mahmoud Abbas, cooperating with Israel and funded by Western nations. In the coming years, Abbas' forces often spent more time imprisoning, torturing or killing their Hamas opponents in the West Bank than they did protesting Israel's continued land theft around Abbas' own 'capital' of Ramallah or its murderous attacks on the Palestinian people of Gaza. What more could Israel have wished?

US and European leaders would visit Israel and the West Bank, waltzing across the Wall to visit the 'democratic' president of Palestine while Hamas was contained inside Gaza, supposedly contaminating its own Palestinian people with 'terror' and fundamentalist Islam. It took Tony Blair almost two years to visit this part of his double-state Palestinian political fiefdom, and even then he chose not to meet any Hamas officials. For Hamas had since 2003 earned itself that most coveted of all Muslim militia awards; it was listed by the US and many others as a 'terrorist organisation'.

There were European politicians who argued that the world should sit down with Hamas and try to lure them into a peace, or even an extended ceasefire, through some form of recognition, and quiet persuasion to abandon its racist charter. Could Hamas not reconsider its refusal to accept the now largely discredited promises of the Oslo agreement? But Israel, whose senior military officers had encouraged Hamas to build its mosques and Islamic networks in Gaza when they wished to destroy Fatah, decided it could never submit to Hamas 'terror'. Unless, of course, they needed to negotiate with Hamas for the release of captured soldiers, in which case it would ignore all these prohibitions and talk to the leaders of 'world terror', before releasing scores of Islamist prisoners who had long been held as hostages for just such an occasion.*

Democracy no longer mattered to either Hamas or Fatah. Demonstrations by either faction in each other's version of 'Palestine' were suppressed. And Palestinian 'democracy' was now as studiously disregarded by the Western world as it was by the two Palestinian leaderships. All along, American and European leaders had claimed that the only real 'democracy' in the Middle East was practised by the nation that had occupied Palestinian land, stolen Palestinian land, besieged two million Palestinian people in Gaza and that would destroy their lives by the thousand. In his State of the Union address in 2007, George W. Bush had praised the supposed advent of democracy in Afghanistan, Iraq and Lebanon, remarking only that the Quartet – the US, the UN, the EU and Russia – was 'pursuing diplomacy to help bring peace to the Holy Land' and 'pursuing the establishment of a democratic Palestinian state'. But 'pursuing' was not the same as fulfilling.

---

* In 2011, for example, Israel released 1,027 Palestinian prisoners, including two involved in the killing of two Israeli soldiers, in exchange for Corporal Gilad Shalit, who had been captured in a cross-border raid more than five years earlier.

It was difficult to identify any kind of serious military 'struggle' against the Israelis, save for the increasing but almost totally ineffective bombardment of Sderot by Hamas. Their Qassam rockets, home-made, inaccurate, propelled by a combination of fertilisers and woefully inferior to anything their enemies possessed, merely allowed the Israelis to claim a right to self-defence, a plausible argument in terms of Israeli casualties but one that became more credible once Sharon had withdrawn Israel's 8,000 colonists from Gaza in 2005. Why should Hamas attack Israel now? Wasn't Gaza at last 'free' and 'independent', its occupation at an end? But its occupation had not ended.

'Disengagement', as the Israelis called the unilateral withdrawal of their settlers from 25 per cent of Gaza, allowed Israel to maintain its occupation by remote control. It remained in charge of the Palestinian enclave's airspace, territorial waters, borders and crossing points. It could cut off water and power and bombard its population at will. A blockade of iron and steel imports, concrete, car repair equipment, lathes and anything else that might enable the inhabitants of Gaza to make guns or rockets was harsh but explicable. Yet other items on Israel's prohibition list proved even more draconian than those prevented from entering Saddam's Iraq after 1990.

Far more eloquent were the casualty figures of each side, grotesquely manipulated though they were to become. The first major 'war' lasted for three weeks in the winter of 2008–9, costing the lives of more than 1,300 Palestinians and thirteen Israelis; in the second, in November 2014, over 2,000 Palestinians and seventy-two Israelis were killed. The figures for Palestinians are less precise because they were compiled under the shells and missiles of Israel's overwhelming land and air power. A fact-finding mission assembled by the Israeli branch of Physicians for Human Rights stated that Israeli casualty figures 'pale in comparison with the consequences of the massive destruction wreaked on Gaza'.

Israeli forces and the politicians who encourage them in their cruelty are responsible for most of the killings and crimes against humanity in Gaza. Those who rightly blame Israel for these outrages, however, must record that Hamas' deliberate rocketing of Sderot and, later, of other Israeli towns and cities, also stains the Palestinian guerrilla force and their allies with crimes against humanity, however pitiful their weapons and despite the grotesque disproportion of Israel's response.

The very inaccuracy of these home-made or cheaply manufactured weapons means that Hamas cannot even make the grotesque claim, so often put forward by Israel, of 'surgical' targeting.

The craven genuflection of the American political elite towards Israel is as shameful as it is unworthy of a great nation. Strength and cowardice do not have to walk hand in hand, but that is the nature of the American–Israeli relationship. US foreign policy in the Middle East belongs to Israel to such an extent that American policy is now Israeli policy. Trump's decision to recognise Jerusalem as the capital of Israel in 2018 was merely an enlarged mirror of all that had gone before.

Proof of this can be found in almost every US foreign policy decision since 1956, when Eisenhower successfully ordered Israeli forces out of Sinai. From then on, any hint of serious criticism of Israel in America would be met with abuse, threats and coercion, either by Israel itself or by its supposed 'friends' in the US. Discussion of the colonisation of Arab land or the immoral siege of Gaza would engender accusations of racism or Nazism or Islamist 'terror'. US senators who have ignored this power have lost their political careers. Neither American Jew nor American gentile would be spared. Every time I visited the United States to talk about the Middle East, the immense and unscrupulous power of Israel's supposed 'friends' has been made clear to me.

Inside the First Congregational Church of Berkeley, the Californian audience had been struck silent. Dennis Bernstein, the Jewish host of KPFA Radio's *Flashpoints* current affairs programme, was reading some emails that he had received from Israel's supporters in America. Each one left the people in the church in a state of shock. 'You mother-fuck-ing-asshole-self-hating Jewish piece of shit. Hitler killed the wrong Jews. He should have killed your parents, so a piece of Jewish shit like you would not have been born. God willing, Arab terrorists will cut you to pieces Daniel Pearl-style. AMEN!!!'

Bernstein's sin was to have covered the story of Israel's invasion of the West Bank city of Jenin in April 2002 for his programme. Bernstein's father was a revered Orthodox rabbi of international prominence but neither his family history nor his origins spared him. 'Read this and weep, you mother-fucker self-hating Jew boy!!!' another email told Bernstein. 'God willing, a Palestinian will murder you, rape your wife and slash your kids' throats.' Yet another, this time to Barbara Lubin, who is also Jewish, the executive director of the Middle East Children's Alliance, a one-time committed Zionist but now one of Israel's fiercest critics: 'I hope that you, Barbara Lubin and all other Jewish Marxist Communist traitors anti-American cop haters will die a violent and cruel death just like the victims of suicide bombers in Israel.'

Bernstein is the first to acknowledge that a combination of Israeli lobbyists and conservative Christian fundamentalists have in effect censored all free discussion of Israel and the Middle East out of the public domain in the US. 'Everyone else is terrified,' Bernstein said, and he was speaking fourteen years before Trump's election. 'The only ones who begin to open their mouths are the Jews in this country. You know, as a kid, I sent money to plant trees in Israel. But now we are horrified by a government representing a country that we grew up loving and cherishing.'

Adam Shapiro was among those who paid a price for their beliefs. A Jew married to an American-born Palestinian, he is a volunteer with the International Solidarity Movement, who was trapped in the spring of 2002 in Yasser Arafat's headquarters while administering medical aid. After telling CNN that the Sharon government was acting like 'terrorists' while receiving $3 billion a year in US military aid, Shapiro was savaged in the *New York Post* as the 'Jewish Taliban', while his family were described as 'traitors'. Israeli supporters publicised his family's address and his parents were forced to flee their Brooklyn home and seek police protection. Shapiro and his wife spoke together at public lectures in America, but were constantly heckled by Israeli 'supporters' and falsely accused of wishing to destroy Israel.

These 'supporters' have no qualms about their alliance with the Christian right in America. The fundamentalists also campaign on their own in Israel's favour, as I discovered for myself when I was about to give a lecture on the media and the Israeli–Palestinian conflict, part of a series of talks arranged partly by Jewish Americans. A right-wing Christian 'Free Republic' outfit posted my name on its website in 2002 and called me a 'PLO butt-kisser'. A few dozen demonstrators turned up outside the First United Methodist Church in Sacramento where I was to speak, waving US and Israeli flags. 'Jew haters!' they screamed at the organisers, a dark irony since many of these were non-Jews shrieking abuse at Jews. The truth did not matter to these people, and nor did the content of my talk. Their aim was to shut me up.

Dennis Bernstein summed it up. 'Any US journalist, columnist, editor, college professor, student-activist, public official or clergy member who dares to speak critically of Israel or accurately report the brutalities of its illegal occupation will be vilified as an anti-Semite.'*

Christian Zionist enthusiasm was to become a foundational stone for Israel in the US, where 20 million American believers could be counted upon to believe that Jesus Christ will return to the Holy Land in a Second Coming. Evangelists have avoided advertising their conviction that Jews must convert to Christianity before Jesus reappears; all those Jews who fail to do so will apparently perish in the Battle of Armageddon. Trump's 2018 decision to move the US embassy from Tel Aviv to Jerusalem probably had as much to do with this widely held American faith in the apocalyptic hereafter as any presidential love of Israel.

This basically anti-Semitic teaching did not stop a cynical 1978 Likud project to encourage fundamentalist churches to give their support to Israel, and within two years there was an 'International Christian Embassy' in Jerusalem. In 1985, a Christian Zionist lobby emerged at a 'National Prayer Breakfast for Israel' whose principal speaker was Benjamin Netanyahu. 'A sense of history, poetry and morality,' declared the future Israeli prime minister, 'imbued the Christian Zionists who, more than a century ago, began to write, plan and organise for Israel's restoration.' In May 2002, the Israeli embassy in Washington arranged a 'prayer breakfast' for Christian Zionists; among the guests was Michael Little, president of the Christian Broadcasting Corporation.

Yet these Christian fundamentalists seemed little interested in their fellow Christians' suffering in Palestine at the time of Israel's creation, when over 50 per cent of Jerusalem's Christians were expelled from

---

* No sooner had Bernstein made this remark in 2002 than pro-Israeli groups initiated an extraordinary campaign against newspapers in America, all claiming that the *New York Times*, the *Los Angeles Times* and the *San Francisco Chronicle* were biased in their coverage of the Middle East conflict. Just how the *New York Times* – which then boasted among its fanatically pro-Israeli columnists William Safire and Charles Krauthammer – could be 'anti-Israeli' is difficult to see, although it was possible that some mildly critical comments found their way into print. When the *San Francisco Chronicle* published a four-page guide to the conflict, its editors had to meet a fourteen-member delegation of local Jewish groups to discuss their grievances although the supplement was a soft sell.

their homes by the Israelis. In Jerusalem itself, a higher proportion of Palestinian Christians than Palestinian Muslims became refugees after 1949, a ratio of 37 per cent of Christians to 17 per cent of Muslims. But most of those who suffered were Arab Christians and thus fell outside the fundamentalists' sympathy zone.

Every congressman and congresswoman knows the names of those critics of Israel who have been undone by the 'lobby', of whom Senator J. William Fulbright is merely – in Israeli eyes – the most disreputable. His 1963 testimony to the Senate Foreign Relations Committee detailed how five million tax-deductible dollars from philanthropic Americans had been sent to Israel and then recycled back to the US for distribution to organisations seeking to influence public opinion in favour of Israel; this cost him the chance of being secretary of state. He was defeated in the 1974 Democratic primary after pro-Israeli money poured into the campaign funds of his rival, Governor Dale Bumpers, following a statement by the American Israel Public Affairs Committee (AIPAC) that Fulbright was 'consistently unkind to Israel and our supporters in this country'. Paul Findley, who spent twenty-two years as a Republican congressman from Illinois, found his political career destroyed after he campaigned against the lobby.

'I do not recall,' James Abu Rizk, an Arab-American of Lebanese origin, told the Arab-American Anti-Discrimination Committee in 2002, 'any member of Congress asking me if I was in favour of patting Israel on the back ... The votes and bows have nothing to do with the legislators' love for Israel. They have everything to do with the money that is fed into their campaigns by members of the Israeli lobby. My estimate is that $6 billion flows from the American treasury to Israel each year.' Within days, forty-two US governors turned up in Sacramento to sign declarations supporting Israel.

It did not need Uri Avnery to claim that resistance to the directives of the 'Jewish lobby' was political suicide. 'If the AIPAC were to table a resolution abolishing the Ten Commandments,' he wrote, '80 Senators and 300 Congressmen would sign it at once.'* By now, the

---

* Avnery could have looked no further than the 2002 Democratic primary in Alabama for proof of his assertion. Earl Hilliard, the five-time incumbent, had committed the one mortal sin of any American politician: he had expressed sympathy for the cause of the Palestinians. He had also visited Libya some years earlier, which was not wise. Hilliard's opponent, Artur Davis, turned into an outspoken supporter of Israel and raised large amounts of

'lobby', the effective smothering of almost all mainstream political condemnation of Israel, became normal. If the injustices visited upon the Palestinians by Israel – the bloodshed, the occupation, the colonial project itself – were now routine, so too was the war-weary fear of addressing them. When through some freak publishing indiscretion authors attempted to expose the lethal military and political relationship between the US and Israel, this could be discussed only when Israel's protectors had condemned the errant writers' work – thus creating a 'controversy'. Like walls, taboos are easy to create but far more difficult to tear down.

This phenomenon took many forms. Even historical events within the United States could lose their perspective. Americans know that Robert Kennedy was assassinated during his 1968 presidential race by Sirhan Beshara Sirhan, who was repeatedly portrayed at his trial as mentally deficient. Yet his motives were perfectly clear. A Palestinian Christian, he had become outraged by Kennedy's promotion of Israel during his presidential campaign and especially his promise to sell fifty Phantom fighter-bombers to Israel if elected. Yet the background to Kennedy's murder largely disappeared from the public's imagination.

The failure of large media organisations to indicate the political bias of pro-Israeli 'commentators' – their use of 'analysts' and 'experts' from the Washington Institute for Near East Policy like Dennis Ross, for example – maintained the same gloss of impartiality on the Middle East that Ross would adopt with his colleagues among the 'peace envoys' whom Washington regularly sent to supervise Israeli–Palestinian negotiations. Columnist Roger Cohen would mischievously suggest during the 2008–9 Gaza war that newly elected President Obama might choose a group of Arab Muslim or Christian figures to represent US efforts for Middle East peace. 'I have nothing against smart, driven, liberal Jewish (or half Jewish) males,' Cohen wrote. 'I've looked in the mirror ... these guys [are] knowledgeable, broad-minded and determined. Still, on the diversity front they fall short.' Avnery was harsher. 'Palestinians may well ask whether among the 300 million US citizens

money from the Jewish community, both in Alabama and nationwide. The Jewish magazine *Forward*, essential reading for any serious understanding of the American Jewish community, quoted a Jewish activist following the race: 'Hilliard has been a problem in his votes and with guys like that, when they're any conceivable primary challenge, you take your shot.' Hilliard lost to Davis, whose campaign funds reached $781,000.

there is not a single non-Jew who can manage this job.' Avnery might
have asked a different question: what would have been Israel's reaction
– and that of its supporters in America – if Muslim Americans had
made up the entire US 'peace' team in the Middle East?

This extraordinary reticence meant that a blanket was thrown over
the most crucial decision-making processes within the Israeli–American
relationship, which affected the long-term future of US servicemen and
women. Just before the 2003 Anglo-American invasion of Iraq, lone
voices warned that Bush had been ill-advised to listen to pro-Israeli
supporters urging regime change in Baghdad who were more interested in destroying Israel's regional enemies than in America's
supposedly patriotic destiny in the Middle East. Only three years after
the invasion did the *New York Times* dare to shine a light beneath the
cloak of the Israeli–American alliance by revealing the bogus advice
given to the Bush administration by Israeli intelligence operatives.

It would be pleasant to record that the influence of Israel's 'supporters' in the US diminishes the further one travels from the North
American continent, but this is not true. The Qatari Al Jazeera channel,
which regularly earned Western praise for its freedom, proved this in
2018 when it declined to air its own exclusive and deeply troubling
investigation of the Israeli lobby in the United States.

An earlier four-part inquiry by Al Jazeera reporters into Israeli influence in the UK had been broadcast in 2017 to journalistic approval.
Clayton Swisher, the head of the network's investigation unit, was to
describe how

> we captured on hidden camera an Israeli official, Shai Masot,
> manipulating domestic British NGOs and threatening to target
> pro-Palestinian MPs. Masot, whose business card read 'Senior
> Political Officer' with the Israeli Embassy in London, threatened
> to 'take down' the Foreign Office's number two, Sir Alan Duncan,
> a critic of Israeli settlements. A British civil servant entertaining
> the plot, who we secretly recorded, was summarily dismissed.

The Israeli ambassador was forced to issue a public apology. The usual
accusations of 'anti-Semitism' followed transmission of the series but
when self-declared friends of Israel complained to the British broadcast
regulator Ofcom, Al Jazeera was cleared of both foul play and racism.

But when the series on the US Israeli lobby was completed, leaders of Jewish American organisations met with the state of Qatar's registered agent in Washington who later told *Haaretz* that 'he was discussing the issue with the Qataris and didn't think the film would broadcast in the near future'. *Haaretz* was also told that 'the Qatari emir [Sheikh Hamad bin Khalifa Al Thani] himself helped make the decision'. These same 'zealots', Swisher was to record, then lobbied Congress 'to pressure the Department of Justice to require our network to register as "foreign agents" under the US Foreign Agent Registration Act'. After unexplained delays, Swisher was promised by Al Jazeera management that the series would be broadcast. It was not.

The Zionist Organisation of America would later boast that it was 'proud and happy to announce that, thanks to their efforts, including long, numerous and detailed discussions by Mr Klein [its president] in Doha, in Qatar, with the Emir and other senior Qatari officials ... [that] Qatar had agreed not to air this viciously anti-Semitic documentary on Al Jazeera'.

An angry and dismayed Swisher took a six-month sabbatical. He had every reason to feel aggrieved. He had been behind the 2011 release of 1,600 Israeli–Palestinian negotiation documents that Al Jazeera shared with the *Guardian*. They provided not just an account of the immense pressures placed on the Palestinian Authority by pro-Israeli US officials but of the PA's effective betrayal of much that Palestinians had stood for over previous decades.

Particularly relevant was the documentary evidence in the Palestine Papers that Mahmoud Abbas had been alerted by Israel in advance of the 2008–9 assault on Gaza. Amos Gilad, the director of Israeli military intelligence, held several meetings with Abbas' advisers about Gaza prior to the attack, the archive showed, information that was not used to warn the two million Palestinian citizens there of their fate.* It was

---

* Swisher already represented a flashing red light for Israel's supporters. His earlier analysis of the Camp David accords in 2000 debunked Dennis Ross's claim that Arafat was the cause of the talks' failure. While Swisher urged students to read Ross's own account, he quoted Ross as mocking Arafat when the latter sought a follow-up summit. Swisher blames the Palestinians' 'abysmal failure to clearly and quickly articulate to the world their positions ...' for the success of the US and Israel in blaming Arafat. A former marine reservist and US federal criminal investigator, Swisher has become one of the foremost political detectives in the dishonourable story of Israeli–Palestinian talks.

clear, therefore, that the Palestinians of Gaza could trust neither the United States nor the Palestinian Authority.

By 2009, *Haaretz* was revealing that every appointee to the American government had 'to endure a thorough background check by the American Jewish community before appointment'. This followed the withdrawal of diplomat Charles Freeman from his new post as chairman of the US National Intelligence Council; he had publicly criticised America's special relationship with Israel and Israel's occupation of Palestinian land.* Barack Obama remained silent.

Gazing across the landscape of propaganda, anxiety and intimidation, it was remarkable to find anyone who emerged unscathed. When US Central Command General David Petraeus told the Senate Armed Services Committee in 2010 that 'the conflict foments anti-American sentiment, due to a perception of US favouritism for Israel', he was pounced on by lobbyist Abe Foxman, head of the Anti-Defamation League, for his 'dangerous and counterproductive' linkage.† Only Bernie Sanders, the Jewish-American candidate for the US Democratic nomination in 2016 who was foolishly persuaded to give way to Hillary Clinton, has effortlessly survived his own critical take on Israel, condemning Israeli assassinations, its colonisation of the West Bank and the destruction of Palestinian homes. When Netanyahu addressed Congress in 2015, Sanders stayed away.‡

★ ★ ★

---

* Typical of Freeman's crimes was his contention four years earlier that 'as long as the United States continues unconditionally to provide the subsidies and political protection that make the Israeli occupation and the high-handed and self-defeating policies it engenders possible, there is little, if any, reason to hope that anything resembling the former peace process can be resurrected.'

† Petraeus tried to wriggle out of his perfectly truthful remarks by suggesting, in an email to a right-wing columnist, that 'it might help to know' he had hosted Elie Wiesel to dinner and would be a speaker at a Holocaust anniversary in Washington.

‡ When non-American critics refused to give way to Israel, they sometimes got away with it. Supported by the Bush administration in naming an interim Iraqi administration in 2004, UN envoy Lakhdar Brahimi – a former Algerian foreign minister and one of his country's most accomplished diplomats – unburdened himself of the unspeakable opinion that 'the great poison in the Middle East is this Israeli policy of domination and the suffering imposed on the Palestinians', along with the 'equally unjust support' of the US. When Israel objected to his critical opinion, Brahimi snapped back that what he said 'was not an opinion – it's a fact'.

Almost three months before the start of the 2008 Israeli bombardment, Brigadier General Gadi Eizenkot, the head of the Israeli army's Northern Command, explained just how ruthless his country's military intentions would be towards civilians. Talking of the destruction of south Beirut in 2006, he outlined to the Israeli newspaper *Yedioth Ahronoth* that 'disproportionality' was now a military doctrine. 'What happened in the Dahiyah quarter of Beirut ... will happen in every village from which Israel is fired on ... We will apply disproportionate force on it and cause great damage and destruction there. From our standpoint, these are no civilian villages, they are military bases. This is not a recommendation. This is a plan. And it has been approved.'

There was nothing new in Israel's willingness to slaughter civilians. Most of the 17,500 victims of its invasion of Lebanon in 1982 were civilians. After the 2006 war in Lebanon, Human Rights Watch had accused Israel of war crimes. Israel had produced its usual excuses. Its enemies lived amid civilians and used them as 'human shields'. Its generals had long raged at the double standards of the West – which would condemn Israel for its bombing 'mistakes' while killing far more civilians in its own wars.

The cross-fertilisation of Israeli and US–NATO operations would become a feature of Middle East wars, the criminal precedents of one conflict justifying the promiscuous use of air power in another. But America's profligate military assistance to Israel, worth $2.3 billion every year by 2005, ensured that it would never suffer from the shortage of munitions that restrained the NATO attacks on Serbia. Under one of its many arms agreements, the Israel WSI-1 (War Reserve Stocks for Allies) programme included 'ammunition owned by the US but intended for Israeli use, overseen by the [US] army and Marine Corps' and located at Ben Gurion International Airport at Tel Aviv, Herzliya-Pituach, Nevatim airfield (air force base 28) and Ovda air base. These vast storage sites allowed Israel to maintain its 2006 bombing of Lebanon for thirty-four days – and its subsequent 2008–9 attack on Gaza for twenty-three days.

In the critical month of June 2008, two events occurred within only five days of each other, events that hold clues to the bloodbath that was to soak Gaza six months later. On 14 June, a Gaza ceasefire was agreed under Egyptian auspices between Hamas and Israel that should have given some confidence to the Palestinians. Since the start of the year, UN agencies had reported the devastating effect of the blockade of food, medicine and fuel imposed on Gaza since Hamas seized power the previous summer.

But exactly five days after the ceasefire announcement, seventy-seven US senators, including future secretary of state Hillary Clinton, sent a letter to President George W. Bush, urging him to block any UN resolution critical of Israel because UN opposition to attacks on Gaza constituted a refusal to 'acknowledge Israel's right to self-defense'. A liberal Zionist group in the US, 'Americans for Peace Now', warned that the letter was designed to build 'a defense, in advance, for a large Israeli military offensive in Gaza'. A March House of Representatives resolution spoke of Hamas using civilians as 'human shields'. Human rights groups agreed that Hamas failed to protect civilians in Gaza, but found no instances of 'human shields'. In September, Congress would vote to send 1,000 GBU-39 air-to-ground missiles to Israel, an important stockpile for the Gaza war.

Far more worrying, however, was an article in *Haaretz* on 28 December 2008, the day after the first air strikes on Gaza began, in which its diplomatic correspondent Barak Ravid disclosed that what was to become Israel's 'Operation Cast Lead' had been prepared over the previous six months. Defence minister Ehud Barak had initiated 'long-term planning, meticulous intelligence-gathering, secret discussions, visual deception tactics and disinformation' just as 'Israel was beginning to negotiate a ceasefire agreement with Hamas'. And so it becomes apparent that in June, the Israelis began planning their Gaza war and US senators set out their country's response to just such a conflict – at the very moment when the Israel–Hamas truce was agreed.

In November, as the ICRC reported that Palestinians were forced by the Israeli blockade to cut their food intake to 'survival levels', the Gaza ceasefire was broken. By Israel. On 4 November, an Israeli military force raided Gaza, killing six Hamas members. The Israelis claimed they were seeking to destroy a tunnel that Hamas planned to use for capturing soldiers on the Gaza border fence. The military attack naturally provoked a flurry of rockets from Hamas into Israel and, six weeks later, a statement from the Islamists that they would not renew the truce. The massive assault on the Palestinians of Gaza was thus based on a lie. The 'outburst' of violence, Bush would tell Americans, was 'instigated by Hamas'. It had staged 'a coup' in Gaza in 2007 and then, after the Egyptian-hosted 2008 June truce, Hamas 'routinely violated that ceasefire by launching rockets into Israel'. In vain did journalists and NGOs try to remind the world of the truth.* Among the most eloquent was the Israeli historian Avi Shlaim, himself a veteran of the Israeli army, who wrote that

> the brutality of Israel's soldiers is fully matched by the mendacity of its spokesmen ... their propaganda is a pack of lies ... It was not Hamas but the IDF that broke the ceasefire. It did so by a raid into Gaza on 4 November that killed six Hamas men. Israel's objective is not just the defence of its population but the eventual overthrow of the Hamas government in Gaza by turning the people against their rulers.

The expression 'war' dignifies Gaza. Like most of the violence there, it was always a confrontation between the least popular and least efficient Islamist militia in the Middle East and the most expensive and best-armed, if least disciplined, army in the Middle East. Though disputed by the Israeli military, the 2008–9 'war' produced a Palestinian death toll of 1,387 – this figure is according to the Israeli B''Tselem human rights group – of whom 773 were civilians. In the same period, four Israelis were killed in Israel by Hamas' rockets, and nine soldiers in Gaza, four of whom were accidentally killed by their own army.

The gravest single potential Israeli war crime in Gaza occurred on 5 January when twenty-one members of the Palestinian al-Samouni

---

* Even the Israeli foreign affairs ministry website had recognised that Hamas had kept its side of the ceasefire agreement, Dominique Vidal, joint editor-in-chief of *Le Monde diplomatique*, told his readers under the headline 'The bigger the lie ...' Rachad Antonius, a sociology professor at the University of Quebec at Montreal, angrily dismissed the editorials and television reports that blamed Hamas. 'Contrary to what has been repeated ad nauseam in the media, it is not Hamas which broke the truce ...' he wrote in a Canadian newspaper above an article co-signed by sixteen academics, journalists and Israel friendship groups which claimed that Hamas 'never stopped' firing rockets during the ceasefire, a variation on Israel's own sophistry. Israel's November incursion into Gaza, wrote Sara Roy, an American Jewish scholar who lost a hundred of her relatives in the Holocaust, was 'no doubt designed finally to undermine the truce ...' Weeks later, Israeli ambassadors were still repeating the false story – in the words of Zion Evrony, ambassador to Dublin – that 'it was Hamas who decided to put an end to the period of calm'.

family were variously done to death by Israeli Givati Brigade soldiers in the Zeitoun district of eastern Gaza. Donald Macintyre spent days investigating and wrote about the al-Samouni family a year later – and then again in his bestselling book on Gaza in 2018.

It is important to remember how Israel spoke of the plight of the Palestinians – and how the world responded to it. The Israeli prime minister, Ehud Olmert, promised at New Year January 2009 'an iron fist' for Hamas but 'silk gloves' for Palestinian civilians. Even in the first hours of the Gaza bombardment, international appeals for peace had a demeaning, cowardly quality about them.

Similarly, the hundreds of journalists who took up camera positions on the low hill north of Gaza only reinforced this fantasy image of the 'war'. Crews could broadcast distant explosions, caused by Israel's American-made fighter-bombers over Gaza, but their only direct contact with violence was with the few victims of the home-made Hamas rockets that crashed into Sderot, or the land of Huj. Nor, for the most part, did the forthcoming Israeli election in February 2009, in which Tzipi Livni and Benjamin Netanyahu were competing in their promises to defeat Hamas, merit much international attention. Did journalists believe that the war and the political ambitions of Israel's politicians had no connection?

Canadian newspaper reporter Patrick Lagacé wrote a series of articles of suppressed fury from Israel during the 2008–9 Gaza war, visited the infamous 'hill' and filed an angry report from Sderot. 'Gaza, over there, so close,' he wrote:

> Beside us, on the hill, the television journalists. One of them carried his flak jacket. It was so ridiculous, given the distance between us and Gaza, it was like going to watch a hockey match wearing a helmet and visor. But that's OK, his mum is going to be excited, I'm sure, when she sees the pictures of her son dressed in a flak jacket. She will, no doubt, show them to her friends at the bingo club with great pride.

Le Monde found a BBC special correspondent who described how Israel had turned Gaza into 'a giant aquarium' for the media. Benjamin Barthe cruelly added that 'to give some thrills to viewers, the "Beeb" reporters slip on flak jackets when they pass the camera', quoting one of them as saying that this was 'thought to be so much more sexy'.

The Israelis would admit that they had been using white phosphorus shells in Gaza, but only after Human Rights Watch had accused them of firing the US-made munitions. The projectiles can cause serious injuries to the liver, kidneys and lungs, and their use in civilian areas is against international law.* Photographs had already appeared in the European press of Israeli soldiers standing beside the shells, marked with the US coding M825A1. The munitions had been fired at the UN headquarters in Gaza City on 15 January and on the Al Quds hospital the same day.

The 'secrecy' that was always supposed to 'shroud' Israeli military planning in the minds of the media was no secret at all. But the 'shroud' was much more seriously ripped apart around two weeks into the Gaza war when foreign minister Tzipi Livni boasted in a radio interview that 'Israel … is a country that when you fire on its citizens, it responds by going wild – and this is a good thing.' 'Going wild' was a phrase picked up by the media, not so much because it evoked some darker, more dangerous side to Israel's military 'personality' but because it appeared so at odds with Israel's insistence that it was the most moral army in the world.

Film and photographs suggested that the Israeli army had indeed 'gone wild', and Israel's supporters therefore decided to propagate a much simpler story, one in which the 'world' would be turned into a gigantic 'Sderot', its inhabitants all trapped in their own towns and cities at the mercy of a gigantic 'terror' organisation. This was to become the repeated text of so many advertisements and newspaper articles that it would be frivolous to suggest that they emerged by chance.

I became as much a newspaper reader as a writer, studying each day how Israel was portraying its conflict against an entire imprisoned Arab people. Israel's response was perfectly encapsulated in an advertisement by the American Anti-Defamation League in the *International Herald Tribune* in mid-January. 'WHAT IF HAMAS WAS IN YOUR NEIGHBORHOOD?' it asked. No country, it concluded, would allow such danger on its border, 'and neither will Israel'. A headline two

* Under Protocol III of the conventional weapons convention of 1980.

weeks earlier above a column in the Toronto-based *National Post* by
Lorne Gunter, asked Canadians: 'What would you do?' Here is the first
paragraph:

> Suppose you lived in the Toronto suburb of Don Mills and
> people from the suburb of Scarborough – about ten kilometres
> away – were firing as many as ten rockets a day into your yard,
> your kid's school, the strip mall down the street and your
> dentist's office … Or maybe you had a home in south
> Vancouver and militants living in Richmond were lobbing
> rockets every day across the Fraser River.

These paragraphs of false equivalence went on and on. Sderot's experience could be compared with 'extremists living in St Boniface
constantly attacking Winnipeg, or Hullois terrorising Ottawa daily or
Dartmouthians menacing Halifax year after year'.

But as usual with such explanations, it was the 'why' question that
was missing. Why on earth would the people in Vancouver fear the
people of Richmond? Why would the Nova Scotians of Dartmouth
wish to attack the Nova Scotians of Halifax? Or why would the good
folk of Calgary endure 'fusillades' from the suburb of Springbank? And
if these continent-wide outbreaks of Canadian civil carnage were really
conceivable, what injustice, land-theft and cruelty could have provoked
them? An unanswerable question, naturally enough, because it might
explain all too clearly what was going on between Israel and Gaza.
Readers should be aware, however, that Gunter's contribution to the
Middle East debate was no isolated example.

French Canadians were not to be spared the Anglophone terrors of
Sderot. 'Imagine for a moment,' wrote sixteen 'open letter' contribu-
tors to *La Presse* in Montreal, 'that the children of Longueuil live in
terror day and night, that businesses, shops, hospitals and schools are
the target of terrorists located in Brossard. What would Quebecois
expect of their governments? No government can tolerate its territory
and people being placed in danger.'

These extraordinary fictions spread to the corners of Europe. In the
Irish Times, for example, the Israeli ambassador to Dublin, Zion Evrony
claimed that he had been asking Irish people a series of questions
'fundamental to any discussion of Israel's action'. His first question was

more than predictable: 'What would you do if Dublin were subjected to a bombardment of 8,000 rockets and mortars similar to that endured by Israeli towns and cities for eight years?'*

If all of the above seems hysterical, there was about it a more distressing message; that Israel was justified in its savage killing of civilians by the same 'fear', 'danger', 'anger' and 'terror-day-and-night' which Westerners would surely feel if attacked by their 'neighbours'. 'We' would also be entitled to 'go wild'. We and the vengeful Israelis would act in just the same way. And all these examples must prove that some elements within the Israeli information apparatus must have circulated the 'what would you do?' story on a large scale to have it replicated so many times.

There were some Israelis who did care deeply about the Palestinians, although opinion polls suggested they were not many. Uri Dan, a security coordinator for a kibbutz only three miles from Gaza, a veteran of the 1967 and 1973 Arab–Israeli wars who blamed Hamas for the outbreak of violence, stoutly demanded that the war should end. 'In Sderot and the area around Gaza, the suffering from rockets is great but it has no proportion at all to what is happening to the Palestinians,' he said. 'We live next to the Palestinians and we will have to continue living with them.' The Sderot leader of a now defunct Israeli-Gaza residents' 'dialogue group', Naomika Zion, received an email from a nine-year-old Palestinian girl saying: 'Help us, don't you understand we are human beings too?' Zion acknowledged that Israel had broken the ceasefire in November 2008, and opposed the subsequent bombardment. She wrote an article on Israel's Y-net website headlined 'Not in my name', claiming that her country's 'monolithic' militaristic public and media language was more dangerous than Hamas' Qassam rockets. 'It was tough to write this,' she told an *Independent* reporter, 'but I said to myself I am ready to pay the price of social isolation, but not of fear. I assume most people think I'm a traitor.'

There was one Palestinian in Gaza, however, whose personal catastrophe was so overwhelming that it embraced Israel, 'Palestine'

---

* The last 'foreign' artillery assault on Dublin had been from the British artillery and from a twelve-pounder aboard the British gunboat *Helga* in 1916. British guns in Irish hands had been used against anti-treaty forces in the Dublin Four Courts at the start of the civil war in 1922.

and the sympathy of the world. He was a much-loved Palestinian
doctor who treated Israelis as well as Palestinians, who spoke fluent
Hebrew and whose work for human rights was respected by Israelis
and Palestinians. And just two days before the destruction of Gaza
ended, Israeli tanks fired shells into his home, tearing to pieces three of
his daughters and a niece, blasting out the eye of another daughter.
And because Dr Izzeldin Abuelaish was a well-known figure in Israel
and because he was reporting for an Israeli station that very night,
everyone in the country and across the West Bank witnessed the
anguish and fury of a truly good man.

Bessan was twenty-one, Mayar fifteen, Aya thirteen. The dead niece
was Nour, who was fourteen. The terribly wounded daughter was
Shatha who was sixteen. A cousin, Ghaida, was fourteen and is perma-
nently disabled. Izzeldin's wife died of leukaemia four months before
her daughters' deaths.

We should take a moment here to tell the 'other side' of this story.
The Israelis claimed first that there were snipers in the home of the
Abuelaish family, which was in the Jabalya refugee camp. This was
untrue. Then they claimed that Hamas fighters were hiding there with
weapons. Untrue, announced the distraught doctor. Then that shrapnel taken from the dismembered young women were from Hamas
projectiles. But this was grotesque; and the Israeli public could scarcely
buy the line that this disaster was yet more 'collateral damage'.
Abuelaish was a gynaecologist at the Israeli Shiba hospital near Tel
Aviv, a well-known figure among both his professional colleagues and
to Israeli television audiences. He went on air minutes after the killing
of his daughters by the Israeli shells. The Israeli Channel 10 correspondent, Shlomi Eldar, his voice breaking, repeatedly reminded Israeli
viewers that Abuelaish worked at the Shiba hospital in Israel, and he
held out his mobile so they could hear the doctor wail into the phone:
'My daughters, they killed them, Oh lord, God, God, God.'

Abuelaish pleaded for help, still crying, with the words 'I want to
save them but they are dead', and Eldar appealed for anyone in the
army who might be watching to allow ambulances to reach the
Abuelaish home in Gaza. Shatha, her eye hanging on her cheek, was
taken to an Israeli hospital, as was one of Abuelaish's brothers. The
doctor would later take reporters on a grim tour of his broken home,
his remarks laced with cynicism at the Israeli army's pitiful excuses:

> These are the 'weapons' – the books and their clothes. These
> were the science handouts. There, you see, these are her
> handouts for the courses that she studies, which is stained with
> her blood ... These are the books – 'weapons' which I equipped
> my daughters with: with education, with knowledge, with
> dreams, with hopes, with loves.

It was the first time Israelis had glimpsed, in real time, the suffering and
death of Palestinian civilians. Abuelaish spoke in Hebrew, his voice
filled with grief, but also with indignation:

> I had left the room seconds earlier. How would gunmen have
> reached the roof? From where would they have entered ... I
> have never done anything wrong in my life. If you don't believe
> Palestinians, ask Israelis who Doctor Abuelaish is. They should
> just admit they made a mistake. There is no shame in making a
> mistake, but don't deceive the nation.

But the nation of Israel, and much of the rest of the world, would go
on being deceived, not just in the next few days, nor in the months of
UN and human rights investigations and reports that would follow the
2008–9 'war', but for years to come. True, there was, as we have seen,
a continual and casual acceptance of Arab suffering in the international
media, not least in Thomas Friedman's columns in the *New York Times*.
In mid-January, he had compared Israel's 2006 bombing of Lebanon
with the bombardment of Gaza. Israel, he wrote, believed that since
Hizbollah 'nested among civilians, the only long-term source of deter-
rence was to exact enough pain on the civilians – the families and
employers of the militants – to restrain Hizbollah in the future'. In
Gaza, he asked, was Israel trying to 'educate' Hamas 'by inflicting a
heavy death toll on Hamas militants and heavy pain on the Gaza population?'

With a far more humanitarian response, the Irish columnist Fintan
O'Toole asked at what stage 'the mandate of victimhood' expires. 'At
what point does the Nazi genocide of Europe's Jews cease to excuse
the state of Israel from the demands of international law and of
common humanity? At the point, surely, when that special pleading
dishonours the memory of the Holocaust itself.' Hamas' campaign of

rocket-firing indiscriminately into Israeli towns was 'a terrorist crime', O'Toole wrote. 'But Israel's response to this terrorism is not merely criminal in exactly the same sense. It adds a further dimension of depravity by playing a game of revenge in which one Israeli life is worth at least twenty Palestinian lives.' In fact, by the second day, the exchange rate was one Israeli for 285 Palestinians. 'Our intention is to totally change the rules of the game,' Israeli defence minister Ehud Barak told Fox News.

Western opponents of the war expressed their frustration by variously re-running Gaza's recent history or by further encouraging the boycott and divestment campaign against Israel. Worldwide protests, in Europe as well as the Muslim world, showed how widely felt was the revulsion at Israel's actions.

And who supported Hamas? If the Islamist group could claim victory, which it inevitably did, it could scarcely do so with much moral credit, or boast of its military prowess. Hamas did indeed survive Israel's destruction of Gaza and continued to fight on by firing its idiotic rockets right through to the January ceasefire. Two of the nine Israeli fatalities on the Israeli side were Israeli Arabs – members of the same Palestinian people living in Gaza but whose families did not flee 'Palestine' in 1948 – and who were working in the fields around Sderot (Huj).* In fact, Hamas accounted for more than thirty Palestinian lives during the war: most of them alleged Palestinian collaborators with Israel who were murdered in their homes or dragged from hospital beds or prisons for street executions by hooded gunmen.†

Yet Hamas was infected by spies – some working for the Palestinian Authority, others for the Israelis – which is why Israel successfully murdered one Hamas leader after another. When Friedman expanded again on his theory that Hamas rockets were 'nested among local civilians' and 'nested among homes and schools', he stated that Israel's

---

* Neither side wished to emphasise this fact, the Israelis preferring to keep the two dead Arabs among the casualties of Israeli identity while Hamas was reluctant to admit that two of their 'Israeli' victims were Palestinians.

† Saleh Hajoj, for example, had been in the Gaza central prison awaiting 'trial' by Hamas judges for collaboration when it was bombed by Israel on 28 December 2008; he had been taken to the Shifa hospital but when his young wife turned up to see him in his fourth-floor room, she was turned away by Hamas. Twenty minutes later, as he lay on a stretcher, he was shot in the left side of the head.

decision to go after them 'without being deterred by the prospect of civilian casualties' provoked a UN investigation into alleged war crimes. While laced with Friedman's usual semantics, his column had at least grasped that Israeli forces had abandoned the old myth of 'purity of arms'.

Yet purity was a quality never claimed by Hamas, whose estimated 1,500 tunnels to Egypt brought in millions of dollars for the Islamist movement. The owner of a newly repaired tunnel in Rafah told Donald Macintyre that he had paid more than $2,000 to the local Hamas-run municipality before the Israeli offensive. NGOs spoke of how Hamas blocked food from entering through the Erez Israeli crossing point to increase their own profits. Even before the Gaza bombardment, Egypt had been building an underground steel wall to prevent smuggling, designed by US army engineers and modelled on structures used to reinforce levees against hurricanes. In 2008, the US had spent $23 million on teaching Egyptian government security cops how to stop arms being smuggled through the tunnels.

For several months, American, British and French diplomats had been informing their respective governments about the behaviour of Israeli forces in Gaza, both before and during the invasion. One of these embassy employees reported that Israeli soldiers had been writing about the Gaza operations in an army college magazine, describing the deliberate murder of Palestinian civilians. On 24 March 2008, a reporter for France Inter, one of the country's major public channels, claimed it had found a written order authorising Israeli forces to fire on Palestinian ambulances.

In the days and weeks to come, such stories would become commonplace. At first, media reports concentrated on the 'new tactics' of Hamas – their maze of tunnels and booby traps – and of Israel's telephone warnings to Palestinian residents to move out of their homes before they were destroyed. But there were clues within the press reports of a more significant and disturbing strategy. In a dispatch from Jerusalem on 11 January 2008, *New York Times* reporter Steven Erlanger switched from a description of Israel's pre-attack leaflet, loudspeaker and telephone warnings to the one-sentence remark: 'But troops are instructed to protect themselves first, and civilians second.' He quoted the commander of an Israeli engineering unit as saying, 'The mindset from top to bottom is fight and fight cruel; this is a war, not a pinpoint operation.'

This might account for the sudden Israeli use of phosphorus shells. Roaming the 'earthquake zone' ruins of Gaza, Donald Macintyre interviewed Mohamed Abu Kalima, who saw his mother descending the stairs with her clothes on fire and who found the body of his father in the hallway 'stuck together' to the bodies of Mohamed's three brothers, aged eight, ten and fourteen. His fifteen-month-old sister Shahed, lying separately, had 'melted away'. Amira Hass, making her own rounds of the wreckage of Gaza, heard ominous stories of a 'different' Israeli army that forced Palestinians to flee their homes in their tens of thousands, 'under fire from helicopters, tanks, drones, behind a heavy screen of smoke produced by white phosphorus bombs'. Israel, Hass perceptively concluded, 'has finally breached the few limits it formerly set up for itself as an occupying state, and defied all the restrictions of international law that would require it to provide for the safety and welfare of the occupied population'.

Haaretz and Breaking the Silence* played a crucial role in revealing the testimony, including further evidence that many Israeli troops had the sense of fighting a 'religious war' against gentiles in Gaza. Military rabbis had distributed a clear message to soldiers, another veteran said: 'We are the Jewish people. We came to this land by a miracle, God brought us back to this land and now we need to fight to expel the Gentiles who are interfering with our conquest of this holy land.' In this context, Tzipi Livni's talk of Israel 'going wild' in Gaza becomes clearer. A later dispatch by Macintyre referred to leaflets at military synagogues stating that 'the Palestinians are like the Philistines of old, newcomers who do not belong in the land'. One rabbi was reported to have told Israeli troops that they were conducting the war as 'the sons of light' against 'the sons of darkness'.

There were more revelations; of Israelis using Palestinians as 'human shields', including an eleven-year-old boy, of further vandalism and the deliberate destruction of infrastructure on a vast scale. A battalion commander was quoted as telling his men that 'if we see something

---

* Veterans of the Israel Defense Forces who object to the brutality of the armed forces in the Palestinian Occupied Territories. It was established in 2004 to enable serving and discharged members of the IDF to recount their experiences.

suspect and shoot, better hit an innocent than hesitate to target an enemy'. What these soldiers revealed, said an *Independent* editorial, was far from a 'scrupulous morality' 'but an almost complete absence of it' and 'a chilling indifference to civilian casualties' made possible by 'the permissive rules of engagement followed by their superiors'. These reports continued into the summer of 2009 and there was further corroboration of Israeli army cruelty in the growing files of Breaking the Silence. Amnesty released two human rights reports on the Gaza killings, Human Rights Watch another four.

So who could save the Palestinians? What human intercession could give them the dignity and justice? What power could survive the intimidation of all who dared oppose Israel's occupation and repression of Palestinian nationhood?

Perhaps because there was no one else, the Palestinian civilians of Gaza were forced to entrust their hopes for justice in the small man who had sought to bring equal justice to the murderous Balkans. Could the appointment of Judge Richard Goldstone, one of the world's most eminent jurists, as leader of the 'United Nations Fact-Finding Mission on the Gaza Conflict' provide those who had suffered with some recognition of their pain?

Could Goldstone – in his own words to me at the Hague more than a decade earlier – demonstrate 'the main purpose of justice'? 'It's to officially acknowledge to the victims what happened to them,' he had told me then. Naturally enough, when he was appointed the UN mission leader in April 2009, I pulled from my files the sixteen pages of notes of my long interview with him on 13 September 1996.

I met Goldstone at the International War Crimes Tribunal in the Hague. While our discussion then was about the Balkan war, some of his remarks might apply all too painfully to the aftermath of the Gaza war. His comments on the almost culpable lassitude of the UN Dutch battalion in failing to protect the Muslims of Srebrenica and his anger at the Americans for refusing to risk the lives of their military personnel in hunting for Serb war criminals only tangentially touched upon his new task as a 'fact-finder' amid the ruins of Gaza. But some of Goldstone's more emotional replies carried a troubling forewarning of what he would encounter in Gaza. I asked him about an earlier Middle East atrocity, the massacre of up to 1,700 Palestinian refugees in the

Sabra and Chatila camps in Beirut in September 1982, murdered by
Israel's Lebanese Christian militia allies – while Israeli troops watched
from surrounding buildings. This was clearly a war crime, I said to
Goldstone, yet – examining our readers' letters at the time – they did
not respond to it as a war crime in the same way they would later
respond to Bosnia because, I said, 'these were a different, coloured
people with an unhappy reputation of being refugees ... as opposed to
being poor, European refugees'. Goldstone interrupted:

> If things happen to people whom you don't consider your
> equals, it's easier to swallow. And this is why the
> dehumanisation process, certainly from what I've learned, is an
> absolute sine qua non of any genocide. You have to reduce the
> victim to a level that's below you. Otherwise it's not going to
> work.

He said, if international criminal leaders 'know that they may be called
to account, it must ... in a substantial number of cases act as a sort of
deterrent'.

But as I read through my notes again, I wondered whether Goldstone
might be an insensitive man in his historical judgements. His reference
to the victims of the Armenian genocide as 'entitled to justice' but
whose 'boat didn't come into their harbour' seemed unnecessarily
callous.

And he was a Jew, who expressed his admiration and affection for
Israel. And thus he held, perhaps, for many in the world, a sacred hope
that his Jewish origin gave him a unique ability to hold Israel to
account. No novel could dream up a more dramatic story of courage;
that of an individual who, squeezed between the colossal power of
Israel and its allies, yet unwilling to excuse the dishonesty of Gaza's
Islamist protectors, must produce a truthful account that might save
thousands of innocent lives.

The Israelis decided from the start that they would give no help of
any kind to Goldstone. At the end of his report, he included his revealing correspondence with Aharon Leshno Yaar, the Israeli ambassador
to Israel's UN office in Geneva. Yaar, while stressing that Israel's decision did not reflect 'on its sincere respect for you personally', objected
to the 'inflammatory and prejudicial language' in which the UN

Human Rights Council's original resolution for the mission was written. The Israelis were right. HRC Resolution S-9/1 had specifically limited the team to enquiries about 'violations' of international law committed by Israel 'against the Palestinian people'. Before accepting to lead the mission, Goldstone had insisted its mandate be changed. It would instead now investigate violations of international law by both Israelis and Palestinians.

But if Goldstone thought that the change in his mission's definition would persuade Israel to help him, he was wrong. While at first placing itself in the dock for declining to assist a now 'impartial' inquiry, Israel's refusal allowed it to set up its own investigations and subsequently claim that Goldstone's conclusions did not take account of theirs – to Goldstone's eventual ruin.

Readers are advised to study Goldstone's exhaustive 452-page report. It investigated the deaths of more than 220 people – at least forty-seven of them children and nineteen adult women – conducted 188 individual interviews and perused more than 10,000 pages of documentation, thirty videos and 1,200 photographs. Despite Israel's stubborn non-participation, Goldstone and his three colleagues investigated Hamas' attacks on Sderot and other Israeli towns, heard evidence from Israeli witnesses in Geneva – when the team could not enter Israel itself – and showed no patience with Hamas' bleak excuses for war crimes. But nor did they demonstrate the slightest bias towards Israel, whose sheer brutality and unlawful killing of Palestinian civilians was catalogued in minute detail. It was the nearest the Israeli–Palestinian conflict had ever come to an impartial international investigation.

It noted the Israeli raid on Gaza on 4 November 2008 when 'the ceasefire began to founder', adding that Israel's 'effective control' of the territory established 'that the Gaza Strip remains occupied by Israel'. Criminal proceedings, the report added, 'have a deterrent function and offer a measure of justice for the victims of violations'.

Goldstone's enterprise contained no journalistic emotions or rhetoric, merely the clinical work of criminal investigators. Of particular concern were the killings of the al-Samouni family, the mass destruction in the area and the air strike that killed twenty-two members of the al-Daya family in the Zeitoun district. The report countered the Israeli argument that it should 'put pressure' on Hamas 'by targeting

292 NIGHT OF POWER

infrastructure to attain its war aims' by stating that 'attacks that are not directed against military or dual use objectives are violations of the laws of war'.* Goldstone dissected the initial attacks on the police barracks, concluding that up to eighty-nine officers and cadets had been killed, but concentrated on the civilian victims.

Like the Israelis, Hamas armed groups and their militant allies were not 'agreeable' to meetings with his personnel, although Goldstone listed numerous occasions when they had placed civilians at risk when firing rockets close to residential housing. However, his report 'found no evidence that Palestinian combatants mingled with the civilian population with the intention of shielding themselves from attack'. So much for the 'human shields' of Israeli propaganda. Equally important was his note that Israel's emergency and ambulance service, in contradiction to the Israeli army, stated that the Palestinian Red Crescent did not use ambulances to transport weapons or ammunition.

Goldstone dismissed many of Israel's pretexts for firing phosphorus shells at the United Nations Relief and Works Agency's headquarters, asking 'how [Israeli] specialists expertly trained in the complex issue of artillery deployment and aware of the presence of an extremely sensitive site can strike that site ten times while apparently trying to avoid it'.

The evidence of civilian deaths was painstakingly catalogued; the al-Samouni slaughter was retold. When Wael al-Samouni took Goldstone around the courtyard of his cousin's home in Gaza, the head of the UN mission found the walls lined with twenty-three photographs framed in black. The Palestinian paused at each picture of the dead to talk about them. 'The pain of loss affected Goldstone deeply,' his biographer would write. 'As Wael completed the tour, neither man

---

* There was a telling reminder in the final report of the tendency of military forces to enlarge the area of civilian targets, quoting an academic study on whether 'new wars' required 'new laws'. The original paper, by Geneva university law professor Marco Sassoli – referenced in the report – argued that if attacks against political, financial or 'psychological' targets proved decisive in war, then 'it may be hospital maternity wards, kindergartens, religious shrines, or homes for the elderly whose destruction would most affect the willingness of the military or of the government to continue the war'. This encapsulated precisely the way in which successive conflicts in the Balkans and Middle East built on the precedents set by successive armies to seek ever more extraordinary excuses for their killing of civilians.

could contain his emotion, and the two clasped each other in a tearful embrace.'

If the accounts of the killings seem shocking now, imagine the effect they had on the UN team. Almost ten years later, a veteran Irish UN and EU peacekeeper Desmond Travers would recall how they responded to their interview with Khalid Abd Rabbo. It was, he said, 'absolutely awful', a meeting that Travers still struggled to describe, especially when he came to the point where the third Israeli soldier emerged from the tank with his Uzi and shot the three children and their grandmother. The family, carrying white flags, had emerged from their home and were waiting for orders from the Israeli soldiers.

Repeatedly, the Goldstone Report would describe eyewitnesses as 'credible and reliable'. Incriminating evidence emerged of exactly how Israeli soldiers used Palestinian men as human shields, forcing them to walk in front of troops to search buildings. The report described an incident in which a civilian was told to enter houses, threatened with execution if he did not warn the Israelis of men who might be hiding there, and constantly 'punched, slapped and insulted'.

Though less dramatic in human terms, the UN mission was evidently shocked by the massive extent of Israel's deliberate destruction of Palestinian infrastructure in Gaza, its factories, orchards, farms, sewage plants and civic buildings. The Fourth Geneva Convention had been breached again, Goldstone's team decided, and 'unlawful and wanton destruction which is not justified by military necessity would amount to a war crime'.

The publication of the Goldstone Report on 15 September 2009 was an earthquake. It spoke of war crimes committed by the Israelis and possible crimes against humanity. It focused on the killing and suffering of Palestinian civilians but did not try to exonerate Hamas, which was also accused of war crimes and crimes against humanity, albeit on nothing like the same scale. The report did not accept Hamas' pathetic claim that it did not wish to target Israeli civilians. Hamas, which declined to reply to the report's demand for investigations, gained no credit from its conclusions.

A short, rather optimistic book that Goldstone had published about war crimes and international justice nine years earlier gave some small clue of what he and his team would produce in 2009. He spoke of the need for tribunals that would provide 'a meaningful blow against impunity', that the world would no longer allow 'serious war crimes to be committed without the threat of retribution', while lamenting the US refusal to participate in an international criminal court. This seriousness of purpose was part of his character – even if it also gave the dangerous impression that he was a resolute man.

Did he not comprehend the original sin he would be committing if he dared – even suggested – that the country for which he felt such affection, so much trust and love, should have its foundational myths shattered before the eyes of its enemies? If Israel was to be asked to lay itself prostrate before a war crimes tribunal then no amount of tanks or F-16s or missiles or, indeed, nuclear weapons could protect it. Goldstone's integrity, his honesty, his reputation as a patently decent and fair man and as an eminent jurist – his very Jewish origins – would not save him. For these were the very reasons why he had to be politically and morally liquidated.

Had Goldstone been a middle-ranking UN official trying to make a name for himself by throwing stones at the Goliath of the Middle East in a hopeless effort to right the wrongs of the Palestinians, he would have been ignored.

But Goldstone simply did not appreciate that his UN report, in the words of his future biographer, 'would make Richard Goldstone the most hated man in the Jewish world'. Less than a month after it was published he gave a penetrating, highly revealing but largely ignored interview to the leftist and progressive Jewish American magazine *Tikkun*. When he first arrived in Gaza, Goldstone told Rabbi Michael Lerner, he was shocked at the scale of destruction, particularly the number of private homes that had been razed:

> And I wasn't prepared for the stories that were told by witnesses
> we considered to be credible. As to the way the Israeli army
> treated them, I felt a great deal of shame and embarrassment
> particularly as a Jew, but also as a human being.

When he investigated the killings in the Gaza mosque, Goldstone said, 'I put myself in the position [of] how Jews would feel if they were attacked in a synagogue when it was full of worshippers.' He was 'a firm believer in the absolute right of the Jewish people to have their home there in Israel,' he said, before adding that 'it's really crucially important for Jews particularly to stand up for Jewish values.'

Again, we witness Goldstone's sense of morality and rectitude, his belief in Jewish values – at a time when he evidently did not comprehend that these characteristics would only increase the abuse he was to suffer. The scale of animosity directed at Goldstone was visceral. That old pro-Israeli warhorse, Harvard lawyer Alan Dershowitz, waited until Israel had made its inept response to the report before denouncing Goldstone as 'a traitor to the Jewish people', adding that his report was 'a defamation written by an evil, evil man'. Many liberal Israelis and non-Israeli Jews have long regarded Dershowitz as a windbag who should not be taken seriously rather than a moral sage, but Tzipi Livni, now the Israeli opposition leader, also said that 'the Goldstone Report was born in sin'. No doubt fearing – correctly, as it turned out – that war crimes charges might be levelled against her outside Israel, she rejected an Israeli commission of inquiry into Gaza 'without ensuring that the sheer establishment of such a commission would protect IDF officers from future lawsuits'.

Mark Regev, the Israeli prime minister's spokesman, adopted Livni's messianic tone. 'This report was conceived in sin and is the product of a union between propaganda and bias,' he said. Other Israeli representatives applied hitherto trusty bandages to the wounds inflicted by Goldstone, but it was difficult to maintain the 'purity of arms' myth when the Israeli army was accused of punishing, humiliating and terrorising civilians. As Norman Finkelstein candidly pointed out, Israel had over thirty years refined its ideological weapons so that any critic of Israel was an anti-Semite, a self-hating Jew or a Holocaust denier:

> But now along comes Richard Goldstone. He's Jewish, he's a Zionist, he says he loves Israel, he says his mother was an activist in the Zionist women's organisation, his daughter went to live in Israel, he sits on the board of governors at the Hebrew University in Jerusalem, he has an honorary degree from the Hebrew University, and he's also a distinguished international jurist … He wrote what he wrote because it is true. And that for Israel is the nightmare scenario.

Israel began producing its own military 'investigations',* but the United States had to take over the task of trashing the Goldstone Report and rescuing the Israeli army. Over the coming months, the Obama administration did everything it could to debunk, undermine and destroy the work of the UN mission in Gaza. US assistant secretary of state and human rights lawyer Michael Posner declared the report 'deeply flawed', criticising its 'methodology and many of its recommendations'. Posner could not be bothered to explain these 'flaws' to Goldstone. 'I would be happy to respond to them, if and when I know what they are,' Goldstone responded. Obama's new UN ambassador Susan Rice spoke of the Goldstone Report's 'lopsided' view of Israel, which she claimed was perfectly capable of investigating possible war crimes, adding that 'our view is that we need to be focused on the future'. She would later tell Congress that she would like the report to 'disappear'.

Congress, which had obligingly prepared the ground for Israel's attack in the summer of 2008, now condemned the 'biased report'. Thirty-two senators signed a letter to Hillary Clinton, praising her State Department's efforts to quash Goldstone's recommendations and claiming that 'legitimising the report sends a dangerous message to countries defending themselves against terrorism'. The Israeli justice system should handle matters of human rights internally, the letter advised.

Clinton herself telephoned British foreign secretary David Miliband, urging him to oppose a UN Security Council resolution. The real fear in Israel and the US, of course, was Goldstone's recommendation that the UN Security Council should refer his report to the International Criminal Court.

---

* The Israelis closed their first 'inquiry' into Gaza deaths, including the killing of a Palestinian mother and two children, only six weeks after hostilities ended, claiming that evidence against soldiers was based on 'hearsay'. In April 2009, the Israeli military closed five more investigations – the public had to accept the army's word that these examinations ever took place – into attacks on civilians, UN staff and compounds. It cited 'lack of evidence'. It conceded that military errors might have caused 'isolated cases' of civilian casualties, but that the army had acted 'within international law'. As it had – or so it claimed – when it fired phosphorus shells into Gaza. Further evidence of the IDF's alleged ability to judge itself for 'war crimes' came in 2012 when an Israeli sniper who in Gaza killed two Palestinian women carrying a white flag was sentenced to forty-five days in prison for 'using a weapon illegally'.

Nor could the report's authors have imagined the deceitfulness of Mahmoud Abbas' Palestinian Authority. After initially welcoming the mission's work, Abbas was intimidated by the Americans into withdrawing his support and delaying any action at the UN for six months. Abbas claimed that he needed time to consult Arab allies; Clayton Swisher's Palestine Papers reveal how Obama's new 'special envoy' for Middle East peace George Mitchell asked Palestinian negotiators to 'refrain from pursuing or supporting any initiative directly or indirectly in international legal forums'.

Palestinians wounded in the Gaza offensive held a press conference to express their outrage at Abbas' obsequiousness. A Palestinian minister resigned. Abbas had ganged up alongside Israel, the Obama-Clinton administration and the US Congress to crush Goldstone's brave work. The report would now lie dormant for at least six months. In reality, forever.

But the political aftershocks of Goldstone's earthquake continued to torment Israel.* Norman Finkelstein believed that Israel's subsequent decision to abandon the use of phosphorus shells was due to Goldstone's report, but the damage to Israel's integrity was not so easily assuaged. Benjamin Netanyahu recognised that 'the most important sphere we need to work in is the sphere of public opinion in the democratic world'. At the Israeli annual Herzliya conference in 2010, I listened to speaker after speaker condemning Goldstone five months after his report was published. Uzi Arad, Netanyahu's 'security adviser', told the great and the good at Israel's regular hasbara meeting that the report had become part of an insidious political campaign to 'delegitimise' the Israeli state.

If in order to tell the truth, Goldstone had been forced to climb the vast rampart of political power behind America's support for Israel, it now seemed that its walls would crash down upon him personally. His report might be misrepresented and torn to pieces by politicians and

---

* NGOs and journalists would not let the Israeli army rest in peace. In September 2009, B'Tselem produced figures – backed by death certificates, photographs and testimonies – showing that 252 children under the age of sixteen had been killed in the Gaza offensive. Five months later, the Goldstone Report's assertion that an Israeli air strike had hit the only working flour mill in Gaza – denied by the Israelis – was proved true when it emerged that a demining team had defused part of a fractured Israeli 500lb Mark 82 aerial bomb, made by US manufacturer Raytheon, in the ruins.

diplomats but the jurist himself had so far survived with his personal life and reputation unscathed. However much mud was flung at his work, Goldstone remained a sentinel tower. So he, too, would have to be broken.

There were persistent rumours, especially in Israel, that Goldstone was now put under personal pressure by his Jewish family. He had complained in April 2010 that local protests would prevent him attending his grandson's bar mitzvah in Johannesburg, a threat that was only withdrawn when he agreed to meet leaders of the South African Zionist Federation and other Jewish organisations. The South African chief rabbi Warren Goldstein claimed in a local newspaper that Goldstone's work had 'unfairly done enormous damage to the reputation and safety of the State of Israel and her citizens', to which the judge had made a feisty reply. He was 'dismayed', he wrote, 'that the chief rabbi would so brazenly politicise the occasion of my thirteen-year-old grandson's bar mitzvah to engage in further attacks on me'. The rabbi's 'rhetoric' about tolerance 'simply does not coincide with how my family and I have been treated'.

South African Jews claimed that the report had put their own sons and daughters in danger if they had chosen to serve in the Israeli military and then return to South Africa, though they never questioned the cruelty of the Israeli army their families might be joining. Within weeks, Goldstone was to come under much more vicious attack by Israeli journalists and politicians for his supposedly unblemished role in South Africa's apartheid courts. Under the headline 'Judge Goldstone's dark past', *Yediot Ahronoth* ran a long article in early May stating that Goldstone had sentenced twenty-eight black defendants to death by hanging and others to 'birching'.

His enemies now exploded in wrath once more. How could a man who was 'a part of the system' of apartheid cruelty demand war crimes trials for Israel's innocent soldiers? Israeli politicians and government officials were delighted with this revelation, forgetting their country's own cosy relationship with the formerly racist regime in South Africa.

Goldstone's biographer, Daniel Terris, did his best to justify the unjustifiable. In South Africa, Goldstone 'believed that the law – perverted though it was – could nevertheless serve the cause of justice,' he wrote. Terris does not quite clear up these events, save for a comforting suggestion that the sentences were not carried out. Though a restrained man in public, Goldstone spoke often of his experiences under apartheid, but he never mentioned the hangings. Nor did he refer to these death sentences in press interviews or in publicity material prior to his appointment in the Hague or his position as leader of the Gaza report. Was penitence now required?

The sword fell, appropriately enough, on April Fool's Day. It was an unworthy, cringeing article which Richard Goldstone published in the *Washington Post* on 1 April 2011. The key lines of this mea culpa read as follows:

> If I had known then what I know now, the Goldstone Report would have been a different document ... Our Report found evidence of potential war crimes and 'possibly crimes against humanity' by both Israel and Hamas ... The allegations of intentionality by Israel were based on the deaths of and injuries to civilians in situations where our fact-finding mission found no evidence on which to draw any other reasonable conclusion ... [T]he investigations published by the Israeli military ... indicate that civilians were not intentionally targeted as a matter of policy.

This astonishing volte-face stunned all who had believed in Goldstone's courage and perseverance. Suddenly, he was suggesting, we must take seriously the very process of Israeli self-examination which no one found credible. Just over six months earlier, Goldstone had himself remarked in the *New York Times* that both Israel and Hamas had 'dismal records' of investigating their own forces. While Israel had begun investigations into alleged violations by its forces in the Gaza conflict, he wrote, 'they are unlikely to be serious and objective'.

But no longer, it seemed. Thanks to Israel's exculpatory noises, Goldstone concluded that 'we know a lot more today' than when his findings were first published. And he proceeded to return to the barbaric killings of the al-Samouni family, seizing upon the report that the deaths were caused by a misread drone image. The Israeli investigations that Goldstone now came to embrace were largely held in secret, their testimony never made public. To accept that Israel, by far the biggest killers in Gaza compared to Hamas, were going to tell the truth took more than a leap of faith. Or was this, in some strange way, what it was about? About the power of faith over the power of reason?

Daniel Terris recalls how Richard Falk, a Princeton law professor and former UN rapporteur on human rights in Gaza and the West Bank, described Goldstone's retraction as 'a personal tragedy for such a distinguished international civil servant'. Terris's book was eminently fair, although he does not give Goldstone the absolution he might have preferred. The Goldstone Report 'brought to the fore the challenging questions about how best to protect civilian lives in the complex circumstances of asymmetric warfare'. Goldstone, Terris wrote, declined to comment during the next Gaza outrage because 'the wounds were still deep'. But what about the wounds of the Palestinians?

Goldstone's family was torn apart by the Gaza report. His daughter Nicole's anguish 'spilled over into rage' and she told her father she was furious that he had allowed himself 'to be used by those who seek to destroy Israel'. Goldstone was later dropped from the board of the Hebrew University.

Desmond Travers, one of the report's three fellow authors, spoke of 'the blatant untruth' in Goldstone's renunciation. 'Our first hostile reaction ... was that Richard had no right to start his preamble by saying "if I knew then what I know now, our findings would have been different".' Travers thought Goldstone had been 'very, very badly emotionally injured' and concluded that 'privately, in the human rights world, Richard is very much a spent force, and he's finished'.

Goldstone's detractors lost no time cashing in on his retraction. Almost immediately, the US Senate asked the UN to rescind the Goldstone Report. Netanyahu announced that 'the fact that Goldstone backtracked must lead to the shelving of this report once and for all'. The Israeli media scourged him all over again. Finkelstein's contention that Goldstone's recantation 'renewed Israel's license to kill', was echoed by Gideon Levy who exclaimed that 'Goldstone has paved the path for a second Gaza war'. It would begin just over four years later, on 8 July 2014 – and this time it would kill well over 2,000 Palestinians.

It is tempting to regard this story as a classical tragedy, but that would be a romantic distortion. It was a historical and legalistic betrayal of the Palestinians. The most accurate of the humanitarian reports on the Gaza conflict had been most scurrilously renounced by its principal author, a good man brought down by a fatal flaw. And thus Goldstone failed all those Palestinians who put their trust in him as a seeker after truth and a teller of truth. He did tell the truth. And then he denied it. And that will be his legacy.

In the years to come, the drama of Gaza appeared to repeat itself in ever tighter circles; Palestinian blood, world outrage at disproportionate slaughter, attacks on UN premises, pitiful UN inquiries and Israeli indignation became a pattern, coarse and vulgar in its retelling.

There was to be no Goldstone-style investigation into the diminutive 2012 Gaza killings – in which only a hundred Palestinian civilians and four Israeli civilians were killed – although the UN trundled out a diminutive copycat version of Goldstone after the graves of Gaza were filled in 2014. This time the UN would count 1,462 Palestinian civilians and seven Israeli civilians among the 2,251 dead, far exceeding the 2008–9 hecatomb.

In 2014, Colonel Ofer Winter of the Givati Brigade – a veteran of 2008–9 in Gaza – told his soldiers that

> History has chosen us to be the bayonet point of battle against the Gazan terrorist enemy which curses, defames and abuses the God of Israel's military campaigns. God, the Lord of Israel, make our path successful, as we are about to fight for Your People, Israel, against an enemy who defames your name.*

If Winter's Holy War was answered, the Palestinian response was almost Goldstone-like in its demand for international justice. 'Palestine' requested to join the International Criminal Court. Naturally, Mahmoud Abbas was condemned for wishing to try Israel for war crimes in Gaza. But in the real world, this should have been the most significant event in more than forty years of the Palestinian–Israeli conflict. The descendants of the PLO wanted to abide by international

---

* As usual, the Palestinians, UN, Israeli and NGO statistics differed. Sixty-seven Israeli soldiers were killed in 2014 and more than 750 members of Palestinian armed groups. Overall, the exchange rate for civilian death was one Israeli for more than 200 Palestinians. In both 2012 and 2014, Hamas distinguished themselves by executing Palestinian 'spies', a total of thirty-one supposed 'informers', including two women, to add to their mythical victory against 'Zionism'.

law. After all their past calls for Israel's extinction, the suicide bombings and two intifadas, the Palestinians were asking to join one of the
most prestigious judicial bodies on earth.

It goes without saying that the US State Department, seeking to
protect any Israeli soldier who might be indicted as a war criminal, was
'strongly opposed' and 'deeply troubled' by the Palestinian application.
According to John Kerry's spokesman, it was 'entirely counterproductive' because it did 'nothing to further the aspirations of the Palestinian
people for a sovereign and independent state'. Israel was outraged.*

Obama had not uttered a word of condemnation after the 2012 killings in Gaza, Ari Shavit of *Haaretz* noted, 'after all the innocent Afghans
and Pakistanis he has killed'. As one lobby group said of this Gaza
'war', 'our [Israeli] press did not adequately expose the huge disparity
between the number of civilian casualties in Libya and Kosovo and the
total lack of NATO casualties'. The cross-fertilisation of wars was a
fruitful business.

In the years to come, even the audacious Israeli soldiers who contributed so much evidence to Breaking the Silence would be defeated.
Veterans who tried to talk publicly were abused, and in some cases
prevented from speaking altogether. 'Breaking the Silence was delegit-
imised by the establishment, with the typical collaboration of the Israeli
media,' Gideon Levy said. 'I'm afraid to say that Breaking the Silence is
crushed today.' Who could withstand this weight of grief and – despite
all the falsehoods, the lies and intimidation – fight on, whatever the
cost?

It was a damp, cold early winter afternoon when I drove across
Toronto to the university medical centre. I was almost six thousand
miles from Gaza but when I telephoned the Palestinian doctor on the

---

* We can only imagine what might have happened if Israel and America had demanded
that Palestine join the International Criminal Court as a qualification for statehood. There
would be war crime accusations against Hamas and Fatah for encouraging suicide
bombings, firing missiles into Israeli towns or executing their own prisoners – and thus
Hamas and Fatah could be indicted for war crimes. Abbas' refusal to do so would then be
further proof of his 'terrorist' intentions. However, the United States – and this did not
feature in the flurry of news reports on the Palestinian application – had itself refused to
join the ICC. And with good reason; because Washington, like the Israelis, was also
worried that its soldiers and government officials would be arraigned for war crimes (Abu
Ghraib, CIA waterboarding, etc). Great minds kill alike.

fifth floor, his accent was still a thick Arabic rather than Canadian, cheerfully agreeing to set his time aside to talk about the worst moments of his life. I knew the questions I wanted to ask. Doctor he may be, but could history really have dictated that the blood of three beheaded daughters should be injected into a vein of hope?

A large coloured photograph on the wall showed Dr Abuelaish's three daughters, Mayar, Aya and Bessan, sitting on a blustery Gaza beach in the early New Year of 2009. Two weeks after this photograph was taken, they were with their father in their Gaza home when the Israeli tank shells came smashing into the house. He told the story eloquently, terribly, unanswerably in the minutes and hours and months afterwards.

Izzeldin is an associate professor of global health and knows all too well the terrible ironies of his life. He was already the first Palestinian to receive a staff position at an Israeli hospital. Could there have been a more appropriate symbol of human trust between two sides? His agony, the affliction of explosives that tore his children and his niece to bits, televised across Israel from the wreckage of Gaza, should have changed everything. But then came the blood of 2012 and the blood of 2014. But despite the fact that he vainly took the Israelis to court for his family's slaughter, he founded the Daughters for Life Foundation to provide scholarships for young women to study at universities in the West Bank, Gaza, Israel, Lebanon, Jordan, Egypt and Syria. Izzeldin wrote a book called *I Shall Not Hate* and is now a Canadian citizen, and much honoured.

He clings to what is perhaps a forlorn hope: that history will always surprise us. 'Did you ever dream that a black guy would be president of the United States?' he asks. 'If I'd told you that fifteen years ago, you'd have told me I'm crazy. Or would you imagine Trump would be president? Can you tell me what will happen tomorrow? Did you think Arafat would ever shake hands with Rabin?' I get the doctor's point: some things are unimaginable, others pre-determined.

'Palestine will never leave me,' he says. 'It's inside me. I go there. I am rooted there. I understand all the challenges and the myths. The land is the determinant of our life. The Jews imagined two thousand years ago that the Jews would go back to Jerusalem and they were all over the world – and they succeeded in establishing their state. [But] we are close [to a Palestinian state]. We are there. We see it. There is a difference between what you want and what is the reality ... This is not a religious conflict. This is a political, colonial conflict.'

The latter is true, but Izzeldin's determination is laced with an innocent pragmatism. He does believe that Palestinians and Israelis should love one another but he places his trust in common sense. This seems to me a dangerous foundation for peace in the Middle East. There can be no 'transfer' of Palestinians from the West Bank, he says. I am not so sure. He has doubts about Abbas, the Palestinian 'president', and then says that as 'Palestine' gets smaller and smaller for Palestinians, so the Palestinian factions want to be bigger and bigger. And then he talks of how Palestinians do not want to 'delete' the Israelis. 'We want to be equal to them. I want to ask Netanyahu: what do Israelis want for themselves and their children?'

'The antidote of hatred and revolution is success and education,' Izzeldin says. 'We must understand the interconnectedness of health and peace. If you are in Gaza, you want to be happy, to be free, to enjoy yourself. This is health. If you are unemployed, you want to have a job. Peace, freedom, justice, education depends on who you are and where you are.'

It must be a hard call, this peace-seeking and peace-believing. He tells me he is pursuing his legal action against the Israelis in an Israeli court. Whatever compensation he wins will go towards Daughters for Life. He should win, I tell him, as we sit in his safe, well-lit doctor's office on that November day in Toronto.

But of course, he did not win. Almost a month later, Justice Shlomo Friedlander will rule against him. Hamas was responsible for the deaths of Bessan, Mayar, Aya and their cousin Noor. Figures on the roof of Izzeldin's house were suspected of being 'lookouts' for 'terror groups', the court is told. Secondary explosions may have been caused by weapons stored in the building. Judge Friedlander's conclusions may seem faintly familiar at the end of this painful chapter. They were, perhaps, preordained, shaped by the history of Gaza that hangs in curtains over the lands of the Palestinians – both Arab and Jew – who lived under the British mandate, and over the lands in which they live today. In many cases, the curtains are heavy with blood.

None more so than that of Izzeldin Abuelaish. 'It is regrettable that the four children who were not involved in the fighting lost their lives,' Friedlander lectured the court. 'However, this is a very unfortunate side effect of the criminal practice of the terrorist organisations to fight Israel out of a civilian population.' It was the same old story. The Israelis killed the innocents but they were not to blame.

One of his surviving daughters had telephoned Izzeldin Abuelaish on the morning of our interview. She had read my article about the village of Huj, and the doctor's face lit up – his grandfather was the mayor of Huj in 1948 and his family came from the village of Huj. And they had been forced from their village by the new Israeli army and abandoned to the camps of Gaza. Izzeldin produced a mobile phone upon which he has photographs of a stone wall that was all that remained of the original Huj village. He had gone to meet the Israelis who lived in Sderot and they had led him to see this little old wall that divided the farming lands of his ancestral home.

He is a tough man, this Palestinian-Canadian doctor who, just a week before we met, had expressed his condolences for eleven Jewish Americans murdered in their synagogue in Pittsburgh. 'I will never give up,' he says to me. 'I will never forget my daughters. I believe one day I will meet them and I am accountable to God and to them, and they will ask me: "What did you do for us?"'

10

How Brave Our
Warships Looked
That Dawn

... I will do such things –
What they are, yet I know not; but they shall be
The terrors of the earth.

William Shakespeare, *King Lear*, Act II, scene 4

The sun is burning through the curtains, and I listen to the telephone ringing in the next room. Sixty years old this morning, the chance to sleep in, and now that low, long, burbling ringing tone. Birthday greetings? A bit early, I thought, even for Lebanese friends. The phone didn't stop. I could hear the cars on the Mediterranean Corniche – fewer than usual for this blistering summer's day in Beirut, a peaceful morning in a peaceful year, 2006, in a largely peaceful city.

True, Rafiq Hariri, Lebanon's former prime minister, had been blown up by a huge bomb more than a year ago, along with twenty-one other innocents. But the last Israeli–Lebanese war had been ten years ago.

I picked up the phone. 'I'm so sorry for you, Robert. What a thing to happen on your birthday! The Hizbollah captured some Israelis on the border – an Israeli tank blew up. They've killed five or six Israeli soldiers.' I walked to the balcony. No wonder the traffic had died down. The Lebanese had a sixth sense about these things. They called their families, ran home, drove home, back to their apartments or hovels, closed their shops, queued in fear at banks and petrol stations. Money, fuel; the siege memory of the Lebanese stretched back to the Lebanon war of 1982, when Beirut was surrounded by the Israeli army.

I sat for a minute on the balcony sofa. A few foreign tourists walked the Corniche – Lebanon had long resumed its role as a tourist destination for both the Westerners and Saudis. Hadn't Hizbollah's chairman, Sayed Hassan Nasrallah, promised the Lebanese a quiet summer? Mobile networks jammed, I kept punching the repeat button on Abed's number. Faithful Abed, comrade of civil war and invasion, of bombardment and militia checkpoints. He was due to come at lunchtime with the morning papers. He must come now. The Israelis would attack Lebanon. And all this, readers must remember, was two years before the great Gaza attack of 2008. This was the rerun of earlier attacks on Lebanon, but it was the trial run for Gaza.

Abed and I made a run south, through Sidon, the banging of anti-aircraft guns from the Palestinian camp at Ein el-Helweh, the polite Lebanese soldiers still at their checkpoints above Tyre, filled with warnings for the crazy journalists heading into a war when all sane souls were driving north to Beirut. There were plumes of black smoke to the east, the pummelling sound of bombs dropped from the air, the smell of oranges from the orchards on both sides of the road; a UN truck careering over the pot-holes near the coast.

Yes, it was a rerun of a movie that I had seen many times before. I had followed this same route in the 1978 Israeli invasion, during the 1982 Israeli invasion, after the 1993 Israeli bombardment, in 1996 and now again in 2006. Only the dead were new. There were three corpses in the Tyre morgue, one without a head. The war had only just begun.

We watched for Israeli gunboats. Their shelling of the coast road was a routine, every bridge a killing field, every fleeing civilian marked down as a 'terrorist'. Once more, Israel intended to 'root out the evil weed of terrorism' but also to cause 'pain' to Lebanon, because the Lebanese government was responsible for the Hizbollah. Of course, the Beirut cabinet had no power at all over the Hizbollah. Hizbollah's fighters were Shiites to a man, as were at least a third of the Lebanese army's soldiers. They were not going to break into their own homes and kill their brothers, fathers or uncles on behalf of Israeli and US policy in Lebanon. Besides, Hizbollah's weapons came through 'sister' Syria, whose loving embrace of Lebanon was still secured by the Shiite militia. Hizbollah's men were more efficient than Israel's soldiers, their confidence matched only by their arrogance and their belief in God.

We would not be back in Beirut until late afternoon and I jotted thoughts into my notebook as Abed raced north up the highway. In the wars of the eighties and nineties, I had scribbled away in the car, knowing that I needed time to punch out tape for the telex machine, wait for the power cuts to end, try to make calls on broken landlines. But now we had laptops and mobile phones that purred away in our hands, colleagues and friends offering advice, repeating what they had heard on the radio, warning of air raids, innocently asking if I was free for dinner on Thursday while I cowered in a ditch to avoid red-hot bomb fragments.

My words spread out over page after page, jogged by the speed of Abed's driving. It's about Syria, I write on 12 July. Had Syria not allowed its Hizbollah friends to cross the UN's Blue Line to attack Israeli forces? Lebanese prime minister Fouad Siniora may have thought he was running his country, but it was President Bashar al-Assad of Syria who could bring life or death to a land that lost 150,000 lives in its 1975–90 civil war. Syria would rely on an old formula; despite all Israel's threats of destroying Lebanon's infrastructure, this war would run out of control until Israel would plead for a ceasefire, ask the Americans for help. The international big-hitters would then turn up in the real Lebanese capital – Damascus, not Beirut – and ask for help. Meanwhile, to get at Hizbollah, Israel must send its soldiers into Lebanon once again.

My mobile phone rang. Lena Saidi of Lebanese television, telling me there might be nine Israelis dead; a Lebanese army colonel trying to clarify the BBC's version of events, Ireland's RTE radio wanting an interview. Was it a war? they wanted to know. Yes, I said. And I slowly patched together what we journalists still call a 'story'. I prefer 'dispatch', even if it has diplomatic overtones. A 'story' is a tale, embroidered perhaps, but a dispatch is a report from the front, every detail, every reaction and a no-holds-barred account of what was really going on.

Well, under the cover of a rocket attack on Israeli towns, Hizbollah men *had* crossed the border fence that morning and had seized two Israeli soldiers inside Israeli territory, killing three others as they did so; an Israeli tank that pursued the captors into Lebanese territory hit a mine, which killed another four Israeli troops; then an infantryman beside the tank was killed. By evening, the UN senior official in

Lebanon, Geir Pedersen, was calling the Hizbollah attack a 'violent breach' of the UN's Blue Line – the hastily constructed version of the international frontier, created in June 2000 by an over-ambitious UN civil servant. But in Beirut, many Lebanese were angered when squads of Hizbollah men drove through the streets of the capital to 'celebrate' the border crossing.

All that night, I heard the jets whispering high above the Mediterranean, waiting for dawn, for it was then that they descended. They came first to the little village of Dweir near Nabatiya in southern Lebanon, where an Israeli plane dropped a bomb on the home of a Shia Muslim cleric. He was killed, along with his wife and eight of his children. Then the planes visited another home in Dweir and disposed of a family of seven. It was a brisk start to Day Two of Israel's latest 'war on terror', a conflict that used some of the same language as George W. Bush's larger 'war on terror'.

This meant not only physical wounds but economic wounds and it arrived at Beirut's gleaming new $450 million international airport just before 6 a.m. on 13 July, as passengers prepared to board flights for London and Paris. From my home, I heard the F-16 that suddenly appeared over the newest runway and fired a spread of rockets into it, ripping up twenty metres of tarmac and blasting tons of concrete into the air before an Israeli *Hetz*-class gunboat fired onto the other runways. Two of Middle East Airlines' new Airbuses were left untouched but, within minutes, the airport was deserted as passengers fled back to their homes and hotels. Apart from me, only a few television crews walked through the terminals. The flight indicators told the whole story: Paris no flight, London no flight, Cairo no flight, Dubai no flight, Baghdad no flight.

By the time I reached home, Israel's threats had grown worse. Israel would not 'sit idly by' after Hizbollah's attack. Everywhere in Lebanon would now be a target, the Israelis announced. If Israel bombed the Beirut suburbs, the Hizbollah roared, it would fire its long-range Katyushas at the Israeli city of Haifa. This certainly frightened Lebanon's Gulf tourists, who packed the roads from the mountain town of Bhamdoun in their 4 × 4s, fleeing for the safety of Syria and flights home from Damascus.

The Israelis attacked the international highway from Beirut to Damascus at dawn on 14 July and dropped a bomb clean through the central span of the Italian-built bridge, sending concrete crashing hundreds of feet into the valley beneath. It had been the pride of murdered ex-prime minister Hariri, the face of a new, emergent Lebanon and now it had become a 'terrorist' target. So Abed and I drove gingerly along the old mountain road towards the Bekaa Valley – the Israeli jets still hissing through the sky above us – turned the corner once we rejoined the highway and found a fifty-foot crater, an old woman climbing down the side on her hands and knees, trying to reach her home in the valley. This too had become a 'terrorist' target. Within twenty-four hours, more than two dozen other road bridges would join this list.

Only two days into their war did the Israelis manage to strike the headquarters of Hizbollah in the Haret Hreik district of Beirut, a real 'terrorist' target. So could the Lebanese not be forgiven for believing that the Israelis had a greater interest in destroying Lebanon than they had in recovering their two soldiers?

Already, European politicians were talking about Israel's 'disproportionate' response to the 12 July military assault on the Israeli army. They had used the same word during Israel's slaughter in the 1982 Israeli invasion. They would use the same word two years later when Israel began its assault on Gaza in 2008 – and here in Lebanon, the word 'war' was also a cover-up. How could there be any excuse for the seventy-three dead Lebanese civilians blown apart now, in 2006? The same applied, of course, to the four Israeli civilians already killed by Hizbollah rockets. But the exchange rate was rising. Now it stood at one Israeli to fifteen Lebanese.

No, I wrote on the night of 14 July, we should not forget that Hizbollah broke international law when it crossed the Israeli border. It was an act of calculated ruthlessness that should never have allowed Nasrallah to grin so broadly at his subsequent press conference; his actions had brought unparalleled tragedy to the innocents of Lebanon. And it led the Hizbollah to fire 170 Katyushas into Israel. But, I asked in my report:

What would happen if the powerless Lebanese government had unleashed air attacks across Israel the last time Israeli troops crossed into Lebanon? What if the Lebanese air force then killed seventy-three Israeli civilians in bombing raids on Ashkelon, Tel

Aviv and Israeli West Jerusalem? What if a Lebanese fighter aircraft bombed Ben Gurion airport? What if a Lebanese plane destroyed twenty-six road bridges across Israel? Would it not be called 'terrorism'? I rather think it would.

Next day, the Israelis found some more 'terrorist' targets – petrol stations in the Bekaa Valley all the way up to the frontier town of Hermel in northern Lebanon and another series of bridges on one of the few escape routes to Damascus. But there was a far more spectacular 'terrorist' target hit that day; the Lebanese would refer to it as the massacre at Marwahin.

Daily reporting can carry the immediacy of bloodshed or battle, but to comprehend the immorality and the sorrow, we have to go back. That's why I return to the massacres of last year or last month. Still I try to discover what really happened in the deserts of the Iran–Iraq war, during the 1982 Sabra and Chatila massacre, across the killing fields of Bosnia and Kosovo. After each Lebanon war, I roam the broken villages of the south and talk to the distraught families, to search for a chronology, a meaning perhaps, behind the terrible events. So, a month after the 2006 Lebanon war ended, I drove with Abed to Marwahin to visit those who survived – and the graves of those who did not.

In antiquity, Pliny wrote of the cliffs of Bayada. The chalk runs down to the Mediterranean in a cascade of white rock, and the view from the top – just below the little Lebanese village of Chama'a – is breathtaking. To the south lies the United Nations headquarters and the Israeli frontier, to the north the city of Tyre. A poorly made road winds down to the shore below Chama'a and for some reason fifty-eight-year-old Ali Kemal Abdullah took a right turn above the Mediterranean on the morning of 15 July 2006. In the open-top pick-up behind him, Ali had packed twenty-seven Lebanese refugees, most of them children. Twenty-three of them were to die within the next fifteen minutes.

Mohamed al-Abdullah understands the reality of that terrible morning because his fifty-two-year-old wife Zahra, his sons Hadi, aged six, and fifteen-year-old Wissam, and his daughters, Marwa, aged ten, and thirteen-year-old Myrna, were in the pick-up. Zahra was to die, as were Hadi and Myrna. Wissam, a vein in his leg cut open by an Israeli missile as he vainly tried to save Myrna's life, sits next to his father as he talks to me outside their Beirut house, its walls drenched in black cloth. 'From the day of the attack until now, lots of delegations have come to see us,' Mohamed says. 'They all talk and it is all for nothing. My problem is with a huge nation. Can the international community get me my rights?'

Marwahin is one of a string of villages opposite the Israeli border and, unlike many others further north, is inhabited by Sunni Muslim Lebanese; they were followers of the now dead Rafiq Hariri rather than the Hizbollah militia. While no friends of Israel, the Sunnis of Lebanon were no threat. Had their parents been born a few hundred metres further south, they would – like the Sunni Muslim Palestinians who lived there until 1948 – have fled to the Lebanese camps when Israel was created; they would have been Palestinians rather than Lebanese.

Mohamed recalls how his wife took his children south from Beirut to their family home in Marwahin on 9 July 2006, just three days before the war began. Survivors describe how they visited two nearby UN posts to appeal for protection, one manned by four members of the United Nations Truce Supervisory Organisation and the other by Ghanaian soldiers of the United Nations Interim Force in Lebanon. Both the UNTSO men and the Ghanaians read the rulebook at the villagers of Marwahin. Ever since the Israelis attacked the UNIFIL barracks at Qana in 1996, slaughtering 106 Lebanese refugees, the UN had been under orders not to allow civilians into their bases.

'When the Israeli soldiers were taken on 12 July, the airport closed down and all the roads became dangerous,' Mohamed says. 'But mobile phones still worked and I had constant conversations with my wife. I asked her what was happening in the village. She said the Israelis were bombing in the fields around the village, but not in the village itself. On 13 and 14 July, we spoke six or seven times. She had heard that Beirut had been bombed so we were worried about each other.'

Mohamed was watching the Arabia television channel on the morning of the fifteenth. 'I heard that the people of Marwahin had been ordered by the Israelis to leave their homes within two hours. I tried to call my wife and children but I couldn't get through. Then after half an hour, Zahra called me to say she was in the neighbouring village of Um Mtut and that people had gone to the UN to seek help and been turned away.' Mohamed insists that while the UN were turning the civilians away, a van drove into Marwahin containing missiles. The driver was a member of Hizbollah, he says. If this is true, it clearly created a 'crisis' – to use Mohamed al-Abdullah's word – in the village. Certainly, once the ceasefire came into place thirty-two days later, there was a damaged van beside the equally damaged village mosque, with a missile standing next to it. Human rights investigators are unclear of the date of the van's arrival but seem certain that it was attacked after Marwahin was evacuated.

In her last conversation with her husband, Zahra told Mohamed that the four children were having breakfast in a neighbour's house in Um Mtut. 'I told her to stay with these people,' Mohamed recalls. 'I said that if all the civilians were together, they would be protected. My brother-in-law, Ali Kemal al-Abdullah, had a small pick-up and they could travel in this.' First to leave Marwahin was a car driven by Ahmed Kassem, who took his children with him. He called a couple of hours later to say the road was safe and that he had reached Tyre. 'That's when Ali put his children and my children and his own grand-children in the pick-up. There were twenty-seven people, almost twenty of them children.'

Ali Kemal drove north from Marwahin, away from the Israeli border, then west towards the sea. He must have seen the Israeli warship, and the Israeli naval crew certainly saw Ali's pick-up. The Israelis had been firing at all vehicles on the roads of southern Lebanon for three days – they had hit dozens of civilian cars as well as ambulances. Where the road descends to the sea, Ali Kemal realised his vehicle was overheating and pulled to a halt. For seven minutes, he tried to restart the pick-up.

According to Mohamed's son Wissam, Ali – whose elderly mother Sabaha was sitting beside him in the front – turned to the children with the words: 'Get out, all you children get out, and the Israelis will realise we are civilians.' The first two or three children had managed to climb out the back when the Israeli warship fired a shell that exploded in the cab of the pick-up, killing Ali and Sabaha instantly. 'I had almost been able to jump from the vehicle,' Wissam says. 'But the pressure of the explosion blew me out when I had only one leg over the railing and I was wounded. There was blood everywhere.' Within a few seconds, Wissam says, an Israeli Apache helicopter arrived over the vehicle, hovering just above the children. 'I saw Myrna still in the pick-up and she was crying and pleading for help. I went to get her and that's when the helicopter hit us. Its missile hit the back of the vehicle where all the children were and I couldn't hear anything because the blast had damaged my ears. Then the helicopter fired a rocket into the car behind the pick-up.'

'I lost sight of Myrna ... Then the helicopter came back and started firing its guns ... I ran away behind a *tell* [a small hill] and lay there and pretended to be dead because I knew the pilot would kill me if I moved. Some of the children were in bits.'

Hadi burned to death in Zahra's arms. Two small girls – Fatmi and Zainab Ghanem – were blasted into such small body parts that they were buried together in the same grave after the war was over. Other children lay wounded by the initial shell-burst and rocket explosions as the helicopter attacked them again. Only four survived, Wissam and his sister Marwa among them.

Wissam's father Mohamed heard on the radio that a pick-up had been attacked by the Israelis at Bayada, perhaps ten kilometres from Marwahin. 'I had another brother in Tyre and I called him. He had heard the same news and was waiting at the hospital. He said it was too dangerous to travel from Beirut to Tyre. He said that my family were only wounded. I spoke to Marwa. She said Wissam was in the operating theatre.'

Anyone who has travelled the roads of southern Lebanon under Israeli air attack cannot underestimate the dangers. But Mohamed and his nephew Khalil decided to make the run to Tyre in the afternoon. 'We just drove fast, all the way,' Mohamed remembers. 'I got to the Hiram hospital and I found my brother waiting for me. I saw Marwa and I asked about her mother and Hadi and Myrna, and she said: "I saw them in the pick-up. When the ship hit us, I was blown out of the vehicle. Afterwards, I saw Mummy and my brother sleeping."'

'Every day is worse than the one before for me,' Mohamed says. And he blames the world. The UN for giving no protection to his family, Hizbollah's 'vanity' in starting a war with a more powerful enemy and the Israelis for destroying the life of his family. 'Is Israel in a state of war with children? We need an answer. We ask for a trial for this Israeli pilot who killed the children.'

On the dirt road to the cemetery on the little hill above the village, there still lies a face mask worn by the young men carrying the decomposing bodies to their final grave. And just to the left of the dead, clearly visible to the Israeli settlers in their homes across the border, the villagers have left the remains of Ali Kemal al-Abdullah's Daihatsu pick-up. It is punctured by a hundred shrapnel holes, burned and distorted. The children in this vehicle had no chance.

Mohamed al-Abdullah weeps beside his wounded son in Beirut. 'I consider this to have been a useless war ... Those who died are resting, but we who are living are paying a price every day.'

A UN investigation was underway into Rafiq Hariri's murder – but five years later, it had produced no results. When I visited Marwahin, an Israeli investigation was about to begin into the disastrous performance of its army during the war. Human Rights Watch investigated the killings of civilians at Marwahin and other locations. 'The Israeli military,' it said in its initial report, 'did not follow its orders to evacuate with the creation of safe passage routes, and on a daily basis Israeli warplanes and helicopters struck civilians in cars who were trying to flee, many with white flags out the windows, a widely accepted sign of civilian status ... On some days, Israeli war planes hit dozens of civilian cars, showing a clear pattern of failing to distinguish between civilian and military objects.' International law states that it is forbidden in any circumstances to carry out direct attacks against civilians and that to do so is a war crime.

Two-year-old Lama al-Abdullah was among the youngest victims of the Marwahin twenty-three. Sabaha was in her eighties. At least six of the children were under ten. The Israeli helicopter pilot's name remains, of course, a secret. And all this was two years before the Gaza war.

I tried to keep a diary during this Lebanon war. Sometimes, if I wasn't too tired, I wrote it up after I'd filed my report to the *Independent* from a basement internet café. Other times, I wrote it on the back of used paper in my library-cum-office at home. On 16 July, obviously frightened, I wrote:

It is the first time I have actually seen a missile in this war. They fly too fast – or you are too busy trying to run away to look for them – but this morning, Abed and I actually saw one pierce through the smoke above us. 'Habibi!' he cries, and I start

screaming 'Turn the car round, turn it round!' and we drive
away for our lives from the southern suburbs. As we turn the
corner there is a shattering explosion and a mountain of grey
smoke blossoming from the road we have just left. What
happened to the men and women we saw running for their lives
from that Israeli rocket? We do not know. In air raids, all you
see are the few square yards around you. You get out and you
survive and that is enough.

In retrospect, that must have been the journey that persuaded Abed
that his life was worth more than the *Independent*. For the first time in
the two decades he had worked for me, Abed declined to go on assignment to the south of Lebanon and he'd only drive me around Beirut.
How could I blame him? He was almost seventy now. Why should a
grandfather squander his life for a reporter who thought he could still
play James Bond at the age of sixty? I would have to find another crazed
traveller to share my journeys of fear and exhaustion.

It streaked out of the heaven like a fiery meteor, crashing onto a truck
and a car, spewing fuel on to the road. An Israeli helicopter shot down
by a Hizbollah missile? Or – as the Israelis claimed – a container that
fell from a military aircraft with nothing more lethal inside than propaganda papers? By the time I got there, the bushes and the very
roadway were on fire and the car upon which this thing had crashed
still contained its partly decapitated driver. Large pieces of metal were
on the road, part of what might have been a cluster bomb on the
verge, and what looked like a rotor blade. Then came the sound of
Israeli jets and a huge explosion. Abed stood next to the car, looking
ostentatiously at his watch. 'Give yourself ten minutes and then we go
– this is the rule *you* invented.' Even in Beirut, Abed was spooked. We
fled.
    We were always fleeing. We drove fast through the southern
suburbs of Beirut, now a haunted place of rubble and fear, we sped past
bomb craters, terrified that the planes would come back. We sprinted
away from Raouche when the ground shook under our feet. Then we
panted like dogs as we ran for the vast palace in which the Lebanese
prime minister held court and where the men from the United Nations
had arrived to bring us peace.

Kofi Annan's special adviser was Vijay Nambiar, brother of the former Indian commander to the doomed UNPROFOR 'protection' force in Bosnia. Vijay had held talks with prime minister Fouad Siniora and his ineffective speaker of parliament, Nabih Berri. There were to be no questions – a bad sign – and parsing his dull statement did not hold out much hope of an immediate end to air raids, killer missiles, piles of innocent dead and the vast packs of lies that had characterised this filthy war ever since Hizbollah crossed into Israel.

As many lies were now falling upon Lebanon as bombs. The explosions were easy to count; the lies were less obvious but just as powerful. The first came from Israeli prime minister Ehud Olmert. Only hours after UN Secretary-General Kofi Annan had asked for a ceasefire and appealed for 'corridors' to allow the movement of humanitarian aid to civilians, Olmert said he would allow such a 'humanitarian corridor' between Cyprus and Lebanon. This had made the headlines on 17 July, but there already was free sea passage between Cyprus and Beirut. What Annan was asking for were land 'corridors' between Beirut and the heavily bombed villages of southern Lebanon. The Israeli army's response was almost immediate; it demanded the removal of all civilians within twenty miles of the Israeli border, an act regarded by the Lebanese as 'ethnic cleansing'. Olmert made no mention of this.

The Israelis were then reported to be planning the dispatch of a large ground force up to the Litani river in southern Lebanon, an offensive that would cost them heavy casualties and would anyway not prevent the Hizbollah from further long-range missile attacks on Israeli territory. Then we had John Bolton, Washington's ambassador to the United Nations, telling another lie. In order to delay a ceasefire and avoid a Security Council vote, he asked how a 'democratically elected state' could have a ceasefire with a 'gang of terrorists'. It was impossible, he said. Either Bolton was cracked, or he was completely ignorant of Middle East history. Twelve years from now, Trump would make him his 'national security advisor'.

For in 1980, after Palestinian Katyushas were fired across the border, Israel – presumably Mr Bolton's 'democratically elected state' – entered upon a ceasefire with Yasser Arafat's PLO guerrillas, whom Israel certainly regarded as a 'gang of terrorists'. The truce was negotiated by Lieutenant General Bill Callaghan, the Irish UN commander in south-

ern Lebanon, and guaranteed by the UN. It was broken two years later
by Israel when it bombarded the PLO because it claimed that Arafat
had ordered an attack on Israel's ambassador in London, Shlomo
Argov.*

Yet still the lies continued. The network reporters were saying that
Israel was ready to lift its 'naval blockade' on Lebanon for those
'humanitarian' supplies, but this was rubbish. Naval vessels evacuating
foreigners from Lebanon had cravenly sought Israel's permission to do
so, but the Israelis withdrew all their warships from Lebanese waters
after Hizbollah struck a gunboat with an Iranian-made missile.
Although the Israelis failed to reveal this, it now emerged that the
Israeli naval vessel almost sank in the Mediterranean after the missile
started fires in the engine room and killed four Israeli sailors.

Again, we were still being told by Olmert that there would be no
prisoners swapped for Israel's two captured soldiers. But if this was
true, why had the Israelis contacted the German security services –
who had negotiated every prisoner swap between Hizbollah and the
Israelis for the past twenty years? Oddly, although the names of the
two Israelis held captive in Lebanon were now known, no interest was
shown in the names of the three principal Lebanese prisoners whose
release had already been demanded by Hassan Nasrallah. The
Hizbollah lie was that these men were being held for their pro-Hizbol-
lah sympathies.†

How brave our warships looked that dawn. Spread over the pale-blue
Mediterranean in front of my home, bristling with missiles and
machine guns and cannons, it was an armada led by the destroyer HMS
Gloucester, the USS *Nashville* and *York* and the sleek French anti-subma-
rine frigate *Jean de Vienne*. They represented Western power, the
military strength of our billion-dollar economies. Who would dare
challenge this naval might?

---

* The Israelis were wrong; it was Arafat's cynical adversary Saddam Hussein who gave
the order in the hope that Israel would falsely accuse Arafat of the crime and invade
Lebanon. The Israelis obliged.

† Equally, Hizbollah had also been inventing Israeli casualty figures – they claimed seven
Israeli soldiers were killed on the border in the previous three days, when the real figure
was four, and that they had destroyed four Israeli tanks. In fact, they destroyed just one in
that period.

It was, our colleagues told us, to be the greatest evacuation since Dunkirk – another cruel lie, which the Lebanese spotted at once. For these mighty craft had not arrived to save the Lebanese; no, they were creeping through the dawn after asking Israel's permission to help their own citizens to flee. These great warships had been sent here by Western leaders, too cowardly to utter a single word of compassion for Lebanon's suffering.

Even British prime minister Tony Blair could only condemn Hizbollah for attacking the Israelis. Margaret Beckett, one of the most ill-informed British foreign secretaries of recent years, repeatedly said on radio and television that 'they [the Hizbollah] started this', without mentioning Israel's latest killing toll of more than 300 Lebanese civilians. No, those ships I watched steaming into Beirut port did not represent Dunkirk. They represented appeasement, total and uncritical support for the powerful over the weak.

Of course, there are various kinds of escape, and one of the most adept of political Houdinis was His Excellency Mr Jeffrey Feltman, US ambassador to Lebanon. For the past few hours, he had to listen as Lebanese prime minister Fouad Siniora desperately appealed for a ceasefire to end the destruction of Lebanon by the Israeli air force.

This was the same Feltman who, just a year earlier, had heaped laurels on Siniora and his democratically elected government for throwing the Syrian army out of Lebanon. But if he were to praise Siniora's words condemning Israel, Feltman would no doubt be summoned back to the State Department in Washington. So what was he to say when asked for a comment on Siniora's speech? It was, he said, 'articulate and touching'.

You could now clearly see the Israeli missiles hurtling like thunderbolts onto the apartment blocks of Ghobeiri. And yes, I suppose we could call this a 'terrorist' target, for in these mean streets stood the Hizbollah's offices. Even the movement's propaganda television station, Al-Manar, now lay ruined, but still broadcasting from a bunker beneath the rubble. The few civilians still above ground ran screaming through the streets, desperate to leave the heaps of broken buildings, the roadways covered in smashed balconies and electrical wires. 'You don't have to help the resistance,' Nasrallah told the Lebanese on his underground television station. 'The Hizbollah are on the front line and the Lebanese are behind them.'

This was untrue, of course. Those who had not fled for Tripoli or to Syria, or who were lucky enough to hold a foreign passport, lived on in their ghost city, sitting in their basements amid power cuts and the hopelessness of all who believed that Lebanon had been emerging from the shadows of its fifteen-year civil war. It was Nasrallah who said that there were 'more surprises to come', and the Lebanese feared that the Israelis had more surprises in store for them, too.

From my balcony, I watched an American-made Apache helicopter turning three times over the Mediterranean before firing a single missile that smacked into Beirut's brand-new lighthouse on the Corniche. Another 'terrorist' target.

In the year AD 551, the magnificent, wealthy city of Berytus, headquarters of the imperial East Mediterranean Roman fleet, was struck by a massive earthquake. In its aftermath, the sea withdrew several miles and the survivors – ancestors of the present-day Lebanese – walked out on the sands to loot the long-sunken merchant ships revealed in front of them. Then a tsunami tidal wall arrived to swamp the city and kill them all. So savagely was the old Beirut damaged that the Emperor Justinian sent gold from Constantinople as compensation to every family left alive.

Some cities seem forever doomed. When the Crusaders arrived at Beirut on their way to Jerusalem in the eleventh century, they slaughtered their way through the city. In the First World War, Ottoman Beirut suffered mass famine. An American woman living in Beirut in 1916 described how she 'passed women and children lying by the roadside with closed eyes and ghastly, pale faces'.

Why does this happen to Beirut? For four decades, I'd watched this place die, rise from the grave and then die again, its apartment blocks pitted with bullets. I lived here through fifteen years of civil war that took 150,000 lives, and two earlier Israeli invasions and years of Israeli bombardments that cost the lives of a further 20,000 of its people. Yet they are a fine, educated, moral people whose generosity amazes every foreigner, whose gentleness puts any Westerner to shame and whose suffering we almost always ignore.

Walking through the deserted city centre of Beirut, it reminded me more than ever of a film lot, a phoenix that had risen from the ashes of civil war. This part of the city – once a Dresden of ruins – was rebuilt by Rafiq Hariri.

The 'Martyr Rafiq Hariri International Airport' had been attacked three times by the Israelis; Hariri's transnational highway viaduct had been broken open by Israeli bombers and most of his motorway bridges had been destroyed. Only this small jewel of a city centre had been spared. The slums of Haret Hreik, Ghobeiri and Shiyah had now been levelled and pounded to dust, sending a quarter of a million Shia Muslims to seek safety in this sanctuary of the rich, with its shuttered Gucci stores and jewellery boutiques. But did the tens of thousands of poor deserve this act of mass punishment? And for a country that boasted of its pinpoint accuracy, what does this act of destruction tell us about Israel?

From out of the past, Ed Cody arrives in Beirut. As an Associated Press correspondent during the Lebanese civil war, he taught me how to survive. A fluent Arabist, a cynical American who never believed what he was told, Cody didn't take kindly to political speeches and talk of sacrifice. He thought the Hizbollah lied. He thought the Israelis lied. So did I. Cody now worked for the *Washington Post*.

Abed is out of the war now, after his gentle, firm refusal to drive south. Cody finds a Shia driver called Hussein – inevitably this costs us $1,000 a day – but he has a dark sense of humour, doesn't panic and has a smart, fast Mercedes. Despite the bombed bridges, he gets us to Sidon in less than twenty minutes.

The Sunni Muslim city that confronts us is under siege from the nation's Shia poor. They are in the schools, in empty hospitals, in halls and mosques and in the streets. They are arriving in Sidon by the thousand, cared for by Sunni Muslims and then sent north to join the 600,000 displaced Lebanese in Beirut. More than 34,000 have passed through here in the past four days alone, a tide of misery and anger. It will take years to heal their wounds, and billions of dollars to rebuild and repair their damaged property. And who can blame them for their flight?

These sentiments provoke some dark questions. Why, for example, can't these poor people be shown the same compassion by Tony Blair as he supposedly felt for the Muslims of Kosovo when they were being driven from their homes by the Serbs? These thousands are as terrified and homeless as the Kosovo Albanians who fled to Macedonia in 1998 and for whom Mr Blair had claimed he was waging a moral war. But for the Shia Muslims sleeping homeless in Sidon, there was to be no such moral posturing – and no ceasefire suggestions from Mr Blair, who had now aligned himself with the Israelis and the Americans.

I travelled south on the next ICRC convoy. The smoke could have been our guide; vast columns of it towered into the heavens, not from the villages but from within Israel itself. Their F-16s turned in the bright sun and their bombs burst over the old prison where the Hizbollah were still holding out; but beyond the frontier, I could see fires burning across the Israeli hillside and the Jewish settlement of Metullah.

In Marjayoun, next to Qlaya – headquarters of Israel's slovenly proxy South Lebanon Army militia before 2000 – Lebanese troops were trying to prevent the Hizbollah using the streets of the Greek Catholic town to fire yet more missiles at Israel. It was the same old story. The Lebanese army, whose primary duty was to protect its citizens, was trying to prevent Lebanon's only fighting force, the Hizbollah, from shooting back at the Israeli enemy which was killing Lebanese civilians.

Sitting in the villages and listening to how US secretary of state Condoleezza Rice planned to reshape Lebanon was a lesson in human self-delusion. Rice was proposing a NATO-led intervention force along the Lebanese–Israeli border for between sixty and ninety days after a ceasefire declaration, the subsequent deployment of an enlarged NATO-led force throughout Lebanon to ensure the disarmament of Hizbollah and the retraining of the Lebanese army before it too deployed to the border.

Did Condoleezza Rice think the Hizbollah wanted to be disarmed? And by NATO? The problem, as usual, was that the United States saw this bloodbath as an 'opportunity' rather than a tragedy, a chance to humble Hizbollah's supporters in Tehran and shape the 'new Middle East' of which Rice spoke so blandly. In subsequent violence, the same rule of thumb would apply: death and suffering provided 'opportunities' for the fulfilment of American–Israeli plans in the region, a chance to cobble together ceasefires and political aims.

Yet from the border of Pakistan to the Mediterranean – with the sole exception of the much-hated Syria and Iran, which might be smothered in blood later – we had turned a 2,500-mile swath of the Muslim world into a hell-disaster of unparalleled suffering and hatred. Our British 'peacekeepers' in Afghanistan were fighting for their lives against an Islamist enemy that grew by the week. In Iraq, our soldiers – and those of the United States – hid in their concrete crusader fortresses while the people they so generously liberated and introduced to the benefits of Western-style democracy slashed each other to death. And now Blair and his American friends were allowing Israel to destroy Lebanon and call it peace. It was perfectly acceptable, it seemed, after Hizbollah staged its reckless and lethal 12 July assault, for the Israelis to destroy the infrastructure of Lebanon and the lives of its innocents. Yet when the IRA used to cross the Irish border to kill British soldiers, Blair and his cronies did not blame the Irish republic's government. They did not order the RAF to bomb Dublin.

But Israel had special privileges afforded to no other civilised nation. It could do exactly what Blair would never have done – and still receive the British government's approbation. It could trash the Geneva Conventions and it could commit war crimes and murder UN soldiers like the four unarmed observers who refused to leave their post under fire outside Khiam.

They wrote the names of the dead children on their plastic shrouds. A thick dust was sweeping through the outdoor mortuary at Tyre and I was standing on tip-toe to read the names, scribbled in Arabic, the ink sometimes skidding on the shiny surface of the body bag. 'Mehdi Hashem, aged seven, Qana,' was written in pen on the plastic sheet in which the little boy's body lay. 'Hussein al-Mohamed, aged twelve, Qana', 'Abbas al-Shalhoub, aged one, Qana'. And when a Lebanese soldier picked up Abbas' tiny body, it bounced on his shoulder as the child might have done on his father's shoulder before his death. The vibration of bombs could be felt under our feet.

In all, fifty-six corpses were brought to the Tyre government hospital and other clinics on 30 July 2006, thirty-four of them children. When the hospital ran out of plastic bags, the small corpses were wrapped in carpets. Their hair was matted with dust, most had blood running from their noses. 'You must have a heart of stone,' I wrote in the *Independent* that night, 'not to feel the outrage [that] those of us watching this experienced ... This slaughter was an obscenity, an atrocity and, yes, if the Israeli air force truly bombs with the "pinpoint accuracy" it claims, this was also a war crime.' And there was no doubt of the missile that killed all those children. It came from the United States,

and upon a fragment of it was written: 'For use on MK-84 Guided
Bomb BSU-37-B'. No doubt the manufacturers would call it 'combat-
proven' because it had destroyed the entire three-storey house in
which the Shalhoub and Hashem families lived. They had taken refuge
in the basement from the enormous Israeli bombardment, and that is
where most of them died.

Israel claimed, inevitably, that missiles had been fired by Hizbollah
gunmen from Qana – the justification for a massacre we would hear so
many times in Gaza. And Israel's prime minister, Ehud Olmert, talked
about 'Muslim terror' threatening 'Western civilisation'. Innocents die
in war. Didn't the Americans and British accidentally kill the innocent
in Afghanistan? Didn't we blow them apart in Iraq? So how could
anyone criticise Israel when it pursued identical tactics in the same
'war on terror'? What hypocrisy, what anti-Semitism, to single Israel
out.

Thousands of protesters attacked the largest United Nations building in Beirut, screaming 'destroy Tel Aviv', and prime minister Siniora,
normally so unflappable, telephoned Condoleezza Rice, ordering her
to cancel her imminent 'peace-making' trip to Beirut. No one could
now forget how Bush, Rice and Blair repeatedly refused to demand an
immediate ceasefire – a truce that would have saved all those lives at
Qana.

Siniora told foreign diplomats in Beirut that his government was
now demanding only an immediate ceasefire and was no longer interested in a political package to go with it. Israeli prime minister Olmert
was defending his war with a familiar argument. 'We could not let the
terror organisation on our border get stronger ... If we had held off,
the day would have arrived when they would have caused unprecedented damage.'

Here, again, was the normalisation of war. Back in 1982, Begin had
claimed his invasion of Lebanon was a 'preventive' war, designed to
destroy the PLO before they became so strong that they would pose an
even greater threat to Israel. George W. Bush and Tony Blair claimed
the same about Afghanistan in 2001; if we didn't fight al-Qaeda now,
they would turn up in America and Britain. But al-Qaeda had arrived
in New York, Washington and Pennsylvania before Bush and Blair set
off on their Afghan adventure. Then both men justified the invasion of
Iraq on almost identical grounds; Saddam had weapons of mass

destruction and would use them if we didn't invade. Having discovered that there were no such arms, Bush and Blair embarked on a repeat performance. No, Saddam, did not have such weapons – but he would have reconstituted them had we not invaded.

More than five years later, the great information bin of WikiLeaks was tipped up to provide a unique view of the war through the eyes and ears of the US embassy in Beirut. This collection of diplomatic documents is somewhat opaque; after all, we see events only through the dim vision of US diplomats, including the abysmal Feltman whose initial sources of information appeared to be confined to the UN, the Lebanese media and a clutch of inevitably Christian politicians and 'a trusted Shia journalist'.

As the carnage of the thirty-four-day conflict grows, we see Lebanese prime minister Fouad Siniora, desperate to protect his own government, physically 'leaning close to the Ambassador' and pleading for assistance. He needs to show his administration's independence from Syria. 'We need help,' he tells Feltman after the first twenty-four hours of bombing. The latter coldly tells Siniora that 'it would be important for the GOL [Government of Lebanon] to credibly distance itself from Hizbollah's assaults if they hoped to temper the severity of Israel's retaliation'. Siniora calls later to say that Israel should lighten its blockade on Lebanon because 'Syria is becoming our lungs ... we can only breathe through the Syrians.'

There are times when Feltman's reports read like an Israeli diplomatic document, referring to Hizbollah's 'outrageous provocation' on the border that may have 'some useful side effects' since it might prompt Christian leader Michel Aoun to reconsider his own relationship with the Shia militia. By 17 July, the embassy was recording the Lebanese Druze leader Walid Jumblatt saying that 'publicly he must call for a ceasefire, but he saw the fighting as an opportunity to defeat Hizbollah'. Incredibly, UN special envoy Terje Rod-Larsen – he who had so hastily drawn the Blue Line along the Lebanese–Israeli border – is quoted as saying that he 'agreed that an Israeli invasion might be positive'.

On 17 July, five days into the almost five-week war, Nabih Berri, the Shia leader of the Lebanese parliament, is reported as suggesting to Feltman that 'the potential for Israel's assault to weaken Hizbollah

militarily and undermine the organisation politically is a positive
development'. Again, we must remember that the above is an
American version of a dialogue in Beirut that may reflect what the US
embassy wishes Washington to hear. Yet there is no escaping the
hypocrisy of Lebanese political opinion nor the outrageous way in
which the UN's 'peacekeepers' place political opportunity ahead of
further human suffering. There are times when this is reminiscent of
Tony Blair's attitude not only towards the 2003 invasion of Iraq but
his own unwillingness to seek an early ceasefire in Lebanon. This,
rather than the Iraq war, would finally destroy his premiership, as
Labour MPs in Britain became revolted at his refusal to demand a
truce in Lebanon.

Reports arrived at the US embassy of the Israeli attack on the UN
post at Khiam on 25 July, in which four UNTSO observers were killed.
Those of us only a mile from the scene had already concluded that the
Israelis had deliberately targeted these military observers. The
WikiLeaks archive reveals how. In lines that might have been written
into a Goldstone-type report, UNIFIL senior adviser Milos Strugar
reported

> that the lethal Israeli attack was deliberate for three reasons.
> First, Israel knew that the long-time UN post was there. Second,
> the four UN observers were killed by two direct hits by precision
> Israeli aerial bombs. It was not a near miss. Third, the UN post
> had been receiving close and direct artillery hits for three days
> and UNIFIL commander Maj. Gen. Alain Pellegrini had warned
> the IDF [Israel Defense Force] that it was hitting a UN post.

By 4 August, Feltman's officials were reduced to complaining about
Israeli air attacks on areas near the diplomatic compound 'that prevents
us from any timely cutting-edge diplomatic efforts'. It was Israel's
American-supplied weaponry, of course, that was 'cutting-edge', and
the embassy's casual remark that 'the Israelis probably can give reasons'
for their strikes in Christian areas spoke for itself.

This was pretty grim stuff, had Cody and I been able to contemplate
it as we drove south yet again on 15 August, the day after the ceasefire,
a truce that was supposed to produce a UN mission 'robust' enough –
Blair's words – to disarm the Hizbollah. However, no militia army

fights for almost a quarter of a century only to surrender its weapons after a successful battle.

It was my old friend Patrick Cockburn who first grasped the extent to which Israel had – within the very last three days of the conflict – sewn this desolate landscape with cluster bombs, US-made munitions that would kill another eighty-three souls within a month of the August ceasefire at a rate of at least four every day.

It was that grand old paper *Haaretz* that originally broke the story, quoting an Israeli rocket unit commander who stated that his army fired around 1,800 cluster bombs into Lebanon in the last three days of the war. 'What we did was insane and monstrous,' he told the paper's reporter. 'We covered entire [Lebanese] towns in cluster bombs.'

Four million bomblets had been fountained across the land in seventy-six hours and at least 30 per cent would not explode. More than four years later, at least forty-five civilians had been killed by cluster munitions since the autumn of 2006, the latest a twenty-year-old de-miner who died in a double cluster-mine explosion while clearing bomblets from a tobacco field near Tyre. By 2015, there were still 704 'hazardous sites' remaining across more than fifteen square miles of Lebanon.

Faced not only with its own military fiasco but the condemnation of the world for its bombardment of civilians, Israel found itself deluged with humanitarian reports that, if they lacked the depth of Goldstone's work on Gaza three years later, nonetheless contained a disturbing amount of detail. One of Amnesty International's reports on the war asked if the destruction of civilian infrastructure was deliberate or 'collateral damage', but Human Rights Watch went further, referring to 'Israel's indiscriminate attacks against civilians in Lebanon' and including an accurate account of the Marwahin massacre. The report provoked from Israel's usual friends in America a campaign of Goldstone-like denigration, not only against a widely respected human rights organisation but against its executive director Kenneth Roth who was, readers will not be surprised to learn, condemned as an anti-Semite.

Perhaps Goldstone himself should have studied this assault on Roth before he undertook his Gaza report three years later. When Human Rights Watch refused to accept that Israel's killing of civilians were 'accidents', Abraham Foxman, national director of the Anti-Defamation

League, described its treatment of 'war crimes' by Israel as 'immorality at the highest level'. Martin Peretz of the *New Republic* claimed that Human Rights Watch had 'utterly destroyed its credibility, at least for me'. And our old friend Professor Dershowitz popped up in the *Jerusalem Post* to say that when it came to Israel, 'Human Rights Watch cooks the books about facts, cheats on interviews and puts out predetermined conclusions that are driven more by ideology than by evidence.'

Roth, who like Goldstone is Jewish and a legal scholar, survived this childish onslaught. Interestingly, the Human Rights Watch director was invited to make his own mea culpa after Goldstone's recantation, a request he found it easy to decline. The pattern, however, had been set. If Israel is accused of war crimes, it is the accusers who must be punished – not the criminals.

What was equally clear, however, was that those governments, presidents and ministers who at first supported Israel during the commission of these crimes were, morally, as guilty as the officers who ordered the shelling or air assault on civilian targets – and as culpable as those who sought to extend the conflict for political 'opportunity'.

Driving across southern Lebanon, the villages could appear undamaged beneath the high, bright sun. But the closer Cody and I got, the more we noticed the vast grey heaps of rubble that were once homes. Some villages had been half-destroyed. The stench was overpowering. They would be pulling out bodies for another month.

Many villagers spoke of how the Hizbollah came 'out of the ground' between the battles, and it became obvious that many had spent the war in underground tunnels, emerging only to ambush their antagonists. I would become familiar with their tunnels less than a decade later, as the fighters of Al-Nusra and ISIS veined their way beneath the surface of Homs and Aleppo and Mosul and Raqqa.

Within months, we would hear how the Israelis, armed with photographic aerial maps of Hizbollah locations in southern Lebanon, had enthusiastically burst into the tunnels – only to find photocopies of their very own maps waiting for them to discover. Having purchased the originals from a spy in Israeli intelligence, the Hizbollah had immediately identified those tunnels of which the Israelis were aware – and realised at once which of their tunnels remained secure.

In the end, the Hizbollah, with hundreds of thousands of dollars physically carried in suitcases into Beirut airport from Iranian flights, paid for the rebuilding of almost every village and town in southern Lebanon, along with south Beirut. And on 16 July 2008, almost exactly two years since the start of Hizbollah's war, Nasrallah was awarded his doubtful victory honours, a grisly day of corpse-swapping as refrigerated human remains were brought across the Israeli border. A series of coffins were soon bathed in the Lebanese flag and golden Hizbollah banners, drawn by a flower-encrusted truck towards Beirut.

There was one man whom the crowds were waiting for. It was for him that the Hizbollah had fought on. Samir Kuntar – twenty-eight years in an Israeli prison for the brutal 1979 murder of an Israeli, his eight-year-old daughter and a policeman – turned up wearing a newly supplied camouflage uniform. A man used to solitary confinement who suddenly found himself idolised by a people he hadn't seen for almost three decades, his eyes moved around the crowd. Nasrallah had promised his release – and he had kept his word.

But it was also a day of humiliation, most of all for the Israelis. After launching their 2006 war to retrieve their two captured soldiers, the Israelis had killed well over a thousand Lebanese civilians, devastated Lebanon, lost 165 of their own people, most of them soldiers – and ended up handing over two hundred Arab corpses and five prisoners, in return for a box of body parts and the remains of the two missing soldiers.

For the Americans who had supported Fouad Siniora's elected government, it was a day of hopelessness. For Siniora himself, along with the president and all the surviving prime ministers and presidents of Lebanon and the leader of the Druze community, and the country's MPs, Muslim religious leaders, senior civil servants and the heads of all the security services were at Beirut airport to grovel before the five living prisoners whom Hizbollah had freed from Israel. In the way of so many Middle East revenge sagas, Israelis would have the satisfaction of learning on 20 December 2015 that Samir Kuntar had been blown to pieces in central Damascus, along with several Hizbollah colleagues. The Syrian government blamed 'terrorists' for the explosion; the anti-Assad 'Free Syrian Army' claimed they were responsible, but Hizbollah believed that Israeli aircraft had launched a missile at the building. Months later, a former Israeli minister and intelligence officer,

Omer Bar Lev, was asked if Israel killed Kuntar. 'Absolutely,' he replied.

After each war I've covered as a journalist, I've looked back and thought of the dead. Usually, I remember the young who have been so carelessly flung from life; the children, for example, who were instructed so innocently to climb from the truck on the road from Marwahin so that they could be seen by the Israelis. Or the little girl in the south Lebanese hospital with her face pitted with the steel of cluster munitions.

But sometimes I think of the innocent adults of war, the 'peacekeepers' and the soldiers who try to protect human beings rather than kill them, but who are blasted away from us forever. That is the hardest kind of soldiering, and I am not sure of its rewards. There are none if they die, as often they do. And so I turn at the end of another chapter 'soaked in the multitudinous seas incarnadine' to five soldiers.

The first four were killed only a mile from me in southern Lebanon, their superior UN officers pleading with the Israelis to cease fire. I saw the Indian UN troops weeping with sorrow after they had collected their comrades, who were in pieces. We will recall how Milos Strugar told the US ambassador of their fate next day, insisting that they had been deliberately killed. They were international soldiers, unarmed military observers from Observer Group Lebanon which has been monitoring the old Palestine–Lebanon truce lines after 1948. Amid the crash of Israeli shellfire, Canadian Major Paeta Hess-von Kruedener, known to his family as 'Wolf', perhaps realised he would not survive. He put through a call to his wife Cynthia in Canada. It was 19.10 in Lebanon but ten minutes past midday in Ontario. When Cynthia's phone rang, she replied:

'Paeta, I can't hear you, there's static, but I love you, if you can hear me I love you. Are you alright? I'm going to have to hang up because I want you to call me back because all I can hear is static, but I don't want to hang up. I love you. I've got to hang up.'

A few minutes later, just before 19.30 an Israeli F-16 pilot dropped a 1,000-pound GPS-guided precision Joint Direct Attack Munition bomb inside the UN compound. In the words of a Canadian reporter who spent weeks investigating this crime, 'Cynthia was walking around with the phone in her hand waiting for Wolf to call back. She turned on the TV just before dinner and the first thing she saw was a picture of Wolf on the news with the caption: "Missing, presumed dead".'*

He died most grievously, along with his three international comrades: Major Hans-Peter Lang from Austria, Lieutenant Senior Grade Jarno Makinen from Finland and Major Du Zhaoyu from the People's Republic of China. UN Secretary-General Kofi Annan's expression of shock, in which he referred to the 'apparently deliberate targeting by Israeli Defense Forces of a UN observer post', evoked more debate about his truthful accusations than horror at the death of his soldiers. It was Annan who would be chastised, not the Israelis.

Not that the soldiers themselves did not feel their own sense of revulsion at what they were witnessing in the last days of their life. 'It is disgusting what [the Israelis] are doing here,' Paeta emailed to Cynthia:

> Yesterday I witnessed an attack helicopter fire missiles at a local school and destroy a brand new hospital. [They] are trying to cripple and destroy the infrastructure of Lebanon. What this has to do with Hizbollah terrorists I have no idea and cannot make the connection. I agree that [the Israelis] have the right to protect themselves, but they are indiscriminately bombing and targeting the civilian population and infrastructure which is a fucking WAR CRIME under the Geneva Conventions.

Irish army commandant Kevin McDonald, who was a UN officer at the time, would describe how 'the biggest place to manoeuvre armour is the Hula valley below Khiam and it is quite possible that [the Israelis]

---

* It is only correct to quote from the report so scrupulously put together years later by award-winning Canadian journalist and war reporter Adam Day, who died at the age of only forty-two in 2017 after covering the Canadian military conflict in Afghanistan. Colleagues said Day was 'fighting his own personal demons' following seven assignments in Afghanistan, during which he was injured when a bomb blew up beneath the armoured vehicle in which he was travelling.

didn't want the UN reporting on their movements up that valley'. None of this, however, was of interest to those whose duty was to seek justice for the lives of the four UN observers.

The then Canadian Conservative premier Stephen Harper – perhaps Israel's closest friend outside the United States – chose to criticise the victims, asking why the UN permitted its Khiam position to remain 'manned during what is now, more or less, a war'. The Israelis said that the UN position had been put on their target list by mistake, but prevented both the UN and the Canadian government from verifying this. A Canadian board of inquiry later reported that both the UN and the Israelis had declined to allow their personnel to be interviewed by authorities. As an organisation, the report concluded, the Israeli military was 'responsible for the death of Major Hess-von Kruedener'. But then – and what else could Harper's pro-Israeli government do to help its friends in the Middle East? – the official inquiry was mysteriously removed from their own government's websites for unexplained 'security reasons'.

Paeta's widow Cynthia, who twice visited Lebanon to commemorate her husband at the place of his death, has not stopped asking questions about the Israeli bombing. Less than two years after Paeta's killing, she asked why the Israelis had offered no explanation for their 'operational error'. Here was a wife speaking for her dead husband. What were the odds, she asked, that two operational errors, land and air, could occur within an hour of each other and in the same place? She demanded that the IDF reveal 'the complete findings of its own internal investigation'. The IDF, she insisted, had lost their 'privilege of secrecy' when they bombed the UN post.

The Israelis have never revealed their secret. Nor did the new Canadian government, under Justin Trudeau, restore the military investigation report to its website. Irish OGL officer Kevin McDonald had helped carry the pulverised bones and flesh of his comrades through the UN's technical fence to Israel for repatriation. 'So was it deliberate targeting?' he would rhetorically ask me a decade later. 'In my opinion it absolutely was.'

Another woman who had to speak for a dead soldier – the sister of Colonel Nagib Wakim, a Lebanese army officer, unarmed and dedicated to restoring the broken electricity lines of his country's capital – wrote to me from America. Was her brother one of the brave soldiers who tried to protect me after the first Israeli attack at Kfar Chima? she asked. When I reached the site of the explosion, three Lebanese army personnel walked beside me up the burning roadway. That night the Israelis bombed the Lebanese logistic unit tasked with repairing the power system. The three soldiers who had stood beside me were among the ten dead.

Was Colonel Nagib Wakim among these soldiers? his sister Jamile wanted to know. I would like to think so, but I replied to Jamile Wakim that I would never be able to answer her question. A year after the war, Jamile wrote to me again from the United States where she is a physician. Her letter was without rancour and self-pity but with much self-questioning and enough doubt to prove her courage. She was searching, she said, for a good reason for Nagib's 'transcendence'. But:

> I have become angry with my brother's courage and tired of his relentless belief in the sovereignty of Lebanon and the human life. I have wept and wept and wept. Then I was angry with myself for leaving Lebanon and leaving him behind in the [civil war] eighties. I could not tolerate the injustices of that war. But Nagib stayed. He believed in Lebanon, he had hope. Nothing made me feel good. Nothing except the one thought that he must have died to save the country he loved so much. I wish I could believe that my brother Nagib's blood is sealing the cracks in Lebanon. I wish I could believe that the Lebanese people understand that their unity is their power.

11

The Awakening

Everyone suddenly burst out singing;
And I was filled with such delight
As prisoned birds must find in freedom ...

Everyone's voice was suddenly lifted;
And beauty came like the setting sun:
My heart was shaken with tears; and horror
Drifted away ... O, but Everyone
Was a bird; and the song was wordless;
the singing will never be done.

Siegfried Sassoon, 'Everyone Sang', 1919

The Egyptian city of Mahalla el-Kubra hides its political history well. It is a place of throbbing twenty-four-hour-a-day blockhouse factories, half-ruined nineteenth-century town houses buried between concrete apartments and a shambling railway station. Only the appearance of a large cockroach scuttling across the floor of the municipality office prompts the council workers to sit up. That and the arrival of the strangest creature of them all: the sweat-soaked correspondent of the *Independent*, asking about an industrial strike that began and ended five years before the revolution that overthrew Hosni Mubarak.

Every time I asked about the strike, the officials asked me if I'd seen Mubarak in his Cairo court cage; they thought I was enquiring about the battles in Tahrir Square eight months earlier, two hundred miles to the south. No, I said. I was here to find out what happened in their

Tahrir Square – in this scruffy town in 2006, long before Mubarak had yielded to the people of Egypt and was wheeled from power by the army in February 2011. Only when one of the heroines of the Battle of Mahalla, Widdad Dimirdach, a scarved woman with a loud voice and a great sense of pride, walked into the room did they understand. Mrs Dimirdach helped to lead one of the first great strikes against the government-owned Misr Cotton Company in 2006. 'It wasn't really political,' she said. 'But we had no choice. Our wages had become so low and the cost of food so high that we could no more afford to eat and live.'

Of the 30,000 cotton workers in Mahalla, 6,000 are female. Men and women work in separate factories, and Widdad Dimirdach spent her days and nights sewing shirts. In 2006, she and her comrades stopped work, refusing to leave until they received a pay increase from $100 a month to $175, making them – still in 2011 – among the lowest paid industrial workers in Egypt.

Back in 2006, the Mubarak government agreed the new salaries within three days. It had no option – Mahalla, the centre of Egypt's export trade, was too big to fight. It was 'The First Cotton Town in the Delta', a rusting sign informed me as I drove past broken pavements, garbage and lines of rickshaws. The city might wear its industrial history lightly but it floated around these decrepit ruins.

The people of Mahalla added yet another footnote to modern Egyptian history on 6 April 2008, two years after their original strike, when they took to the streets again. They negotiated with a Mubarak government minister for better working conditions and salaries – Widdad Dimirdach was one of two women among the seven workers' negotiators – while withstanding the violence of the state police. Adel Dora, a local journalist, described to me how he watched the baltagi – pro-government street thugs armed with crowbars – lining up to beat the protesters. 'They attacked us terribly and the police used tear gas, but we got people to come in and support us from the countryside by using Facebook.' Only two Arab satellite channels carried stories about the battle. 'Our press simply lied about us – they printed everything the Mubarak government wanted.' The protesters held out for a week, camping in the small midan which, like the great concrete plain in central Cairo, is also called Tahrir Square. In 2009, they tried again, but this time people were frightened. 'They were afraid of the police, of being killed, of more violence, of what the government might do to them.'

Dora told his story with considerable anger but little sense of the precedent his city had set.* Here in dingy Mahalla in 2006 and in 2008 was a miniature version of the revolution that would overwhelm the Egyptian government in February 2011. The unity of ordinary men and women, the use of Facebook, the city centre encampment, the baltagi and the tear gas-firing cops were all to reappear later. And in that Tahrir Square, my colleagues and I had found, only days before Mubarak's departure, men and women workers from Mahalla. Yes, they knew how to overthrow a dictator.

A few days later, in Beirut, I went back through my files and my diary for the Mahalla unrest. I had a few clippings from the Egyptian press about 'foreign' influence in the strikes and the supposed involvement of the Muslim Brotherhood, but I had largely ignored these reports. Israel was destroying Lebanon. Iraq was burning. In 2009, Obama addressed the Islamic world from Cairo, but I had no interest in rural strikes. Millions of Iranians were protesting against the re-election of their mildly insane president Mahmoud Ahmadinejad. We did not care about Egyptian trade unions.

The Egyptian-French journalist Alain Gresh was among the first to realise that the workers may have been the 'forgotten actors' of the Egyptian revolution. He recorded how one Egyptian industrial reporter responded to his questions in Cairo by asking: 'Why, up till now, have the rebellions in Libya, Yemen and Bahrain failed?' He might later have added Syria to the list. But it was in Tunisia that the Tunisian General Workers Syndicate finally brought down its dictatorship. In President Zine al-Abidine Ben Ali's final days, its call for a general strike was the ultimate blow to the regime. Nor were the men and women of Mahalla the only workers to crush Mubarak's power.

---

* Cotton was introduced to Egypt through Napoleonic industrialisation but the later economic importance of Mahalla and the far larger textile city of Kafr el-Dawar was all too evident to the British. Allenby, as high commissioner for Egypt and Sudan, crushed textile factory occupations in the Delta, partly instigated by the Egyptian Communist Party, in 1924. Under General Naguib, Nasser's vain predecessor, 10,000 textile workers again struck in Kafr el-Dawar in 1952. The Egyptian army shot several trade unionists dead. When Mubarak tried to raise food prices in 1984, Kafr el-Dawar workers threw stones at the police and occupied parts of their city. The violence spread to Mahalla.

The Suez cement factory complex workers began another political strike against Mubarak in February 2011.

In the aftermath of the Arab revolutions, local 'activists' and the Western media fell in love with the concept that modern communications technology had played a leading role in the Arab uprisings. Once the internet became a religion, it was difficult to convince anyone that there were other factors, playing a role in events. Socialism and secular trade unions were no longer sufficiently romantic to capture attention. The story was supposed to be Islamism versus dictatorial stability, upset by the gadfly of social media.

As for the workers of Syria, Libya, Yemen, they had long ago been co-opted, Baathised, Green Booked or tribalised, socialism being an unhappy inspiration to dictators. So was it by chance that in Arab countries where unions maintained some support among the people – Tunisia and Egypt, for example – that the violence accompanying social change was less bloody? These questions may now seem academic. Which revolution, save for tiny Tunisia, has ended in anything but tragedy? I never called it a 'spring' in 2011 – that was a media fixation. If the uprisings had mostly started in the spring of 2011, the old colonial borders ensured that the seasons followed their own course of fruition and destruction.

Only when they became violent did the uprisings become internationalised. Thousands of foreign fighters, not just from the Arab world but from China, Burma, the Philippines and from Europe, would crisscross the old Sykes–Picot frontiers of the Middle East to assault the surviving regimes or their successors, often paid and supported and armed by Western nations and their Arab proxies in the Gulf. If al-Qaeda sounded out of date by 2011, the newly emergent Islamist groups in the Middle East adorned themselves with Qur'anic titles, ever larger and more garishly publicised supermarkets of martyrdom.

So what happened to the dignity, honour and justice that the Arabs had demanded on the streets of Cairo, Tunis, Damascus, Bahrain and Libya? How did the courageous young people of these cities allow their cause to be betrayed? How could the heroic Egyptians of 2011 stand in the same streets just over two years later and demand a military coup d'état by a field marshal and soon-to-be president who would turn upon his own people with such hideous repression that Mubarak's dictatorship might be recalled as a mild autocracy?

Was there something absent in the moral, religious, cultural and educational upbringing of these people? How could a risen people in Egypt suddenly re-infantilise themselves and their society and accept the same patriarchal fantasy world of pseudo-democratic tyranny that they thought they had destroyed? Surely the sad, cowed, foolish figure of Egypt's only elected president, Mohamed Morsi, could not have brought about this transition? Surely the Muslim Brotherhood of Egypt could not so frighten the people, or the army that ultimately decided their fate?

I recall writing in the days after Mubarak's fall that this was 'the happiest story I have ever covered in the Middle East'. I was naive, of course, but this was true. In a part of the world that had long been synonymous with geriatric kings and emirs, uneducated generals and sectarian killer-presidents, we could be forgiven for believing that some good must now bless millions of Arabs who had suffered decades of cruelty. Had they not earned this reward?

Looking back, all this seems faintly absurd. It is almost ten years since the American media literati told us that the Arab 'spring' of 2011 had turned into bloody winter. I saw that truism being constructed in the summer of the same year. But the history that followed moved at incredible speed.

What we saw was in many ways more important than what we heard. Like the hideous execution videos that ISIS would force upon us, the Arab world since 2011 has been one at which we must gasp in awe, our incomprehension directed at images. In 2011, we went from the conceptual to the physical, from vague hope to ecstasy – and then to despair and fear.

Since the Second World War, in the West, where our life has been one of steady improvement in health, education and security, this seemed an aberration. For Muslims it was, I suspect, like a path to paradise that at the very last moment reveals not the blossoms of human freedom but a hooded executioner standing by the roadside, impatient for his next decapitation.

How does one describe a day that may prove to be so giant a page in Egypt's history, I asked in the *Independent* after twenty-four hours on the streets of Cairo. 'It might be the end,' I wrote. 'It is certainly the beginning of the end.' Maybe, I suggested in that dispatch of 28 January

2011, 'reporters should abandon their analyses and just tell the tale of what happened from morning to night in one of the world's most ancient cities'.

I think all of us journalists were acutely aware of the language we ourselves were using. The 'giant page in Egypt's history' it would truly turn out to be, and there are times when even the humble journalist must aspire to carry these events on our shoulders. If this seems a trifle pompous, then this is the result of our obedience to that old, stale maxim: that we are the first witnesses to history.

For when the water cannons were switched off and the cops bathed the crowds on Gaza Square in tear gas, something remarkable happened. From the gaunt housing complexes and dingy alleyways, from neighbouring streets, hundreds and then thousands of Egyptians swarmed onto the highway leading to Tahrir Square. This was the one tactic the police had decided to prevent. To have Mubarak's detractors in the very centre of Cairo would suggest that his rule was already over. The government had cut the internet, isolated Egypt from the world and closed down all the mobile phone lines. It made no difference.

'We want the regime to fall,' the crowds screamed again and again, until these words drowned out the pop of tear gas grenades. That's when the first baltagi arrived, pushed to the front of the police ranks in order to attack the protesters. They had metal rods, police truncheons and sharpened sticks. One man whipped a youth over the back with a long yellow cable. Across the city, we found the cops standing in lines, the sun glinting on their riot visors. They looked oddly like hooded birds. Then the tens of thousands of Egyptians reached the west bank of the Nile. A few tourists found themselves caught up in this spectacle, but the police decided that they must hold the eastern end of the fly-over. Then the tear-gassing began in earnest, hundreds upon hundreds of canisters raining onto the crowds. It stung our eyes and made us cough till we were gasping. Men knelt on the pavement to vomit.

With Swedish Radio's veteran Middle East correspondent Cecilia Udden, I took refuge in the old Café Riche off Talaat Harb Square, a tiny restaurant and bar of blue-robed waiters; and there, sipping his coffee, was the Egyptian novelist Ibrahim Abdel Meguid, right in front of us. It was like bumping into Gorky at the height of the 1917 Russian revolution. 'There has been no reaction from Mubarak!' Meguid exalted. 'It is as if nothing has happened. But they will do it – the people will do it!'

We couldn't get back to western Cairo over the bridges. The gas grenades were still soaring off the parapets into the Nile. But a cop eventually took pity on us and led us to the bank of the Nile. And there was an old Egyptian boat, the tourist kind, with plastic flowers and a cheerful owner. So Cecilia and I sailed back to the journalists' Nile-side hotel, watching the grenades spinning off the bridges above us as the crowds struggled with the baltagi.

This was, for the moment at least, a statement of mass revulsion at what had gone before. Observing this titanic upheaval, it was necessary for us to remember the mass arrests, the torture, the decades of imprisonment and death sentences of the Mubarak era, all the way back to the 1990s. The horrors endured by those Egyptians who opposed the regime were not distant memories. The state's wickedness was known to all who came onto the streets in 2011. To understand their courage, you must remember that we in the West admired them for their resolution in confronting the security police on the streets of Egyptian cities, an event we could witness in person or on our screens. But their bravery was far more nuanced; among these thousands of people, many knew from personal experience what they would suffer if they failed.

For the West, Mubarak was tyrant-lite, an elderly and boring autocrat whose people lived in poverty rather than fear. But to those who actually opposed the regime – politically or violently – Mubarak's fury was Saddam-like in its pain and sadism, his torturers as professionally cruel as those who worked for the Iraqi despot. It is a mistake to believe that we can divide up dictators into moderates and madmen.

At first, the army turned up around the square in old Vietnam-era M60 Patton tanks crewed by reservists. Their soldiers were friendly, accepted food from the people in Tahrir, shared their military rations and even allowed protesters to write slogans on their tanks – though references to Mubarak were not permitted. Then a new and more mechanised army unit arrived in the square. That's when I saw an elderly lady in a red scarf standing inches from the front of a modern American-made M1A1 Abrams tank of the Egyptian Third Army. Its soldiers were paratroopers, their 102 mm gun barrel pointed across the midan, a heavy machine gun mounted on the turret. 'If they fire on the Egyptian people, Mubarak is finished,' the lady said. 'And if they don't fire on the Egyptian people, Mubarak is finished.'

Shortly before dusk on 31 January 2011, four F-16 fighters screamed over the square. 'They are on our side,' the cry went up from the crowds. But those new tanks, fourteen of them, their soldiers sullen and apprehensive, had not come, as the protesters forlornly believed, to protect them.

But when I talked to the officer on the first tank, he smiled. 'We will never fire on our people – even if we are ordered to do so,' he shouted. I wasn't so sure. There was a report that Mubarak was at military head-quarters, that the old wolf would still bite. Others said it didn't matter. 'Can he kill 80 million Egyptians?'

But the army fired no guns at all. There had been extraordinary scenes between protesters and the crew of one M60 tank that appeared to be guarding a group of water cannon trucks.

I found the man of the moment – Mohamed ElBaradei, not Mubarak – sitting in his garden chair near a small swimming pool. It was the last day of January, warm, windy, dusty. Egypt's favourite Nobel Prize-winner sometimes looked like a friendly, shrewd and bespectacled mouse, and it was a delight to hear him dissect the bigger mice of the White House and the State Department. 'Do you remember how on the second day, all we heard was that they were "monitoring the situation"?' he asked. 'On the second day, Secretary [Hillary] Clinton said: "We assess the situation as stable." It was funny yesterday, too, to hear Clinton say that "we have been urging ... Mubarak for thirty years to have democratic reform"; but if you have been urging a dictator for thirty years to move on this – and he moved backward – how on earth can you still ask him to introduce democratic reform?'

He had heard the stories of policemen who had 'taken off their uniforms and gone about looting, and everybody says they have been ordered to do that by the regime or by the ministry of interior ... When a regime withdraws the police entirely from the streets of Cairo, when thugs are part of the secret police, trying to give the impression that without Mubarak the country will go into chaos, this is a criminal act. Somebody has to be accountable. And now, as you can hear in the streets, people are not saying Mubarak should go, they are now saying he should be put on trial. If he wants to save his skin, he better leave.'

Less than two years later, we would observe ElBaradei's temporary appointment as an Egyptian vice president after supporting General Abdel Fattah al-Sisi's military coup d'état against the government of Mohamed Morsi, the only elected president in the history of Egypt.

Even as ElBaradei was speaking in his garden, however, Mubarak's senior policemen were preparing a counter-revolution a few miles away in Giza. It smashed into Mubarak's opponents in Tahrir Square the next morning, in a barrage of stones, cudgels, iron bars and clubs. It was vicious, ruthless and bloody – and well planned – a vindication of Mubarak's critics and an indictment of Obama and Clinton for their failure to denounce this faithful ally of America and Israel. The fighting around us in Tahrir was so ferocious that we could smell the blood.

The men and women who were demanding the end of Mubarak's thirty-year rule fought back with immense courage which later turned into a kind of awful cruelty. Some dragged Mubarak security men across the square, beating them until blood broke from their heads and splashed down their clothes. The Egyptian Third Army could not – or would not – cross Tahrir Square to help the wounded.

And where, amid all this hatred and bloodshed, was the West? Reporting its shameful response each day could induce insomnia. Sometime around 3 a.m. that same morning, I had watched former British prime minister Tony Blair as he struggled to explain in his role as a Middle East 'peace' envoy our need to 'partner the process of change' in Egypt. For years to come, he would toady up to dictators while encouraging war against Iran; he would befriend Sisi after his military coup. But in 2011, he was dispensing his advice to the antagonists of the Egyptian revolution. There were three elements at play, he informed his audience: 'a government that's not elected according to the system of democracy we espouse' and 'Islamist groups that would take the situation in a completely different direction', a clear reference to the Muslim Brotherhood.

And – this being Blair – there were 'well-intentioned people' who needed 'time to get organised'. These were clearly the millions of courageous young people who wished to get rid of a government that was not elected according to the system Blair and his countrymen 'espoused' and were risking their lives to do so. Blair talked of a 'plan of action' for this 'partnership'. In other words, he wished the young people of Egypt to take advice from the grown-ups, from the wreckage of Mubarak's own regime, from the West, from him.

That there were Salafists among the protest groups was understandable. Once the revolution appeared to be potentially successful, those who had suffered most grievously under his tyranny had every right to join the protesters. The Muslim Brotherhood, whose greed and desire for political power played their usual role, avoided Tahrir Square until they sensed the weakness of the regime – and then privately joined in talks with the very same authorities to prepare for their own possible role in a future government. It was Mohamed Morsi, soon to be the elected president, who promised on 4 February that 'The people have brought down the regime and we see no point in any dialogue with an illegitimate regime.'*

Yet next day, the Brotherhood announced that it would participate in just such a dialogue with Mubarak's sinister and newly appointed seventy-five-year-old vice president Omar Suleiman, the country's top intelligence agent and Egypt's principal interlocutor with Israel. And Morsi was one of the Brotherhood delegates who went to talk to him. On 6 February, as protesters in Tahrir were angrily denouncing the Brotherhood's tawdry covenant with the regime, Suleiman appeared on CNN with a message that might have been Mubarak's – and not unlike the line peddled by Blair. Suleiman was undertaking 'a process starting with national dialogue ... we want young people to know that [to] all your requests we will respond positively ... We don't want chaos in our country.' 'I'm an old man,' Suleiman admitted. 'I did a lot for the country and have no interest to be president of this country. When the President [Mubarak] asked me to be vice-president, I accepted immediately, just to help him in this critical time.'

Far from convincing 'young people', Suleiman's promises were bound to infuriate them. The wounded but unrepentant Egyptian

---

* In one sense, the Brotherhood, the Ikhwan, helped dictatorships to survive because it was Islamist enough to act as a threat to 'Westernised' tyrants but corrupt enough to offer the same regimes support in return for electoral power. Thus Mubarak could accept their presence in parliament as 'independent' candidates. Sisi would try to persuade the world, Egyptians, and perhaps even himself, that the Brotherhood and ISIS were interchangeable, if not the same. In a Middle East where every citizen had now become a real or potential 'terrorist' – unless they happened to be the president – you could stick any label on a political enemy, charge them with state crimes and sentence them to death.

people in Tahrir Square were exhausted by the old canard of Islamic-inspired unrest, foreign plots and impending chaos – these were tales to frighten schoolchildren or American presidents.

All their lives, Egyptians had been forced to live in an infantilised world of fake elections, fake parliaments, fake newspapers and fake public opinion. Any breaking of the rules would necessitate a visit to the police station, with all that this entailed. But everyone knew that obedience and loyalty would be rewarded with bread, cash, status, secure employment and the maintenance of the conservative, patriarchal family discipline that would always gain the wholehearted support of half the population: the men.

But suddenly, these schoolchildren had grown up. Again, I do not believe we should give too much credit to Facebook, Twitter and YouTube. This may have increased the speed of events, but it did not provide the inspiration. A social revolution had taken place within Egyptian society; and it included all classes. When I first visited the University of Cairo in 1977, few of its students spoke English, and even the engineering department library was contained in a small room. When I gave a talk at the same university in 2010, most students spoke foreign languages, and their campus included an ambitious multi-disciplinary library. Satellite television had shown the poor that richer, more pluralistic nations existed outside Egypt.

This was a slow and incremental social process that did not emerge through social media.* But it made its appearance within a short space of time, and I suspect it had something to do with the behaviour of the Arab autocrat towards his own family. Most Arab tyrants portrayed themselves as fathers of their nation; it was when it became apparent that the father of the nation intended to pass on the nation not to his people but to his biological children that the whole system began to break apart.

----

* Scholars have also suggested that the emphasis on social media within popular uprisings has been misplaced, partly because of the West's bias towards its own technology. In an essay on the Egyptian revolution, Canadian political scientist Genevieve Barrons argued that communications 'did not constitute the revolution itself, nor did they instigate it'. Focusing solely on social media 'diminishes the personal risks that Egyptians took when heading into the streets to face rubber bullets and tear gas, as well as more lethal weapons. Social media was neither the cause nor the catalyst of the revolution ...'

Visiting Egypt shortly before the revolution, I was told that
Mubarak's security police were tearing down pictures of his businessman son Gamal from the walls of the Cairo suburb of Mohandesin.
Graffiti had been written across many of the posters. Arab kings and
emirs made no secret of their medieval system of succession, but it did
not have much purchase on the popular imagination. If there was a
bargain between a people's servility and the 'monarch-type figure' who
ruled them, this did not include the restoration of a caliphate.

Yet within the space of just a few years, this is what the leading autocratic families of the Middle East were planning. Gaddafi intended his
son Saif to become the owner of Libya. Ben Ali was already spreading
his nation's wealth through his family. Hafez al-Assad posthumously
bequeathed Syria to his son Bashar and an extraordinary meeting of the
Syrian Arab Baath party was called to lower the age of Syria's constitutional president after the father's death so that the young Bashar could
ascend to his caliphate. Gamal Mubarak already held senior positions
in Hosni's National Democratic Party when his father was toppled. It
was this familial betrayal by the autocracy that helped to provoke the
Arab awakening. They arose from their oppressive beds to discover
that they did not have to be afraid or believe in children's nightmares.

Vile rags were now hanging in the corner of the square, the last
clothes worn by the martyrs of Tahrir, their pictures strewn above the
crowds. On day sixteen of the revolution, 8 February, the people
honoured their dead in their tens of thousands in their largest ever
march against the dictatorship, a sweating, pushing, shouting, weeping, joyful people, fearful that the world may forget their courage.
High above us, a ghostly photomontage flapped in the wind: Mubarak's
head superimposed upon the terrible picture of Saddam Hussein with
a noose round his neck.

The father of the Egyptian people had brought forth a new back-to-
work government in the hope that the nation might slide back into its
old, autocratic torpor; gas stations open, banks handing out money,
ministers sitting to attention on state television as the man who promised to remain king lectured them on the need to bring order from
chaos. But Issam Etman proved him wrong.

Shoved and battered by the thousands around him, he carried his
five-year-old daughter Khadiga on his shoulders. 'I am here for my
daughter,' he shouted above the protest. 'It is for her freedom that I

want Mubarak to go.' And all the while, the little girl sat on Issam Etman's shoulders and stared at the crowds in wonderment.

Thousands of new protesters had come here for the first time. The soldiers of the Third Army must have been outnumbered 40,000 to one and they sat meekly on their tanks, smiling nervously; a military force turned to impotence by an army of dissent. Many said they had come because they feared the world was losing interest in their struggle, because the crowds had grown smaller in recent days, because camera crews had left for other tragedies, because the smell of betrayal was in the air. If the Republic of Tahrir dried up, the national awakening was over. It was easy to forget how the regime could persuade the 'moderates' among the people to debase their only demand.

Regimes grow iron roots, and so it was in Egypt. The ministry of interior thugs, the state security cops, the dictator who gives them their orders, were still in operation. It was easy to accuse the hundreds of thousands of naivety, of over-reliance on the internet. Sometimes I felt that the young of Egypt came to believe in the screen rather than the street – so that when they took to the streets, they were deeply shocked by the state violence and the regime's continued brutal strength. But how can a people who have lived under dictatorship for so long plan their revolution? Egypt was a thunderstorm without direction, an inundation of popular expression that did not fit neatly into our revolutionary history books or our political meteorology. Less than twenty years earlier, we had rejoiced at the fall of communist dictatorships, but now we sat glumly observing the extraordinary events in Cairo with the same enthusiasm as many east European dictators watched the fall of their allied Warsaw Pact regimes.

If we, the outsiders, really believed in the regime-or-chaos theory that still gripped Washington, London and Paris, the secular, democratised nature of this great protest would also be blighted. The iron fingernails of this regime, I wrote in that night:

> have long ago grown into the sand, deeper than the pyramids, more powerful than ideology. We have not seen the last of this particular creature. Nor of its vengeance.

*   *   *

Everyone suddenly burst out singing, laughing and crying, shouting and praying, kneeling on the road and kissing the tarmac, praising God for ridding them of Hosni Mubarak. It was as if joy could smother the decades of dictatorship, pain and humiliation, hopelessness and blood. Forever it would be known as the Egyptian Revolution of 25 January – the day the rising began.

It was already dark on that night of 11 February when Nelofer and I arrived at the edge of the square. We were exhausted after spending five days in the square, every hour waiting for the announcement of Mubarak's departure. A day earlier, he had appeared on the huge television screen above Tahrir, calling the protesters his 'children', warning of 'terror' and talking of his past heroism as an Egyptian air force officer in the 1973 war. The crowds had roared their defiance across Egypt, and men and women took off their shoes and held the heels to the great screens in contempt.

But now the impossible became the possible – and in less than five seconds. At the very moment when the thousands around us heard the news, they became transfigured, possessed, transformed. It was as if, despite the darkness, dawn had shone upon their faces. Those who prayed had seen the proof of their belief, a discovery that good can conquer evil, that courage must be recognised as a human faculty that cannot be diminished or destroyed in the torture chamber.

Arabs had been portrayed as weak, mendacious, obedient to power, fearful of violence, frightened for their lives when confronted by Western invasion. The people were shocked by their own ability to give the great wheel of history a shove and to find that it moved.

Nelofer's camera moved in circles and caught the bearded, middle-aged man standing beside me who suddenly knelt and kissed the road. The Egyptians were humble in their victory. When Mubarak had refused to leave the previous night, they had roared their anger. In many countries, they would have burned government buildings after a speech of such hubris; in Tahrir Square, they staged poetry readings. And now they heard that their wretched antagonist had gone.

If the connections between the insurrections in Tunisia and Egypt were inspirational – we might later add Bahrain and subsequently Syria – the response of the state authorities was almost identical. The cops in Cairo had obviously seen tape of the cops in Tunis bludgeoning the government's opponents and responded in the same way. Uniformed police confronted the demonstrators, their ranks parting for the baltagi to run forward and strike protesters with sticks, stones, coshes and crowbars. They would retreat back to police lines while the crowds were doused in tear gas; whereupon the protesters overwhelmed the state security forces and their mafiosi.

But what happened when I turned on Al Jazeera in the coming days to see where I should travel next? There on the streets of Yemen were state security police baton-charging crowds of Sana'a's pro-democracy demonstrators and then parting ranks to allow plain-clothed men to attack the people with sticks, iron bars and pistols. When the cop-criminals retreated, the Yemeni authorities poured tear gas canisters over their opponents. A few minutes later I watched Algerian police baton-bashing the crowds in Algiers city, permitting the state criminal gangs to take over before spraying the streets with tear gas. Then I watched the scenes in Bahrain where precisely the same routine is performed.

This sequence of events acquired its own tedium, as if the opposing sides advanced and retreated on cue, each aware of their role in the drama of rebellion. This should not have been surprising. For decades the secret services of these Arab countries had been visiting each other's capitals and exchanging tips from each other's practical experience of state repression. In Cairo, it was said that the Egyptians at the Lazoughli Street interrogation centre learned how to use electricity more effectively on the tongues and genitals of prisoners after a visit from their opposite numbers at the Chateauneuf police station in central Algiers. When I was reporting in Algiers in December 2010, the head of Tunisian state security paid an official visit to the country. Almost overwhelmed by their Islamist enemies in 1994, Algerian security men had travelled to Damascus to learn how Hafez al-Assad dealt with the 1982 Muslim uprising in Hama: slaughter the people, blow the city up, leave the corpses of innocent and guilty for the survivors to see.

In this infernal, open university of torture, there was a constant round of conferences and first-hand 'interrogation' accounts by the sadists of the Arab world, with the support of the Pentagon and its scandalous 'strategic cooperation manuals'. The Palestinian Authority security apparatus would learn from the Israelis and from their

American security assistance colleagues. The Arab world in revolt might still be divided by its old borders, but the universe of torture knew no such post-colonial frontiers.*

So it was crucial to understand not only the power of the army that had supported Egypt's autocrats since 1952 but its relationship with what one Egyptian woman, daughter of a senior military officer, was already calling the 'deep state'. Omar Suleiman was admired by the Americans and Israelis; and with good reason, since he had agreed more than a decade earlier to the US 'rendition' programme in which prisoners were sent to Cairo for interrogation-by-torture. Field Marshal Mohamed Tantawi and his staff thus kept a subtle distance from the old man, yet all senior military officers had achieved their positions under Mubarak and could not have done so without his consent. Among the millions of protesters, no one objected when the army command dissolved parliament, since Mubarak's assembly elections were so transparently fraudulent. The suspension of the constitution left most Egyptians unmoved. And the army announced that it would hold power for only six months.

But a clear divergence emerged almost at once between the young men and women who brought down the Mubarak regime and the concessions that the army appeared willing to grant them. On 13 February, a small rally at the side of Tahrir Square distributed a series of printed demands that included the suspension of Mubarak's old emergency law and freedom for political prisoners. On this last demand, the army had remained suspiciously silent. Was this because there are prisoners who know too much about the army's involvement with the previous regime? Or because escaped and newly liberated prisoners were now returning to Cairo and Alexandria from desert camps with terrible stories of torture and executions by military personnel?

Five days later, with his usual inexhaustible detective work, Donald Macintyre revealed that watchtower guards at the Egyptian al-Qatta prison had opened fire on some of the 3,500 inmates who had staged a

---

* Thus in November 2016, General Jamil Hassan, the head of Syria's horrific Air Force Security intelligence service, personally confirmed to me in Hama that his government had just received a delegation of Egyptian mukhabarat officers who had been sent to Damascus on the personal instructions of Field Marshal-President Abdel Fattah al-Sisi to share their experiences with the Syrians.

'revolution' inside the walls. When a senior prisons inspector, General Mohamed el-Batran, had earlier arrived to tell the prisoners they would be freed and that guards would be put on trial for torturing them, he himself was shot dead by one of the prison staff – who then turned their guns on the inmates.

And even if they no longer supported the rais – the leader – the Egyptian military's high command were men of the old order. Most of the army's highest ranking officers had long ago been sucked into the nexus of regime power and benefited from huge business contracts – why should the high command give up these lucrative perquisites?

Just before I returned to Beirut, I visited a tatty gift shop on the Cairo island of Zamalek and asked the owner if he could sell me a photograph of Saad Zaghloul. Out from a paper bag at the back of the shop came a portrait of the father of Egypt's real independence struggle, the Wafdist hero of 1919 when the Egyptian people marched in street demonstrations and staged industrial strikes to demand the end of British rule.

The spread of strikes across Egypt, the cutting of railway lines, the brutality of repression – by British soldiers in 1919, using live rounds like the bullets and tear gas of Mubarak's goons – was an almost fingerprint-perfect copy of what would happen in Cairo a century later. But in 1919, President Wilson also did an Obama. Instead of supporting the Egyptian democrats and adhering to his gospel of self-determination for all races, Wilson immediately recognised the British protectorate over Egypt.

Zaghloul's towering bronze figure at the west end of the Qasr El Nil Lion's Bridge over the Nile was wreathed in the trailing smoke of tear gas grenades when the pro-democracy crowds fought off the cops and their plain-clothes mafia on 28 January. In the photograph I bought in Cairo, he is sitting on an ornate pseudo-Louis XV chair. Back in Beirut, my picture-framer wanted to encompass him in a grandfatherly thick brown frame, which made him look like a dead family member.

Over the previous thirty-five years, I usually hated my assignments to Cairo, but I had suddenly begun to enjoy the city. Its people had re-awoken from the hibernation of dictatorship with a courage and maturity and humour that proved how wrong were the Westerners who believed that a surfeit of dictatorships made Egyptians politically comatose, obedient, hopelessly condemned to exist in the shadows of their country's history. Zaghloul was proof that even in the age of imperialism, this was not true.

To be romantic about the present is excusable, but to be nostalgic about the past is not. Zaghloul was a shrewd leader of the nationalist Wafd ('Delegation') party, but his desire for power allowed him to compromise with the British and accept their protectorate status in Egypt – to the fury of Huda Shaarawi, one of Egypt's most prominent and wealthiest feminists. She and Zaghloul's wife Safiya had campaigned for women's suffrage and equal rights, but Shaarawi was outraged when Zaghloul pointedly refused to invite her women's group to the opening of the Egyptian parliament. Most women's leaders were educated and middle class and visited Europe, and were happy to enlist poorer women in the nationalist struggle. But they made less effort to mobilise socially the millions of Egyptian women who lived in squalor and under male domination in the city slums.

Shaarawi, at one remove from the squalor of Cairo, created an army of female 'Cadettes', including two of her cousins – 'a kind of nimble army of volunteers to take welfare to the doors of the poor', as Shaarawi's biographer daintily put it – and to report back 'about the lack of potable water, muddy streets and other problems'. Perhaps the most prominent 'woman of letters' among the early Arab feminists was the Lebanese-Palestinian poet and essayist May Ziadeh, who maintained a long correspondence with the Lebanese poet Kahlil Gibran. In a Cairo lecture in 1914, she proclaimed that 'the civilisation of the future does not belong to man alone. It is the civilisation of humanity, for women are slowly [sic] ascending to their true station alongside men ... here in Egypt, the chains that had for ages past bound women are beginning to shatter.' In the early twenties, it was fashionable for Egyptian women's rights campaigners to take off their traditional veils in public – which Huda Shaarawi and Safiya Zaghloul did very ostentatiously. These early pioneers would initiate laws to protect women workers in factories and encourage female students to enter university. But it would be almost a century before Egyptian women would actively participate in trade union or popular revolutionary protest.

Could one return to those earlier days and discover what went wrong? On the very day when 50 million Egyptians were waiting to hear if they had elected Mohamed Morsi as president, the best I could do was to go to the great man's home eighty-five years after his death. 'The House of People', it was called, and even now it muffled the roar of cars and buses from Qasr el-Aini Street and the nearby Metro station which bears Zaghloul's name. Unlike Morsi, Zaghloul wanted to live in a modern, progressive, secular Egypt. One could see why in 2013, he might be missed, after an election campaign in which the words 'Islam' and 'security' seemed interchangeable platitudes. But Zaghloul was not a perfect man. He had failed to make any impression on the delegates to the Versailles peace conference and he had failed to prevent the British separating Sudan from Egypt. From that moment, Arab leaders – in Syria, in Palestine and Jordan, in Lebanon – would have to accept similar imperial partition of their lands. After an assassination attempt at Cairo railway station, Zaghloul kept the grey jacket he was wearing when he was shot. It hangs outside his bedroom, his blood still staining the material.

Morsi was a Muslim Brotherhood bag-carrier who would only just win the poll in June 2013 over Ahmed Shafiq, a Mubarak bag-carrier whom the military might have preferred. The former was no revolutionary, no feminist, not much of a nationalist, but the 'deep state' represented by his opponent receded, for a short time, and Zaghloul would have approved.

How swiftly the army appeared to move centre frame. Instead of the young, fearful, brave protesters of Tahrir, Egyptian television viewers were suddenly confronted with the unsmiling super-patriot generals of the Supreme Council of the Armed Forces (SCAF). The prosaic reality was that the Egyptian military, since the Naguib–Nasser coup of 1952, had been the institutional bedrock of political power in Egypt. From a defeated rabble after the 1967 war to the victorious legions which crossed the Suez Canal in 1973, the army had become softened by privilege and wealth, its generals accomplished businessmen who protected billions of dollars of real estate and foreign investments. But after 2011, these same generals had to learn how to mind their property and their position, how to 'manage' events so that no one could dispute the necessity of their guiding hand.

Within days of Mubarak's departure to Sharm el-Sheikh, it became evident to Egyptians that something had gone badly wrong with their revolution. The SCAF began toadying up to the middle-aged Muslim

Brothers and the Salafists, the generals chatting to the pseudo-Isla-mists while the young, the liberal, poor and wealthy who brought down the dictator were ignored. The economy was collapsing. Anarchy crept through the streets of Egyptian cities each night. Sectarianism flourished in the darkness. The cops were going back to their dirty work.

You only had to walk the streets of Cairo in the summer of 2011 to understand what had happened, to wander again across the acres of Tahrir Square and listen to the tired Kerenskys insisting on democracy and freedom as the old men of the Mubarak regime clung on. Tantawi's elderly head was now framed in posters around Tahrir, and the old January–February cry was back: 'We want the end of the regime.'

On the traffic island, the groupuscules of the revolution now had their tents with tiny carpets and plastic chairs on the dust floor, debat-ing Nasserism, secularism and the Christian civil rights movement, 'The Mass Bureau Youth Movement'; the Brotherhood and the Salafists were not there. These were the debates the democrats should have held before the revolution. 'We've got sick of the Military Council which is using the same tools as Mubarak,' a twenty-six-year-old Cairo University veterinary student called Fahdi Philip told me as we sat amid the summer heat. 'The judgement on the guilty is slow in coming. The state of insecurity is still with us.'

According to an official government commission, 846 civilians were killed by Egypt's security police and snipers in the revolution and only one policeman had been tried, in absentia, for killing demonstrators. When a mass protest by the families of the 'martyrs' poured into the streets in June, the cops reverted to form. In front of television cameras, they threw stones at the protesters, beat them with sticks and – in one extraordinary incident – danced towards them waving swords. More than 1,100 civilians were injured. Fearful of further violence, the SCAF announced a new fund of $15 million to compensate the families of those killed or wounded in the revolution. But no sooner did I open my morning Cairo newspapers than I saw a coloured photograph of Field Marshal Tantawi appointing a new 'minister of information'. Only months earlier, he had announced the total scrapping of the infor-mation ministry. Just as the young vet said, Tantawi was using Mubarak's old tools.

But despair was best summed up by essayist and poet Youssef Rakha, who wrote a profoundly eloquent article in the *Al-Ahram* newspaper prior to a 'corrective' protest demonstration:

> Tomorrow is 'the second revolution'. The demands of the first revolution, which were more or less willingly left to the army to respond to and have therefore not been met, will be made more forcefully, once again. It is as if the revolutionaries are suddenly discovering that the army had been part of the regime all along ... The stepping down of Mubarak is, as if for the first time since 17 February, seen for what it actually was: a significant enough concession to the social-political transformation ... but one that could not in itself lead to democracy.

By talking of a 'second revolution', Rakha was a little premature. That particular event, however distorted, would be organised two years later by Sisi himself. The author did seem to understand, however, why the 'transformation' did not produce 'democracy'. The advantage of the January–February 2011 revolution was that it had no leaders, and thus no one to arrest. But its disadvantage was that it had no leaders, and thus no one to take responsibility for the revolution once it was over. Only the Egyptian military could be the ultimate 'responsible' power.

At the same time, there was a perverse humour to all of this. Mubarak did not build statues to himself, but his name had graced a vast number of educational and urban projects in Egypt. There were 381 Hosni Mubarak schools, another 160 named after his half-English wife Suzanne and one after the president-who-might-have-been, Gamal Mubarak. The Mubarak Police Academy and the Suzanne Mubarak Specialised Hospital lost their names. Crowds changed the Mubarak metro sign to Martyrs of the January 25 Revolution Station. Newspapers that once ran photographs of the leader on their front pages now published snapshots of the twenty SCAF generals, often sitting opposite the carefully groomed figure of Mohamed Morsi.

When the first free Egyptian parliamentary elections were held between November 2011 and January 2012, the Brotherhood's Freedom and Justice Party and other Islamic groups won a large majority of parliamentary seats, almost guaranteeing that a member of the

Brotherhood would become the next president. Although the legitimacy of this new assembly would be both denied and then reconfirmed
over the next two years, the vote was both free and fair. In the last
parliamentary elections in 2010, boycotted by the Brotherhood,
Mubarak's National Democratic Party had claimed a tiresomely
predictable victory of 83 per cent. In the 2011–12 post-revolution parliamentary elections, the Islamist parties won a more honest 71 per cent
of the vote. In the June 2012 presidential poll, Morsi would receive only
51.7 per cent, a credible result. Sisi's post-coup presidential victory in
2018, however, naturally returned to the autocratic comfort of 97.08
per cent.

Yet long before Morsi was elected president, the Egyptian army's
operations became ever more oppressive in a series of violent incidents
that included street killings, mass arrests and the beating of young
women. The behaviour of the Egyptian military in this period was
often ignored out of interest in the 'democracy' that the SCAF had
promised to patronise. Since this was a time of great political uncer-
tainty, we should avoid the temptation to regard the army as a corrupt
and monolithic creature bent only on its own economic survival and
running a 'deep state' that could control the nation.

Tens of thousands of Egyptian soldiers had responded to the revolution with great restraint and even tacit support; other Arab armies
would prove a good deal less compassionate in the coming months. If
the Egyptian military command sometimes appeared blundering and
divided, this may have reflected the truth. There was no military
'mastermind' behind the orders of the defence ministry. But was there
a class among the army officers who sought to eliminate, one by one,
those groups that would oppose a military regime, rather than destroying them in a single violent onslaught? And if these senior officers
wished to prune the branches of the revolution, the participation of
women was something that could not be tolerated.

Was this why there suddenly occurred, without apparent reason, a
spate of sexual attacks by soldiers that were clearly intended to frighten
young women off the streets? The latter revealed a side to the Egyptian
military that none of us had hitherto recognised: a misogynistic and
shocking display of brutality towards women that could not have been
the work of a few indisciplined units. Thousands of women demonstrated in December 2011 after military police officers kicked, beat,

partially stripped and stamped on the breasts of a young Muslim woman protester. The attack was clearly a sexual assault by military personnel, a disgraceful act that was only the latest of a series of attacks by soldiers on unguarded women in Tahrir. The heroes of the 1973 war had become molesters.

Far more sinister had been the virginity tests to which young women arrested in Tahrir were subjected by the army in March 2011, often in front of male personnel. They could thus, so we were supposed to believe, make no future rape claims against soldiers. CNN quoted an anonymous 'senior general' as explaining that 'the girls who were detained were not like your daughter or mine. We didn't want them to say we had sexually assaulted them or raped them, so we wanted to prove that they were not virgins in the first place. These were girls who had camped out in tents with male protesters in Tahrir Square and we found in the tents Molotov cocktails.' The first 'tests' were conducted after plain-clothes police attacked protesters while the army cleared the square. Amnesty International found that eighteen female detainees had been threatened with prostitution charges; former women prisoners spoke of electric torture and of being forced to strip in front of cameras. General Abdel Fattah al-Sisi, the Egyptian army intelligence head whom Morsi would appoint minister of defence in August 2012, defended the virginity tests. 'The procedure,' he said, 'was done to protect the girls from rape as well as to protect soldiers and officers from rape accusations.'

These events briefly caused international uproar, although the outrage expressed by Western leaders failed to address the political purpose behind these acts, which was, surely, to disenfranchise Egyptian women from physical political protest. They were tolerated when they broke up the paving stones to help the demonstrators defend themselves from Mubarak's goons, but not when they opposed the post-revolution military.

A statement by twelve Egyptian human rights groups published in November 2011, including at least two women's groups, accused the SCAF of employing 'extrajudicial killing, torture, arbitrary arrest, forced virginity tests and military trials' against 'media professionals, bloggers, liberals, leftists, or rights activists' while leaving untouched 'those religious groups [which had] committed crimes which threaten the social peace between Muslims and Copts'. The army, the groups said, were now 'adopting the very methods of the Mubarak regime by repressing protests and sit-ins, using excessive force against peaceful demonstrators, killing dozens of unarmed civilians, carrying out arbitrary arrests'.

The statement also noted that 'following several promises to issue a law guaranteeing the freedoms of trade unions and workers, the proposed law was never issued and implemented. Rather, after issuing a decree to dissolve the General Federation of Trade Unions of Egypt, another decision was issued to return it to work once more.' In other words, the tens of thousands of industrial workers who had rallied to Tahrir must return to their factories and abide by the old government puppet trade union instituted by Mubarak. If the army of women was to be neutered within months of the uprising against the dictatorship, the army of independent trade unions and workers would be ruthlessly emasculated over the coming months and years.

As for the youth of the revolution, they quickly realised the army was no longer on the streets to protect them. On 9 March 2011, soldiers had fought demonstrators alongside club-carrying men in civilian clothes, pulling down tents and beating young men. By the end of May, peaceful protesters, many now arguing that the army had become a new dictatorship, were being tried in front of military courts – as many as 5,600 in two months.

Yet the Islamists continued to bathe in the embrace of the army. Major General Mohamed al-Assar, a SCAF general, told a Washington audience in July that 'day by day, the Brotherhood are changing and are getting on a more moderate track. They have the willingness to share in the political life.' Even the Brotherhood objected when their electoral Salafist allies took over a Tahrir rally that forced thirty political parties and secular groups to abandon the square at the end of the month. To find the slogan 'lift up your head – you are an Egyptian' replaced by 'lift up your head – you are a Muslim' was too much even for Mohamed Beltagy, a prominent Brotherhood politician.

But the Brotherhood's Freedom and Justice Party was equally jealous when Turkish prime minister Erdogan arrived to support the Egyptian revolution in September. Western nations had already begun naively urging Arabs to regard Turkey as a role model for future 'democracy' in the Middle East, apparently forgetting the Turks' treatment of their Kurdish minority and the country's continued refusal to recognise the 1915 genocide of the Armenians. Less than five years later and after a failed coup d'état against him, Erdogan would lock up more political detainees than did Sisi after his successful coup in 2013.

But the army had one spectral performance to distract the Egyptian masses: the much promised August trial of Mubarak, along with his sons, at the police school outside Cairo. Look carefully, and you could even see that part of the sign saying 'Police Academy' had been gently eased from the wall. Until its namesake turned up for his day in court, it had of course been the 'Mubarak Police Academy'.

So just when the remaining Arab dictators desperately needed to drink the cool waters of an Arab summer, along came the Egyptian army to poison the well. In front of their satellite television screens, tyrants could see a flickering, enmeshed face, fragile fingers playing over its nose and mouth, but, for just a few brief moments, they could see the same old arrogant eyes. Then the heavy black mic appeared in the man's left hand. 'I am here, your honour,' said a chillingly strong voice. 'I have not committed any such crimes.'

And so Egypt put its wretched, ancient autocrat on trial, along with his effete, sullen sons. The lawyers screamed their clients' pain; of torture, of snipers, of the murder of Egypt's own people in the January–February uprising, of the brutality of the security forces. And to whom did these terrible charges also apply? Damascus came to mind. And the Libyan capital of Tripoli. And the Bahraini capital of Manama. And Rabat, Algiers and Riyadh.

But across the vast, arid wastelands of the Arab despots, their own government television stations continued to show friendly crowds, all of whom loved their presidents and kings and potentates who could never be accused of these awful crimes. Outside Egypt, the only live national coverage of the trial was broadcast by post-revolutionary Tunisia and by Hizbollah's Al-Manar television in Lebanon.

Egyptians – and the West – were supposed to take this seriously. History, we believed, would place these scenes in the police academy in whole chapters; it was the moment when a country proved not only that its revolution was real but that its victims were real, its people's suffering forensically described. Could the Arab infection be stopped, we asked ourselves, the poisoned waters cleansed? If this was a bonbon affair, a toffee or two to humour the masses, it promised by close of play to be a much more serious matter. 'Are you Mohamed Hosni Sayed Mubarak?' asked Judge Ahmed Refaat. Defence and prosecuting lawyers shrieked their demands, Mubarak's men trying to draw out the trial for weeks, months, years, for thousands more pages of evidence and subpoenas of all the men around the sundered president.

And then the lawyers for 'civil rights claimants' shouted out the names of the victims. They had walked and were shot down in the streets of Cairo and Alexandria and Giza, dying in astonishment as Mubarak's thugs took aim at them.

Ex-interior minister Habib al-Adly, blue-suited and ignored by Gamal and Alaa Mubarak, hovered on his side of the cage to receive yet more charges of corruption and violence. He had already received a sentence of twelve years and appeared a pathetic figure behind the iron bars and wire mesh of the court prison cage. Long ago, I asked him for an interview to discuss his business affairs – and was told I would be arrested if I asked again.

'I deny all the charges,' announced Gamal. 'I deny everything,' declared Alaa. There was even a demand to subpoena General Tantawi, which was surely taking things too far. From Damascus and Amman and Rabat and Manama and Riyadh, there came only silence. And then the cameras, too, were cloaked when sixty-nine-year-old Judge Refaat ordered that live television coverage of the trial must cease 'in the public interest'. True, the lawyers postured for the cameras, working themselves into a frenzy as if to make a name for themselves, but the military had decided that the masses had consumed enough of this gruel.

The trial continued over five months of delays, muddled witness accounts and legal postponements. Mubarak, the chief prosecutor Mustafa Suleiman claimed in January 2012, 'deserves to end in humiliation and indignity: from the presidential palace to the defendants' cage and then the harshest penalty'. The two sons had already circulated a plea for leniency in a letter carried from their prison by Oman's most prominent businessman, in which they lamented that 'we have been through rounds of politically motivated investigations that resemble more of a witch hunt directed at our family at large'. The media were manipulated, the two men complained, the investigations 'corrupted', the charges 'manufactured' and their lawyers slandered. There was, no doubt, an element of truth in all this; but since their father's regime had routinely practised just such illegalities, their smuggled letter was unlikely to purchase much sympathy.*

In Egypt, injustice could now be acknowledged. As Mubarak's trial dragged on, new videotapes were collected, along with eyewitness evidence of the shooting of demonstrators by Mubarak's security services. In 2012, he was sentenced to life imprisonment for the killing of protesters, but in November 2014, more than a year after Sisi had staged his coup against Morsi's elected government, the Cairo Criminal Court dismissed charges of conspiracy to kill against Mubarak. Embezzlement accusations against him were also dropped. There was a retrial, but in 2017 the courts again acquitted him of the 2011 killings and he was released from prison.†

When young demonstrators calling for Tantawi's resignation confronted police outside the American University in Cairo, thirty-three civilians were killed. Much anger had already been generated by the military's attempt to keep the defence budget secret and separate from the national budget, since it was involved in up to 40 per cent of the country's economy.

Groups of middle-ranking officers began to call for Tantawi's dismissal. Three young officers appeared on a balcony over Tahrir, shaking their fists in support of the protesters. An army major who identified himself to the *Guardian* as Tamer Samir Badr proclaimed that he 'wanted people to know that there are officers who are with them'. Many other officers had been attending the protests in civilian clothes, he said. And when people were killed in the square a week earlier, the army had issued orders to its soldiers not to intervene.

Within two months, Major Badr was in a military prison, awaiting trial, along with more than twenty other officers who had joined the revolution in January. His contention that army officers in plain clothes

---

* Nor was their outrageous defence of the killing of anti-Mubarak demonstrators: 'Who in his right mind could believe that Hosni Mubarak with his history of fighting for the dignity of his people ... would even contemplate committing such a crime? In fact, he decided to step down [*sic*] to prevent violence from escalating.' At no point did the Mubarak sons show the slightest sympathy for the hundreds of protesters killed in the uprising against their father. They blamed the Muslim Brotherhood for their predicament.

† Mubarak's sons Gamal and Alaa were freed from prison in October 2015 because time had already been served for their own embezzlement offences.

had been among the protesters in Tahrir was correct. Several months later, in the summer of 2012, I was to meet one of them, a young man who approached me in the square and said that he wished to talk to me urgently. Morsi had been elected president only a few days earlier* and I was extremely suspicious of this man, but he showed me his army military intelligence card, gave me his phone number and asked me to meet him in his home city of Alexandria, in a parking lot behind a supermarket not far from the port.

I took the desert road to Alexandria and there was my contact, dressed now in jeans and sneakers. We shook hands. We would sit on a bench close to the sea, he said. Yes, I could take notes, but he had little time. And under no circumstances could I reveal that I had met any member of the army's intelligence service. And then he told me a story of rigged elections, of a mini-revolution in the army's intelligence service, of the secret killing of Egyptian soldiers by government forces. There was no way I could check this information. Worse still, how could I explain to readers of the *Independent* that my military contact had given me information which – if it could not be independently proved – must surely be taken seriously?

Driving back to Cairo that afternoon, I brooded on this problem. Even if I could hint at the source of my story, the army would quickly be after him. About two hours south of Alexandria, I was looking westwards towards the lowering sun when I saw a fox running between the dunes. He raced over the sand, visible for only a few seconds. In Arabic and Persian poetry, the fox emerges as both wise and cunning, a slightly dodgy creature but worthy of respect.† And it occurred to me that I might use a 'fox' as my source, that anyone who read my report would understand at once that the animal represented a creature which knew many things, even if his life depended on the act of dissembling. And so, sitting in the Marriott Hotel beside the Nile, I wrote one of the

---

* Morsi officially won the final round of the June 2012 Egyptian presidential election with exactly 51.73 per cent of the vote, defeating his rival Ahmed Shafiq, Mubarak's last prime minister and the army's alleged favourite, who gained 48.27 per cent. Morsi collected 13,230,131 votes against Shafiq's 12,347,380.

† Kahlil Gibran wrote a short poem of a hungry fox who begins his day looking for a camel for lunch but who by midday would settle for a mouse. Some scholars believe the Egyptian god Anubis, lord of the underworld, was a fox rather than a wolf or a man with a canine head.

more curious reports of my life, an Aesop fable about the Egyptian revolution:

There is a fox in Tahrir Square. Bushy tailed and thickly furred, he claims to hear everything. And this is what he says: that 51.7 per cent of Egyptian voters cast their ballot for Mubarak's former prime minister, Ahmed Shafiq, in last month's elections; that only 48.3 per cent voted for Mohamed Morsi ... but that the military were so fearful of the hundreds of thousands of Brotherhood supporters who would gather in Tahrir Square that they gave the victory to Morsi.

Now foxes can be deceitful. But this is a well-connected fox and he claims that Morsi actually met four leading members of the Supreme Council of the Armed Forces in Egypt four days before the election results were proclaimed and that he agreed to accept his presidency before the constitutional court rather than the newly dissolved parliament – which is exactly what he did [last] Saturday ...

Now behind this piece of Reynard-like gossip is a further piece of information – shattering if true – that the Egyptian army's intelligence service is outraged by some members of the SCAF (in particular the four who supposedly met Morsi) and wants a mini-revolution to get rid of officers whom it believes to be corrupt. These young soldiers call themselves the New Liberal Movement – a different version of the Free Officers Movement which overthrew the corrupt King Farouq way back in 1952.

Many of the present young intelligence officers were very sympathetic to the Egyptian revolution last year – and several of them were shot dead by government snipers long after Mubarak's departure during a Tahrir Square demonstration. They admire the current head of military intelligence, soon to retire ...*

I have to say that all Cairo is abuzz with 'the deal', and almost every newspaper has a version of how Morsi got to be President

---

* The 'current head of military intelligence' was General al-Sisi, who would resign to become Morsi's minister of defence a month after my meeting with the 'fox'. And would later become Egypt's new dictator.

– though I must also add that none have gone so far as the fox. He says, for example, that the military intelligence services – like some of the SCAF officers – want a thorough clean-out of generals who control a third of the Egyptian economy in lucrative scams that include shopping malls, banks and vast amounts of property ...

There is also much talk of great tensions between the military intelligence and the staff of the interior ministry, some of whom are fearful that another mini-revolution will have them in court for committing crimes against Egyptian civilians during the anti-Mubarak revolution.

There are persistent rumours that the plain-clothes baltagi thugs who were used to beat protesters last year were [also] employed to prevent Christians voting [for Morsi] in some Egyptian villages. Interestingly, when [president of the electoral commission] Farouk Sultan ran through Egyptian election irregularities before announcing the presidential winner ... he said he didn't know who prevented the village voters getting to the polling station.

All of which is quite a story. Not the kind that can be confirmed ... But one fact cannot be denied. When he wanted to show he was a revolutionary animal, the fox held out his back paw. And there was a very severe year-old bullet wound in it.

Many of the Tahrir veterans nursed the same battle wounds as the army intelligence man, one of whose back legs was indeed deeply scarred by a bullet. It was a symbol of the sickness that had infected the security forces that many protesters were shot in the face, most notoriously by an eye-sniper identified as police Lieutenant Mahmoud al-Shinnawi. There was even, it later transpired, an eye-sniper's unit among the cops whose duty was to blind street demonstrators.

Far from being cowed by their defeat in the first months of 2011, the security authorities appeared to have become bolder. Just as civilians had lost their fear of armed police in the 2011 revolution, so it now seemed that the intelligence services had lost any previous inhibitions they may have felt on the streets of Cairo and other cities. If I had characterised the intelligence officer I met in Alexandria as a fox, the cops were now wounded tigers, backs against the wall and ready to fight ever more ferociously to protect their role and privileges.

Now that we have long grown used to the return of Egypt's military autarchy, it is worth re-examining the events that took place as Mohamed Morsi was voted into power as the country's first democratically elected president. Even as the run-off poll was taking place in June 2012, a decision by the Egyptian Supreme Constitutional Court, still packed with Mubarak's appointees, disbanded the five-month old parliament now controlled by Islamists, most of them Freedom and Justice Party members. Another ruling in mid-June granted the army new powers of arrest and investigation, a proxy extension of Mubarak's old emergency laws. There would be a new constitution drafted by a panel of men selected by the SCAF, who would insist that it must be in accordance with 'the principles safeguarding the higher interests of the country'. As Cairo newspaper *Al-Masry Al-Youm*'s front page put it, 'the military transfers power to the military'.

The army was therefore prepared to welcome the new emperor of Egypt. It would be able to veto any presidential declaration of war – essential, of course, for the security of Israel – and would delete any future article in the constitution that was not in the 'national interest'. Morsi would be expected to have no influence over foreign policy nor on relations with Washington, which continued to give an annual gift of £1.3 billion to the Egyptian military. In its desire for power, the Brotherhood had knelt before the army, just as it had done before Mubarak's departure when it negotiated with Omar Suleiman. Grotesquely, Hillary Clinton now announced that 'there can be no going back on the democratic transition called for by the Egyptian people'.

Tens of thousands of Muslim Brotherhood followers trooped into Tahrir on 22 June to wait for the presidential results and to demand that the army return to barracks. I had spent so long in this square over previous months that it was a shock to see so many beards. There were even postcards of Guevara for sale, along with Nasser and Sadat and Saddam and Osama bin Laden. There were glorious photo-montages of Tantawi holding a baby Hosni Mubarak in his arms, and a row of ex-dictators, Mubarak and Ben Ali and Gaddafi, begging for dollars on an Egyptian roadside, but it was all a little too late. The Islamists should have spent their time studying the Egyptian press, which now demonised the Brotherhood and Morsi as the state's most frightening enemies, claiming that the group would plunge the country into chaos if its candidate did not win the election.

The cover of the weekly *Al-Mussawar* showed a picture of Morsi planting a kiss on the head of the Brotherhood's spiritual leader Mohamed Badie, a gesture of reverence and submission. 'We will not be ruled by the murshid,' the paper declared in red print.

In Tahrir that day I came across a distant relative of the lawyer-rebel Saad Zaghloul. Ahmed Reda Saad Mohamed Zaghloul, member of the tiny Coalition of Youth group, had the same slim face as his ancestor. 'We are a sentimental people,' he said. 'We adore our religion – but not the terrorism way of religion. There are two scenarios for this crisis situation. Morsi is like a hat you cannot wear. The other – well, if Shafiq is president, there will be blood, though only for a limited time … the big generals in the army will never be able to govern Egypt. Every home here in Egypt has a soldier in the army – and they will never allow these old men to govern. The army is on the side of the people.'

But Shafiq lost the election and fled to Abu Dhabi, and Egypt would wear the hat of Morsi; and the big generals – one of them in particular – did come to govern Egypt just over twelve months later, even more harshly and with more bloodshed than Ahmed Zaghloul could have imagined. Morsi set off down the road to Egyptian democracy with no constitution, no parliament and no right to command his own country's army, but he did have the Palestinians behind him. If Hamas was the daughter of the Muslim Brotherhood, some of its leading figures had been granted Egyptian citizenship through their parents' nationality. Mahmoud al-Zahar, one of the founders of Hamas whose son, a member of the movement's military wing, was killed by the Israelis in 2008, was an Egyptian national because his mother was born in Egypt. So was the mother of the speaker of the Palestinian parliament, Hamas member Aziz Dwiek. Many Hamas activists were educated in Cairo. In Palestinian eyes, Morsi was the first Islamist president to become an Arab president, and his sympathies, like those of the Freedom and Justice Party, had always been with Hamas, Gaza and the Palestinian cause. Many Egyptians still believed that Mubarak's 2009 refusal to open the Gaza–Egyptian border for aid and medicine during Israel's murderous bombardment of the Palestinians was another reason for the hatred manifested against him in 2011.

Morsi was an intelligent, honourable, obtuse, arrogant and naive man whose twelve months' rule began with the kind of platitudes that might satisfy secular revolutionaries and Western governments, but which were bound to infuriate the army. Promising to respect 'the constitution and the rule of law', he told the crowds in Tahrir that he would 'look after the interests of the people and protect the independence of the nation and the safety of its territory'. But his declaration that 'there is no power but people power' was hardly subtle. And while he said that Christians and Muslims would enjoy a 'civil, nationalist, constitutional state', his later references to a cleric jailed in America and to demonstrators imprisoned by the Egyptian army were surely calculated to enrage the military. 'I see the family of Omar Abdel-Rahman [in Tahrir],' he said. 'And I see the banners of the families of those who have been jailed by the [Egyptian] military.'*

He might have intended to placate a population desperate for freedom, an army suspicious of his Brotherhood credentials and millions of party supporters anxious to see some indication that the new Egypt would be Islamist rather than nationalist. But his confusing message did nothing of the kind. The men and women who had fought in Tahrir and other Egyptian cities were not going to be fobbed off with talk of the 'rule of law'. The army generals were insulted by his apparent support for 'terrorism', and the Freedom and Justice Party looked for more than moral support for their imprisoned members. In a more nuanced speech at the non-aligned summit in Tehran, Morsi said that Egypt's 'solidarity with the struggle of the Syrian people against an oppressive regime that has lost its legitimacy is an ethical duty and it is a political and strategic necessity … We all have to announce our full solidarity with the struggle of those seeking freedom and justice in Syria.' This would scarcely please Syria's great ally Iran, but – if it involved sending Egyptian Islamist fighters to Syria – would cause even more shockwaves in the Egyptian armed forces. It was also clear

---

* Omar Abdel-Rahman, one of Mubarak's fiercest Islamist opponents whom I had interviewed in New York, was sentenced to life in 1996 for plotting to blow up the George Washington Bridge, the Lincoln and Holland tunnels and the UN headquarters on the East river. Morsi pledged himself to free both the prisoners in Egyptian custody and Abdel-Rahman – who died in a North Carolina prison in 2017, four years after Morsi himself was put behind bars by the military and joined the inmates he had promised to liberate.

that 'Palestine', especially Gaza, would now receive political and at least humanitarian help from Egypt across the Sinai border, an area which the army had hitherto regarded as its own preserve. Wasn't Washington's largesse to the Egyptian military its reward for safe-guarding Israel's southern borders?

The new president threw open his palace to the people, and his wife Naglaa rejected the title of 'first lady' in favour of 'first servant'. But was Morsi the real president of Egypt? There were growing rumours that he would interrupt cabinet meetings to seek advice on govern-ment decisions from the Brotherhood leadership; and opposition groups, including some who had fought in Tahrir, asked whether it was not the Muslim Brotherhood which really controlled the presi-dency. Within months, Morsi would adopt sweeping powers to control the streets, giving the military the right to detain civilians, abusing activists as tools of 'third parties' and warning, after the arrest of eighty people, some of whom he claimed were armed, that an investigation would discover who was 'pulling the strings'.

And all this after Morsi had taken steps that he thought would neuter the military's power over his presidency. For at ten in the morning on Sunday, 12 August 2012, minister of defence Tantawi and chief of staff Sami Anan were summoned to the presidential palace. Neither Anan, the nominal head of the SCAF, nor Tantawi suspected anything out of the ordinary when they were shown into a high-security room in which they were unable to use their mobile phones. At the same moment, elsewhere in the palace, Morsi was welcoming the army's intelligence commander Abdel Fattah al-Sisi, declaring him to be his new minister of defence. Only hours earlier, Egypt's official gazette had announced that the constitutional programme adopted by the SCAF after the parliamentary elections was no longer valid. Morsi then walked to the sealed room in which Tantawi and Anan were waiting, to tell them that they had been fired.

It was a serious strategic error. Morsi did not understand the army's internal disputes. While Sisi must have already indicated his acceptance of the defence ministry, Morsi could not grasp that Tantawi was as much a protection for him as the ambitious Sisi was a danger. By throwing two old army lions out of the palace, Morsi had introduced a wolf into his cabinet who would, when the time came, devour his pres-idency, the Freedom and Justice Party and the entire Muslim

Brotherhood leadership in Egypt, let alone the crippled democracy of the nation itself.

Morsi rested more upon his prestige as the first freely elected president of his country than on his deeds. So the moment he appeared to expand his control, the less democratic he seemed to be. After a December referendum produced a constitution that placed him largely above the law, he allowed the now Islamist-dominated Shura Council, the upper house of parliament whose speaker was one of his own relatives, to prepare new assembly elections, 'regulate' the press and fight 'corruption'. Among Morsi's appointees to the council were forty-two fundamentalists and nineteen Islamist 'independents', which in effect gave the Brotherhood 75 per cent of the seats. This was a rerun of Mubarak's old tactic of stuffing the council with regime loyalists.

Morsi's arrival at the presidential palace coincided with the mass killing of sixteen soldiers in the Sinai desert, ambushed as they shared their evening Ramadan meal at a frontier post close to the Gaza–Israeli border at Rafah. Armed men, variously described as jihadists or 'terrorists', tried to escape towards the Israeli border, where one of their stolen jeeps blew up while the other was bombed by the Israeli air force. The Egyptian army later claimed they had 'found' the bodies of several of the attackers. The Israelis suggested they may have been Hamas members, which Hamas denied, but there were also suggestions that they may have been part of a militant Muslim Brotherhood group.

It may also have marked the first stage of an assault on Egypt's eastern lands by al-Qaeda and what was to become ISIS, a pattern of bloodshed which was to be repeated over the coming years in Sinai until it reached Cairo itself. The Egyptian army under Sisi's post-coup presidency would then find itself at war with the cult which had already captured large areas of Iraq and Syria. At the time of the August 2012 attacks, however, the killing of the security officers appeared to be part of the post-revolution chaos that accompanied Morsi's first days in office, occurring exactly a week before Morsi sacked Tantawi and Anan, appointing Sisi in Tantawi's place as his defence minister.

At the Cairo funerals of the dead soldiers and policemen, crowds shouted 'You killed them, you dogs!' at the few Muslim Brotherhood officials who attended, including Morsi's prime minister Hisham

Qandil. Morsi was noticeably absent.* And after his overthrow a year later, Sisi would slowly conflate the identity of Morsi and his fellow Islamists with ISIS itself.

More damaging still for Morsi was the growing conviction among young secular Egyptians that he was allowing the security apparatus to adopt the same murderous tactics of the Mubarak regime against his own domestic political enemies. The most notorious example was that of Mohamed el-Gindy, a twenty-eight-year-old from a middle-class family in Tanta who ran a tour business in Cairo and supported a leftist group protesting against Morsi's Islamist government. On television, Gindy promised in January 2013 to support a revolt against the president if he tried to recreate the old Egyptian police state. Within a week, he was found dead on a street ramp near the Egyptian Museum in Cairo, bleeding from a head wound. The authorities said he was the victim of a hit-and-run accident, but both the autopsy report and the testimony of an ambulance crew were invented by the government. A report by three doctors concluded that the dead man could not have been killed in a car accident. Rumours circulated that he had been kidnapped and tortured. Gindy's mother lamented that 'I voted for them [the Islamists]. Is this the reward? For them to kill my son?'

The West slowly lost its sympathy for Morsi's 'democracy'. The president inexplicably allowed the authorities to persecute American-based 'democracy-promotion' groups. Some of their activities undoubtedly angered the nationalist sentiments of Egyptians who felt contempt for all foreigners who supposedly interfered in their country's politics. But when in early June 2013 an Egyptian court gave jail terms of between two and five years to forty-three Americans, Europeans, Egyptians and other Arabs, Obama's secretary of state John Kerry denounced the trial as 'politically motivated' and 'incompatible

---

* Morsi's apparent indifference to suffering was demonstrated in November 2012 when fifty-one children were killed in a school bus collision with a train near Assiut. Their parents were awarded government compensation of around $500 for each loss – 'less than the price of an iPhone', as one critic complained – and Morsi did not bother to offer his condolences, even though he had condemned Mubarak ten years earlier when a train fire killed 383 passengers. The children's families' anger turned to rage, however, when the local press claimed that more than $1.3 million had been spent on Morsi's security at Friday prayers in Cairo – and $28.5 million on the garish refurbishment of Ramses Street Station in the city, rather than on an updated railway signalling system.

with the transition to democracy'. Some of the Americans had taken refuge in the US embassy.*

While increasingly concerned, so it claimed, at Morsi's failure to create 'political inclusivity', the US was also frustrated by his stewardship of the economy. The IMF had offered a $4.8 billion loan agreement worth $15 billion if Egypt introduced a plan to phase out subsidies and a sales tax law. Morsi, unwilling to force austerity measures on Egyptians when his popularity was already so battered, declined to increase food prices but, in an effort to augment the Brotherhood's influence in his cabinet, replaced the planning and finance ministers who were involved in the IMF talks with Islamist economists.

It is important to recall Morsi's disdain and lack of responsibility in government, since the subsequent coup has bestowed on his brief reign an almost romantic aura. His demise was accompanied by such terrifying violence by the state security authorities that his overthrow has come to be regarded in isolation, as if the vast number of Egyptians who sought his resignation had mentally regressed into the old traps of lethargy and state patriarchy.

By the time Morsi was forced from office, he was very unpopular. The Brotherhood had failed to transform themselves into a political party capable of forming alliances; the Freedom and Justice Party remained a front for the ikhwan and thus allowed the army, police and judiciary to remain faithful to the society that supported the Mubarak regime. Shockingly, Morsi also planned to shackle the newly free trade unions that had supported the 2011 January revolution; in parliament, Brotherhood members rejected a proposed law guaranteeing the right of workers to hold free elections for independent unions, and now wanted to 'control' strikes.

Sisi had accepted Morsi's offer of the ministry of defence without the slightest hesitation; he was not now going to allow Morsi to damage his leadership of the Egyptian army. But Sisi must have known when

---

* Morsi even managed to alienate Egyptian art lovers by appointing a culture minister who immediately fired the head of the Cairo Opera House. Staff at the institution went on strike, cancelling Verdi's *Aida*, while an Islamist parliamentary member called for the abolition of ballet performances on the grounds that they were 'immoral' and 'nude art'. A Russian dancer at the opera expressed her astonishment at demands that it cut the love scene from *Romeo and Juliet*.

he became Morsi's top soldier that his relationship with the president could not be sustained.

So as early as January 2013, a mere five months after Morsi entrusted him with the defence portfolio, Sisi began to make pointed references to the powerlessness of the president, warning that the continuing violence in Egypt could 'threaten the future of coming generations'. On 29 January, he went so far as to post his remarks at a military academy on the Egyptian army's Facebook page, stating that 'the continuation of conflict, and the differences among the various political groups on the management of the country's affairs, may lead to the collapse of the state'. Fearful though Sisi claimed to be at the imminent ruin of his country, in some cases he stood aside and allowed his soldiers to observe, rather than intervene to prevent further civil disorder.

Like many of the Egyptian army's ambitious new generals, Sisi had been awarded an American military fellowship, writing a thirteen-page paper on 'Democracy in the Middle East' for the US Army War College in Carlisle, Pennsylvania, five years before the 2011 revolution. While theoretically supporting 'transition towards democratic forms of government', it contained the usual Arab leadership stereotypes of uneducated populations that needed 'time' to learn the principles of democracy. We shall never know if Morsi later read Brigadier General Sisi's college paper, but he should have done.

The army would later have the world believe that it was Morsi's attendance at a packed Islamist rally on 15 June calling for holy war in Syria that doomed him. Sunni clerics at the meeting used the word 'infidels' to condemn both the Shiites fighting for Bashar al-Assad and for non-Islamists opposed to Morsi in Egypt – a fatal combination. Morsi himself called for foreign intervention in Syria against Assad. As president, he was constitutionally the supreme commander of the Egyptian army, but Sisi insisted that the military should remain master of its own destiny. Here was the critical moment, surely, when nation should have come before 'ruling party'. When Egypt's leader encouraged his own people to fight abroad, he had 'crossed a national security red line'.

Sisi gave Morsi four days to settle his differences with the opposition – or the army would have to protect 'the will of the people'. If Morsi's ill-judged appearance at the anti-Syria rally provided the army with the excuse to stage a coup d'état, Sisi had only been waiting for the Egyptian president to stage such an ill-judged performance. Not only had Morsi himself crossed a 'red line', but the swelling chorus of contempt against him could now be mobilised to support his over-throw by the military. And it needed only these millions of Egyptians to sanction what the army could present as the second stage of the country's revolution.

As Tahrir Square filled with hundreds of thousands of anti-Morsi demonstrators, the events of January 2011 could now be replayed in Sisi's favour. The original mass revolt against Mubarak was to be followed, in the summer of 2013, by The Egyptian Revolution Part 2, an epic whose production values included a cast of millions and a loyal army safeguarding their future before civil war engulfed the nation. Since there would be no presidential elections to follow this drama for ten months, the sheer number of those who demonstrated against Morsi and the Brotherhood became the army's mandate.

These statistics, which did not in fact exist, became the critical factor in the army's legitimacy to rule, a mass support large enough to dwarf any previous expression of Egyptian popular feeling, the biggest, most powerful, most overwhelming, most prodigious multiplier in history, however ridiculous it might seem. The tens of millions, who rallied for the army against Morsi, became a 'fact' simply because so many people heard these preposterously exaggerated figures and lamely accepted that they must have some basis in truth.

The pictures came first. Live international coverage of Tahrir, the anti-Morsi crowds dancing to bands and cheering wildly at the military helicopters that swooped above them, fireworks lighting up the night sky, the images supporting the claim that far larger crowds were calling for Morsi to leave than ever demanded the end of Mubarak's regime. The amorphous Tamarod ('Rebellion'), whose roots subsequently turned out to have connections to the army's intelligence service, announced that it had gathered more than 22 million signatures demanding Morsi's resignation. But where did this extraordinary score-card come from?

The military had first announced 14 million protesters on the streets of Egyptian cities, 'the biggest protest in Egypt's history,' it claimed, only to be followed by coup supporters publicising this epic as 'the largest demonstrations in human history' with 'between 14 million and

33 million'. When asked later if the coup would provoke the Obama administration to cancel a planned shipment of F-16s to Egypt, the State Department spokeswoman Jen Psaki declared that the US could not reverse the will of the '22 million people who spoke out and had their voices heard'.

On 30 June, the billionaire tycoon and Tamarod supporter Naguib Sawiris informed his nearly one million Twitter followers that the BBC had reported 'the number of people protesting today is the largest number in a political event in the history of mankind'. The BBC Arabic service later said it could find no such statistic. A real BBC report spoke of only 'tens of thousands of people' massing in Tahrir. Egypt's Dream TV then 'quoted' a CNN report that '33 million people were in the streets today'. No such number was ever broadcast by CNN. But when a former Egyptian general appeared on CNN to repeat the claim, he was not contradicted.

Appropriately, Tony Blair interposed himself into this fantasy of exaggeration. 'Seventeen million people on the street is not the same as an election,' Blair wrote in the *Observer* and *Guardian*. 'But it is an awesome manifestation of people power.' Blair's source turned out to be an anonymous military spokesman quoted by the Egyptian newspaper *Shorouk*. The Muslim Brotherhood, he would tell us six months later, 'tried to take the country away from its basic values of hope and progress. The army have intervened at the will of the people.'

The BBC declared on 15 July that it could find no legitimate source for the claims of 14, 17 or 33 million protesters. More convincingly, the Egyptian blogger Shereef Ismail calculated that the maximum number of demonstrators who could fit into the streets and squares in Egyptian cities was at most 2.8 million.

Too late. The myths had been created in order to avoid one crucial word. The fraudulent numbers, the false context of civilisational history, was intended to stifle, smother and effectively asphyxiate the use of the word 'coup'. Sisi had obeyed the will of the people, the nation rather than the party, in order to continue, renew and reshape the revolution.

Essential to this disingenuous story was Sisi's 24 July claim to have warned two Brotherhood leaders that the situation had become 'dangerous' and that reconciliation was necessary between government and opposition. The two men, he said, replied that 'armed groups' would be able to resolve any problem – a proposal that Sisi said he denounced.

According to Sisi, the president had initially agreed to a 'national dialogue' but told him the next day to cancel the invitation. Confronted on Monday 1 July, Morsi is said to have exclaimed 'Over my dead body!', a remark that gains credibility in the context of his actual words in his televised address just before midnight on 2 July, when the army was preparing to take the powerless president of Egypt to his imprisonment in a Republican Guards barracks:

> If the price for safeguarding legitimacy is my blood, then I am prepared to sacrifice my blood for the cause of safety and legitimacy of this homeland … I adhere to legitimacy and only legitimacy. The constitution and only the constitution.

But the army and their 'millions' had already undermined this precious 'legitimacy', and the 'will of the people' was now more powerful than any election.

Those credulous or vain enough to believe this helped Sisi form an unelected civilian 'ghost' government to which, lamentably, Mohamed ElBaradei immediately lent his name as 'interim vice president'. Adly Mansour, an old Mubarak appointee to the Supreme Constitutional Court, became 'president', the whole contrivance invariably supported by the Grand Imam of Al-Azhar, Ahmed el-Tayeb, and the Coptic pope, Tawadros II. Field Marshal Sisi, commander in chief of the armed forces, of course, remained minister of defence, no longer loyal to Morsi but to himself and the phantom administration he and the army had created.

But 'legitimacy' was what the Brotherhood now held as sacred, even if they still believed that the even more sacred Islam was 'the answer'. But if the army's first task was to protect 'the people', how could it also protect 'the people' who still insisted that Morsi was the 'legitimate' president? And if the army, as ElBaradei told me in 2011, was 'part of the people', which 'people' would they now defend?

The circumstances of Morsi's detention were initially unclear – but they were critical to the avoidance of the word 'coup'. In November 2013, lawyer Mohamed Damati read on Egyptian television what he said was a letter from the deposed president in which Morsi allegedly stated, 'that I have been kidnapped forcibly and against my will since 2 July and until 5 July in a Republican Guard house until I and my aide were moved again forcibly to a naval base belonging to the armed forces for four full months'.

Less than two years after the coup-that-wasn't, Egyptian émigrés sympathetic to the Brotherhood sent me tapes of Egyptian generals apparently plotting to persuade the world that Morsi had been held in a civilian rather than a military prison after his detention in 2013 – and was thus not the victim of a military coup d'état. The tapes appeared to provide valuable evidence that Morsi was deposed unconstitutionally; if his confinement was illegal, Sisi could no longer deny that he staged a coup.

The tapes themselves were uproariously funny, as generals and senior officials working for Sisi argued over the need to construct an entire prison wing beside an army jail – with a civilian police signpost over the door to fool lawyers and judges. Although Sisi denounced the tapes as fabricated, they provided graphic proof of how the new regime feared that the military coup might be revealed. At one point, a man identified as General Mamdouh Shahin, Sisi's assistant defence minister 'for legal and constitutional affairs', asks an official to pre-date the day of Morsi's detention, adding that 'I need you to mention a building but we will not mention it is inside a military unit.'

On the tapes, Sisi's men made panic-stricken and hilarious demands to hide the location of Morsi's prison, which was in fact the Abu Qir naval base on the Mediterranean.* At one point, voices could be heard suggesting that 'we can put a shelter anywhere within two days, even at the path to the military unit, not at the [exact] place ... and a separate door with "Ministry of Interior" written on it or something like that'. This was satire that almost obscured the dark consequences of this comedy.

And so, as Sisi's most servile supporters might have said, for the first time in world history, a coup was not a coup. The army took over the country, deposed and imprisoned the democratically elected president, suspended the constitution, arrested the usual suspects, closed down television stations and massed their armour in the streets of the capital, yet Obama could not bring himself to call this a coup. He asked the

* Opposite 'Aboukir Bay' where Nelson fought the Battle of the Nile in 1798.

Egyptian military 'to return full authority back to a democratically elected civilian government … through an inclusive and transparent process' – without explaining which particular 'elected civilian government' he had in mind. Hillary Clinton's spokeswoman Jen Psaki, who had earlier parroted the ridiculous figure of Egypt's '22 million' anti-Morsi protesters, limply announced that 'we're on neither side … we're on the side of the Egyptian people'.*

It scarcely mattered. Sisi was in a hurry. He wanted, at once, the very same 'legitimacy' that had so obsessed Morsi in his last presidential address. For this, he desperately needed a cast of millions, the president's arrest as a criminal and the world's silent acceptance that this was not an army coup d'état. He got what he wanted in time for the Brotherhood to be smashed by a thunderclap so sudden and so shocking that Morsi's supporters were struck down in their thousands before the world could react. The very corpses that piled up in the squares, mosques and mortuaries of Cairo would be physical proof of Field Marshal Sisi's legitimacy. For who would now dare question his power or his right to act according to 'the will of the people'?

---

* Obama and Hillary Clinton cravenly failed to use the words 'coup d'état' because US law would then have required the administration to cut aid to Egypt, including the $1.3 billion to Sisi's army. British prime minister David Cameron caught the same verbal infection, avoiding the word 'coup' but seeking 'a genuine democratic transition' in Egypt.

12

The Wounded Tiger

I am in blood
Stepp'd in so far that, should I wade no more,
Returning were as tedious as go o'er

William Shakespeare, Macbeth, Act III, scene 4

Aiman Husseini was lying by the wall. Khaled Abdul Nasser's name was written in black ink on his white shroud to the left of the door. There were thirty-seven bodies in the room. The doctors had blood on their shirts. There were swathes of it, dark brown, even on the walls. The field hospital next to the Rabaa al-Adawiya mosque was packed with weeping men and women. Many of them talked about God. 'These people are in the sun,' a doctor told me. 'They are with God. We are just in the shade.'

Most of the dead had been shot in the face, several in the eyes. A massacre? Most certainly – although small compared to the days to come. And these were a mere fraction of the dead on 27 July 2013. These killings took place in the hours before dawn. The police, everyone said, opened fire as Brotherhood members paraded close to the tomb of President Anwar Sadat, not far from the Rabaa al-Adawiya mosque where they maintained a vast sit-in demanding Mohamed Morsi's restoration. Who fired first? Well, all the dead were Muslim Brothers or their friends. There were no dead policemen.

The Brotherhood said their people were unarmed, which may well be true, although I recalled that a man guarding a car park near the mosque who directed me to the hospital was holding a Kalashnikov rifle. In Beirut, I had grown used to seeing guns in the hands of young men but I was a little shocked to see this man in a blue T-shirt holding an automatic weapon. But he had been the only armed man I saw.

Dr Ahmed Habib told me that he had used up two weeks' worth of medical equipment in just a few hours. 'Look at the blood on my clothes,' he shouted at me. Doctors lay outside the room of the dead, sleeping on the dirty floor, exhausted after trying to save lives all morning. 'We are told we are a minority now, so we don't deserve to live,' another doctor told me. I didn't like the propaganda line, but these were dramatic minutes in a room packed with dead bodies. They were taken from the room on stretchers under the flash of cameras and inserted into ambulances that queued beside the mosque in the midday heat.

Many people said the things people always say when confronted by tragedy; that they would never give way, that they would die rather than submit to military rule and that God was greater than life itself, certainly greater than Sisi. Dr Habib even insisted to me that there was an afterlife, which I asked him to prove. 'Because we are not animals to eat food and drink water all our lives,' he replied. 'Do you think that is the only reason for our being?'

Behind the hospital were many men who had been wounded, some of them groaning with pain. But it was the dead who caught our attention, so newly killed that their faces had not yet taken on the mask of death. I remember as I walked through this little charnel house that I was unable to comprehend the number of bodies around me. I had seen death by the hundred, by the thousand, in Lebanon, in Bosnia, in Algeria. But here? This was not the familiar Egypt I had visited so many times. This terrifying violence, unleashed so swiftly and so obviously pre-planned, was astonishing. How could a people so imperturbable, so forbearing, so apparently resigned, inflict upon themselves such pain and at such speed? And this was just a foretaste of what was to come.*

Morsi's supporters made no secret of their intention to oppose the coup. They would demand the return of their president. Had he not

---

* The Egyptian interior minister would claim that only twenty-one Brotherhood members had been killed. Human Rights Watch would later state that seventy-four pro-Morsi supporters were killed by riot police and armed plain-clothes men on 27 July.

been democratically elected, they repeatedly asked us on the streets of Cairo. If Morsi's enemies could demonstrate in Tahrir, then 'millions' of Muslims could also stand loyally by their president.

The old argument for free elections in the Arab world was simple: if Islamists were allowed to win at the polls, let's see if they could govern. But Morsi's government had frittered away its time imposing a Brotherhood-style constitution, allowed ministries to stage their own mini-revolutions and promoted laws that would shut down human rights groups and arrest foreign NGOs. Morsi's 51 per cent victory was not sufficient, amid the current chaos, to make him the president 'of all Egyptians'. The 2011 revolution's demand for bread, freedom, justice and dignity had gone unanswered. But could the army satisfy these calls any more than Morsi, just by calling the pro-military demonstrations 'glorious'? Politicians may be rogues, but generals can be killers, especially when they have an increasingly pliant media to fawn over them. Journalists who had extolled the freedoms bestowed on them by the 2011 revolution suddenly reverted to their earlier Mubarakite obsequiousness. Some went even further. When Sisi staged his coup, the entire journalistic staff of one popular local television channel turned up onscreen in full military costume, journalistic servility on an unheard of scale. So when Sisi decided to destroy the huge Muslim Brotherhood camp with its thousands of Morsi supporters outside the Rabaa mosque in Cairo, he could rely on a largely faithful media to support the subsequent massacre.

After several warnings to the protesters whose tent 'homes' covered at least a square mile around the mosque, Sisi's heavily armed Central Security Forces and Special Forces acted with utter ruthlessness. Did these civilians believe that the Islamic house of prayer behind them would protect the innocent? It was named in honour of the eighth-century Iraqi female Sufi saint Rabia al-Adawiyya al-Qaysiyya, born a century after the Prophet Mohamed's death, who in an ancient text was described running through the streets of Basra with a jug of fire and a bucket of water. 'I want to put out the fires of Hell and burn down the rewards of Paradise,' she supposedly announced.

At 6.30 on the morning of 14 August, Sisi's paramilitaries stormed into the square, firing live rounds into the thousands of families camping there. The army did not shoot, but they allowed government snipers to enter their base and failed to prevent the slaughter that went on for all of twelve hours. Despite earlier promises of 'safe passage', soldiers prevented the traumatised and wounded protesters from leaving the square. Early reports indicated that at least 817 Egyptian civilians – including women and children, and local journalists, even a British Sky News cameraman – fell to the guns of the Egyptian 'security' forces.*

No attempt was made to hide the extent of the massacre. Other news organisations, including the BBC, freely reported the carnage. This was Sisi's response to the Brotherhood's demand that Morsi must be restored. His supporters must be liquidated, along with anyone who got in the way. In a futile attempt to defend themselves, some threw stones at the security police. Later figures showed that well over a thousand people were killed, far more than died in the whole of the 2011 revolution.

The faces of the dead were concealed beneath the knots in the cellophane, their ghastly but invisible presence alleviated from time to time by the pairs of feet still wearing cheap rubber-soled shoes poking from the bottom of the stretchers. Down a side street, I found Abeer Saady, a reporter of the *Shorouk* newspaper, watching the crowds before she searched for the body of a colleague, twenty-seven-year-old Ahmed Abdul Dawed, a Muslim Brotherhood supporter who worked for the government newspaper *Al-Akhbar*. 'The Brotherhood wants the figures of dead to be high, the government wants the figures low,' she said sadly. Other Arab journalists had paid the same price as Ahmed Dawed. Habiba Ahmed Abd Elaziz worked for Gulf News but was officially on leave when she was shot dead near the Rabaa mosque.

Brotherhood supporters long ago abandoned any affection for local journalists but still had time for the infidels of the foreign press. Even so, they were distant in their replies to me. Who is this? I asked of a youth standing beside a body covered in a big kuffiya scarf. 'What does

---

* Mick Deane, who had worked for Sky News for fifteen years, was hit on the left side of his chest by a single round. A colleague standing next to him later told a British coroner's court that he thought 'he was targeted ... I don't know why they shot him, the only other people around were some women sitting on the floor reading the Quran, there was nobody standing next to us ... I didn't hear the shot being fired, the first I knew about it was when Mr Deane turned to me and said, "I've been shot" and I could see blood coming through his shirt ...' The crew's flak jackets had been confiscated from them when they arrived at Cairo airport.

it matter to you?' came his reply. I muttered that the dead man deserved a name, and the man shrugged. An old man sitting on the lid of a coffin said that a man called Adham lay inside the box. I persisted. 'Mahmoud Mustafa,' another man shouted at me when I pointed to the ice that crushed the mound of his dead son. Yet another man told me he was guarding the corpse of Mohamed Fared Mutwali, who was fifty-seven when he was killed. Slowly, the names brought the dead back to life. Until a few hours ago, these people had identities, ages, jobs.

A smart young man who wanted to speak in English put his hand on my arm and pointed to another cellophane shape. 'This was my brother,' he said. 'He was shot yesterday. He was a doctor. His name was Dr Khaled Kamal and he trained in medicine in Beni Suef in Upper Egypt.'

You could not see these things and believe that Egypt's tragedy would be buried with the dead. That Friday morning, the Brotherhood would remember the dead in the mosques of Cairo and Egyptians would wait for the government's reaction, the police reaction, the army's reaction, the response of Field Marshal Abdel Fattah al-Sisi. Of course, you could try to balance the pain that was so visible outside the mortuary with the normality that the government wanted us all to enjoy in Cairo. But there were small things about the place of the dead that stayed in the mind. The cheerful bright blue plastic that lined one coffin and the incongruity of seeing an Etihad Airways label pasted to one end.

This was a place that exhausted you with the inexplicable. It should have been comforting to return to the comparative safety of the old Marriott Hotel, but it was not. No sooner did I reach my favourite Cairo haunt than I learned that Ra'ad Nabil – a tourist policeman who often greeted me with a wave – was walking home across the river in Mohandesin a few hours earlier when a group of local men threatened him. He drew his gun and fired it in the air. One of the men seized the weapon and pointed it at Ra'ad, a harmless man in his early fifties, and shot him in the heart.

And after the Rabaa massacre came the Ramses Square massacre beside the Al-Fath mosque. Beneath its towering minaret, the tallest in Cairo and the third highest in the world, we would watch the last open Brotherhood revolt against Sisi's regime. What we saw was a most

shameful chapter in Egyptian history. The police, some of them wearing black hoods, shot down into the crowds from the roof of the
Ramses Street police station. They even fired at traffic on the airport
highway.

To understand their terrible work, you had only to climb the pink
marble steps of the Al-Fath mosque and see the acre of wounded lying
on deep-woven carpets inside and, in a remote corner, twenty-five half-
shrouded corpses. Dr Ibrahim Yamani gently lifted the bandages: shot
in the face, shot in the head, shot in the chest. The police were sharp-
shooters, brought into the city centre to make these people suffer. You
could hear their gunshots crackling over the square from inside the
mosque, sometimes followed by screams.

What was so extraordinary was to see some of the faces of the killers. There was a man with a moustache and close-cropped hair on the
roof of the police station, waving a pistol in the air and shouting
obscenities to crowds below. To his left, a policeman wearing a black
hood, crouching by the wall and pointing his automatic rifle at the cars
on the highway. I was standing on the road with my driver Adel when
one of the cop's bullets passed between us and whizzed off into the
square.

An hour earlier, I had been chatting to the security police at the
burned-out Rabaa mosque – the scene of the massacre two days before
– and one of them cheerfully told me that 'we do the work, and the
army watches'. This was an important truth. For I was to see the army
a mile from the slaughter in Ramses Square, sitting atop their clean
armoured vehicles, far enough away to be out of range. There would
be no blood on their uniforms.

Even amid the bloodshed, no one had any excuse to be romantic
about the Brotherhood, and I rather think those cops I saw on the roof
were as fearful as some among the crowds. Cynicism aside, the
Brotherhood probably needed those corpses in the mosque. A day
without 'martyrdom' might suggest that the fire of ideology had been
dampened down by bullets, that the Salafists might take their place as
the only truly Islamist right hand of the state, albeit in collaboration
with the army.

But there was no excuse for the police. Their behaviour was not
undisciplined. They had been told to kill, and kill they did. In the centre
of one of the greatest cities in the world, known to billions, scarcely a

mile from the magnificence of Tutankhamun's tomb, only two hundred metres from the Egyptian courts of justice, the police shot into thousands of their own citizens with the simple aim of killing them. And as they did so, the baltagi, the drug addicts and ex-cops with the clubs and iron bars, turned up with rifles beside the Ramses Street police station.

Needless to say, the dead, too, became 'terrorists' in the Egyptian media. A massacre of twenty-six Egyptian police cadets, handcuffed and executed in Sinai allowed the government to conflate the Brotherhood with the most violent of Islamist groups: ISIS. Brotherhood members, dead or alive, were now slandered in the Cairo press as 'terrorists', guilty, according to Gamal Zayed of *Al-Ahram*, of 'systematic and deliberate acts of treachery, betrayal, killing, torture, perjury, ingratitude and deception'. A few journalists expressed their outrage. 'Everyone has the right to call for disbanding this group,' wrote Emad Eddin Hussein in *Shorouk*, 'but no one has the right to annihilate them.' His was a lone voice.*

Sisi himself never uttered a single word of regret at the mass killing of so many Brotherhood supporters across Egypt. The silence of normally moderate politicians, intellectuals, artists and authors was alarming, since they should have represented the moral conscience of the nation. Mohamed ElBaradei, sickened by the slaughter at Rabaa, resigned as interim vice president, writing that 'I cannot be responsible before God for a single drop of blood.' He had warned against any government violence but then claimed that 'extremist groups' – in other words the Brotherhood – would profit from the subsequent mass killings at Rabaa. Having therefore expressed his disgust at the violence of the administration he had so rashly joined, Egypt's Nobel Prize-winner flew off to Vienna with his virtue intact.

Over the coming days, weeks and years, the atrocities committed by

---

* The statistics of the Egyptian Centre for Economic and Social Research made solemn reading. It stated that 1,295 Egyptians were killed between 14 and 16 August, 1,063 on the first day alone – including 983 civilians, fifty-three security personnel and twenty-eight bodies found under the platform of the Rabaa mosque. Thirteen policemen and three civilians were reportedly killed in an attack on a police station in Kerdasa, twenty-four civilians in Alexandria, six in Sherqeya, six in Damietta, thirteen in Suez, forty-five in Fayoum, twenty-one in Beni Suef and sixty-eight in Minya. This was a national rather than just a Cairo tragedy.

the Egyptian security forces on the Brotherhood's supporters and its
legitimacy would be revealed by NGOs, by foreign media investigations, by Amnesty International and Human Rights Watch. The killing
of fifty-one Morsi supporters at a protest outside the army's Republican
Guard Club on 8 July 2013 had brought forth an angry demand from
Amnesty that a judicial inquiry should investigate the 'intentional
lethal force against people who were posing no risk to the lives of security forces'. A year later, Human Rights Watch published a 195-page
report that found that the Egyptian police and army at Rabaa 'systematically and deliberately killed largely unarmed protesters on political
grounds' on a scale 'unprecedented in Egypt' and which 'likely
amounted to crimes against humanity'. Human Rights Watch spoke of
the massacre as a premeditated attack equal to the Tiananmen Square
killings in China in 1989.

We all knew what President Mohamed Morsi would say when he faced
his judges for the first time in November 2013. 'I am the President of
the Republic,' he shouted. And as the court descended into uproar,
Egyptian journalists shrieked at Morsi and his six co-accused over and
over again. 'Execute them! Execute them!' they chorused, and of
course the cops did absolutely nothing to end this monstrous circus.
Maybe they agreed with the journalists, but at one point lawyers for
Muslim Brotherhood defendants were fighting on the court benches
with Egyptian reporters and policemen while Morsi and his former
comrades – who were meeting for the first time since the July military
coup – watched placidly from within their iron cage.

It might have been easy to joke about this carnival of a court, its
police officers pleading with mobs of reporters and advocates to stop
fighting while Egypt's former president stood in his business suit, occasionally bear-hugging his fellow prisoners, all behind bars at the end of
the wooden-panelled courtroom. This was part of Egypt's post-revolutionary tragedy, an elected leader facing charges of incitement to kill,
an accusation which might cost him his life.

No one believed it would. The journalists would not have bayed for
his hanging if they thought he would be sentenced to death, but it was
essential for Morsi to claim he was still president of Egypt in case he did
hang. This historically unprecedented hearing was about whether
post-revolutionary Egypt could have a working democracy.

For Sisi, however, Morsi's trial was intended to place the final seal upon the legitimacy of his overthrow. What mattered was that Morsi was tried in a criminal court for inciting people 'to commit crimes of deliberate and premeditated murder' and of inciting others to 'the use of violence, thuggery, coercion, possession of firearms, ammunition ... and unlawfully arresting, detaining and torturing peaceful demonstrators'. These charges referred to violence outside the presidential palace eleven months earlier when five civilians were killed – but they could have been made, with far more justification, against the cops and baltagi thugs who ran amok among the Brotherhood on an infinitely greater scale at the Rabaa and Al-Fath mosques the previous August.

The criminality of Morsi and the Brotherhood was all-important. Legality could only be conferred upon what was indeed a coup if Morsi could be found guilty of criminal acts, a process that would continue right up to the day upon which he suffered a fatal heart attack – still in his court cage – almost six years later. The most important act of legitimacy, of course, was to be Sisi's election to the presidency in 2014 with that fraudulent 96.91 per cent of the vote.

The portents for Morsi's first trial appearance were not good. The cops on the gate shook our hands, smiled, took our passports and mobiles, handed out laminated plastic identity numbers, bussed us to the court, prowled respectfully through our files, books and handbags. When we reached the courthouse, hundreds more cops filled the front seats, the side aisles, the seats at both ends of the benches, the dais behind the judge's chair, with another three dozen crammed into an adjacent iron cage.

We hadn't seen Morsi since the coup but he looked fit enough, maybe a trifle plumper, speaking animatedly to his colleagues who were wearing prisoners' white jumpsuits. His party crony Mohamed Beltagy was there and we could see Essam el-Erian, the Brotherhood leader, and I think it was he who shouted that a criminal court should not be trying their case, that the hearing was 'illegal ... unfair, unjust, unconstitutional'.

Six of the prisoners had been held at the police academy since dawn and El-Erian went on bellowing that they had been 'tortured' and deprived of lawyers since their arrest. The lawyers themselves complained that they had been given no time to prepare their cases. They demanded to know why plain-clothes men suddenly emerged behind the judge with cameras, but the judge Sabri Youssef chose not to explain who these strange men were. Lawyers for Morsi and his colleagues held up their hands in the four-finger 'Rabaa' symbol of the Brotherhood, along with sketches of a pro-Brotherhood journalist killed in Tahrir Square. They were met with hoots of derision from Egyptian reporters and some of the cops.

The judge read out the name Mohamed Mohamed Morsi – it was, of course, for him that we had all come to this very odd court. Ahmed Abdul-Ali, another of the defendants, told reporters through the cage wire that Morsi had seen none of his assistants since July, which is why we could see him in earnest conversation with his former colleagues, undoubtedly the first serious meeting of the Freedom and Justice Party since the coup.

When he interrupted Judge Youssef, Morsi's voice sounded loud and confident. 'I am the President of the Republic,' he stated. 'The coup is a crime. The court is held responsible for this crime. Everything that is happening here is a cover for the coup. It's a tragedy that Egypt's great judiciary should be a cover for the coup.' Morsi had grasped exactly the same point that El-Erian had made. The court was intended to expunge the fact of the coup. As he was shouted down by Egyptian journalists, Morsi could be heard saying: 'Don't let it fool you ... this is all in the interests of the external enemy.'

It was unclear to which 'external enemy' he was referring. Israel? The Americans? Or the Sisi regime? He said that he respected the members of the court, but that it had no constitutional right to try a head of state. 'I am the president of the state, and I am being held against my will.' And that was why Morsi insisted he was still the president – because if he was not, the court might be entitled to try him.

He struggled on. As the sound men ramped up the volume on the judge's microphone to drown out Morsi's words, he could be heard pleading: 'Give me something [a microphone] so I can speak to you.' 'Not now,' the judge snapped. If a court can show the divisions of a nation, this one did. Morsi had sound legal grounds to object to the hearing – but far too many Egyptians believed that he should never have been elected, that he never acted as their president and was thrown from power in ignominy because he was planning a coup of his own.

Outside the academy, riot police were fixing gas canisters to their guns opposite hundreds of pro-Morsi demonstrators. A gang of armed government thugs began to chase men across the car park. All in all, a disgraceful day, to be followed by many others. Morsi would struggle on for years, before a series of mass trials would entrap him and his Brotherhood colleagues and, quite literally, exhaust him to death.

He would be charged with breaking out of the prison to which he had been dispatched by Mubarak during the 2011 revolution, but he was now alleged to have been freed with the help of armed Palestinians of the Hamas movement from Gaza. So he could be portrayed as a Hamas 'leader' rather than an Egyptian president – and thus receive a twenty-year sentence for being a member of a 'terrorist' organisation freed by another 'terrorist' organisation. In 2015, Morsi was charged with espionage and treason over the same prison release. Most of the Brotherhood's leadership had already received heavy prison terms or death sentences. Mohamed Badie, the Brotherhood's 'Supreme Leader', appeared in court in the red jumpsuit; the Egyptian judiciary was to sentence him to death twice and to life imprisonment six times.

The crushing of the Brotherhood was now a security matter. Morsi and his colleagues were daily condemned as 'terrorists' on a level with the Islamists of Sinai, who were already coalescing into ISIS. Qatar withdrew all its financial assistance from Egypt; Saudi Arabia, which had funded the Egyptian Salafists, stepped in to bankroll Sisi's regime. Sisi himself called the Saudi King Abdullah 'King of the Arabs', adulation to which the king wisely did not respond. But the Brotherhood could still be dragged out of its grave to frighten voters. Almost a year after Morsi's overthrow, the walls of the Brotherhood stronghold of Kerdasa, south-west of Cairo, were still decorated with stencilled pictures of Brotherhood 'martyrs' and of Morsi himself, 'the legitimate president'. This was the town where mobs took revenge for the Rabaa killings by attacking the police station, killing thirteen officers and mutilating their bodies.

If the Brotherhood was buried as a political party, it could still be resurrected when Sisi thought it necessary. A week before his triumph in the 2014 presidential elections, he repeated several times that this was not the time for demonstrations or 'freedom of expression'. The most important objectives, he said, were the restoration of 'security' and the war against Muslim Brotherhood 'terrorists'. If some of the artistic, middle-class intellectuals who initially threw their support behind the army now had to purchase ever darker sunglasses to obscure the colour of blood, European leaders showed themselves ever more accommodating to the new dictatorship, even before Sisi was elected president.

Only days after the August massacres in Cairo, British foreign secretary William Hague described the bloodshed that left hundreds of civilians dead as 'turbulence'. And while the UK government did not approve of 'military interventions in democratic processes', he believed Sisi's overthrow of Morsi was not illegal; it was, he said, a 'grey area'. After several Muslim Brotherhood officials sought refuge in the UK, prime minister David Cameron took the extraordinary step in April 2014 of ordering an inquiry into the Brotherhood's activities in Britain so 'that we understand ... what its beliefs are in terms of the path of extremism and violent extremism'. This was clearly going to be difficult – there had never been any evidence that Brotherhood refugees in Britain ever indulged in violence. Besides, British officials had frequently met with Morsi during his presidency and would surely have indicated to the Foreign Office any suspicion that his Brotherhood mentors were involved in 'terrorism'.

Yet Cameron asked Sir John Jenkins, the British ambassador to Saudi Arabia, to lead the inquiry. The Saudis, who wanted Sisi to crush the Brotherhood, were now funding $5 billion of a $12 billion Gulf economic assistance package to make up for Cairo's loss of a $5.5 billion financing package from Qatar. Sir John would, Cameron said, draw up a report on its 'philosophy and values' and 'alleged connections' with violence. Since Saudi Arabia had itself denounced the Brotherhood as 'terrorists', Jenkins could scarcely be expected to have much first-hand experience of the organisation, although Cameron's spokeswoman claimed he had 'deep knowledge' of the Middle East. Sir Richard Dearlove, the former head of MI6, reportedly described the Brotherhood as 'at heart a terrorist organisation' – again without any evidence.*

---

* Interestingly, Cameron's inquiry team also included his national security adviser, Sir Kim Darroch – whose leaked ambassadorial reports from Washington on US President Trump's 'dysfunctional' administration led to his resignation in 2019. After his own retirement, ex-ambassador Jenkins would become a defender and apologist for Crown Prince Mohamed bin Salman – after Saudi Arabia's assault on Yemen, but prior to the dismemberment of journalist Jamal Khashoggi in the Saudi consulate in Istanbul.

In public, the UK government always emphasised the assistance which the Saudis gave British intelligence authorities, variously declaring that Saudi 'information' had saved British lives or that any damage to UK relations with Saudi Arabia might end its intelligence-sharing relationship and thus cost British lives.

But there were other costs involved in the UK's relationship with the Saudis. In February 2014, less than two months before Cameron publicly announced his 'security' inquiry into the Brotherhood, the UK arms company BAE Systems settled a deal for the sale of seventy-two Typhoon fighter jets to Saudi Arabia for $7 billion. The earlier Al-Yamamah sale by British Aerospace of British fighter jets to the Kingdom was worth $45 billion by 2005. A subsequent UK fraud inquiry into the transaction was closed down by prime minister Tony Blair on the grounds that its continuation would not be in the 'national interest'.* By 2019, Saudi–UK joint ventures were worth $17.9 billion. By ignoring the massacres perpetrated against the Brotherhood and by expressing its suspicions about the victims of the Egyptian coup d'état and their leader Mohamed Morsi, David Cameron was in effect denying the integrity of the man who had been legally elected president less than two years earlier. Cameron's decision was not just a cowardly submission to Britain's commercial interests; he was aiding Sisi's dictatorial regime.

Needless to say, Cameron's team of sleuths could come up with no evidence of the 'terrorist' nature of the Brotherhood and, almost a year after he announced his investigation, he was forced to announce that it would not be published. But like the 'coup' debate, it no longer mattered. The Egyptian military regime had received international support for its erasure of the Muslim Brotherhood. Less than three months after Cameron pulled his own inquiry, Sisi was elected president.

And so on 3 June 2015, only a day after Morsi was sentenced to death in Cairo, the Egyptian government announced that President Sisi was to make an official visit to Britain. Cameron's invitation was accompanied by UK assurances that 'no issues are off the table', although the

---

* When the Serious Fraud Squad inquired into charges of bribery and corruption in Al-Yamamah, the Saudis complained that it might impugn the reputation of leading figures in the Kingdom. The transfer of Saudi intelligence information to the UK could end if the police continued their work, and reports spoke of 'British lives' at risk if the police accused Saudi officials of accepting massive bribes from BAE.

effect was somewhat spoiled by the statement that these 'issues' included those that were important 'to the UK's national interest'. It is important to catalogue this infernal combination of commerce, 'security' and dictatorship, since it opened the way for further approaches from France and Germany. The Cameron invitation followed a BP investment agreement with Egypt worth $12 billion. The British response to Sisi's ascension in Egypt and the empty promise of a report into the Brotherhood that would please Saudi Arabia illustrated the same imbalance that existed between Europe and America and their client dictators and kings in the Middle East. Were these Arabs to be treated as trusted allies or greedy customers?

Sisi said on election day that 'Egyptians are coming out to write their history and chart their future', but a three-hour drive around the polling stations of Cairo on 28 May 2014 produced no evidence of such enthusiasm. In Giza, the schools that opened for voters were deserted. On the island of Gezira, home to the literati and the fallen business leaders of Cairo, three soldiers and two cops lounged outside the polling station. In one district, I found an armed soldier wearing a black ski mask; but he, too, was guarding an empty building. Even in Heliopolis, where Sisi himself lived, there was not a single voter to be found. I drove round to the very electoral station where Adly Mansour, the 'interim president', had voted two days earlier, in a well-appointed street of small mansions. It was the same story: four soldiers, three policemen, armed plain-clothes cops, but not one voter to be seen.

News shows had denounced those who would not vote as 'traitors to their country', and Ibrahim Mahlab, the 'interim prime minister', announced that the law requiring eligible voters to go to polling stations would be fully implemented. It made no difference. The official result of 93.3 per cent was quite literally incredible. Less agreeable to Sisi was the turnout: a mere 45 per cent, representing only 23.3 million voters rather than the 80 million he confidently expected; and this was 6 per cent less than the voter turnout in the final round of the 2012 presidential election which Morsi won.* The rival candidate in

---

* The Brotherhood had regarded the poll as a farce, although a twenty-year-old interviewed by *Le Monde* probably caught the popular mood before the election. 'We know the result already,' he said. 'He's going to win. So what's the point in voting?'

2014, the luckless journalist Nasserist Hamdeen Sabahi, supposedly gained the support of a mere 3 per cent of voters.

Sisi's face continued to adorn the lamp-posts of Cairo over the following weeks, but it was impossible to miss the posters of his only real opponent; not Sabahi, but the immensely popular Algerian singer Cheb Khaled who packed the house on 8 May in Cairo. Sisi's supporters gathered in Tahrir to celebrate the victory of a president who overthrew his predecessor in a military coup and then sought popularity with vague policies of austerity, family values and appeals to patriotism and security – without even bothering to stage an election campaign.

Sisi was an impatient man. The suppression of his internal enemies – and then all those who might oppose him – commenced long before he gained the presidency. Before the election, an independent website, Wiki Thawra, claimed that 41,163 Egyptians had been arrested in the eleven months after Sisi's coup, between 3 July 2013 and 15 May 2014.[*] Underwritten by an increasingly slovenly US administration, Sisi decided to crush all dissent, starting with students. Egyptian police were given special powers to enter university campuses, allegedly to prevent violence between pro-Morsi and pro-Sisi supporters; thirty-eight Al-Azhar university students were sentenced to eighteen months in jail. A new anti-protest law allowed police to arrest three of the most prominent leaders of the 2011 revolution. They were sentenced to three years' hard labour. In November 2013, sentences of eleven years were handed out to fourteen young female supporters of Morsi. There were new restrictions on public demonstrations on gatherings of more than ten people. Pro-democracy activists were seized in their homes and sent to court for participating in protests.

In demonstrations across Egypt to mark the third anniversary of the 2011 overthrow of Mubarak, held by both pro-Morsi and secular anti-Sisi activists, security forces killed forty-nine protesters. In a grotesque

---

[*] Statistics of state coercion can be as banal as they are terrifying. While 2,076 were detained after the Rabaa mosque killings and 2,240 before and after the siege of the Al-Fath mosque – many of those who might otherwise have been arrested at Rabaa had probably already been shot dead – almost 40,000 Egyptians were taken to prison. According to the website, there were 837 military trials for civilians during this period, most of the hearings in Marsa Matruh on the north-western border with Libya.

miscarriage of justice in March 2014, a Minya provincial judge sentenced to death 529 alleged supporters of the Brotherhood for killing a single police officer the previous summer. Judge Saeed Youssef Elgazar gave the prisoners only a few hours to defend themselves, reportedly exclaiming: 'Don't talk about the constitution – I don't want to hear about that in my court.'

Less than four months earlier, Egyptian 'foreign minister' Nabil Fahmy had insisted that 'the Egyptian people are aspiring for a democratic system ... irrespective of the fact that we may have some cultural variations here and there in terms of our traditions'. Egyptians were now finding out what these 'cultural variations' would involve. When a fifteen-year-old schoolboy took to school a ruler bearing the four-finger symbol of the Brotherhood, his father was arrested and two of his teachers faced charges of 'spreading chaos among school students'.

As Sisi's dictatorship asserted itself, humour of even the most innocuous kind was suppressed as surely as political dissent. Satire would disappear as swiftly as the state's enemies. One of the few privately owned newspapers still trying to report the truth shocked its readers in the summer of 2015 with a seven-page condemnation of the police for theft, torture, rape, kidnapping and inhuman conditions of detention. *Al-Masry Al-Youm* blamed the security forces, the interior ministry and parliament – which, in the absence of an elected parliament, meant Sisi. The semi-government National Council for the Rights of Man noted that 1,500 men had now been condemned to death and that 124 prisoners had died in custody through lack of medical care, torture or ill treatment.*

Lawyer Karim Hamdi, for example, turned up in January 2015 at the Matareya police station – known locally as 'the abattoir' – to make a routine complaint on behalf of a client. He died inside the police post, in a working-class area where there had been many pro-Morsi demonstrations and arrests. According to a colleague, his autopsy revealed that 'his tongue had been cut out and that he had wounds to his genital organs and broken ribs'. Ahmed Gamal Ziada, a photo-journalist

---

* Sensing the frisson of concern at these atrocities that were now touching even his middle-class supporters, Sisi issued an unusual – and highly revealing – public address to his cops: 'I say to all our sons in the police or any other government agency [*sic*] that they must keep in mind that they are dealing with human beings.'

acquitted after 496 days of detention at the Abu Zabel jail north of Cairo – the same institution outside of which thirty-seven prisoners had been burned to death in the summer of 2013 – talked of the 'slow death' of inmates held in the isolation section, known as 'the tomb of the living'. By November 2015, nine Egyptian journalists were behind bars.

Foreign NGOs had even less influence. When Kenneth Roth, the Human Rights Watch director, arrived at Cairo airport to present the organisation's report on the Rabaa massacre a year after the killings, he was immediately deported. The Carter Center closed its Egypt office because it could no longer monitor elections. Among more than a thousand death sentences passed by June 2015 was one against Emad Shahin, a former Harvard scholar and now a visiting Georgetown professor, who was accused of 'espionage' but was thankfully out of the country when he was condemned.

But Egypt's executioners were kept busy. In the six years that followed Sisi's coup, they hanged 179 men, many of them tortured before confessing to murder, bomb attacks or other acts of 'terrorism'. But those who claimed that Sisi had returned the country to a Mubarak-style dictatorship were wrong. In the seven years of his own war against the Brotherhood, between 1990 and 1997, Mubarak's hangmen had executed only sixty-eight Islamists and locked up 15,000 others. By 2019, in the six years since the coup, Sisi had jailed 60,000 political prisoners.

This was a sign of fear as much as it was evidence of determination to stamp out 'terror'. Sisi now had three separate conflicts on his hands: his suppression of the Brotherhood on the grounds that they were themselves violent 'terrorists'; a campaign by Islamist extremist groups against Egypt's minority Christian Copts; and, most frightening of all, the very real al-Qaeda–ISIS war against Sisi's own regime.

Violent assaults on Egypt's Christian minority had begun under Sadat and continued throughout Mubarak's almost thirty-year rule. Only days before the start of the January 2011 revolution, an armed man killed nine worshippers at a midnight mass in upper Egypt, a sectarian attack followed by the murder of twenty-one Christians and others outside a church in Alexandria, for which al-Qaeda was widely blamed. More than two years later, after Sisi deposed Morsi, Copts were again targeted in a series of killings and church-burnings and looting of Christian property, some of the attacks clearly committed out of revenge by Brotherhood supporters. In northern Sinai, two masked men shot dead a village priest. The World Council of Churches protested. The bishop of Minya in upper Egypt insisted that 'we must pray for those who wrong us, for they know not what they do', but this Christ-like blessing had no effect.

Muslim–Christian antagonism, inflamed in the past by family disputes over marriage or kidnapping, transformed itself into sectarian violence once Christians were seen to have given their allegiance to Sisi and his army. When Islamist groups joined in this killing spree, Sisi's hope that he could treat his enemies as one and the same was fulfilled. Muslims themselves even conflated the new Sisi regime and the Copts with Egypt's pharaohs, just as Sadat's killers had done in 1981. 'Yes to Islam,' was daubed on the walls of the Mallawi Museum of antiquities in upper Egypt after it was burned and looted. 'Sisi, we are coming.' The museum's antiquities, however, included gold and jewels from the time of the seventh-century Omayyad dynasty to the twelfth-century Fatimids. Both before and after the coup, the security forces often turned up far too late to catch the culprits. Was their delay deliberate? Were the authorities trying to show Egyptians the chaos they would endure if they did not support Sisi? Or had government intelligence agents instigated the attacks for the same reason? However unlikely, these stories floated around Egypt.

So did the casualty lists for Sisi's soldiers in the Sinai peninsula: a hundred killed in the ten weeks following Sisi's coup d'état, nine killed in a double suicide car bombing in early September. The Sinai battle extended to the borders of Gaza as Egyptian troops renewed their duties of protecting Israel by closing down 152 smuggling tunnels used for transporting food and weapons to the Palestinians. The Islamists of Sinai – and soon ISIS itself – were already penetrating Cairo. By late November, more than a thousand soldiers and policemen had been killed.

Journalists and NGOs were now forbidden to visit Sinai; had they done so, they would have been able to report that large areas of the vast 23,000-square-mile desert had fallen into the hands of Islamist fighters, soon to declare themselves allies of ISIS.* When ISIS men

---

* The original Sinai battles were explained away by the authorities in Cairo as armed

stormed six military bases near Sheikh Zuweid close to the Israeli border in late June 2015, they killed sixty-four soldiers, some of them executed after they had been captured. Sisi sent in the air force to bomb the town.

So after dozens of grotesquely unfair trials of his enemies, Sisi was now going to 'amend' whatever laws protected the accused, to speed up his peculiar form of 'justice'. The Brotherhood continued to claim that it remained a non-violent movement that believed in fair elections. But with its ranks smashed by Sisi's programme of arrests, torture and death, 'experts' in Washington suggested that a younger generation of supporters had abandoned their slogan of 'our peacefulness is stronger than bullets'. This sounded logical enough, but those who remained in contact with Morsi's ex-ministerial colleagues described a more nuanced – and more terrifying – scenario.

To share a prison cell and a jail truck with jihadis is both a journalist's dream and a journalist's nightmare; which made Mohamed Fahmy a unique figure. An Egyptian with Canadian citizenship, he was the Al Jazeera English channel reporter who spent almost two years in Sisi's prison system, locked up with two colleagues for being a pro-Brotherhood 'terrorist', fabricating news and endangering the 'security' of the state. The charges were lies and the trials that followed were a mockery of justice. But extracted at last from the depths of his incarceration, he was able to travel to Canada and to write an extraordinary account of his time in captivity.

As Qur'anic recitations echo through the Tora prison's verminous 'Scorpion' section, and Fahmy mumbles half-remembered verses, 'my rational, Western educated mind rises up in protest – it is, after all, a group of incarcerated Islamists with whom I pray. I feel self-conscious. Silly almost … But a few of the prayers I learned as a young boy return

---

attacks by smugglers or impoverished tribes angered by the central government's neglect of their region. But as the Egyptian army boasted of killing hundreds of Islamists, this excuse was no longer credible. And with hundreds of Egyptian troops dying in the subsequent battles, Sisi's promises of stability became even less sustainable. When thirty-two soldiers and police were killed in four separate attacks in January 2015, their corpses were returned by air to Cairo. ISIS kidnapped twenty-one Egyptian Christians working in Libya, cutting their throats on a Mediterranean beach in February 2015, while filming their last agonising moments on video as the tide flowed red across the sand.

and wash over me, drawing me along in their tide.' On arrival in his cell, he discovers that he is imprisoned with men whom he was interviewing for Al Jazeera only a few months earlier when they were members of the Morsi government: Essam al-Haddad, Morsi's executive aid who had met Barack Obama; Khaled al-Qazzaz, Morsi's foreign affairs adviser.

Much to his distress, a number of other prisoners shout their support for Al Jazeera, which had at the time – to Fahmy's horror – been carrying pro-Brotherhood material on its 'live' Egypt network. 'You journalists have been sent here to see the truth,' a man shouted. 'There is a reason why God led you here.' And then Fahmy discovers that some of his fellow Islamist prisoners had themselves filmed for the Al Jazeera 'live' channel – no wonder he was in his cell.

Fahmy meets Mohamed al-Zawahiri, brother of Ayman, the man appointed al-Qaeda's leader after Bin Laden's assassination. 'We are not bloodthirsty merciless killers,' he assures Fahmy. 'We merely defend ourselves … demand our rights of establishing a governance based on Islamic Sharia.' When Fahmy asks whether his connections in Sinai might have led to his imprisonment, a man beside al-Zawahiri shouts: 'What Sinai! Those are legitimate resistance fighters. Whose side are you on?'

Whose side indeed? In August 2014, ISIS released a video of the beheading of American journalist James Foley. When he is taken for further interrogation, Fahmy finds himself in a police truck amid the Cairo traffic and his companions whoop with delight when the driver's radio tells of three policemen killed at a checkpoint. ISIS promise to kill another reporter, Steven Sotloff, if the US continued to bomb their positions in Iraq. Fahmy was a friend of Sotloff. 'He must be a spy,' the prisoner handcuffed to Fahmy spits out. 'Why would an American put himself in such danger otherwise?' Fahmy knows why: risking one's life to get the story. He listens, aghast, as another man says that 'he's just one American. What about the thousands of Iraqis killed by the US?'

Then it is Sotloff's turn. Fahmy sees the next video. 'Steven, head and beard shaved, wears an orange jumpsuit … His small glasses, the round curves of his warm face, and the kind smile … are nowhere to be seen … I pray that his mind and heart were calm.' Fahmy is enraged 'that this hideous man who killed Steven and I are being labelled with the same name: terrorist'. But on the eve of his release from prison, he shakes hands with a man under sentence of death. 'For the past six months,' he would write, 'these men, some of them jihadists who call death and destruction down on the world for an inhumane ideology, have generously shared their food and meagre possessions.'

Fahmy remained convinced that the torture and prison regimes of the Middle East were universities for future jihadis. He also feared for the future of his own profession, quoting Adel Iskandar, a Canadian professor of Egyptian origin, on Al Jazeera's coverage of Egypt during the military coup: 'Al Jazeera picked a side in the conflict and ran with it, and when the station was unable to deliver coverage from the ground, they relied on footage and reports produced by Islamist opposition groups and armed militia factions. This technique became their modus operandi in Syria where the stakes and the costs are extremely high – especially to journalists.'

Fahmy, like his Al Jazeera colleagues imprisoned with him, was a victim of Qatar's support for the Brotherhood and its hostility towards the Sisi regime. As soon as Qatar withdrew its massive financial support for Egypt, anyone connected to the Gulf emirate was forfeit. If Qatar had abandoned the Brotherhood, its international correspondents in Cairo would have been protected. But the network's own duplicity in airing the work of Fahmy and his colleagues on the live and anti-Sisi channel was a form of journalistic betrayal of which the Egyptians took full advantage. This also meant that the most terrible ISIS assaults on Egypt in the coming years went without any first-hand reporting on the most widely viewed English-language Arab satellite channel in the world.

This was a relief for Sisi, whose anti-'terrorist' credentials were now looking tarnished. Sinai itself was beginning to acquire the feel of the hinterland of Mosul and Fallujah in Iraq and eastern Syria, an insurrectionist playground in which Egyptian forces were ever more on the defensive. Just as the Israelis used fighter-bombers in their regular assaults on Gaza, and just as the Syrians and Russians would air-bomb eastern Aleppo, the Egyptians sent F-16s to assault their targets in Sinai. The precedents set by Israel and the Americans were being followed most precisely.*

---

* In July 2015, an Islamist website showed an Egyptian naval vessel on fire off the coast of Sinai after what appeared to have been an ISIS missile attack. The military authorities in Cairo chose not to admit the virtual destruction of one of their ships.

Inside Sinai itself, civilians found themselves in the familiar valley of the shadow of death: trapped in poverty between barbarous Islamists and murderous soldiers. The Egyptian army was already executing prisoners, a war crime in which ISIS had indulged for several years. But the carnage caused by the five-truck assault group of ISIS killers who surrounded a Sufi mosque at Bir el-Abed in the Sinai on 25 November 2017 showed just how seriously the perverted theocratic ideas of the group had infected their supporters in Egypt.* Some forty attackers would kill 305 Muslim worshippers, including twenty-seven children. They even carried the black ISIS flag with them, surrounding the Al-Rawda mosque, placing armed men outside the entrance and all twelve windows, and then shooting down every man, woman and child who tried to escape. Entire families were killed. It was the deadliest attack of its kind in Egyptian history – here, at least, was a figure that could not be exaggerated. Sisi uttered his standard promise of revenge with 'an iron fist', engaged in the biggest battle fought in Sinai since the 1967 Arab–Israeli war.

If his army was now constantly challenged inside the borders of Egypt itself, Sisi would allow nothing to interfere with its unlicensed and undocumented economic profits. The only challenge to the army's monopoly over shopping malls, real estate sales, hotels, resorts, apartment blocks, villas, construction companies, factories and petrol stations could come from the workers who produce Egypt's exports. The potential army of women had already been destroyed by the military's obscene behaviour in Tahrir; the army of workers must now be emasculated. For if Sisi imagined himself loved for his ascetic habits, nothing should interfere with the financial security of his military officers.

---

* Claims of a mystical union with God were bound to attract the animal fury of ISIS. So was the Sufi contention that human imagination could bring believers closer to God, and that those who based their belief on dogma were, as a Persian expression would have it, 'standing on wooden legs'. Like the Christians, the great Sufi families tended now to support their local dictators. Exactly thirteen months before the Bir el-Abed attack, an elderly and prominent Sufi sheikh in Sinai, Suleiman Abu Heraz, was kidnapped by ISIS, accused of practising magic and then decapitated. The commander of the group's 'morality police' declared some weeks later that its 'first priority was to fight polytheism, including Sufism'.

We have already seen how Egyptian trade unions, with their long anti-colonial tradition, staged the first 'revolution' against Mubarak and gave their support to the protesters of Tahrir in 2011 by travelling down from the cotton city of Mahalla and other factory towns in the Nile Delta. The workers' taste for independent action continued after Morsi's election. Around 20,000 workers at the spinning and weaving companies in Mahalla called an eight-day strike for better conditions in July 2012. But Sisi's protection of the army's financial monopoly meant that Egyptian workers must no longer dream of controlling the 'means of production', let alone challenging government authority. This is why the army's right to try civilians in military courts was so important to the regime.

Article 174 of Sisi's new 2013 national constitution authorised military judges to try any workers employed by army-controlled commercial companies for striking, occupying factories or committing acts of 'civil disobedience'. The constitution, of course, made no mention of the army's monopoly of so many economic assets. A Supreme Administrative Court decision in April 2015 effectively outlawed all strikes by declaring that the right to strike 'violates Islamic Sharia' and 'goes against Islamic teachings'. Employees were public servants and could not deprive citizens of services. Islamic rules, the court decided, meant that a refusal to 'obey orders by seniors at work' was 'a crime'.

How could this be, trade unions and a former deputy prime minister asked, when it was the Muslim Brotherhood that had attempted to mix religion with the state? Whoever said that striking was against Sharia law? This ruling was supported by the court when they claimed that even international agreements on workers' rights signed by Egypt had to be 'conditioned on its consistency with Islamic Sharia'. Independent trade union and human rights activist Kamal Abbas protested that 'what we are witnessing is the retreat of all the gains we made as workers following the 25 January revolution' of 2011.

In the first four months of 2016, thousands of industrial workers participated in almost 500 strikes, pickets and demonstrations across Egypt in protest at rising prices, low wages and delayed payments. Jabali al-Maraghi's official Egyptian Trade Union Federation filed a lawsuit to criminalise unofficial trade unions. But when independent unions complained to the International Labour Organization that government delegates to its Geneva conference were illegitimate, the ILO expressed only its 'concern', before duly adding Egypt to its blacklist for states that violate workers' rights.

There was something both droll and uninspiring about Sisi's dictatorship. It was brutal, overpowering, oppressive and deadly, but it had a framework of both farce and tragedy that some might regard as comic. He called the people 'the light of my eyes' but he could also act the role of angry father to his indolent children. 'I will not sleep and neither will you,' he announced in a television interview. 'We must work, night and day, without rest.' The job of the president was improving public morals and 'presenting God' correctly. He would, he promised, take legal action against personal insults.

But Sisi's rule contained an essential element of buffoonery, more Mussolini than Nazi tyrant. Prior to his first presidency, street portraits would show him bedecked with medals, yet he had seen no military combat – unless his now forgotten defence of virginity tests on female Tahrir demonstrators counted. He graduated from military academy only after the 1973 war, yet after his coup, he did nothing to prevent Egyptian shopkeepers selling cakes and sweets bearing his likeness.

Adoring Egyptians passed around fake hundred-dollar bills with Sisi's portrait Photoshopped over the engraving of Benjamin Franklin. It was the same picture we had seen on the streets, in full dress uniform. On the reverse side, over the White House, he was on a kind of throne, in camouflage fatigues this time, baseball cap on his head, arm raised to his chin as he thought, no doubt, of Egypt's stable future. Sisi did not instigate this hero worship, but he did nothing to stop it. A voice in a dream, Sisi told a journalist confidant in a leaked recording, had told him: 'We will give you what we have given to no other.' But if the new president-for-life regarded himself as blessed by such unearthly promises, how come the Egyptians who so courageously fought down Mubarak's 'deep state' had gone along with this fraudulent promotion of their new leader? Was this, as I sometimes feared, the re-infantilisation of the people? Or had some more sinister fears taken hold in Egypt?

After television viewers in early 2016 observed Sisi travelling in a motorcade along a four-kilometre red carpet, there was an outcry,

THE WOUNDED TIGER 401

even in newspapers that had long ago adopted reverence for the man who was officially still a field marshal. The army was forced to respond that the carpet had been used before and had not been purchased by Sisi. Far more disturbing for Egyptians was Sisi's decision to give to the Saudis two strategic Red Sea islands – for which Egyptian soldiers had given their lives in the 1967 war – in return, presumably, for the billions of dollars that the Kingdom had given Egypt since the coup.

Sisi fought his over-generous gift through the Cairo courts and through parliament, where normally subservient MPs complained that no one had the right to hand the country's sovereign territory to a foreign nation. For many Egyptians, their favourite general – the man who promised to protect their homeland from Islamist 'terrorists' and 'foreigners' – was selling off the islands of Tiran and Sanafir as a bribe. 'Come, come my Pasha,' satirist Bassem Youssef announced. 'The island is for a billion, the pyramids for two, with two statues free.' There were street demonstrations in Cairo, swiftly crushed by the police. Parliament and courts grudgingly cleared the transfer. It was one thing, it seemed, to see Sisi's neatly iced face appear on chocolates – quite another to eat them.

Those who dared to criticise Sisi's rule would find their personal criticism condemned as treachery. This time it was the Egyptian Actors' Syndicate, yet another official trade union, who would wield the knife. Amr Waked and Khaled Abol Naga were accused of 'high treason to the country and the people of Egypt' because they publicly condemned the Egyptian government at a US congressional hearing. Waked and Naga, both prominent actors, were banned from acting in Egypt.

Naga had described a country whose people were either imprisoned or lived in fear of arrest. Waked said that Sisi's regime had developed an 'allergy' to the truth, a claim that contained its own painful irony. For both men had naively supported the 2013 Sisi coup. Waked, whose criticism of Sisi's government had already earned him a sentence of eight years in an Egyptian prison – in absentia, because he was living in Europe – believed the union's prohibition hardly mattered, since 'if I go back to Egypt, I won't even have time to act'. Because, of course, he would be locked up at once. If all this seems a little clownish, it would be as well to recall an infinitely more terrible event that overtook a young man who showed too close an interest in the army of workers whom Sisi and the military so feared.

On 3 February 2016, the gruesome remains of an Italian student's body were found in a concrete ditch on the outskirts of Cairo. Giulio Regeni's half-naked corpse bore the terrible evidence of his torture: seven broken ribs, broken bones in his hands and feet, cuts and scratches all over his body, smashed teeth, signs of electrocution to his penis and a brain haemorrhage caused by blows to the head. When his parents held a news conference in the Italian Senate, they thought of handing out photographs of their dead twenty-eight-year-old son, a PhD student at Cambridge University, before deciding that the images were too horrible to show.

Regeni studied at high school in the United States, travelled in Latin America, Germany and Austria, and had lived in Egypt since November 2015. For his PhD thesis, he was researching the Egyptian trade union movements – which was both the reason he was in Cairo and the probable motive for his murder. A few weeks before his death, Regeni had written presciently that 'the [Egyptian] unions' defiance of the state of emergency and the regime's appeal for stability and social order – justified by the "war on terror" – signifies … a bold questioning of the underlying rhetoric the regime uses to justify its own existence and its repression of civil society'.

Regeni had just attended a meeting in Cairo at which workers from all over Egypt had called for a committee to organise a national campaign for trade union freedom. As the German journalist Alexander Stille was to write, Regeni and his Cambridge supervisor, the Egyptian academic Maha Abdelrahman, understood that the independent trade union movement seemed 'to threaten a military regime determined to repress autonomous sources of power'. Far more threatening for Regeni, however, were the suspicions, fears and delusions of the Egyptian security services who quickly learned of the student's work and even persuaded themselves that he might be a British spy.

These men had inherited a system of police and prison barbarity that had long existed within Mubarak's 'deep state'. The chaos of Morsi's presidency and the 'corrective' revolution had if anything increased their desire to use cruel and lethal measures to crush those who would destroy the state that protected them. Some of these men had developed their own form of sadism, while police officers under Sisi were found to have developed the habit of carving initials into the bodies of their victims. Regeni's corpse bore just such letters.

In his last article for the Italian communist daily *Il Manifesto*, published posthumously, Regeni pointed out that Sisi controlled 'the highest number of police and military personnel in the history of the country' but that 'in an authoritarian and repressive context under General Sisi, the simple fact that there are popular and spontaneous initiatives that break the wall of fear is itself a major spur for change'. In a few words, he had hinted at a truth largely hidden from those who believed only in the panorama of dictatorship-versus-Islamists: that one of the greatest dangers to the Egyptian regime came from the secular, socialist opposition, symbolised by the tough and independent trade union movements.

In the days following the discovery of Regeni's body, Sisi's cops variously announced that he had been the victim of a traffic accident, kidnapped and murdered by a 'criminal gang' of thieves or was the victim of a lover's quarrel. The Italian government exploded in anger over Regeni's death, suspecting that the 'criminal gang' were Sisi's own state security police.*

Italian and British news organisations named a Mubarak-era police general, Khaled Shalabi, as the man in charge of the CID in Giza governorate where Regeni's body was found. It was Shalabi who first stated that the student had been killed in a road accident – surely the first ever traffic violation in which the victim had previously been tortured with electricity. The Italian media quickly discovered that Regeni had left his Cairo apartment on 25 January 2016, on the fifth anniversary of the 2011 revolution, to attend the birthday party of a friend. Reuters was the first to report that he had been arrested near the Nasser metro station in central Cairo and taken to a security compound. The agency

---

* The Foreign Office in London only clip-clopped into complaining about the Cambridge student's murder after it had received 10,000 signatures of protest from within the UK. In apparent contrast, the European parliament voted by a 588 majority that Egypt must cooperate with Italy's enquiries into Regeni's death, adding that this was not 'an isolated case' among the country's growing human rights violations and that weapons should no longer be sold to Egypt if they could be used against 'the opposition or civil society'. The Italian foreign ministry said Italy must be involved in the investigation because 'we want the truth to come out, every last bit of it'. But the 'last bit' never did come out.

said its sources included three police officers and three members of the security services.

The journalist Stille's own investigation revealed that Regeni's area of academic enquiry included the independent union of street vendors, who were in constant contact with protesters. Many of the vendors also worked for the police as poorly paid spies. In 2015, Regeni learned of a £10,000 grant issued by a British foundation to fund a development project that might aid his PhD research. One of the Egyptian union leaders took an interest in this and a video emerged of him asking Regeni whether this money might be used by his syndicate. A Western diplomat from a neutral nation whom I met by chance in Cairo not long after Regeni's death had seen the video, in which the student appeared embarrassed as the union man pressed him for cash. Regeni, he said, was 'out of his depth'. But for the police, this must have appeared far more sinister. What was a well-funded foreigner doing talking to an army of near beggars in Cairo?

The Egyptian ministry of interior announced that Regeni's killers were a gang of four men 'specialised in impersonating policemen, kidnapping foreigners and stealing their money'. All had been shot dead by the police 'in an exchange of fire'. The government produced a tray of objects belonging to Regeni: his Italian passport, his Cambridge University ID and his credit card. But Italian investigators found no credit card transactions registered after Regeni's disappearance. This was surely another first: a professional gang of thieves who killed a captive but had not once used his credit card.

The details of this individual case were as terrifying as they were revealing. If this was the fate of an innocent foreign student in Egypt, what happened to the thousands of ordinary Egyptians who were being 'disappeared' by the Sisi police state? An anonymous email received by La Repubblica newspaper claimed that Regeni had been put under surveillance by General Shalabi, and when questioned by police, he had refused to answer unless an Italian diplomat and an interpreter were present. That was when the torture began. The email said this included electric shock treatment to his 'delicate parts', being stripped naked and left in a room in which the floor was under water and which was 'electrified' every half-hour.

We now know that the Egyptian prison administration under Sisi is layered, with forty-two 'official' prisons but a parallel system of detention in which tens of thousands of citizens are held in military-run jails, tortured and brutally interrogated by Sisi's national intelligence service. Journalist and author Tom Stevenson named some of the secret prisons as Maskar Zaqaziq, Al-Azouly and Agroot – all outside Cairo – in which victims were routinely stripped, electrocuted, beaten on the soles of the feet and lashed with leather straps.

The inmates, according to Stevenson, included students, labour activists and socialists as well as suspected Muslim Brothers, all treated 'as an army would regard captured combatants in a world without Geneva protocols'. This, Stevenson reported, 'was the essence of military dictatorship: a vision of the state and the population it rules as two opposing armies, the first better equipped but smaller than the second, which makes brutality an indispensable tactic.' We may lament the plight of Al Jazeera journalists locked up by Sisi. 'But worse happens every day to people whose names we will never know.'

Regeni's death was naturally more important to Europeans than the thousands of Egyptians who were dying amid the violence of Sisi's military regime.* Nor would Regeni's family receive justice. To this day, Sisi denies all responsibility for the Italian's murder. Nor did he make any comment on the demise of his most important prisoner on 17 June 2019.

Mohamed Morsi's death was utterly predictable, truly outrageous and arguably a case of murder. When you die in a dictator's prison or at the hands of a dictator's security services, you are murdered. It did not matter if it was the solitary confinement, the lack of medical treatment or the isolation, nor if Morsi was broken by the lack of human contact with those whom he loved. According to Amnesty, he was allowed only three family visits in almost six years of solitary confinement, and

---

* Not that Italian interest in their own martyr maintained its moral cause. By the summer of 2019, the spread of right-wing political power in the country prompted mayors – including Massimiliano Fedriga, the new mayor of Udine, Regeni's hometown – to take down or obscure banners publicising the student's fate. Fedriga claimed it was necessary to 'disconnect' his murder from the 'political arena' and end controversy about the case. The mayor's Facebook, however, contained hundreds of vicious comments about Regeni, calling him a communist, an Islamist and a British spy. As Professor Mario Del Pero was to write, Regini's 'was a different world from the one that is now becoming reality in Italy and elsewhere, inhabited by those who – out of fear or hatred – prefer nationalist autocrats to a student of the world like Regeni'.

was denied access to his lawyers or a doctor. It is of no relevance that
the courts were unfair, the charges frivolous, the sentence mortifying.
The evidence suggested that Morsi's death must have been much
sought after by his jailors, his judges and the one man in Egypt who
could not be contradicted. You don't have to be tortured with electricity to be murdered.

Not that Morsi was himself a visionary figure. His presidency was
shambolic, uninspiring, occasionally brutal and very arrogant. The
Muslim Brotherhood always suffered from a kind of vanity, which is
why it stayed away from the 2011 revolution until Mubarak's fall was
certain – and why Morsi himself began talking to the army before the
violence had ended. But symbolism becomes all-important when the
first and last elected president of a country dies in front of his own
judges and is denied even a public funeral. The sixty-seven-year-old
diabetic was speaking to his judges – on trial for his life yet again, this
time for espionage – when he fainted to the floor.

One could only imagine the response of the judges when Morsi
collapsed. To be prepared to sentence the man to the gallows, only to
witness him meeting his maker earlier than planned, must have
provoked a unique concentration of judicial minds. But could they
have been surprised? Human rights groups had long complained of
Morsi's ill treatment, but the world's media and the world's statesmen
largely ignored these denunciations.* Morsi was now a has-been, his
court reappearances a bore. All that might have been surprising to his
judges was that he managed to talk for all of five minutes before he
departed their jurisdiction forever.

The headlines were muted on inside pages; the only Western newspaper to give a friend of the dead man a chance to speak was the
Washington Post, which allowed Egyptian-Canadian physician and
academic Wael Haddara, a pre-election adviser to Morsi, room to
demand that Egypt must answer for the ex-president's death.

If he could navigate Egypt towards democracy, Morsi had remarked
to Haddara, he expected to be assassinated. Assuming executive
authority, he had earlier told an Egyptian television anchor, was a 'kind
of suicide'. At a last meeting before he became president in June 2013,

---

* Save for Turkey, Malaysia, Qatar, Jordan, Hamas, the Muslim Brotherhood-in-exile and
other suspects.

Haddara asked Morsi to autograph an Egyptian flag for him. And this is what Morsi wrote: 'The Egypt that lives in my imagination: an Egypt of values and civilisation; an Egypt of growth and stability and love. And its flag, ever soaring above us.' Would that Sisi possessed such eloquence, or such honour.

Morsi's family were refused permission to inter him in his home town in the Nile Delta, so he was buried at 5 a.m. in a furtive and heavily guarded ceremony in eastern Cairo, attended only by his wife and sons. *Al-Masry Al-Youm* was the sole Cairo newspaper to place his death on its front page, although the headline failed to mention that he had been a president of Egypt, let alone the only one to be genuinely elected. A leaked audio recording from one of his court appearances in 2017 allowed the world to hear his voice for the last time. 'I don't know where I am,' he could be heard pleading. 'It's steel behind steel and glass behind glass. The reflection of my image makes me dizzy.'

13

'Dear Moussa ...'

We'll have thee, as our rare monsters are,
Painted on a pole, and underwrit,
'Here may you see the tyrant'

William Shakespeare, Macbeth, Act V, scene 8

'The uprisings here,' Cat Stevens began. And the Lebanese audience went wild. They stood and shouted and clapped. That one word 'uprisings' had not a magical but a cathartic effect, perhaps a kind of drug: it touched everyone. Stevens stood on the Beirut stage, scarcely an hour's drive from the Syrian border, an hour and a half from Damascus. No one needed the message spelled out.

His decision to sing 'My People', well over two decades old, one of the original great civil rights songs, perfectly reflected these times of excitement and terror in the Middle East. It might have been written for them:

My People
When you gonna leave
My People?
Give them room to breathe

The Lebanese knew all about Stevens' conversion to Islam, his deportation from Israel because he supposedly gave funds to Hamas and his denial of entry to the US because of 'concerns of ties he may have had to potential terrorist-related activities'. But even if true, being deported from Israel is, for most Lebanese, the equivalent of a music award. No wonder they wept to those words:

All they need is dignity
A chance to be free ...
Let them out of jail
My people
[...]
Stop pointing guns at
My People

Civil rights was one thing; now this song contained an extraordinary prescience. Let them out of jail. Who among the audience could not now think of prisons in Egypt or Syria? Who could not think of the people 'in the square' without remembering a place called Tahrir? Stevens loved the whole gig, but the great man had to be made to talk about the uprisings. Yusuf Islam was exhausted, but I buttonholed him with the enthusiasm of a cub reporter. Anything to tell us about the 'Arab awakening'? 'I'm inspired,' he replied. 'But I'm also afraid – because of the lack of defined leadership. Dictatorship is easy, but democracy is about consensus – and that's hard. But it's like the sun coming up.'

By February 2012, the sun shone blood-red over the Middle East. The earthquake of the past year had been the most tumultuous political experience since the fall of the Ottoman Empire. The docile, supine, cringing Arabs of Orientalism had transformed themselves into fighters for the freedom, liberty and dignity which we Westerners had always assumed it was our unique role to play in the world. In his last days, as we have seen, even Bin Laden was forced to suggest there was some divine content in these profoundly secular movements.

But so long after Bin Laden's death did his last messages emerge that they were no longer worthy of derision. For a darker and even crueller Islamist element would by then have infected the wounds of the Arab world. By early 2012, the revolutions had not produced the happy endings which Western – and Middle Eastern – audiences enjoy. Those who cried for freedom had been shot down in Syria, Libya, Yemen, Bahrain. We in the West helped to turn the Libyan revolt into a blood-bath, but when the Saudis staged their mini-invasion of the 'Kingdom of Bahrain', we were silent. The Yemenis might have learned a lesson from this grim Saudi intervention.

Yet Cat Stevens' choice of location for his concert was inspired. It was here in Lebanon, less than seven years earlier, in 2005, that the first real Arab revolution was staged, in the aftermath of the assassination of prime minister Rafiq Hariri. Most of the hundreds of thousands who gathered in Martyrs' Square blamed the Syrians for murdering their prime minister. Never before had we seen anything like it in Lebanon, or in the modern Arab world. This was not just a game of power. Nor was it a 'democratic revolution'. It was an insurrection by the people against the lies and corruption of government as well as the foreign control that they had lived under for twenty-nine years.

Yes, they wanted the Syrian army out, but they also wanted their pro-Syrian president Emile Lahoud to resign. They wanted no more compliant Lebanese governments led by weak old men; and most of them were demanding the truth about Hariri's murder. Let us, for a moment, avoid the fact that the largest minority in Lebanon, the Shia Muslims, were absent.

There was an ocean of Lebanon banners. And never before had those flags appeared so magnificent. It wasn't just the green cedar tree in the centre, but the fact that it was raised in protest at dishonesty and murder. It was the young of Lebanon, so often courted by the elderly and guilty men of this country, who were using their flag to get rid of them. They were happy and laughing; some even brought picnics or marched to trumpets and drums. Many were the children whose parents had sent them to be educated abroad during the civil war, returned now and anxious to rid themselves of the sectarian past. The Lebanese troops who stood around the square ostentatiously carried their rifles reversed over their shoulders, barrels pointed to the ground.

This indomitable courage would last – even through the Israel–Hizbollah war of 2006 – and be tragically restaged almost a decade and a half later when yet another generation insisted that Lebanon's sectarian leaders must resign and its corruption be brought to an end. Once more the old Lebanese zaim – leader – tried to stay in power, protecting their overseas bank accounts and their leadership of this financially decomposing country. But even this 2019–20 demonstration proved that the Lebanese revolution could outlive the fires of al-Qaeda. It was perhaps inevitable that the Arab awakening began in Lebanon, which remains the most educated, cynical, brave and internally dangerous of Arab nations. This seductive place – iron covered in gold leaf – survived even the neighbouring fires of Syria as the revolution ruthlessly visited the rest of the Arab world.

And even in 2005 – in the revolution, which no one at the time acknowledged to be a revolution – the Lebanese managed to force the Syrian army out of their 4,036 square miles of territory. And 'the people in the square' felt their own power for the first time. Many chose to ignore the importance of UN Security Resolution 1559, supported by the United States, the principal international power behind Syria's departure.

The Lebanese slept in tents on the pavements. It was tempting for them to believe that they were part of a great movement for democracy in the Middle East. Of course, there were some wearying signs; Christians tended to keep to their eastern side of Martyrs' Square and Muslims to the west. But so many Lebanese told us reporters that they were demonstrating for their children. There was a large and cruel cartoon of the Shia Hizbollah leader, Sayed Hassan Nasrallah, one of his arms tugged by Lebanon, the other by Syria, with the words 'Make up your mind!' above it. Bashar al-Assad had already made up his own mind.

As the last Syrian troops moved through the storms and blizzards of Mount Lebanon into the Bekaa Valley, they passed beneath the glowering statue of Bashar's brother Basil, the man who would have been president of Syria had he not died while driving too fast to Damascus airport. Seated astride his favourite horse, his effigy had been guarded for the past decade by pairs of equally glowering Syrian intelligence officers. Soon, they would arrange to cart Basil's foppish statue back to Damascus. The last Syrian positions in the mountains were abandoned in the early hours of 14 March 2005 as one of its largest air surveillance radar bases at Mdeirej was dismantled. Only a few trucks were left on the lower slopes. It did not look like an army in retreat, I wrote at the time, but its departure on this bleak, cold morning provided an astonishing contrast to its arrival in June 1976. I had been in Chtaura when they came, hundreds of armoured vehicles pouring down the international highway towards Beirut. 'It is always nice to have visitors,' a shopkeeper observed archly to me at the time. 'And it is always nice when they go home again.'

Lebanon treated its journalists to every nuance of irony. And true to form, the very same shopkeeper walked up to me as I watched the Syrians drive back through the town all those years later and asked if I remembered him. It was good to see the 'visitors' going home again, he smirked. It was the lowest point in the history of the Syrian army, a sly retreat over the snows with rusting tanks and demoralised soldiers, crippled by the corruption of Lebanon over almost three decades.

The Lebanese revolution was incomplete – it always would be – but 'people power' had forced the Syrian army to leave Lebanon. Yet it was not the simple victory which the Bush administration and American newscasters liked to portray. Half a million Lebanese Shia Muslims also came to Beirut from the Bekaa and from southern Lebanon to say they rejected America's plans in Lebanon and demanding to know who killed Rafiq Hariri. But this was more an anti-American demonstration than a demand for freedom; and Hizbollah, whose formidable organisational skills brought about this little counter-revolution, were providing a nationalist and pro-Syrian voice. The whole vast rally was handled in the usual Hizbollah way: maximum security, lots of young men in black shirts and frightening discipline. Assad's sarcastic remark about the Hariri protesters needing a 'zoom lens' to show their numbers had been answered by a demonstration of Shia power. Lebanon could no longer be taken for granted – neither by Bush nor Assad.

★   ★   ★

First the Iranian cop screamed abuse at Mir Hossein Mousavi's supporter, a white-shirted youth with a straggling beard and unkempt hair. Then he smashed his baton into the young man's face and kicked him in the testicles. It was the same all the way down to Vali Asr Square. Riot police in black body armour and black helmets and black riot sticks, most on foot but followed by a flying column of security men on bright red Honda motorcycles, tearing into the shrieking youths running for their lives. They would not accept the results of Iran's 2009 presidential elections. They did not believe that Mahmoud Ahmadinejad had won 62.6 per cent of the votes. The Lebanese were not the only Middle Eastern people prepared to confront their oppressors.

It has long been fashionable to confine the Muslim struggle for enlightenment and freedom to the Arab world. Save for the corrupted,

Wahhabi-Saudi pseudo-monarchy, Iran was the only nation in the region to claim God as its inspiration. Ayatollah Khomeini's bequest to Iranians – permanent religious rule and the thin tissue of parliamentary democracy – was as unique as it was arrogant. The 2009 poll would inevitably explode when a brave people went in their millions to voting booths because they wanted a say in how their country was governed. Not since the post-invasion Iraqi elections and a Lebanese election five days earlier had a Middle East people so staunchly demonstrated their right to be heard.

However, it was not a new Iran we were about to see. Whether the unbalanced Mahmoud Ahmadinejad clung to power or whether the old, reliable Iran–Iraq wartime prime minister Mir Hossein Mousavi won the ticket, Iran would be a little bit stronger than it was before.

The thick skin of clerical rule that covered Iran would remain, scratched occasionally perhaps, but unable to bleed or to reform a nation which so badly needed the change that only Mousavi dreamed of. Khomeini gave Iran government for and by the dead, symbolised in the 'Supreme Leader' ethos that the old man constructed before his death almost twenty years earlier. Mousavi at least had the support of the saintly ex-president Mohamed Khatami. The West's rejection of Khatami's rule brought us the triumph of the oddball Ahmadinejad, another victory for the Americans in their demonisation of the Islamic Republic.

This was the president who once claimed that a cloud emanated over his head, a halo no less, when he addressed the United Nations – then denied he'd ever said such nonsense. So could Ahmadinejad really be re-elected? He would later claim that the 'Israeli regime' should be 'wiped off the map' and that Iran would batter on with its nuclear technology, however much Israel and America may threaten to bomb them. Now he was constantly demanding democracy while threatening on the very eve of the election to jail his opponents because of what he claimed were their 'Hitler-like' lies. Opponents swiftly nicknamed Ahmadinejad the 'Democrator'.

Iran's political life has always produced a burlesque combination of sacred old men and smart economists, occasionally acting in highly unsacred coalition, so perhaps Mousavi's steady hand during the dreadful Iran–Iraq war would add to his popularity. Of the four candidates – the others were former Revolutionary Guards commander Mohsen

Rezaee and Mehdi Karroubi, a reformist cleric and former speaker of parliament – voters on the streets of southern Tehran openly talked to me of their support for him. 'I was not going to vote,' Mariam Amina said. 'But then I thought my silence would help someone who is not qualified to be president of Iran. And I thought my one vote would be worth it and that the person who becomes president would be a good president.' Could there be a better reason for any democrat in the world to vote?

For this was also a protest against the regime. There was much conversation among the crowd at the Issar School voting booths in Shaeed Mozaffarikhah Street about the permanent crust of Islamic rule which Khomeini had placed over the people. A man called Ehsan thought this accounted for the failure of the Khatami government, the failure of demonstrations at Tehran University in 1997 in favour of civil law, 'the chain over us,' he called it. 'The key roles are always taken by the Supreme Leader [now Ayatollah Ali Khamenei], the expediency council, the judiciary, the intelligence services. There are people surrounding the Supreme Leader and they are all in line with him.'

The judiciary authorities had just closed down the reformist pro-Mousavi newspaper *Hayat-e-No* ('Resurgence'). Ahmadinejad's lads were already at work. And as I drove to the poverty in the south of the city there were the juvenile posters of the ever-smiling boy. Here at least was a common denominator with Iran's fellow Muslims to the west. Assad Senior and Junior were portrayed in military uniforms, Saddam in Kurdish costume. But no one was ever taken in by these absurd portraits. In the Hasrat Rasoul mosque voting station I even found a Basiji, Asghar Naderzadeh, one of the religiously inspired warriors who fought Saddam in the trenches of Shalamcheh, who would vote for Mousavi. 'The war veterans all know him as a good person,' he said. 'He managed the war perfectly and controlled infla-tion during this period.'

I write of these people to show how their desire for freedom was as courageously expressed as the demands which the Lebanese made of their Syrian masters four years earlier. Kubra, a nurse in a scarf and purple coat, wanted to re-elect Ahmadinejad. Her brother died in the Battle of Shalamcheh, the same killing field to which Naderzadeh had been sent as a child soldier. But, she suddenly added, she approved of Barack Obama's speech in Cairo six days earlier, when the US president had acknowledged Washington's baleful interference in Iranian history. 'I think Obama is approaching Iran properly and this will be accepted in our society. We don't respect a special person – but we respect someone who respects our beliefs. We want other people in other countries to acknowledge us as human beings.'

Just at that moment, an army lieutenant who had been listening to our conversation approached me, AK-47 rifle over his shoulder. He was unshaven but with hard, strong eyes. 'We are persuading these elements that we are having a democracy in Iran,' he began. 'But democracy is for people who know their own intentions. Iranian people don't know what they want. Democracy will not work here.' I replied that I didn't think you could filter out the poor from the educated and let only the rich and the powerful rule. I guessed the soldier was an intelligent man, but then up came a man from the interior ministry and a man from the governorate and told the soldier he was not allowed to talk to journalists.

And so it was that when Iranians heard that Ahmadinejad was given 62.63 per cent of the votes but that Mousavi had won a mere 33.75 per cent – their two rivals together less than 3 per cent – they came onto the streets across the country to denounce a massive electoral fraud. Or, as the crowd round Fatimi Square chorused as they danced in a circle: 'Zionist Ahmadinejad – cheating at exams!'

Many of the protesters – some of them now wearing green scarves over their faces, the colour of Mousavi's campaign – were trying to reach the interior ministry where the government's electoral council were busy counting (or miscounting) the huge popular national vote. I descended into the basement of this fiercely ugly edifice, where cold chocolate lattes and strawberry fruitcake were on offer to journalists. Burly individuals handed out free copies of the execrable newssheet *Iran*. 'Ahmadinejad,' the headline read. '24 million votes. People vote for honesty, success and the battle against corruption'.

On the Tehran streets, I was watching scenes that would become frighteningly, wearyingly, desperately familiar in the Arab world in less than two years. The Iranian cops had now dismounted from their bikes and were breaking up paving stones to hurl at the protesters, many of them riding their own motorbikes between the rows of police. I saw one immensely tall officer smashing up stones with his baton, breaking them with his boots and chucking them at the Mousavi men. A middle-aged woman walked up to him and shouted an obvious question: 'Why are you breaking up the paving stones of our city?'

My own Persian translator was beaten three times on the back. The cops brought their own photographers to take pictures of the protesters – hence the green scarves over their faces – and overfed plain-clothes men were now mixing with them on the streets. I arrived outside the interior ministry as the police brought their prisoners back from the front line down the road. The first was a youth of perhaps fifteen or sixteen who was frog-marched by two uniformed paramilitary police to a van and thrown onto the steel floor, before one of the cops climbed in and set about him with his baton. Behind me, more than twenty policemen were sitting on the steps of a shop, munching through pre-packed luncheon boxes.

We watched as the next unfortunate was brought to the van. In a shirt falling over his filthy trousers, he was beaten outside the vehicle, kicked in the balls and then beaten onto a seat at the back of the vehicle. Another cop climbed in and batoned him in the face. The man was howling with pain. Another cop came to repeat the performance – and this, remember, was in front of dozens of other security men and with many women on the opposite pavement, all staring in horror. Now a third policeman, in an army uniform, boarded the vehicle, tied the man's hands behind his back with plastic handcuffs, took out his baton and whacked him across the face. The prisoner was now in tears but the blows kept coming until more young men arrived for their torment. Then more police vans arrived and ever more prisoners to be beaten. All were taken in these caged trucks to the basement of the interior ministry.

Another break now from these outrages, because this was the moment Mousavi's printed statement arrived at his campaign headquarters. It was strong stuff:

> The results of these elections are shocking. People who stood in the voting lines, they know the situation, they know who they voted for. They are looking now with astonishment at this magic game of the authorities on the television and radio. What has happened has shaken the whole foundation of the Islamic Republic of Iran and now it is governing by lies and dictatorship. I recommend to the authorities to stop this at once and return to

law and order, to care for the people's votes. The first message
of our revolution is that people are intelligent and will not obey
those who gain power by cheating. The whole land of Iran
belongs to them and not to the cheaters.

This was a most courageous and eloquent call for freedom, as bold as
anything we had witnessed in Beirut four years earlier and equal to the
demands we would hear from Tunisians and Egyptians and Libyans
and Syrians two years later. Mousavi's talk of the 'magic game' and the
insistence that the country must 'return to law and order', with its
clear implication that the leadership had deviated from the principles
of the Islamic Republic, were essential parts of this message. He never
called for a counter-revolution, which is why his supporters adopted
the Islamic colour green. But the essence of his message was contained
in the word 'magic'. The Islamic Republic of Iran – like all the Arab
nations to the west – must be owned by their people, not by their leaders. Reformism, which Mousavi represented, ultimately meant a
separation of church and state. But not a separation of Islam from the
Iranian people.

Iranians are a sophisticated, educated people who understand
Westerners far better than we understand them. But Ahmadinejad's
appearance before the press was almost that of an Arab 'Democrator'
in its insouciance, its naivety, its righteousness. Of course, there was a
vital difference between this 'president' and his opposite numbers elsewhere in the Middle East. They were hated not just as oppressors but
as tools of outside powers. Without America, Mubarak could not
survive. Nor Jordan. Nor Lebanon, perhaps. Nor the monarchies of the
Gulf. Nor – as we would discover soon – could Assad survive without
the Russians. But in Iran, the religious leadership was blessed by the
hatred of America. And thus their internal enemies could be contaminated as stooges of the Great Satan. The one thing Arab tyrants needed
was America's support. The one thing Iranian autocrats needed was
America's hatred. Obama's Cairo speech caused a slight problem in
this equation, although Trump would later correct the balance in Iran's
favour by tearing up his country's solemn nuclear agreement with the
Islamic Republic.

But Ahmadinejad's little speech was highly instructive. His
Humphrey Bogart jacket was open, his special smile clearly visible

behind his whiskers. There were prayers. Then came the man. The Iranian people won the elections. It was their role to rule. Iran loved all peoples. It would help all peoples. Iranians loved each other. They were unified. They would always stand together.

The man had clearly read carefully through the Obama Cairo speech and some of his 'change' motifs fitted rather well with the new US administration. Bullying was in the past, he assured us. We needed dialogue with all issues on the table. Post-Second World War political systems had proved anti-humanitarian. 'The time when a handful of countries came together to decide the fate of a smaller country was over. It is finished.' But there was a sinister undertow to this little speech, a mixture of immense conceit and potential brutality, childish praise and physical threat. The viciousness of the police – which I had just witnessed at first hand – suggested that, once the authorities had cleared the streets, there might be little mercy for Ahmadinejad's enemies.

It was Iran's day of destiny and day of courage. A million of its people marched from Engelob Square to Azadi Square – from the Square of Revolution to the Square of Freedom – beneath the eyes of the riot police, the crowds singing and laughing and abusing Ahmadinejad as 'dust'. Mir Hossein Mousavi was among them, riding atop a car amid the exhaust smoke and heat, unsmiling, lost, still unaware of the size of this epic demonstration. He may have officially lost the election, but this was his victory parade through the streets of Tehran. It was to end, predictably, in gunfire and more blood.

Not since the 1979 revolution had massed protesters gathered in such numbers through the boulevards of this torrid, despairing city. They jostled and pushed and crowded through narrow laneways to reach the main highway and then found the police in steel helmets and batons lined up on each side. The cops, now horribly outnumbered by these tens of thousands, smiled sheepishly and nodded their heads towards the men and women demanding freedom. The bravery of these people was all the more staggering as many had already learned of the savage killing of five Iranians on the campus of Tehran University the previous day, done to death, according to students, by pistol-firing Basiji. When I had reached the gates of the college, many of the students were weeping behind the iron fence of their campus, shouting 'massacre' and throwing a black cloth over the iron fence.

At times, Mousavi's victory march threatened to crush us against walls of chanting men and women. They sang in unison: 'Tanks, guns, Basiji, you have no effect now.' As the government's helicopters roared overhead, these thousands looked upwards and bayed above the clatter of rotor blades: 'Where is my vote?' Could these words muzzle the arrogance of power? In chorus, they sang: 'They have stolen our vote and now they are using it against us.' Behind us, stones began to burst onto the road as the Basiji turned their attention to the Sharif University. One man collapsed on the road, his face covered in blood. But the great mass of people moved on, shouting with joy at the thousands of Iranians who waved at them from the rooftops.

A woman who must have been ninety waved a green handkerchief on the balcony of an old people's home and an even older man emerged and waved his crutch in the air. The thousands below them shrieked back with joy. A strange fearlessness possessed them all. Who would dare attack them now? What government could deny a people of this size and determination? By dusk, the Basiji were being chased by hundreds of protesters in the west of the city and shooting was crackling around the suburbs.

It was a perilous darkness, prefigured by a grey cloud which approached us as we drew closer to Azadi Square. Then it rained and soaked us. There is a faint rainy season in mid-summer Tehran but it had arrived early, sunlight arcing through the clouds like the horizon in a biblical painting. Moin, a student of chemical engineering at Tehran University, the same campus where blood had been shed a few hours before, was walking beside me and singing in Persian as the rain pelted down. I asked him to translate. 'It's a poem by Sohrab Sepehri, one of our modern poets,' he replied.

We should go under the rain.
We should wash our eyes,
And we should see the world in a different way.

Moin grinned at me and at his two student friends. We were tripping over manhole covers and street kerbs hidden beneath men's feet and women's chadors. For these were not just the trendy young. The poor were here, the street workers and middle-aged ladies in full covering, a few holding babies on their shoulders or children by the arm.

The vast Azadi monument appeared through the grey light like a spaceship, and after walking for four miles Moin, his friends and I spent an hour squeezing through a body of humanity so dense that we thought our chests might be crushed. Around the monument, the Shah had long ago built a grass rampart and we struggled to its height and there, suddenly, was the breathtaking nature of it all. Amid the great basin of grass and concrete that surrounds the Shah's bleak concrete architecture were a thousand souls, moving and swaying and singing in the fresh post-rain sunlight. There may have been three million people around us; it was like a vast animal, a great heaving beast that breathed and roared and moved sluggishly beneath that monstrous arrow of concrete.

It was not frightening. Moin and his friends lay on the grass, smoking cigarettes. They asked each other if the Supreme Leader Khamenei would understand what this meant for Iran. One of Moin's friends insisted he would have to hold fresh elections. I wasn't so sure that the fathers of the 1979 revolution would look so kindly upon this self-evident demand for freedom. True, the Supreme Leader had agreed to enquire into the election results, but Ahmadinejad was a tough man in a tough clerical environment. His glorious predecessor, Hojatoleslam Mohamed Khatami, was somewhere down there in the crowds, along with Mousavi and, so they said, Mousavi's wife Rahnavand. But they could not protect these people. Government is about state and political power, a frightening combination even in a democracy, let alone a necrocracy, and unless those wanly smiling riot police moved across to the opposition, the weapons of the Islamic Republic remained in the hands of Ahmadinejad's administration and his spiritual protectors.*

What came next was predictable, ruthless, alarming, intended to put the fear of God into his enemies. 'The time for competition is

---

* A day later, thousands of Iranians walked in silence through Tehran to mourn those students killed at the university and, afterwards, in Azadi Square. A young commercial lawyer among them had studied psychology. 'If we let go now, we are going to face someone like Pinochet – and our dictators here are not even up-to-date dictators,' she told me without a trace of a smile. 'My psychological training is very useful. Ahmadinejad has a classic psychosis problem. He lies a lot and he's hallucinatory and the problem is, he thinks he's related to someone up there!' And here the lady pointed in the general direction of heaven. Years later, trying to elevate his most trusted lieutenant to his private office, Ahmadinejad found his friend accused of sorcery and witchcraft. This was the world of occultism which Khomeini had managed to frame for his Islamic state.

over,' the Supreme Leader told us. 'If street protests don't stop, there will be other consequences.' Ayatollah Ali Khamenei had become Thomas Cromwell, praising those he loathed with just enough directness for the recipient to know that a Supreme Leader's anger could embrace a senior cleric or two. And when he confirmed that 'those who voted for these four candidates will have their rewards in heaven', you knew that most would not be rewarded with the president of their choice.

I was standing only a few feet from this all-powerful divine. If the people took to the streets once more, 'terrorists might be hiding among the masses'. It was a sliding scale from there. Perhaps some of these people were working for foreign espionage services, for the Zionists, for that 'most treacherous enemy', the British. But where did this leave Mousavi and the million Iranians who marched through Tehran and many other cities? They were about to become enemies of the people, enemies of the revolution. It was one thing to say that they were protesting only against a fraudulent vote and Ahmadinejad, but now the demonstrators would be made to pay for their 'terrorism'.

As the internet faltered and journalists' visas were curtailed, the international press departed and the frightful aftermath of this Iranian 'awakening' was relayed outside Iran by social media, eyewitnesses and the Iranian diaspora, which had in past decades distorted many of the critical events that transformed this country after its revolution. Thus the pitiful story of twenty-six-year-old philosophy student Neda Agha-Soltan, shot dead by a Basiji during a demonstration on 20 June, blood streaming from her nose and mouth, was perverted by the authorities who would claim that she was shot by the CIA.

While the government tried to persuade Agha-Soltan's parents to blame the opposition for her death and banned memorial services for her in mosques, the most nauseous photograph to emerge from this tragedy was a Reuters picture of former crown prince Reza Pahlavi, 'fighting back tears' in Washington, as he declared that Neda Agha-Soltan was 'now forever in my pocket'. Taking immediate and shameful advantage of the woman's killing, the son of the merciless late Shah announced that 'I have added her to my list of daughters.' So belittling a statement was followed by vast coverage in the Western media where this innocent woman was ennobled as an 'Islamic Joan of Arc'.

The street demonstrations continued in Iran but detained supporters of Mousavi were beaten and tortured – and in some cases raped – by
government interrogators. There was public revulsion at the trial of a
hundred people, many of them prominent in the reform camp, on
charges of fomenting a revolution. As Ahmadinejad was formally
sworn in on 3 August, the wife of Mohamed Abtahi, theologian scholar
and chief of staff to Khatami during his presidency, claimed that her
husband had been tortured into a confession of guilt. Within days, the
Iranian police chief General Ismail Moghaddam admitted that detainees had been tortured in Kahrizak prison in Tehran. Human rights
groups identified three men who had died under torture. Opposition
protesters were now regularly confronted by Ahmadinejad supporters
and beaten on the streets. From the safety of the US, the Iranian philosopher and intellectual Abdolkarim Soroush accused the Supreme
Leader of ordering the rape of women prisoners.

This was more than just the 'kick in the balls' punishments which
we had witnessed. The Iranian parliament would later reveal the scandal of Kahrizak prison and identify the country's chief prosecutor,
Saeed Mortazavi, as the culprit. He was moved aside to run the country's counter-smuggling agency, although no punishment was meted
out to Iran's deputy police chief, General Ahmad Reza Radan, who
was said to have supervised torture sessions in which prisoners were
sprayed with water and then beaten with electric cables.

During the mass street protests against Ahmadinejad's re-election in
the summer of 2009, many Iranians, knowing that I lived in Beirut and
had witnessed the mass demonstrations against Syria, asked me how
the Lebanese mobilised their rallies. I would emphasise to them that
the Shiites of Lebanon had carefully aligned themselves with those
who demanded the truth about Rafiq Hariri's murder while still regarding Syria as a friend. But I stressed that many of the Lebanese security
forces sympathised with the Lebanese crowds, personally agreed with
their demands and had no reputation for brutality against their own
people. But the enemies of the 'green' movement in Iran were not
occupiers or soldiers of a foreign country; Iranian protesters were
opposing their very own government.

If the Iranians took any inspiration from their opposite numbers in
Lebanon, the repression of Ahmadinejad's enemies in 2009 also held
vital lessons for Arab dictators who might one day confront similar

civil unrest in their own cities. Syrian president Bashar al-Assad would soon find his own country burning in an uprising far more dangerous than any which confronted the Islamic Republic. The Assad regime watched carefully how the Islamic Republic crushed the opposition and the Syrian president was one of the first foreign leaders to visit Tehran to congratulate Ahmadinejad. The Iranian news agency IRNA reported that Assad 'condemned the interference of foreign countries in Iran's internal affairs'. This same admonition would become canon law among Syrian government officials and newspapers once revolution reached Syria two years later.

★   ★   ★

> I left with a feeling of bitterness towards a system which devoured its own children. When I chanced to cross the path of a former detainee, I pretended not to recognise him. He did the same ... All the regrets I have will do nothing to wipe clean what happened. Now it's my turn to be tortured. I turned towards God, but his forgiveness is easier to obtain than that of ordinary people; it's impossible for me to find the words to beg for it.

Distraught but self-pitying, this former Tunisian policeman, sixty-eight now, was still too frightened to give his name six years after the overthrow of President Zine al-Abidine Ben Ali. A ministry of interior cop and torturer, he was one of the little men who knew how to inflict pain. They exist in their thousands in every Arab regime. When he eventually agreed to tell his story in 2017 to a small circulation francophone magazine, he chose the name 'Ridha' which means 'contentment', a peace of mind he clearly could not enjoy. He had been a carefree young man when he joined the police school in the 1970s, unaware, he claimed, that he was part of a system of repression.

When they taught him how to question suspects, torture was not mentioned. His first act of violence, he said, was against an accused paedophile. 'How can you not slap about a rapist who's destroyed a child's life? Is this torture?' His superiors had learned from their German occupiers in the Second World War, he said, how to use electricity on prisoners. 'We were neither perverted nor sadistic, or at least we didn't think of ourselves like that, even if some of us were more cruel ... we [were] convinced we were in a struggle against the forces

of darkness who were trying to bring our country to its knees.' Small
squads of policemen would interrogate two or three detainees, humiliating them to break their resistance, 'forcing them to undress and to
stand in degrading postures, hitting them with rubber hoses and whips,
leaving as few traces as possible, asking the same questions over and
over'. Then, Ridha said:

> there were more sophisticated methods like the 'chicken on the
> spit', where [the prisoner] was held naked over a fire, beaten and
> had electric shocks administered to sensitive parts of his body, or
> had his head shoved into a container of water, chemicals and
> shit, or even made to impale himself on a bottle. There were
> variations on this, more or less disgusting, depending on … the
> degree of cruelty of the police squad. We were caught up in the
> system.

Suspects would confess to crimes they knew nothing about, 'but we
would pass these on to our superiors and they would submit them to
the juge d'instruction [examining magistrate]. These barbarous methods taught the victims never again to oppose the regime.' The prisoners
were not criminals but were treated as worse than murderers, Ridha
said. He was promoted and now gave verbal orders to others to torture
prisoners, gathering information about Islamists from Omar Suleiman's
Egyptian intelligence service. Thus he progressed from an enthusiastic
police recruit with a safe government job to a retired interior ministry
torturer, a late middle-aged man terrified that his crimes would be
discovered now that the twenty-three-year tyranny of Ben Ali had been
destroyed.

His life reflected the vicious careers of his opposite numbers in
Egypt, Libya, Syria, Yemen and Bahrain and every other Arab state.
Once the police treated the people as the nation's enemies, they have
initiated a necessary routine of humiliation in which the most powerless would inevitably be treated as unworthy of respect. This is what
happened to the now legendary martyr Mohamed Bouazizi, the unemployed street vendor in central Tunisia who set fire to himself after a
policewoman confiscated his vegetable cart and allegedly slapped him
in the face, 'striking the match that literally sparked the Arab Spring'.
Before he died eighteen days later, Ben Ali would hasten with photogra-

phers to Bouazizi's bedside, brows furrowed with concern for the twenty-six-year-old, hospital staff rigid with fear at the presence of the dictator. Too late. The young man became the symbol of the country's self-sacrificing resistance; in the age of jihadi suicide-attackers, his self-immolation was unique for it was intended to cause only his own death. Even this would be ignored in the months to come, for history would treat poor Bouazizi mercilessly once he had expired.*

His story had been told so many times that his posthumous ejection from the Tunisian hall of revolution was probably inevitable. Amid the 42,000 souls of an economically depressed town like Sidi Bouzid, heroes must retain their humility if they are to be honoured. By the time Irish journalist Mary Boland arrived in the town in November 2011, when Bouazizi was being globally credited with starting the entire Arab awakening, his grave had been whitewashed, a plaque to his memory torn down, his act of suicide demeaned by accusations that he had been drinking and had set himself on fire by accident. When Bouazizi's mother accepted Ben Ali's state compensation of $13,000 and moved her family to the coastal resort of La Marsa, she was condemned for abandoning the people of Sidi Bouzid.

The Americans had provided the Tunisians with the moniker of the 'Jasmine Revolution' – as they had bestowed upon the Lebanese the 'Cedar Revolution' – although, as Tunisian geographer Habib Ayeb, caustically noted, 'residents of Sidi Bouzid have probably never seen any jasmine in their lives'. The West preferred to concentrate on those who had died for this daintily named rising without reflecting on how many lives might be destroyed in the vast revolutions that were swiftly unleashed across the Middle East. When I later asked the Lebanese lawyer representing the exiled Ben Ali about Tunisia's most famous martyr, he replied that 'the body of Bouazizi will either be a light in this part of the world, or he will be the fire that will consume it'.

As Tunisia's 'martyrs' increased in number, Bouazizi became more of a statistic while the wealth and corruption of Ben Ali's Trabulsi

---

* In the first weeks of the revolution, Bouazizi's memory was burnished by the retelling of his sacrifice by intellectuals. Tunisian author and psychoanalyst Fethi Benslama, for example, would claim that Bouazizi 'has become an example ... of how each man is reduced by qahr – a word we might translate as "total powerlessness" – and who prefers total annihilation rather than a life as a nobody. I believe that he heralds, or reveals, a change in the role model of the "martyr" in the Arab world.'

family was an obscenity almost as infamous as the list of those his regime had killed. Much of the money was invested by Ben Ali's second wife and her Trabulsi family, members of whom owned or controlled many of the country's biggest financial institutions. Tunis courts, in convictions decided after only a few hours with neither witnesses nor lawyers for the defendant, sentenced the absent tyrant and his wife to a total of fifty years' imprisonment.*

Hosni Mubarak, only days from his own dethronement, watched the fate of Ben Ali with appalled fascination. He, too, had sent his purloined wealth abroad. And like Mubarak, the Tunisian dictator had fed his people election results so fraudulent as to invite open mockery. In 1999, the Tunisian padrone had officially won 99.48 per cent in the presidential election, but in 2004 he gained only 99.44 per cent. Ben Ali, while imprisoning and torturing political opponents, lawyers, journalists, human rights activists, trade unionists and supporters of political prisoners, exhorted his citizens to recall Tunisia's 'three thousand years of history', to remember Hannibal and Ibn Khaldun, 'an inspiration for every loyal Tunisian in this land of openness and tolerance'.

During the 2017 truth commission hearings in Tunis, Sami Brahim, an academic researcher, described his arrest and torture for suspected Islamist sympathies when he was a student two decades earlier. He described how prisoners were forced to sexually abuse each other – precisely the same outrage as Mubarak's prisoners were compelled to perform at the Tora prison complex in Cairo – and of how a doctor then poured ether over his groin, burning his genitals. His treatment was worse, he said, than that perpetrated by the Americans at Abu Ghraib during the occupation of Iraq.

Like Mubarak, Ben Ali became head of Tunisia's general security department; 'a cop to his very soul, he never fully matured' in the words of a former companion. He gave rare interviews to the foreign

---

* Ben Ali, who was seventy-four, died in his Saudi exile eight years later. A story, subsequently investigated by *Le Monde*, said that he and his family had not 'fled' to Saudi Arabia on 14 January 2011 but had travelled to Jeddah for an official 'holiday' visit on a Tunisair flight. The crew, walking into the airport's VIP suite, apparently saw an Al Jazeera newscast claiming that their president had run away to Saudi Arabia. At which point, the aircraft's captain, Mahmoud Cheikhrouhou later revealed, called his airline boss and decided to leave his president behind in Jeddah, taking his plane and crew straight back to Tunis after only two and a half hours on the ground.

press, never held press conferences, yet sometimes revealed his character even to political enemies.

Eric Rouleau, a masterly *Le Monde* correspondent and later diplomat, described how Ben Ali would play games with foreign emissaries in Tunis. He was obsessed, Rouleau recalled, with communications technology – supplied by France – and when the French ambassador paid a courtesy visit to Ben Ali, the president 'asked me with white hot anger why I regarded him as a CIA agent who was eaten up with endless ambition. And he quoted, as evidence of what he said, nearly word for word, the confidential telegrams that I had sent to the Quai d'Orsay ... The ambassador had thus not escaped the intelligence net of [Ben Ali's] spy centre.'

To understand how Tunisians regarded Ben Ali after the revolution, we could study Roger Zerbo's cartoons, in which the president and his family and sycophants are always coloured imperial purple. Ben Ali's bloated relatives were depicted flaunting their new shopping malls while the people – 96 per cent of whom were always said to be Ben Ali's secret police – were beaten by thugs in black uniforms and shades.

No sooner had I bought Zerbo's volume of cartoons than I was driving through the suburbs of the capital with a Tunisian journalist friend who insisted that of all books now published in Tunis, 92 per cent were Islamist. I had no way of checking this figure, but the little town of Sejnane west of Bizerta witnessed, very briefly, the existence of an 'Islamic Emirate' at the end of 2011, when around two hundred Salafists took control of it and turned government buildings into prisons for 'sinners'. Women began to wear the niqab, men to grow beards and wear Afghan-style clothes. A shop selling CDs of Western songs in Arabic was set on fire and a self-proclaimed Islamist judge announced to the owner that 'if you try once more to distract Muslims from the mosque, it will be your home and all those in it who will burn'.

Was this sudden emergence of what we would soon call jihadism the result of outside influence or a natural response to the twenty-three years of political and mental stagnation that millions of Tunisians had been forced to endure under Ben Ali? There is more than one way for a population to set itself on fire. You can burn your body – or you can burn your mind.

Serious investigation strongly suggested that Bouazizi was not alone in his martyrdom. Journalist Olivier Piot, for example, discovered that two other youths had killed themselves in an identical fashion, one in the coastal city of Monastir in March 2010 and the other at Metlaoui in the south-west of the country eight months later. As long ago as 1998, Piot wrote, a study by the burns unit of a major Tunis hospital estimated that 15.1 per cent of admissions were 'suicide by fire'.

As founder and leader of the largest post-revolution party in Tunisia, Ennahda, Rached Ghannouchi initially spent much of his time trying to persuade his fellow citizens – and the West – that he did not want to create an Islamist state. The day before we met well over a year after the revolution, he had just been excoriated by law professor Jamil Sayah (in Zerbo's old target newspaper *La Presse*), who accused him of wanting to 'Islamicise modernity while Tunisians want to modernise Islam'. I suspected that Ghannouchi had not read the article, but he went for the bait:

> I don't believe Tunisians want to change Islam but they want to be modern while being Muslims. Islam is a modern religion. We don't need any surgery on Islam to make it modern. From the beginning, Islam was a pluralistic religion. From the beginning, Islam believed in freedom of religion and conscience, and in the legitimacy of the state in a contract between the citizens and the state.

Then what about the mysterious video, I asked, which surfaced early in 2012, which showed Ghannouchi greeting Salafist leaders and which caused an avalanche of condemnation? There had been a big debate in Tunisia about Sharia law, he replied. The Salafists had held demonstrations in favour and the secular elites in the country felt threatened. Even within Ennahda, there were divisions and its seventy-one-year-old leader claimed that he had to react 'forcefully' to this. He held meetings with the Salafists. He had to convince them that Sharia had been 'linked to many other applications that went wrong in Afghanistan'.

To his immense credit, Ghannouchi was able to avoid both the perils of Morsi-like subservience to opponents within his own party and obedience to the secular-conservative middle classes who wanted to suppress the Salafists. And by remaining leader of Ennahda while refusing any government office for himself, he became an intellectual rather than a political leader of Tunisia. He was not prepared to recreate Ben Ali's archipelago of prisons for opponents of the regime:

> We must be firm with those who break the law ... but some of our opponents, they want us to adopt the same methods as Ben Ali, opening prison camps, arresting thousands of people and using torture and kangaroo courts just because they belong to this group. We say that the law looks at people as individuals, not just as groups. If a driver doesn't stop at a red light, he should not be asked what his ideology is, but told he has broken the law.

★   ★   ★

The man I watched more than three decades ago solemnly saluting a phalanx of black-uniformed frogmen as they flippered their way across Green Square on a torrid night in Tripoli was on the run at last, pursued – like the dictators of Tunis and Cairo – by his own furious people. And in his case by NATO as well.

The YouTube and Facebook pictures told the story with a grainy reality, fantasy turned to fire and burning police stations in Benghazi and Tripoli, of corpses and angry men, of a woman with a pistol leaning from a car door, of a crowd of students breaking down a concrete replica of his Green Book.* Quite an epitaph for a regime we all, Americans and British and Russians, from time to time supported or fawned upon.

Gaddafi was in a class of his own. He wrote another book – appropriately titled, in his present unfortunate circumstances, *Escape to Hell and Other Stories* – and demanded a one-state solution to the Israeli–Palestinian conflict which would be called, so he decided, 'Isratine'. Shortly thereafter, he threw half a million Palestinian residents of Libya out of the country and told them to walk home to their lost land. He stormed out of the Arab League because he deemed it irrelevant – a brief moment of sanity there, one had to admit – and arrived in Cairo for a summit, deliberately confusing a lavatory door with that of the conference chamber until led aside by Mubarak, who wore on his face a thin, suffering smile.

---

* Published in 1975, Gaddafi's thin volume sets out his political philosophy.

Surely now we would be able to rifle through the Tripoli files and read the Libyan version of the Berlin disco bombings, for which a host of Arab civilians and Gaddafi's own adopted daughter were killed in America's 1986 revenge raids. And of the 1988 Lockerbie plane bombing – and the grotesque deportation of its convicted plotter, and the 1989 UTA Flight 722 plane bombing, and of his IRA arms supplies and of his assassination of opponents at home and abroad, and of the murder of a British policewoman in London, and of his invasion of Chad and of the mass killings in his prisons. And – here, yet again, we must draw breath – the secret agreements which Western countries concocted with Gaddafi to help him crush his political enemies and to deliver unto him those whom he would torture for years. And if some profound and terrible files remain undiscovered, the utter hypocrisy of our immediate policy towards Libya would be revealed in a series of creepy memoranda between the UK's own intelligence services and the brutal men who served Gaddafi.

We knew all about Tony Blair's supine 2004 visit to this hideous old man.* Gaddafi was already an addled figure whose 'statesmanlike and courageous' gesture – a phrase emanating from the home secretary Jack Straw when the Libyan leader promised to hand over the nuclear knick-knacks that his scientists had failed to turn into a bomb – allowed Britain's leader to claim that, had we not smitten the Saddamites with our justified anger because of their own non-existent weapons of mass destruction, Libya, too, would have joined the 'axis of evil'. Only days after the infamous Blair kiss and handshake, the Saudis accused Gaddafi of plotting to murder Britain's ally, King Abdullah.

As with all Middle East stories, a historical tale must precede the pageant of Gaddafi's fall. For decades, his opponents tried to kill him. They rose up as nationalists, as prisoners of his torture chambers, as 'stray dog' exiles, as Islamists on the streets of Benghazi, the focus of the final revolt against his rule. And he smote them all. This venerable city had achieved its martyrdom status in 1979 when Gaddafi publicly hanged dissident students in its main square. Yet it was important to remember that, forty-two years earlier, the British Foreign Office had no objection to a coup against 'a weak and unpopular king' by a young

---

* Blair was an official Middle East envoy when travelling on Gaddafi's private jet.

and dynamic military officer who spoke, according to the acting British ambassador, with 'remarkable authority'.

Somehow, until the end, Gaddafi managed to avoid the international opprobrium visited upon fellow despots in Egypt, Syria or Yemen. Just as we regard Mussolini as a buffoon rather than the devil, Gaddafi's narcissism allowed us to indulge in mockery rather than hatred – until we were encouraged to Hitlerise him just before and during NATO's 'humanitarian' attack in 2011.

A Canadian reporter captured this phenomenon perfectly when that year she reviewed the outlandish portraits of a leader who was 'clearly in love with his own exceptionalism'. The faces of Gaddafi, Rosie DiManno wrote, were

> smiley, somber, beatific, pensive, assured, glamorised, imperious ... On horseback and clanging with military medals, crop tucked inside his elbow; turbaned and swaddled in Bedouin clothes; khaki-clad and kepi-capped; saluting in Che Guevara beret and John Lennon tea glasses ... semi-divine, rays of light radiating from his head like a saintly halo ... blessed and blessing, the singular font from which all beneficence springs ... the palpable vanity of an ageing eccentric ... This business of being immortalised has freeze-framed his features in perpetual middle age ... No adoration, however contrived, can ever be quite sufficient.

At the end we saw the tyrant laid out to rot on a concrete floor in a meat locker in Misrata, a lying in state 'so gruesome that the Libyans who formed lines to see him had to wear face masks to filter the odour of putrefaction', the blood washed off his face, eyes closed, a single bullet wound visible under his now lank hair, but other wounds on his body. He would be buried secretly in the desert. 'If that sequence of images inspires the first chapter of the post-Qaddafi era,' wrote Alan Cowell in the *New York Times*, 'then the new Libya will be founded on a legend not of the heroism of its liberators – the militias who resisted the onslaught of pro-Qaddafi forces – but of moral ambiguity and dubious authority, of recourse to untruth in the face of unpalatable evidence.' There had been summary executions, apparently by anti-government militias, in Gaddafi's home town of Sirte.

And like Saddam, tried and executed only for the massacre of Shiites twenty-one years before the Anglo-American invasion of Iraq, Gaddafi might have taken his secrets with him.* But human rights groups pounced on Libyan government archives packed with correspondence between Gaddafi's security services and MI6, who with the CIA had delivered up his enemies for torture. In the end, NATO saw to his death – even though 'regime change' was not supposed to be the purpose of its intervention. A fighter-bomber, believed to be French, attacked his convoy as it left Sirte, wounding Gaddafi; video footage showed him being taunted, beaten and abused by his rebel captors, dragged from a vehicle's bonnet and pulled to the ground by his hair. The camera moves away as gunshots are heard.

His demise was a long time coming. The Arab 'awakening' in Libya began, like the protests in Tunisia and Egypt and subsequently in Syria, with mass street demonstrations by students, academics, defecting government soldiers, lawyers and local families. Western news coverage, already weaned on the dictator-versus-the people storyline which it had adopted in Tunisia and Egypt, dwelt upon the courage of the Libyan rebels rather than the tribalism of the country and, far more importantly, upon the Islamist groups that swiftly emerged among the fighters. The 'Islamic Fighting Group' and the '17 February Brigade' were clearly evident on the streets of Benghazi, but few hints of their existence appeared in news reports when civil war broke out in early February 2011.

Gaddafi's initial ravings – that his real enemies were al-Qaeda and the US, UK and France – contained some substance, but his security forces embarked on a series of killings and then threatened to smash their way into Benghazi, which was now the centre of an opposition 'government'. The story of Gaddafi's hatred for his enemies in Benghazi, whom he vowed to hunt down 'inch by inch', led perhaps inevitably to NATO's intervention. As a later UK House of Commons committee report made clear, European leaders were still haunted by 'the appalling events at Srebrenica' and the West's failure to save the

---

* It is hard to avoid the impression, Cowell concluded, 'that in the murky worlds of intelligence agencies that first tracked Colonel Qaddafi as a sponsor of terrorism, then collaborated with him after his Pauline conversion to cooperation with the West less than a decade ago, there may have been relief that he was denied an opportunity to unburden himself of his manifold secrets'.

Muslim civilians of the Bosnian town sixteen years earlier. But they knew little about the participants in the rebellion, nor the exaggerations and lies which Gaddafi's opponents spread in order to rally Western opinion. And once the US, Britain and France began bombing Gaddafi's tanks, it became 'their' story.

My colleague Patrick Cockburn, now reporting from the front lines in Libya, was almost alone in warning readers of the misleading news reports that characterised this new war. How well, he asked, were journalists performing as the Arab world was convulsed by uprisings against the police states that had ruled it for so long? The reporting in Libya, Cockburn feared, was crudely simple-minded:

> Saddam was once condemned as the source of all evil in Iraq just as Gaddafi is today demonised as an unrelenting tyrant. This picture fosters the lethally misleading belief that once the Satanic picture is removed everything will fall into place, and, whatever the failings of the new leadership, it is bound to be better than what went before.

In February, many journalists – taking their cue from the swift destruction of the Tunisian and Egyptian regimes – believed that Gaddafi's rule would last only a few more days. Brave civilian protesters were driven from the streets of Tripoli, where a handful of journalists were allowed to stay in the Rixos Hotel under close guard from the regime. Up to 15,000 men, many of them Egyptian workers desperate to leave the country, were beaten back by police goons at Tripoli airport as they tried to buy tickets out of the country. Newly arrived and wealthy Libyans bribed immigration officials to allow them a few hours in the city and a safe exit the same day. Tripoli itself appeared about to fall. Would it collapse before the rebels of Benghazi arrived? It would not. Gaddafi's army and paramilitary forces fought back.

Patrick Cockburn was relentless in his criticism of how the war was portrayed. The story that most compellingly illustrated the evil nature of Muammar Gaddafi, he wrote in June:

> is the allegation that he ordered his troops to rape women who oppose him and his acquisition of Viagra-type medicines to encourage them to do so. This tale had been around for some

time, but gained credibility when the International Criminal
Court's prosecutor, Luis Moreno-Ocampo, said he had evidence
that the Libyan leader had personally ordered mass rape. This
week the US Secretary of State Hillary Clinton said she was
'deeply concerned' by reports Gaddafi's troops were engaged in
widespread rape as a weapon of war.

No doubt, Cockburn added, individual rapes had occurred. The one
substantive piece of evidence for mass rape came in May in a survey by
Dr Seham Sergiwa, a child psychologist working with children traumatised by the fighting. She said she distributed 70,000 questionnaires to
Libyans in refugee camps and received 59,000 responses, finding 259
raped women and interviewing 140 of them, some assaulted in front of
their families. But Cockburn recounted how when Diana Eltahawy,
Amnesty International's Libya expert, asked if Amnesty could meet
any of the women, Dr Sergiwa replied that 'she had lost touch with
them and she was the only one who said she was directly in touch with
victims'. Eltahawy told Cockburn that 'we spoke to women, without
anybody else there, all across Libya, including Misrata ... None of them
knew of anybody who had been raped. We also spoke to many doctors
and psychologists with the same result.' She said that she had found no
evidence of rape as a policy. Nor, Cockburn wrote, could Human
Rights Watch find evidence of mass rape.

   All of us journalists were familiar with the atrocity stories that circulated about the West's enemies in the Arab world. They were easy to
believe, often impossible to refute; merely to question them would
provoke accusations from colleagues that the sceptical journalist was
biased or prejudiced towards the wicked regime or indifferent to the
suffering of its victims. Cockburn made no excuses for Gaddafi's brutality, but pointed out that so far 'the only massacre by the Gaddafi
regime ... which is so far well-attested' was the killing of 1,200 prisoners at Abu Salim prison in Tripoli in 1996. But he decided that in Libya,
journalists

have been over-credulous and Western governments self-
serving in pumping out atrocity stories about the Libyan
government regardless of whether or not there is any evidence
for them.

When stories turned out to be untrue or exaggerated, Cockburn wrote, they gained 'scarcely a mention'.*

War reporting, Cockburn added, 'has reverted to what it was during imperial skirmishes in the nineteenth century, with the world getting only a partial and often misleading account of what is happening in Libya.'

The corollary was obvious. Western nations looked with favour upon the 'mysterious self-appointed group' in Benghazi as the leaders of Libya. This enthusiasm, as Cockburn realised, was 'probably motivated' by expectations of commercial concessions and a carve-up of oil fields, the same motives which had led Blair, French president Nicolas Sarkozy and others 'to kow-tow humiliatingly to Gaddafi' prior to the uprising. 'A foreign no-fly zone and limited no-drive zone to defend Benghazi against Gaddafi's tanks could be justified in the early stage of the war, but this rapidly changed into a dubious decision to overthrow Gaddafi.' With considerable prescience, *Independent* columnist Adrian Hamilton described the summit held in Paris in September 2011 in which leaders and foreign secretaries of thirty countries belonging to the so-called 'Friends of Libya' would discuss how they could help a post-Gaddafi Libya. 'In reality,' Hamilton wrote, 'the thirty countries attending, along with twenty aid agencies and international organisations, will be there to see what they can get out of it ... [But] will the West pressure the interim government to keep the Islamists at bay?'†

---

* Our journalistic response to all reports of atrocities in the Middle East was heavily influenced by the history of propaganda warfare. After reports of German outrages against Belgian civilians in 1914 – some of them true, but grossly exaggerated – were used to inflame Allied anger against the Kaiser, British and American officials doubted initial accounts of the Holocaust which reached them in 1942. These turned out to be not only true, but a gross underestimation of the evil committed by Nazi Germany against the Jews of Europe and other minorities. After the Second World War, armies regularly publicised atrocity stories about their enemies, and journalists – unwilling to repeat those initial expressions of disbelief at Nazi war crimes – readily accepted almost any accusation of massacre, mass rape or torture alleged by Western military or political leaders.

† Within weeks, widespread Islamist violence would become a routine part of the Libya war. In early October, more than 200 heavily armed, uniformed and bearded Salafists attacked a Tripoli mosque and smashed the tombs of two imams. Pneumatic drills were used to destroy two Muslim cemeteries near the capital. In Benghazi five months later, Commonwealth and Italian military graveyards from the Second World War would be desecrated.

   The West's policies towards Libya, both before and after Gaddafi's fall, were secretive, ignorant, greedy and lethal – an indictment that its leaders scarcely bothered to conceal, but which the world easily forgot once the Syria war provided more innocent blood for us to gaze upon. Besides the queue of Western politicians seeking Gaddafi's friendship once the Iraq war turned into catastrophe, the UK itself not only serviced the brutal Libyan security regime by providing it with intelligence about Gaddafi's enemies, but organised the kidnapping of the regime's opponents and with the help of the CIA sent them as captives to Libya for torture and interrogation. This shameful policy was inaugurated under Blair's premiership and primarily uncovered by Human Rights Watch in the abandoned offices of Gaddafi's former intelligence commander and later foreign minister, Moussa Koussa. Documents revealed a scandal of international dimensions, proving the complicity of the UK government in the rendition of one of Gaddafi's most prominent Islamist enemies from Malaysia.

   The story of Abdul Hakim Belhaj, founder and emir of the 'Islamic Fighting Group', was to become infamous. Supposedly granted asylum in the UK, he and his pregnant wife Fatima flew from Kuala Lumpur to Bangkok for a transfer flight to London. But by arrangement with MI6, CIA and Thai officials met them in Bangkok and dispatched them to Gaddafi's secret police in Tripoli. Belhaj was to describe six years of torture in the Abu Salim prison as senior MI6 officers badgered Moussa Koussa's office for news of any revelations their victim may have given up. British intelligence operatives handed the Libyans the names of Gaddafi's opponents in the UK, putting pressure on asylum seekers to cooperate with the regime. MI6 sent three of its personnel to visit Belhaj in jail and ask him if he had links to al-Qaeda. When he indicated to them the torment he was undergoing, the British visitors did nothing about it.

   The MI6 'director of counter terrorism', Sir Mark Allen, played a woeful role in this vile relationship, arranging meetings between the UK and Libyan secret services and sharing intelligence information about the regime's enemies and their supposed links to al-Qaeda. The sheer amiability of the UK correspondence is quite staggering. 'Greetings from the British Security Service,' begins one note from 2003. 'We wish to extend our thanks to you for the detailed and very useful information that you have been sharing with us.' On 24

December of the same year, Sir Mark Allen sent the following astounding message to his opposite number:

> Tomorrow is our feast of Christmas. I end by sending you every best wish to you, your family and the people of your Service. Your achievement realising the Leader's initiative has been enormous and of huge importance. It has been a real privilege working with you and I have enjoyed it greatly. At this time sacred to peace, I offer you my admiration and every congratulation. I hope to see you soon. We want you to come to lunch at our Office.

Sending Christmas greetings to Gaddafi's torturers surely demonstrated how polluted had become the Western response to 9/11, and how gravely and morally distorted was our struggle against al-Qaeda. Belhaj's 'rendition' to Libya would follow almost at once; in March 2004, Allen congratulated Koussa's officers on the prisoner's 'safe arrival', adding that his rendition 'was the least we could do for you and for Libya to demonstrate the remarkable relationship we have built over recent years'. Belhaj would later receive £500,000 in compensation from the British government, with prime minister Theresa May acknowledging in 2018 that he had suffered 'appalling treatment'. A UK judge had earlier struck out his case against the British authorities on grounds of 'national interest'. Blair repeatedly denied any memory of the affair.

Just how this disgraceful relationship between British state agencies and the Libyan regime led to the release of the man jailed for the Lockerbie bombing remains something close to a state secret.* Abdelbaset Ali al-Megrahi, one of two Libyan intelligence officers handed over by Gaddafi, was the only man to be convicted of the destruction of a Pan Am airliner over Lockerbie in Scotland on 21 December 1988. His trial, imprisonment, early release and death have

---

* Readers might start their search for the truth of this mysterious but tragic mass killing by studying *Megrahi: You Are My Jury – The Lockerbie Evidence* (2012) by journalist John Ashton, who was a researcher with the legal team representing Megrahi. While it contains its own flaws, several reviewers and the campaigning MP Tam Dalyell were convinced that Ashton's 497-page investigation provided convincing evidence of Megrahi's innocence.

been the subject of legal investigations, public appeals and books, many of which suggested that the case against him was illegally concocted by the CIA to avoid blaming those who were really responsible. Even a Scottish criminal review commission reported that Megrahi 'may have suffered a miscarriage of justice'.*

Megrahi's lawyers lodged an appeal, for a full legal inquiry that would have revealed documents from foreign sources, including evidence from the German police. But by 2009, Megrahi, suffering from terminal prostate cancer, wanted to return home to Libya under a prisoner transfer – which would mean that he would drop his appeal. A mountain of evidence also showed that the Labour government now led by Gordon Brown feared that BP would lose substantial interests in Libyan oil if Megrahi died in a UK prison. Libya had warned the British that such an outcome would have a 'catastrophic' impact on UK–Libyan relations. And it turned out that Brown's predecessor, Tony Blair, had also discussed Megrahi's case with Gaddafi in 2004. So the sick prisoner's release solved two problems: it maintained the UK's trade relations with Libya, and it closed down forever the devastating information that might have been disclosed at a formal legal appeal. Megrahi's grotesque public welcome back in Tripoli was accompanied by a promise from Saif Gaddafi that friendship between Libya and the UK would 'be enhanced forever'.

As for Moussa Koussa, he fled Libya in March 2011, in the early days of the rising against Gaddafi, travelling to Tunis and then, on a Swiss-registered private jet, to Farnborough airfield in England. David Cameron's foreign secretary William Hague said the ex-intelligence commander had been his personal 'channel of communication to the regime in recent weeks', and was now 'voluntarily talking to British officials' in London. The EU lifted sanctions against him and he subsequently flew to Qatar, denying all allegations of torture or responsibility for the deaths of prisoners.

---

* Syria alone in the Middle East was capable of finding the operatives capable of destroying an American aircraft. Yet the moment Syria sent its tanks to defend Saudi Arabia after Saddam Hussein invaded Kuwait less than two years later, all the MI6 truth-telling was switched off. Syria was now an ally of the United States. So the spies and diplomats – and the man from the *Daily Telegraph* – suddenly peddled a new and far less likely story. It was not Syria but Colonel Gaddafi who had destroyed Pan Am Flight 103 over Lockerbie.

Cameron himself boasted in September 2011 that Britain had played a moral as well as military role in removing Gaddafi. The Libyan dictator, he said, was 'a monster'. He was 'responsible for appalling crimes ... and I think the world will be much better off without him'. Cameron chided critics who claimed the UK would run out of bombs during the campaign against Gaddafi. And, in the most wretched prediction of the year, he added that 'people who said this is all going to be an enormous swamp of Islamists and extremists, they were wrong'.

The NATO bombing campaign against the Libyan regime had begun on 19 March, but within two months former British military personnel were warning of the haste with which the UK and its allies had plunged into the war. Their decision was based on UN Security Council Resolution 1973 – which theoretically demanded an immediate cease-fire, an end to attacks against civilians and potential crimes against humanity, a no-fly zone and tightened sanctions. It did not call for the overthrow of Gaddafi. Christopher Parry, a former senior UK Ministry of Defence rear admiral, was among the first to remark that the conflict was 'a classic example of how to act in haste and repent at leisure'. In its concentration on getting rid of Gaddafi, he wrote, 'too little attention has been paid to what happens afterwards'. So short of ordnance was NATO that by June it had run out of 'smart' bombs. The US had to resupply its forces. Washington was also requested to refuel British and French aircraft and furnish the European powers with electronic surveillance. Despite Cameron's reassurances, the French were reduced to using non-explosive 'exercise' bombs to smash tanks and buildings; among their targets – a sign of just how EU nations had been arming Gaddafi since the 1980s – were seven French-made Libyan patrol boats.

Although this near-fatal collapse of European NATO firepower has now been largely forgotten, it was no secret at the time. In June 2011, Obama's defense secretary Robert Gates publicly reminded NATO of its chronic under-investment during the Afghan war, and rebuked the alliance for its performance in Libya. 'The mightiest military alliance in history,' he told a 'security' conference in Brussels, 'is only eleven weeks into an operation against a poorly armed regime in a sparsely populated country – yet many allies are beginning to run short of munitions, requiring the US once more to make up the difference.' But whence came the intellectual underpinning for NATO's war-on-the-cheap, a 'shitshow' according to Obama?

Any account of France's involvement in Gaddafi's demise must include the role of Bernard-Henri Lévy. This philosopher and public intellectual phoned Nicolas Sarkozy from Benghazi and over a patchy line persuaded the French president to recognise the Libyan opposition. And to meet them. He took Mustafa Abdul Jalil, the rebel leader and now head of the 'Transitional National Council' to Paris, where he met both Sarkozy and Hillary Clinton on 14 March. Thus was laid the path to UNSCR 1973 and NATO's assault on the Gaddafi regime. Lévy has never denied his involvement and claims he told Sarkozy that 'if there's a massacre in Benghazi, the blood of the dead will stain the French flag'. To which – again, according to Lévy – Sarkozy replied: 'I don't want to be French president for a second Srebrenica.' Lévy would admit, months later, that the Libyan rebels were 'no angels', and he regretted Gaddafi's killing. But his justification for his own involvement contained a unique form of egoism. 'I'm not elected,' he said:

> I'm not a diplomat. I didn't have any legitimacy in the traditional sense of the word. My legitimacy was that which I gave myself, and which [Sarkozy] then recognised.

But legitimacy of this kind is the same claim to self-entitlement that every dictator bestows upon himself; elections had nothing to do with this. French foreign minister Alain Juppé was understandably outraged at this interference from a man whom he personally disdained and who saw himself as an intellectual of the standing of George Orwell or André Malraux. But in none of his subsequent interviews did Lévy give any indication that he understood the complex tribal realities of Libya that were one of the sources of Gaddafi's 'legitimacy'.* In May, he published a joint letter from 'sixty-one tribes across Libya' who demanded 'a free, democratic and united Libya … once the dictator has gone', hopefully describing themselves as 'a single and united tribe … of free Libyans'. But it was for his presumed leadership of the Western tribes of NATO that Lévy would be most vilified. For more

---

* He would have done well to read the work of Patrick Haimzadeh, a former French diplomat in Tripoli. He has written at length of the Libyan tribes who, for political as well as geographical reasons, supported both Gaddafi and the rebels. Some different allegiances – those of the Zintan and the Machachiya, for example – went back to the period of Italian colonisation. Tribes from Bani Walid, Tarhouna and the Fezzan were loyal to Gaddafi.

than any other individual, Lévy squeezed the physical protection of Benghazi into a quite different direction: the crushing of Gaddafi.

In September 2011, representatives of sixty nations met in Paris to shower symbolic blessings on the 'new Libya', ready to demand the rapid release of $110 billion of frozen Libyan assets to help the newly consecrated Transitional National Council. My Paris colleague John Lichfield reported tongue-in-cheek that 'avoiding "another Iraq" in the "new Libya" – a descent into factional or tribal civil war – was the unspoken purpose of the Paris meeting'. Three years later, Patrick Cockburn noted that David Cameron had not returned to Benghazi since he appeared there in 2011 to tell a crowd that 'your city was an example to the world as you threw off a dictator and chose freedom' – words which he 'evidently wants to forget' as 'warring militias reduce Libya to primal anarchy'. Foreign governments and media alike, Cockburn added, 'have good reason to forget what they said and did in Libya in 2011 because the aftermath of the overthrow of Gaddafi has been so appalling'. In January 2012, aid groups reported that supporters of Gaddafi had been tortured to death; Médecins sans Frontières withdrew from Libya after patients were brought to them by officials between torture sessions.

Asked later whether British policy in Libya in 2011 was civilian protection or regime change, Lord David Richards, then chief of the UK defence staff, told the House of Commons Foreign Affairs Committee that 'one thing morphed almost ineluctably into the other'. In fact, he told an interviewer in May 2011 that 'we now have to tighten the vice to demonstrate to Gaddafi that the game is up and he must go'.* The Americans had much earlier been far more explicit about their aims. Admiral Mike Mullen, chairman of the Joint Chiefs of Staff, testified to the US Congress on 31 March that 'the policy of the President is one to see Qadhafi out, to see regime change'.

★   ★   ★

* On behalf of the UK government, Richards – still the head of the defence staff – also drew up plans to train and equip a 100,000-strong Syrian rebel army to overthrow Assad, a scheme later abandoned by the British cabinet. After his retirement in 2013, Baron Richards of Herstmonceux would become an adviser to the United Arab Emirates government and the American arms company DynCorp.

'Massacre – it's a massacre!' the doctors were shouting. Three dead. Four dead. One man was stretchered past me in the emergency room, blood spurting onto the floor from a massive bullet wound in his thigh. A few feet away, six nurses were fighting for the life of a pale-faced, bearded man with blood oozing out of his chest. 'I have to take him to theatre now,' a doctor screamed. 'There is no time – he's dying!' Others were closer to death. One poor youth – eighteen, nineteen years old, perhaps – had a terrible head wound, a bullet hole in the leg and a bloody mess on his chest. The doctor beside him turned to me, weeping. 'He has a fragmented bullet in his brain and I can't get the bits out, and the bones on the left side of his head are completely smashed. His arteries are all broken. I just can't help him.' The wounded were not militiamen; they were mourners returning from a funeral, Muslims shot down by their own security forces. But this was not Libya.

Nor were Western leaders calling for the overthrow of the autocrat who ran Bahrain, a king who insisted on being addressed as 'His Majesty' even though his pocket-size emirate was more than two thousand times smaller than Libya. Nor was NATO about to defend the unarmed demonstrators who were at the mercy of the local king's police and soldiers. They were Shiites confronted by a monarch representing a Sunni minority. And while Libya now lay open to anarchy and the West's greed, King Hamad bin Isa Al Khalifa of Bahrain had an insurance policy that any Arab nation might envy: a guarantee of its little kingdom from its Sunni Saudi neighbours, a headquarters for the US Fifth Fleet with more than 4,000 American military personnel, and a base for the Royal Navy. This was not the moment for Obama's liberalism and Cameron's moral triumphalism to hinder the suppression of Shiite Bahrainis demanding freedom, a 70 per cent majority whose only sympathetic ally – and then only notionally – was Iran.

Outside the Salmaniya Medical Complex on 18 March 2011, a hospital orderly was returning with thousands of other men and women from the funeral of one of the demonstrators who had been killed at Pearl Square the previous day. 'We decided to walk to the hospital because we knew there was a demonstration,' he told me. 'Some of us were carrying tree branches as a token of peace which we wanted to give to the soldiers near the square, and we were shouting "peace, peace". There was no provocation – nothing against a government.

Then suddenly the soldiers started shooting. One was firing a machine gun from the top of a personnel carrier. There were police but they just left as the soldiers shot at us. But you know, the people in Bahrain have changed. They didn't want to run away. They faced the bullets with their bodies.'

The protests now occurring at the hospital had already drawn in thousands of Shiites – including hundreds of doctors and nurses from all over the Bahraini capital of Manama, still in their white gowns – but their anger turned to near-hysteria when the dying and wounded were now brought in. Up to a hundred doctors had crowded into the emergency rooms, shouting and cursing their king and their government as paramedics fought to push trolleys loaded with the latest victims through screaming crowds. One man had a thick wad of bandages stuffed into his chest but blood was already staining his torso, running down his jeans, dripping off the trolley. 'He has a live round in his chest – and now there is air and blood in his lungs,' the nurse beside him shouted at me amid the confusion. 'I think he is going.'

Rumours burned like petrol in the little island of Bahrain that evening and many medical staff were insisting that up to sixty corpses had been taken from Pearl Square the previous day, and that police were seen by crowds piling bodies into lorries that were driven across the causeway to Saudi Arabia. It was easy to dismiss such ghoulish stories; the entire 'revolt' and its aftermath, including state torture, in reality cost the lives of only forty-six Bahrainis. But why had the royal family of Bahrain allowed its security forces to open fire at peaceful demonstrators? To turn on Bahraini civilians – Shiites as well as Sunnis were a well-educated, intellectual people – with live fire seemed like an act of lunacy. It allowed seven Shiite political societies to call the deaths 'a heinous massacre', which was clearly an exaggeration. But the government inquiry was to accept that the protests represented 'a cross-section of Bahraini society' and those of us who covered this tragedy found ourselves interviewing poor Shiites from the villages, students, lawyers, intellectuals, trade unionists, doctors, clerics, even airline pilots.

The demonstrators had decided they would turn Bahrain's Pearl Roundabout – a highway interchange dominated by the monument of a giant pearl to represent the fishing heritage of the old village of Muharraq – into their 'Tahrir Square', complete with tents, a 'media centre' and a handful of kebab shops. Originally, their demands were simple enough, a constitutional monarchy but an elected prime minister – although this would almost certainly have taken the executive out of the hands of the Khalifa family in favour of a Shiite leader. King Hamad had just granted every Bahraini family a bequest of $2,600 and expressed his regrets at the first deaths. At the start of the protests, Crown Prince Salman spoke to opposition leaders – he was a popular man who had helped rid the monarchy of the more sinister and cruel apparatchiks who had countered earlier Shiite opposition with torture and banishment. One young woman told me she and her friends would gladly carry the crown prince on their shoulders around the square if he would come and talk to them. Such goodwill did not last long.

For the dull, heavy, inescapable power of Saudi Arabia lowered over the island of Bahrain. The Saudis were fearful that the demonstrations in Manama and in the towns outside might kindle equally provocative fires in the east of their kingdom, where a substantial Shia minority lived in Dhahran and other cities close to the Kuwaiti border. The Sunni princes and sheikhs of the Arabian peninsula were all agreed that they would tolerate no Egyptian-inspired revolutions, especially in a tiny kingdom with an overwhelming Shia majority ruled by a Sunni minority which included the royal family. Inevitably, what had started as a 'moderate' revolution demanding only a constitutional monarchy and an elected prime minister turned – after more state killings and the usual torture of detainees – into a rebellion against the king. Less than a month later, Saudi troops would enter Bahrain to crush the rebellion.

King Hamad bin Isa Al Khalifa, whose clan connections with Bahrain dated back to 1796 and whose family's rule was cemented by a treaty with Britain in 1820, might not have been in danger had his 'reforms' – much publicised by his Western public relations companies – really allowed the Shia a greater say in government. But the Khalifas' rule had been disruptive, embittered by family disputes, British arrogance and an abiding fear of both Saudi Arabia and the majority Shia. Bahrain possessed a giant refinery to service the Saudi oil industry but spent its energies constructing an international financial centre which provided a refuge for the banks fleeing the Lebanese civil war. For visitors who did not drive beyond Manama to the poor Shiite villages to the south, it seemed a secure, hot, almost tropical island ruled by a socially anglophile tribe.

King Hamad went to school at Godalming and Cambridge before attending the British army's officer staff college at Aldershot. Crown Prince Salman gained a master's in history and philosophy at Queen's College, Cambridge. There was a habit among Western correspondents of regarding Bahrain – with its wealthy Sunni elite, its earnings from banking and tourism, its largely British ex-patriots and its friendly Gulf Air crews – as a rather cosy little Ruritania, as novelettish in its pretensions as it was welcoming to its European and American visitors. Its hotels and nightclubs – before Dubai became an alternative oriental fantasy city – provided women and alcohol to a clientele of visiting financiers, diplomats, bored US and European naval personnel and expatriate bankers. And thousands of whisky-starved Saudi tourists.

The British vouchsafed Bahrain its 'independence' in 1971 and secured a treaty of friendship with the Al Khalifas' statelet, but a combination of British security officials, London department stores and English road signs turned the centre of the capital into Bahrain-on-Thames. Its friendly immigration officials smiled at Western visitors.

Even when I arrived just after the start of the February 2011 protests, the immigration officer at Bahrain International Airport did little more than glance at my passport. Was I the Robert Fisk who wrote books about the Middle East? he asked. I was indeed, I beamed ingratiatingly. In that case, he said with an equally warm smile, he would like a copy of *The Great War for Civilisation* – in Arabic. And of course, I had that very edition in my hand baggage – for exactly this moment. The visa was immediate. Welcome to Bahrain. Like Shiite forbearance, this amiable reception would not be forthcoming much longer.

For beneath Bahrain's membrane of urbane tolerance, there lay constantly the 'undemocracy' of Bahrain. To maintain its family power and its status as a Saudi satellite, the Khalifas had to suppress their Shiite majority. In 2011, we forgot the earlier, longer and equally violent Shiite uprising of the 1990s in Bahrain when both leftist nationalists and Islamists together protested over the lack of human rights and demanded a return to the 1973 democratic constitution. They had good reason to demonstrate. The emergency laws allowed imprisonment without trial, widespread torture, deportation and loss of citizenship. Britain regularly but mildly complained, not least when Bahraini opposition politicians – who did not need a visa to enter the UK – were bundled onto flights to London and then, after their arrival, deprived of their citizenship. But Britain's involvement in the suppression of Bahraini dissent went much further than this.

Ian Stewart MacWalter Henderson had torturers on his staff in Bahrain. By 1996, he was the most feared of all secret policemen in the Gulf, the director general of security and head of Bahrain's State Investigation Department, a sixty-seven-year-old former British Special Branch police superintendent whose officers routinely tortured prisoners, both in the basements of their headquarters and in the al-Qalaa prison. According to witnesses, they maimed inmates with power drills, sexually abused prisoners and sent child detainees home in body bags. For thirty years, Henderson was the colonial power behind the throne of Sheikh Isa, and clearly the perfect man for the job. As a police officer in Kenya, he had fought the Mau Mau and was twice awarded the George Medal by Queen Elizabeth for suppressing the native uprising. Perhaps his greatest achievement was the capture of Dedan Kimathi, the Mau Mau leader who led the armed struggle against colonial rule and who was executed by the British in 1957.

Moving to Manama as a servant of Britain's Bahraini ally, Henderson quickly established himself as a most frightening individual. Shiite villages were ransacked in much the same way as Kenyan hamlets sympathetic to the Mau Mau had been destroyed. Bahrain's political opponents called him 'the Butcher of Bahrain'.

In late 1995 and early 1996, I spent weeks travelling in Lebanon, Syria, Qatar and the UK, interviewing former Bahraini prisoners who provided consistent – and, as we journalists like to say, compelling – evidence of severe beatings and sexual assaults, all carried out under Henderson's responsibility. A leading Shia clergyman described to me how he was beaten with a cane by a Jordanian Special Investigation Service colonel called Adel Flaifl, who was also Henderson's interpreter. The same man was accused of torturing a young Shia woman in 1985 by tying her to a pole in the SIS headquarters and beating her insensible with his fists. One former prisoner claimed that in the 1980s, he was sexually abused in Henderson's headquarters by another British officer who forced a bottle into his anus in an attempt to persuade him to reveal the names of Shia opponents of Sheikh Isa's regime. The man identified the Briton by name – and I confirmed that a British officer of the same name worked for Henderson at the time.

This tale of cruelty – insignificant as it might appear against the epic savagery meted out at the time to prisoners in the jails of Saddam Hussein or Hafez al-Assad – was part and parcel of the same uprising which confronted King Hamad in 2011. Many of the middle-aged men who participated in the Pearl Roundabout protests told us they had been tortured in Bahraini prisons in the 1990s. Some even mentioned Henderson and Flaifl. For these ex-prisoners, the 'Arab Awakening' of 2011 was part of a continuing thirty-year struggle for freedom, electoral representation and equal rights.

Henderson himself was a bespectacled, almost avuncular figure whose politeness was as legendary as his staff's brutality. He never personally harmed a prisoner – nor, so far as it was known, had he been present at torture sessions – and his fourth-floor offices and archive rooms in Bahrain's SIS headquarters suggested the workplace of a hard-pressed civil servant rather than that of a secret policeman. Those who visited these rooms thought that Henderson regarded himself as a bit of both. His wife was his personal secretary, a woman in her mid-sixties who, dressed in a brown, one-piece suit – 'like any English housewife,' as one ex-detainee described her – ushered prisoners into her husband's office for interrogation. Sometimes, Henderson preferred to meet important prisoners at the Al Hidd headquarters of the Bahraini interior ministry Special Forces whose all-Pakistani units smartly saluted Henderson on his arrival and guarded him during his daily swim near the Bahrain dry-dock complex. Local newspaper photographs of Henderson, which never identified him by name, invariably showed him next to the interior minister, Sheikh Mohamed al-Khalifa, and the ministry's director of training, Colonel Hassan Issa al-Hassan.

Sheikh Khalil Sultan, a prominent Shia clergyman, met Henderson twenty times in 1995 during a series of negotiations that briefly halted the insurrection against Sheikh Isa – talks which proved that the former British colonial police officer played a personal role in dealing with opposition demands for the return of parliament and constitutional democracy. 'I was arrested at my home at midnight of 1 April ... during the unrest in the villages outside Manama,' Sheikh Khalil said:

There was no warrant for my arrest. I was blindfolded and
handcuffed. I was taken to SIS headquarters where Colonel Adel
Flaifl came into my cell and attacked me with his cane, whipping
me six times on the head, face and thighs. He was furious. He
said: 'I don't have time for you because we are busy with the
other [prisoners]. Tonight is the finish of you – all of you.' Then
he left. But nothing happened.

Up to 2,000 more prisoners were incarcerated by Henderson's security
police as rioting and disorder continued in Bahrain. Sheikh Khalil, now
invited to meet the interior minister, was then told that he and two
other Shia leaders could offer proposals for an end to the unrest to
Henderson in person. They were taken to the top floor of the SIS building where Henderson's wife told them to go into his room:

There were others present, including another Briton whose
name was 'Brian' ... Henderson had receding hair and a chalk-
white face; he was wearing a suit and tie. He was very courteous
and shook hands with each of us. He could say "Ahlan wa
sahlan" [welcome] in Arabic, but he couldn't speak the language
– Colonel Adel Flaifl translated for him.

Sheikh Khalil and his two colleagues suggested that the protests in
Bahrain could be ended by releasing all non-sentenced prisoners, an
amnesty for sentenced prisoners, the return of deportees, work for
Bahrain's unemployed, freedom of expression, the restoration of the
constitution and parliamentary elections – which at one point would
be the very same demands of the 2011 protesters. In 1995, Henderson,
according to Khalil, said these proposals would solve the crisis. But the
talks continued without effect for four months. Then, after the Shia
prelate agreed to end opposition propaganda against the government
– he recalled that he 'spoke in mosques, urging people to be calm, and
they obeyed' – he was freed. He travelled to London to talk to the
exiled opposition, only to hear that the interior minister had reneged
on the agreement.

There were further mass arrests, followed by beatings at the SIS
headquarters. Three Shia clergymen – Sheikhs Ali Salman, Haidar Fikri
and Hamze Deir – were forced to stand for hours without sleep and

refused medication by Flaifl, according to Khalil, and then deported. And here again, is a direct link to the events of 2011; for it was Sheikh Ali Salman, now secretary general of the Al-Wefaq National Islamic Society, the largest political party in Bahrain, who spoke at Friday prayers on 4 February that year before an estimated crowd of 5,000 to compare these 2011 protests with those in Tunisia and Egypt and to demand peaceful elections. Two weeks later, Salman was prepared to lead Friday prayers at the Pearl Roundabout in the presence of the crown prince as a gesture of reconciliation. The king's son appeared on state television to state that talks with the opposition had begun and that 'a new era' had started in the history of Bahrain, one in which 'this nation is not for only one section – it is not for Sunnis or Shias. It is for Bahrain and for Bahrainis.' And so after two days of bloodshed, tens of thousands of Shiites – a few Sunni trade unionists and Bahraini journalists among them – ran back into the square on 19 February, chanting, singing and waving roses.

Yet by the afternoon, many of those who had stormed joyously back towards the Pearl monument from which they had been driven by the police and army were now going further in their aspirations, demanding the abolition of the monarchy itself. Many held posters of Saddam and Mubarak and Ben Ali, all of the portraits crossed out in black alongside a portrait of King Hamad and the words 'Down, Down Hamad'. Crowds sang 'Go away Khalifas' and told us journalists that only a new constitution and the trial of police and soldiers who had fired at them with live ammunition would end the protests. Men and women in the square asked us how Bahraini troops could have shot at their own citizens. But a proportion of the 'Bahraini' troops turned out to have been Pakistani soldiers employed by the Bahraini security authorities. And most of these Pakistanis had shown no hesitation at all in shooting at their own fellow citizens as well as the Taliban in the massive offensives against Islamists in Pakistan itself over the past three years. Speaking Urdu, Pushtu and even Baluch, these men also constituted a core unit of the Emirates army. And if Obama was now insisting that there should be no more violence by the Bahrain security forces, I wrote in my report to London, 'you can be sure that the Saudis would have been advising the opposite'. Why couldn't the Bahraini authorities accept democratic elections if the protesters were prepared to have a constitutional monarchy? I asked a junior member of the royal family next day. He smiled at my innocence. 'The Saudis would not permit this,' he replied.

Nor would the Saudis have been worried by Obama's squeamish words when it came to King Hamad. At the UN, the American president praised recent 'reform and accountability' in the kingdom and declared that Bahraini 'patriotism' was more powerful than 'sectarianism'. He did not mention the thousands of Bahrainis 'protesting peacefully, standing in the streets, dying for the same values that this institution is supposed to stand for' as he did with Syria. The Friday prayer meeting with the crown prince was cancelled by Sheikh Ali Salman when the former declined to say in advance how far he would go in meeting the Shia demand for reform. There was also a distinct note of anger against America when men and women in the square found – amid the debris of the protesters' camp destroyed on 17 February – dozens of tear gas rounds imported from the US.

The actions of the Khalifa regime over the next few days in Bahrain were almost identical to the system of sadistic but ultimately useless repression which Henderson, Flaifl and his men used a decade and a half earlier – but on this occasion, the monarchy also enlisted the army of Saudi Arabia and the Emirates. Not that they had much choice. On 14 March, Saudi troops in armoured vehicles and soldiers from the United Arab Emirates – the latter necessary to give the flavour of an international Gulf project to the Saudis' arrival – crossed the causeway and entered Bahraini sovereign territory. The Khalifas claimed they had invited the Saudis to come, although their own army contained 30,000 men. 'This is not an invasion of a country,' a White House spokesman insisted, thus deliberately avoiding any parallels with Saddam Hussein's 1990 invasion of Kuwait.

So the protests were doomed. According to the official investigation which appeared the following November, the Bahraini authorities feared Iranian 'intervention' in the country although there was no sign of such a prospect, save for the condemnation of the government's actions by the Iranian foreign ministry. But there had been serious sectarian violence and, as the crowds again grew in number, 'armed' men were seen on the streets, albeit carrying only knives or iron bars. Pakistani expatriates were attacked, two fatally. Then on 16 March, two days after the arrival of the Saudis, thousands of Bahraini soldiers and tanks advanced on the Pearl 'square' behind clouds of tear gas. At least four protesters were shot dead and two policemen were run over and killed. Mass arrests started at once. The official November report – which might have been written about Henderson's men in the 1990s – stated that 'arrested individuals were ... transported to police stations where they were subjected to various forms of mistreatment the most common of which were beating, kicking, slapping, lashing with rubber hoses and verbal insults directed in particular at Shia religious beliefs'.

In an obviously planned campaign of destruction, Bahraini security forces with the help of Asian workers proceeded to demolish fifty-three Shia religious structures in towns and villages. Despite government claims that the destroyed buildings had been erected without official permission, at least five had been given a royal deed and an official building permit. Bulldozers and cranes were used to turn mosques into rubble; the Momin mosque had been a place of worship for 400 years. In Nuwaidrat, the grave of a Shia holy man called Mohamed Abu Kharis, who died 200 years ago, was dug up and his bones scattered. This was not just an anti-Shia pogrom, it was a Wahhabist assault every bit as devastating as the Saudi campaign against shrines and graves.

Throughout their inevitably hopeless uprising, the Shiites insisted on demonstrating their allegiance to Bahrain. Their 'revolutionary' banner was the red and white Bahraini flag. The protesters included some of the best-educated Bahrainis in what was the best-educated state in the Arab Gulf. Ali al-Ekri, a distinguished pediatric orthopaedic surgeon, was arrested on 17 March and sentenced to five years' imprisonment for treating injured protesters, released only in 2017. A twenty-year-old student poet, Ayat al-Gormezi, claimed she was beaten with electric cables after reciting a poem criticising the monarchy at a pro-democracy rally. It contained the line: 'We will kill humiliation and assassinate misery.'

Local Bahraini newspapers naturally biased their coverage in the government's favour – one journalist who reported the protests was even fired by the editor who had sent him to cover the events – and carried many letters and articles supporting the regime by writers with English names who identified themselves as UK expatriates or British-born naturalised Bahrainis. Most condemned the Western media, repeated sectarian slanders against the island's Shias and praised King Hamad. 'Blood has been spilled here in Bahrain and the vultures are swarming here to feast,' one article announced, referring to newspaper and television reporters as 'self-centred journalists being spoon-fed a diatribe of anti-government propaganda', 'bloodhounds' and 'blood-hungry hacks … salivating at the prospect of the next scoop of the hour'. An Anglo-Bahraini woman attacked Sky News' coverage of the wounded protesters in the Salmaniya Medical Complex, insisting that 'Bahrain is a shining beacon to the world that multiculturalism can and does work … His Majesty has been incredibly patient … the people [sic] of Bahrain will continue to stand unstintingly behind their leadership'. A British woman reader in Bahrain wrote personally to me, abusing Dr Ekri while claiming that Shia citizens 'have families of thirty children and four wives'.

Far more whimsical was the decision by the Bahrain government's information office to ask the British Press Complaints Commission to condemn me for 'pursuing an agenda to attack and smear the government of the Kingdom of Bahrain' and accusing both myself and Patrick Cockburn of covering the protests in a 'grossly oversimplified' manner. The Independent responded by publishing the original Bahraini complaint and subsequently urging readers to acquire the official investigation into the violence – which was far more devastating in its revelations of government abuses and torture than anything Cockburn or I had written.

Britain itself was now the target of growing criticism, both for its arms sales to Bahrain and the work of the UK National Policing Improvement Agency – a title containing its own disparaging message – which had helped train the Bahrain police force, as well as those of Libya, Qatar and Saudi Arabia. Britain's defence – insisting that human rights elements were incorporated into its overseas police training programmes (which presumably included the Tunisian police torturer 'Ridha') – looked ridiculous when armed UK-trained Bahraini police squads were attacking democracy demonstrators. Until the protests began, Britain had been supplying Bahrain with assault rifles, sub-machine guns, shotguns, sniper rifles and hand grenades, earning £6.4 million in arms sales in the year ending 2010.

Yet far from now demanding freedom for the majority of Bahrain's population, British prime minister David Cameron in May 2011 invited the Bahraini crown prince for an official visit to the UK, exchanging a warm handshake with Sheikh Salman outside 10 Downing Street as the latter set out to repair his kingdom's reputation for violence. There were obvious reasons for what the *Independent* called Britain's 'morally offensive' selective blindness. The Royal Bank of Scotland alone revealed that it had £302 million of loans tied up in Bahrain, and in April 2011, the Bahrain British Business Forum looked back on what it called 'a record year'. Yet in that same month of May, Cameron's foreign secretary William Hague was organising EU sanctions against Syria after Assad's troops fired on protesters.

We do not know how Ian Henderson, Bahrain's former security boss, reacted to the 2011 uprising. He had retired to his Dartmoor home in the English west country fifteen years earlier, weighed down with honours from the monarchy he so faithfully served. He was to die in 2013, untroubled by the numerous accusations of brutality made against him by human rights groups. In 2000, Scotland Yard's Serious Crimes Branch organised a lacklustre investigation of Henderson's outrageous behaviour in Bahrain but no charges were ever levelled against the most trusted of the king's foreign servants – despite evidence from disfigured torture victims who were able to identify him.

In July 2002, British Carlton Television broadcast a half-hour documentary on Henderson's career in Bahrain, 'Blind Eye to the Butcher'. It disclosed a Foreign Office report which mentioned Henderson – and was probably written by Sir Anthony Parsons, a former political agent at the British embassy in Bahrain in the late 1960s and later ambassador to Iran. An extract from the document describes how 'over the past three years [Bahrain] Special Branch under the able leadership of Henderson has established a dominating position over the subversive [*sic*] groups'.

Nor, in those sensitive days immediately following its publication, was the Bahraini royal family bereft of advice from another experienced former British police officer. For in early December 2011, the Bahraini monarchy hired 'Yates of the Yard' to advise on the reform of its security services. John Yates had been Assistant Commissioner in the London Metropolitan Police Service, holder of the Queen's Police Medal for coordinating the police response to the 2004 tsunami in the Indian Ocean. Yates ran the British 'Special Inquiry Squad', investigating cash-for-honours accusations in the UK, but retired in 2011 after severe criticism of his handling of a re-investigation of the *News of the*

World phone-hacking scandal. Lord Justice Leveson would refer to Yates' approach during the later inquiry as an 'inappropriately dismissive, defensive and closed-minded attitude'. This obviously did not worry his new employers in the Bahraini royal palace who hired Yates less than six months after his resignation from the Met.

He arrived in Bahrain, in his own words, 'to reform the practices of the police force' along with former US police chief John Timoney, an Irish-born officer who had transformed the Miami police department – with a reputation for recklessly shooting civilians – into a force which did not fire a shot for almost two years. The *New Yorker*, no less, described Timoney as 'one of the most progressive and effective police chiefs in the country'. But confronting protests against a 2003 trade summit in Miami, Timoney was bitterly criticised for organising the extensive use of pepper spray, rubber bullets, tasers and batons against protesters.

Neither Yates nor Timoney were accused of encouraging the brutalisation or torture of Bahraini prisoners, but even after the arrival of the two police 'experts', condemnation by human rights groups continued. The Bahrain Centre for Human Rights logged thirty documented cases of Bahrainis dying after confrontations with the police or security forces between November 2011 and March 2012. Reports persisted in 2012 of Shiites accused of plotting with Iran to overthrow the monarchy. The Anglo-Danish Redress NGO complained in 2013 that detainees from the 2011 protests had still not been released, that policemen were never charged with torture – but with 'assault resulting in death'. In early 2013, a prestigious medical ethics conference in Bahrain was cancelled by Médecins Sans Frontières after the authorities failed to give written permission for the meeting at a Manama hotel to go ahead. Jonathan Whittall of MSF in the Middle East said that the conference had been intended to 'restore trust in the health system of Bahrain' because health facilities in Bahrain had become a battleground during the 2011 protests. The Irish president of the Medical University of Bahrain resigned. He had received a verbal assurance from the crown prince that the event would go ahead – 'I want this conference to happen,' he apparently told the university president – but the necessary written permission never arrived.

Only months later, the Washington-based Human Rights First movement called on the Obama administration to withhold arms sales because King Hamad had not fulfilled his promised reforms. In January 2014, Shia crowds fought police after a twenty-three-year-old died in custody. The Bahrain justice minister sought to suspend the Shia Al-Wefaq party; then the government ordered Tom Malinowski, the US assistant secretary for human rights, to leave Bahrain after he met leaders of Al-Wefaq, including Sheikh Ali Salman. The Obama administration failed to react, although the State Department devoted forty-nine pages of its 2014 report on human rights to Bahrain, detailing arbitrary detention, torture, prison overcrowding and constraints on free speech.

Incredibly – an overused word which in this case is justified – many of these abuses were almost identical to those I was writing about two decades earlier. The reports of torture and deaths in custody after the 2011 demonstrations were interchangeable with my own files of Amnesty International records of equivalent events in the 1990s. In November 2014, an inmate was beaten senseless by Bahraini security police and thrown into solitary confinement where he died from his wounds. In the summer of 2016, the Bahraini government closed down Al-Wefaq, stripped Bahrain's Shia spiritual leader, Ayatollah Isa Qassim, of his citizenship and doubled a prison sentence on the veteran opposition leader Sheikh Ali Salman, the secretary general of Al-Wefaq. The sheikh – once, of course, a detainee of Henderson and now an essential figure in the theatre of the absurd which Bahrain constructed around his existence – is, at the time of writing, still in prison. Sentenced to four years in 2015 for speeches he made in 2012 and 2014 – he had then dared to call for a peaceful settlement of the 2011 demonstrators' demands and the arrest of those committing human rights abuses – Ali Salman was arraigned yet again after a successful appeal court hearing in 2018, and sent to prison for life. The evidence for this latest travesty in justice was based on a telephone call Salman made to the Bahrain prime minister, Khalifa bin Salman Al Khalifa, eight years earlier. Nothing, in other words, had changed.

But amid Bahrain's rule of repression, detention and death, there was one unique opera bouffe performed by the royal family and its faithful retainers: to persuade the world – despite all the evidence to the contrary – that Bahrain was just an ordinary, freedom-loving, peaceful little kingdom in the Orient, as beloved by its Western friends (and Saudi Arabia) as it was suffering only from occasional troublemakers and unspecified 'activists' on the streets. The key word was normality – demonstrated most potently by the holding of the Bahrain Grand Prix in 2012, only a year after it was cancelled because of the Arab uprising in Manama. The island was safe for this great international sporting event, the Khalifas insisted; more than that, it was a symbol of national unity. Sport – however much a parody its physical expression might be in the circumstances – was supposed to be above politics. The UK Foreign Office urged fans to stay away, but the crown prince turned the arguments round. Having decided to stage the race, he announced that 'cancelling just empowers extremists' – thus proving that sport had a good deal to do with politics, especially of the violent kind.

He did not have to worry. Those kings of motor-racing Jenson Button and Lewis Hamilton were only in it for the sport, they announced. 'I think it's a lot of hype,' declared German driver Sebastian Vettel. The Formula 1 boss Bernie Ecclestone said it was 'business as usual', arguing that 'the press should just be quiet and deal with the facts rather than make up stories' – as if the death and torture of protesters in Bahrain was fiction. Suppose, I asked in the *Independent*, if Bashar al-Assad had been hosting the Formula 1 weekend. Would Ecclestone have been dining out in Damascus, happy to give the regime a soft sporting cover for its oppression? But none were as convinced of Bahrain's integrity – nor more loyal in upholding its government – as the writer of a long and sometimes bitterly argued post-Grand Prix article which appeared in the *Daily Telegraph* on 24 April 2012 under the self-pitying headline: 'Bahrain is bewildered by the world's hostility'.

Yes, terrible 'things' had happened in 2011 and the king had acknowledged this; some of the thirty-five deaths had been at the hands of the security forces. But there was to be a new police ombudsman, 500 extra 'community police officers', a new police 'code of conduct' and the CID was being reformed, the article promised. 'I am not an apologist for what happened last year,' the writer lamented, but 'like many Bahrainis and expats ... I am bewildered by the level of criticism aimed at a nation that has acknowledged its mistakes'. This small nation had been left amazed at the level of ignorance about what is really happening here, at the level of animosity and bile, at the media bias. And bewildered that so many in the UK ... could so readily swallow everything opposition groups and activists were saying ... Headlines suggested that the country was in flames ... I do not wish to trivialise the situation in Bahrain. There remain difficulties [sic], all of which require political solutions. But this is not Syria ...

Henderson would have approved. The article was written, the *Telegraph* explained, by 'the former UK Head of Counter-Terrorism', John Yates – 'Yates of the Yard'.

14

The Men in White Socks

... I think too of
The conquered condition, countries where [...]
Courts martial meet at midnight with drums,
And pudgy persons pace unsmiling
The quays and stations or cruise the nights
In vans for victims, to investigate
In sound-proof cells the Sense of Honour ...

W. H. Auden, from *The Age of Anxiety: A Baroque Eclogue,*
Part One (Rosetta), 1947

Waiting in Aeroflot's Moscow lounge for a flight back to Beirut, I was attracted by a Russian magazine containing a feature on the Prophet Mohamed. I cannot read Russian, but the article was illustrated with an extraordinary sixteenth-century oil painting of the Prophet riding up to heaven on the Night of Power, his face covered with a veil, his horse Buraq galloping up to the seven heavens for Mohamed's ultimate arrival at the throne of God. In the painting, his journey was surrounded by gouts of golden fire that curled and writhed across a pitch-black surface. It crystallised the fearful, magnificent, brave and terrible events that I was witnessing with my own eyes across these lands of super-history.

And never would there be more golden fire and darkness as in Syria. I had been visiting this country for three and a half decades. And the moment I heard in 2011 of civil unrest and anti-Assad demonstrations in Damascus and then Daraa, I knew what to expect. In my Beirut

archives, I searched back to some of my first reports from Syria after I
arrived in the Middle East as a correspondent for *The Times*. I had
almost forgotten one series of dispatches, which I filed from Aleppo in
1980 – all of thirty-one years before the civil war broke out. These
telexed reports of mine were a ghostly template of what I would be
writing as the civil war reached Aleppo in 2012. Were it not for the
rusting staples and the creased old paper I might have been persuaded
this was an aberrant version of my current reports. But sure enough,
on 26 March 1980 I reported from northern Syria on how the country's
deputy interior minister had

> just sent a report to his superior on the violence in Aleppo and
> the central city of Hama. Usually, the minister's weekly report is
> just half a page in length but this document covered five full
> pages and listed outbreaks of rioting and shooting not only in
> Aleppo and in Hama but in the towns of Deir ez-Zor on the
> Euphrates, Idlib and at Maarat al-Numan where the army
> maintains a well-guarded barracks. More significantly, the
> document gave the casualty toll as eighty dead in Hama – nearly
> all of them Baath party officials – and almost a hundred dead in
> Aleppo, most of them civilians.*

And all this was almost a year before the mass Islamist uprising in
Hama in February 1982, which I witnessed and wrote about at the
time. I had over decades written dozens of long analyses of Syrian
history, its treatment by the Ottomans and then by the French, whose
colonial instincts were to infect Syria as surely as they spread the virus
of sectarianism. Syria, I often recalled, was always accused of being
expansionist, yet its experience was one of territorial amputation and
loss. First came the one-armed French general Henri Gouraud, who
tore Lebanon from Syria in 1920 and gave it to the pro-French
Christians. Then Paris handed the Syrian coastal city of Alexandretta to
the Turks in 1939, in the hope that Turkey would join the allied Entente

---

* Turkey was accused of plotting with the regime's opponents. Necmettin Erbakan's
National Salvation Party – to which a youthful future Turkish president, Recep Tayyip
Erdogan, belonged, and which called for a less secular, more Islamic government in
Ankara – was reported to be plotting against Hafez al-Assad's regime. The parallels with
his son Bashar's war – far in the future – were suffocating.

against Hitler.* Then in the Six-Day War of 1967, Syria lost the Golan Heights, subsequently annexed by Israel. After Rafiq Hariri's assassination in 2005, the Syrian Baath party's cynical twenty-nine-year attempt to re-dominate Lebanon had ended in bitter withdrawal.

Now, in 2011, the Damascus regime of Bashar al-Assad would be driven out of more than half of Syria itself. The terrifying civil war was therefore not only about the survival or destruction of a brutal regime. It was also an attempt by the country's rulers to prevent the final division of Syria at the hands of Turks, Kurds and Americans and, indirectly, Saudi Arabia and the other Gulf kingdoms. They would use ISIS and other Islamists in an effort to destroy Assad. His allies would come from the Shiite Lebanese Hizbollah, Shiite Iran and the Shiite militias of Iraq and Afghanistan, and from Russia.

These were heady days. Gaddafi was still on the run in Libya, Egypt was in post-revolutionary chaos, Bahrain's uprising only recently crushed, and Yemen, after weeks of bloodshed, now possessed two governments. Syria's war had only just begun. I could even sympathise with the chairman of the US Joint Chiefs of Staff, Admiral Mike Mullen, when he expressed his feelings at a Washington news conference earlier in 2011. 'Never,' he said, 'have I seen so much happening so quickly in so many different places at once.' Perhaps Syria would be different. Assad had himself told the *Wall Street Journal* in January 2011 that despite events in Tunisia and Egypt, Syria would remain 'stable'. Scarcely a year earlier, I was listening in Abu Dhabi to a discussion among Sweden's Middle East ambassadors. In the light of later events, Stockholm's man in Damascus was especially intriguing. He talked of Syria's 'dwindling oil resources' and the need for a competitive economy 'if the regime is to survive', but concluded that Syria was 'a politically stable country in the middle of an unstable region'.

In its condemnation of Middle East dictatorships, the West has usually judged these corrupt and cruel autocracies according to their usefulness to the West. If the tyrants were allies, we would describe them as 'strongmen' who imposed an 'iron rule' over their people but who remained 'loyal friends'. Ben Ali, Mubarak, the Shah of Iran and the monarchies of the Gulf fitted this description. So, from time to time, did Saddam Hussein – when he was invading Iran rather than Kuwait

---

* The Turks obliged – but not until 1945, nine weeks before Hitler killed himself.

– and even Gaddafi, when he was offering up his nuclear playpen to our intelligence authorities. Those who fell outside this pliable category were monsters; Saddam, for example, after he had invaded Kuwait, or Iran's new leaders after they dethroned the Shah. And, save for a few smiles from the Nixon and Carter administrations and a French president or two, the Assad père et fils slotted neatly into the role of despots.

The strongman/tyrant routine also depended on the amicable nature of the 'loyal' dictators towards Israel. Mubarak, Ben Ali and the Gulf Arabs and King Hussein of Jordan passed this test with almost full marks.* Saddam's hatred for Israel could sometimes be accommodated, depending on his equal hatred for the Iranians and his relationship with Saudi Arabia. Ruling over a land containing almost 150 billion barrels of the world's oil reserves also helped. Petty miscreants who did not own a state, 'revolutionaries', secessionists or irredentists might be forgiven – even admired – if they acquiesced in the power of the West's friends, although this could induce vertigo in the chosen few. Arafat's transition from super-terrorist in Beirut in the 1980s to super-diplomat after making peace with Israel in the 1990s and then back into super-terrorist after he refused Israel's truncated version of an independent 'Palestine' in 2000 was enough to induce paroxysm.

But the Assad caliphate was, in that most unimaginative of Baathist rhetoric, steadfast. The regime of Hafez and Bashar was the 'beating heart of Arabism', the 'rock of Palestinian resistance', the 'mortal enemy of Zionism' and, inevitably, the true friend of the Soviet Union and its somewhat truncated, but equally tyrannical successor. Unless Kissinger needed a ceasefire on Golan or Obama could arrange direct negotiations with Israel, Syria and its Shia Alawite leaders were untrustworthy, barbaric, sadistic, terrorists, murderers and executioners.

For those of us who lived in the region and were burdened with the cursed privilege of visiting these torture states, it was impossible to persuade visitors that a certain perspective might be adopted if anything like reality was to colour their view of evil incarnate.

There was an unhappy tendency to excuse the father's ruthlessness as mere pragmatism. Hafez al-Assad always regarded Arafat as 'a conniving politician who was rarely true to his word'. Years later, he

---

* The Plucky Little King Mark 2, Hussein's son Abdullah, took the throne after his father's death in February 1999.

would tell his adviser Bouthaina Shaaban that 'I saved Arafat from three assassination attempts. In looking back, I don't know if what I did was right!' But with internal dissent, Hafez did not display such humour. He was prepared to negotiate via intermediaries after the Aleppo violence in 1980, even after the slaughter of Alawite army recruits. But two years later, faced with a campaign by the Brotherhood around Hama, he crushed the revolt in blood and executions. 'Death a thousand times to the Muslim Brothers,' Assad jeered. So what would Hafez have done if confronted by the Syrian war of 2011? Bashar's diplomats and soldiers would tell me they asked this question of each other many times.

Since the Brotherhood in the 1980s was regarded in the West as an Islamist danger – al-Qaeda was then an unthinkable future nightmare, the ISIS apocalypse unimaginable – there was little international reaction to the Hama massacres, save for the usual condemnation of Amnesty and other humanitarian organisations. The Brotherhood was seeking freedom and independence from the Assad family – but it never demanded democracy. This was the all-purpose jewel for which the US and Europe might be prepared to support potential allies in the Arab world.

It was easy to satirise Syria's wearying five-year economic plans, its pitiful pro-government rallies, its peasant fealty to the Assad family, its servile parliament and genuflecting members. Presidential speeches at these miserable sessions in Damascus would be interrupted ad nauseam by the 'people's representatives', shrieking their eternal love for Hafez or Bashar, and their willingness to sacrifice their blood and soul for them. I only came across the like of this in one other city; not in Cairo, nor in Tripoli, but in Washington. When Israel's prime minister Netanyahu addressed a joint session of the US Congress in 1996, he was interrupted by applause fourteen times; in 2011, he received twenty-nine standing ovations from American Representatives; in 2015, Netanyahu was interrupted thirty-nine times by rounds of applause. US Congress members might not be ready to shed their blood for Israel, but they were prepared to sacrifice their souls.*

---

* Palestinian human rights lawyer Raja Shehadeh has scornfully compared the Syrian parliamentarians' response to Bashar with 'these venerable senators and members of Congress … exhibiting the herd-like mentality of sheep, rising on their hind quarters and clapping their hooves for this inveterate warmonger'.

Bashar's intelligence operatives, however, were no laughing matter. State security, military intelligence, Baath party security, Air Force Intelligence, the Presidential Guard information centre and Ministry of Interior intelligence were supposed to spy on each other; but this was a slightly imaginative confection distributed by regime underlings to gullible journalists and diplomats. There were indeed powerful rivalries between the Syrian interior and defence agencies, but a skein of trusted officers were given Bashar's attention. Some controlled the 'Lebanese file', while others spread their influence and protection through the separate espionage groups of the Palestinian movements based in Syria. These most senior officers had no interest in physical brutality, but they worked hard on suspicion and theory. Many of them had been in service for more than two decades.

When ISIS struck at the heart of the regime with suicide bombs in Damascus in July 2012, one of the most feared figures in the Syrian intelligence network, Bashar's brother-in-law Assef Shawkat, was assassinated. The Christian defence minister Daoud Rajiha died with him. But the senior mukhabarat network did not perish. It was a shock, yet since the early days of Hafez al-Assad, the Baath could absorb almost any earthquake. Its Alawite-tribal core and the loyalty of the old army officer class was the reason why Bashar could survive the longest and most terrible civil war in the Arab world. And it was the Syrian army that would finally save him, along with Russia's ruthless military campaign.

The depth of Bashar's information authorities, however, gave him both self-confidence and a dangerous contempt for America's own vast intelligence operation in the Middle East. The Americans, Bashar would tell a group of US congressmen on 30 December 2009, possessed a 'huge information apparatus', but lacked the ability to analyse the information they gathered. 'You're failing in the fight against extremism,' Bashar crowed to them. 'While we lack your intelligence capabilities, we succeed in fighting extremists because we have better analysts.' The Syrian president praised his then close cooperation with Turkey's state security police and the information with which this provided him. 'In the US, you like to shoot [terrorists],' he said. 'Suffocating their networks is far more effective.' In fact, 'suffocating' these networks in the tunnels they groined through the living rock beneath Syria's cities would become a vital part of the strategy of destroying the country's opponents.

Bashar was perhaps the only Arab leader who shared the Iranians' ability to understand the Americans better than the Americans understood them. Hafez the father was a man of short temper but infinite patience, an apparent contradiction but one that allowed him to act with fierce emotion while encouraging the dreary paternalism of cabinet meetings at which vainly ambitious ministers would assent to anything that avoided change. Syrian foreign policy towards Israel would be to maintain precisely the same policy as Hafez followed: land for peace, but the return of land before peace. The Israelis wanted to enjoy peace before ceding a square mile of territory – and both Hafez and Bashar understood what this would mean. They had watched Arafat betray the Palestinians by agreeing to exactly this Israeli demand. They would not do the same.

This taught Bashar that, however insurmountable his antagonists might appear and whatever threat his external enemies might present, their wish did not constitute the deed. If he was utterly divorced from Syrian public opinion at the start of 2011, Bashar understood very well the most flagrant error of his enemies: wishful thinking. Repeatedly in the early years of the civil war, the utter conviction of European and American leaders that Bashar al-Assad would be overthrown was based not on any objective criteria; it was founded on the romantic notion that because he should be destroyed, he could and therefore would be destroyed, ending his days in exile like Ben Ali, in a hospital like Mubarak or preferably cut down in horror like Gaddafi.*

Horror was a word that always pertained to Syria's torture chambers although, as we have seen, Western nations were prepared to secretly collude in their pain by submitting questions for the victims to answer, courtesy of Syria's interrogators. Under Hafez, the brutal suppression of freedom in Syria provoked Human Rights Watch to publish an entire book on the frightfulness of the country's prisons and torture chambers in 1991. My own archives on human rights abuses in the country are shelves in length. They include a twenty-page Amnesty

---

* Béchir Ben Yahmed, the Tunisian journalist who founded the inestimable French weekly *Jeune Afrique*, was the first to grasp that Obama, Hillary Clinton, François Hollande, Sarkozy, Cameron and numerous media correspondents had made fools of themselves 'because we took our desires for reality'. Politicians and writers failed to take account of the regime's allies – Iran, the Hizbollah and Russia, and of its determination to survive.

file on the continued imprisonment of physicians since 1980, a sixty-four-page Human Rights Watch document on the suppression of Syrian Kurds and thousands of pages of individual appeals for political prisoners, some of them in their eighties. With Bashar's succession in 2000, a 'Syrian Spring' was supposed to have arrived as the former optometrist followed his obsession with the internet by permitting the country to go online, a privilege that ended for some with arbitrary arrests. Government officials would remind journalists, unofficially, that Bashar had now forbidden all torture – an assurance undermined for me when a mukhabarat officer whose family I knew remarked to me offhandedly 'unless it is really necessary'.

The Amnesty and Human Rights Watch reports dwindled in the first half of 2000, the former welcoming the release of 600 political prisoners in November, but within five months it was recording the arrest of Hassain Daoud, 'interrogated and tortured continually' about Kurdish activists after being forcibly returned to Syria from Germany following a failed asylum request. Riyad al-Turk, a seventy-one-year-old lawyer who had been incarcerated for eighteen years under Hafez al-Assad for opposing the government, was in September 2001 taken to the Adra prison just after heart surgery, because he was a leading member of the National Democratic Alliance. Some very elderly prisoners were freed after only a few weeks in the summer of 2003, but this did not indicate any compassion on the part of the security police. In the same month, Khalil Mustafa, a Kurdish activist, died after torture in the military detention centre in Aleppo. His body was returned to his family with a leg broken in two places – and a missing eye. In 2004, more than thirty Syrian Kurds were killed by government agents in sectarian football riots in Qamishli.

Again in 2004 – seven years before the Syrian uprising – Amnesty was reporting that 'the authorities have arbitrarily arrested scores of Islamist activists including nationals from other countries', at least fifty of whom had been arrested during night raids across Syria. Amnesty identified fifteen of the detainees but it was unclear why the Syrian mukhabarat decided to launch this campaign of arrests. These men did not appear to be Brotherhood supporters. So were these 'nationals from other countries' the same 'foreign fighters' who had been attacking American occupation forces in Iraq? Had the US asked the Syrians to seize these men?

But the seizure of non-violent and respected figures in the unofficial Syrian opposition continued, as the old intelligence generals of Hafez al-Assad's era frightened Bashar into suppressing all signs of dissent. Why, we might ask, did the Syrian security services have to arrest Dr Alfred Thoma, Dr Yasser al-Aiti, Jabr al-Shufi, Fayez Sara, Ali al-Abdulla and Rashed Sattouf in December 2007, only days after they – along with 163 other Syrians – had attended a meeting of the 'Damascus Declaration for Democratic Change'? They never called for the end of the regime. The delegates had elected Dr Fida al-Hurani as head of the organisation. She, too, was detained and her husband, Dr Gazi Alayan, a Palestinian who had lived in Syria for eighteen years, deported to Jordan.

As they say in police reports, the net spread wider. The Syrian artist Talal Abu Dana was arrested in Aleppo, his studio trashed and his paintings destroyed. Then in February 2008, Kamel al-Moyel from the hill town of Zabadani was picked up by the men in white socks.* Already sentenced and in prison was Michel Kilo, a prominent Christian intellectual who helped to found the 'Declaration' movement. But when the detainees were at last brought to the Palace of Justice, Ali al-Abdulla appeared to have bruises on his body. Judge Mohamed al-Saaour, the third investigative judge in Damascus, presided over the case at which the prisoners were accused of 'spreading false information', forming a secret organisation to overthrow the government and for inciting 'sectarian and racist tendencies'.

So why all this sudden anger towards these self-declared democrats? It subsequently turned out that on 4 December 2007, just before the first arrests, President George W. Bush met at the White House with former Syrian MP Mamoun al-Homsi, with Ammar Abdulhamid, an exiled Syrian author who had already called for the overthrow of the Assad government, and Djengizkhan Hass, a Kurdish opposition activist. Nine days later, an official 'source' leaked the meeting to the media, which is when the men in white socks pounced.

The Damascus newspaper *Tishrin* demanded to know why Washington was showing such concern for human rights in Syria. Was

---

* Almost all Middle East mukhabarat men wear white socks. Perhaps there is a clothing emporium with a concession for the region's secret policemen. The only ones who do not wear white socks are the Israeli variety, who wear old baseball hats.

not the American-supported Israeli blockade of a million and a half Gaza Palestinians a violation of the rights of man? Had not the Arabs seen all too clearly Washington's concern for the rights of man in Abu Ghraib and Guantanamo? But in that case, why on earth did Syria feed America's campaign against it, with regular arrests of middle-aged academics and even, it transpired, the vice dean of the Islamic Studies Faculty at Damascus University?

Bashar, like his father, could indulge the nationalists of Syria – but not those who would question his legitimacy or point out the sectarian nature of this nationalist autocracy. But he also felt obliged to indulge the corrupt foundations of his own family, as his relatives enriched themselves through the banks, shopping malls, land deals, mobile phone companies and the degraded army which returned in disgrace from Lebanon – a country whose venality contaminated the Syrian military leadership as soon as they arrived as 'peacekeepers' in Beirut in 1976.

The system of billionaire family nepotism has been researched at length, but the personal dangers of its power were frightening. One of Bashar's deputy prime ministers told me later that after his appointment, Rami Makhlouf – Bashar's maternal cousin and a billionaire Syrian businessman who controlled the country's mobile phone concession, Syriatel – personally congratulated him:

In the evening, when I got home to Malki, there was a knock on the door. 'This is for you,' a man said, and there was a brown envelope. I opened it and there was a set of diamond jewellery inside – all diamonds. I closed it. I called Rami Makhlouf to thank him – and asked him to send the same man back to pick up the gift. [Then] I talked to the president. 'Mr President,' I said. 'Your cousin has just sent me a gift to bribe me.' And Bashar Assad replied: 'If you had accepted, he would own you.' Then Rami Makhlouf called. 'You refused the gift,' he said. 'But why did you have to tell the president?' Bashar Assad trusted me. 'No one dares to say a word about your integrity,' he told me.

It was clear that Bashar understood that a close member of his own family might try to purchase one of his ministers – but he clearly could not break free of the corruption that threatened his regime. It embraced the entire security system and the Baath party. Most damning of all was that Bashar allowed this all-consuming poison in the body politic to continue at a time when Syria was enduring its harshest economic crisis in a generation.* In his January 2011 interview with the *Wall Street Journal*, Bashar was reported to have told reporter Jay Solomon that Syria was 'immune' to the uprisings in the Middle East, but he never used that word. He described Syria as 'stable' and compared it favourably to Egypt, which had 'been supported financially by the United States, while we are under embargo by most countries of the world'. Syrians 'do not go into an uprising,' he said, because they possessed something more important than their own problems and the need for economic reform. 'It is about the ideology, the beliefs and the cause that you have.'

But socialism and nationalism were not enough when corruption existed alongside mass pauperisation. Remarkably, Assad seemed well aware of the dangers he faced, and he expressed them in a largely ignored passage of his interview. Wherever one travelled in Syria, he said:

> you have poverty and the situation is getting worse day by day and we have five years of drought ... So, we will have less wheat; we used to export wheat and cotton every year but this year we have problems ... This year, three million Syrians out of 22 million Syrians will be affected by the drought.

Only nine months after Assad was bemoaning an economic situation 'getting worse day by day', Michel Kilo, one of the 'Declaration' prisoners, explained that the Assad government's 'liberal' reforms had destroyed the sources of income of the rural and small-town populations in Syria, the very people from whom the regime 'derives

---

* Makhlouf was as loyal as he was corrupt. In 2011, he told his 80,000 Syrian employees they would be fired if they protested against the regime. He would only be brought low in 2019 when Bashar sent the mukhabarat to demand millions of dollars of unpaid 'tax' from his billion-dollar business empire, including Syriatel. In a pitiful Facebook appearance addressed to the president in 2020, Makhlouf even complained of Syria's 'inhumane' security forces!

protection ... for the military security order'. In some regions, 12 per cent of Syrian farmers abandoned their lands or transformed 15 per cent of their farmlands into feed for livestock – along with drought, here was a primary reason for the lack of wheat. Expropriation of land 'for public purposes', impoverishment and forced migration, Kilo would write, meant that refugees were 'drawn to tin-roofed shanty towns in the suburbs of the cities'.

And these were the very slums where the opposition was to rise against the regime. Watching the Tunisian and Egyptian revolutions on their televisions, Syrians, wrote Kilo, 'could see with their own eyes how weak and unarmed people could defeat a security state'. They concluded that the regime's nationalism 'was nothing but the nationalism of regulation and control, suppression and division'. And all this, Kilo added, while a few lived in 'aristocratic opulence' and youth unemployment, officially estimated at 7 per cent, could be as high as 70 per cent. Like the Western governments, however, Syria's protesters would premise their confidence on moral rather than material grounds. It was the same old fatal equation: that the regime that had crushed its people for four decades could and would be destroyed because it should be destroyed.

The 'crushing' of the people continued right up to the moment of revolution. Could there have been a more pathetic symbol of humiliation than the nineteen-year-old Syrian girl dragged into a Damascus security court in February 2011 to be sentenced to five years' imprisonment for using the internet 'to reveal information to a foreign power that should remain secret'. Tal al-Mallouhi's real crime was to ask for a role in shaping the future of her country and to complain that Obama should do more for Palestinians.

By chance, Khaled Yacoub Oweis, the Reuters correspondent who had bravely covered al-Mallouhi's pitiful court appearance, followed a reporter's instinct by heading a few days later to southern Syria to interview the penniless local gravedigger at Tisia, the farmer forced to turn wheat crop into animal feed, the old man trying to survive in the abandoned Roman city of Bosra. 'You cannot keep pressuring people like this,' the old man told Oweis. This was the only journalism that counted in a revolutionary world: the shoe-leather reporter on the ground who went after the story. Just two weeks later, the Syrians withdrew Oweis' accreditation for his 'unprofessional and false coverage of events'.

And in the months that followed, no foreign correspondents could enter the country and the few Lebanese journalists working for international news agencies were harassed by mukhabarat agents. The regime hoped to stifle the uprising by controlling news reports of the protests. But by denying foreign reporters the opportunity to cover events themselves, the regime obliged overseas news organisations to rely on the technology of its opponents. There was no way of verifying their social media websites and mobile phone footage of violent confrontations but since this was the only reportage available, it was disseminated around the world. If there was a propaganda war to be won, Syria lost it from the first day.

We cannot even be sure on which day the Syrian revolution began. Was it in the southern town of Daraa where in early March 2011 the security police arrested a group of school pupils for writing anti-Assad slogans on a wall? Around fifteen of the teenagers were taken to the local police station, routinely beaten and mistreated for up to a month. Some were said to have had their nails torn out; one was reported to have been killed and then dumped outside his family's front door. Another more credible report would have it that the boy was shot dead in a demonstration in the days that followed. In any case, it was the kind of cruelty that came naturally to those with the arrogance of power, not least the local head of the 'Political Security Directorate', Atif Najib, who was a cousin of the president.

Or did the revolution begin more than a month earlier, on 26 January, when Hasan Ali Aqlah, a Syrian in Hasakah, a city in the far north-east of the country, set himself on fire with gasoline in protest at government policies? Here surely could be observed the incendiary influence of Mohamed Bouazizi's self-immolation in Tunisia. But there had already been a torchlight demonstration in Raqqa by crowds angered at the killing of two local Kurds. In Damascus in February, shopkeepers spontaneously ran to the defence of a young man being assaulted by police.

Syrian friends of mine arriving in Beirut would speak excitedly of the unprecedented feeling of rebellion in the country, although their remarks were often accompanied by the conviction that Assad must be unaware of his own government's repression. This was preposterous; these men and women were, I felt, unconsciously hoping to avoid the violence of Egypt – and especially Libya – by somehow persuading themselves that

Bashar could be 'uncoupled' from his own security apparatus. The idea that the white knight of Baathism could obtain transubstantiation into protector of the Syrian people was a romantic but dangerous illusion.

Bashar did release thousands of non-political prisoners, and promised jobs to all university graduates. But this was tokenism. There was no great enthusiasm among Syrians to enjoy the presence of newly freed thieves on their streets, any more than Assad and his coterie wished to share their power with educated opponents of the whole ramshackle state – which was why political prisoners remained in their cells. Nor was there an obvious desire on anyone's part to open the prison doors for members of the Muslim Brotherhood. But there was a growing and visceral determination to share the apparent freedoms won by Tunisians and Egyptians. Why should Syrians not deserve – and share in – this same honour and dignity?

Honour and dignity were certainly at stake in the traditionally rebellious Hauran, in the south of which stood the ancient Canaanite city of Daraa.* When the mothers of the schoolchildren held in captivity turned up at the police headquarters in the city to demand their release, they were abused. Then, much more seriously, a group of tribal elders went to see the city's governor, Faysal Kalthum, to demand an explanation for the behaviour of the police. According to a Syrian Druze friend of mine who said he was present, each of the men placed his turban on the governor's desk as a traditional gesture of negotiation. But Kalthum took the turban of the most prestigious sheikh, threw it on the floor of his office and stamped on it. The people of Daraa came out in their thousands to protest. Bashar – playing, I suppose, the role of protector – hastily dismissed his governor. As always, too late.

AFP reported on 20 March that one man had been killed, a hundred others wounded. Christians joined their Muslim fellow citizens in demanding an end to the government's violence. The Baath party headquarters in the city were burned, along with Rami Makhlouf's regional Syriatel mobile phone offices. Bashar now sent his deputy foreign minister Faisal Mekdad, a native of Daraa, to face the bereaved families of the city.

---

* Hitherto known as a scruffy station on the old Ottoman Haj railway line from Damascus to Medina, its buildings were principally famous as the location of T. E. Lawrence's supposed sexual humiliation at the hands of Turkish officers in 1917.

It was another eight months before I could question Mekdad about his role. A bespectacled, academic figure in his late fifties, a former Syrian diplomat at the UN, Mekdad sat in the sparkling new Starship Galactica foreign ministry in Damascus, arguing that 'the old Syria will never come back ... it will be a country free for the press'. This did not sound reassuring to me, but Mekdad put on a brave face. The demonstrations in Daraa had been peaceful, he agreed:

> What happened should never have happened. I was sent to
> Daraa to give condolences for the dead. I faced angry people. I
> told them the president did not want this to happen, that the
> president had nothing to do with it. I gave them the president's
> condolences and they said they knew mistakes were made ... He
> fired the governor and he established an independent judicial
> committee to investigate. What I do know is that armed groups
> are killing demonstrators.

The videos uploaded to YouTube from Daraa had told a different story. Mekdad's account of the bereaved parents' acceptance of the president's innocence and his assertion that an 'independent' committee would investigate the killings were on a par with the claim that 'armed groups' were killing the protesters.

The first two innocents to be shot dead by Assad's men were Mahmoud al-Jawabra and Husam al-Ayash, and when crowds then protested outside the Omari mosque, another eight men were shot dead by state security cops. No shots were fired against government forces in this period, but a state television clip of the early demonstrations clearly showed a man with an automatic rifle strapped to his back, standing behind the crowds. Peaceful street protests broke out in many Syrian cities, crushed with ever increasing savagery by military special forces, security agents and militiamen. As accounts emerged of the further murder of unarmed protesters in Damascus, Daraa and other Syrian cities, there sometimes emerged stories of how fear was injected into the people. A report published in the *Independent* contained an eyewitness account of routine thuggery in a city police station, recounted by a man who had been arrested for filming a street demonstration. The corridor in the security building, the witness said, was fifteen metres long, and in the middle, seated at a desk, was a general in green military fatigues while

> all around him, people huddled on the floor, most of them young men with the same anxious look. There were about fifty, some of them from Daraa … The biggest group of prisoners was crouched in a heap next to the curtain. One looked as though part of his right eye had been gouged out; another missing a section of his nose. Both were probably no more than sixteen years old … Soon, an enormous man in a white T-shirt and pyjama bottoms emerged from behind the curtain. He seized a young teenager and took him behind the barrier. He was there for about three minutes … All I could hear was his screams. When he was brought back out, his head was covered in blood. They had tried to slice half of his face off. The general, who sat at his table drinking herbal tea and listening to a Lebanese singer on a stereo, said nothing.*

In Beirut, I was receiving similar accounts from opposition protesters. One young man I knew emailed me from Amman after fleeing his home in Damascus in April with an account of his travails at the hands of state security.† His anger at events in Daraa and in the Alawite 'capital' of Latakia boiled over in his message:

---

* The *Independent*'s source for this story was impeccable – and in Damascus, Alastair Beach, our stringer in Cairo, had persuaded the Syrians that he was a tourist. He had completed a year's Arabic language course in Damascus in 2010, his passport contained plenty of Syrian entry stamps, and his excuse – to be returning 'to see my old friends' in Damascus – was good enough for the Syrian visa officer. But in order to avoid discovery once he reached Syria, Beach used the pseudonym of 'Khalid Ali' as his own by-line. And he could only identify the terrified man whom he interviewed as 'Mohamed'.

† Saad Ajmal had rashly tried to videotape a demonstration in Marjeh Square in Damascus – where the Syrian interior ministry is located – to find more than a hundred security cops in the street, shouting praise for Bashar al-Assad. He hid his video-phone, but found himself surrounded by dozens of government agents shouting 'he is taking video!!' 'Five guys hold me … and started beating me … they took my phone, my identification card and my money … they said why are you taking video bastard?? We will kill you all enimies [sic] of assad, Syria belongs to assad not to you bastard people!! Immediately I said "I am with you guys!! We all follow president assad even to death!" They said then why are you taking video? I said because I am happy there is demonstration calling for the greatest leader assad, they let me go [but] there was one man (looks like officer) caught me and slapped me … I don't know how I could escape it was a miracle.'

[W]ill Assad hang his brother Maher because he killed thousands people during the last years and recently in Deraa? The gang in Lattakia are Alawiyeen gang belong to Assad family, we all know them in Syria they are called shapeeha [shabiha], the people in Lattakia were demonstrating against the government and afterwards the secret service, police and army brought these shapeeha to scare people and kill them. In Syria we are not demonstrating for food or money, we want to change the whole system and hang all Assad family …

This was the first time I had come across the word 'shabiha', which, loosely translated, means 'ghosts', a pro-government killer militia whose existence the regime always denied. The shabiha included Sunni as well as Alawite-Shia fighters, originally created by the Assad family in the 1970s to control smuggling and protection rackets.

On 22 April, Alastair Beach was reporting the shooting to death of at least forty-nine protesters across the country, a day after Assad had lifted a forty-eight-year-old 'state of emergency'. Since the first killings in Daraa, rights groups in Damascus were claiming that 220 civilians had died. Among the reliable sources at this early stage of the war was Nadim Houry, Human Rights Watch's senior researcher on Syria. 'It's clear that the Syrian security forces are prepared to go very far to quell this,' he told me at the time. 'But people need to brush up quickly on the history of Syria. There is no easy path to transition there – there are no independent institutions. The youth movements are controlled, the unions are controlled by the Baath party.'

Assad's predicament was already clear. Having gazed with two faces at Daraa – first, the physiognomy of rage and then the paternal gaze of suspicious love – he was now at his most vulnerable. Every dictator knows that when he starts making concessions, he is in the greatest danger of being overthrown. Each concession, each balancing act, each freeing of prisoners, and the crowds demand more. Had he not lifted the state of emergency for Syrians? Had he not allowed them permission to protest peacefully and released more prisoners? Had he not scrapped the hated security courts? In Damascus, in Hama and in Banias and Latakia and Daraa, they still came out in their tens of thousands. They wanted 6,000 more political prisoners freed, they wanted an end to torture, an end to the mukhabarat. And they wanted Bashar to go. 'Nothing is more corrosive than blood,' wrote Issa Goraieb, the editor of *L'Orient-Le Jour*, that traditional voice of the Lebanese Christians. 'And nothing is more perishable than a concession offered only under pressure from the street.' Perhaps sensing that the Syrian-supported Shia militiamen of Hizbollah might soon have to fight for Assad, one of Goraieb's colleagues reminded readers that the Iranian-funded movement boasted of its struggle for 'the liberation of Arab peoples' but that its good intentions had 'stopped short at the gates of Syria'.

These bloody events were now assuming a macabre quality all their own. In several cities, snipers would attack crowds – and would then shoot at mourners attending the funerals of the dead. On the following day, government forces would return to open fire on the mourners attending the funerals of the mourners shot dead the previous day. Still waiting for a visa, I would sit in my darkened front room in Beirut, watching Syrian state television's nightly newscasts. They were a horror show. Naked corpses with multiple bullet wounds, backs of heads blown away. But these were not murdered protesters. They were Syrian soldiers, the television insisted, murdered by 'the treacherous armed criminal gangs' near Daraa.

These pictures showed the bodies, newly washed for burial, taken from the Tishrin military hospital in Damascus. Their ranks and identities were read out as they were carried in flag-draped coffins from the army's mortuary by military police. They were from Tartous, Banias, Aleppo, Damascus. When the funeral cortege of a soldier called Nida al-Hoshi was passing up the Mediterranean coast road to the north, the newsreader added, the mourners were ambushed by 'an armed gang'. It was easy to be cynical about these images and the gloss put on their deaths. Shooting at funerals, after all, had hitherto been the prerogative of the government's own 'armed gangs'. And Syrian television had shown not a single dead civilian or civilian funerals after the killing of 320 demonstrators in more than a month.

But if these dead soldiers were victims of revenge killings by outraged families who had lost their loved ones at the hands of the secret police, it meant that there was an opposition prepared to use arms against their aggressors. And if there really were armed groups roaming Syria, then Assad's regime was indeed on the road to civil war.

According to those who were bravely trying to send news out of Syria – although not from Daraa, where the telephones and internet had now been shut down – the bodies were those of Syrian troops who refused to shoot at their own people and who were immediately punished by execution by the shabiha. Wasn't that typical of a brutal sectarian regime that was liquidating its own people to remain in power? Or did there now exist, among the unarmed protesters, 'armed civilians' who were fighting back in a systematic fashion?

Then, suddenly, hundreds of Syrians, most of them women and children, began to flee into the far north of Lebanon across an old stone bridge that marked the border between the two countries. They were escaping from the Syrian town of Tel Kalakh, twenty miles from Homs, whose population had just begun staging demonstrations against their government. Tel Kalakh had now been surrounded by the Syrian army, whose troops we could see across the narrow Nahr al-Kabir river.

My driver Abed was back with me again, now nearly eighty years old but filled with excitement. He raced his dark-red Mercedes up into the valleys of the Akkar in the north of Lebanon, driving too fast as always. Only when we approached the hilltops above the plain of Homs – just inside Lebanon but close enough to see into Syria – did he slow down, crawling between the olive orchards as if he had just caught sight of Dracula's castle.

Something terrible had happened in the town of Tel Kalakh, where as many as 28,000 people had been living, including Christians, Alawites and Sunnis. About 4,000 of the Syrian Sunnis made it to the safety of Lebanon and the tiny village of Arida to be given food, shelter and blankets by relatives and total strangers, and they were there when I arrived – eighty living in one house alone, scarcely twenty metres from Syria, desperate to praise the kindness of the Lebanese, ferocious in their resentment towards Assad. There had been a massacre, so these people told us. There had been arrests, and panic. One man described how detainees from the town had returned home with nails ripped out and beards burned off. 'For forty years, we have not been able to breathe,' he said.

These people cried tears of fear and frustration. They said that there were shabiha gunmen among the soldiers, dressed in black and who spent some time tearing the veils off girls and trying to kidnap them. Even before the shooting started, they said, military and plain-clothes officers had spent time separating Sunnis from Alawites, telling the latter to stay in their houses. Then they shot into the crowds, sometimes from a machine gun mounted on an armoured vehicle. The refugees claimed that their revolt started two months earlier, which suggests the first rural protests in Syria may have begun two weeks before the Daraa shootings. Some of the refugees said they had been protected because of the intercession of the respected imam of the town's mosque, Sheikh Osama Akeri. But on 27 April, they said, armed men took the sheikh from his home – which brought thousands of Sunni Muslims into the streets again.

At least forty civilians were killed in this bloodbath. And here are the words of one man who spoke to me anonymously:

> We were shouting 'independence – give us freedom and
> independence' and they came in tanks and opened fire, the
> shabiha shooting at the men at the front; everyone started
> running but they went on shooting at us from the tanks and
> people fell everywhere. The tanks completely surrounded the
> town. People were running away into the fields, the babies
> screaming, trying to get to Lebanon.

In sight of Arida, many women and children were stopped at a military checkpoint, but it appears that men from Tel Kalakh set the roadblock on fire. For three days, Sunni Muslims had been escaping from the town, creeping from their houses at night as shooting continued across the streets. Tel Kalakh, just like Daraa, was not only surrounded, but electricity and water supplies were cut. I could see several Syrian soldiers on the other riverbank, watching the movement of the refugees.

Some in the town were too frightened to attend the funerals of the dead, another man told me. 'We didn't want to risk being killed … the close families of the dead went to the cemeteries, and some old people. That was all.' Perhaps these people had heard of the fate of the mourners in Daraa. One of the dead was named as Muntaser Akeri, a cousin of the arrested sheikh. Other villagers, both men and women, said that the shooting continued for twenty-four hours, that it was only after a day that some of those who had been dragged away by the mukhabarat in buses and cars came back. 'There were so many soldiers and plain-clothes police and thugs that we couldn't escape,' I was told. 'The Alawis didn't join our protest. We were alone.'

No one could explain to me why so many soldiers were being killed in Syria although they said that no armed men were among the protest-ers. Yet shooting was heard after dark on the Syrian side of the frontier, a phenomenon that had persuaded the Lebanese army to send out night patrols on the border. Those Syrians I spoke to insisted that there had never in the past been any sectarian violence in Tel Kalakh.

The inhabitants did own guns – this was smuggling country – so had these weapons been used against government forces? Or were there other men in Tel Kalakh who were fighting the Syrian army? If so, they were not far away. So close to Syria were the refugees that while I was talking to them, my Lebanese mobile phone repeatedly switched from Beirut to Rami Makhlouf's Syriatel mobile system in Damascus, the message 'ping' constantly drawing my attention to the words: 'Welcome to Syria ... For Tourist guide, dial 1555. Enjoy your stay.'

Back in my Beirut apartment, I received a call from an Al Jazeera camera crew. Would I meet them in a coffee shop in Hamra Street? They knew I'd been up on the Syrian border. In fact, Ali Hashem and his crew had been filming only a few hundred metres from the refu-gees I interviewed. And they had not only managed to take footage of Syrian troops – but also of armed men shooting at the government soldiers. As we sat over our coffee, they turned on their camera screen. I could see one of the fighters running behind the wall of a breezeblock house, a man with a Kalashnikov rifle firing round the side of the building at an unseen target. Hashem worked for Al Jazeera's Beirut bureau and said that three weeks earlier, he had witnessed armed groups entering Syria with rifles and rocket-pro-pelled grenades.

So those courageous and unarmed protesters in Daraa and Damascus, Latakia and Tel Kalakh were not the only enemies of the Assad regime. There was, it seemed, an armed component to the Syrian revolution – even as early as April 2011. Ali Hashem sent his footage to Al Jazeera's head office in Qatar for the next news bulletin. It was important for the world to know that men with weapons were now in action against Syrian forces. But to my astonishment, he told me that the Qatari satellite channel had refused to broadcast his footage. Mohamed Fahmy of Al Jazeera – readers will remember the story of his imprisonment in Cairo's jails – also later contacted Hashem, who said the Qatari channel had told him to 'forget there are armed men' in Syria. Fahmy believed this showed how Al Jazeera supported Qatar's anti-Assad policy; and how it was shaping rather than reporting the story, and thus 'potentially contributing to the intractable situation in Syria'. The channel was happy to emphasise the Egyptian government's cruelty towards its opponents but, as I noticed in Bahrain, Al Jazeera was not at all eager to give air time to the Gulf state's Shia opponents during the kingdom's own miniature revolution.

The violence in Tel Kalakh continued for at least another week. In mid-May, a Syrian woman had died in a Lebanese hospital, along with a Syrian soldier. In Daraa, a mass grave containing at least twenty-six bodies was discovered, including the decomposing remains of a sixty-two-year-old man and four of his children, along with a woman, another child and six men. As US sanctions were imposed on Assad and several of his senior security staff, the president said forlornly that the crisis was coming to an end, adding, farcically, that poorly trained police officers were to blame. Syria's torturers were by any standard very well trained indeed.

Suleiman al-Khalidi, a Reuters correspondent detained in Damascus at the end of May after reporting in Daraa, was taken to a mukhabarat headquarters where he saw a young man

dangling upside down, white foam saliva dripping from his mouth. His groans sounded more bestial than human ... the blindfold was removed for a few minutes. That allowed me ... to see a hooded man screaming in pain in front of me. When they told him to take down his pants, I could see his swollen genitals, tied tight with a plastic cable ... To my horror, a masked man took a pair of wires from a household power socket and gave him electric shocks to the head.

Al-Khalidi recalled that his interrogator, who had been screaming at him that he was 'a dog', took a call on his mobile phone. 'His tone became immediately warmer and affectionate: "Of course, my dear, I'll get you whatever you want," he said, switching from professional torturer to indulgent father.'*

And all the while, reports of mass killings flooded out of Syria. AFP reported from Damascus that thirty-three civilians had been killed in one day by Syrian security personnel: twelve in Homs, fifteen in Idlib province, two in Daraa and another four in Damascus, Latakia, Deir ez-Zor and Hama. Tens of thousands of demonstrators packed the squares of cities across the country. There was no doubt that these mass protests took place, but the absence of international reporters inside Syria produced a confusing picture of what was happening. Human rights 'activists' were claiming that 1,310 people had been killed by 21 June – but reporters could find no way of confirming this figure.

In the *Irish Times*, the paper's Middle East correspondent now referred for the first time to 'armed civilian elements' who had 'opened fire on internal security forces and troops' in Syria. When Syrian political opposition leaders met in Istanbul, Haitham El-Maleh, a prominent human rights defender, was specifically asked if an 'armed rebellion' was underway; he insisted that 'the only armed groups are those of the shabiha', the regime's militiamen. He knew, he said, families whose fathers and sons were paid no more than 1,000 Syrian pounds (around $20 at that time) to attack protesters or join pro-regime demonstrations.

Repeatedly, news organisations outside Syria found themselves relying on social media, with few ways of checking their information. Reports from Syria, for example, were seriously undermined when a young and supposedly lesbian blogger called 'Gay Girl in Damascus', whose vivid accounts of life in the capital transfixed much of the international media, turned out to be a hoax. After a claim that 'Amina Abdallah Aral al Omari' had been arrested by the mukhabarat, the blogger was revealed to be a forty-year-old married American male

---

* The *Independent*'s Alastair Beach came close to sharing al-Khalidi's experience when he travelled on a bus from northern Lebanon to Aleppo in the early autumn of 2011. The taxi driver who picked him up at the bus stop, he recalled, 'was a nasty rat-faced fellow who ended up shopping me to the local mukhabarat. During questioning they were particularly interested in (and not a little befuddled by) my iPod. Was it really a device for listening to music? Or could it also double as a not particularly subtle listening device?' Syrians asked by security agents to explain their Apple technology found their questioners equally ignorant.

called Tom MacMaster, studying for a Master's degree at Edinburgh University in Scotland. 'She' had fooled the BBC, the *Guardian* and *Time* magazine, which had called the fake blog 'an honest and reflective voice of the revolution'. Syrian bloggers exploded with fury at MacMaster's falsehood, pointing out how much damage it would cause to Syrian truth-telling.

This fiasco, wrote *Toronto Star* columnist Thomas Walkom, 'should serve as a warning to those enamoured with social media … To say that mainstream newspapers and television have a love affair with social media is to engage in understatement. Conventional media are desperate to be hip.' But Western reporters then seemed more interested in exploring why MacMaster perpetrated his lies than how they had been fooled by them. He put this down to his 'vanity' and because – almost unbelievably – he said he wanted to expose 'the often superficial coverage of the Middle East'. In one sense, he had already done that. There was no noticeable change in the response of foreign journalists towards Syrian social media, save for a pointless and repeated boilerplate warning that content 'could not be verified'.

History, I often thought, provided more clues to current events than all the bloggers in Syria. So in that summer of 2011, I asked *Independent* readers if they recognised a scenario in which

> Syrians were shot down in the streets of cities across their country, tanks surrounding the major cities of Syria, soldiers killing unarmed and largely Sunni Muslim demonstrators as the authorities protest that 'armed gangs' are themselves killing troops. In northern Syria, citizens barricade their cities from armed assault by the authorities, and Syrian nationalists carrying weapons and demanding freedom are preparing to move into Homs and Hama. Local troops are said to be deserting en masse to the people while others, many of them Alawis of the Shiite Muslim sect, are loyal to the authorities in Damascus. The uprising is infecting neighbouring Lebanon while a British diplomat writes from Damascus that the authorities have 'instituted nothing less than a reign of terror … This will surely spread throughout the whole Middle East.'

Readers may have found this familiar. I intended that they should. But
the scene I was describing was Syria in May of 1945. The regime doing
the shooting was that of Charles de Gaulle, and the nationalists were
the grandfathers of the young men now protesting so bravely on those
same streets against the Assad regime. The British diplomat was
Terence Shone, formerly the 'minister plenipotentiary' in Egypt and
then tasked by British foreign secretary Anthony Eden to honour the
promise – made by Anglo-French forces when they liberated Syria and
Lebanon from Vichy France in 1941 – to give full independence to
both countries. To the horror of Shone and Eden – and Churchill as
well – the French went on to fire shells into the Syrian parliament
building and strafed the Hamidiyah soukh in central Damascus from
the air.

Eventually, the French were persuaded to abandon their former
mandated territories and the Sunni nationalists, led by redoubtable
men like Jamil Mardam Bey, declared victory. Syria was independent.
Or so they believed. These ironies hung like dark candelabras over the
new battle for Syria. Yesterday's 'armed gangs' were now 'terrorists',
and the nationalists were carrying weapons again. Soldiers were deserting and the regime was re-enacting the 'reign of terror' once imposed
by France. Instead of Terence Shone, we now saw the US ambassador,
Robert Ford, expressing his opprobrium of the Syrian regime – along
with his French counterpart – by visiting Hama. Here he would
encourage the protesters not to negotiate with Assad who would, he
assured them, shortly flee Damascus. But it would soon be the
European and American embassy staff who would flee Damascus,
cutting themselves off from the regime they thought was doomed and
leaving the tens of thousands – nay, millions – of civilians opposed to
Assad to face the dictator alone.

This was the first critical moment in the Syrian revolution. Could
the protest of the Syrian people retain the 'purity' of its political intentions by allowing its people to die undefended? During the Egyptian
revolution, Syrian regime opponents sent anti-Mubarak demonstrators
tips on how to use Facebook and tweets. Now the Egyptians tried to
help their comrades in Syria. An Egyptian, who said he 'adored' Syria,
sent advice to them on the 'Syrian News Network'. Remain united, he
said. Shout the same slogans. Make sure that Muslims and Christians
march together. 'Don't give any excuse to the [Syrian] authorities to

divide you on sectarian or ideological grounds.' And, surely most important of all:

> Don't ever attack the security forces. Your movement must remain peaceful at all costs. Refuse to carry weapons, even if you are attacked.

It was advice that could never be heeded. For those who were urging the peaceful protesters to break off all contact with the Assad regime – the Americans and Europeans and their Arab allies – were already arming the dictator's enemies for their own benefit.

Ever a weathervane of passing fortunes, Walid Jumblatt now sensed that Bashar might not survive, and feared for his own Druze people in Syria as well as Lebanon. While not yet calling for the dictator's removal, he observed that 'some' in the Syrian Baath party were trying to impede Bashar's promised reforms that there should be punishment for crimes committed against 'the Syrian people' and the freeing of all political prisoners. And – another hint of the unmentionable – he condemned 'all armed attacks targeting … the Syrian army'. He did not suggest who was behind these attacks. The Syrian government certainly used these 'armed attacks' as an excuse for a veritable massacre in Hama when around one hundred civilians were reported killed. The state news agency described how Syrian troops entered Hama to stop armed groups who were 'shooting intensively to terrorise civilians', a claim to which a US embassy spokesman in Damascus responded at once. 'There is one big armed gang in Syria,' he said, 'and it's named the Syrian government.'

There can be no doubt that these mass killings occurred in Hama at the end of July 2011; years later, residents would repeat these accounts to me at considerable risk to their personal safety. But Reuters was now regularly including in its dispatches a paragraph that would soon become a permanent addition to almost all its reporting from Syria: that the absence of independent journalists made it 'difficult to verify reports of violence and casualties'. One source to which many international media now referred was called the 'Syrian Observatory for Human Rights', run from a house in Coventry in the UK by a longstanding opponent of the Syrian regime known as Rami Abdulrahman.

The more outraged the 'international community' became, the more it turned up the rhetorIc against the regime. A day after King Abdullah of Saudi Arabia pulled his ambassador out of Damascus, the Kuwaitis and Bahrainis dutifully followed his example – although none drew attention to Bahrain's suppression of its own little civil revolt. The Arab League pitifully called for Assad to 'immediately stop' the violence. Even Turkey, according to Erdogan, had 'run out of patience'. The UN roared, though it managed to smear Syria's protesters by calling for both sides to 'exercise restraint' – as if the demonstrators also possessed tanks.

A YouTube video emerged from Hama showing troops in military uniform on top of a Syrian armoured vehicle, defecting soldiers cheering demonstrators. This kind of footage was a dodgy witness to history, I remarked in the *Independent*, 'but there can be little doubt that, faced with state violence on such a scale, civilians have armed themselves to protect their families, to take revenge on the regime, to keep the Syrian [government] militias out of their cities'. This was a romantic version of reality for me to have construed.

Yet it was pathetic to listen to the jaw-jaw of the West's leaders. Obama said that Assad must 'step down', but Damascus did not tremble. In any case, the US president had only chosen to go this far after condemnation of Bashar al-Assad by Saudi Arabia, Qatar, Kuwait, Turkey, Jordan, the Palestinian Authority and the EU.* Cameron, Sarkozy and Angela Merkel followed up Obama's words a few minutes later. Hillary Clinton spoke of new sanctions against Assad 'and his cronies' and 'strong economic sanctions', but Damascus did not bother to respond.† UN Secretary-General Ban Ki-moon had no sooner demanded an 'immediate' end to 'all military operations and mass arrests' than Bashar told him a straightforward lie: that 'all military and police action' had stopped.

---

* The odd nation out was Israel, which remained uncharacteristically silent; cogently waiting, no doubt, to see if Assad's replacement might prove even worse than the present incumbent.

† If the latter suggested a mere freeze on petroleum products of Syrian origin, it meant little since Syria could scarcely produce enough oil for itself, let alone for export. At the Swedish ambassadorial meeting I had attended in the Gulf, a Stockholm government agency concluded that Syria was largely unaffected by the world economic crisis because it really didn't have an economy.

Outside Syria, the stories of horror were overwhelming. How could we as journalists not react to the report which began to circulate at the end of July that eight newly born babies had died in their incubators in a Hama hospital after government forces had deliberately destroyed the electrical generators that powered the facility? Those of us who covered Saddam Hussein's invasion of Kuwait remembered all too well the reports of Iraqi troops throwing babies out of incubators in Kuwait City in August 1990. It garnered enormous support for the forthcoming Western liberation of Kuwait, but the story was fiction. So when CNN broke the new incubator story from Hama, I noted that its source was the Coventry-based 'Syrian Observatory for Human Rights'.

The reports had been illustrated by a photograph of still-swaddled babies, all apparently lying dead at the al-Hourani hospital. In his own website, Rami Abdulrahman, SOHR's 'director', quoted an anony- mous hospital employee as saying that the electricity supply was cut 'in a renewal of the campaign of military oppression'. But Egyptians who saw the picture recognised that it had been used in an Egyptian news- paper to illustrate overcrowding and poor conditions in the maternity ward at the Shatby Pediatric Hospital in Alexandria. An Egyptian colleague warned me of this revelation and told the *Independent* that the entire story from Hama appeared to be untrue, yet the account did not die.

These lies did not excuse the cruelty of the Syrian government, though the gullibility of the international media was certainly reducing the credibility of reports coming from inside Syria. Amnesty's August report on 1,800 deaths of protesters and detainees contained fearful accounts of torture or execution in custody. Some prisoners had their necks broken. Thirteen-year-old Hamza al-Khatib was returned to his parents in Daraa with marks of torture and with his penis cut off. Like the international press, Amnesty was not allowed into Syria but the details were, in the language of modern journalism, compelling.

At the same time, further reports came from Syria that deserting soldiers were forming their own units to fight the government army. But Obama, still deeply involved in his war in Libya, had no intention of going into battle for the protesters of Syria. When twenty-six-year- old Ghiyath Matar, a prominent leader of the demonstrations in the Damascus suburb of Daraya, was murdered in custody, the American and French ambassadors made another very public journey from their diplomatic compounds to offer their condolences to Matar's family. But when Syrian opposition groups announced their 'unity' after a long conference in Istanbul and asked for international help, there was no Bernard-Henri Lévy to arrange international recognition for them. A Syrian government-in-exile in Turkey was a country too far. And this would remain so even when, a year later, a heavily armed opposition force took over half of Aleppo as their own 'Benghazi capital', en route – so they thought – to Damascus.

Individual assassinations were a pattern of what most of us now called the Syrian civil war, although this definition was shunned by both the Assad government and its enemies. Sariya Hassoun, the twenty-two-year-old son of the Syrian grand mufti Ahmed Badreddin Hassoun, an Assad loyalist, was shot down by 'armed terrorists' in Idlib province. A prominent Kurdish leader was murdered in the north of Syria by four masked men, presumably government agents. Yet still the UN's officials, now putting Syria's fatalities at 3,000 in seven months, said only that they 'feared' civil war in the country.

Even in Lebanon, you could see the groundwork for Syrian civil conflict. Weapons were now being smuggled in large amounts from northern Lebanon. There were cross-border Syrian tank incursions to search for 'armed gangs'. The Lebanese army stopped a truckload of ammunition and rocket-propelled grenades near Halba in the far north of the country. It emerged that even before the abduction of the elderly Syrian politician Shibli Aysami, three Syrian members of the Jassem family were seized near a police station in east Beirut, having been seen handing out flyers calling for 'democratic change'. The kidnappers' vehicle belonged to the Syrian embassy in Beirut, according to the head of the Lebanese Internal Security Forces, Major General Ashraf Rifi. Syrian forces had briefly crossed the frontier and fired shells into the village of Ersal because they believed 'subversive armed elements' were hiding there.* They killed an innocent man, who turned out to be Syrian. Western ambassadors in Beirut had earlier in the year complained to the Lebanese government when the Lebanese army

---

* They may have been correct. Years later, Ersal would be seized by ISIS and other Islamists who captured Lebanese soldiers in the town and cut the throat of several of their captives.

sent back to Damascus three Syrian military deserters. Fearing that the latter were not welcomed home by their officers, the ambassadors warned that this could amount to a crime against humanity. A whole unit of Syrian army deserters appeared on a website shortly afterwards, claiming they were several thousand strong.

And there began the vast mass rallies in Damascus in favour of Assad, a million strong said his admirers, above which flew Syrian military helicopters carrying massive national flags of Russia and China – Syria's two friends in the Security Council who vetoed more UN sanctions in early October.

I had crossed the dirty old Syrian frontier post at Al-Jdeideh so many times that the broken walls, the crowds of destitute Shia pilgrims, the signs suggesting that any visitor with a complaint should call a telephone number in Damascus, had years ago lost their quaint charm. The immigration officers were the same tired middle-aged men I had met so many times. At last, my visa had been granted – but for all of three days. There was, of course, a 'small problem'. A mukhabarat warning had popped up on the top right of the immigration computer screen. Robert Fisk was forbidden to enter. I called Reem Haddad at the information ministry. She called the mukhabarat. She then called the chief immigration officer. The mukhabarat then called the immigration officer. 'Welcome to Syria,' he said.

I drove to see Reem Haddad at what I had subversively deemed the Temple of Truth in the early years of the Assad regime. The obsessive desire to know every journey undertaken by foreign journalists had disappeared. Keeping the façade of 'control', however, cast a deep shadow over the true-to-form communist-style building, the shabby banality of its clunky elevators, dreary corridors and its equally tiresome 'foreign press' office. I wanted to see the funeral of soldiers killed by the so-called 'armed gangs'? Call the army. I did.

Turn up at the Tishrin military hospital at 9.30 a.m., I was told. The guards on the gate will have my name. They did. And Sergeant Jassem Abdul-Raheem Shehadi and Private Ahmed Khalaf Adalli of the Syrian army were sent to their graves with the ceremony their families would have wished: coffins draped with the Syrian flag, trumpets and drums and wreaths held by their comrades and the presence of their commanding officer. Shehadi was nineteen, Adalli was twenty.

I realised that the army, the mukhabarat, government officials – even old Syrian friends who might have sought privacy before they talked to me – were now involved in the gravest crisis of their lives. Death had been associated with Syria's wars with Israel. But now Syria was fighting itself. Under shellfire, with sectarian killers roaming the villages, with 'armed gangs' and squads of soldiers shot down and shabiha killers, with mass graves uncovered and executions in battle, the inhabitants of this proudest of Arab countries were facing their own annihilation.

Whether they believed the government hated them, tortured them, imprisoned them, protected them, loved them or represented them, Syria had embarked on a pathway into the desert which none could have foreseen. In hundreds of interviews and conversations over eight years and more, I found not a single Syrian who had predicted this. They all said, quite directly, that they could never have imagined what would happen to their country. And if there had been a dream of freedom, it would become a disaster for all who struggled within its framework.

Everything I learned that day would add a little more to this panorama of collapse. Shehadi and Adalli were both shot dead in Daraa – by snipers, according to their commanding officer, Major Walid Hatim. Hatim and a fellow officer told me that 1,150 soldiers had been killed in Syria in the past five months. So this was a war – civil or international would vary in the years to come – a bloody conflict in which the army was now fully engaged. Military casualties in Syria are a state secret but in the years to come, the army's officers would tell me the total dead in their battles. By the end of 2018, the Syrian military had lost more than 65,000 soldiers, including five generals. But here we were in the autumn of 2011, and more than a thousand had been killed. Add this to the UN's figure of 3,000 dead and the total was already around 4,500, perhaps 5,000.

Major Hatim wanted to talk about the army's losses. On Zawi mountain near Idlib, he said, thirty Syrian soldiers had been killed in an ambush. Shehadi and Adalli had been based in Daraa for six and four months respectively; so the army was not moving its battalions around, a commonplace tactic in the military if it does not trust its soldiers. It was a sign of the times that Major Hatim arrived at this Damascus funeral in civilian clothes. Why was he not wearing his uniform? I asked him. 'It is easier,' he replied. Because of the dangers driving from Daraa to Damascus? 'Maybe,' he replied. That, too, told its own story.

Both of the dead soldiers had lost their fathers years ago and their two uncles had travelled from Raqqa to escort the bodies home. Salim Abdullah Shehadi was on the edge of tears. 'My nephew had three brothers and two sisters and they are very poor. His mother Arash will now have to be looked after by us. Those killers have killed the hope of our family. Behind Salim Shehadi, Syrian troops stood in full battle-dress as the coffins were brought from the hospital mortuary. All Syria's military dead – if their bodies are recovered – leave from the concrete portals of the Tishrin hospital in the suburbs of Damascus.

Major Hatim himself was a twenty-five-year army veteran. 'When I joined the army, we did not distinguish where our soldiers came from, from which region – and we do not do so now.' This was his way of saying that the religious origins of soldiers did not matter. But I persisted. What was the dead men's religion? A doctor interrupted. 'The national religion,' he said. 'They were Sunnis.' An odd phrase, the 'national' religion. And for all the government talk of 'foreign hands' behind the violence in Syria, Major Hatim admitted to me that – so far as his own dead soldiers were concerned – 'unfortunately the killers are Syrian'.

Bouthaina Shaaban, the government adviser so loyal to the ruling family that she was writing an academic account of her years as Hafez al-Assad's translator, said what every other Syrian in Damascus was saying to me: that the situation in Homs was terrible, that the army was being attacked all over the country. Anyone with a military regis-tration plate on their car was a target.

It was a familiar political narrative to hear from the regime. Violence was being directed at the army, at public buildings and cities. It had nothing to do with political demonstrations. 'This violence is the most dangerous thing happening now in Syria,' Shaaban continued. 'Syrians all want to live in peace, to press ahead with pluralism and reforms. There is obviously a sector which is interested in conflict and not in reforms. They are all given money to shoot at demonstrators – or they are extremist fundamentalists.'

Surely, I said to Shaaban – those terrible YouTube pictures of demonstrators being shot in Daraa, Homs and Hama were real. One even showed Syrian soldiers turning and firing on the man who was

filming them with his mobile camera. We all knew how brutal the
intelligence services could be. Shaaban watched me intently and then
went on to defend 'the army and police and security services who paid
terrible sacrifices but they were told not to shoot at demonstrators. I
really don't know why people should make things up.' I tell Shaaban
that I've spent hours talking to Syrian refugees in Lebanon who told
terrible stories of the shabiha militia and the brutality of the intelligence services in their village of Tel Kalakh. Surely she doesn't believe
these people were all inventing these events?

Instead, she talked about the 'armed groups' and that she was much
aggrieved at the reporting of Al Jazeera, which was anyway banned in
Syria. But then almost all foreign correspondents were banned from
Syria – and this was on the advice, according to her associates, of
Shaaban herself.

And so what was one to make of yet another pro-Assad demonstration in Umayyad Square? This one grew from 10,000 to perhaps 50,000
and it might have reached 200,000 by midday. They were only a quarter the size of the Syrian opposition protests. There were old veiled
women, middle-aged women, children with 'Syria' painted on their
faces. Most held red-white-and-black Syrian banners. Some carried the
flags of Russia and China.

Sure, this was organised by the government. The idea that all these
people had produced identical flags was nonsensical. I had been kept
awake in my bed in the early hours by tape-recorded cheers, as government workers repeatedly tested the deafening sound system for the
demonstration to come. I had last heard such false applause at an
equally fraudulent Syrian presidential referendum. Yes, I remembered
the election of 2007 – when poor Muhsen Bilal, a surgeon by trade, a
former ambassador to Spain and then minister of information, had to
announce that Bashar's 99.82 per cent victory demonstrated what he
called 'our own style of democracy'.

So how truly did all these people believe in their pseudo-democracy?
How many would be sacrificed for the rather effete optometrist whose
portraits were mercifully outnumbered by Syrian flags? I followed a
crowd of demonstrators out of the square. I walked with them way up
Mount Qasioun above Damascus. Some of the people invited me into
their homes to drink tea with them. These people were poor as well as
middle class; there were young people sporting Christian crosses

among their Muslim neighbours. I did not believe that they all felt paternal love towards the rather thin and diminutive Alawite who promised to lead them into the broad sunlit uplands of peace, and who was already refusing to talk to any form of political opposition. No doubt the mukhabarat were around. I rather suspected that some of those 'armed civilian elements' were also there. But despite the demonstrations of mass courage that were staged against Assad across Syria, a lot of men and women had turned out for him in Damascus that day.

When I talked to them privately in their homes, they were more frightened than inspired. Yes, they expressed their loyalty to Assad, but in a routine way. But they talked about the army. Almost everyone in Damascus had a father, brother, uncle, cousin, son in the army. These people knew all about the army's casualties. They told me the armed men killing the soldiers were maybe Bedouin who smuggled drugs to Saudi Arabia, 'Islamists' from Iraq or 'people who think there is just no other way of getting rid of the regime'.

Fear was clearly at work: but fear of change, fear of chaos, 'Islamists', 'terrorists' and the government had obviously done much to encourage this sense of alarm. Everyone told me of the rumours they had heard from the countryside outside Damascus. In Idlib province, so they said, everyone was armed. Weapons had arrived in Homs and Hama from Lebanon, a story that made sense to me. Damascus was still safe; but Damascus was not the rest of Syria. The city lived in a bubble, but everyone knew how fragile was its skin.

Despite the daily claims of Assad's imminent overthrow, it was also becoming clear to me that the war was not going to end soon. Both sides believed they could win, which ensured that the war would continue. But people were talking. Many of the apparatchiks and ministry 'minders' who had in the past tormented the lives of foreign journalists had been sent off to fight in the war. I knew of several mukhabarat officers who had been transferred to the regular Syrian army. A few sought a kind of redemption in this mutation, and it must have been a considerable psychological experience for them: to fight for their countrymen instead of torturing them.

In Beirut, the Lebanese morning newspapers I bought each bright winter dawn to read beside the Mediterranean should have had a health warning attached to them. 'New bloodbath in Syria: at least thirty-six civilians killed'; 'Forty-seven dead in twenty-four hours among loyalists and rebels'; 'onslaught kills forty protesters'; 'Armed rebels begin to defend neighbourhoods, says Homs activist'. The headlines were tall, the cautionary note – 'claims could not be independently verified' – usually printed at the end of the reports. The *New York Times* carried a dispatch that anti-Assad military defectors were operating out of southern Turkey under the command of a former Syrian army colonel, Riad Asaad, calling itself the 'Free Syrian Army'. Yet while they encouraged a few senior officers to transfer their allegiance, the 'FSA' could not win a revolution with Kalashnikov rifles. They would need a tank brigade or two to defect en masse. And this did not happen.*

Unfortunately, we paid less attention to the connections which continued between Damascus and Moscow. The Russians, we all knew, maintained a marine base in the Syrian port of Tartous. Less obvious was the continued supply of weapons to the Syrian army and air force. Just nine days after Russia and China vetoed a UN Security Council resolution condemning Syria, the joint director-general of the federal Russian service of military cooperation said there would be 'no restrictions at all on arms' deliveries to Syria'. In my report to the *Independent* I wrote:

> It's Putin's Sukhois and Migs that are setting the pace in the terrible Syrian war. And amid lands where human rights count not a jot for most of the regional dictators, there's been scarcely a whimper about the Kremlin … Even America's blitz on ISIS didn't really get under way until Putin sent his own fighter-bombers to Syria – at which point, many Arabs were asking why Washington hadn't managed to destroy the cult.

Go back to the Arab revolutions, I suggested, and you see Obama and his hapless secretary of state Hillary Clinton goofing again, failing to realise that this massive public awakening in the Arab world was real and that the dictators were going to go – most of them, at least. In

---

* Like several defecting army officers, Asaad's new career did not last long. Protesters abused him for remaining loyal to the regime in the early days of the Syrian uprising; and he went on to make alliances with Islamist groups which angered the FSA's original foreign supporters.

Cairo in 2011, about the only decision taken by Obama was to evacuate US citizens from the Egyptian capital. At the same time, Assad was welcoming the Russian Orthodox patriarch Kirill to Syria, an important prelate in an Arab nation whose population was 10 per cent Christian. Assad expressed his 'admiration for the Russian people and their authorities, who have placed themselves at the side of the Syrian people'. Kirill, who knew how to sing from the same hymn book, described Assad's Syria as 'a model of Islamic-Christian cohesion'.

We Westerners have a habit of always looking at the Middle East through our own pious cartography, but tip the map ninety degrees and you appreciate how close Syria is to Russia's Chechen Muslim irredentists. No wonder Moscow watched the rebellion in Syria with the gravest of concern. Quoting Napoleon, who once said, 'If one wants to understand the behaviour of a country, one has to look at a map', my Israeli friend Uri Avnery wrote that 'geography is more important than ideology, however fanatical. Ideologies change with time. The most fanatically ideological country in the twentieth century was the Soviet Union. It abhorred its predecessor, Tsarist Russia. It would have abhorred its successor, Putin's Russia. But lo and behold – the Tsars, Stalin and Putin conduct more or less the same foreign policy.' I wrote that Russia is back in the Middle East. Iran is securing its political semi-circle of Tehran-Baghdad-Damascus-Beirut. And if the Gulf Arabs – or the Americans – want to reinvolve themselves, they can chat to Putin.

As Western embassies in Damascus prepared to reduce their diplomats in the city, their intelligence services were already offering military assistance to the FSA. The French secret service (DGSE – Direction générale de la sécurité extérieure) and British MI6 operatives were speaking to their Turkish opposite numbers about a no-fly zone and a five-mile wide 'cordon sanitaire' along a strip of northern Syria in which 8,000 FSA personnel might be protected. A DGSE unit was tasked to train these men in guerrilla warfare before returning them across the frontier. A DGSE officer would later disclose that the British and French were the first to make contact with FSA rebels – but had already noticed political divisions among them. French foreign minister Alain Juppé had concluded that the Turks feared the start of a full-scale civil war on their southern frontier and sought the absence of their voisin dictateur.

I wrote in the *Independent* that Russia and America have always suffered an addiction for obedient military rulers; and Putin, who only retired from the KGB with the rank of lieutenant colonel – against Al-Sisi's field marshal status – understands all too well how a 'deep state' works. Patriotism, nationalism and corruption are a potent blood group for autocratic survival in the Arab world. Along with amoral economics. I was referring to Putin's visit to Cairo for talks on new rubles-only trade deals, the sale of billions of dollars' worth of guns and tanks, and a new 'anti-terrorist' alliance of the kind Russia already boasted in Syria. Al-Sisi will remember, I wrote 'that Bashar al-Assad himself sent a congratulatory telegram to him when he crushed the Brotherhood ... and since Putin has demonstrated that he has no qualms about the brutalities committed by his Syrian ally, a few thousand broken bodies in the Egyptian Islamist camp are not going to keep [him] awake at night', and he would be content to 'bring Egypt into a triple Cairo-Damascus-Moscow alliance against "terror"'.*

We were sitting in the dining room of one of Istanbul's ancient hotels, the fifteenth-century Malatya tower looming over us. The Ottomans would have understood Khaled Khoja, a Syrian Turkman, eyes watching me to see if I admired his grasp of English. Or his cynicism.

> If Bashar al-Assad is caught in Damascus, he will not be treated like Gaddafi. But what if he was caught in Homs? We don't want Mr Bashar al-Assad to face this end. But as Mr Erdogan says, he has to think what happened to Gaddafi and to Saddam Hussein. The youth now are crazy. All revolutions are created by crazy men, not by wise men.

---

* Al-Sisi has met Putin before, I wrote, in Moscow, and a Russian leader known for his cynicism can only enjoy meeting a military autocrat who was elected president after staging a successful coup d'état against a previously elected president – even the old Soviet Union could never quite achieve that. The Egyptian president oversaw the shooting massacre of hundreds of Brotherhood supporters in 2013. The Russian president oversaw the bloody occupation of parts of eastern Ukraine a year later. They will have much to talk about.

Always fearing for their own empire, the Ottomans knew how to destroy those of others. Khoja was sitting back in his chair, enjoying the idea of incipient power. Was he to be counted among the mad? Or would he be the man to resolve the Syrian mess before the lunatics took over?

Khoja, a dark-haired family doctor in his forties, was one of the most senior representatives of the exiled Syrian National Council, recognised only by post-Gaddafi Libya as the representative of Syria. And like all exiles, he basked in a strange world of fantasy and reality. We were approaching the last chance, he said. Otherwise it would be a sectarian conflict. And Assad? 'I give him six months to a year.' Here was the fantasy. The chaos in Homs was already a sectarian conflict.

Yet Khoja had the kind of curriculum vitae every Syrian opposition leader craved. He knew all about the men in white socks. For his refusal to countenance Hafez al-Assad, his father had been imprisoned at Tadmor military prison (Palmyra) for fourteen years, his mother sentenced to five years, Khaled himself for two years at the age of fifteen – including one year in the cells of the intelligence headquarters in Damascus. Of his three uncles, one was hanged; two, according to Khoja himself, were shot in the street.

And then, without warning, Khoja admitted to me that he had met the armed insurgents of Syria. He had talked to them in Antakya:

> They said they are organising themselves and that the rebellion
> started in Jisr al-Shughour in Idlib. They trained the youth there.
> They are getting guns from Lebanon – and somehow guns from
> Iraq. The 'buffer zone' – this scenario will be the next step if
> Bashar al-Assad continues killing people. Most refugees will try
> to evacuate to a buffer zone. A no-fly zone would help the Free
> Syrian Army to organise themselves in the buffer zone without
> any military intervention.

So there it was. A Turkish army buffer zone. As a member of the SNC's 'foreign affairs committee', Khoja had been urged by fellow exiles to visit the Gulf and Tripoli – and had arrived in the Libyan capital the day after Gaddafi was murdered. But the SNC's ambitions did not end with mere political support. With coordination from King Abdullah:

there could be another buffer zone in Daraa so that the Syrian regime will be stuck like Saddam in 1990 – with buffer zones in north and south. But there could be a solution without any military intervention. The Syrian army can reorganise itself.

Here the fantasy was taking over.* In the early days of the Syrian uprising, Khoja remarked, the United Arab Emirates foreign minister had visited Syria – just as he had visited Saddam Hussein before the 2003 invasion and Hosni Mubarak before his 2011 overthrow. And when the UAE was involved, it meant there was an offer to the Assad family. They could go to Saudi Arabia, Malta. 'It would be a good solution. We don't want to take revenge on the Assad family – especially if this will help avoid a civil war.' There was a smile on Khoja's face now. Hafez, he added, would have handled the Syrian crisis better than his son Bashar. He talked vaguely of 'a civil, democratic, pluralist Syria' in almost exactly the same way that Bashar al-Assad spoke of the country. But he had no illusions about Moscow:

> The Russians talk to us. They are trying to convince us to have a compromise with Bashar al-Assad and give him a chance. They will not change – they will support Bashar to the end.

And here Khoja was correct.

---

* When I suggested to Khoja that almost three decades of exile had led him into mythology rather than history, he replied: 'I can think very clearly, even in exile – but I'm not facing the tanks. I'm not facing the bullets of the regime.' This was the same old problem faced by every political exile in the Arab world.

15

The Surgeon with the Bloodstained Hands

Meanwhile the Turks enter the village ... where there are
only women and children, and, when they leave, we see
only a few corpses, large and small. And public opinion?
What does it do? What does it say? Nothing ... These
catastrophes are a 'misfortune' ... Six or seven major
powers conspire against a small people. What is this
conspiracy? The most cowardly of all. The conspiracy of
silence ... But thunder it's not. The thunder comes from
above and, in the language of politicians, it's called the
thunder of revolution.

Victor Hugo on the massacre of Greek civilians by Ottoman Turks in
Crete, 17 February 1867, *Kleio* newspaper, Trieste

Just over a year after the start of the Syrian war, Goya came to Beirut.
To transport *Disasters of War*, his terrifying nineteenth-century sketches
of rapine and torture and execution, to the Middle East showed great
trust by the Beirut Cervantes Institute. This was, in effect, a display of
Lebanon's own sadism and masochism in the 1975–90 Lebanese civil
war. But I feared that those who came to explore this greatest of anti-
war manifestos must have looked at these obscenities and thought of
countryside and cities 250 miles further east, where such atrocities
were taking place by the hour. Would that Francisco de Goya could
return to us and visit Hama or Homs.

In these sketches was the savagery unleashed on a people who dared
to challenge Napoleon after he installed his brother Joseph as king of

Spain in 1808. The eighty-two prints are so unspeakable that Goya scarcely talked about them. I had last seen Goya's images of war in Lille, but here in Lebanon they had a far more terrible effect.

Two weeks before Goya's prints arrived in Beirut, *Paris Match* published the photographs of an American photo-journalist Robert King, who had just spent seven weeks in a secret clinic in al-Qusayr near Homs, filming the work of Dr Kassem al-Zein as he cared for the victims of Syrian army gunfire. One of his pictures showed a little girl with a mangled hand, another a four-year-old boy called Mustapha whose blood-encrusted face was a mask of pity and violence. 'I didn't try to hide the reality or embellish it,' King said in an interview. 'On the contrary I wanted to show its brutal ugliness. I think it is scandalous to go to a war to make art photos.'

So what did Goya do almost 200 years earlier? I continued to walk around the sketches. A priest about to be garrotted, a woman taken away to be sexually assaulted, men chopped up and pinioned on a tree, a figure hauled up the steps of a gallows, a man hanging beside a self-satisfied French officer. These pictures were unseen until thirty-five years after Goya's death. What proof of barbarity will we see next from Syria? I asked myself. Little could we have imagined that out of the deserts would come that which would use art as the antithesis of humanity and those who would believe that violence in its most appalling conception should be deployed as a form of psychotic art.

Yet long before ISIS, the winter of 2011–12 was one of unrestrained carnage in Syria, mass cruelty whose details seeped like blood over its frontiers, the regime's continued refusal to tolerate all but a few journalists only emphasising to the world its desire to keep secret its own guilt. A UN investigation concluded that Syrian forces had killed 256 children up to 9 November 2011, including a two-year-old girl who was shot dead in Latakia on 13 August by an officer who said that he 'did not want her to grow into a demonstrator'. The UN, which defined a child as anyone under eighteen, said it had interviewed 233 surviving victims and witnesses.

The Arab League threatened the suspension of Syria if it did not end violence against protesters, withdraw its armour from Syrian cities, free political prisoners and begin talks with the opposition. Back fumed the lion of Damascus: Syria had already implemented the League's 'peace plan', while its potential suspension was an attempt to 'provoke foreign intervention in Syria, as it did in Libya'. Shiite Iraq abstained at the League, while Yemen and Lebanon voted against.* The League would subsequently freeze Syria's membership – but the opposition Syrian National Council was not permitted to take its place, merely to anticipate in meetings on an 'exceptional basis'. An ill-chosen and underfunded delegation of Arab League 'monitors' arrived in Damascus, with their communications confiscated by the regime the moment they arrived at the Jordanian–Syrian border. Its worthless report spoke of the injustice and oppression endured by Syrian citizens, recorded the condemnation of government forces by the opposition and denounced the use of bombs and anti-tank missiles against government forces by 'armed groups'.

But how many 'armed groups' were now roaming across Syria? Photographs of Syrian troops who had defected to the FSA now filled YouTube footage, many of them posing in front of the opposition black-white-and-green flag, which would become so familiar in Syrian streets in the years to come. The group claimed responsibility for the attack on a Syrian air force bus on the main highway between Homs and Palmyra in November 2011, an ambush in which six pilots, an officer and three other military personnel were killed. As I was talking about the incident to a Syrian army major months later, he turned and shouted at me: 'What do you think our pilots feel when their comrades are murdered?' It might have been a fair reply were Syria's barrel bombs not dropped on civilians.

Yet some attacks on the government were clearly not the work of the FSA. After suicide bombings targeted two state security offices in central Damascus in late December 2011, the regime blamed al-Qaeda; the FSA had never used suicide teams and al-Qaeda were specialists in self-immolation. One of the bombs exploded at the Syrian military intelligence headquarters in the Kafr Soussa district, killing fifteen people. In all, forty men and women were killed and another 150 wounded. But a new argument was then heard. The Syrian govern-

---

* The Lebanese, fearful that Assad's promise of an 'earthquake' might fracture their own national territory, remembered another League 'peace plan' in 1976, which sent a 'peacekeeping' force of 30,000 largely Syrian troops into Lebanon (along with a few battalions of Saudi, Sudanese and Emirati soldiers). The Syrian military had stayed for the next twenty-nine years – and still held Lebanon, even after its official departure, in its sisterly embrace.

ment, it was claimed, had staged the bombings in order to frighten the Arab League monitoring mission. An opposition 'activist' named as Omar Idlibi announced that the regime must have staged the explosions 'because they happened in heavily guarded areas that are difficult to penetrate by car'.

This would become a familiar refrain in the years to come; that any guerrilla attack which caused mass civilian casualties among Assad's supposed supporters was perpetrated by the government. Journalists in the region had heard this explanation many times. In 1982, the Israelis would often accuse the Palestinians of setting off bombs which were intended to kill their own people in order to elicit international sympathy. Yet in May 2012, after at least another fifty-five people were reported killed in two more huge car bomb explosions at an intelligence headquarters in the capital, the opposition again claimed that the bombs were set off by the government. This and previous bombings, however, had actually been claimed – in the words of one Middle East correspondent – 'by an organisation calling itself al-Nusra Front for the Protection of the people of Syria, believed to be associated with al-Qaeda'. Slowly, this Qaeda affiliate would move into our reporting of the Syrian war.

In early 2012, the regime concentrated its firepower on Homs. In previous months, there had been continuous friction between Alawite and Sunni parts of the city but the FSA decided to create a bastion in the Sunni district of Baba Amr, an unpretentious suburb of cement apartment blocks on the city's southern outskirts next to the main highway between Damascus and Aleppo.

At enormous personal risk, several Western journalists and photographers managed to enter Homs with the help of regime opponents. Their reports told of a battle in which the innocent suffered most terribly, in which the smallest children had become casual victims of the Syrian bombardment. Their words could not be dismissed as mere rebel propaganda. Paul Wood of the BBC wrote a classic account of the siege which combined both immense sympathy for the suffering civilians and a fearful account of executions by FSA men. Most of the casualties he saw in hospitals were civilians and many were children. An eleven-year-old boy was brought in. Most of his face had been torn off in an explosion. Everything below the mid-point of his nose was gone, bloody shreds hanging over a hole where his jaw and mouth had been. Bombs were continually falling outside. People were screaming in the corridor. The boy was still conscious. We caught a glimpse of eyes wide with shock ... the boy died of his wounds the following day.

Wood discovered civilians who had become hysterical after 'hundreds of shells, mortars and rockets had fallen'. One man walked back and forth shouting that the Syrian army was about to use chemical weapons and that ground troops were advancing into the suburb. Neither was true, Wood added.

State television denied there was a bombardment. It told the inventive lie that residents were setting fire to rubbish on their roofs to give the impression of an attack. The official media also said that most of the violence was caused by the rebel fighters of the Free Syrian Army.

As Wood wrote, 'Free Syrian Army' was 'more a name used by local militias rather than a single organisation with a coherent command structure' – a significant and dangerous state of affairs when the West was already sending weapons to the Syrian opposition. The BBC man watched a video taken two months earlier in which a dozen men in Syrian army uniform were lined up facing a wall, one of whom turns to the camera looking petrified. 'We killed them,' an FSA man told Wood, 'that is the policy for shabiha.' Wood was shown a film which, he was told, had been taken from the mobile phone of a captured government militiaman:

Prisoners lay face down on the ground, hands tied behind their backs. One by one, their heads were cut off. The man wielding the knife said, tauntingly, to the first: 'This for freedom.' As his victim's neck opened, he went on: 'This is for martyrs. And this is for collaborating with Israel.'

Such things, Wood added, would give Western governments pause 'as they decide whether ... to help the rebels. If they help the rebels, will they fuel a civil war or, worse, a sectarian war?'

But as we now know, foreign governments spent little or no time 'pausing' before they began their gun-running operations into Syria. And even at this early stage of the conflict, there was disturbing evidence that the FSA was divided. Some of its fighters appeared to hold strongly Islamist sympathies. A Western NGO worker who was in Homs in mid-February 2012 recalled how the armed men who drove him through Baba Amr 'would stop at each dangerous road junction, push a tape into their car cassette player and broadcast Islamic music loudly with many prayers as they raced across the intersections'. On one occasion, the same NGO worker had to calm a group of opposition fighters who intended to execute a Westerner for drinking whisky.

But human misery lay at the heart of the events in Baba Amr. When a baby wounded by shrapnel was brought to a poorly equipped make-shift medical centre, Marie Colvin, veteran war correspondent of the *Sunday Times*, gave a devastating account of the child's last moments to CNN. The baby's death, she said:

> was just heartbreaking, possibly because he was so quiet. One of the first shocks … was that the grandmother had been helping … in the emergency room, and just started shouting, 'That's my grandson, where did you find him?' And then the doctor said 'there's nothing we can do'. We just watched this little boy, his little tummy heaving and heaving as he tried to breathe. It was horrific. My heart broke.

The boy's house had been hit by a shell, Colvin told the CNN commentator Anderson Cooper, who asked why she thought it important that the public should see these images of the dying child. Colvin believed, she said, that the baby would move more people to ask: 'What is going on, and why is no one stopping this murder in Homs that is happening every day?' There were no military targets where she was located, she said:

> There is the Free Syrian Army: heavily outnumbered and out-gunned – they have only Kalashnikovs and rocket-propelled grenades. But they don't have a base. There are more young men being killed, we see a lot of teenaged young men, but they are going out to just try to get the wounded to some kind of

medical treatment. So it's a complete and utter lie that they [the regime] are only going after terrorists. There are rockets, shells, tank shells, anti-aircraft being fired in parallel lines into the city. The Syrian Army is simply shelling a city of cold, starving people.

Hours later, a Syrian shell exploded beside Colvin and her French colleague, photographer Rémi Ochlik. They died instantly.

Already, Syrian 'citizen journalists' were dying in their attempts to report the revolution in their country. But little did we think that a Lebanese would be among the first in the list of martyr journalists. Ali Shabaan was now one of those – unknown in the West, but loved in his little south Lebanese village, not least by Fatima Atwi to whom he was to become engaged on the day they buried him.

Fatima clung to the railings of the balcony over the road from the beautiful village cemetery, tears splashing on her blouse. Shabaan had worked the past weekend on the Lebanese–Syrian border so that he could have the following weekend off for his engagement ceremony. He worked for Lebanon's New TV channel, generally sympathetic to the Syrian regime, and had driven to the border and been ordered to turn back by Syrian troops. That is when they shot him. A quick death. And a quick funeral, of course, according to Muslim tradition.

But why did Shabaan die? He and his crew had passed the Lebanese customs post at Wadi Khaled to film the border and shouted across to the Syrian immigration officers that they were filming for New TV from the Lebanese side of the frontier. The story from his colleagues was straightforward: after they had identified themselves, the crew began filming and were told to stop by uniformed Syrian troops. The crew was reversing its car when the fusillade of bullets crashed into it, and Shabaan was hit by the first round. He had never entered Syrian territory. Thanks to the old French mandate, the exact line of the border was not delineated as carefully as it might have been. But that was no reason to kill a journalist. Ahmed Shabaan watched the body of his only son placed in the earth. And Syria, to the disgust of the mourners, sent its official condolences.

★　★　★

No regime mouthpiece, no public relations outfit, could wash the blood off the streets of Syria's cities. In February, Human Rights Watch published another report on the torture of children; it covered much the same ground as the previous year's UN investigation but included details of the burning of thirteen-year-old children with cigarette butts and electric shocks. How could Russian foreign minister Sergey Lavrov defend Moscow's veto at the UN Security Council by repeating promises of fresh Syrian elections when the civilian death toll in Homs was reported to be eighty on 6 February, over one hundred in forty-eight hours a day later?

By the end of February, the Syrian government was talking of 'cleaning' Baba Amr, a chilling expression which in military parlance almost always precedes mass killing.* Then we learned that the International Red Cross had still not been given access to Baba Amr. For the West, the 'right to protect' was utterly lost amid the clamour by leaders who refused to interfere in Syria. But interference, there certainly was. The Lebanese army reinforced Ersal after a pro-Syrian minister in the Beirut government had complained of al-Qaeda infiltration of the border town. In early February, two men were brought before the military tribunal in Beirut for shipping weapons into Syria via the Bekaa Valley. In the far north-east of the country I found a truckload of Lebanese soldiers at the border station, big, burly men with automatic weapons. Lebanese Red Cross ambulances, their Syrian wounded from Homs lying inside, were allowed through. But for the sad, pathetic creatures walking down the road with neither bags nor documents, there was no easy passage. I felt the temptation, when I wrote about these people that night in late March 2012, to recall other refugees at another time in another place, the neutral Swiss border with Nazi Germany.

All was not quite as it seemed at al-Qaa. A few hundred metres from the customs house were a cluster of homes and a rocky path that ran low behind an olive grove. A woman and her husband who lived beside it welcomed me cautiously and asked me not to print even their

---

* The Israelis would use the same word in English when they stormed into Lebanon in 1982. Five months earlier, when the Syrians were finishing off the Muslim insurgents of Hama, they said – in the words of the then Syrian information minister – that they were 'searching' the area. 'Bahath' was the word he used. The British spoke of 'mopping up' in the Second World War. In the same conflict, SS Major Juergen Stroop referred to the 'cleansing' of Jewish streets in Warsaw.

first names. 'At night, they all come this way, along the path,' she said. 'Nobody stops them. They are [Syrian] opposition moving into Lebanon, and Syrian refugees. Whoever they are, we don't ask and we just say "God help them". Many civilians are Christians running away.'

I saw something else along this path. Broken shoes and boots with their soles ripped off and filthy socks, all torn. They belonged to desperate people who had walked into Lebanon at night, people who could not see and in the dark must have fallen on the unseen rocks and slithered in the mud. A silent people making their way into an unknown future. The word in al-Qaa was that Bashar al-Assad's men were trying to cut off the last escape routes. No wonder these people fell in the darkness.*

Just what they were fleeing was clear from a stream of grisly video footage of dead civilians, apparently filmed in the Karm el-Zeitoun and al-Adawiye districts of Homs. The pictures showed the bodies of at least twenty-six children and twenty-one women, some of whom had been raped before being murdered, according to 'Syrian militants' – this designation from the Beirut daily *L'Orient-Le Jour* – while others had been stabbed by shabiha militiamen. The Syrian information ministry in Damascus acknowledged that a mass grave had been found but stated, inevitably, that they were the victims of 'terrorists gangs' intent on rousing international opinion against Syria. Saudi Arabia and

---

* Just how Syria's sectarian demography touched its neighour was all too visible in the Lebanese city of Tripoli, just forty miles over the mountains from Homs. The Lebanese army was forced to position its old French-made armour around the enclave of Jabal Mohsen, where up to 40,000 Alawites have their homes, after Mohamed Bathish, a Sunni, was shot in the head by a sniper in mid-February 2012 in the longest gun battle the city had witnessed in many years. To reach the front line below the crusader castle of Saint Gilles was easy. I had only to follow the hundreds of black-white-and-green Free Syrian Army posters on the walls. To protest the onslaught on Homs, Sunni inhabitants had raised over the main street a huge sheet which depicted Assad as a giant pig. This image of the most unclean of animals in Islam did not, needless to say, commend itself to the inhabitants of Jabal Mohsen. After the Alawites had plastered their balconies with pictures of Assad – as a man, not a pig – volleys of rifle and rocket fire echoed across the Abu Ali river. In Jabal Mohsen, I later discovered portraits of Assad alongside those of Jesus and Mary, at least one of whom should surely not have been there. The Alawites of Tripoli originally came not from Homs but from the Syrian coastal city of Latakia. In the 1930s, Alawites had moved into the centre of Damascus, Sunnis to the suburbs of the Syrian capital, many of them with extended families inside Lebanon. Before the French mandate and its colonial borders, Homs and Tripoli were so close that families would cross the mountains between them for weekends.

Qatar were helping these groups, the government said. The opposition 'Syrian National Council', equally inevitably, called for 'urgent international and Arab military intervention'. The NATO secretary-general, Anders Fogh Rasmussen, told Reuters in Turkey five days later that 'we have no intention whatsoever to intervene in Syria'. He even rejected logistical support for 'humanitarian corridors' to besieged towns and cities; if a UN mandate was provided for NATO to take action in Syria as it had in Libya, this would change nothing, 'because Syria is also a different society, it is much more complicated ethnically, politically, religiously'.

There you had it. Syria was not too dangerous for international intervention, but it was too complicated for NATO. We will not go to war for Syria, I wrote in my report. 'In Kosovo, we bombed from the air until Milosovic was told by Yeltsin's Russia that he was on his own. But Putin's Russia is not going to tell Assad he's on his own. And besides, we don't have NATO armies waiting on the Syrian border to invade the country if Assad surrendered.'

The war was infecting ever larger areas of the country. There were fierce battles between the Syrian army and armed groups – not just the FSA – in the northern province of Idlib, adjacent to the Turkish border. This would become the hardest battlefield in the entire war. Idlib almost broke the Syrian army and would finish as the garbage tip of every Islamist jihadist group in the war. In the following years, the Western television networks and mainstream media continued to talk of the US president's 'red lines' and 'options on the table' and all the other Obama-isms. I wrote that 'we can also forget "red lines" because both sides in Syria have, I suspect, used gas and we didn't go to war … But we didn't go to war for Kurds when Saddam gassed them in 1988 – it became one of the smaller excuses for the Blair–Bush invasion of Iraq fifteen years later. And after suggesting the Russians have just dropped gas in Idlib province, you can be sure we are not going to war with Moscow. So amid the anguish of Syria's people … it's time we stopped lying to the people of the Middle East. And it's time we stopped lying to ourselves.'

Journalists were now travelling into northern Syria and speaking directly to rebel groups which despised the FSA but were regularly fighting government forces in Idlib. AFP, for example, interviewed members of the 'Abu Sulieman Combat Group' amid olive orchards and Roman ruins in northern Syria and found that its thirty-five-year-old leader distrusted the Syrian army deserters.* There were other signs of dissatisfaction. Fadwa Sulieman, the accomplished Syrian actress, an Alawite who pleaded for Sunnis and Alawites to unite in resisting Assad's power, was forced to seek safety in Paris in March 2012. She said she was 'ashamed to see that the revolution is not going in the right way, that it's in the process of arming itself ... that the country is moving towards a sectarian war'. In late April, a major report on Syrian refugees in *Time* magazine was describing the political and military opposition as 'hapless and disorganised'.

You could identify the growing anarchy in the Syrian countryside by chance details. Armed men turned up at the ICARDA agricultural research station at Tel Hadya twenty miles from Aleppo and stole vehicles along with farm machinery and computers.† But there were other, more sinister patterns emerging. Two Syrian helicopters attacked the small Sunni town of Haouch, forcing its 7,000 residents to abandon their homes. They had been shelled by government forces for two weeks. The authorities claimed that rebels were in these locations, but there was a growing suspicion that this was also part of a Baathist policy to prepare Syria for partition if Damascus fell. The 'frontier' between Alawite and Sunni towns here matched almost precisely the eastern border of the old 'State of the Alawites' – created by the French mandate which had chopped Syria up into sectarian mini-states.

The stories of sadism and cruelty that emerged from the Sunni villages to the West of Hama are so terrible that any author must pause at the details. Al-Qubayr (between seventy-eight and a hundred dead), Tremseh (between sixty-eight and 150), in Bayda and villages outside

---

* One of the guerrillas told AFP that he 'travelled three times to Turkey to see its boss, Riad Asaad. I asked him to give us money, weapons. He did nothing. He's a liar. What he wants is to take the place of Bashar in his palace, and nothing else!'

† As the 'birthplace of agriculture' – the Euphrates flows only seventy miles to the east of Aleppo – the city was also headquarters to the International Centre for Agricultural Research in Dry Areas, one of the finest institutions of its kind in the world, which increased food production in Asia and Africa in an area containing a billion people, half of whom earned their living from agriculture. Donors included Britain, Canada, the US, Germany, Holland and the World Bank. Mercifully, ICARDA's gene bank had been duplicated outside Syria. The Syrian government later moved an army checkpoint closer to the Tel Hadya research station – then abandoned the village altogether.

the coastal city of Banias ('at least' 248) – in some cases soldiers were among the dead, in most cases civilians and almost always Sunnis. But the name of Houla stands out, not because of the number of dead but because the UN put experienced soldiers into the village to gather evidence. And because an equally experienced British correspondent, Alex Thomson of Channel 4 News, went with them.

Weeks later, in Europe, I spoke at great length to one of the senior UN officers who gave me an emotional account of the civilian dead, 'a little girl with her brain missing, shot through the front of the skull, men shot through the head, all Sunnis, and their killers – without a shadow of doubt – the Alawi shabiha gangs'. The UN found a mass grave containing a hundred bodies, mostly women and children. Its subsequent report would hold the Syrian government responsible. But a far more memorable account is contained in Thomson's own report. He and his crew found themselves mobbed by 'people shouting and crying in a mixture of relief, shock and anger', then physically pulled from house to house. Within minutes, he reported:

> we meet twenty-five-year-old Younis, lying in a room with two gunshot wounds in his torso. He's telling us, weakly, how he was trying to help an eleven-year-old boy on Friday when he was injured. The boy was shot dead. A fifteen-year-old girl lies on another bed not ten yards away describing how she witnessed the Shabiya militia crouching behind a window as she tried to flee. She too was shot ... Whether we like it or not, we were pretty much dragged onto the streets again. On one hand an eight-year-old boy shot in the arm, next to him a man showing us a video on his telephone of two children, their throats slit so deeply they are virtually decapitated.

A man speaking good English approaches Thomson and his crew, talking in 'cold, measured anger'. He describes the intense shelling of Houla before the shabiha entered, around a hundred of them in military uniforms. He and other villagers agree they came from Alawite villages to the south and west and they went from house to house, slaughtering Sunni families. 'When this is all over,' the man says:

we will be victorious. And we will go there. And we will find them out and we will slaughter them and we will kill them. We will kill their men, women and children as they killed our men, women and children.

Thomson rhetorically asks his audience what he can offer an elderly man called Abdul Hamad 'who knows not only that his daughter was killed but that her throat was hacked with a knife, it seems, wielded by men who live just a few miles distant'.

Briefly in Damascus, my colleague Patrick Cockburn suggested that the Houla massacre may have been 'carried out by regime forces in revenge for the killing of a government informant in the nearby Alawite village of Kabu a month earlier'. Syrian friends gave me a different account: that the throat-cuttings of Houla might have been a reprisal for the attempted poisoning of Assad's brother-in-law Assef Shawkat, one of the regime's most important security figures, claimed by the FSA a few days earlier.* The UN Supervision Mission tried to continue its investigations into other village massacres but came under fire when it sought to enter Al-Qubayr, apparently from Syrian troops. One dying man in the village managed to make a mobile phone call to his brother, and told him that the shabiha had just cut off his hand. The brother, hiding in a neighbouring village, later reached his family home. 'We started pulling the corpses from the house,' he said. 'All of them were mutilated, cut with knives. There were bodies of children and women everywhere.' The man did not find his brother.

Reading one's old dispatches can be a miserable exercise. So often we journalists get it wrong. The weight of evidence can be so awesome that we become utterly convinced of the conclusion of any series of events. When the Oslo agreement was first disclosed, there was an almost childish desire on the part of the 'international community' to convince themselves that there would finally be 'peace' between

* Preparing a meal for Shawkat (and for the two other men who would die with him in the July Damascus explosion), an enthusiastic cook apparently put fifteen poison tablets into their food rather than the prescribed five – and they didn't eat it because they thought the food was bad.

Israelis and Palestinians; an end to war in the Middle East. Enough of blood and tears, Yitzhak Rabin had said. Anyone who opposed this storyline became not only an object of derision, but of personal abuse.

But after years in the saddle, you get to spot the mirages in the desert, the happy endings which will inevitably turn into tragedy, the 'justice' which must be accompanied by dishonour; in other words, the reports you would like to write as opposed to the reports you must write. And so after Houla and the other bloodbaths, I filled my column with warnings that many readers would not want to hear. Bashar al-Assad, I wrote, will get away with it.

> He got away with Daraa. He got away with Homs. And he'll get
> away with Houla. Yes, this may be the critical moment, the
> eponymous 'tipping point' of horror, the milli-second of
> revolutionary fission, when Baathist collapse becomes inevitable
> rather than probable … But the Middle East is littered with a
> hundred Houlas, their dead children piled among the statistics,
> with knives and ropes as well as guns among the murder
> weapons.

What if Assad's soldiers let their Alawite militia do the dirty work? I asked. Didn't the Algerian FLN regime use 'home guard' units to murder their opponents in the 1990s? Didn't Gaddafi have his loyalist militias … and Mubarak his jailbird drugged-up cops, the baltagi? Didn't Israel allow its Lebanese Phalangists into the Palestinian camps in 1982 where they raped and eviscerated and murdered civilians? Was this not also 'rule by murder'? At Bentalha in Algeria, as many as 200 villagers were destroyed in one night in 1997, babies' heads bashed into walls, women raped and mutilated to death with machetes, men decapitated with knives. The killers may have been Islamists. Or government militiamen – the village had voted in elections for opponents of the government – and certainly the army refused to help the victims. Today, the West treats Algeria as a bulwark against 'terror'. 'For Houla, read Bentalha, a place we have all forgotten,' I wrote in my article in May 2012. 'As we will forget Houla.'

The international demands for the destruction of Assad tyranny grew in almost inverse proportion to the willingness of the West to bring this about.* In late 2011, Obama's defense secretary Leon Panetta said in Tel Aviv that Assad's fall was 'only a question of time'. But two months later, again in Israel, Panetta was walking backwards. 'It is tragic, obviously that there are people who are dying,' he said lamely, 'but the key right now is to put pressure on him … [for us] to make the effort to replace Assad … Let's give that some time.' A month later, French president Nicolas Sarkozy demanded Assad's resignation, since the regime's activities had 'produced disgust around the world'.

It was like a children's dancing lesson, each politician more enthusiastic to show off their ability to move with the music, to mark time, to step back when required to do so. The noisier the rhetoric, however hollow, the more satisfied were the statesmen who awaited the collapse of the tyrant. Even when Assad was accused of using chemical weapons, the British – unwilling like all other 'civilised' nations to become militarily involved – were still happy to write off Assad's regime with words. 'I think it is unthinkable that President Assad can play any part in the future government of his country,' British prime minister David Cameron said at the G8 summit in the summer of 2013. Just days later, US secretary of state John Kerry likened Assad to Adolf Hitler and Saddam Hussein.† Obama would subsequently make the

---

* Long before the Syrian war, Assad's opponents had been over-hastily predicting his departure. '… Bashar is going to fall – the people are going to overthrow him,' Abdul Halim Khaddam, Assad's former vice president, boasted in 2006 from his exile in Paris. By the summer of 2011, a former Israeli intelligence operative (Professor Mordechai Kedar of Bar Ilan University) was announcing that if the Alawites lost control, 'the worst will transpire for them'. In which case, 'frenzied Sunni masses will descend on Alawi neighbourhoods in Damascus, Homs, Hama and Aleppo, ready to detach Alawi heads from their necks.' This was indeed what many Alawites feared. Local Arab papers, especially the stridently anti-Assad *L'Orient-Le Jour* in Beirut, proclaimed that the time had come for the Syrian president 'to pack his bags with a minimum of dignity'. Nadim Khoury, Human Rights Watch's researcher, was hoping that 'if the regime falls', many of the mukhabarat's 'well-guarded secrets' – including the fate of Lebanese detainees in Syrian prisons – would be revealed. It was not to be.

† This was a potent mix. Saddam had been compared to Hitler by US presidents in the 1990s – even though Saddam's dictator-hero was Stalin – but now both men were thrown in together because of their use of gas. But it was an unhappy combination since many of the precursors for Saddam's chemical weapons came from America. Kerry's remarks were somewhat in advance of Hillary Clinton's observation in March 2011 – four days after Syrian demonstrators were being shot down – that 'there is a different leader in Syria now. Many of the members of Congress of both parties who have gone to Syria in recent

case for 'tailored, limited strikes' on Syria, a 'shot across the bow', as he put it in his weary imperial vocabulary.

It was infectious, this form of impotent fury. Eleven Western and Arab countries solemnly reaffirmed at a meeting of the 'Friends of Syria' in London that Assad had 'no role' in the future Syrian government. The joint statement, however, did reveal the nations' 'growing concern at the increase in extremism and extremist groups' inside Syria. The Islamic State of Iraq and the Levant – soon to be ISIS – along with the Nusra front, seeded from al-Qaeda, 'threaten moderate forces as well as territorial integrity, and regional and international security'. This was in itself intriguing. The regime had all along, for its own purposes, promoted these Islamist groups as the enemies of Syria. Now the US, Europe and their Arab allies saw them as a threat not to the Assad regime but to the 'moderate forces' which the West was already arming in order to destroy Assad.

Two years into the uprising and already Syria was a battleground for the old cold war enemies. I wrote in the summer of 2013 that 'today's superpowers are now fighting in Syria; Russia wants to prove its international power and crush an Islamist uprising close to its border. The West wants to counter Russian's power in the Middle East by giving guns to the rebels while at the same time preventing the Islamists taking over Syria. It means we don't really care to end the war.' Grafted onto this phantom West-versus-Russia conflict, there was the Sunni–Shia struggle, in which the Sunni – the Gulf monarchies, Jordan, Turkey, Egypt (up to a point) and much of north Africa – aligned themselves against the Shia: the Iranians, the Alawites, Iraq's majority population, the Hizbollah representing the largest Shia community in Lebanon, and Bahrain, and a minority Shia population in Saudi Arabia.

Had there ever been, one wondered, a Middle East war of such hypocrisy, of such moral cowardice, of such false rhetoric and such public humiliation? Obama and Clinton still hoped for a 'democracy' in a post-Assad Syria. Yet when Qatar and Saudi Arabia, the West's allies, armed and funded the rebels of Syria, Washington uttered not a word of criticism. Qatar was a royal autocracy and Saudi Arabia among the most pernicious of caliphate-kingly dictatorships in the Arab world. Rulers of both states inherited power from their families – just as

months have said they believe [Assad] is a reformer.'

Bashar al-Assad had done – and the Saudis were allies of the Salafist-Wahhabi groups in Syria, just as they were once loyal supporters of the 'medieval' Taliban in Afghanistan.

Even Walid Jumblatt's excoriation of the Syrian regime, year after year and ever more apoplectic, appeared comparatively sane in comparison to the record of the world's statesmen and stateswomen. In February 2012, the Lebanese Druze leader was urging Moscow to exile Assad to 'the far end of Siberia'. 'The life of tyrants is short!' he cried a year later, urging the West to find a solution 'without Assad'. Then he began speaking of the 'banality of evil' in Syria, the expression used by Hannah Arendt of the Nazi war criminal Adolf Eichmann. She had described him as 'neither perverted nor sadistic' but 'terrifyingly normal'. And there Jumblatt might just have had a point.

That the despot might one day even declare victory over those who planned to liquidate his regime was a suggestion as unthinkable as his continued existence. But while I too originally believed that Daraa and the atrocities which followed had doomed Assad, I instinctively felt that this was too easy a conclusion. In early 2012, I began to express my own doubts about Assad's imminent flight. He was not about to go, I wrote in the *Independent*:

> Not yet. Not, maybe, for quite a long time. Newspapers in the Middle East are filled with stories about whether this is Assad's 'Benghazi moment' – these reports are almost invariably written from Washington or London or Paris – but few in the region understand how we Westerners can get it so wrong. The old saw has to be repeated and repeated: Egypt was not Tunisia; Bahrain was not Egypt; Libya was not Yemen. And Syria is very definitely not Libya.

Hatred cascaded into my email inbox. I was supporting Assad, giving my blessing to his diabolical regime. How much was the Syrian government paying me to write such lies? To attempt to tell the truth – that Assad was not likely to be overthrown, perhaps not even for years – was deemed identical to endorsement of a ruthless dictatorship. Merely to imply that Assad might survive longer than we anticipated was to give moral succour to the regime. A personal friend of mine, Sammy Katz, the AFP Beirut bureau chief, provoked a similar reaction when

he reached the same conclusions. 'I was at the war correspondent's
award ceremony at Bayeux,' he told me. 'My colleagues were not
abusive, but they were aggressive. That is the only word I can think of:
agressif.'* The French writer and academic Fabrice Balanche, greatly
respected for his knowledge of Syria and the Alawites, was condemned
as 'a defender of the Assad regime' when he said during an interview in
France in 2011 that the regime was not 'ripe' to fall and that Syria was
heading towards a civil war.

It was as if the whole Arab awakening, that massive struggle for
dignity and justice, could only have a happy ending – and must thus be
reported according to a format laid down in presidential speeches,
'expert' analyses and editorials. It had started years before, a plague
given renewed emphasis by George W. Bush's hollow language, where
everyone in the region was supposed to be fighting – or fleeing from
– 'terror'. It became clear that if anyone's views no longer synchro-
nised with the overwhelming insistence upon a beneficial outcome of
events – the fall of Assad, for example – they were to be rejected,
condemned, reviled, cursed and denounced. It mattered not how carefully the offender tried to explain that a cool assessment of the likely
conclusion of a war might not match the high hopes of rebels, freedom
fighters, democrats and unarmed innocents, let alone the promiscuous
assessment of politicians. To utter these heresies was to invite calumny.
Social media contained more than slander and defamation. Anonymous
'readers' told me they hoped my throat would soon be cut by my
'friends', the shabiha.

Almost exactly five years before his death, my long-standing Israeli
friend, author and philosopher Uri Avnery, wrote of the 'fatal faults' of
so many popular movements for democracy, liberty and social justice.
They were, he thought, 'the faults of a generation brought up on the
"social media", the immediacy of the internet, the effortlessness of
instant mass communication. These fostered a sense of empowerment

* I had been through this routine so many times before – in Northern Ireland when I
wrote about the brutality of the British army, in the Kosovo war when I wrote about the
innocent Serb victims of NATO bombing, in Gaza when I wrote of Israel's Palestinian
victims, in Iraq when I wrote of American as well as jihadist cruelty – that I was even able
to guess the words in which the abuse would be couched. I was 'pro-IRA' or approved
Serb 'ethnic cleansing' or supported 'terrorism'. The abuse, especially on social media, was
intended not to clarify the truth but to inhibit my reporting.

without effort, of the ability to change things without the arduous process of mass-organisation, political power-building, of ideology, of leadership, of parties. A happy and anarchistic attitude that, alas, cannot stand up against real power.'

Avnery was clearly thinking of the dissatisfaction of Egyptian protesters with the Muslim Brotherhood – because they were faced with a party which possessed all that they lacked: 'organisation, discipline, ideology, leadership, experience, cohesion'. In the case of Syria, however, the force that confronted the protesters also possessed tanks, artillery and air power. If the Syrian revolution was to continue, these protesters, too, would have to build political power. But they would also have to be heavily armed; which would be the end of the peaceful revolution. At this point, Assad's opponents had to decide whether those who wished to arm them intended to help them destroy the regime – or whether they were more interested in destroying Syria.

Nikolaos Van Dam, a genuine expert on Syria and a former Dutch diplomat in Damascus, eloquently expressed the dichotomy behind this problem in his indispensable work on the destruction of the country. He noted how academics and journalists who observed that the opposition

> was not only peaceful but also occasionally used violence and attacked the [government] army and security forces with arms were strongly criticised by the opposition and others, if only because that might give some credibility to the regime's story of its being attacked by 'armed terrorists' and could help shatter the image of the strictly peaceful opposition, a peacefulness which provided the opposition with a strong kind of moral legitimacy. Criticism of the violent Islamist radicals who started to overshadow the peaceful opponents of the regime was easily interpreted as criticism of the whole opposition, including those who were peaceful.

Sami Moubayed, a sane Syrian scholar and historian (and no Baathist), described how senior Syrian opposition figures were sceptical of the Nusra front when it announced itself in 2012 because they were

desperately trying to prove that no Islamists existed in the Syrian
rebel community – only secular soldiers who had defected from
the Syrian army. If Jabhat al Nusra was real, then it threatened
to do away with all they had been working for since March 2011.

In the middle of July 2012, a young Syrian turned up at a smart office
block in Beirut. Without giving his name, he said he wanted to speak
to another Syrian who worked in the building, a well-educated, middle-
class Sunni man from Damascus, a friend of mine, who had defected
several months earlier after occupying a high post in the regime. The
visitor was taken upstairs and introduced himself. 'I was sent to you by
the shebab,' he said – meaning he worked for the Syrian opposition –
'and we need your help.' His story was as revealing as it was frightening.
Damascus was about to be attacked. But the rebel fighters were out of
control. 'Some of our people are on drugs,' the visitor said. 'They will
take anyone out. We can't guarantee what some of these men will do.
If they went into [the suburb of] Malki, we couldn't protect any of the
people who lived there. We are against the Salafists who are fighting
– there are good Syrians – Druze and Ishmaelis [Alawites] are with us.
If we capture Damascus, we don't know how to run a small town, let
alone a country.'

It was a true civil war story. There were bad guys among the good
guys and good guys among the bad. But sectarianism was biting into
the Syrian revolution. The prominent Syrian in Beirut knew all this. He
was taking notes and he gave his visitor the following advice: 'Organise
neighbourhood committees, well-dressed men who must be clearly
identified, who must protect everyone, Christian, Druze, Sunni,
Alawites, everyone in each neighbourhood.'

The storm was about to break. On 18 July, they went for the jugular.
The brother-in-law of the president, the defence minister and a senior
adviser dead, the wounding of the interior minister, a massive bomb
inside the military headquarters run by Assad's own brother; assassinations take time to plan, but this was on an epic scale. Bashar al-Assad's
sister Bushra had lost her husband in the explosion in the very centre
of Damascus. There was talk of the 'decisive battle' and there would be
massacres to come.

Days later, I would meet a young Syrian officer who witnessed the
fighting on the streets. 'It was merciless, it was a butchery,' he said.

Assad had called in his brother Maher, whose own legion – a branch of the army's 4th Armoured Division – was sent in to the city. Their tanks quartered off the capital. 'They shot all the armed men dead,' the officer told me. 'When they surrendered, they shot all the prisoners. I saw the bodies, they were piled up on top of each other. I have never seen anything like it.'

The shooting could be heard inside the presidential palace. These were historic, unprecedented days for the regime, not least for Bashar al-Assad himself. Did he think of leaving?* When the presidential jet left Damascus on the evening of 18 July, it turned out to be carrying his brother-in-law's body for burial near his native city of Tartous. Assad's supporters fled in mile-long convoys of family cars to Lebanon. More than 30,000 Syrians crossed the border in two days. Inside Lebanon, Sunnis were celebrating Shawkat's death; he was believed to have ordered the murder of their Sunni ex-prime minister Rafiq Hariri in 2005 and appeared in a UN document as a suspect – until the UN itself censored his name from the page.

In street fighting in both Damascus and Hama, the army won back almost all the ground lost to the rebel fighters in their grand attack on the capital. The reports of scores of dead were as unverifiable as they were probable. A video which surfaced, apparently from the southern town of Herak, showed the bodies of dead children lying on a blood-smeared floor.

Even four years since the great rebel attack, artillery still murmurs outside the walls of the Mezze prison in Damascus. Unlike his fellow inmates, Hamoud Saleh Hamed does not wear leg shackles when he is pushed in a new wheelchair into the Syrian prison governor's guest room at the military jail. Impossible, since his trousered right stump and the missing lower half of his left leg mean that the thirty-seven-year-old Saudi maths teacher from Mecca cannot escape. He speaks with great calmness, an intelligent man with long hair, large, sunken eyes and a wispy beard who recounts his life as a Nusra Front platoon

---

* Even if Assad thought of departing, this would have been impossible. 'Suppose our Alawite president decides to flee,' a former Syrian soldier had said to me earlier. 'He will be driven to the airport by an Alawite colonel. What do you think the colonel will think? Will he let [the president] go [to the airport]? I doubt it.'

commander and an executioner who fired four shots into the head of a
Syrian government 'collaborator'.

For all these years, I have waited to speak to an Islamist who fought
to capture this city in 2012 and now here he is, insisting that we record
his words, happy to have his photograph taken by Nelofer who sits
beside me. Here is one of the 'foreign fighters' of whom the regime
spoke so frequently, one of the jihadists whom we heard so much
about but never saw. He is a thoughtful man who sometimes pauses
for recollection, but whose words are precise and uttered with a
disturbing confidence. Hamoud Hamed says he regrets killing the fifty-
year-old man whose name he never knew, but he recounts with pride
his weapons' training and his role in the bloody July 2012 Battle of
Damascus when he and his comrades, from Nusra and the FSA and
Liwa al-Islam and other groups vainly tried to capture the capital of
Syria.

'Frankly,' the governor's balding intelligence officer admitted to us
before the prisoner was brought into the room, 'I'm very surprised
they are going to let you meet this man.' But I could well understand
why 'they' did. Hamoud Hamed was a Saudi who fought against the
Syrian regime alongside other Wahhabi Sunni Saudis, admitting he
was misled about the Syrian war by the internet and by the Qatari Al
Jazeera channel, describing in detail how he was groomed in Saudi
Arabia for his jihad by a friend who arranged his passage through
Turkey into the Syrian killing fields. Terribly wounded, he was
captured by Syrian troops in 2015 while trying to escape to Idlib. He
was one of the few who were left. Some had got away. Many –
although he did not say so – had been executed.

Hamoud Hamed smiled a lot during our interview, his words occasionally interrupted by the rumble of shellfire from the darkness
outside. The governor and his security officer left the room at our
request and Hamed insisted he wished to speak, even when we assured
him he could relax and drink the glass of orange juice beside him. He
had never met a foreign journalist before but he enjoyed talking, he
said.

Many Islamists have expressed a fascination with mathematics, but
Hamed said he gained his MA because he had good teachers in
'respected Mecca' where he married a Saudi woman and was father of
a son and four daughters. His own father, now dead, had been muez-

zin at a Mecca mosque. 'The Syrian war had started and there were many protests,' he said. 'The internet and the television channels like Al Jazeera said that the Syrian people were asking for help. Jihadi slogans spread, and the jihadis outside Syria began to call for help to defend the people and stop the brutality of the Assad regime. The idea of going to Syria and to participate grew in my mind. Some sheikhs and religious leaders in Saudi Arabia spoke on television and in the mosques and encouraged us.'

A Syrian friend in Mecca whom he called 'Abdul-Rahman al-Suri' (Abdul-Rahman from Syria) organised his Saudi Airlines flight to the Turkish city of Antakya although his departure was kept secret for fear that the Saudi intelligence service would find out. 'They were refusing to allow people to go to Syria,' Hamed said, 'but for political reasons, nothing to do with Islamic sharia.' Taken across the border and to the Syrian town of Atme in a car, Hamed reached a 'guest house' where their identity papers and passports were taken from them for 'safekeeping'. After two more days, they were taken to a Nusra/al-Qaeda military training camp where they were taught to use AK-47 rifles, RPG B-7 anti-tank rocket launchers and mortars. The teachers were Egyptian, their instructor Turkish. After a month, Hamed was sent to the eastern countryside of Deir ez-Zour with seven men, an Egyptian, a Qatari and five Saudis, where they met the Nusra leader of eastern Syria, 'Emir' Abu Maria al-Qahtani, who would later be demoted by the Nusra leadership during a dispute over relations with ISIS. 'After we met,' Hamoud Hamed said, 'we pledged our loyalty and obedience and prayed that we would accept good times and bad times and would not question the orders of our commander as we sought to see those who are infidels in the sight of God. We were taken to the city of Deir ez-Zour which was under siege and there was fierce fighting.'

From Deir ez-Zour, in a convoy of cars, vans and jeeps, Hamed said, he was taken with seven more men to the Damascus suburb of Ghouta where, staying in 'a great house', he was told to train on mortars for another month; after which he was sent to the district of Jobar. One of Hamed's leaders, 'Abu Bakr al-Urduni' [Abu Bakr from Jordan]:

pinpointed our targets. I was to fire at the Abbasiyyin stadium
and the Panorama war memorial area.* I was given the target
points from Google maps. The idea was to separate the
defending Syrian soldiers, to confuse them. The plan was for
seven suicide car bombers to enter Damascus. Zero hour for me
was 9 a.m. on 15 July [2012] and we started shelling.

Hamed admits he did not know who was inside his target areas, but
says that his own home-made mortars began to explode. One was hit
by Syrian army fire and he was eventually forced to escape as government forces advanced. 'There had been mistakes by our leaders, one of
the car bombs exploded on the road into the city.' As his men shelled
Ghouta, which was now under siege by the army, Hamed retreated yet
again, to al-Teibi and then to the village of Marj al-Sultan. And here, a
Nusra man invited him to marry his niece as a second wife. She would
later bear him two children.

Hamed was driving a vehicle in the company of his new brother-in-
law when a Syrian army rocket hit the vehicle, blowing off his left leg
and severing his right leg at the knee. There followed months of medical operations in makeshift rebel hospitals and four days of surgery.
Hamed smiled as he spoke of his injuries. Was it worth it? I asked. 'It
was fate,' he said:

> I will tell you about an incident. There was a man in the Ghouta
> area who had been caught signalling targets to the Syrian army. A
> religious judge, a mufti, condemned him to death. They asked me
> if I would kill him. It was outside, and the man was kneeling on
> the ground. He confessed before several of the leaders who were
> there. Then I shot him in the back of the head. I did not know his
> name. The others told me to keep shooting and I shot him three
> more times. I felt nothing. If this man was a Muslim and had
> made a sin, when I killed him I purified him from his sins.

---

* An interesting choice of targets. The Abbasiyyin stadium, a 30,000-seat athletics arena
where Pope John Paul II conducted mass in 2001, had been invested by government army
troops several months earlier, and bordered the Jobar district where Hamed commanded
his mortar teams. The Panorama war memorial four miles to the west contained an
exhibition on the battle for the Syrian Golan Heights in the 1973 Middle East war – and
was an honoured location for soldiers and veterans of the conflict.

This horrifying admission was followed by a long silence. Hamoud Hamed talked again about fate, of further months of medical operations and then of his regrets. 'It was fate,' he said again:

> In Ghouta, the siege was worse and people were very hungry. When the people wanted us to go, it gave me great pain. The people who we wanted to help didn't want us anymore. And it was painful to me when fighting broke out between the different rebel groups, between Muslims, between the Free Syrian Army and Nusra and Daesh.

And so he had mentioned Daesh at last. The 'Islamic State' had arrived to infect every jihadi. ISIS was grotesquely sectarian, its duty to destroy its Sunni Muslim, Christian, Alawite adversaries, pro-regime, anti-regime, Yazidi, innocents and spies. And it would almost win.

'Strange, isn't it, how every time we have a "crisis" in the Middle East, the Russians step in to take advantage of it?' I wrote in the *Independent* in March 2015:

> No sooner have we identified ISIS/the Islamic Caliphate/Daesh as the most apocalyptic, end-of-the-world antagonist since Hitler/Napoleon/Nero/Genghis Khan, than old Mother Russia stretches out her bear's claws and tickles a former Soviet Republic, namely Ukraine. While the ISIS boys consolidated in Raqaa and Mosul, the Russians took over the Crimea.

In Syria, weapons poured in to help the Kurds in Kobani while the Ukrainians pleaded for more guns. Moscow's 'experts' regularly appeared on television – many had an odd habit of flapping their hands in front of the screen – to tell us that 'our' war was in fighting Islamist 'fascism' in Syria and Iraq (and, I suppose, Afghanistan). I remarked:

> Flashback now to the forgotten war in Chechnya – forgotten by us, that is. We were indulgent when Boris Yeltsin fought the first Chechen war in the mid-1990s, and when Vladimir Putin was concluding Russia's second war in Chechnya in 2002, we

were far too preoccupied with our new adventure in
Afghanistan and our forthcoming 'liberation' of Baghdad to
worry about the poor old Chechens again.

Ruffle the pages of our history books a little further, however, and we
find another far more momentous self-negation in 1956. For no sooner
had the British and French connived with the Israelis to go to war over
Suez – and drive Nasser out of power – than the Soviets sent their
tanks into the streets of Budapest to suppress the Hungarian
Revolution. The supreme disregard for international law demonstrated
by both the Soviet forces and the Anglo-French armies flattened out
each other's outrageous conduct. And although the Soviet tank
bombardment of Budapest was long in the planning and thus more
likely to have been timed to coincide with the Suez invasion, it was
difficult to condemn the Russians for taking advantage of our European
aggression in Egypt.

'And who are the winners of this decades-long burlesque?' I asked.
Well, the Arabs for one, I wrote in my report. Field Marshal President
al-Sisi of Egypt fêted Putin in Cairo, but is happy to host UK businessmen to assist his pharaonic projects for a new Egyptian administrative
capital (total cost around $45 billion) and a 'new' Suez Canal. And
President Bashar al-Assad can count on Putin's support in his war
against the rebels of Syria while benefiting from US air strikes on his
ISIS enemies. And there's Israel. Its alliance with the US as strong as
ever despite Bibi Netanyahu's tomfoolery on Capitol Hill, Israel was
offering to mediate between Russia and Ukraine – an interesting
proposal, since Israel has plenty of experience of occupying other
people's land. And remember, Putin once praised the political career of
Soviet-born Israeli foreign minister Avigdor Lieberman – who believes,
ISIS-like, that disloyal Arab-Israelis should have their heads axed off –
as 'brilliant'. At least the dictators and racists of the Middle East
understand the hypocrisy of the superpowers.

Hypocrisy was on display aplenty in Syria. I kept a diary from which
I wrote a daily 'notebook' for readers of the *Independent*, a scrabble of
news items, horror stories, unbelievable claims, rumours and military
secrets. And the account of the UN's miserable departure.

Behind the walls of the original French barracks down from
Umayyad Square, the burned wreckage of the latest truck bomb lay

below a wizened tree. Was it aimed at the run-down caserne which the Syrian army still uses? Or was it a little trick for the UN officers in the Dama Rose Hotel across the road? The last hundred military observers were already packing for the journey to Beirut. 'We are defunct in five days,' I heard one of the UN officers say in the lobby.

You could hardly blame them for leaving. In Aleppo, the UN soldiers had started off travelling within a thirty-mile radius of the city but in the space of months, their government escorts would not venture beyond the last government checkpoint on the municipal limits. The rebels were less friendly to the UN; several of the international observers told me they saw 'foreigners' among the Free Syrian Army. Phone calls arrived for FSA men, tracked by the UN's own intelligence unit, from dialling codes in Qatar and Saudi Arabia.

Some warnings were more direct. Just a week before, a security man working for the UN, formerly a Syrian government security agent, was kidnapped, tortured and then murdered near his home north of Damascus. They found twenty bullet wounds in his body. UN officers, who were permitted to talk to both sides in the conflict, spoke to me of Kfar Zita near Hama, and executions carried out by men with rifles using 7.62 mm rounds, brain matter on the wall beside the embedded bullets. The Syrian military in the district were using T-72 tanks, S-5 rockets from Hind helicopters, Mig-23s and tiny planes that looked little larger than Piper Cubs. And drones, always followed by the Hinds. A Salafist on the state television told his audience that his enemies were 'Alawites and Shiites and Christians'. The UN soldiers tended to agree. Like every foreign army to enter the Levant in recent times, they had long ago worked out the sectarian patterns.

The UN's commander in Damascus, Senegalese general Babacar Gaye, bid a miserable goodbye to his mission on 18 August 2012, unconvincingly claiming that the UN would not abandon Syria – but in fact turning the country into a free-fire zone the moment his last soldiers began their retreat. After UN troops had arrived on 21 April to monitor the withdrawal of heavy weapons and a ceasefire, violence declined, Gaye told us. But 'by the middle of June, it was clear that the parties were no longer committed to the ceasefire'. UN observers had tried 'to facilitate pauses in the fighting' to assist humanitarian work and Gaye called upon 'all parties to stop the violence which is causing such suffering to the Syrian people'. When I asked the general how he felt about the failure of his mission, he said he was 'comforted by the fact that the UN will stay in Syria'. But this was fantasy. Save for a tiny UN office with perhaps only ten staff, the only UN observer mission left in Syria was the post-1967 UNTSO force which was supposed to keep the Israeli–Syrian peace on the Golan Heights. Very soon, it would be sheltering from Syria's civil war shellfire.

We were left to ponder why Gaye's UN troops were pulled out, even before the Algerian diplomat Lakhdar Brahimi had arrived to take up his role as UN envoy. Were there some in UN headquarters who knew from the start that the assignment was not intended to succeed? Or was it because the Western nations and Gulf sponsors did not want UN observers snooping into the amount of new weaponry which they might be planning to send to the FSA and its more bearded allies in those parts of Syria?

Outside the UN's hotel, in the hot Damascus afternoon, the often empty streets spoke of lassitude rather than disaster. The regime did not appear to be on the verge of collapse, but the signs of dislocation were everywhere. Soldiers were now billeted in the old Ottoman Haj station in central Damascus – from which no trains had left in months. The main highways to the north had been cut and phone lines to Aleppo had collapsed; most travellers chose to fly to the city from Damascus, even though the road from Aleppo airport to the city centre was itself dangerous.

We found the Syrian Arab Airlines' main ticket office opposite the Haj station packed with passengers, all seeking flights out of the country or pleading for overbooked seats for relatives on planes out of Aleppo. There were murderous gun battles in that old Silk Road city, until now spared by the war. This was a new front in the conflict. If the Syrian army lost Aleppo, they would give their rebel opponents a new capital from which they could claim to dominate Syria. Nelofer and I decided to join the queue at that packed airline ticket office. There were plenty of seats to Aleppo on the Syrian Arab Airlines' flight. The ticket clerk, nonchalantly telling us it was impossible to book a return, glanced at our Western passports without interest, as if we were tourists on our way to enjoy the ancient souks of Aleppo, visit the great Citadel or relax at the Baron Hotel. Only when he said 'good luck' did I see a reflection of concern in his eyes.

The Airbus 320 had only a dozen passengers. But the crew went through the flight safety routine – as if ensuring that our table-tops were safely fastened would somehow guarantee our little adventure. We landed before dusk. The travel posters on the walls, their colours already blued-out, the ill-kempt security man pointed to a small office where an airline official told us to wait for the airport's military manager. He eventually arrived, and in vain tried to call Damascus. He shook his head with amazement that two Western journalists had turned up to watch the war in Aleppo and then led us to the abandoned airport car park in which a solitary yellow taxi stood. 'Take these people to a good hotel,' he told the driver. Then he looked at Nelofer and said, 'You should wear a scarf. It will be safer for you.' That's when we realised that we would have to travel through rebel-held territory to reach the west of Aleppo.

Journalists who crossed the Turkish border into Syria had already reached the eastern suburbs. Their reports spoke of rebels looking at the Citadel. We would be looking at the other side of this same fortress which Christopher Marlowe's Tamburlaine destroyed in 1400. Destruction is what Aleppo will be known for again, its ancient city even now, in the summer of 2012, awaiting its re-demolition. The annihilation of Syria itself and its cities and towns and villages, its mosques and churches and most of all its people, will now be part of our terrible story.

August 2012. Is Aleppo, we ask ourselves, really now participating in the Syrian conflict after those almost incredible months in which the largest city in the country remained haughtily aloof from the Arab awakening? We know it is true when the airport taxi driver turns off the motorway into Aleppo. A halo of brown smoke embraces the horizon and the driver knows better than to follow the motorway signs from the airport. He turns left, bouncing over the broken median rail and between two vast piles of rocks, aware of what we are about to see. In front of us is a sea of ruins, burned houses and wrecked cars through which we drive very slowly, the accelerator cutting out as we slink past two garbage trucks, upended to form a roadblock.

But these are phantom checkpoints. There are no gunmen, no militiamen, no Free Syrian Army, no al-Qaeda and not a civilian soul, because this battle is over. This is the suburb of al-Baz, retaken by the

government army, we are told later, although we see not a soldier for
miles. The army has come and it has gone, and the buildings on each
side of the road are shell-smashed and bullet-scarred. We drive on
through these ghost streets. Electric cables droop from their pylons.
There is even, on our right, a spectral police station, its giant wall-por-
trait of Bashar al-Assad intact but above each window the black stain of
fires, the building gutted, the fire station next door abandoned. A fire
truck has been driven into a wall. In all of four miles, I spot one forlorn
child in the ruins and a mother carrying a baby across an acre of dust.
Only when the Citadel appears to our right are there people on the
streets, families, small girls in their Eid dresses, a shwarma café.

'We cleansed these streets,' a Syrian officer will tell me later. Yes,
that word again. We found the Aleppo Palace Hotel in the centre of
the city, government soldiers lounging in the park opposite, a smart
Armenian desk manager and cramped, dirty rooms with broken
windows. I wasn't so sure about the men we would meet, Assad's
soldiers, privates and officers. It was a strange sensation, to sit in a
private house commandeered by the Syrian army in Aleppo and talk to
generals accused of being war criminals. I was, so to speak, in 'the lair
of the enemy'. An immensely tall, balding major general who
commanded Saif al-Dowla had much to say about the war his soldiers
were fighting and the contempt with which they regarded their
enemies. 'Mice,' the general called them. 'They snipe at us and then
they run and hide in the sewers. Foreigners – Turks, Chechens,
Afghans, Libyans, Sudanese ...' And Syrians, I said. 'Yes, Syrians too,
but smugglers and criminals ...' A machine gun puttered away at the
bottom of the street.

I did not believe in the international list of 'Terrorists Inc.', although
I would change my mind somewhat in the weeks to come. And the
Syrian generals were to change their description of the 'smugglers and
criminals', the FSA deserters whom, of course, they knew. The fifty-
three-year-old major general had thirty-three years in the Syrian
military behind him, two sons, two grandsons and two bullet wounds
from the July battle in Damascus. He told me he could 'clean' this part
of Aleppo from 'terrorists' in twenty days. Nelofer and I hoped we
would meet this general later when – we were sure – his pledge would
remain unfulfilled. And sure enough, three years later, in Palmyra –
recaptured by the army from ISIS, lost again to ISIS and retaken once

more by the army with the Russians' help – we did meet him again. What about those twenty days? we asked him. He didn't realise when he met us in 2012, he admitted, the 'nature' of the enemy.

Bullets whizzed as we ran across the old highway towards the fortress. The huge medieval iron and wooden gate, its ornamented hinges and supports, a defence-work that had stood for seven hundred years, had been torn apart. I clambered over carbonised wood and hunks of rock bearing delicate Qur'anic inscriptions. Hundreds of bullet holes had pitted the stonework of the inner gate. For me, a visitor to Aleppo who had marvelled at its architectural treasures for well over three decades, the shock of finding these pitched battles amid this world heritage site, a place of museums and mosques, was a matter of infinite sorrow. But the devastation suffered by its civilians would be immeasurable in words. In a note to a colleague in 2018, I wrote that 'maybe Putin's bombardment of Grozny should've been a warning to us of another flat-out barrage against another city in Syria'. And in the years to come, the very citadel, the iron heart of this city, occupied, destroyed and rebuilt by iron-hearted men, was to witness the neutering of its power once more.

Yet in 2012, the Syrian soldiers liked to boast. Thirty rebels dead, only eight soldiers wounded – I saw one of them, but that did not prove the statistics to be true. With his soldiers, we trotted past the wreckage of the beautiful old Carlton Hotel, where a 1930s Renault remained on the forecourt. But across several roads, we ran for our lives and it was clear that the Syrian army no longer controlled this part of the city. For fifteen minutes, we took shelter with a group of officers in a small house above an abandoned tourist store. When we had walked into it, we noticed a queue forming in front of a bakery in the square opposite the Sissi Hotel. But when we left, there was no more queue and so many bullets were criss-crossing the square that we had to run down a neighbouring alleyway.

In the west of Aleppo, Nelofer and I would leave our central hotel and simply wander the streets. Shells exploded across the rooftops and a hollow-sounding cannon fired into the east from behind the artillery college. The rich had already left, the middle classes stayed at home and the poor suffered, largely because they came from the slums around the east of the city, ribbons of concrete neglect in which units of the FSA and Islamist groups now made their little fortresses.

The poor, of course, were everywhere. Take the three families of nineteen souls we met when we walked through the park beside Saddallah al-Jabiri Square. They lay in the shade of a scrawny tree, their only cover since they came here a month ago from the eastern suburb of Haydariya. There is a father in his mid-forties who refuses to give even his first name but is prepared to tell the family's story. 'The Free Army came to our mosque and an imam told us to "go out of your homes". This was his advice. And then we heard bombs and bullets so we left our homes.' The father was a Syrian-Kurd, it turned out, and he referred to the gunmen opposing the Assad regime as the 'Free Army'. We had to strain to hear his words above the sound of a helicopter.

'Almost everyone was leaving our area – it was the beginning of Ramadan – although some families stayed in their homes,' the man shouted. There was the crack of bullets hitting a street two or three blocks away. Another rebel fighter had sniped into the Quwatli Street area and the Syrian army had called for an air attack and now the helicopter gunner was banging away. But the father would not stop:

> The imam was from the other side of Haydariya, we knew who he was, he wore a sheikh's clothes, he was not a foreigner. As we were leaving, our nephew Hassan got out of the car to buy some bread. That's when the sniper shot him, yes, one of the 'Free Army'.

Hassan is lying beside us on an old carpet, in pain, his left arm bandaged at the wrist and shoulder. 'Now the charities [here] come and feed us but we have nowhere to stay.' Then a young man approached, a thirty-two-year-old tailor who said his name was Bakri Toufnakji. He had a home in Bab Jenin in the Old City and was there when the rebels arrived. 'The families were all in the street and I went to speak to the "Free Army" people,' he said. 'I said we have families here and women and children and a man with a heart problem. I said: "Please go away and take your guns with you." And the "Free Army" said they would go. But then the [government] army came and the fighting began.'

In a revealing interview with a Reuters correspondent, a local insurgent commander would give a largely analogous account of these events. He complained that although he and his men had 'liberated the rural parts of this province' earlier, 'we waited and waited for Aleppo to rise and it didn't. We couldn't rely on them to do it for themselves so we had to bring the revolution to them.' Another fighter told the Reuters reporter that 'we had to start the battle to encourage Aleppo and get the residents accustomed to being part of the uprising ... there are even people, unfortunately, who still support the regime.'

Aleppo was an 'army town' and Allepines willingly allowed their sons to be conscripted. But the city had always possessed an ascetic core of Islamists who have sometimes moved down to the 'Idlib triangle' along the Turkish border, widely regarded in Syria as an al-Qaeda centre; men from Idlib were among those believed to have moved into the Palestinian camp of Nahr el-Bared in Lebanon in 2006, provoking a miniature Islamist uprising north of Tripoli. In 1994, an Egyptian architectural student paid two visits lasting several weeks to Aleppo, studying its buildings and history: Mohamed Atta would later lead the 9/11 hijackers.

I sat down to tea with a middle-aged Syrian who wanted to tell me why he hated the regime. He was a mildly spoken person who met me in a downtown Damascus café. 'My brother was part of the [Muslim Brotherhood] revolution of 1980 and even my family didn't know this,' he said:

> Then one day the mukhabarat intelligence men came in three cars to arrest him. Nobody knows where they took him – not even now, thirty-two years later. Official documents said my brother was alive, but in 1996 we got some news from ex-prisoners who said they had seen my brother, and that he had been hanged or shot in Tadmor [Palmyra] prison. For me, the revolution started a long time ago, when my brother was arrested. Now my revolution is getting bigger ... What happened is that if you have a balloon and keep putting a lot of air in it, it will explode. When the people started to protest last year, the government used force to stop them and arrests – drip, drip, drip – there was an explosion.

The people, this man told me, 'got outside of silence' – in itself a remarkable expression – and 'started to use a little bit of violence against the government'. But would he accept a truly democratic

parliament with real elections even if Bashar al-Assad stayed? 'We have
known this government for forty years,' he replied. 'You cannot trust
them to give you the correct temperature during the day. Democracy
and violence don't meet together.'

In 2016, in a public attempt to show the 'soft' hand of the regime,
267 inmates – more than half of them held at the police headquarters
in Damascus – were freed on Assad's orders. My colleague, Sammy
Kaz, met some of them as they were freed in the capital, filthy, beaten
and each forced to sign a document in which he said he regretted his
'action' and promised 'not to take part in any more unauthorised
demonstrations'. A thirty-six-year-old identified only as 'Ahmad' said
that he had first been abducted and shot in the legs by the FSA for
giving information about its members to the regime, was found by
government soldiers who took him to hospital – and then imprisoned
by the mukhabarat for two months. Ahmad had no money for a taxi
home. And no shoes.

Agency reporters were still, with great care, able to operate inside
what they now called 'rebel-held territory' and visit the sites of Syrian
air attacks on civilian homes in Tal Rifaat and Azaz; small images of
horror would appear in their dispatches along with complaints from
freelance rebel commanders that 'war crimes ... have risked giving the
opposition as bad a reputation as Assad'.

While Western leaders continued to emphasise Assad's calamitous
loss of power, direct reports of growing Islamist influence continued to
surface. In November 2012, Reuters journalist Erika Solomon was
reporting the fear of 'foreign powers' that 'arms sent to shadowy
groups may simply fuel carnage – or even be turned against their
owners'. In a separate dispatch, she wrote of 'the bodies of four
uniformed [Syrian] soldiers, lined up in a garden, all shot in the head'
and commented that 'more and more instances of executions are
coming to light, including a video ... that showed rebels in another
part of Idlib ... lining several soldiers up against a wall and gunning
them down, an act the United Nations has said could constitute a war
crime.'

When Orthodox priest Fadi Jammil Haddad sought the release of a
kidnapped Christian doctor south of Damascus, he was himself
abducted and shot dead; at his funeral, a bomb exploded killing two
civilians. In the same week, al-Qaeda's leader, Ayman al-Zawahiri,

asked Muslims living in countries neighbouring Syria to join the revolt against Assad. On the same day that a Nusra suicide bomber killed at least fifty government troops near Hama, stories emerged of Syrian rebels turning against their own commanders. Writing about 'a cause that has been increasingly hijacked by Islamists', AFP reporter Jennie Matthew interviewed an FSA commander near Aleppo, a former religious student who called himself 'Sheikh Omar' and who blamed defectors in Turkey for their failure to destroy the regime. 'There are two types of defectors – those who stay in Syria and fight and then the other type who stay in fancy hotels in Turkey,' he said. 'They are dreaming of when the regime falls ... These are people who just think of personal benefit ... they are weak people.'*

By this stage, even the Americans had begun to realise that something was going very wrong with the Syrian-people-versus-tyrant story upon which they had publicly based their policies. Hillary Clinton was now speaking of Islamist foreign fighters who had 'hijacked' the Syrian revolution, demanding that the Western-supported 'Syrian National Council' opposition enlarge its membership to include more resistance groups. She was worried, it transpired, at growing 'extremism' in Syria. After viewing another video of the execution of government troops, the UN High Commissioner for Human Rights described the images as probably being 'a war crime'. The pictures showed twelve wounded Syrian soldiers lined up on the ground and shot dead with automatic weapons while the killers described them as 'dogs of Assad's shabiha'. After encouraging Syrians to rise against their dictator – as we did in Iraq in the 1990s – the West would abandon Syria to the purgatory of its sectarian war and the torment of the same regime which they wanted to escape in the first place. Just as the catastrophic Anglo-American invasion of Iraq brought an end to epic Western military adventures in the Middle East, so the tragedy of Syria ensures that there will be no more Arab revolution, I wrote. And it's taken just thirteen blood-soaked years – from 2003 to 2016 – to realign political power. Russia

---

* The growing number of 'cowards in exile' whom FSA commanders loathed also annoyed their American hosts in Turkey. One US diplomat complained bitterly to me that his distaste for the opposition there finally turned to contempt when many declared they would only fly to peace talks in Rome if they were given business class airline tickets from Istanbul.

and Iran and the Shia Muslims of the region are now deciding its future. So much for our promise of 'freedom' and 'democracy'!

Events unprecedented in the modern Middle East were now occurring in Syria almost every day; a report from Damascus, for example, that the government was systematically razing the battle-smashed houses and damaged neighbourhoods of families sympathetic to the insurrection – thus ensuring that they could never return home. And there emerged the very first accounts of fighting between rebels and government troops inside the eleventh-century Grand Mosque of Aleppo. This, at least, had survived – for now. But, cruel though the expression may be, these were mere buildings. The colossal sadism of this conflict would shadow the minds of even the most neutral observers for much of their lives. Irish UN troops serving in the United Nations Disengagement Observer Force peacekeeping mission on Syrian Golan would be haunted for years by the massacres which they saw in village streets. They would, in the cold words of one UN eyewitness, come across 'remains of beheadings, hangings openly displayed in streets and off trees and bridges, innocent civilians and families slaughtered'.

POSTSCRIPT

by Nelofer Pazira-Fisk

Failure to distinguish between absolute evil, semi-evil, corruption, cynicism and hubris, produced strange mirages. Regimes which we favoured always possessed 'crack' army divisions, 'elite' security units and were sustained by fatherly and much-revered ruling families. Regimes we wished to destroy were equipped only with third-rate troops, mutineers, defectors, corrupt cops and blighted by ruling families.

Egypt, with its political prisoners, its police torture and fake elections, was a tourist paradise. Syria, with its political prisoners, police torture and fake elections, would like to be a tourist paradise. Iraq, with its political prisoners, police torture and fake elections, was not – and did not wish to be – a tourist paradise.

These were the last two paragraphs that Robert wrote before his death on 30 October 2020. They were part of the final chapter to this book – and on the subject of the Western media's coverage of the Middle East and their relationship to the Western political elite. 'The problem is that there is an osmotic relationship between journalists and power and they feed on each other. If they betray that osmotic relationship, they will be thrown out of the press pack. Not only by government but by the other journalists,' Robert told Eva Salinas of Open Canada on 8 November 2019. 'One of the reasons I get an awful lot of flak on the stories I write is that if I don't keep to the general journalistic version of what's going on, I am [seen as] betraying [others].'

Robert wrote about the responsibility of journalists and the manipulation of language in reporting which skewed the truth. He wrote of the Western media's deliberate use of language to accommodate its double standards: 'When protesters in Libya, Syria and Iran are being shot at, it is a "massacre"; but when protesters are shot at in Bahrain or Saudi Arabia or Egypt under Sisi, it is a "crackdown".' The mainstream media in the West dances around words, obfuscating their meaning simply to avoid controversy or offending 'centres of power'.

> In the Western context, power and the media is about words –
> and the use of words. It is about semantics. It is about the
> employment of phrases and clauses and their origins. And it is
> about the misuse of history; and about our ignorance of history.
> More and more today, we journalists have become prisoners of
> the language of power.

Israeli journalist Amira Hass was one of the greatest influences in Robert's life. He often quoted her as saying that the job of a journalist is to 'challenge centres of power'. Holding powers to account and challenging their authority, Robert argued that governments and politicians don't have a monopoly over 'truth', yet they act as if they do.

Robert took his readers seriously and wrote back to each and every one, spending hours replying to their letters and emails. He welcomed their criticism or divergent points of view so long as they were willing to engage in a dialogue. But he didn't waste his time on abusive attacks which he said were designed to silence criticism of the West's powerful elite and their wrongdoings in the Middle East rather than an attempt to debate the issue. The anonymity offered by the digital online platforms made the nature of these attacks more vicious and frequent.

> This has now become a feature of much hate comment on the
> internet. Be it anti-Semitic abuse or Islamophobia or gender
> hatred, slogans are displacing argument. Thus, baldly and
> unsubtly, accusation has replaced debate. Every politician,
> journalist, 'activist', every prime minister, editor and clergyman
> (of whichever variety) now has to disprove the accusations
> made against them – however outlandish – in order to prove
> their innocence. They are guilty until proved innocent, the latter
> a happy outcome but one almost impossible to achieve since

their guilt is already an internet 'fact', only put in doubt by responding to the contrary – and thus becoming part of the hate discussion. There is no point in blaming technology for our plight ... It is the use to which we allow that technology to be put which now confronts us over social media. Journalists – and we should speak up for ourselves – do not deserve, nor should we tolerate, the filth and slander which is thrown at us for doing our job by those people who, far from being worthy of attention, need serious medical help.

In chronicling the West's mistreatment and betrayal of the Middle East, Robert compiled an archive of documents and individual testimonies – a catalogue of the West's failures and the effect on people's lives in the lands of 'great history and suffering'. From the Anglo-American invasion of Iraq, Israel's illegal and open-ended occupation and colonisation of the Arab lands, Western governments' continued cosy relationship with the Gulf monarchies and the dictators in Egypt and Turkey, to the US and NATO's catastrophic campaigns in Libya, Syria and Afghanistan – they are innumerable accounts of human anguish, sorrow, hope and defeat.

The Syrian army kills civilians but claims to take every care to avoid 'collateral damage'. The Israelis say the same. The Brits say the same, the Americans and Russians and the French. Maybe the International Court in the Hague will one day name Syrian soldiers responsible for such crimes – be sure they won't touch the West's warriors. A German court did put two Syrian security officers on trial in 2020 for torture and sexual assault against prisoners nine years earlier. But the US had withdrawn from the International Criminal Court in 2002 lest it tried to prosecute US service members or officials.

Letting Western governments and their allies get away with war crimes set a new, dangerous precedent: the normalisation of such crimes. Robert warned that this pattern and the language used to cover up the deliberate targeting and killing of civilians, and then the blaming of victims for their own death and destruction, not only weakened the West's moral stand against tyranny, but allowed dictatorships and autocrats around the world to use it as a justification for their own war crimes.

This couldn't have been more true than in the case of Syria, or more accurate than in the case of the Russian invasion of Ukraine. I'm often asked what Robert would have said about the latest war in Europe. His dispatches would have viewed the current crisis in the Middle East, the Balkans and Europe from the perspective of history and from a Middle Eastern point of view, pointing out Western governments' double standards and hypocritical attitude towards the suffering of people in the region. America's constant refusal to sign up to the International Criminal Court has compromised the West's ability to upbraid Putin for his crimes against humanity. How could the European Union, in the weakest and most uninspiring moment in its history, hold Putin to account when the language he and his foreign minister Sergey Lavrov use is matched word for word by that of Benjamin Netanyahu and the Israeli defence and foreign ministries, and is routinely adopted by the White House and the media?

Making a deal with the Taliban, the United States and NATO hurled Afghans, especially women, under the rule of a militant group that has been killing unarmed civilians – suicide bombing hospitals and schools – and kidnapping and torturing women protesters. The glaring hypocrisy of the West is impossible to hide, even behind the language of its usual cowardice. How could Joe Biden have the audacity to speak about the rights of Iranian women to freedom, when he presided over the snatching of the same rights from women in Afghanistan? America's once created, then abandoned and recently rebranded new ally in Afghanistan, the Taliban, is the only government in the world that bans women and girls from attending school.

Blighted by conflict since the Soviet invasion in 1979 and the protracted proxy, civil and religious wars that followed – in part thanks to the Americans' backing of the Afghan mujahidin and the Taliban's predecessors – Afghanistan was forgotten by the West. Afghans can't be blamed for thinking the real goal of the West was the break-up of the Soviet Union, not their freedom or independence. And now they can enjoy 'democracy' under the Taliban, who also indulge Putin's imagined influence and power. It is not so different from the situation in Syria, where rebel forces have been discarded to the dustbin of Idlib, and protesters' dreams of 'freedom' and 'democracy' have been aban-

doned as a Western 'project'. The American goal of overthrowing
Assad may not have been achieved, but there are other power politics
to consider.

Letting Assad remain in power, after all, is the price the US administration is prepared to pay to prevent an Israeli–Iranian war. No
question could be asked about Israel's role in the Syrian war as its army
randomly attacked Syrian and Iranian targets in Syria since 2013,
though curiously never ISIS. There is credible video and eyewitness
evidence of wounded Nusra fighters being evacuated and treated in
Israeli hospitals. In 2018, the Trump administration recognised Israel's
illegal annexation of the Golan, the Syrian territory captured in the
1967 war.

In February 2021, the US secretary of state Antony Blinken stated
that 'as a practical matter, the control of the Golan … I think remains
of real importance to Israel's security'. He told CNN that 'legal questions are something else and over time if the situation were to change
in Syria, that's something we look at, but we are nowhere near that'.

'Somewhere over the Atlantic,' wrote Robert, 'there is a giant glass
curtain through which Americans view the Middle East, which utterly
distorts their vision.' Embedded in that view is an arrogant colonial attitude that only the West and Europeans truly appreciate democracy. The
West offered the Middle East democracy in the form of military operations – overt or covert, either directly or with the help of its regional
allies – but no one should expect the people in these countries to fully
understand or value democracy because they were not Europeans.

A Syrian refugee, Dr Hamza al-Kateab, from Aleppo, living in exile
in the UK, offered advice to the Ukrainians in 2022: they 'should not
expect any kind of red lines to be respected. Or any humanitarian law
to be respected in this invasion. Do not expect that [this situation] is
going to change in the next couple of weeks; it's a long-lasting war. Do
not expect that the world is going to stand beside you for a long time.
People tend to forget. Media tend to shift to the next hot point or to
the next conflict area. And the two million refugees now, that number
is going to increase in the days [to come], and suddenly the narrative is
going to be, "You're stealing our jobs. You should have stayed to fight
for your country, and what are you doing here?"'

When Robert took the job of Middle East correspondent for
The Times of London in 1976 and made Beirut his home, he also made a

decision. Conscious of Western colonial attitudes, he would never buy or own property in Lebanon or anywhere else in the Middle East because the Arab lands belonged to the Arabs, not to the Europeans. For forty-four years, he lived in the same rental apartment, with the same landlord. He argued that the Western armies and their self-serving governments should leave the Middle East alone. *Night of Power: The Betrayal of the Middle East* is both his plea for an end to Western interference and an account of human suffering due to the folly of war and propped-up dictators. The media's inadequate representation of the people in the Middle East is an extension of the same mindset that once colonised those lands.

During the Covid lockdown, as Robert continued his research and writing of this volume, we discussed the worsening conditions in the Middle East and the need for more investigative reporting. Robert didn't live to witness and write the next chapter of this great tragedy called the Middle East. But he reminded his readers of the 'tarnished rays', in the words of Faiz Ahmed Faiz, that great Pakistani poet we often read and admired. The dawn which Robert wished to see break across these epic lands didn't arrive; the promised light between the curtains flickered and gave way to more darkness; and the night is still soaked in innocent blood:

> This is not that Dawn for which, ravished with freedom,
> we had set out in sheer longing ...
> Friends, our blood shaped its own mysterious roads.
> When hands tugged at our sleeves, enticing us to stay,
> and from wondrous chambers Sirens cried out
> with their beguiling arms, with their bare bodies,
> our eyes remained fixed on that beckoning Dawn ...
> Now listen to the terrible rampant lie:
> ... See our leaders polish their manner clean of our suffering:
> Indeed, we must confess only to bliss;
> we must surrender any utterance for the Beloved – all yearning
>   is outlawed.*

---

* Faiz Ahmed Faiz, 'Dawn of Freedom', 1947, translated from the Urdu by Agha Shahid Ali.

Overlooking the Mediterranean, our balcony faced the Corniche seafront, where the Crusaders once passed through; the French mandate named it 'Avenue des Français', a reminder of the greed and failed military campaigns of the past. Future generations will have to struggle for freedom from their own dictators, despots, corrupt presidents, stalemate in sectarian political systems and freedom from military bases and their operations. In 2020 there were more US and NATO military bases in the region than at any other time in history. Why? One might ask if another iron curtain is being drawn as the Russian army retreats, ghosts of the past lingering again in darker lairs. The rise of fascism, Islamophobia, anti-Semitism, nationalism and dogma of all varieties in Europe is yet again threatening civil liberties and tolerance, while the earth we occupy is edging towards extinction as a result of our exploitation and wars. And Syria? I asked Robert just days before his death. He handed me one of his articles: 'Gulf Arabs – particularly Qatar – are said to be interested in financially rebuilding Syria. So if they would not surrender militarily, can the Idlib "rebels" be bought off? Not least by the Arab nations which supported them in the first place. These are early days. But all wars come to an end. And that's where history restarts.'

NOTES

Preface

xviii *first revealed to the Prophet Mohamed*: My preferred spelling is Muhammad, but to be consistent with *The Great War for Civilisation* I've kept this spelling (Mohamed) in *Night of Power*, except for a couple of occasions when it is spelled differently in a written original document.

1: Legacy

1 *For little Sayef*: interview with the parents of Sayef Mohamed, and with Dr Samira Alaani, Fallujah, 6 and 7 March 2012

4 *When children died in a plague of cancers*: Fisk, *The Great War for Civilisation* pp. 895–913; no 'peer reviewed epidemiological data', Doug Henderson letter dated 22 December 1998

6 *Its vice president, Tariq al-Hashemi, had just fled*: see Reuters, 17 February and 1 April 2012, and AP, 3 April 2012

7 *There was a massacre every night*: records of the Baghdad dead, mortuary statistics and witness statements in these pages are in my personal notebooks 2003–5 and subsequently reported in the *Independent*. See especially the paper's editions of 19, 21, 22, 25 September 2003; 17, 27, 31 December 2003; 7 January 2003; 3 April 2003; 14, 27 July 2003; 2 January 2004; 27, 29 March 2004

21 *in 2004 when David Brooks announced*: see *International Herald Tribune*, 13 April 2004, 'The battle for Iraq is not over', by David Brooks

21 *But when Thomas Friedman announced*: see *International Herald Tribune*, 10 December 2004, 'People of mass destruction', by Thomas L. Friedman

22 *Brooks wrote of*: see *International Herald Tribune*, 3 November 2006, 'Same old demons', by David Brooks; see also *Independent*, 11 November 2006, 'Here come the odious excuses', by Robert Fisk

22 *Peters was more to the point*: see *USA Today*, 3 November 2006, 'Last gasp in Iraq', by Ralph Peters

22 *'It was impossible to tell'*: Mansour, *Inside Fallujah*, p. 173

2: The Age of the Dictator

24 *Sadat – America's new friend*: David Hirst and Irene Beeson, *Sadat* (Faber, 1991), pp. 345–7

25 *By November 1983, the White House was being briefed*: US State Department memorandum to secretary of state 'Iraq use of Chemical Weapons', 1 November 1983, National Security Archives, cited in Biological and Toxin Weapons Convention and Iraq: A report for Parliament on the British government's response to the US supply of biological materials to Iraq, 18 October 2004, p. 4

25 *Howard Teicher, a staff member*: US District Court, Southern District of Florida: 'The Teicher Affidavit: Iraqgate', 31 January 1995, cited in Geoffrey Holland, 'United States exports of biological materials to Iraq: Compromising the credibility of international law', June 2005, p. 9

25 *A 1994 US Senate report by Donald Riegle*: Riegle's report to the US Senate, 25 May 1994, cited in Holland, 'United States exports of biological materials to Iraq', p. 5

25 *Years afterwards, the British Foreign Office*: Hansard, 10 March 2003, cited in Holland, op. cit., p. 5

25 *The destinations for the anthrax bacilli*: Riegle report, cited in Holland, op. cit.

26 *In 2011, UK armed forces minister Nick Harvey admitted*: see *Guardian*, 14 November 2011, cited in *CADU* (Campaign Against Depleted Uranium weapons) *News*, Issue 37, Autumn 2011

26 *In the 2003 invasion, US and UK forces*: *CADU News*, Issue 34, August 2010

29 *According to one semi-official transcript*: see *New York Times*, 23 September 1990

29 *interview with the Saudi-owned daily Al-Hayat*: see *Al-Hayat*, 15 March 2008, 'Saddam summoned me requesting that I should notify the president "not to be alarmed … there is no case for concern"'

30 *Robert Gates, later*: *London Review of Books*, 22 July 2010, 'Worth It', by Andrew Cockburn

30 *The American official asked to calculate*: see *Independent*, 23 April 1992, 'US demographer sacked for exposing Iraqi civilian deaths', by Simon Jones

31 *During the massacre of Shiites*: The Islamic Union of Iraqi Students & Youth (Britain and Ireland), undated, probably 1992, 'Saddam launches ruthless campaign to wipe out Marsh Arabs'

31 *In a six-week period in April to May 1999*: Amnesty International 'Urgent action' reports 19 May and 18 August 1999 (Index nos AMR 51/81/99 and AMR 51/133/99

33 *The Washington Post had already reported*: see *Washington Post*, 2 March 1999, 'US spied on Iraq via UN', by Barton Gellman

34 *More than 70 per cent of Arabs in Egypt, Jordan and Lebanon*: see *The Monthly* (Beirut: Issue 11, May 2003) recording a poll carried out in February 2003 by Information International of Beirut and Zogby International; see also *Independent*, 12 March 2003

37 *in Berkeley journalism professor Mark Danner's expression*: see the *New York Review of Books*, 21 December 2006, 'Iraq: The war of the imagination', by Mark Danner

37 *Right-wing American intellectuals*: Christopher DeMuth, president of the American Enterprise Institute, quoted in *State of Denial* by Bob Woodward, cited in Danner, ibid.

38 *But how to convince Iraqis*: see *Time* magazine, 25 May 2003, 'The sum of two Evils', by Brian Bennett and Michael Weisskopf

40 *Ruud Lubbers of the UN High Commission for Refugees*: see *Independent on Sunday*, 27 July 2003, 'We keep asking ourselves who's next', by Robert Fisk

41 *Saddam's formal interrogation by the FBI*: see *Independent on Sunday*, 5 July 2009, 'The Saddam files: His final interviews', by David Connett

45 *In a fair trial, wrote Gwynne Dyer*: see *Jordan Times*, 22 December 2003, 'The trials of Saddam', by Gwynne Dyer

46 *Yet the shock of Saddam's appearance*: see *Le Figaro*, 19 October 2006, 'Le procès raté de Saddam Hussein en Irak', by Thierry Oberlé

46 *More serious was American financial and technical support*: *Toronto Star*, 30 December 2006, 'Storm rages over trial, sentence', by Olivia Ward

46 *Amnesty International, describing the hearings*: see the *Globe and Mail* (Toronto), 1 January 2007, 'Critics blast Iraq's rush to kill Hussein', by Estanislao Oziewicz

47 *Even when three of Saddam's closest aides*: agencies cited by *L'Orient-Le Jour* (Beirut), 'Operation Anfal: "Ali le Chimique" condamne a mort'

47 *Most damning of all*: see the *Globe and Mail*, 'Critics blast Iraq's rush to kill Hussein'

47 *Sitting only a few feet away*: BBC World News, 5 November 2006, report by John Simpson

48 *The World Health Organisation and the Iraqi Ministry of Health*: see *New York Times*, 9 January 2008, 'WHO finds increased civilian death toll in Iraq', by Nick Cumming-Bruce; see also *Le Monde*, 11 January 2008, '150 000 morts en trois ans en Irak: l'OMS révise à la baisse le bilan du "Lancet"'

48 *In early 2008, the British-based*: agencies cited by *L'Orient-Le Jour* (Beirut), 31 January 2008, 'Plus d'un million d'Irakiens tués depuis l'invasion de 2003'

49 *Ten days after his execution*: see *New York Times*, 8 January 2007, 'Saddam's voice hovers over reopening of war crimes trial', by John Burns

50 *in the few months before Saddam's hanging*: see *Le Canard Enchainé*, 3 January 2007, 'Le Bagdad du pendu', by Louis-Marie Horeau

50 *Sickened by the evidence*: interviews by author 2003 to July 2008 with former trial translators and investigators who requested anonymity

51 *One of these was Samar Sa'ad Abdullah*: see Amnesty International Report, 31 August 2009, p. 8

52 *an Egyptian newspaper reported*: see the *Egyptian Mail*, 20 August 2013, 'Iraq executes 17 people: ministry'

52 *In a statement passed to me in Beirut*: see *Independent*, 9 February 2007, 'Iraqi insurgents disclose their conditions for ceasefire', by Robert Fisk

52 *he was dubbed 'the last chance general'*: see *Le Monde*, 24 January 2007, 'Le général de la dernière chance', by Patrice Claude

3: Walking on Windows

58 *I found a Humvee*: see *Independent*, 19 September 2003, 'Another day, another death-trap for the US', by Robert Fisk

58 *The anonymous soldier's story*: see *Independent*, 5 December 2003, 'How an American war hero is taking his battle over Iraq to Washington', by Andrew Buncombe, and 'Samarra: soldier's e-mail devastates Pentagon's account'

59 *US soldiers used sledgehammers, crowbars*: AP, 18 December 2003, 'US troops smash into homes, shops in major raid to hunt for guerrillas in turbulent city', by Aleksander Vasovic

59 *Three months after the Samarra battle*: see *Independent*, 23 March 2004, 'Finnish civilians join list of fatalities as 14 British soldiers hurt in Basra', by Robert Fisk

59 *Newsweek brought the American dead back to life*: see *Newsweek*, 2 April 2007, 'Voices of the fallen: The Iraq War in the words of America's dead'

61 *But not only the dead talked*: see *New York Times*, 19 August 2007, 'The war as we saw it', by Buddhika Jayamaha, Wesley D. Smith, Jeremy Roebuck, Omar Mora, Edward Sandmeier, Yance T. Gray and Jeremy A. Murphy

61 *Take Benjamin Busch*: Busch's letters home from May and July 2005 were originally sent to me by his friend Benji Rogers. Details of Busch's subsequent book, *Dust to Dust: A Memoir*, appear in the bibliography

62 *building up a ferocious reputation*: see Ricks, *Fiasco*, pp. 313–17

62 *In words spookily similar*: see Zaki, *Mesopotamia*, pp. 126–7: and Zaki reference to S.H. Longrigg, *Four Centuries of Modern Iraq*, first published 1925, further edition (Reading (UK): Garnet, 2002)

63 *Lieutenant Colonel Gareth F. Brandl*: BBC News, 7 November 2004, Paul Wood

63 *'because we're a Christian nation'*: see *Los Angeles Times*, 16 October 2003, 'General casts war in religious terms', by Richard T. Cooper; see also NBC Nightly News with Tom Brokaw, 1 October 2003

63 *'You have to understand the Arab mind'*: see *New York Times*, 7 December 2003, 'Tough new tactics by US tighten grip on Iraq towns', by Dexter Filkins

64 *had revealed US and Israeli military intelligence contacts*: Vane letter in *Army Magazine* (Arlington, Virginia), July 2003. The journal states that articles are 'expressions of personal opinion' but adds that it is a 'professional journal … representing the interests of the US Army'

64 *'active and secret help in the war'*: see *New Yorker*, 15 December 2013, 'Moving targets: Will the counter-insurgency plan in Iraq repeat the mistakes of Vietnam?', by Seymour M. Hersh

65 'Those who have to deal with like problems': see Los Angeles Times, 22 November 2003, 'US seeks advice from Israel on Iraq: As the occupation grows bloodier, officials draw on an ally's experience with insurgents', by Esther Shrader and Josh Meyer

65 Joe Klein wrote cynically: see Time magazine, 5 February 2003, 'How Israel is wrapped up in Iraq', by Joe Klein

66 In 1978 Lieutenant Daniel Pinto: see Jonathan Randal, The Tragedy of Lebanon: Christian Warlords, Israeli Adventurers and American Bunglers (London: Chatto and Windus, 1983), p. 217

66 Israeli troops who killed seven Palestinians: see Robert Fisk, Pity the Nation: Lebanon at War (London: OUP, 1992), pp. 423–8

67 Garner co-signed a letter in 2000: see New Statesman, 7 April 2003, 'The weird men behind George W. Bush's war', by Michael Lind

68 I first noticed the huge number: see Independent on Sunday, 28 March 2004, 'Occupiers spend millions on private army of security men', by Robert Fisk in Baghdad and Severin Carrell in London

68 Blackwater: see Scahill, Blackwater (2006)

68 Blackwater's thugs with guns: see Independent, 4 July 2004, 'So this is what they call the "new", free Iraq', by Robert Fisk

68 In mid-2007, Reuters reported that 933 'contractors' had died in Iraq: see Reuters, 3 July 2007, 'In outsourced US wars, contractor deaths top 1,000', by Bernd Debusmann

69 'the mercenary firms offer a privatised alternative': see Scahill, Blackwater, p. 365

69 at a price: see Independent on Sunday, 28 March 2004, 'Occupiers spend millions on private army of security men', by Robert Fisk in Baghdad and Severin Carrell in London

72 His was a ferocious narrative of disaster: see Independent, 28 April 2006, 'Seen through a Syrian lens: "Unknown Americans" are provoking civil war in Iraq', by Robert Fisk

73 It included a high-risk counter-insurgency operation: see Independent, 11 April 2007, 'Divide and rule: America's plan for Baghdad', by Robert Fisk; see also Independent, 'Myth of Tal Afar, beacon of American "success"', by Patrick Cockburn

74 He was highly sceptical: correspondence with the author from George W. Appenzeller Snr, 18 February and 20 March 2007

75 Shia Muslim leaders feared that the militiamen: see Independent, 25 March 2008, 'Death toll for US troops in Iraq hits 4,000', by Patrick Cockburn

75 No wonder American officers: see New York Times, 11 June 2007, 'US arming some Sunni groups to fight Al-Qaeda', by John F. Burns and Alissa J. Rubin

75 In a world grown tired of Iraq: see Dr Abdul Kareem al-Obeidi, chair of the Iraqi Association for Child Mental Health, to UN Secretary-General, 13 June 2007; for coverage, see Independent, 15 June 2007, 'Conflict "will create a violent generation"', by Colin Brown

76 *Janina Struk, a freelance*: Janina Struk, *Private Pictures*, pp. 168–70

77 *what had she not found?*: see *Independent*, 6 March 2006, 'The shocking truth about the American occupation of Iraq', by Robert Fisk

77 *The military jury convicted Welshofer*: see AP, 23 January 2006, 'Officer convicted in Iraqi's death sorry', by Jon Sarche; see also *Independent*, 18 March 2006, 'The farcical end of the American dream', by Robert Fisk

78 *The last letter of a young soldier*: Daniel Somers' last letter was first published in the *Phoenix New Times* and then appeared on the Gawker. com blog. Howard and Jean Somers wrote of their family's tragedy in the *New York Times* on 11 November 2013 ('On losing a veteran son to a broken system') but made no mention of Daniel's reference to war crimes. Former Republican congressman Ron Paul quoted briefly from the 'war crimes' section of Somers' letter in his Institute for Peace and Prosperity newsletter of 24 June 2013, but wrote only about his anger at those who send American soldiers 'to suffer and die in unnecessary wars'

4: Painting Othello Black

81 *In the initial stages of the war*: correspondence of Tom Geddes to UK Ministry of Defence, 28 October 2008 and 12 March 2009; and of Ministry of Defence (Directorate of Operations, Iraq Operations Team) correspondence to Geddes, 20 January 2009 (ref: TO4839/08) and 6 July 2009 (ref: TO2330/2009)

83 *the Chilcot Inquiry into the Iraq war would later reveal*: see *Independent*, 1 July 2010, 'Documents lay bare how Goldsmith changed his advice on legality of war', by Kim Sengupta

84 *'binary distinction', I wrote*: see *Independent*, 30 January 2010, 'Tony Blair and his oh-so-clean conscience', by Robert Fisk

85 *You only had to listen to Blair's language*: Blair interview with Andrew Marr, BBC 2, 1 September 2010

85 *Among the sourest and most Dickensian*: see *Independent*, 22 January 2011, 'You can catch an eel by the tail but it can still bite you in the face', by Simon Carr

86 *The AP ran a blunt story*: see AP, 1 January 2004, 'Iraq hunt may hinder other U.S. aims', by Dafna Linzer

87 *Just as Bush and Blair claimed they did not wish to invade Iraq*: see Fisk, *The Great War for Civilisation*, pp. 1193–4

87 *ample evidence that their invasion would follow a remarkably similar path*: John Newsinger in *Race and Class*, Vol. 49, No. 3, January–March 2008, who quotes from Trevor Lloyd, *The General Election of 1880* (London, 1968), pp. 14, 22; Sir Edward Malet, *Egypt 1879–1883* (London, 1909); William Laird Clowes, *The Royal Navy*, Vol. 7 (London, 1903); John Morley, *The Life of William Ewart Gladstone*, Vol. 3 (London, 1904), p. 85; William Scawen Blunt, *Secret History of the English Occupation of Egypt* (New York, 1922), p. 9; J.L.Garvin, *The Life of Joseph Chamberlain*, Vol. 1,

(London, 1935), p. 455; R.A.J.Walling (ed.), *The Diaries of John Bright* (New York, 1931), pp. 487–8; Sir William F. Butler, *An Autobiography* (London, 1911), pp. 253–6; Reverend Arthur Male, *Scenes Through the Battle Smoke* (London, 1901) pp. 453–4; Norman Kelvin, *The Collected Letters of William Morris 1885–1888*, Vol. 3 (Princeton, 1987); Timothy Mitchell, *Colonising Egypt* (Berkeley, 1991), p. 97

89 *'to redeem something from the tragedy of death'*: see Tony Blair, *A Journey* (London: Hutchinson, 2010)

89 *Major General Tim Cross, sent to Washington to monitor*: see *Independent*, 8 December 2009, 'Blair "ignored call to delay Iraq invasion"', by Michael Savage

90 *'blind spot' over post-war planning*: see *Independent*, 2 December 2009, 'Britain "did not plan for the fall of Saddam"', by Michael Savage

90 *Eight years later*: see *Financial Times*, 12 February 2011, 'Are we better off now? You bet', by Gideon Rachman

90 *General Wesley K. Clark*: interviewed by Amy Goodman on *Democracy Now!*, 2 March 2007

91 *As the US Defense Department released further evidence*: see AP, 6 April 2007

91 *Blair was revealed to have had three telephone conversations*: see *Independent*, 22 July 2011, 'Labour accused of hypocrisy over Murdoch contacts', by Andrew Grice

91 *increase in the warnings*: see *Independent*, 21 July 2010, 'Former MI5 chief demolishes Blair's defence of the Iraq war', by Andy McSmith

91 *My colleague Patrick Cockburn and I had railed*: see *Independent*, 19 March 2008, 'This is the war that started with lies, and continues with lie after lie after lie', by Patrick Cockburn

91 *I would still have thought it right to remove him*: Blair interview with Fern Britton, BBC 1, 13 December 2009

92 *'that you should prosper'*: The Proclamation of Baghdad by Lieutenant General Sir Stanley Maude, 19 March 1917; see also Fisk, *The Great War for Civilisation*, pp. 170–3

92 *In 2006, a growing circle of US ex-generals*: see *New York Times*, 14 April 2006, 'More retired generals call for Rumsfeld's resignation', by David S. Cloud and Eric Schmitt; *New York Times*, 13 October 2007, 'Ex-commander Calls Iraq Effort "a Nightmare"', by David S. Cloud

93 *'It may be hoped that the weary centuries of misrule'*: William Ewing, *From Gallipoli to Baghdad*, pp. 297–8

93 *a beautiful volume of paintings by Donald Maxwell*: Donald Maxwell, *A Dweller in Mesopotamia*, pp. 4–14, 117, 121–4

93 *Ewing lectured*: Ewing, *From Gallipoli to Baghdad*, p. 234

94 *In July 1918, the Admiralty's oil expert*: see Helmut Mejcher, *Imperial Quest for Oil: Iraq 1910–1928* (London: Ithaca Press, 1976) pp. 35–42, quoting Admiral Sir Edmund Slade's paper on the 'Petroleum situation in the British Empire', 29 July 1918, PRO CAB 21/119

95 *In 1995, for example, the CIA asked Congress*: see *New York Times*, 12 April 1995, 'CIA asks congress for money to rein in Iraq and Iran', by Elaine Sciolino

96 *Let me just deal with the oil thing*: see Hansard (Commons), 15 January 2003

96 *In 2011, however, secret memoranda revealed*: see *Independent*, 19 April 2011, 'Secret memos expose link between oil firms and invasion of Iraq', by Paul Bignell; see also Greg Muttitt, *Fuel on the Fire*, pp. 43–5

97 *Oil is slippery stuff*: see *Independent*, 1 October 2003, 'Oil, war and a growing sense of panic in the US', by Robert Fisk

97 *Even after the war began, a detailed analysis*: see *Le Monde diplomatique* (English edition), April 2003, 'No war for whose oil?', by Yahya Sadowski

98 *It was not long before major Bush election campaign donors*: see the Center for Public Integrity report, 30 October 2003, 'US contractors reap the windfalls of post-war reconstruction'

99 *A month later, Paul Krugman asked*: see *New York Times*, 23 July 2004, 'Accounting and accountability', by Paul Krugman

99 *'too many oil-rich countries go down the road of unaccountable government'*: see Christian Aid (London) report, 28 June 2004, 'Fuelling suspicion: The coalition and Iraq's oil billions'; see also Christian Aid news release of 28 June 2004

99 *The father of seven was a senior auditor in Iraq's new Industry Ministry*: see *Independent*, 16 July 2004, 'Coffin bomb ends another macabre day in "new" Iraq', by Robert Fisk

102 *'It was our duty'*: Muttitt, *Fuel on the Fire*, p. 76

102 *As one NGO investigation pointed out*: see Platform, 'Crude designs: The rip-off of Iraq's oil wealth', by Greg Muttitt, 22 November 2005

102 *'The USA was liberator not coloniser'*: see Muttitt, *Fuel on the Fire*, p. 247

103 *Muttitt traced the original US plans*: see 'Mission accomplished for big oil? How an American disaster paved the way for big oil's rise – and possible fall – in Iraq', by Greg Muttitt, 2012

103 *Klein believes that James Baker's Iraq Study Group*: see Naomi Klein, *The Shock Doctrine*, p. 453, quoting James A. Baker III, Lee H. Hamilton, Lawrence S. Eagleburger et al., Iraq Study Group Report, December 2006, p. 57

103 *Muttitt took the view that the new contracts*: see Muttitt, 'Mission accomplished for big oil?'

103 *'the nature of a resource war in the twenty-first century'*: see *Independent*, 22 April 2011, 'Greg Muttitt: Big oil firms are still in the driving seat when it comes to the resource war', by Phil England

104 *'the rapidity of the process'*: see Muttitt, *Fuel on the Fire*, pp. 328–30

104 *One MP, Shatha al-Musawi, tried to bring a legal case*: see ibid., p. 346

104 *'didn't want an oil law to put multinationals'*: Jonathan Pickering interview with Greg Muttitt, 26 June 2013, 'Dissecting oil and politics and beyond'

105 *'found that almost all the American money set aside to rebuild Iraq'*: see *London Review of Books*, 6 September 2007, 'Burn rate', by Ed Harriman

105 'handing out truckloads of dollars': see *London Review of Books*, 7 July 2005, 'Where has all the money gone?', by Ed Harriman

105 *The trail of 'lost' money*: see *Independent*, 28 July 2010, 'US unable to account for billions of Iraqi oil money', by Patrick Cockburn

106 *By 2006, foreign and local mercenaries accounted*: see *Globe and Mail* (Toronto), 28 December 2006, 'A true accounting of US "forces" in Iraq', by Barry Lando

106 *'"America," columnist Frank Rich wrote'*: see *New York Times*, 21 October 2007, 'Suicide is not painless', by Frank Rich

106 *'the non pareil war profiteer'*: see *New York Times*, 24 March 2008, 'The private sector's tramping in Iraq'

106 *By March 2010, 207,553 mercenaries*: Feinstein, *The Shadow World*

107 *In October 2011, Exxon Mobil*: see *Independent*, 9 December 2011, 'Exxon's deal with Kurds inflames Baghdad', by Patrick Cockburn

107 *A company with close ties to George W. Bush*: see *New York Times*, 3 July 2008, 'Panel questions State Department role in deal', by James Glanz and Richard A. Oppel Jr

107 *'questions on unhelpful topics would not be tolerated'*: see *Independent on Sunday*, 8 December 2003, 'Iraqis find US zone in Baghdad a parallel universe', by Phil Reeves

107 *henceforth, they could only plant seeds*: see *Current Concerns* (Zurich), August 2005, 'Iraq and Washington's "seeds of democracy"', by F. William Engdahl

107 *to admit that 190,000 rifles and pistols*: see *Independent*, 7 August 2007, 'Pentagon admits 190,000 weapons missing in Iraq', by Rupert Cornwall

109 *By 2007, the financial toll of America's wars*: see *Guardian*, 14 November 2007, 'Afghanistan and Iraq wars cost $1.6 trillion', by Julian Borger

109 *President Barack Obama was asking Congress*: AP, 13 January 2010, 'Obama wants $33 billion more for wars'

110 *David Brooks wrote*: see *New York Times*, 25 January 2007, 'Breaking the clinch', by David Brooks

110 *When I saw with my own eyes*: see *Independent*, 5 June 2003, 'Raiders of the Lost Iraq', by Robert Fisk; see also *Independent*, 17 September 2007, 'It is the death of history', by Robert Fisk; see also Peter G. Stone and Joanne Farchakh Bajjaly, *The Destruction of Cultural Heritage in Iraq* (Woodbridge (UK): Boydell, 2008)

5: 'You Have Your Mission – And I Have Mine'

114 *It took me weeks to persuade*: see *Independent*, 6 June 2006, 'The face of the enemy', by Robert Fisk

117 *I watch as they pull corpses*: see *Independent*, 18 March 2004, 'Car bomb attack on Baghdad hotel leaves 17 dead', by Robert Fisk

118 *I long ago reached the conclusion*: see, for example, *Pity the Nation* (Fisk), esp. pp. 478–522 and 561, 610–1; see also *The Great War for Civilisation* (Fisk), esp. pp. 580–90, 1039–42

119 *When I went to see Samir again two years later*: author's interview with
    Samir Jarrah, Houch, Lebanon, 6 November 2003

121 *Nor was he respected because he was a mass killer*: see *Independent*, 13
    September 2001, 'They can run and they can hide. Suicide bombers are
    here to stay', by Robert Fisk

121 *By 2006, over the mosques of Sidon and Tripoli*: see *Independent*, 7 July 2006,
    'Lebanese salute their "martyrs" in Iraq war', by Robert Fisk

123 *I spent a month trowelling through official statistics, Arabic-language*: see
    Independent, 14 March 2008, 'The cult of the suicide bomber', by Robert
    Fisk; newspapers and archives consulted during March and early
    April 2008 included *As-Safir* (Beirut), *An-Nahar* (Beirut), *Sharq al-Awsat*
    (London), *Al-Ahram Weekly* (Cairo), *L'Orient-Le Jour* (Beirut), the *Middle
    East Reporter* (Beirut), AP and Reuters

126 *US military figures showed that*: see AP, 6 June 2008, 'Women bombers
    show shifting insurgent tactics in Iraq', by Kim Gamel

126 *One of the most fearful female suicide bombings*: see AP, 2 February 2010,
    'Female suicide bomber hits Iraqi pilgrims, kills 54'

126 *Nothing could better illustrate the lack of knowledge*: see Reuters, 28 March
    2007, 'US blames Syria for letting bombers into Iraq', by Sue Pleming

127 *In 2008, the US military estimated that 40 per cent of jihadis*: see *Los Angeles
    Times*, 17 March 2008, 'A profile of Iraq's foreign insurgents', by
    Alexandra Zaris

128 *a long cherished ambition*: see Atwan, *After Bin Laden*, p. 16

129 *'I was stunned by his [Fisk's] question'*: see Najwa and Omar bin Laden and
    Sasson, *Growing Up bin Laden*, p. 225

130 *because he was not a fan of photography*: ibid.

132 *The Saudi regime, he said, had 'lost its legitimacy'*: see Fisk, *The Great War for
    Civilisation*, pp. 23–4

133 *this secret Pakistani account*: see The Abbottabad Commission, 2013 (32
    chapters) by Justice Javed Iqbal (president), Abbas Khan, Ashraf Qazi and
    Lt Gen. (retired) Nadeem Ahmed (members), revealed by Al Jazeera,
    July 2013. Until a published copy is available, readers must refer to the Al
    Jazeera website to obtain a copy: http://www.aljazeera.com/indepth/
    ·spotlight/binladenfiles/2013/07/201378143927822246.html. References in
    this book come from pp. 1, 36, 37–40, 41, 43, 45, 47, 50, 52, 54, 56–62, 65,
    67, 70, 72, 75–6, 77, 101, 105–6, 108–24, 145, 170–1, 174, 188–9, 190–2, 195–6,
    207, 208, 211, 218, 244–5, 253, 279, 287, 304, 334

137 *A big man in a white robe*: see *Independent*, 21 May 2011, 'Uneasy times in
    Lebanon as Syrian revolt simmers', by Robert Fisk

138 *The documents that the Americans released*: see Osama bin Laden &
    Al-Qaeda: Documents Captured At Abbottabad Compound, Original
    Arabic Transcriptions, English Translations and Annotations, available
    from BACM Research (www.PaperlessArchives.com), 264 South La
    Cienega Boulevard, No. 1142, Beverly Hills, CA 90211. Quotations in
    these pages are taken from the following files and pages: SOCOM-2012-

0000003, p. 3; SOCOM-2012-0000004, pp. 1–21; SOCOM-2012-0000007, p. 1; SOCOM-2012-0000009; SOCOM-2012-0000010 pp. 1–5, 8, 10; SOCOM-2012-0000011; SOCOM-2012-0000018, pp. 2, 408; SOCOM-2012-0000019, pp. 2–6, 9–10, 12–13, 18–20, 22, 22–4, 30–2, 34–7, 44–6, 48

139 *'a new fundamentalist organisation even more morbid than al-Qaeda'*: see *Al-Ahram Weekly* (Cairo), 24–30 January 2008, 'Jockeying for the militant mandate', by Khalil El-Anani

147 *We could not forget amid the burning cars*: see *Independent*, 19 November 2013, 'Beirut bomb blasts … Iranian embassy is the target in a widening war between Shia and Sunni', by Robert Fisk

148 *On the night before the bombings*: see *Independent*, 25 November 2013, 'Suicide attack in Beirut: Tragedy is spreading from Iran's western border to the Mediterranean', by Robert Fisk

149 *Mouin Abu Dahr was born into a mixed Sunni–Shia family*: see *L'Orient-Le Jour* (Beirut), 25 November 2013, 'Après l'identification des kamikazes de Jnah, la chasse aux instigateurs'

149 *The commander of the 'Abdullah Azzam Brigades'*: see *New York Times*, 5 January 2014, 'Militant tied to bombing in Lebanon dies in jail', by Ben Hubbard and Hwaida Saadjan

150 *An acquaintance of Mohamed's family*: see *Daily Star* (Beirut), 25 November 2013, 'Who were the Beirut Bir Hassan bombers?', by Mohamed Zaatari

6: 'The Gloves Are Coming Off, Gentlemen …'

151 *Now General Richard Myers*: see *New York Times*, 12 August 2005, 'Officials see risk in the release of images of Iraq prisoner abuse', by Julia Preston

152 *How then to explain the testimony of Haj Ali*: see Klein, *Shock Doctrine*, p. 446

152 *'the shock of the torture chamber'*: Klein, *Shock Doctrine*, p. 443

153 *We didn't know, Hersh told a lecture audience*: Fisk, *Age of the Warrior: Selected Writings by Robert Fisk* (London: Fourth Estate/HarperCollins 2008), p. 307, citing ACLU Membership Conference Keynote Speech by Seymour Hersh, 8 July 2008

153 *They studied a Pentagon press conference*: US Defense Department news transcript of briefing with defense secretary Rumsfeld and General Pace, 29 November 2005

153 *A Pentagon investigation revealed that at Guantanamo, Mohamed al-Qahtani*: see *Independent*, 15 July 2005, 'Guantanamo degredation revealed', by Rupert Cornwall

154 *'stands in sharp contrast to my own experiences as an interrogator'*: see *Washington Post*, 9 February 2007, 'An Iraq interrogator's nightmare', by Eric Fair

154 *When the American massacre was revealed*: see *Independent*, 3 June 2006, 'On the shocking truth about the American occupation of Iraq', by Robert Fisk

154 *The murders only came to light*: see *Independent*, 5 September 2011, 'US troops did execute civilians, leaked letter claims', by Donald Macintyre and Jerome Taylor

155 *'It's the one that just happened to be uncovered'*: see the *Sunday Times*, 2 March 2008, 'Patriot missiles: Iraq veterans against the war', by Ariel Leve

155 *Within ten years of the invasion*: see *Daily Star* (Beirut), 6 August 2007, 'US soldier gets 110 years behind bars for rape, murder of Iraqi girl and family', quoting AFP report from Washington; *Le Monde*, 13 July 2007, 'Un soldat américain condamné a 13 ans de prison pour l'assassinat de trois prisonniers irakiens', quoting AFP from Washington; *National Post* (Toronto), 31 March 2009, 'US soldier gets life for killing Iraqi prisoners', by William Ickes, quoting AFP; *Independent*, 17 November 2004, 'Marines will investigate claims of war crimes', by Andrew Buncombe

155 *Among many incidents Washburn was to recall*: see *Winter Soldier*, p. 20

156 *'holed up in hotels, hemmed in by drivers and translators'*: see Hedges and Al-Arian, *Collateral Damage*, p. xvii

157 *Sami al-Haj walks with pain on his steel crutch*: see *Independent*, 25 September 2008, 'Six years in Guantanamo', by Robert Fisk

161 *US intelligence operative Captain Ponce*: see Klein, *Shock Doctrine*, p. 443

161 *become 'socialised to atrocity'*: see *Collateral Damage* by Hedges and Al-Arian, p. xiii

162 *'coarse insensibility to suffering … the influence of licensed cruelty'*: see *Roman Society from Nero to Marcus Aurelius* by Samuel Dill, pp. 234–5 (London: Macmillan, 1904)

162 *Mark Twain wrote a deeply*: see *A Pen Warmed Up in Hell: Mark Twain in Protest*, edited by Frederick Anderson (New York: Harper & Row, 1979), pp. 97–100, 'Grief and Mourning for the Night', by Mark Twain

163 *'common methods of war'*: see, for example, Redress, August 2013, (Redress Trust, London) 'Torture in the Middle East: The law and practice', p. 4

165 *'This moves laterally across the Arab world'*: see *Independent*, 19 March 1997, 'Mubarak's gadfly prophecies a peaceful Islamic revolution', by Robert Fisk

168 *the 'Five Techniques'*: see *Cruel Britannia: A Secret History of Torture* by Ian Cobain (London: Portobello, 2013), pp. 129–34

169 *The last time he saw his son*: see *Independent on Sunday*, 4 January 2004. '"The British said my son would be free soon. Three days later I had his body"' by Robert Fisk; *Independent*, 19 December 2004, 'The army had not a word of compassion for the dead man, nor for his orphaned sons', by Robert Fisk; *Independent*, 9 September 2011, 'Robert Fisk: It's not the brutality that is "symptomatic". It's the lying about it'

170 *It took the British defence ministry*: see *Independent*, 11 July 2008, 'Family of Iraqi man killed by soldiers gets £3m payment', by Beverley Rouse; see also Cobain, *Cruel Britannia*, p. 311

171 *Punching the prisoners*: see Janina Struk, *Private Pictures*, p. 126

171 *British lawyers felt the same*: letter to author from Phil Shiner, 9 July 2009

172 *After an eight-year campaign*: see *Independent*, 9 September 2011, 'Kicked and punched to death by cowards', by Nina Lakhani

172 *Were combatants unaware*: see *RCRC, The Magazine of the International Red Cross and Red Crescent Movement*, issue 2 – 2004, pp. 24–5, 'What makes people behave the way they do in war?'

173 *During the UK military inquiry*: see *Independent*, 14 July 2009, 'Baha Mousa enquiry shown video of soldier abusing Iraqi detainees', by Robert Verkaik

173 *A glance at the childish*: see *New York Times*, 21 November 2003, 'As Bush and Blair speak, they find many ways to say, "We must fight terror"' (partial transcript)

174 *US officers in Baghdad*: see *New York Times*, 19 March 2006, 'In secret unit's "black room", a grim portrait of US abuse', by Eric Schmitt and Carolyn Marshall

174 *'One reason why'*: author's telephone interview with Justin Huggler, 21 February 2015

174 *In August 2004, the use of torture*: see *Independent*, 12 August 2004, 'Evidence gained by torture allowed by British judges', by Robert Verkaik

176 *Discovering that several dictatorships*: see *The Spokesman* (ed. Ken Coates), No. 95, 2007, pp. 12–48, 'An indictment of Tony Blair, and the failure of the political process', by Judge E.W. Thomas

176 *The history of sending Arabs*: see *Guardian*, 18 August 1972, 'Britain delays decision on Rabat rebels', by Patrick Keatley; see also *The Times*, 19 August 1972, 'Government accused of ill-judged haste in sending rebel officers back to Rabat', by John Groser; *The Times*, 19 August 1972, 'Extradition by another name' (editorial); and *The Times*, 8 November 1972, '11 officers to die for plot against King Hassan' (Reuters report)

177 *Researching the life of his grandfather*: see *Independent*, 6 December 2007, 'Henry's war: One man's fight against rendition', by Patrick Cockburn

177 *George W. Bush openly told the world*: see *New York Times*, 14 March 2009, 'Tales from torture's dark world', by Mark Danner; see also *New York Review of Books*, 30 April 2009, 'The Red Cross torture report: What it means', by Mark Danner

178 *Take the case of Mohamed al-Zery and Ahmed Agiza*: see *Le Monde diplomatique*, April 2005, 'United States: Trade in torture', by Stephen Grey

178 *Three years after the UK Court of Appeal*: see European Parliament Justice and Home Affairs report, 14 January 2007, 'CIA activities in Europe: European Parliament adopts final report deploring passivity from some member states' (rapporteur Giovanni Claudio Fava); see also *Independent*, 24 January 2007, 'Hoon criticised over CIA's secret flights', by Stephen Castle

179 *The five were seized with the help of Albanian police*: see *Washington Post*, 11 March 2002, 'US behind secret transfer of terror suspects', by Rajiv Chandrasekaran and Peter Finn

179 *Secret CIA documents held by the British Foreign Office*: see *Independent*, 5 February 2009, 'US accused of blackmail over terror trial evidence', by Robert Verkaik; see also *Independent*, 11 February 2010, 'Britain did know CIA tortured suspect', by Nigel Morris; *Independent*, 20 February 2010, 'Secret service face fresh claim of complicity in torture', by Robert Verkaik; *Daily Mail*, 27 February 2010, 'Torture: The shame of MI5', by James Slack

180 *Human rights groups had for many years*: see Amnesty International report MDE 24/02/95 of April 1995, 'Syria – Repression and impunity: The forgotten victims'; Human Rights Watch report, Vol. 8, No. 2 of April 1996, 'Syria's Tadmor Prison: Dissent still hostage to a legacy of terror'; Amnesty report MDE 24/01/2001 of September 2001, 'Syria – Tadmor Military Prison: Torture, despair and dehumanisation'; author's interview with former Tadmor prisoner, Boston, USA, February 2003

180 *Aamer was to testify that two MI5 or MI6 officers*: see *Independent*, 1 March 2009, 'Guilty: Second Britain: Whitehall colluded in my torture', by Robert Verkaik; see also, *Independent*, 17 November 2010, 'Bill for settling Guantanamo Bay "torture" cases could top $30m', by Robert Verkaik and Nigel Morris

181 *In November 2003, Amnesty International produced two urgent reports*: see Amnesty International reports MDE 24/042/2003 of 11 November 2003 on Hasan Mustafa and MDE 24/038/2003 of 4 November 2003 on Abdullah Almalki

182 *Those who find this tale incredible*: author's interview with Abdullah Almalki, Ottawa, Canada, 22 February 2009; Almalki's notes for seminar 28 January 2009 (copy in author's possession); see also *Independent*, 14 March 2009, 'The West should feel shame over its collusion with torturers', by Robert Fisk; The Commission of Inquiry into the Actions of Canadian Officials in Relation to Maher Arar, 18 September 2006, Frank Iacobucci (Canadian Privy Council, Ottawa); Kerry Pither, *Dark Days*

184 *Not only were the RCMP again accomplices*: see *New York Times*, 1 February 2004, 'Misconduct charges sully image of Canadian police', by Clifford Krauss; see also *Toronto Star*, 6 November 2007, 'Ottawa's invisible inquiry', by Tonda MacCharles; *Globe and Mail*, 19 October 2007, 'Several US congressmen apologize to Arar', by Paul Koring

185 *Years after Arar, and Almalki*: see *Toronto Star*, 1 April 2009, 'CSIS "defies orders on torture"', by Tonda MacCharles

186 *Bob Herbert, an old op-ed stalwart*: see *New York Times*, 18 February 2005, 'Our friends, the torturers', by Bob Herbert

186 *Yet there were heroes*: see *New York Times*, 6 July 2008, 'The Truth Commission', by Nicholas D. Kristof

187 *Five years after 'water-boarding' had become routine*: see *New York Times*, 1 November 2007, 'Nominee's stand avoids tangle of torture cases', by Scott Shane

187 *It is true that some of those who abused their prisoners*: see *Washington Post*, 9 February 2007, 'An Iraq interrogator's nightmare', by Eric Fair

187 *Libyan intelligence officers … were allowed to visit Guantanamo*: see *Independent on Sunday*, 24 April 2005, 'Snakes, beatings, sexual assaults: The tale of one British resident's life in Guantanamo', by Severin Carrell

188 *Al-Saadi was to endure six years in prison*: see Cobain, *Cruel Britannia*, pp. 272–5

188 *Then he surrendered and*: see *Toronto Star*, 18 February 2009, 'Ex-Guantanamo detainee surrenders', by Ahmed al-Haj (Reuters)

188 *Thomas White, the former US Army Secretary*: see McClatchy Newspapers, 15 June 2008, 'America's prison for terrorists often held the wrong men', by Tom Lasseter

189 *This became obvious when in November 2005*: see *New York Times*, 2 July 2009, 'Grand jury inquiry on destruction of tapes', by Mark Mazzetti

189 *Nothing could have more painfully symbolised the moral depths*: see *Public Library of Science (PloS) Medicine*, 26 April 2011, 'Medical complicity in torture at Guantanamo Bay: Evidence is the first step toward justice'; see also *Independent*, 27 April 2011, 'US doctors "hid signs of torture" at Guantanamo', by Steve Connor

190 *The most obtuse of these writers, Bruce Anderson*: see *Independent*, 15 February 2010, 'We not only have a right to use torture. We have a duty', by Bruce Anderson

190 *The 528-page document was as blunt as it was gruesome*: Senate Select Committee on Intelligence report on the Central Intelligence Agency's Detention and Interrogation Programme, 9 December 2014; see also *Washington Post*, 9 December 2014, summary of Senate committee report by Greg Miller; see also *Independent*, 28 April 2012, 'Waterboarding and "enhanced interrogation" shown to be ineffective', by David Usborne

191 *The horror … was in the detail*: see *Globe and Mail*, 10 December 2014, 'We thought it was bad. It was worse' (editorial)

191 *The turnover of US prisoners throughout the world*: see *San Francisco Chronicle*, 18 November 2005, 'US has detained more than 83,000 in war on terror', by Katherine Shrader (AP)

191 *When prisoners tried to commit suicide*: see *London Review of Books*, 2 August 2007, 'The least worst place', by Colin Dayan

191 *There were times … when torture seemed to be more about linguistics than pain*: see *Independent*, 14 December 2014, 'Once again language is distorted in order to hide US state wrongdoing', by Robert Fisk

192 *There would be no accountability for Arab torturers*: see *Daily Star (Beirut)*, 13 December 2014, 'Can the Middle East debate torture?', by Rami G. Khouri

193 *Without implying sympathy*: see *Independent*, 10 December 2014, 'CIA torture report: These depravities are not going to infuriate the Muslim world – they've been enraged about them for years', by Robert Fisk

7: The Dog in the Manger

198 *The British dispatched*: see *The Arab Awakening* by Antonius, pp. 267–8

198 *It wasn't even original*: see *Oxford Illustrated History of the Holy Land* (Oxford: OUP, 2018), pp. 276–8 in Chapter 10, 'From Napoleon to Allenby: The Holy Land and the wider Middle East', by Robert Fisk

199 *After serious inter-Jewish rioting and then Arab attacks in Jaffa*: see Hansard, House of Commons Debates, 14 June 1921, cc 265–334

199 *These explanations, however*: see *The Balfour Declaration: The Origins of the Arab-Israeli Conflict* by Jonathan Schneer, pp. 347–61

200 *Churchill's repeated promises*: see *Winston S. Churchill* by Martin Gilbert, Vol. 5, Companion Part 3 Documents, 'The Coming of War' (London: Heinemann, 1982), pp. 602–6, Churchill evidence to the Palestine Royal Commission, 12 March 1937

201 *Churchill ... Red Indians*: see Dockter, *Churchill and the Islamic World*, p. 178

202 *'You assured me that our conversation'*: see *Winston S. Churchill* by Gilbert, p. 624, letter from Churchill to Peel, 16 March 1937

203 *But the late nineteenth-century origin*: see *Oxford Illustrated History of the Holy Land*, pp. 276–8

203 *But Herzl ... 'viewed'*: see *The Iron Wall* by Avi Shlaim, p. 4

204 *Today, the Palestinians commemorate*: see *Palestine Before 1948: Not Just Memory: Khalil Raad (1854–1957)* (Beirut: Institute for Palestine Studies, 2013); see also *Independent*, 7 April 2013, 'Khalil Raad's Palestinian pictures chart the history – and the tragedy', by Robert Fisk

205 *When did the modern Jewish–Arab conflict begin?*: see *L'Orient Littéraire* (Beirut), 1 June 2017, 'Sykes-Picot: les accords du désaccord', James Barr interviewed by Jean-Claude Perrier

206 *When the 1936–39 Arab Rebellion*: see *Picture Post* (London), 5 November 1938, 'War in the Holyland'

207 *In 1937, Churchill was also imagining*: see Fisk, *The Great War for Civilisation*, p. 451, quoting Winston Churchill, *Step by Step: 1936–1939* (London: Odhams, 1947), 'Palestine Partition', 23 July 1937

208 *There are no armed guards*: see *Independent*, 11 February 2010, 'State of denial: Robert Fisk searches for peace in Israel'

208 *Avi Shlaim, a distinguished Israeli scholar*: see Shlaim, *Israel and Palestine*, pp. 60–1

209 *Young Major Derek Cooper*: see *Irish Times*, 9 December 1997, 'From Ballintemple to the Bedouin camps', by Robert Fisk; see also John Baynes, *For Love of Justice: The Life of a Quixotic Soldier* (London: Quartet, 1997), pp. 60–1

209 *The remains of some of those Palestinian Arab casualties*: see Al Jazeera, 3 June 2013, 'Mass Palestinian grave found in Tel Aviv', quoting AFP report of 31 May 2013

209 *Which brought me to the Tel Aviv seafront*: see *Independent*, 2 December 2012, 'Both Jew and Arab lived in the original Palestine. Why, Ruth Dayan

asks, can't they do so again?', by Robert Fisk; see also author's notes of interview with Ruth Dayan, Tel Aviv, 23 November 2012

211 *Shlomo Sand is a caltrop*: see Shlomo Sand, *The Invention of the Jewish People*, pp. 112–13, quoting Moshe Dayan's *Living With the Bible* (New York: William Morrow, 1978)

211 *Moshe's 'such bad taste in women'*: see *Time* magazine, 26 February 1973, 'Israel: Life with Moshe'

211 *Uri Avnery, that most steadfast*: see *Haaretz* (Tel Aviv), 7 June 2013, 'Occupation? What occupation?', by Uri Avnery

212 *Sand contends*: Sand, *The Invention of the Jewish People*, p. 239

212 *Avnery wrote that*: from Avnery's weekly column in the Gush Shalom website, 30 March 2018, 'Pour Out Your Wrath'

212 *Miko Peled, whose father*: see 'The General's Son', speech by Peled at San Diego University, 30 November 2011

213 *Dorothy Thompson, the influential*: see Peter Kurth, *American Cassandra: The Life of Dorothy Thompson* (Boston: Little, Brown and Company, 1990), pp. 161–2, 281–5, 423, 537–8

214 *On the eve of Begin's fund-raising visit*: see *New York Times*, 2 December 1948

214 *There was nothing new*: see Victor Klemperer, *I Will Bear Witness: A Diary of the Nazi Years 1933–41* (New York: Random House, 1998), Vol. I, pp. 23, 68–9; Vol. II (1942–1945) (Random House, 1999), p. 88

215 *She was, her biographer wrote*: see Kurth, *American Cassandra*, p. 425

215 *It was 2006 before Pappe*: see Ilan Pappe, *The Ethnic Cleansing of Palestine*, pp. xii–xv

216 *But Morris, who had first revealed*: see *Haaretz Magazine*, 9 January 2004, Ari Shavit interview with Benny Morris on his book *The Birth of the Palestinian Refugee Problem Revisited* (Oxford: OUP, 2004)

218 *The Palestinians were not the only ones*: see Amos Oz, the Bruno Kreisky Forum for International Dialogue (Vienna), Annual Report 2005

220 *For Netanyahu and his supporters*: see *Haaretz*, 11 November 2013, 'Netanyahu's rage at Iran nuclear deal is fueled by 1938 western betrayal at Munich', by Chemi Shalev

220 *Surely this is the predicament which Dorothy Thompson*: see Kurth, *American Cassandra*, p. 425

220 *But when Hitler's victims*: see *Courrier International*, 3–16 May 2018, 'Hébraïser les noms'; see also *Courrier International*, 19–25 February 2009, 'Les raciness russes d'Israël', quoting article in *Ogoniok* (Moscow) by Vladimir Baider

221 *The idea that the colonisation of Palestine*: see *L'Humanité* (Paris), 22 January 2016, 'Shlomo Sand: "Quand je lis Finkielkraut ou Zemmour, leur lecture de l'Histoire, je suis effrayé"', interview by Pierre Barbancey

221 *The destruction of Arab villages continued*: see *L'Orient-Le Jour* (Beirut), 29 May 2014, 'À Capharnaum, Rai célèbre une messe pour les Libanais réfugiés en Israel'; see also Walid Khalidi, *All That Remains*, pp. 460–1

221 *When I talked over many years*: see Walid Khalidi, *All That Remains*, p. xxxii

222 *They wear their wounds well*: author's notes of interview with Raphie Etgar, Jerusalem, 25 September 2011; see also *Independent*, 27 September 2011, 'Palestine, yes, but Israelis draw the line at Jerusalem ...', by Robert Fisk

224 *So have UN Security Council Resolutions*: see *Independent*, 20 December 2008, 'One missing word sowed the seeds of ...', by Robert Fisk

229 *Keys must always be the symbol*: see *Independent*, 14 June 2018, 'I spoke to Palestinians who still hold the keys to ...', by Robert Fisk

8: The Israeli Empire

231 *The Catholic Gaelic Irish*: see Robert Kee, *Ireland: A History* (London: Weidenfeld and Nicolson, 1980), p. 41

231 *George Hintlian*: see *Independent*, 30 January 2010, 'Israel can no longer ignore the existence of the first Holocaust', by Robert Fisk; author's notes of interview with Hintlian, Jerusalem, 26 January 2010

233 *'a leader who subordinated humanitarian'*: see *Haaretz*, 1 May 2015, 'How Herzl sold out the Armenians', by Rachel Elboim-Dror

234 *Here is the response of Israeli-Irish writer*: see *Irish Times*, 26 July 2018, letter from Ronit Lentin

235 *'Palestine,' as Edward Said wrote*: see Eqbal Ahmad, *Confronting Empire: Interviews by David Barsamian*, preface by Edward Said, p. xxviii (Cambridge, USA: South End Press, 2000)

236 *Writers, academics, journalists*: see *Guardian*, 8 February 2005, obituary of Michael Adams by David Gilmore

236 *The hatred for Australian Jewish journalist*: see Antony Loewenstein, *My Israel Question* (Melbourne: Melbourne University Press, 2006), p. x

236 *Within five years*: see *Guardian*, 22 March 1972, 'Israel stakes firm claim to West bank', by Walter Schwarz; *The Times*, 19 October 1972, 'Annexation indicated in Dayan speech', by Eric Silver; *Guardian*, 27 April 1972, 'Bulldozing through Arab history', by David Hirst

237 *It is instructive to note that when Dayan*: see *Guardian*, 28 June 1973, 'Dayan bars "sandwich state" plan', by Eric Silver

240 *Sharon's 2005 closure*: see the *Economist*, 18 January 2014, 'What if he had bulldozed on?'; Donald Macintyre, *Gaza: Preparing for Dawn*, pp. 45–52; *New York Review of Books*, 21 December 2006, 'The Enigma of Ariel Sharon', by Jonathan Freedland; *New York Times*, 21 August 2005, 'The Dispossessed', by Elie Wiesel; *Independent*, 16 May 2006, 'Crack of Israeli bullets ends activists' protest against barrier', by Donald Macintyre; Amnesty International, 'Enduring occupation: Palestinians under siege in the West Bank', June 2007, p. 5 (AI Index: MDE 15/033/2007)

241 *'Area C' doesn't sound very ominous*: see *Independent*, 30 January 2010, 'In the West Bank's stony hills, Palestine is slowly dying', by Robert Fisk; UN Office for the Coordination of Humanitarian Affairs, occupied Palestinian territory, December 2009 Report, 'Restricting space: The planning regime applied by Israel in Area C of the West Bank'

242 *Jewish scholars in both Israel and America*: see *Haaretz*, 9 March 2006, 'How the "Accidental Empire" was born', by Aryeh Dayan; Gersham Gorenberg, *The Accidental Empire: Israel and the Birth of the Settlements, 1967–1977* (New York: Henry Holt, 2007); *London Review of Books*, 10 April 2008, 'Grab more hills, expand the territory', by Henry Siegman; *London Review of Books*, 2 August 2007, 'Imagined Territories', by Yonatan Mendel; *L'Humanité* (Paris), 20 April 2015, 'L'architecture comme arme d'occupation de la Palestine', by Léopold Lambert

243 *And so each Palestinian attempt to end the colonisation*: see *Independent*, 7 June 2008, 'Israel cuts off Palestinian tax funds as relations hit new low', by Donald Macintyre; *Independent*, 11 July 2008, '"This is like apartheid"', by Donald Macintyre; *Independent*, 8 November 2008, 'Israel razed homes "while US voted"', by Donald Macintyre; *Independent*, 27 April 2009, 'Israel's secret plan for West Bank expansion', by Ben Lynfield; *Independent*, 6 March 2009, 'Plan for tourist theme park raises Jerusalem tensions', by Donald Macintyre; *Independent*, 12 October 2008, '"The Arabs are a filter through which we find our way to land"', by Donald Macintyre; *Irish Times*, 3 March 2009, 'Peace group claims Israel planning more settlements', by Mark Weiss; *Independent*, 14 May 2009, 'Pope challenges Israel to give Palestinians homeland', by Donald Macintyre; *Daily News Egypt*, 19 May 2009, 'Israel issues tenders for West Bank settlement: radio' (AFP); *Independent*, 29 May 2009, 'Israel rejects US plea to halt settlement building', by Rupert Cornwell; *Independent*, 3 June 2009, 'Netanyahu cites secret deal with Bush to justify more settlements', by Donald Macintyre

244 *In east Jerusalem, there stood*: see Fisk, *The Great War for Civilisation*, pp. 437–48; *Independent*, 25 July 2009, 'Israel uses Hitler picture to sell its settlement expansion', by Donald Macintyre; *Guardian*, 9 June 2011, 'Irving Moskowitz demolishes part of Jerusalem hotel to build settler housing', by Harriet Sherwood; Gilbert Achcar, *The Arabs and the Holocaust*, pp. 141–2 and 142n; Ma'an News Agency, 31 July 2009, 'East Jerusalem settlement plans Israeli message to Obama', by Israeli human rights group Ir Amin; Rabin and Schwanitz, *Nazis, Islamists, and the Making of the Modern Middle East* (London: Yale University Press, 2014), p. 254; Sean McMeekin, *The Berlin-Baghdad Express: The Ottoman Empire and Germany's Bid for World Power 1898–1918*, p. 360–1; *Independent*, 6 July 2014, 'Dumping blame for the Holocaust on a Palestinian is an insult to its six million victims', by Robert Fisk; transcript of Benjamin Netanyahu speech at 37th Zionist Congress, Jerusalem, 20 October 2015 (Office of the Israeli Prime Minister); *Haaretz*, 21 October 2015, 'Netanyahu: Hitler didn't want to exterminate the Jews' (AFP report); *Guardian*, 21 October 2015, 'Anger at Netanyahu claim Palestinian Grand Mufti inspired Holocaust', by Peter Beaumont; Gush Shalom, 30 October 2015, 'Adolf, Amin and Bibi', by Uri Avnery; Gush Shalom, 28 July 2018, 'Adolf and Amin', by Uri Avnery

247 *Whether it was the bias of columnists*: see *Des Moines Register*, 10 April 2002,
'Arafat evidence demands a verdict', by Cal Thomas; *Sunday Times*
(London) 17 September 1972, 'Addicts of terror', by Brian Moynahan;
Daily Mail (London), 13 November 2004, 'Grief from the barrel of a gun as
Arafat is sent to his grave', by Ross Benson; *Iowa City Press Citizen*, 10 April
2002, 'Israel tried peace; Palestine answered with war', by Mona Charen

248 *the deliberate, unstoppable expansion*: *L'Orient-Le Jour* (Beirut), 9 March 2010,
'Israel donne son feu vert à 112 nouveaux logements dans une colonie
de Cisjordanie'; AFP, 13 March 2010, published in *Dawn* (Karachi), 14
March 2010, 'Hillary rebukes Israel over settler homes'; *National Post*
(Toronto), 24 March 2010, '"Jerusalem is not a settlement"', by Stephen
Collinson; *Chicago Tribune*, 9 May 2010, 'Israel's fated bleak future', by
John J. Mearsheimer; *Independent*, 7 July 2010, 'Israeli settlement policy
undermining two-state solution, report finds', by Catrina Stewart and
David Usborne; *Daily Star* (Beirut), 4 August 2010, 'Israeli settlement
watchdog finds 492 "freeze" violations' (agencies); *Toronto Star*, 24 June
2010, 'Building homes for the enemy', by Linda Gradstein; *Financial
Times*, 11 October 2010, 'America should fund Israeli settlers to leave',
by Diana Buttu; *L'Orient-Le Jour* (Beirut), 12 October 2020, 'Le cabinet
israelien pour un referendum avant un retrait du Golan et de Jerusalem-
Est'; *Irish Times*, 11 November 2010, 'Clinton rebukes Israel over plan
on settlements', by Mark Weiss; *Irish Times*, 15 November 2010, 'Israeli
ministers given details of plan to get Palestinian talks back on track',
by Mark Weiss; *Independent*, 15 November 2010, 'Israelis weigh up
US incentive plan to re-start peace talks', by Donald Macintyre; *New
York Times*, 21 November 2010, 'Palestinian leader insists on halt to
settlements', by Isabel Kershner; *Al Ahram Weekly*, 1 December 2010,
'Washington rolls over', by Khaled Amayreh; *Daily Star* (Beirut), 5
April 2011, 'Israel approves 942 new settler homes in East Jerusalem
(AFP, Reuters); AFP, 24 May 2010, 'Netanyahu tells Israel lobby no
going back to old borders', by Gavin Rabinowitz; *Independent*, 17 July
2011, 'Jewish settlers are terrorizing Palestinians, says Israeli general',
by Catrina Stewart; *Guardian*, 16 August 2011, 'Settler homes go-ahead
for West Bank hits peace prospects', by Harriet Sherwood; transcript of
Mahmoud Abbas speech at UN General Assembly, 23 September 2011;
Daily Star (Beirut), 11 February 2012, '42 reasons to dismiss Susan Rice's
rage', by Rami G. Khouri; transcript of President Barack Obama's speech
to UN General Assembly, 21 September 2011; *Haaretz*, 21 September
2011, 'Palestinians disappointed by Obama's UN speech', by Natasha
Mozgovaya and Reuters; *Independent*, 23 September 2011, 'A President
who is helpless in the face of Middle East reality', by Robert Fisk; *Haaretz*,
22 September 2011, 'A harbinger of a dying status quo', by Yael Sternhell

249 *But not 'delicate' enough*: see *Daily Star (Beirut)*, 23 February 2012, 'Israel
approves 500 homes in West Bank settlement, legalises 200 already built
(AFP); Peace Now, 23 June 2012, 'Our Muslim Brothers', by Uri Avnery

250 *Jewish settlers were now regularly attacking*: see *New York Times*, 23 September 2012, 'Amid statehood bid, tensions simmer in West Bank', by Ethan Bonner; *L'Orient-Le Jour*, 4 August 2012, 'Un village palestinien en lutte incessante contre les colons pour la terre' (AFP); *L'Orient-Le Jour*, 4 October 2011, 'Les colons incendient une mosquée; Netanyahu "furieux"' (AFP); *Irish Times*, 14 December 2011, 'Jewish settlers attack Israeli base', by Mark Weiss and Michael Jansen; *Irish Times*, 16 December 2011, 'Jewish settlers set fire to mosque in Ramallah', by Mark Weiss; *Daily Star* (Beirut), 23 October 2012, 'Israel and Palestine after Oslo Accords', by Daoud Kuttab; *Irish Times*, 28 October 2013, 'Israel to free 26 Palestinian militants', by Mark Weiss; *Guardian*, 31 July 2015, 'Israeli government's talk is cheap on "price tag" violence', by Harriet Sherwood; *Independent*, 20 May 2011, 'Lots of rhetoric – but very little help', by Robert Fisk

251 *There were times*: see author's notes of interview with Professor Yeshayahu Leibowitz, Jerusalem, 5 September 1993; email to author from Walid Jumblatt, 18 and 21 August 2018 and 3 September 2018; *Independent*, 20 August 2018, 'Uri Avnery, the Israeli optimist who played chess with Yasser Arafat', by Robert Fisk; Gush Shalom, 2 November 2013, '90 years from now', by Uri Avnery; Gush Shalom, 3 March 2018, 'Because there is nothing', by Uri Avnery; author's email to Holly Baxter at the *Independent*, 20 August 2018

253 *And not without reason*: see *Irish Times*, 1 December 2012, 'UN vote on Palestine likely to kick off Israeli settlement building spree', by Mark Weiss; *Irish Times*, 21 December 2012, 'Israel approves start of new West Bank settlement', by Mark Weiss; *L'Orient-Le Jour* (Beirut), 31 May 2013, 'Un millier de nouveaux logements juifs à Jérusalem-Est' (AFP); Al Arabiya, 13 August 2013, 'Kerry urges Palestinians "not to react adversely" to Israeli settlements' (AFP); *Daily Star* (Beirut), 5 April 2014, 'Kerry: US reconsidering role in Mideast talks' (AP, AFP)

253 *If only Obama and his secretary of state*: see *Libération*, 26 September 2016, 'Poison', by Alexandra Schwarzbrod and 'Au debut, ce n'etaient que des tentes', by Nissim Behar; *Guardian*, 22 January 2017, 'Israel reveals plans for nearly 600 settlement homes in East Jerusalem', by Peter Beaumont; *Irish Times*, 25 January 2017, 'Israel to build 2,500 new settlement homes' (Reuters); *Irish Times*, 31 January 2017, 'Israel's parliament to vote on approval for West Bank settlements', by Mark Weiss

255 *It's like a silver wedding*: see *Independent*, 4 October 2018, 'I watched a Palestinian family lose their land 25 years ago – and this week I returned to find them', by Robert Fisk; see also 'From Beirut to Bosnia Part 2: The Road to Palestine', Channel 4 and Discovery Channel, 1993

256 *But it is Chaim Silberstein's land*: see *Independent*, 24 September 2018, 'In the West Bank, some are unsure about whether Trump is a friend of Israel or not', by Robert Fisk; *New York Times*, 21 September 2018, 'Why the "Jordanian option" won't die', by Shmuel Rosner

259 *I am no longer shocked*: see *Independent*, 20 September 2018, 'I asked Israel's only journalist in Palestine to show me something shocking – and this is what I saw', by Robert Fisk; *Haaretz*, 14 September 2018, 'Israel's intention was never peace nor Palestinian statehood', by Amira Hass

260 *Jewish academics were among*: see New *York Review of Books*, 23 October 2003, 'Israel: The alternative', by Tony Judt

9: 'Going Wild'

262 *One Saturday afternoon*: see Walid Khalidi, *All That Remains*, pp. 102–3, quoting Benny Morris, *The Birth of the Palestinian Refugee Problem 1947–1949*, pp. 129, 152–3; see also *Independent*, 26 November 2012, 'The suffering of Sderot: How its true inhabitants were wiped from Israel's maps and memories', by Robert Fisk

264 *Thus what I called this 'unlovely hiatus'*: see Edmund Blunden, *Undertones of War* (London: Four Square, 1962), pp. 132–3

265 *One of the most verdant and peaceful locations*: see Macintyre, *Gaza*, pp. 3–4, 8–9

269 *Inside the First Congregational Church*: see *Independent*, 29 July 2002, 'Stars and strife: A strange kind of freedom', by Robert Fisk; see also *Toronto Star*, 19 February 2009, 'Obama's role, and outs, in the Mideast', interview with Naomi Klein by Haroon Siddiqui; *Al-Aqsa* journal (UK), Vol. 10, No. 2, Spring 2008, 'Palestinian-Christian/Muslim relations: Myths, propaganda and realities', by Ben White

273 *This phenomenon took many forms*: see *Gulf Today* (Sharjah, UAE), 8 June 2008, 'Obama's pro-Israeli turn dismays peace advocates', by Michael Jansen; *New York Times*, 11 January 2009, 'Mideast dream team? Not quite', by Roger Cohen; Gush Shalom, 27 July 2013, 'Under the table', by Uri Avnery

274 *This extraordinary reticence*: see *Daily Star* (Beirut), 31 January 2003, 'Imperial America is about to strike', by Patrick Seale; *New York Times*, 9 January 2006, 'Where spying starts and stops: Tracking an embattled CIA and a president at war', by James Bamford; see also James Risen, *State of War: The Secret History of the CIA and the Bush Administration* (Free Press, 2006); *Independent*, 6 December 2003, 'Israel accused over dud Saddam reports', by Justin Huggler

274 *It would be pleasant to record*: see *The Forward* (New York), 8 March 2018, 'We made a documentary exposing the "Israeli lobby". Why hasn't it run?', by Clayton Swisher; *Le Monde diplomatique* (Paris), September 2018, 'Lobby israelien, le documentaire interdit', by Alain Gresh; *L'Orient-Le Jour* (Beirut), 17 September 2018, 'Lorsque Al-Jazira's autocensure', by Julie Kebbi; see also Clayton Swisher, *The Palestine Papers: The End of the Road?* (Hesperus, 2011), pp. 27, 53, 64

275 *Swisher already represented*: see The Electronic Intifada, 10 November 2004, 'Challenging Camp David mythology, four years on' (interview with Clayton Swisher); see also Clayton Swisher, *The Truth about the*

Collapse of the Middle East Peace Process (Nation Books: New York, 2004), esp. p. 362

276 *Gazing across the landscape*: see *New Statesman*, 5 July 2010, 'General Petraeus's leaked emails about Israel', by Mehdi Hasan; *Irish Times*, 28 April 2004, 'Negroponte spells out limits of sovereignty to be ceded to Iraq', by Conor O'Clery'; *Le Monde*, 28 April 2004, 'Lakhdar Brahimi, "super-pompier" de l'ONU', by Corine Lesnes

277 *Almost three months before the start*: see Reuters, 3 October 2006, 'Israel warns Hezbollah war would invite destruction', by Joseph Nasr (see also Mohamed Ali Khalidi, 'Five lessons I learned from the Israeli attack on Gaza', Institute for Palestine Studies, 15 April 2015); *Haaretz*, 27 June 1999, 'IDF's honour prevents Israel's normalcy', by Zvi Barel; *Le Monde*, 8 September 2007, 'Human Rights Watch accuse Israel d'avoir commis des "crimes de guerre" en 2006 au Liban', by Michel Bole-Richard; William M. Arkin, *Code Names: Deciphering US Military Plans, Programs, and Operations in the 9/11 World* (New Hampshire, USA: Steerforth Press, 2005), p. 137

277 *in the critical month*: see *Independent*, 3 March 2008, 'Gaza, a matter of life and death for a whole people', letter from Ruth Tenne; *Independent*, 1 May 2008, 'Gaza "on point of explosion" warns UN', by Donald Macintyre; Middle East Policy Council, Vol. XVII, No. 1, Spring 2010, 'The Gaza war, congress and international humanitarian law', by Stephen Zunes; *Haaretz*, 28 December 2008, 'IAF strike followed months of planning', by Barak Ravid; *Independent*, 14 November 2008, 'With crossing closed, food aid runs out for Gaza', by Donald Macintyre; *Independent*, 15 November 2008, 'Chronic malnutrition in Gaza blamed on Israel', by Donald Macintyre; Centre for Research on Global Action, 8 January 2009, 'War and natural gas: The Israeli invasion and offshore gas fields', by Michel Chossudovsky; White House Radio, 2 January 2009, 'President's radio address', George W. Bush; *Guardian*, 7 January 2009, 'How Israel brought Gaza to the brink of humanitarian catastrophe', by Avi Shlaim

279 *Even the Israeli foreign affairs ministry website*: see *Le Monde diplomatique*, February 2009, 'Plus le mensonge est gross …', by Dominique Vidal; *La Presse* (Montreal), 31 December 2008, 'Israel est l'aggresseur', by Rachad Antonius; *London Review of Books*, 1 January 2009, 'If Gaza falls …', by Sara Roy; Hot Press (Dublin), 18 March 2009, 'Return to Zion', interview with Zion Evrony by Jason O'Toole

280 *Canadian newspaper reporter*: see *La Presse* (Montreal), 8 January 2009, 'Boum, boum, boum …', by Patrick Lagacé; *La Presse* (Montreal), 'Elections et guerre des medias', by Jooneed Kahn, quoting *Los Angeles Times* blog, 29 December 2008, 'GAZA STRIP: In praise of Al Jazeera', by Ashraf Khalil; *Le Monde*, 9 January 2009, 'La presse, tenue a distance, rumine sa frustration', by Benjamin Barthe; *Independent*, 9 January 2009, 'Children found next to dead mothers', by Donald Macintyre; *Independent*, 15 January 2009, 'Push for ceasefire intensifies', by Donald

Macintyre; *Independent*, 27 September 2018, 'Here's what I found when I spent the day with Israel's most controversial journalist, Gideon Levy', by Robert Fisk; *Irish Times*, 6 January 2009, 'Arabs criticize Obama's "deafening silence" on crisis', by May Fitzgerald; *Time* magazine, 19 December 2008–6 January 2009, 'The Interview: Person of the Year Barack Obama'

281 *But the 'shroud' was much more seriously ripped*: see *Independent Magazine*, 12 December 2009, 'Gaza: One year on', by Donald Macintyre

281 *I became as much a newspaper reader*: see *International Herald Tribune*, 12 January 2009, 'What if Hamas was in your neighbourhood' (AIPAC); *National Post* (Toronto), 29 December 2008, 'What would you do?', by Lorne Gunter

282 *French Canadians were not to be spared*: see *La Presse* (Montreal), 31 December 2008, 'Tel Aviv n'a pas le choix' (co-signed letter); *National Post* (Toronto), 3 January 2009, 'Israel v. Hamas: Civilization vs. Terror', by Robert Fulford; *New York Times*, 3 January 2009, 'Israelis united on Gaza War as censure rises abroad', by Ethan Bronner

282 *These extraordinary fictions*: see *Irish Times*, 6 January 2009, 'Israeli offensive in Gaza', letter to editor from Zion Evrony; *The Times*, 23 February 1974, 'Provisional IRA fights cross-border battle with Army', by Robert Fisk; *National Post* (Toronto), 2 February 2009, 'Why Israel can't afford to hold back' (editorial); *National Post* (Toronto), 23 February 2009, 'Stop downplaying Hamas', by James Kirchik; *Independent*, 21 January 2009, '"I watched an Israeli soldier shoot dead my two little girls"', by Donald Macintyre; *L'Orient-Le Jour* (Beirut), 20 January 2009, 'Les securistes à la recherche de corps ne connaissent pas de repit', by Mehdi Fedouach (AFP); Katherine Butler, personal email to the author, 17 January 2019

283 *There were some Israelis*: see *Independent*, 17 January 2009, 'Plea to stop war from victims of rocket salvos', by Ben Lynfield

283 *There was one Palestinian in Gaza*: see Democracy Now! (New York), 19 January 2011, interview with Izzeldin Abuelaish by Amy Goodman, which includes earlier recorded interview by Amjali Kamat and Jacqui Soohen with Democracy Now!; *Independent*, 19 January 2009, '"My daughters, they killed them": TV doctor shows Israelis horrors of war', by Ben Lynfield

285 *But the nation of Israel*: see *New York Times*, 13 January 2009, 'Israel's goals in Gaza?', by Thomas Friedman; *Irish Independent* (Dublin), 7 January 2009, 'Israel's problems are due to its enlightened founders', by Kevin Myers; the *Economist*, 7 February 2009, 'Temper tantrums'; *Irish Times*, 6 January 2009, 'Israel must be held to account over Gaza action', by Fintan O'Toole; *Guardian*, 10 January 2009, 'Enough. It's time for a boycott', by Naomi Klein; *Independent*, 8 January 2009, 'Why we care about Israeli inhumanities', letter to the editor by John Kennett

286 *And who supported Hamas?*: see Bruno Stevens, *Ground* (Brussels: Lanoo Books, 2010), foreword by Robert Fisk; *Independent*, 31 December 2008,

'The self-delusion that plagues both sides in this bloody conflict', by Robert Fisk; *Independent*, 22 January 2009, 'Hamas admits killing "Israeli collaborators"', by Donald Macintyre; *New York Times*, 26 June 2010, 'War, timeout, war, time …', by Thomas Friedman; *Independent*, 22 January 2009, 'Smugglers back at work in tunnels beneath Gaza', by Donald Macintyre; *Irish Times*, 11 December 2009, 'Egyptians building wall under ground at Gaza', by Michael Jansen; *Independent*, 8 January 2010, 'Gaza: hope betrayed', by Fares Akram

287 *For several months*: see *Le Canard enchaîné*, 25 March 2009, 'Obama et Sarko inquietent un peu Israel', by Claude Angeli

287 *In the days and weeks to come*: see *New York Times*, 10 January 2009, 'A Gaza war full of traps and trickery', by Steven Erlanger; *Independent*, 24 January 2009, 'White phosphorus blamed for family's pain', by Donald Macintyre; *Independent*, 24 January 2009, 'Palestinians wait for answers on Israeli war in Gaza', by Donald Macintyre; *London Review of Books*, 26 February 2009, 'Return to Gaza', by Amira Hass; *Independent*, 20 March 2009, 'Israel's dirty secrets in Gaza', by Donald Macintyre; *Independent on Sunday*, 1 March 2009, 'Israel's death squads: A soldier's story', by Donald Macintyre; *Independent*, 21 March 2009, 'Israelis told to fight "holy war" in Gaza', by Donald Macintyre; *Independent*, 15 July 2009, 'Israeli soldiers reveal the brutal truth of Gaza attack', by Donald Macintyre; *Independent*, 20 March 2009, 'Israel must root out the canker of military brutality' (editorial); *Independent*, 24 March 2009, 'UN accuses troops of using boy, 11, as human shield', by Donald Macintyre; Human Rights Watch (New York), 13 August 2009, 'White flags deaths: Killing of Palestinian civilians during Operation Cast Lead'; *Guardian*, 13 August 2009, 'Israeli soldiers killed unarmed civilians carrying white flags in Gaza', by Peter Beaumont

290 *But as I read through my notes again*: author's letter to Shameem Bhatia, 17 September 1996 (author's collection)

290 *The Israelis decided from the start*: see UN Human Rights Council, A/HRC/12/48, 'Human Rights in Palestine and Other Occupied Arab Territories: Report of the United Nations Fact-Finding Mission on the Gaza Conflict' (henceforth: Goldstone Report), pp. 434–50; Goldstone Report, pp. 68, 73, 76, 89, 91, 99, 102, 111, 119, 121, 138, 139, 142, 143, 146, 153, 155, 159, 163, 165–6, 187; Daniel Terris, *The Trials of Richard Goldstone* (New Brunswick, USA: Rutgers University Press, 2019), p. 235

293 *Repeatedly, the Goldstone Report*: see Goldstone Report, pp. 184–7; interview with Desmond Travers, January 2018

293 *Incriminating evidence emerged*: see Goldstone Report, pp. 227–32, 242, 255, 199; interview with Desmond Travers, January 2018

293 *A short, rather optimistic book*: see Richard Goldstone, *For Humanity: Reflections of a War Crimes Investigator* (New Haven, USA: Yale University Press, 2000), pp. 126–30; Terris, *The Trials*, p. 241; *Tikkun* (Berkeley, USA), 2 October 2009, 'Tikkun's interview with Judge Richard Goldstone', by Rabbi Michael Lerner; *Jerusalem Post*, 1 February 2010, 'Dershowitz:

Goldstone is a traitor to the Jewish people' (staff reporters); *Guardian*, 17 September 2009, 'Israel rejects UN criticism over Gaza war', by Rory McCarthy; *Revolve* magazine, 2010/11, interview with Norman Finkelstein in November 2009 by Adwan Mohamed and Uffa Kauls Ayring

296 *Israel began producing*: see Reuters, 29 September 2009, 'US urges Israel to probe Gaza crimes to boost peace', by Stephanie Nebehary; AFP, 22 October 2009, 'Goldstone challenges US to spell out Gaza report flaws; *New York Times*, 21 September 2009, 'A US envoy makes a case for the UN', by Neil MacFarquhar; Zunes, 'The Gaza war, congress and international humanitarian law'

296 *Congress, which had obligingly prepared*: see Zunes, 'The Gaza war, congress and international humanitarian law'; Swisher, *The Palestine Papers*, pp. 66–7; *Daily Star* (Beirut), 5 October 2009, 'Palestinians angry as Abbas drops Gaza war crimes case', by Mohammed Daraghmeh' (AP); *Daily Star* (Beirut), 13 August 2010, 'Israeli sniper to get 45 days for killing two Palestinian women' (AFP)

296 *The Israelis closed their first 'inquiry'*: see *Toronto Star*, 31 March 2009, 'Israel rules out charges in Gaza deaths' (AP); *Irish Times*, 24 March 2009, 'Civilians not targeted in Gaza, says Israel', by Mark Weiss; *Independent*, 17 October 2009, 'Israel loses UN vote on Gaza "war crimes"', by Donald Macintyre; *Haaretz*, 1 February 2010, 'Two IDF officers disciplined for using white phosphorous in Gaza offensive', by Anshel Pfeffer

297 *But the political aftershocks of Goldstone's earthquake*: see *Independent*, 23 September 2009, 'American jewry [*sic*] and Israel's interests', by Don [*sic*] Macintyre; *Independent*, 11 March 2010, 'State of denial: Robert Fisk searches for peace in Israel'; *Independent*, 2 February 2010, 'Israel feels under siege. Like a victim. An underdog', by Robert Fisk; *Independent*, 23 November 2012, 'One of Israel's great leftist warriors wants peace with Hamas and Gaza – but does the Knesset?', by Robert Fisk

297 *NGOs and journalists*: see *Independent*, 9 September 2009, 'Israel's war on Gaza killed 252 children, report claims', by Donald Macintyre; *Independent*, 2 February 2010, 'Holes are shot in army's denial of Gaza attack', by Donald Macintyre

298 *There were persistent rumours*: author's interview with Uri Avnery, Tel Aviv, Israel, 23 November 2012; *New York Times*, 25 April 2010, 'A South African judge's Jewish critics relent', by Barry Nearak; *Yediot Ahronoth*, 7 May 2010, 'Judge Richard Goldstone served Apartheid regime in South Africa sending at least 28 Black Africans to the gallows and sending others to the lash', by Zadok Yehezkeli; Terris, *The Trials*, p. 272, quoting *Yediot Ahronoth*, 10 May 2010, 'Judge Goldstone's dark past', by Tehiya Barak; Terris, *The Trials*, p. 56; *London Review of Books*, 10 June 2010, '"J'accuse" Dreyfus in our Times', by Jacqueline Rose

299 *The sword fell*: see Norman Finkelstein, *Gaza: An Inquest into its Martyrdom*, University of California Press, 2018, p. 118; *Washington Post*, 1 April 2011, 'Reconsidering the Goldstone Report on Israel and war crimes', by

Richard Goldstone; *New York Times*, 17 September 2009, 'Justice in Gaza', by Richard Goldstone; Finkelstein, *Gaza*, p. 129; *Haaretz*, 7 April 2011, 'Goldstone has paved the path for a second Gaza war', by Gideon Levy

300 *Daniel Terris recalls*: see Terris, *The Trials*, pp. 300–7, 92, 259–60, 290–1, 295; *Independent*, 3 January 2019, 'Judge Richard Goldstone suffered for turning his back on Gaza – but not as much as the Palestinians he had betrayed', by Robert Fisk; Democracy Now! 19 January 2018, Norman Finkelstein interview with Amy Goodman; author's telephone interview with Desmond Travers, 10 January 2018; author's personal interview with Travers, Blackrock, Ireland, 11 January 2018; Travers' email to author, 12 January 2018; Israeli Ministry of Foreign Affairs, 3 April 2011, 'Behind the headlines: The Goldstone Report refuted – by Goldstone himself'

301 *In 2014, Colonel Ofer Winter*: see *Times of Israel*, 12 July 2014, 'IDF commander seeks God's help to fight "blasphemous" Gazans'; *Jerusalem Post*, 14 July 2014, 'Religious overtones in letter from IDF commander to his soldiers draws criticism, support', by Jeremy Sharon; *Independent*, 4 June 2015, 'When will Palestinians learn? Turning to international law isn't the answer – just ask America and Israel', by Robert Fisk; *Times of Israel*, 22 July 2014, 'Dermer: IDF deserves Nobel Peace Prize for "unimaginable restraint"', by Raphael Ahren; Al Arabiya News, 31 December 2014, 'US "strongly opposes" Palestine ICC membership' (AFP); UNHR Office of the High Commission, Geneva, 22 June 2015, 'UN Gaza Inquiry finds credible allegations of war crimes committed in 2014 by both Israel and Palestinian armed groups'; *Haaretz*, 23 June 2015, 'Head of UN Gaza probe tells Haaretz main message is Israel can't drop one-ton bomb on a neighbourhood', by Barak Ravid; *Times of Israel*, 23 June 2015, 'Shame on you, Mary McGowan Davis', by David Horowitz; *Irish Times*, 23 June 2015, 'War crimes committed in Gaza conflict – UN' (Reuters)

302 *Obama had not uttered*: see *Haaretz*, 22 November 2012, 'Operation rectification', by Ari Shavit; *Jerusalem Post*, 22 November 2012, 'Irresponsibility even in war', by Yisrael Medad and Eli Pollak (of 'Israel's Media Watch')

302 *In the years to come*: see Washington Report on Middle East Affairs, May 2018, p. 47, 'The Zionist tango: Step left, step right', by Gideon Levy; *Independent*, 3 June 2005, 'We killed police for revenge, Israeli soldiers confess', by Donald Macintyre; *Independent*, 19 April 2008, 'Our reign of terror, by the Israeli army', by Donald Macintyre; *Independent*, 9 June 2009, 'Bound, blindfolded and beaten – by Israeli troops', by Ben Lynfield; *Jerusalem Post*, 1 February 2010, 'Women soldiers claim abuses against Palestinians', by Ben Hartman; *Paris Match*, 16–22 September 2010, 'Israel: Quand les officiers brissent le silence', by Catherine Schwaab; *Irish Times*, 15 September 2012, 'Israeli soldiers' new occupation: opening up a closed conflict', by Derek Scally'; *Irish Times*, 19 June 2014, 'Israeli soldiers speak out on abuse of Palestinians', by Kitty Holland; *Irish Times*, 24 June 2014,

'Breaking the Silence' letter to editor from Breaking the Silence executive director Yuli Novak

302 *It was a damp, cold early winter afternoon*: see *Independent*, 8 November 2018, 'Izzeldin Abuelaish's three daughters were killed in Gaza – but he still clings to hope for the Middle East', by Robert Fisk; *Toronto Star*, 28 December 2010, 'Gaza doctor sues Israel over deaths', by Oakland Ross; *Toronto Star*, 1 October 2015, 'The domestic fallout of Harper's foreign policy', by Haroon Siddiqui; *Times of Israel*, 3 December 2018, 'Court rules against Gaza doc who sued over IDF shelling that killed 3 daughters'

10: How Brave Our Warships Looked That Dawn

308 *My words spread out*: see *Independent*, 13 July 2006, 'Beirut waits as Syrian masters send Hezbollah allies into Lebanon', by Robert Fisk

309 *This meant not only physical wounds*: see *Independent*, 14 July 2006, 'From my home, I saw what the "war on terror" meant', by Robert Fisk; *Independent*, 15 July 2006, 'What I am watching in Lebanon each day is an outrage', by Robert Fisk

311 *In antiquity, Pliny wrote of the cliffs*: see *Independent*, 30 September 2006, 'The anatomy of a massacre', by Robert Fisk; *Independent*, 16 July 2006, 'A gripping diary of one week in the life and death of Beirut', by Robert Fisk; *Independent*, 18 July 2006, 'Blow up my city and I'll blow up yours', by Robert Fisk

320 *In the year AD 551*: see *Independent*, 19 July 2006, 'Paradise Lost: Robert Fisk's elegy for Beirut'; *Independent*, 24 June 2006, 'A war crime', by Robert Fisk

323 *They wrote the names of the dead children on their plastic shrouds*: see *Independent*, 31 July 2006, 'How can we stand by and allow this to go on?', by Robert Fisk; *Independent on Sunday*, 6 August 2006, 'Slaughter in Qana', by Robert Fisk; *Independent*, 8 August 2006, 'Crocodile tears of leaders as Beirut burns', by Robert Fisk; for a full account of the 1996 Qana massacre, see Fisk, *Pity the Nation* (2001 edition), pp. 669–89; for Blair on 'Saddam would have become a threat again', see RTE (Dublin), *The Late Late Show*, Tony Blair interviewed by Ryan Tubridy, 3 September 2010

325 *As the carnage*: within the very large WikiLeaks archive on US embassy traffic from Beirut during the 2006 Lebanon war, see especially the 2006 diplomatic reports to secretary of state Rice dated 12, 13, 14, 17, 18, 19, 20, 23, 24, 26, 28 July and 4 August; for details of the Hizbollah attack on the Hanit, see *Le Point* (Paris), 19 October 2006, 'Tsahal: Proces d'un fiasco', by Jean Guisnel

327 *It was that grand old paper*: see *Haaretz*, 12 September 2006, 'IDF commander: We fired more than a million cluster bombs in Lebanon', by Meron Rappaport; *Independent*, 18 September 2006, 'Deadly harvest: The Lebanese fields sown with cluster bombs', by Patrick Cockburn; *Daily Star* (Beirut), 26 October 2010, 'Cluster-bomb fragments kill mine clearer in south Lebanon; Al Jazeera, 13 August 2015, 'Life among Israeli cluster

bombs in Lebanon', by Joseph Ataman; see also Cluster Munitions in Lebanon, 2005 (Landmine Action, UK)

327 *Faced not only with its own*: see Amnesty International report 22 August 2006 (Index no: MDE 18/007/2006), 'Lebanon: Deliberate destruction or "collateral damage"? Israeli attacks on civilian infrastructure'; Human Rights Watch report, Vol. 18, No. 3 (E), 'Fatal strikes: Israel's indiscriminate attacks against civilians in Lebanon'; *London Review of Books*, 2 November 2006, 'The attack on Human Rights Watch', by Aryeh Neier

328 *Within months*: author's interviews with Lebanese security officers and Hizbollah officials, December 2006; see also *Independent*, 9 March 2007, '"Olmert planned Lebanon war before soldiers' kidnap"', by Donald Macintyre; *Jerusalem Post*, 29 September 2009, '"Hizballah had better intel than Israelis in 2006"', by Yaakov Katz

331 *Not that the soldiers*: Day, 'One martyr down'

331 *Irish army commandant*: see *Independent*, 25 July 2016, 'It is 10 years since UN peacekeepers were killed in southern Lebanon – and it could happen again', by Robert Fisk

331 *It is only correct to quote*: see *Legion*, Canada's military history magazine, 2 January 2013, 'One martyr down: The untold story of a Canadian peacekeeper killed at war', by Adam Day; *Ottawa Citizen*, 11 July 2017, 'Adam Day, Canadian war correspondent, friend – Rest in peace', by David Pugliese

332 *The Israelis have never revealed their secret*: author's email from Comdt Kevin McDonald, 21 July 2016; see also Peacekeeping on the Edge: Observer Group Lebanon and the 2006 Israel-Lebanon War, a personal account by Comdt. Kevin McDonald: https://www.academia.edu/27311015/PEACEKEEPING_ON_THE_EDGE

332 *Another woman*: letters to the author from Jamile Wakim-Fleming, 13 October 2006 and 4 June 2007

11: The Awakening

334 *The Egyptian city of Mahalla el-Kubra*: see *Independent*, 6 August 2011, 'The city and its workers who first took on Mubarak', by Robert Fisk; *Le Monde diplomatique*, July 2011, 'L'Egypt en révolution', by Alain Gresh; *Libération*, 5 February 2011, 'Esraa Abdel Farrah, la lutte originelle', by Claude Guibal; see also Marwan Bishara, *The Invisible Arab*, pp. 103–7; Roger J. Cottrell 1994 research paper (in author's possession) 'Class struggle in Egypt: The revolt at Kafr el-Dawar, 42 years on'; *Guardian*, 10 February 2011, 'Trade unions: The revolutionary social network at play in Egypt and Tunisia', by Eric Lee and Benjamin Weinthal

338 *How does one describe a day*: see *Independent*, 29 January 2011, 'A people defies its dictator, and a nation's future is in the balance', by Robert Fisk; *Independent*, 31 January 2011, 'How much longer can Mubarak cling on?', by Robert Fisk

341 *I found the man of the moment*: see *Independent*, 1 February 2011, 'Mohamed El-Baradei: The man who would be President', by Robert Fisk; author's notes of ElBaradei interview, Giza, Egypt, 31 January 2011; *Independent*, 3 February 2011, 'Blood and fear in Cairo's streets as Mubarak's men crack down on protests', by Robert Fisk

343 *Yet next day, the Brotherhood*: CNN, 6 February 2011 Omar Suleiman interviewed by Christiane Amanpour

344 *Scholars have also suggested*: see *Contemporary Arab Affairs* (Centre for Arab Unity Studies, Beirut), Vol. 6, No. 1, Jan–March 2012, pp. 54–67, 'Suleiman: Mubarak decided to step down ... examining the use of social media in the 2011 Egyptian revolution', by Genevieve Barrons

347 *Everyone suddenly burst out singing*: see *Independent*, 12 February 2011, 'A tyrant's exit. A nation's joy', by Robert Fisk

349 *But a clear divergence*: see *Independent*, 14 February 2011, 'Is the army tightening its grip on Egypt?', by Robert Fisk

349 *Five days later*: see *Independent*, 19 February 2011, 'Prison guards accused of killing dozens of jail inmates in Egypt', by Donald Macintyre

351 *To be romantic*: see Sania Lanfranchi, *Casting off the Veil*, pp. 109, 159; Laura Bier, *Revolutionary Womanhood*, pp. 29, 39–40; Tarif Khalidi (ed.), *An Anthology of Arabic Literature*, pp. 131–2, extracts from a lecture in Cairo in 1914 by May Ziadeh

355 *Yet long before Morsi*: see Amnesty International, 31 May 2011, 'Egypt: Admission of forced "virginity tests" must lead to justice'; *Independent*, 21 December 2011, 'Cairo's women take to the streets and tell the military: no more beatings', by Alastair Beach; *Daily Star* (Beirut), 1 June 2011, 'Egypt general defends virginity tests' (Reuters, AP); *Guardian*, 3 September 2012, 'From virginity test to power', by William Wilson; Joint statement by 12 Egyptian human rights organizations, 25 November 2011, Crisis of Human Rights in Egypt: The Bitter Results of Ten Months in the Grip of the Military; *Independent*, 10 March 2011, 'Thirteen killed as violence returns to Tahrir Square', by Alastair Beach; *Independent*, 27 May 2011, 'The revolution will be televised', by Phil England; *Jeune Afrique*, 10–16 July 2011, 'Hussein Tantawi: Gare à vous, maréchal!', by Tony Gamal Gabriel; AP, 26 July 2011, 'Egypt's generals, protesters moving to open clash', by Hamza Hendawi; *Daily Star* (Beirut), 30 July 2011, 'Parties quit Egypt rally over Islamist "hijacking"' (Reuters)

357 *But the Brotherhood's*: see *Al-Ahram Weekly*, 3–9 August 2011, 'Les dissensions au grand jour', by May Al-Maghrabi; *Daily Star* (Beirut), 15 November 2011, 'Egypt's Islamists warn Erdogan on regional role' (Reuters); *Courrier International*, 22–28 September 2011, 'Erdogan a déçu les islamistes du Caire', extract from London online newspaper *Elaph* by Sabri Hassanayn; *International Herald Tribune*, 7 July 2011, 'Hundreds protest release of 7 Egyptian police officers' (AP); *Egyptian Gazette*, 10 July 2011, 'Blood keeps Egypt's revolution alive', by Amr Emam; *Independent*, 14 July 2011, 'Hundreds of police officers purged' (AP)

358 *So just when*: see *Independent*, 4 August 2011, 'Once untouchable, the old despot and his sons faced the wrath of the nation they had terrorised', by Robert Fisk

359 *And then the cameras, too, were cloaked*: see *Independent*, 16 August 2011, 'Judge deprives Egyptians of Mubarak trial TV broadcasts', by Alastair Beach; *Independent*, 4 January 2012, 'Mubarak deserves humiliation and indignity, court told' (AP); *Tehran Times*, 27 June 2011, 'Commentary: SOS from Mubarak sons', by Arnaud de Borchgrave; BBC News Middle East, 2 June 2012, 'Mubarak jailed for protest deaths'; Al Arabiya television, 6 February 2014, 'In rare interview, Mubarak says Egyptians want Sisi'

360 *As Mubarak's trial dragged on*: see *L'Orient-Le Jour* (Beirut), 6 September 2011, 'Le procès Moubarak reprend' (agencies); *Independent*, 22 November 2011, 'Dozens die, the cabinet teeters – and chaos rules', by Alastair Beach; *Irish Times*, 26 November 2011, 'Respect for army fades as people judge it to have failed reforms', by Patrick Bury; *Independent*, 22 November 2011, 'Mubarak was nothing compared to military', by Nada El-Gamma; *Daily News Egypt*, 28 November 2011, 'Tantawi warns against "foreign hands", says crisis must end ahead of vote' (AP); *Guardian*, 26 November 2011, 'Tahrir Square stands united after bloodshed', by Jack Shenker; *Libération*, 27 November 2011, 'Manifestants égyptiens: la désunion nationale', by Marion Guénard

362 *There is a fox in Tahrir Square*: see *Independent*, 2 July 2012, 'President Morsi, a rigged ballot and a fox's tale that has all of Cairo abuzz', by Robert Fisk

363 *Many of the Tahrir veterans*: see *Egyptian Gazette*, 1 December 2011, 'Police "eye sniper" turns himself in: official'; *Independent*, 6 June 2012, 'In Cairo, they know revolutions don't always pan out quite as they wanted', by Robert Fisk; *Guardian*, 6 March 2013, 'Eye Sniper of Tahrir Square is in jail, but has anything changed?', by Patrick Kingsley; *Economist*, 22 December 2013, 'The net widens – Clampdown in Egypt'; *Los Angeles Times*, 23 December 2013, 'In Egypt, activist's death is new blow to revolution', by Amro Hassan and Laura King; *Egyptian Gazette*, 27 November 2012, 'A new name for Mohamed Mahmoud Street?', by Marwa Shaalan

364 *Tens of thousands*: see *Independent*, 23 June 2012, 'Late for the Revolution, Muslim Brotherhood takes over Tahrir', by Robert Fisk; *New York Times*, 22 June 2012, 'Showdown in Egypt escalates in fight for power', by David D. Kirkpatrick; *Egyptian Gazette*, 24 June 2012, 'Papers demonise Muslim Brotherhood', by Hamza Hendawi (AP); *Al-Ahram Weekly*, 27 June 2012, 'Hamas heartened by apparent Musri victory', by Khaled Amayeh

366 *Morsi was an intelligent*: see Reuters, 30 June 2012, 'Egypt's Musri takes symbolic oath to people', by Saimaa Fayed; *Daily Star* (Beirut), 1 September 2012, 'Egypt's refreshing return to sovereignty', by Rami Khoury; *Irish Times*, 7 December 2012, 'Morsi offers no concessions to the opposition', by Michael Jansen; *Le Monde diplomatique*, November 2012, 'Egypte, de la dictature militaire à la dictature religieuse?', by Alain Gresh

368 *Morsi rested*: see *Irish Times*, 11 December 2012, 'Morsi vests power of detention in military', by Michael Jansen; *Irish Times*, 24 December 2012, 'Egypt claims constitution approved by voters', by Michael Jansen; *Irish Times*, 27 December 2012, 'President hails new Egyptian constitution', by Michael Jansen; *L'Orient-Le Jour* (Beirut), 9 August 2012, 'Les sables mouvant du Sinai', by Christian Merveille

369 *More damaging still for Morsi*: see *New York Times*, 21 April 2013, 'Activist's death in Egypt spurs charges of police abuse', by David D. Kirkpatrick; Reuters, 4 June 2013, 'Egypt sentences 43, including Americans, in NGO case', by Shaimaa Fayed; Reuters, 7 May 2013, 'Egypt's Mursi brings more Islamists into cabinet', by Tom Perry and Yasmine Saleh; *Economist*, 30 March 2013, 'Egypt's economy: Going to the dogs'; *Financial Times*, 9 June 2013, 'Morsi advisor blames IMF for delaying Egypt $4.8 billion loan agreement', by Rhoula Khallaf; *Le Monde diplomatique*, August 2013, 'En Egypte, la révolution à l'ombre des militaires', by Alain Gresh, quoting Middle East Research and Information Project (Washington DC), 10 July 2013, 'Egypt in year three'

369 *Morsi's apparent indifference*: see *Le Monde*, 26 November 2012, 'Mohamed Morsi, le syndrome du pharaon', by Christophe Ayad; Reuters, 7 November 2012, 'In Egypt streets, Islamists throw weight around', by Yasmine Saleh

370 *Morsi even managed*: see *Daily Star* (Beirut), 1 June 2013, 'The battle of the Cairo Opera house', by Aya Batrawy (AP); *Le Monde diplomatique*, August 2013, 'Les cygnes du Caire', by Mona Abouissa

371 *So as early as January 2013*: see *Globe and Mail* (Toronto), 30 January 2013, 'Showdown with army looms for Morsi', by Omar El Akkad

371 *Like many of the Egyptian army's ambitious new generals*: see Democracy in the Middle East by Abdelfattah El Sisi [*sic*], Strategy Report Project, US Army War College, Carlisle Barracks, Carlisle, PA, 15 March 2006, (project adviser: Stephen J. Gerras); Reuters, 23 August 2013, 'In small American town, a window into Egyptian general's past', by Phil Stewart

371 *The army would later*: see Reuters, 2 July 2013, 'Morsi role at Syria rally seen as tipping point for Egyptian army', by Yasmine Saleh and Tom Perry; Reuters, 23 June 2013, 'Egypt's army says ready to act to prevent conflict'

372 *The pictures came first*: see Reuters, 10 October 2013, 'Special report – The real force behind Egypt's "revolution of the state"', by Yasmine Alsharif and Yasmine Saleh; Reuters, 20 February 2014, 'Activists who backed Mursi's fall turn against military', by Yasmine Saleh; Abouissa, 'Les cygnes du Caire', quoting *Le Figaro*, 30 June 2013; Al Jazeera, 19 July 2013, 'People, power, or propaganda? Unraveling the Egyptian opposition', by Max Blumenthal; *Guardian*, 30 June 2013, 'Tony Blair backs Egypt's government and criticizes Brotherhood', by Patrick Kingsley; *Independent*, 4 August 2013, 'Millions take to the streets of Egypt in an ever-growing media fantasy', by Robert Fisk

373 *Essential to this disingenuous story*: see *Daily News Egypt*, 25 July 2013, 'Al-Sisi calls for green light to fight "terrorism"', by Nouran El-Behairy; AP, 5 July 2013, 'Egypt's first freely elected president found himself isolated and abandoned by allies as even his guards stepped away', by Hamza Hendawi and Maggie Michael

374 *The circumstances of Morsi's detention*: see Reuters, 13 November 2013, 'Morsi says he was kidnapped before being removed by army', by Hadeel Al Shalchi; author's telephone interview with Rodney Dixon QC, 20 February 2015; transcriptions of tapes 1, 2 and 3 of Messers Shahin, Mohamed Ibrahim, Mamdooh Higazy and Shahin Any and J.P. French Associates, report, 21 January 2015, 'in the matter of Mamdou Shahin, Report on Forensic Speaker Comparisons' (authors: Peter French and Sam Hellmuth); Obama transcripts, The White House, Office of the Press Secretary, 1 and 3 July, 2013; *Guardian*, 3 July 2013, 'US in bind over Egypt supporting Morsi but encouraging protesters', by Dan Roberts; *Independent*, 4 August 2013, 'Millions take to the streets of Egypt in an ever-growing media fantasy', by Robert Fisk

12: The Wounded Tiger

377 *Aiman Husseini was lying by the wall*: see *Independent*, 28 July 2013, 'Eyewitness in Egypt: "Most were shot in the face – only one in the back"', by Robert Fisk

378 *Morsi's supporters made no secret*: see *Independent*, 1 July 2013, 'Demands of 2001 revolution were not met … but the army does not hold the answers', by Robert Fisk

379 *At 6.30 on the morning*: see *Washington Post*, 22 August 2014, 'Why Egypt's military orchestrated a massacre', by Amy Austin Holmes; *Guardian*, 4 September 2015, 'Sky News cameraman was shot in Egypt after his flak jacket was confiscated' (Central News); *Independent*, 15 August 2013, 'Cairo massacre: The Muslim Brotherhood's silent martyrs lie soaked in blood', by Robert Fisk; *Independent*, 16 August 2013, 'The police keep firing: The bodies pile up. In Cairo, bloodbaths are now a daily occurrence', by Robert Fisk; *Independent*, 18 August 2013, 'Exclusive; Cairo at war – under siege inside the Al-Fath Mosque', by Alastair Beach

383 *Sisi himself never uttered*: see *Al-Ahram Weekly*, 22–28 August 2013, 'Departing the scene', by Mohamed Abdel-Baky; *Al-Ahram Weekly*, 21–27 August 2013, 'ElBaradei sur la sellette', by May Al-Maghrabi; *Al-Ahram Weekly*, 15–21 August 2013, 'Same old scapegoat', by Khaled Dawoud; Anwar Sadat public statement, 19 August 2013, 'Response to the US & EU: "Enough With Scare Tactics, Deliver Pragmatic Solutions Instead"', 21 August 2013, 'Response to the *Washington Post* Editorial: "Saving Egypt from Syria's fate" and 20 August 2013, 'Review of the Muslim Brotherhood Legal Status'; *Independent*, 23 August 2013, '"People think they made a big mistake, electing Morsi … they hate the Brotherhood"', by Robert Fisk

384 *We all knew*: see *Independent*, 5 November 2013, 'Morsi trial: If a court can exemplify the divisions of a nation, this one did for Egypt', by Robert Fisk; *Independent*, 4 November 2013, 'As Mohamed Morsi goes to trial, General Sisi should remember: Egypt is a dangerous place to rule', by Robert Fisk

387 *He would be charged*: see AP, 21 April 2015, 'Egyptian court sentences Morsi to 20 years in prison', by Hamza Hindawi; *Independent*, 30 May 2014, 'Robert Fisk on Sisi poll: All hail the Egyptian Emperor – but what about that missing 7%?'; *Daily News Egypt*, 27 May 2014, 'As Egypt votes, pro-Morsi town, Kerdasa, testifies to brutal divide' (AFP); *L'Orient-Le Jour* (Beirut), 24 May 2014, 'La presidence Sissi [*sic*] ne sera pas un retour au regime Moubarak. Ce sera pire!'; *Daily Star* (Beirut), 23 August 2013, 'The Egyptian generals got a free ride', by Michael Glackin; BBC News, 1 April 2014, 'David Cameron orders inquiry into activities of Muslim Brotherhood', by Nicholas Watt; *The Arab Uprisings and Foreign Assistance* (Routledge, 2018), 'International assistance to Egypt after the 2011 and 2013 uprisings: More politics and less development', by Khaled Amin; Reuters, 4 April 2014, 'Muslim Brotherhood urges Britain not to yield to foreign "pressure" over review'; BBC News, 16 March 2015, 'David Cameron pulls Muslim Brotherhood report', by George Parker; BBC News, 18 June 2015, 'The government insists "no issues are off the table" when Mr Cameron hosts the president in Downing Street'

390 *Sisi said on election day*: see *Independent*, 30 May 2014, 'Robert Fisk on Sisi poll: All hail the Egyptian Emperor – but what about that missing 7%?'; *L'Orient-Le Jour* (Beirut), 30 May 2014, 'En Egypte, le retour (force) en arrière' (AFP); *Daily News Egypt*, 29 May 2014, 'Human Rights Watch warns of underlying repression marring presidential elections', by Ali Omar; *L'Orient-Le Jour* (Beirut), 29 May 2015, 'Avec Sissi, la stabilité, mais jusqu'a quand et a quel prix …', by Anthony Samrani; *Daily Star* (Beirut), 14 October 2016, 'Growing jurisdiction of Egypt's military courts', by Sahar Aziz; *Al-Ahram Weekly*, 7–13 November 2013, 'Gatekeepers', by Reem Leila; *Daily Star* (Beirut), 28 November 2013, 'Egypt orders arrest of symbols of anti-Mubarak revolt' (Reuters)

391 *In a grotesque miscarriage of justice*: see *Globe and Mail* (Toronto), 'Kangaroo courts'; *Al-Ahram Weekly*, 7–13 November 2013, 'Kerry's Cairo conciliation', by Ezzat Ibrahim; Reuters, 15 December 2013, 'Egypt prosecutor targets father of boy arrested over "pro-Morsi" ruler: lawyer', by Maggie Fick

392 *As Sisi's dictatorship asserted itself*: see *Le Monde*, 10 June 2015, 'L'Egypte renoue avec les violences de l'Etat policier', by Hélène Sallon; *Le Monde diplomatique*, November 2015, 'La presse egyptienne mise au pas', by Aziz El Mossassi; *L'Orient-Le Jour* (Beirut), 29 December 2013, 'Le pouvoir autoritaire de retour en Egypte?'; *Libération*, 13 August 2014, 'Un an après le massacre de Rabaa, les ONG honnies par Al-Sisi', by Jenna Le Bras; Reuters, 16 October 2014, 'US democracy watchdog quits Egypt as political noose tightens'; *L'Orient-Le Jour* (Beirut), 6 June 2015, 'Les

condamnés à mort d'Egypte', by Omar Ashour (Project Syndicate);
Al-Ahram Weekly, 3–9 August 2011, 'Un dictateur pris au depourru', by
Chaimaa Abdel-Hamid; Reuters, 31 July 2019, 'How Sisi's Egypt hands
out "justice"' (Reuters staff)

393 *Violent assaults*: see *Al-Ahram Weekly*, 25–31 July 2013, 'Copts under
attack', by Michael Adel; *Al-Ahram Weekly*, 15–21 August 2013, 'Paying
the price', by Dina Ezzat; *Al-Ahram Weekly*, 22–28 August 2013, 'The War
on Egypt's Copts', by Michael Adel; *Al-Ahram Weekly*, 15–21 August 2013,
'Les coptes au coeur de la tourmente', by Samar Al-Gamal; *Daily Star*
(Beirut), 3 September 2013, 'History goes up in smoke at sacked Egyptian
museum', by Mohamad Ali Harissi; AP, 11 September 2013, 'Suicide
bombs hit Egyptian military in Sinai, kill nine', by Ashraf Sweilam;
Daily Star (Beirut), 16 September 2013, 'Egyptian forces secure Gaza
Strip border' (Reuters); *Daily Star* (Beirut), 22 October 2013, 'Egypt's
Christians stunned after shootings'; Reuters, 7 October 2013, 'Grenades
fired in Cairo, troops killed near Suez Canal after protesters die', by
Shadia Nasralla and Yara Bayoumy; *Gulf News* (UAE), 19 November 2013,
'Gunmen kill officer who was due to testify against Mursi', by Ramadan
Al Sherbini; *Financial Times*, 1 September 2015, 'Egyptian troops killed
in militant attacks', by Kristen McTighe; *L'Orient-Le Jour* (Beirut), 26
January 2016, '"Ce sont les idées que le pouvoir egyptian combat, pas la
terrorisme"', by Jenna Le Bras

394 *The original Sinai battles*: Reuters, 30 January 2015, 'Egypt's Sisi cuts short
Ethiopia visit after 32 killed in Sinai', by Maggie Fick and Yusri Mohamed;
Daily Star (Beirut), 3 April 2015, 'Egypt jihadis kill 15 soldiers and two
civilians in Sinai checkpoint attacks' (AFP); *New York Times*, 5 August
2015, 'Push for retribution in Egypt frays Muslim Brotherhood', by David
Kirkpatrick and Mayy El Sheikh

395 *To share a prison cell*: see Mohamed Fahmy, *The Marriott Cell: An Epic
Journey from Cairo's Scorpion Prison to Freedom* (Toronto: Random House,
2016), pp. 10–16, 66–7, 125–6, 131–2, 143, 161, 165, 178, 189, 192, 241–3,
293–5, 337; *Guardian*, 23 June 2014, 'Al-Jazeera journalists' stiff sentences
prompt international outrage at Egypt', by Patrick Kingsley; *Independent*,
31 December 2016, 'What one journalist's time in an Egyptian prison tells
us about the fight against Islamist jihad', by Robert Fisk

397 *In July 2015*: see *Independent*, 20 July 2015, 'What a choice for Egypt – a
megalomaniac president or the madness of Isis', by Robert Fisk

398 *Inside Sinai itself*: see *New York Times*, 24 November 2017, 'In Egypt,
furious retaliation but failing strategy in Sinai', by Declan Walsh and
David D. Kirkpatrick; *Le Monde*, 26 November 2017, 'En Egypte, carnage
dans une mosquée de Sinai', by Hélène Sallon

399 *In the first four months*: see AP, 11 June 2016, 'Hard times in Egypt
stoke labour unrest, showdown ahead', by Brian Rohan; Amnesty
International, 30 May 2018 report, 'Egypt: Government accused of
interfering in labour union elections'

400 *There was something both droll*: see *New York Times*, 24 May 2014, 'Egypt's new strongman, Sisi knows best', by David D. Kirkpatrick; *Independent*, 5 November 2013, 'Abdul Fattah al-Sisi: Egyptian general is idolised for deposing former President Mohamed Morsi, but can his popularity last?', by Robert Fisk; *Daily Star* (Beirut), 9 February 2016, 'Giant red carpet for Sisi motorcade sparks uproar (AP); *Guardian*, 28 February 2014, 'Egypt's military leaders unveil devices they claim can detect and cure Aids' (AP); *Courrier International*, 7–14 May 2014, 'Tu peux être fier d'avoir le sida!', quoting Mada Masr (Cairo), 18 April 2014, by Amani Massoud; Reuters, 24 June 2017, 'Egypt's Sisi ratifies deal ceding Red Sea islands to Saudi Arabia', by Ahmed Abulenein; *L'Orient-Le Jour* (Beirut), 22 June 2016, 'Une decision de justice indépendante sera-t-elle sans conséquences?' (interview with Prof. Ibrahim Awad of American University of Cairo, by Lina Kennouche); CBS *60 Minutes*, 6 January 2019; *Washington Post*, 27 March 2019, '"It's become a farce, really": Egyptian actors who criticized Sisi in Washington are kicked out of union', by Emily Tamkin; *Middle East Eye* (London), 27 March 2019, 'Egypt actors' union expels Amr Waked and Khaled Abol Naga for Sisi criticism'; *Independent*, 28 March 2019, 'Egypt's brutal crackdown on workers' rights runs far deeper than the fate of two actors', by Robert Fisk

402 *On 3 February 2016*: see *Irish Times*, 11 April 2016, 'Italy frustrated by investigation into student's killing', by Paddy Agnew; *Independent*, 17 April 2016, 'Murdered Italian student Giulio Regeni paid the ultimate price for his investigation into Al-Sisi's Egypt', by Robert Fisk; *Politico* (Virginia, USA), 4 October 2016, 'Who murdered Giulio Regeni?', by Alexander Stille; Red Pepper (London), 7 February 2016, 'In Egypt, a second life for independent trade unions', by Giulio Regeni, reprinted from *Il Manifesto* (Rome); Reuters, 1 June 2016, 'After university crackdown, Egyptian students fear for their future', by Amira Ismail; *Le Monde*, 12 March 2016, 'Le Parlement européen épingle l'Egypte sur les droits de l'homme', by Hélène Sallon; *New York Review of Books*, 22 February 2018, 'Toughing it out in Cairo', by Yasmine El Rashidi; *London Review of Books*, 19 February 2015, 'Sisi's way', by Tom Stevenson

405 *Regeni's death was naturally*: see Reuters, 5 April 2019, 'Egypt kills hundreds of suspected militants in disputed gun battles', by Reuters staff

405 *Mohamed Morsi's death*: see *Independent*, 18 June 2019, 'Egyptian democracy died yesterday in a prison cage alongside Morsi', by Robert Fisk; *Independent*, 20 June 2019, 'The West is silent over the death of a man it once called the great hope of Arab democracy', by Robert Fisk; *Washington Post*, 18 June 2019, 'Egypt's regime must answer for Morsi's death. Other dictatorships are watching', by Wael Haddara; *New York Times*, 18 June 2019, 'Egypt quietly buries former president Morsi, muting coverage of death', by Declan Walsh

405 *Not that Italian interest*: see *Politico*, 10 July 2019, 'Killing Giulio Regeni – again', by Mario Del Perod

13: 'Dear Moussa ...'

408 *'The uprisings here ...'*: see *Independent*, 22 February 2012, 'If only Hague and Clinton would listen to Yusuf Islam', by Robert Fisk

410 *Most of the hundreds of thousands*: see *Independent*, 2 March 2005, 'Lebanese are united flag of "cedars revolution"', by Robert Fisk; *Independent*, 10 March 2005, 'Half a million gather for pro-Syrian rally to defy vision of US', by Robert Fisk; *Independent*, 11 March 2005, 'Syrian ally returns as Lebanese prime minister', by Robert Fisk; *Independent*, 15 March 2005, 'The people make a stand over the lies of Lebanon', by Robert Fisk

412 *First the Iranian cop screamed abuse*: see *Independent*, 14 June 2009, 'Iran erupts as voters back "the Democrator"', by Robert Fisk; *Independent*, 13 June 2009, 'A divided country united by the spirit of democracy', by Robert Fisk; *Daily Star* (Beirut), 9 June 2009, 'Mousavi puts Ahmadinejad's "halo" beneath spotlight' (AP, AFP); *Kayhan* (Tehran), 13 June 2009, 'The leader of the nation has the last word: the election of the president in Iran has turned into the top story of the news'; *Iran* (Tehran), 13 June 2009, 'Ahmadinejad 24 million votes – people voted for progress, justice, honesty and the fight against corruption'; *Tehran Times*, 13 June 2009, 'Astonishing turnout surprises all'; Etemad-e-Melli (Tehran), 14 June 2009, 'The ministry announced Karoubi as No 5: Minister says from the 39 million ballots, Mahmoud Ahmadinejad was elected president based on 24 million votes'; *Kayhan*, 14 June 2009, 'The election of Ahmadinejad once again is world news'; *Courrier International*, 25 June–1 July, 'Silence in the day, "Allah Akbar" at night', quoting Kalameh Sabz, diary of Ebrahim Raha, 16 June 2009; *Independent*, 16 June 2009, 'Claims of student massacre in Tehran spread', by Robert Fisk; *Independent*, 14 June 2009, 'Ahmadinejad whips crowd to frenzy as opposition muzzled', by Robert Fisk

418 *It was Iran's day of destiny*: see *Independent*, 15 June 2009, 'Iran's day of destiny', by Robert Fisk; *Independent*, 18 June 2009, *Independent*, 19 June, 2009, 'The dead of Iran are mourned – but the fight goes on', by Robert Fisk; *Independent*, 20 June 2009, 'Khamenei is fighting for his own position as well as Ahmadinejad's', by Robert Fisk; *Toronto Star*, 23 June 2009, '"Stay with me, Neda!"', by Cathal Kelly; *National Post* (Toronto), 23 June 2009, 'The bloodied face of Iran's uprising: video of dying angel seen around the world', by Araminta Wordsworth; *Independent*, 10 July 2009, 'Shots fired to clear streets as Iranians defy ban on protests', by Katherine Butler; *Guardian*, 31 July 2009, 'Tens of thousands defy ban to take to Tehran streets on day of remembrance for Soltan', by Saeed Kamali Deghan

422 *The street demonstrations continued*: *Independent*, 4 August 2009, 'As Ahmadinejad is anointed, his victims show the price of dissent', by Katherine Butler; *Guardian*, 10 August 2009, 'Iran admits election demonstrators were tortured', by Simon Tisdall; *Guardian*, 11 January 2010, 'Iran's parliament exposes abuse of opposition prisoners at Tehran jail', by Robert Tait; *Independent*, 19 September 2009, 'Iran's great

divide shows on a day of protests', by Nasser Karimi (AP); *Libération* (Paris), 19 September 2009, '"Le pouvoir a commis une très grave erreur"', by Jean-Pierre Perrin; *Independent*, 3 December 2009, 'Mystery surrounds poisoning of doctor who exposed torture', by Lee Keath (AP); *Independent*, 10 December 2009, 'Torture, rape and violence meted out to opposition supporters after Iranian election, says Amnesty', by Katherine Butler; *Toronto Star*, 27 June 2009, 'Demonstrators must die, Iranian cleric demands', by Thomas Erdbrink (*Washington Post*)

423 *Syrian president Bashar*: see Reuters, 19 August 2009, 'Assad meets Ahmadinejad, condemns "foreign interference" in Iran'

423 *'I left with a feeling of bitterness …'*: see *Jeune Afrique*, 29 Jan–4 February 2017, 'Confession d'un tortionnaire', interview with 'Ridha', by Frida Dahmani; *Le Monde*, 6 January 2011, 'Les défis de la révolution', by Gilles Keppel; *Irish Times*, 25 November 2011, 'Death of Arab Spring "martyr" which led to uprisings may not be all it seems', by Mary Boland; *Independent*, 2 September 2011, 'How revolution turned sour in the birthplace of the Arab Spring', by Kim Sengupta; *Egypt Independent*, 21 June 2012, 'Resolutions bred from poverty', by Dina K. Hussein; *Independent*, 9 July 2011, 'A dictator's trial that even his enemies questioned' (interview with Akram Azoury) by Robert Fisk

425 *In the first weeks of the revolution*: see *Jeune Afrique*, 20–26 February 2011, 'Fethi Benslama: "Le geste de Bouazizi a changé le modèle du martyr"', by Renaud de Rochebrune

426 *Hosni Mubarak, only days from*: see Reuters, 2 May 2011, 'Swiss reveal funds stashed by Gaddafi, Mubarak, Ben Ali', by Stephanie Nebehay; *Courrier International*, 28 October–4 November 2004, 'À Tunis, rien de nouveau', by Ali Lmrabet, quoting *El Mundo* (Madrid); *Le Monde*, 25 May 2002, 'L'inconnu', by Jean-Pierre Tuquoi

426 *During the 2017 truth commission hearings*: see *New York Times*, 22 April 2017, 'Tunisia's truth-telling renews a revolution's promise, painfully', by Carlotta Gall; *Independent*, 24 October 2012, 'Rached Ghannouchi says he doesn't want an Islamic state in Tunisia. Can he prove his critics wrong?', by Robert Fisk; *Le Monde diplomatique*, February 2011, 'Souvénirs d'un diplomat', by Eric Rouleau; *Révolution! Des années mauves à la fuite à carthage* by 'Z', (Tunis: Cérès, 2011); *Independent*, 21 February 2012, 'Poisoned spring: revolution brings Tunisia more fear than freedom', by Robert Fisk; *Le Monde diplomatique*, February 2011, 'Tunisia: Diary of a revolution', by Olivier Piot; *La Révolution Tunisienne: Dix jours qui ébranlèrent le monde Arabe* by Olivier Piot (Paris: Les petits matins, 2011); *La Presse* (Tunis), 16 October 2012, 'Le "frère" Rached ou "Echeikh" Ghannouchi: qui faut-il croire?', by Jamil Sayah

426 *Ben Ali, who was seventy-four*: see *Middle East Eye*, 31 January 2017, 'Tunisie: la fuite de Ben Ali racontée par son pilote'

429 *The man I watched*: see *Independent*, 22 February 2011, 'Muammar Gaddafi, tyrant of Tripoli', by Robert Fisk; *Independent*, 25 March 1994,

'Welcome to Gaddafi's mad, mad world', by Robert Fisk; *Independent*, 22 December 2003, 'Straw reinvents despotic little killer Gaddafi as courageous statesman', by Robert Fisk; *Qaddafi and the Libyan Revolution* by David Blundy and Andrew Lycett (London: Corgi, 1988) pp. 71, 75; *Toronto Star*, 13 June 2011, 'Every Gadhafi picture tells a story', by Rosie Dimanno

431 *At the end we saw*: see *New York Times*, 28 October 2011, 'Libya's history lesson yet to be deciphered', by Alan Cowell; *Independent*, 22 October 2011, '"Gaddafi cannot hurt his people any longer"', by Kim Sengupta; *Daily Star* (Beirut), 26 October 2011, 'Desperate in hiding, Gadhafi believed people still loved him', by Karin Laub; House of Commons Foreign Affairs Committee, 'Libya: Examination of intervention and collapse and the UK's future policy options', Third Report of Session 2016–17; *Independent on Sunday*, 24 April 2011, 'Ghosts will haunt Libya for decades', by Patrick Cockburn

433 *Patrick Cockburn was relentless*: see *Independent on Sunday*, 19 June 2011, 'Lies, damn lies, and reports of battlefield atrocities', by Patrick Cockburn; *Independent*, 24 June 2011, 'Human rights groups cast doubt on Nato justification for going to war', by Patrick Cockburn; Cockburn email to the author, 15 March 2020; *Independent on Sunday*, 26 June 2011, 'Don't believe everything you see and read about Gaddafi', by Patrick Cockburn; *Independent on Sunday*, 31 July 2011, 'Why the West is committed to the murderous rebels in Libya', by Patrick Cockburn; *Independent*, 11 August 2011, 'Libya's ragtag rebels are dubious allies', by Patrick Cockburn; *Irish Times*, 20 August 2011, 'Destiny calls Libya's man of the moments', by Chris Stephen; *Independent*, 30 May 2011, 'Gaddafi snatch squads took hundreds of men and boys from Misrata', by Ruth Sherlock; *Guardian*, 27 July, 2011, 'Libyan rebel forces rescue 100 hostages from behind enemy lines', by Chris Stephen; *Independent*, 1 September 2011, 'Intervention is never simply humanitarian', by Adrian Hamilton

435 *Within weeks*: see *L'Orient-Le Jour* (Beirut), 11 October 2011, 'Une mosquée attaquée et saccagée par 200 à 300 hommes à Tripoli' (AFP); Al Jazeera, 5 March 2012, 'World War II graves smashed in Libya'

436 *The West's policies towards Libya*: see *New Yorker*, 3 September 2011, '"Dear Moussa": Libya and the CIA', by Jon Lee Anderson; *Independent*, 2 September 2011, 'Rebel military chief says he was tortured by CIA', by Patrick Cockburn; *Independent*, 6 September 2011, 'The tide may be turning against systematic abuses of prisoners', by Patrick Cockburn; *Independent*, 6 September 2011, 'Claims about complicity in torture that refuse to go away' (editorial); *Le Figaro*, 4 September 2011, 'Belhaj, l'ex-djihadiste rallié à l'Occident', by Adrien Jaulmes; *Le Monde*, 5 September 2011, 'M. Belhaj: "Nous voulons un État civil en Libye. Nous ne sommes pas d'Al-Qaeda"', interview by Christophe Ayad; BBC News, 10 May 2018, 'Abdul Hakim Belhaj: The documents trail that nailed UK's secret role in rendition', by Dominic Casciani

437 *Just how this disgraceful relationship*: see *Independent*, 21 May 2012, 'Abdelbaset al-Megrahi: The only man convicted of involvement in the Lockerbie bombing' (obituary) by Tam Dalyell; *Independent*, 22 August 2009, 'For the truth, look to Tehran and Damascus – not to Tripoli', by Robert Fisk; *Independent*, 15 August 2009, 'Awkward questions over Lockerbie won't go away', by Richard Ingrams; *Independent*, 20 August 2009, 'Free to die: Bitter legacy of the Lockerbie bomber', by Andrew Grice; *Independent*, 22 August 2009, 'Lockerbie: Now it's payback time', by Chris Green, Andrew Grice, Oliver Duff and Jonathan Brown; *Independent*, 31 August 2009, 'Straw: We did talk about Megrahi', by Andy McSmith; *Independent*, 2 September 2009, 'Brown "did not want Megrahi to die in Britain"', by Andy McSmith and Nigel Morris

439 *Cameron himself boasted*: see *Independent*, 3 September 2011, 'Cameron revels in UK's role in overthrow of Gaddafi', by Nigel Morris; *Guardian*, 23 May 2011, 'Nato must rethink Libya strategy or risk anarchy, warns admiral', by Nick Hopkins; *Le Canard enchaîné*, 1 June 2011, 'Des bombes gratuites pour se payer Kadhafi', by 'J.C.'; *Globe and Mail* (Toronto), 11 June 2011, 'Nato too reliant on US military might: Gates', by Dan De Luce (AFP); *Irish Times*, 17 December 2011, 'Mr President, I have something to tell you', by Ruadhan MacCormaic

440 *He would have done well*: see *Le Monde diplomatique*, September 2011, 'Libye, les conditions de l'unité nationale', by Patrick Haimzadeh; *Le Monde diplomatique*, December 2011, 'Qui a gagné la guerre en Libye', by Patrick Haimzadeh; Committee on Armed Services United States Senate, 'Operation Odyssey and the Situation in Libya', 31 March 2011

441 *In September 2011*: see *Independent*, 2 September 2011, 'World powers put aside their differences to hail "new Libya"', by John Lichfield; *Independent on Sunday*, 2 November 2014, 'The West is silent as Libya falls into the abyss', by Patrick Cockburn; *Independent*, 27 January 2012, '"Free" Libya shamed by new torture claims', by Portia Walker; House of Commons Foreign Affairs Committee, 'Libya', para 47; Committee on Armed Services United States Senate, 'Operation Odyssey and the Situation in Libya'

442 *'Massacre – it's a massacre!'*: see *Independent*, 19 February 2011, '"They didn't run away – they faced the bullets head-on"', by Robert Fisk

446 *Ian Stewart MacWalter Henderson*: see *Independent*, 18 February 1996, 'Britain at the heart of Bahrain's brutality rule', by Robert Fisk; *Guardian*, 30 June 2002, 'Britain silent on "Butcher of Bahrain"', by Tony Thompson

448 *There were further mass arrests*: see *Independent*, 20 February 2011, 'Blooms replace bullets in Bahrain while the region hits boiling point', by Robert Fisk; *Independent*, 14 June 2011, 'I saw these brave doctors trying to save lives – these charges are a pack of lies', by Robert Fisk; *The Atlantic* (Washington), 21 September 2011, 'Obama's UN address and the Bahrain exception', by Max Fisher; *Guardian*, 14 March 2011, 'Saudi Arabian troops

enter Bahrain as regime asks for help in quelling uprising', by Martin
Chulov; Bahrain Independent Commission of Inquiry report, Bahrain, 23
November 2011, p. 151

452 *Far more whimsical*: see letter to the UK Press Complaints Commission
from the Information Affairs Authority of Bahrain, 25 July 2011, and PCC
letter to *Independent* editor (Langham to Blackhurst), 27 July 2011 (copies
in author's possession)

452 *Britain itself was now the target*: see *Independent*, 19 February 2011, 'How
Britain taught Arab police forces all they know', by Jerome Taylor;
Independent, 22 April 2011, 'A blind eye in the West to repression in the
Gulf' (editorial); *Independent*, 20 May 2011, 'Cameron embraces tyranny',
by Andy McSmith

453 *In July 2002*: see Carlton Television (UK), 3 July 2002, 'Blind Eye to
the Butcher'; Leveson Inquiry (UK), 'An Inquiry into the Culture,
Practices and Ethics of the Press by the Rt. Hon. Lord Justice Leveson',
November 2011, Vol. 1 (Part E), p. 418 (section 12:15); *New Statesman*, 17
April 2012, 'Why is former Met police commander John Yates working
for the brutal Bahraini regime?', by Mehdi Hasan; *Daily Telegraph*, 24
April 2012, 'Bahrain is bewildered by the world's hostility', by John
Yates; *New Yorker*, 26 February 2007, 'Miami Blue: The testing of a
top cop', by Elsa Walsh; *Guardian*, 16 February 2012, 'John Timoney:
The notorious police chief sent to reform forces in Bahrain', by Ryan
Devereau

454 *Neither Yates nor Timoney*: see *Guardian*, 16 February 2012, 'John Timoney:
The notorious police chief sent to reform forces in Bahrain', by Ryan
Devereau; *Le Monde*, 12 February 2012, 'A Bahreïn, les chiites sont
accusés du complot au bénéfice de l'Iran', by Laure Stephan; Redress
(London and Copenhagen), April 2013, 'Bahrain: Fundamental reform
or torture without end?', p. 45; author's notes of interview with Prof.
Tom Collins, Beirut, 21 March 2013; *Independent on Sunday*, 24 April
2013, 'Bahrain hit by doctors' desertion', by Robert Fisk; MSI and Royal
College of Surgeons in Ireland agenda for 10–11 April 2013 conference
at the Intercontinental Hotel, Bahrain, 'Medical ethics and dilemmas in
situations of political discord and violence'

454 *Only months later*: *Daily Star* (Beirut), 16 November 2013, 'Rights group
urges US rethink on Bahrain strategy' (AFP); Reuters, 28 February 2014,
'Bahraini police clash with protesters after funeral', by Farishta Saeed
and Rania al Gawal; *Independent*, 8 July 2014, 'Bahrain moves to expel
"unwelcome" US official for meeting Shia opposition group', by Patrick
Cockburn; *New York Times*, 8 July 2015, 'Losing leverage on Bahrain', by
Sayed Ahmed Alwadaei; Reuters, 23 June 2016, 'Bahrain gambles with
security by launching crackdown on Shiites'; Amnesty International,
4 November 2018, 'Bahrain: Opposition leader Sheikh Ali Salman
unlawfully convicted'; Amnesty International, 28 January 2019, 'Bahrain:
Verdict on opposition leader bitter blow to freedom of expression'

455 *But amid Bahrain's rule*: see statement by Crown Prince Salman of
Bahrain, 20 April 2012; BBC Sport, 28 March 2012, 'Bernie Ecclestone has
no doubt about holding Bahrain race', by Andrew Benson; *Independent*, 21
April 2012, 'This is politics not sport. If drivers can't see that, they are the
pits', by Robert Fisk; *Daily Telegraph*, 24 April 2012, 'Bahrain is bewildered
by the world's hostility', by John Yates

14: The Men in White Socks

458 *And never would there be*: see *The Times*, 27 March 1980, 'Aleppo riots
blamed on Turkish political group aiming to bring down the Assad
regime', by Robert Fisk; *The Times*, 26 March 1980, 'Crack troops watch
riot-torn Aleppo', by Robert Fisk
460 *These were heady days*: see US Department of Defense news briefing, 1
March 2011, Mullen reply; *Wall Street Journal*, 31 January 2011, 'Interview
with Syrian President Bashar al-Assad', by Jay Solomon; author's notes
of address by Niklas Kebbon, Swedish ambassador to Syria, Swedish
diplomatic forum, Abu Dhabi, 8 December 2009
461 *There was an unhappy tendency*: see Bouthaina Shaaban, *Damascus Diary*,
p. 75; Nikolaos Van Dam, *The Struggle for Power in Syria: Politics and
Society under Asad and the Ba'th Party*, p. 116; Thomas Friedman, *From
Beirut to Jerusalem*, p.101; *The Atlantic*, 24 May 2011, 'Netanyahu's speech in
Congress and the politics of clapping', by Uri Friedman; *Counterpunch*, 6
March 2015, 'Netanyahu's congressional pep rally', by Ben Norton
462 *Palestinian human rights*: see Raja Shehadeh, *Occupation Diaries*, (London:
Profile Books, 2012), p. 134
463 *The depth of Bashar's information*: see US Embassy Damascus account of
meeting between US senators and President Assad on 30 December 2009
(wrongly dated 2010 in original document), WikiLeaks http://wikileaks.
org/cable/2010/01/10DAMASCUS8.html
464 *Horror was a word*: see Human Rights Watch, *Syria Unmasked: The
Suppression of Human Rights by the Asad Regime* (New Haven: Yale
University Press, 1991); Amnesty International, 19 June 1995, 'Syria,
forgotten victims: Health professionals imprisoned in 1980'; Human
Rights Watch, October 1996, Vol. 8, No. 4(E), 'Syria: The silenced Kurds';
Amnesty International, 16 November 2000, 'Syria: Amnesty International
welcomes the release of political prisoners'; Amnesty International,
26 April 2001, 'Syria: Hussain Daoud, age 30'; Amnesty International,
3 September 2001, 'Syria: Riad al-Turk, aged 71, lawyer'; Amnesty
International, 11 July 2003 and 30 July 2003, 'Syria: Abd el-Razaq Shoullar,
aged 81'; Amnesty International, 4 September 2003, 'Syria: Khalil
Sulayman', including torture and death of Khalik Mustafa; Amnesty
International, 2 April 2004, 'Mass arrests/unlawful killings/torture and
ill treatment: Hundreds of Syrian Kurds'; Amnesty International, 9 July
2004, 'Syria: Arbitrary detention and torture of Islamist activists must
stop'

466 *But the seizure of non-violent*: see *Independent*, 15 March 2008, 'Silenced by the men in white socks', by Robert Fisk; letter and fax to the author from Mrs Wafa Akram Al-Hurani (sister of Dr Fida Akram Al-Hurani), 6 January 2008 and 11 March 2008; interview with Syrian former minister, Beirut, November 2013, for Bashar al-Assad obituary (unpublished to date) to *Independent*, 3 December 2013

468 *It was clear that Bashar understood*: see Solomon, 'Interview with Syrian President Bashar al-Assad'; *Contemporary Arab Affairs* (Centre for Arab Unity Studies, Beirut and London), October 2011, Vol. 4, No. 4, pp. 435–9, 'Syria … the road to where?', by Michel Kilo

468 *Makhlouf was as loyal*: see *Independent*, 7 May 2020, 'This is what the sudden fall of Syrian businessman Rami Makhlouf, the cousin of Bashar al-Assad, means', by Robert Fisk

469 *The 'crushing' of the people*: see Reuters, 14 February 2011, 'Syria jails schoolgirl blogger for 5 years', by Khaled Yacoub Oweis; *Independent*, 19 February 2011, 'Dark humour in a time of dictatorship', by Robert Fisk; Reuters, 10 March 2011, 'In Syria's parched farmlands, echoes of Egyptian woes', by Khaled Yacoub Oweis; *Guardian*, 28 March 2011, 'Reuters journalists missing in Syria', by Roy Greenslade

470 *Or did the revolution*: see Van Dam, *Destroying a Nation*, p. 192n.; *Independent*, 15 April 2011, 'The Arab awakening began not in Tunisia this year, but in Lebanon in 2005', by Robert Fisk; *Independent*, 23 November 2011, 'Egyptian crisis gives Syria time to talk about democracy', by Robert Fisk; author's notes of interview with Faisal Mokdad, Damascus, 24 October 2011; *Independent*, 4 May 2011, 'Syrians brave tactics of terror that have kept a nation in check', by 'Khalid Ali'

473 *In Beirut, I was receiving*: see emails from 'Saad Ajmal' to the author, 13 April 2011; *Independent*, 23 April 2011, 'Bloodiest day in Syrian uprising as Assad troops kill "at least 49"', by 'Khalid Ali'; author's notes of telephone interview with Nadim Houry of Human Rights Watch, 24 April 2011; *Independent*, 25 April 2011, 'Shifting blame to Lebanon may be the method in Assad's madness', by Robert Fisk; *L'Orient-Le Jour* (Beirut), 20 April 2011, 'Rokon Abadi à l'USJ: il n'y a pas de véritable opposition en Iran'; *Independent*, 23 April 2011, 'Every concession makes the President more vulnerable', by Robert Fisk; *L'Orient-Le Jour* (Beirut), 23 April 2011, 'Un Golgotha syrien', by Issa Goraieb; *L'Orient-Le Jour* (Beirut), 19 April 2011, 'Le projet universaliste du Hezbollah stimulé par la houle arabe', by Philippe Abi-Akl

473 *The Independent's source*: Alastair Beach emails to the author, 17 May 2020 and 20 May 2020

475 *These bloody events*: see *Independent*, 27 April 2011, 'If the rumours and conspiracies are true, then President Assad's regime is on the road to civil war', by Robert Fisk; *L'Orient-Le Jour* (Beirut), 29 April 2011, 'Des centaines de Syriens fuient à pied leurs villages pour se réfugier a Wadi Khaled'; *L'Orient-Le Jour* (Beirut), 30 April 2011, 'Le ralentissement

du mouvement de réfugiés syriens à Wadi Khaled n'occulte pas les manifestations de masse à Talkalakh', by Jeanine Jalkh; *Independent*, 2 May 2011, 'We will never cease our struggle until we bring down Assad', by Robert Fisk

479 *But to my astonishment*: see Fahmy, *The Marriott Cell*, p. 335; *Daily Star* (Beirut), 15 May 2011, '2 Syrians die in hospital after flight to Lebanon', by Antoine Amrieh; *L'Orient-Le Jour* (Beirut), 17 May 2011, 'À Deraa, l'horreur après la dècouverte d'une fosse commune'; *Independent*, 18 May 2011, 'Woman and child among 26 bodies "found in mass graves" near Syrian city', by 'Khalid Ali'; *Independent*, 19 May 2011, 'Assad admits Syrian regime's "mistakes" as sanctions are imposed', by 'Khalid Ali'; Reuters, 26 May 2011, 'Shattered humanity inside Syria's security apparatus', by Suleiman al-Khalidi; *Gulf Times* (Doha), 21 May 2011, 'Syrian forces kill at least 34 protesters' (AFP); *Irish Times*, 21 June 2011, 'No reforms if protests continue, Assad warns', by Michael Jansen

480 *When Syrian political opposition leaders*: see *Courrier International*, 21–27 July 2011, '"Le régime sera étranglé par l'économie"', republished interview by Thaer Abbas in *Asharq al-Awsat* (London)

480 *Reports from Syria*: see *Globe and Mail* (Toronto), 14 June 2011, 'Author apologizes for Syrian blog hoax', by Jill Lawless; *Toronto Star*, 15 June 2011, 'Hoax reminds us to question social "news"', by Thomas Walkom; *Guardian*, 13 June 2011, 'Syrian lesbian blogger is revealed conclusively to be a married man', by Esther Addley; *Guardian*, 13 June 2011, 'Gay Girl in Damascus hoaxer acted out of "vanity"', by Esther Addley

481 *History, I often thought*: see *Independent*, 16 July 2011, 'Now the Arab Spring becomes an Arab Summer', by Robert Fisk; A. B. Gaunson, *The Anglo-French Clash in Lebanon and Syria 1940–45* (London: Macmillan, 1987), esp. pp. 171–4; *L'Orient-Le Jour* (Beirut), 22 June 2011, 'Avis aux Syriens: conseils et astuces de la place Tahrir', by Rania Massoud

483 *Ever a weathervane*: see *L'Orient-Le Jour* (Beirut), 25 July 2011, 'Joumblatt: Les responsables des crimes contre le peuple syrien doivent être sanctionnés'; *Daily Star* (Beirut), 25 July 2011, 'Jumblatt: Some in Syria impeding reform'; *L'Orient-Le Jour* (Beirut), 16 November 2009, 'Le corps de Johnny Nassif, porté disparu le 13 octobre 1990 à Yarzé, restitué à sa famille', by Patricia Khoder; *L'Orient-Le Jour* (Beirut), 13 November 2006, 'Ils croyaient leur fils détenu en Syrie, on le retrouve dans une fosse à Yarzé', by Patricia Khoder; *Daily Star* (Beirut), 1 August 2011, 'Massacre in Hama' and 'International condemnation of Syrian "atrocities"' (agencies); *Independent*, 9 August 2011, 'This slaughter will end only when words of condemnation are acted on', by Robert Fisk

484 *Yet it was pathetic*: see *Independent*, 19 August 2011, 'Obama leads diplomatic push against Assad regime', by David Usborne, Oliver Wright and 'Khalid Ali'; *Independent*, 19 August 2011, 'It is his fast disappearing billions that will worry Assad, not words from Washington', by Robert Fisk; *L'Orient-Le Jour* (Beirut), 2 September 2011,

'Le régime syrien accusé d'avoir provoqué la mort de 30 nouveau-nés
à Hama'; Amnesty International, 31 August 2011, 'Deadly detentions:
Deaths in custody amid popular protest in Syria'; *L'Orient-Le Jour*
(Beirut), 14 September 2011, 'Le régime syrien intensifie partout sa
violence'; *L'Orient-Le Jour* (Beirut) 14 September 2011, 'Funérailles de
Matar: l'armée tire sur la foule une fois les ambassadeurs américain et
français partis'; *L'Orient-Le Jour* (Beirut), 3 October 2011, 'L'opposition
syrienne se regroupe et demande de l'aide'

486 *Individual assassinations*: see *L'Orient-Le Jour* (Beirut), 15 October 2011,
'LONU met en garde contre une guerre civile en Syrie'; *L'Orient-Le Jour*
(Beirut), 17 October 2011, 'Le trafic d'armes vers la Syrie a le vent en
poupe'; *Daily Star* (Beirut), 13 October 2011, 'Rifi kidnapping remarks
spark call for probes', by Van Meguerditchian; *Daily Star* (Beirut),
14 October 2011, 'Hard evidence backs up Rifi's emarks on abducted
Syrians'; *L'Orient-Le Jour* (Beirut), 10 October 2011, 'Le Liban puni à Ersal
pour n'avoir pas soutenu à fond Assad à l'ONU', by Philippe Abi-Akl;
Independent, 17 October 2011, 'Assad, his raids on Lebanon, and Syria's
slow slip into civil war', by Robert Fisk

487 *Turn up at the Tishrin*: see *Independent*, 26 October 2011, 'Assad's army
remains defiant as it buries its dead', by Robert Fisk; *Independent*,
27 October 2011, 'Syria slips towards sectarian war', by Robert Fisk;
Independent, 28 October 2011, '"The army was told not to fire at
protesters"', by Robert Fisk; *Sunday Telegraph*, 30 October 2011, 'Bashar
al-Assad: I won't waste my time with Syrian opposition', by Andrew
Gilligan

491 *In Beirut, the Lebanese morning newspapers*: see *L'Orient-Le Jour* (Beirut), 29
October 2011, 'Nouveau bain de sang en Syrie: au moins 36 civils tués';
L'Orient-Le Jour (Beirut), 31 October 2011, 'La Ligue arabe de plus en
plus ferme avec Damas'; *Daily Star* (Beirut), 12 November 2011, 'Armed
rebels begin to defend neighbourhoods, says Homs activist', by Lauren
Williams; *New York Times*, 27 October 2011, 'In slap at Syria, Turkey
shelters anti-Assad fighters', by Liam Stack; *L'Orient-Le Jour* (Beirut),
14 November 2011, 'La Russie continue de livrer des armes à la Syrie';
Independent, 16 November 2011, 'Assad will only go if his own tanks turn
against him', by Robert Fisk; *Le Canard enchaîné*, 23 November 2011, 'Une
intervention "limitée" preparée par l'Otan en Syrie', by Claude Angeli;
author's notes of interview with Khaled Khoja, Istanbul, 14 November
2011; *Independent*, 25 November 2011, 'Exile dreams of a bloodless return
after a life spent opposing Assad regime', by Robert Fisk; *Independent*, 9
February 2015, 'A meeting of minds in Cairo: Billion-dollar arms deal on
table as Putin and Abdel Fattah al-Sisi seek closer trade links and alliance
against terror', by Robert Fisk; *Independent*, 10 November 2016, 'It is
not Donald Trump who matters now in the Middle East – it's Putin',
by Robert Fisk; Gush Shalom, 4 November 2017, 'Who is Afraid of the
Iranian Bomb?', by Uri Avnery

15: The Surgeon with the Bloodstained Hands

497 *Just over a year*: exhibition Goya, Chronicler of All Wars: The Disasters
and the Photographs of War, Villa Audi, Beirut, July 2012; *Independent*,
16 July 2012, 'Where is a Goya who could chronicle today's conflict?',
by Robert Fisk; *L'Orient-Le Jour* (Beirut), 3 July 2012, 'Goya, chroniqueur
de guerre et precurseur du photojournalisme, à la villa Audi', by Zena
Zalzal; *Paris Match*, 14–20 June 2012, 'Les enfants broyés de Syrie', Robert
King recorded by Alfred de Montesquiou; Report of the Independent
International Commission of Inquiry on the Syrian Arab Republic,
United Nations General Assembly Human Rights Council, Seventeenth
special session, 23 November 2011; *Independent*, 13 November 2011,
'Arab League's "roar" at Syria shows how tiny Qatar is starting to flex
its muscle', by Robert Fisk; Van Dam, *Destroying a Nation*, p. 77; *Foreign
Policy* (Washington), 31 January 2012, 'Leaked Syria observers report
details failings of mission', by Colum Lynch

499 *But how many 'armed groups'*: see *Libération*, 26 November 2011, 'Contre
Bachar al-Assad le choix des armes', by Jean-Pierre Perrin; *Irish Times*, 24
December 2011, 'Twin bomb attacks in Syria kill at least 40', by Michael
Jansen; *Irish Times*, 11 May 2012, 'Damascus bomb blasts most deadly
since start of rebellion', by Michael Jansen

500 *In early 2012, the regime concentrated*: see Karl Baedeker, *Palestine et Syrie*
(Leipzig and Paris: Karl Baedeker, 1912), p. 364; *Observer* (London), 12
February 2012, 'Homs from the frontline: Never-ending shelling and
a child buried in the night', by Paul Wood; CNN, 22 February 2012,
'Transcript: Marie Colvin's final CNN interview'; *Independent*, 11 April
2012, 'Shot in the heart – the journalist Assad made into a martyr', by
Robert Fisk

504 *No regime mouthpiece*: see Human Rights Watch, 3 February 2012, 'Syria:
Stop torture of children'; *Independent*, 1 March 2012, 'The regime calls it
"cleaning", but the dirty truth is plain to see', by Robert Fisk; *Independent*,
7 March 2012, 'Is Homs an echo of what happened in Srebrenica?', by
Robert Fisk; *Daily Star* (Beirut), 8 February 2012, '2 Lebanese accused of
arms smuggling to Free Syrian Army'; *Independent*, 28 March, 2012, 'On
Lebanon's border, silent Syrians are flocking to an unknown future',
by Robert Fisk; *L'Orient-Le Jour* (Beirut), 11 February 2012, 'Reprise des
affrontements entre pro et anti-Assad à Tripoli, l'armée se déploie en
force'; *Independent*, 12 February 2012, 'Ethnic conflict spreads over the
mountains', by Robert Fisk; *L'Orient-Le Jour* (Beirut), 13 March 2012,
'Massacre à Homs: des femmes et des enfants égorgés et carbonisés';
Reuters, 18 February 2012, 'NATO to stay out of Syria even if UN
mandate emerges', by Simon Cameron-Moore and Tulay Karadeniz

505 *Just what they were fleeing*: see Reuters, 14 March 2012, 'On the Turkish
border, a stream of fleeing Syrians', by Jonathon Burch; *L'Orient-Le Jour*
(Beirut), 20 March 2012, 'De la montagne rebelle d'Idleb, les maquisards
défient le régime syrien' (AFP); Reuters, 23 March 2012, 'Ambushed,

outgunned, Syrian rebels plead for arms', by Jonathon Burch; *L'Orient-Le Jour* (Beirut), 30 March 2012, 'Fadwa Suleimane, icône de la révolution, voit venir "la guerre confessionnelle"' (AFP); *Time* magazine, 23 April 2012, 'Flight of the Syrians: The refugees escaping Assad's horrors tell their stories', by Rania Abouzeid; *Independent*, 21 April 2012, 'Counter-revolution – the next deadly chapter', by Robert Fisk (quoting Rami Khouri in the *Daily Star*); *Independent*, 5 August 2016, 'Same old story, different war', by Robert Fisk

507 *You could identify*: see International Centre for Agricultural Research in Dry Areas (ICARDA), 16 July 2012, New Developments at ICARDA; author's interview with Dr. Mahmoud el-Solh, director general of ICARDA, Beirut, 21 July 2012; *Independent*, 23 July 2012, 'If Alawites are turning against Assad then his fate is sealed', by Robert Fisk

507 *The stories of sadism*: see Van Dam, *Destroying a Nation*, p. 193, n. 12; author's interview with UN colonel (Houla witness), 7 July 2013; *New York Times*, 8 June 2012, 'UN monitors in Syria find grisly traces of massacre', by Rick Goldstone; *Channel 4 News*, 30 May 2012, 'The searing grief of Houla's survivors', by Alex Thomson; *Independent*, 28 May 2012, 'Assad regime blames murderous onslaught on Houla's rebel army', by Patrick Cockburn; *L'Orient-Le Jour* (Beirut), 20 July 2012, '"Après l'attentat de Damas, le régime pourrait viser des intérêts du Golfe ou Occidentaux au Liban"', by Emilie Sueur, interviewing Fabrice Balanche; *Daily Star* (Beirut), 9 June 2012, 'United Nations frets about "sitting duck" monitors in Syria', by Tim Wicher of AFP; *Daily Star* (Beirut), 8 June 2012, 'Survivor tells of horrific carnage in Syrian village; *Independent*, 29 May 2012, 'The West is horrified by children's slaughter now. Soon we'll forget', by Robert Fisk; *L'Orient-Le Jour* (Beirut), 8 June 2012, 'De Washington à Moscow, le massacre d'al-Koubair unaniment condamné'; Syrian Arab News Agency (SANA) (Damascus), 4 June 2012, 'Speech of Bashar al-Assad to Syrian parliament'; *Financial Times*, 15 June 2012, 'Bashar al-Assad: Behind the mask', by Roula Khalaf

510 *The international demands*: *L'Orient-Le Jour* (Beirut), 4 October 2011, 'Marches de soutien à travers le pays au "Conseil national syrien"'; US Defense Department, 2 December 2011, news transcript, 'Remarks by Secretary of Defense Leon E. Panetta at the Saban Center'; *Irish Times*, 4 January 2012, 'French president accuses Syrian regime of massacres', by Michael Jansen; *Le Monde*, 28 January 2012, 'Le Caire est le nouveau sanctuaire des opposants syriens', by Claire Talon; *L'Orient-Le Jour* (Beirut), 18 March 2013, 'Fabius précise déjà quels seront les destinataires des armes françaises'

511 *It was like a children's dancing lesson*: *Irish Times*, 19 June 2013, 'Cameron claims credit for seven-point Syria plan', by Dan Keenan; *Daily Star* (Beirut), 5 September 2013, 'US policy on Syria: Wishful thinking, misjudgments', by Bernd Debusmann; *Daily Star* (Beirut), 5 September 2013, 'It may be curtains for Bashar Assad', by Michael Young; *L'Orient-Le*

Jour (Beirut), 23 October 2013, 'Assad "ne jouerait aucun role" dans un future gouvernement syrien'; *L'Orient-Le Jour* (Beirut), 21 February 2012, 'Joumblatt presse Moscou d'exiler Assad "au fin fond de la Sibérie"'; *L'Orient-Le Jour* (Beirut), 19 March 2012, 'Joumblatt: "C'est la fin d'Assad"'; *Daily Star* (Beirut), 17 March 2012, 'Syrian uprising flag in Mukhtara', by Maher Zeineddine; *L'Orient-Le Jour* (Beirut), 17 March 2013, 'Joumblatt sur la Syrie: La vie des tyrans est courte!'; *L'Orient-Le Jour* (Beirut), 23 August 2013, 'Joumblatt dénonce la "banalisation du mal" en Syrie'; *Independent*, 14 July 2013, 'By taking sides within sides, Rifkind risks a repeat of Balkans mistake in Syria', by Robert Fisk

511 *Long before the Syrian war*: see *Le Nouvel Observateur*, 12–18 January 2006, '"Bachar va tomber"' (interview with Abdul Halim Khaddam by Jean-Paul Mari); *Globe and Mail* (Toronto), 15 June 2011, 'Dissecting Syria', by Patrick Martin; *L'Orient-Le Jour* (Beirut), 5 September 2011, 'L'éspoir en bémol', by Nagib Aoun; *L'Orient-Le Jour* (Beirut), 14 October 2011, 'Avec la révolte en Syrie, l'éspoit des proches de disparus grandis au Liban'

513 *That the despot might*: see *The Australian*, 13 October 2011, 'For democracy to thrive, Assad needs a chance', by Paul Stenhouse; *Independent*, 7 February 2012, 'Without a nudge from NATO, Assad will stay put', by Robert Fisk; Van Dam, *Destroying a Nation*, p. 206n., quoting Syria Comment, 30 November 2013, 'The Work of Fabrice Balanche on Alawites and Syrian communitarianism', by Nikolaos Van Dam; Van Dam, ibid., p. 120; Uri Avnery newsletter, 24 August 2013, 'Cry, Beloved Country'; Sami Mobayed, *Under the Black Flag*, p. 70; *L'Orient-Le Jour* (Beirut), 31 July 2012, 'À Alger, les réfugiés syriens évitent de parler politique par peur des "moukhabarate"' (AFP); *Independent*, 30 July 2012, 'For the minorities, even neutrality is unsafe', by Robert Fisk; author's telephone interview with Patrick Cockburn, 2 June 2020

516 *In the middle of July 2012*: see *Independent*, 22 July 2012, 'Sectarianism bites into Syria's rebels', by Robert Fisk; *Independent*, 19 July 2012, 'Syria rebels will not claim their greatest prize', by Robert Fisk; *Daily Star* (Beirut), 20 July 2012, 'More than 30,000 Syrians cross into Lebanon in 48 hours', by Rakan al-Fakih; *Daily Star* (Beirut), 25 July 2012, 'Syria names post-bombing security supremo' (AFP); *L'Orient-Le Jour* (Beirut), 19 July 2012, 'L'appareil sécuritaire syrien en partie décapité'; author's interview with Syrian resident from Damascus, 24 July 2012; *Independent*, 26 July 2012, 'Yes, there's violence, but some Syrians think it's time to return', by Robert Fisk; *Independent*, 1 July 2016, 'Inside Bashar al-Assad's Syrian jail, an Islamist prisoner talks of the regret for his killing', by Robert Fisk; *Independent*, 15 March 2015, 'Which superpower will win the battle of hypocrisy', by Robert Fisk

523 *You could hardly blame them*: see *Independent*, 18 August 2012, 'Damascus: A deserted city, a deserting UN, and a storm about to break', by Robert Fisk; subsequent reports by the author can be found in the *Independent* 18 August 2012 ('UN leaves Syria to its bloody fate'), 22 August 2012 ('"No

power can bring down the Assad regime because God is on our side"'),
21 August 2012 ('"They snipe at us and then run and hide in sewers"'),
4 November 2012, ('The case of the Swedish weapons in Syria'), 20
August 2012 ('In the lair of loyalists still killing in Aleppo'), 23 August 2012
('"Rebel army? They're a gang of foreigners"'), 24 August 2012 ('Aleppo's
poor get caught in the crossfire of Syria's civil war'); Reuters, 29 July 2012,
'Rural fighters pour into Syria's Aleppo for battle', by Erika Solomon;
Daily Star (Beirut), 1 August 2012, 'Rebels claim successes in Aleppo';
Reuters, 30 July 2012, 'Arab Islamist fighters eager to join Syria rebels', by
Suleiman al-Khalidi

530 *267 inmates*: see *Daily Star* (Beirut), 3 September 2012, 'Barefoot but free:
Syrian prisoners released across the country' (AFP by Sammy Katz);
Reuters, 8 August 2012, 'Neighbours pull dead from Syria house rubble',
by Hadeel al-Shalchi; *Daily Star* (Beirut), 14 August 2012, 'Syrian rebel
atrocities on video spark outrage' (AFP by Serene Assir); *Daily Star*
(Beirut), 13 August 2012, 'Revolutionaries carve out enclave in north
Syria' (AFP by Ben Hubbard); Samar Yazbek, *A Woman in the Crossfire:
Diaries of the Syrian Revolution* (London: Haus Publishing, 2012), pp. 86–7;
Observer, 28 June 2012, 'Samar Yazbek: "Syria has been hung, drawn
and quartered"', by Andrew Hussey; *Daily Star* (Beirut), 9 August 2012,
'Civilians first to fall in Aleppo attack' (AP by Ben Hubbard); *New York
Times*, 9 April 2013, 'A very busy man behind the Syrian civil war count',
by Neil MacFarquhar; *L'Orient-Le Jour* (Beirut), 15 August 2012, 'Assad
"ne controle plus que 30% de la Syrie"'; Reuters, 8 November 2012,
'In Syria, siege is test for new rebel order', by Erika Solomon; Reuters,
8 November 2012, 'Syrian rebels kill prisoner as war fuels hatred', by
Erika Solomon; *L'Orient-Le Jour* (Beirut), 14 August 2012, 'Jetés d'un toit,
égorgés, mitraillés … par des rebelles' (AFP); Reuters, 25 August 2012,
'Cartoonist Ali Farzat says fear defeated in Syria', by Marwa Awad

532 *Events unprecedented*: see *Wall Street Journal*, 28 November 2012, 'Fighting
to hold Damascus, Syria flattens rebel "slums"', by Sam Dagher; *Daily
Star* (Beirut), 5 October 2012, 'Fierce fighting damages historic mosque in
Aleppo's Old City'; *Irish Times*, 15 July 2020, 'Veterans sue over ambush
in Syria', by Conor Gallagher

Postscript

533 *The problem is that*: Open Canada, 8 November 2019, 'Five Questions with
Foreign Correspondent Robert Fisk', by Eva Salinas

534 *In the Western context*: excerpt from Robert's talk at the fifth annual Al
Jazeera Forum, May 2010

534 *This has now become a feature*: Independent, 13 July 2019, 'Hitler, tweets and
Trump: What do they have in common?', by Robert Fisk

535 *The Syrian army kills*: Independent, 27 August 2012, 'The Syrian Army
would like to appear squeaky clean. It isn't', by Robert Fisk; unpublished
paragraph in final chapter, the *Night of Power*, Robert Fisk, September 2020

537 *In February 2021, the US secretary of state Antony Blinken stated*: Reuters, 8 February 2021, 'Blinken stops short of endorsing Trump recognition of Golan Heights'

537 *'Somewhere over the Atlantic'*: *Independent*, 1 June 2017, 'Iran and Syria and Iraq: Reality check', by Robert Fisk

537 *A Syrian refugee, Dr Hamaz al-Kateab*: *Channel 4 News*, 12 March 2022, Dr Hamza al-Kateab

539 *'Gulf Arabs – particularly Qatar – are said'*: *Independent*, 26 July 2018, 'Even the White Helmets have been rescued from Syria – so are we about to see the final battle of the war?', by Robert Fisk

SELECT BIBLIOGRAPHY

A bibliography is a difficult animal to tame. The Middle East no more lends itself to political order in its literature than it does in life, so the reader must forgive some casuistry in the way I have listed the books below. Israel and 'Palestine' today fall naturally into the same category – though there are many who would disagree – and it seems obvious that Lebanon and Syria should be combined, for historical as well as political reasons. The conjunction of Afghanistan and Pakistan speaks for itself – the Taliban and pilotless drone aircraft eliminate borders – though this does not acknowledge the existence of 'Pushtunistan'. If I had permitted them to do so, the black-uniformed ghouls of the 'Islamic State' (or *Daesh*) might have persuaded me to push Syria and Iraq together.

In the libraries of new books on Iraq, there are brilliant academic studies and mawkish, self-serving memoirs, most of them by Western participants in this bloody pantomime. Layers of official enquiries, and the mendacity of many of their participants, have only served to obscure the moral turpitude that lay behind the illegal Anglo-American invasion of 2003. Bibliographies of the future will, I suppose, also have to include Hollywood's awful contribution to this dubious battlefield, the patriotic conclusion of *The Hurt Locker* leaning heavily against *Rendition*, that penetrating but predictably unsuccessful movie on torture and George W. Bush's 'war on terror'.

Israeli history divides its readers as much as its historians. One of its tragedies is that Benny Morris and Ilan Pappe, the two Israeli academics who have done more than any others to break open the sealed box of the Palestinian catastrophe of 1948, should now be bitter antagonists, the former believing that the 'ethnic cleansing' of the Arab population did not go far enough, the latter convinced that the crimes committed by Zionist forces in 1948 have been buried beneath the very landscape of modern Israel. So much has been written about this kernel-moment in the Israeli–Palestinian story – and so many untruths propagated – that, in the words of that eminent Arab Christian writer George Antonius, too much reliance should not be placed on the vast body of literature available. The world's press, he wrote in 1938, is 'largely amenable' to Zionist propaganda when confronted with the 'primitive and infinitely less successful' Arab propaganda. A kind of balance is slowly being established, although a glance today at Western press reporting and comment when Israel goes to war shows how much further truth still has to travel to be effective. Read Finkelstein and Dershowitz on Israel, and you will have to take sides. They truly hate each other.

I have largely avoided the self-serving autobiographies of those 'statesmen' and generals who have so fatally dominated Western policy – or 'discourse' as we are enjoined to call it – in the Middle East today. So, too, the 'think-tank experts' who have vapoured away on our television screens about the 'war on terror' – or 'evil' – over the past twenty-five years. A bibliography is no place for such liars and mountebanks.

But I have included sometimes short, largely unknown monograms or articles whose authors have shown an originality and freedom of thought which their better-known (and better paid) 'peers' long ago abandoned. That fine Israeli historian Avi Shlaim and Pakistani journalist Ahmed Rashid are represented in this bibliography, for example, and so is Naomi Klein. But so are Bruce Lawrence's collection of Osama bin Laden statements and those of Hizbollah leader Sayed Hassan Nasrallah by Nicholas Noe. Typical of the 'unknown' documents to be found here are Geert von Kesteren's extraordinary compendium of amateur private snapshots of the war in Baghdad taken by Iraqi families. The likes of Samuel Huntingdon and Francis Fukuyama. Those who believe that the Middle East conflict is a clash of civilisations must look elsewhere for guidance.

I have chosen to avoid both novels and poetry, with specific exceptions: two works of fiction on 'honour' killing – because there are so few documentary texts available – and three recent Algerian novels which represent the horror and sordid nature of the 1990s civil war and its aftermath, about which local reporters and historians still cannot write in detail without fear of censorship or arrest; I have also listed Lawrence Durrell's *Judith* which remained – amazingly – unpublished until 2012, a pro-Israeli novel set in 1948 Palestine and a sad near-contemporary of the populist Zionist epic *Exodus* of Leon Uris.

Controversially, perhaps, I have largely refused to use websites or internet reviews or Google as sources in the text of this book. The same applies to this bibliography. The reason is simple. I am no Luddite, nor do I despise technology. But many internet sources used by writers have subsequently disappeared from the web or – much more disturbingly – have later been doctored for political reasons. The Israeli army's 2008 website, for example, was later changed to delete all reference to an Israeli military attack in Gaza – an operation which took place during an agreed Hamas–Israeli ceasefire and therefore undermined Israel's claim that Palestinians had broken the truce. Similarly, many internet contributions, especially on the Middle East, are inaccurate, racist or slanderous. The printed word imposes a responsibility upon a writer; they must be liable in law as well as in honour.

As an old-school journalist, I love books and the patina of age, the 'foxing' of paper, the smell of print – rather than the websites and blogs which have now, insidiously, become part of the academic as well as the journalistic world. My old handwritten notebooks, typed and telexed pages, even my hard-copy dispatches of reports from Afghanistan, Iraq, Lebanon and Egypt, piled up around me as I wrote this book. And, working amid my own beautiful library over the sea, shelf after shelf of loved volumes over which I run my fingers as I check and re-check quotations and dates and memories, there is a sense of permanence, of reliability, of – although I rather distrust this word – the responsibility of print. Lecturing at UCLA, I was asked by a member of the audience which websites I would recommend on the Middle East. Websites? I asked. What's wrong with books? And the student audience immediately applauded. The academic staff in the front row were silent.

Why so, I wondered, given the factual unreliability of internet information, the vast network of hate which it often represents, the eternally changing websites that are now cluttering the bibliographies of reference books long after the sites have been taken down or changed utterly or simply edited out of recognition? Books are supposed to last. They represent an impermeable sense of trust and continuity, to be re-used and re-read, a source upon which to build new histories with new written sources. Authors have to stand by the printed word; which is what this bibliography recognises. Abandon all 'writing tools', those who enter here.

The following, however, is not a recommended reading list. It includes books I admire and books I loathe about the lands in which I work and the terrifying policies which are destroying them. It does not claim to be comprehensive.

General

Cobain, Ian, *Cruel Britannia: A Secret History of Torture* (London: Portobello Books, 2012)

Danner, Mark, *Stripping Bare the Body: Politics, Violence, War* (New York: Nation Books, 2009)

Ehrenreich, Barbara, *Blood Rites: The Origins and History of the Passions of War* (London: Granta, 2011)

Fatih, Lieutenant Mehmed, *Gallipoli 1915: Bloody Ridge (Lone Pine) Diary* (Istanbul: Denizler Kitabevi, 2003, English edition presented by Hasan Basri Danisman)

Klein, Naomi, *The Shock Doctrine: The Rise and Fall of Disaster Capitalism* (Toronto: Knopf, 2007)

Levene, Mark, *The Crisis of Genocide*, Volume I, *Devastation: The European Rimlands 1912–1938*; Volume II, *Annihilation: The European Rimlands 1939–1953* (Oxford, 2013)

LeVine, Mark, *Why They Don't Hate Us: Lifting the Veil on the Axis of Evil* (Oxford: Oneworld, 2005)

Lieven, Anatol, *Chechnya: Tombstone of Russian Power* (London: Yale University Press, 1997)

Maalouf, Amin, *Disordered World: Setting a New Course for the Twenty-first Century* (London: Bloomsbury, 2011)

Mehta, Vijay, *The Economics of Killing: How the West Fuels War and Poverty in the Developing World* (London: Pluto Press, 2012)

Polman, Linda, *War Games: The Story of Aid and War in Modern Times* (London: Viking, 2010)

Rees, Phil, *Dining with Terrorists: Meetings with the World's Most Wanted Militants* (London: Macmillan, 2005)

Roy, Arundhati, *The Chequebook and the Cruise Missile* (interviews with David Barsamian, preface by Naomi Klein) (London: Harper Perennial, 2004)

Summers, Anthony, and Robbyn Swan, *The Eleventh Day: The Full Story of 9/11 and Osama bin Laden* (London: Doubleday, 2011)

The 9/11 Commission Report: The Attack from Planning to Aftermath (new afterword by Philip Zelikow, executive director 9/11 Commission) (New York: W.W. Norton, 2011)

Todorov, Tzvetan, *Hope and Memory: Reflections on the Twentieth Century* (New Jersey, USA: Princeton University Press, 2003)

Vidal, Gore, *Dreaming War: Blood for Oil and the Cheney-Bush Junta* (New York: Nation Books, 2002)

Walker, Christopher J., *Islam and the West: A Dissonant Harmony of Civilisations* (Stroud, UK: Sutton Publishing, 2005)

Wikan, Unni, *In Honor of Fadime: Murder and Shame* (Chicago: University of Chicago Press, 2003)

Middle East

Achcar, Gilbert, *The People Want: A Radical Exploration of the Arab Uprising* (London: Saqi, 2013)

Anderson, Scott, *Lawrence in Arabia: War, Deceit, Imperial Folly and the Making of the Modern Middle East* (London: Atlantic Books, 2013)

Antonius, George, *The Arab Awakening: The Story of the Arab National Movement* (Beirut: Librarie du Liban, 1969, with permission of Hamish Hamilton)

Al-Aswany, Alaa, *The Dictatorship Syndrome* (London: Haus Publishing, 2019)

Atwan, Abdel Bari, *After Bin Laden: Al Qa'ida, The Next Generation* (London: Saqi, 2012)

——*Islamic State: The Digital Caliphate* (London: Saqi Books, 2015)

Ball, Warwick, *Out of Arabia: Phoenicians, Arabs and the Discovery of Europe* (London: East and West Publishing, 2009)

Barr, James, *A Line in the Sand: Britain, France and the Struggle for the Mastery of the Middle East* (London: Simon & Schuster, 2011)

Barry, Michael, *Homage to Andalus: The Rise and Fall of Islamic Spain* (Dublin: Andalus Press, 2008)

Benjamin, Medea, *Drone Warfare: Killing by Remote Control* (New York: OR Books, 2012)

Bin Laden, Najwa and Omar and Jean Sasson, *Growing Up bin Laden: Osama's Wife and Son Take Us Inside Their Secret World* (New York: St. Martin's Press, 2009)

Bishara, Marwan, *The Invisible Arab: The Promise and Peril of the Arab Revolution* (New York: Nation Books, 2012)

Clark, Victoria, *Allies for Armageddon: The Rise of Christian Zionism* (London: Yale University Press, 2007)

Dockter, Warren, *Churchill and the Islamic World: Orientalism, Empire and Diplomacy in the Middle East* (London: I.B. Tauris, 2015)

Edgar, Iain R., *The Dream in Islam: From Qu'ranic Tradition to Jihadist Inspiration* (New York: Bergahn Books, 2011)

Fawaz, Leila Tarazi, *A Land of Aching Hearts: The Middle East in the Great War* (Cambridge, Mass.: Harvard University Press, 2014)

Feinstein, Andrew, *The Shadow World: Inside the Global Arms Trade* (London: Penguin, 2012)

Filiu, Jean-Pierre, *From Deep State to Islamic State: The Arab Counter-Revolution and its Jihadi Legacy* (London: Hurst & Co., 2015)

Filkins, Dexter, *The Forever War: Dispatches from the War on Terror* (London: Bodley Head, 2008)

Fisk, Robert, *The Great War for Civilisation: The Conquest of the Middle East* (London: HarperCollins 2005, updated Fourth Estate 2006; New York: Knopf, 2005)

Friedman, Thomas L., *From Beirut to Jerusalem* (New York: Farrar, Straus and Giroux, 1989)

Gardner, David, *Last Chance: The Middle East in the Balance* (London: I.B.Tauris, 2012)

Gelvin, James L., *The Arab Uprisings: What Everyone Needs to Know* (Oxford: OUP, 2012)

Gerges, Fawaz, *Obama and the Middle East: The End of America's Moment* (New York: Palgrave Macmillan, 2012)

Gilbert, Martin, *In Ishmael's House: A History of Jews in Muslim Lands* (Toronto: McLelland & Stewart, 2010)

Glen, Alec, *In the Front Line: A Doctor in War and Peace* (Edinburgh: Birlinn, 2013)

Hersh, Seymour M., *The Killing of Osama bin Laden* (London: Verso, 2016)

Kassir, Samir, *Being Arab* (London: Verso, 2006)

Keay, John, *Sowing the Wind: The Seeds of Conflict in the Middle East* (London: John Murray 2003)

Khadr, Omar, *Omar Khadr, Oh Canada* (ed. Janice Williamson) (Montreal: McGill-Queen's University Press, 2012)

Khairallah, Shereen, *Railways in the Middle East 1856–1948* (Beirut: Librarie du Liban, 1991)

Khalidi, Tarif (ed.), *An Anthology of Arabic Literature: From the Classical to the Modern* (Edinburgh: Edinburgh University Press, 2016)

Lawrence, T. E., *Seven Pillars of Wisdom: A Triumph* (London: Jonathan Cape, 1973)

Maass, Peter, *Crude World: The Violent Twilight of Oil* (London: Allen Lane, 2009)

Makdisi, Ussama, *Faith Misplaced: The Broken Promise of U.S.-Arab Relations: 1820–2001* (New York: Perseus Books, 2010)

Mango, Andrew, *Ataturk* (London, John Murray, 1999)

Mansel, Philip, *Levant: Splendour and Catastrophe on the Mediterranean* (London: John Murray, 2010)

Mazower, Mark, *Salonica City of Ghosts: Christians, Muslims and Jews 1430–1950* (London: HarperCollins, 2004)

McMeekin, Sean, *The Berlin-Baghdad Express: The Ottoman Empire and Germany's Bid for World Power, 1898–1918* (London: Allen Lane, 2010)

Mernissi, Fatima, *Islam and Democracy: Fear of the Modern World* (New York: Addison-Wesley Publishing, 1992)

Milton, Giles, *Paradise Lost, Smyrna 1922: The Destruction of Islam's City of Tolerance* (London: Hodder & Stoughton, 2008)

Moubayed, Sami, *Under the Black Flag: At the Frontier of the New Jihad* (London: I.B. Tauris, 2015)

Napoleoni, Loretta, *Merchants of Men: How Kidnapping, Ransom and Trafficking Funds Terrorism and Isis* (London: Atlantic Books, 2016)

Nasrallah, Ibrahim, *Balcony of Disgrace* (Arabic: *Sharafa al-Ahr*) (Beirut: Editions El-Ikhtilef/Arab Scientific Publishers, 2010)

Noueihed, Lin, and Alex Warren, *The Battle for the Arab Spring: Revolution, Counter-Revolution and the Making of a New Era* (London: Yale University Press, 2012)

Ottoway, Marina, and Julia Choucair-Vizoso (eds), *Beyond the Façade: Political Reform in the Arab World* (Washington: Carnegie Endowment for International Peace, 2008)

Phillips, Joshua E.S., *None of Us Were Like This Before: American Soldiers and Torture* (London: Verso, 2010)

Pither, Kerry, *Dark Days: The Story of Four Canadians Tortured in the Name of Fighting Terror* (Toronto: Viking, 2008)

Primakov, Yevgeny, *Russia and the Arabs: Behind the Scenes in the Middle East from the Cold War to the Present* (Philadelphia, SA: Basic Books, 2009)

Reid, Walter, *Empire of Sand: How Britain Made the Middle East* (Edinburgh: Birlinn, 2013)

Rihani, Ameen F., *The Pan-Arab Movement* (essays and speeches) (Washington: Platform International, 2008)

——*The Riyani Essays* (essays and speeches) (Washington: Platform International, 2010)

Riva, Rocío da, *Lawrence of Arabia's Forerunner: The Bizarre Enterprise of Leo Frobenius, aka Abdul Kerim Pasha, in Arabia and Eritrea (1914–1915)* (Vienna: Im Selbstverlag des Instituts für Orientalistik, 2009)

Rosen, Nir, *Aftermath: Following the Bloodshed of America's Wars in the Muslim World* (New York: Nation Books, 2010)

Shlaim, Avi, *Lion of Jordan: The Life of King Hussein in War and Peace* (London: Allen Lane, 2007)

Soueif, Ahdaf, *Mezzaterra: Fragments from the Common Ground* (London: Bloomsbury, 2004)

Tyerman, Christopher, *God's War: A New History of the Crusades* (London: Allen Lane, 2006)

Tyler, Patrick, *A World of Trouble: America in the Middle East* (London: Portobello Books, 2009)

Warde, Ibrahim, *The Price of Fear: Al-Qaeda and the Truth behind the Financial War on Terror* (London: I.B. Tauris, 2007)

Weddady, Nasser, and Sohrab Ahmari (eds), *Arab Spring Dreams: The Next Generation Speaks Out for Freedom and Justice from North Africa to Iran* (New York: Palgrave Macmillan, 2012)

Wint, Guy, and Peter Calvocoressi, *Middle East Crisis* (London: Penguin, 1957)

Z, *Révolution! Des années mauves à la fuite de Carthage* (Tunis: Cérès Éditions, 2011)

Zenko, Micah, *Between Threats and Wars: US Discrete Military Operations in the Post-Cold War World* (Stanford, California: Stanford University Press, 2010)

Zogby, James, *Arab Voices: What They Are Saying to Us, and Why it Matters* (New York: Palgrave Macmillan 2010)

Zulfo, 'Ismat Hasan, *Karari: The Sudanese Account of the Battle of Omdurman* (London: Frederick Warne, 1980)

Afghanistan and Pakistan

Ahsan, Aitzaz, *The Indus Saga and the Making of Pakistan* (Islamabad: Army Press, 2008)

Bonosky, Phillip, *Afghanistan: Washington's Secret War* (New York: International Publishing, 1985)

Brooke-Smith, Robin, *Storm Warning: Riding the Crosswinds in the Pakistan-Afghan Borderlands* (London: Radcliffe Press, 2013)

Bury, Patrick, *Callsign Hades* (London: Simon & Schuster, 2010)

Fergusson, James, *Taliban: The True Story of the World's Most Feared Guerrilla Fighters* (London: Bantam Press, 2010)

Gul, Imtiaz, *The Most Dangerous Place: Pakistan's Lawless Frontier* (London: Penguin Books, 2010)

Jaunarena, Eugenia, *Afghanistan Chooses a New Road* (Moscow: Novosti Press Agency, 1986)

Muñoz, Heraldo, *Getting Away With Murder: Benazir Bhutto's Assassination and the Politics of Pakistan* (New York: W.W. Norton & Co., 2014)

Rashid, Ahmed, *Jihad: The Rise of Militant Islam in Central Asia* (London: Yale University, 2002)

Tanner, Stephen, *Afghanistan: A Military History from Alexander the Great to the War against the Taliban* (Philadelphia: Da Capo Press (Perseus Books), 2003)

Turse, Nick (ed.), *The Case for Withdrawal from Afghanistan* (London: Verso, 2010)

Van Linschoten, Alex Strick and Felix Kuehn (eds), *Poetry of the Taliban* (London: Hurst & Co., 2012)

Zaeef, Abdul Salam, *My Life with the Taliban* (eds Alex Strick van Linschoten and Felix Kuehn) (London: Hurst & Co., 2010)

Algeria

Boudjedra, Rachid, *Les figuiers de barbarie* (Algiers: Barzakh, 2010)

Brace, Richard and Joan, *Ordeal in Algeria* (New Jersey, USA: D. Van Norstrand, 1960)

Chenouf, Aissa, *Les Juifs d'Algerie ... 2,000 ans d'existence* (Algiers: Editions el-Maarifa, 2004)

Cherif, Mustapha, *L'Émir Abdelkader: Apôtre de la fraternité* (Paris: Odile Jacob, 2016)

Evans, Martin, *Algeria: France's Undeclared War* (Oxford: OUP, 2012)

Meddi, Adlene, *La prière du maure* (Algiers: Barzakh, 2008)

Meziane Cherif, Abderrahmane, *La guerre d'Algérie en France: Mourepiane: L'armée des ombres* (Algiers: Edif, 200; Paris: Editions Publisud, 2010)

Morgan, Ted, *My Battle of Algiers: A Memoir* (New York: HarperCollins, 2005)

Zaoui, Amin, *La Chambre de la vierge impure* (Algiers: Barzakh, 2009)

Armenia

Akcam, Taner, *A Shameful Act: The Armenian Genocide and the Question of Turkish Responsibility* (New York: Metropolitan Books, Henry Holt, 2006)

——*The Young Turks' Crime Against Humanity: The Armenian Genocide and Ethnic Cleansing in the Ottoman Empire* (Princeton: Princeton University Press, 2012)

Arsenian, Hagop, *Towards Golgotha: The Memoirs of Hagop Arsenian, a Genocide Survivor* (Beirut: Haigazian University Press, 2011)

Babkenian, Vicken, and Peter Stanley, *Armenia, Australia & the Great War* (Sydney: NewSouth Publishing, University of New South Wales, 2016)

Balakian, Grigoris, *Armenian Golgotha: A Memoir of the Armenian Genocide, 1915–1918* (trans. Peter Balakian) (New York: Random House, 2006)

Bogosian, Eric, *Operation Nemesis: The Assassination Plot that Avenged the Armenian Genocide* (New York: Little, Brown, 2015)

Cheterian, Vicken, *Open Wounds: Armenians, Turks, and a Century of Genocide* (London: Hurst & Co., 2015)

Duckett, Ferriman, *The Young Turks and the Truth about the Holocaust at Adana in Asia Minor, during April 1909* (Yerevan: Armenian Genocide Museum-Institute, 2009)

Fernandes, Desmond, *The Kurdish and Armenian Genocides: From Censorship to Denial and Recognition?* (Spanga, Sweden: Apec, 2008)

Fethiye Cetin, *My Grandmother: A Memoir* (London: Verso, 2008)

Galichian, Rouben, *The Invention of History: Azerbaijan, Armenia, and the Showcasing of Imagination* (London: Gomidas Institute, 2009)

Ihrig, Stefan, *Ataturk in the Nazi Imagination* (Cambridge, Mass.: Belknap Press of Harvard University Press, 2014)

——*Justifying Genocide: Germany and the Armenians from Bismarck to Hitler* (Cambridge, Mass.: Harvard University Press, 2015)

Kevorkian, Raymond, *The Armenian Genocide: A Complete History* (London: I.B. Tauris, 2011)

——*Les Arméniens: La Quête d'un refugé 1917–1939* (edited by Kevorkian, Levon Nordiguian and Vahe Tachjian) (Beirut: Presses de L'Université Saint-Joseph, 2007)

Koundakjian, Armine Carapetian, *The Repression of Armenian Repatriates during the Stalin Era* (Yerevan: self-published, 2012)

——*What Was Written in Iran during Armenian Genocide Years* (Yerevan: self-published, 2012)

Kouyoumdjian, Bardig, and Christine Simeone, *Deir-Zor: On the Trail of the Armenian Genocide of 1915* (Paris: Actes sud, 2005; English version privately published by the author and photographer 2010)

Leverkuhn, Paul, *A German Officer During the Armenian Genocide: A Biography of Max von Scheubner-Richter* (London: Gomidas Institute, 2008)

Maronian, Bared and Maggie Mangassarian-Goschin, *Orphans of the Genocide* (Florida: Signalman Publishing, 2012)

Marsoobian, Armen T., *Fragments of a Lost Homeland: Remembering Armenia* (London: I.B. Tauris, 2015)

Natalie, Shahan, *The Turks and Us* (Nagorno-Karabagh: Punik Publishing, 2002)

Panian, Karnig, *Goodbye, Antoura: A Memoir of the Armenian Genocide* (Stanford, California: Stanford University Press, 2015)

Reiss, Tom, *The Orientalist: Solving the Mystery of a Strange and Dangerous Life* (New York: Random House, 2006)

Suny, Ronald Grigor, *They Can Live in the Desert but Nowhere Else: A History of the Armenian Genocide* (Princeton: Princeton University Press, 2015)

Tchamkerten, Astrig, *Les Gulbenkian à Jerusalem* (Lisbon: Fondation Calouste Gulbenkian, 2006)

Torossian, Captain Sarkis, *From … Dardanelles to Palestine: A true story of five battlefronts of Turkey and her allies and a harem romance* (Boston: Meador Publishing, 1947)

Waal, Thomas de, *Great Catastrophe: Armenians and Turks in the Shadow of Genocide* (Oxford: OUP, 2015)

Watenpaugh, Keith David, *Bread from Stones: The Middle East and the Making of Modern Humanitarianism* (Oakland, California: University of California Press, 2015)

Yotnakhparian, Levon, *Crows of the Desert: Memoirs* (Tujunga, California: Parian Photographic Design, 2012)

Egypt

Aburish, Said K., *Nasser: The Last Arab* (London: Duckworth, 2004)

Alwan, Yasser (preface and introduction), *Imagining Egypt: The Photographs of Lehnert and Landrock* (Cairo: Lehnert and Landrock, 2007)

Amin, Galal, *Whatever Happened to the Egyptian Revolution?* (trans. Jonathan Wright) (Cairo: American University in Cairo Press, 2013)

Al-Aswany, Alaa, *The Republic 'As If': A Novel* (London: HarperCollins, 2020)

Bier, Laura, *Revolutionary Womanhood: Feminism, Modernity, and the State in Nasser's Egypt* (Cairo: American University in Cairo Press, 2011)

Cook, Steven A., *The Struggle for Egypt: From Nasser to Tahrir Square* (New York: Oxford University Press, 2012)

Fahmy, Mohamed (with Carol Shaben), *The Marriott Cell: An Epic Journey from Cairo's Scorpion Prison to Freedom* (Toronto: Random House Canada, 2016)

Idle, Nadia, and Alex Nunns, Tweets (editors), *Tweets from Tahrir: Egypt's Revolution as it Unfolded, in the Words of the People Who Made It* (New York: OR Books, 2011)

Kandil, Hazem, *Soldiers, Spies and Statesmen: Egypt's Road to Revolt* (London: Verso, 2012)

Lanfranchi, Sania Sharawi, *Casting off the Veil: The Life of Huda Shaarawi, Egypt's First Feminist* (London: I.B. Tauris, 2012)

Mehrez, Samia, *Egypt's Culture Wars: Politics and Practice* (Cairo: American University in Cairo Press, 2010)

Nasser, Tahia Gamal Abdel, *Nasser: My Husband* (Cairo: American University in Cairo Press, 2013)

Pargeter, Alison, *The Muslim Brotherhood: From Opposition to Power* (London: Saqi, 2013)

Rifaat, Mohamed (Pasha), *The Awakening of Modern Egypt* (Cairo: Palm Press, 2005)

Sabry, Mohannad, *Sinai: Egypt's Linchpin, Gaza's Lifeline, Israel's Nightmare* (Cairo: American University in Cairo Press, 2015)

Smith, Simon C. (ed.), *Reassessing Suez 1956: New Perspectives on the Crisis and its Aftermath* (Aldershot, UK: Ashgate, 2008)

The Gulf

Barr, James, *Setting the Desert on Fire: T.E. Lawrence and Britain's Secret War in Arabia, 1916–18* (London: Bloomsbury, 2006)

Al-Bishr, Mohammed (editor), *Saudis and Terror: Cross Cultural Views* (Riyadh: Ghainaa Publications, 2005)

Mitchell, Timothy, *Carbon Democracy: Political Power in the Age of Oil* (London: Verso, 2011)

Trofimov, Yaroslav, *The Siege of Mecca: The Forgotten Uprising* (London: Allen Lane, 2007)

Iran

Ahmadi, Albertine, *Carnets d'Iran: Recit* (Sainte Croix, Switzerland: Editions Mon Village, 2001)

Ansari, Ali M., *Iran: A Very Short Introduction* (Oxford: OUP, 2014)

Bellaigue, Christophe de, *Patriot of Persia: Muhammad Mossadegh and a Very British Coup* (London: Bodley Head, 2012)

Diba, Farhad, *Mohammad Mossadegh: A Political Biography* (London: Croom Helm, 1986)

Hashemi, Nader, and Danny Postel (eds), *The People Reloaded: The Green Movement and the Struggle for Iran's Future* (New York: Melville House, 2010)

Milani, Abbas, *The Shah* (New York: Palgrave Macmillan, 2011)

Moqadam, Afsaneh, *Death to the Dictator! Witnessing Iran's Election and the Crippling of the Islamic Republic* (London: Bodley Head, 2010)

Ritter, Scott, *Target Iran: The Truth about the White House's Plans for Regime Change* (New York: Nation Books, 2006)

Iraq

Ali, Tariq, *Rough Music: Blair/Bombs/Baghdad/London/Terror* (London: Verso, 2005)

Amirian, Nazanin, *Los Kurdos: Kurdistan: el pais inexistente* (Barcelona: Flor del Viento Edicciones, 2005)

Bellavia, David (with John Bruning), *House to House: An Epic of War* (London: Simon and Schuster, 2007)

Blix, Hans, *Disarming Iraq: The Search for Weapons of Mass Destruction* (London: Bloomsbury, 2004)

Busch, Benjamin, *Dust to Dust: A Memoir* (London: HarperCollins, 2012)

Chandrasekaran, Rajiv, *Imperial Life in the Emerald City: Inside Baghdad's Green Zone* (London: Bloomsbury, 2007)

Cockburn, Patrick, *The Occupation: War and Resistance in Iraq* (London: Verso, 2006)

——*Muqtada Al-Sadr and the Fall of Iraq* (London: Faber & Faber, 2008)

——*The Jihadis Return: ISIS and the New Sunni Uprising* (New York: OR Books, 2014)

Duelfer, Charles, *Hide and Seek* (London: Perseus Books, 2010)

Ewing, William, *From Gallipoli to Baghdad* (London: Hodder and Stoughton, 1917)

Ferguson, Charles H., *No End in Sight: Iraq's Descent into Chaos* (New York: Perseus Books, 2008)

Galbraith, Peter W., *The End of Iraq: How American Incompetence Created a War Without End* (New York: Simon and Schuster, 2006)

Gardner, Lloyd C., and Marilyn B. Young (eds), *Iraq and the Lessons of Vietnam: Or How Not to Learn From the Past* (New York: New Press, 2007)

Gordon, Joy, *Invisible War: The United States and the Iraqi Sanctions* (Cambridge, Mass.: Harvard University Press, 2010)

Hedges, Chris, and Laila Al-Arian, *Collateral Damage: America's War Against Iraqi Civilians* (New York: Nation Books, 2008)

Al-Jezairy, Zuhair, *The Devil You Don't Know: Going Back to Iraq* (London: Saqi, 2009)

Kesteren, Geert von, *Baghdad Calling* (Rotterdam: Episode Publishers, 2008)

Khudayyir, Muhammad, *Basrayatha: The Story of a City* (London: Verso, 2008)

Mansour, Ahmed, *Inside Fallujah: The Unembedded Story* (Gloucestershire, UK: Arris Books, 2009)

Maxwell, Donald, *A Dweller in Mesopotamia: Being the Adventures of an Official Artist in the Garden of Eden* (London: John Lane, Bodley Head, 1921)

Muttitt, Greg, *Fuel on the Fire: Oil and Politics in Occupied Iraq* (London: Bodley Head, 2011)

Nixon, John, *Debriefing the President: The Interrogation of Saddam Hussein* (London: Penguin Random House, 2016)

Oborne, Peter, *The Rise of Political Lying* (London: Free Press, 2005)

Packer, George, *The Assassin's Gate: America in Iraq* (New York: Farrar, Straus and Giroux, 2005)

Rai, Milan (chapter by Noam Chomsky), *War Plan Iraq: 10 Reasons Why We Shouldn't Launch Another War Against Iraq* (St Leonard's-on-Sea, UK: Arrow Publications, 2002)

Ricks, Thomas E., *Fiasco: The American Military Adventure in Iraq* (New York: Penguin, 2007)

——*The Gamble: General Petraeus and the Untold Story of the American Surge in Iraq* (London: Penguin, 2010)

Rosen, Nir, *In the Belly of the Green Bird: The Triumph of the Martyrs in Iraq* (New York: Simon and Schuster, 2006)

Rutledge, Ian, *Enemy on the Euphrates: The British Occupation of Iraq and the Great Arab Revolt 1914–1921* (London: Saqi, 2014)

Al-Safi, Haider, *Iraqi Media: From Saddam's Propaganda to American State-Building* (Cambridge: Askance Publishing, 2013)

Saleh, Zaki, *Mesopotamia (Iraq) 1600–1914: A Study in English Foreign Affairs* (Baghdad: Al-Ma'aref Press, 1957)

Scahill, Jeremy, *Blackwater: The Rise of the World's Most Powerful Mercenary Army* (New York: Nation Books, 2007); updated as *Blackwater: From the Nissour Square Massacre to the Future of the Mercenary Industry* (2008)

Scheer, Christopher, and Robert Scheer, and Lakshmi Chaudhry, *The Five Biggest Lies Bush Told Us About Iraq* (London: Seven Stories Press and Akashic Books, 2003)

Short, Clare, *An Honourable Deception? New Labour, Iraq, and the Misuse of Power* (London: Simon and Schuster, 2004)

Simons, Geoff, *Iraq Endgame? Surge, Suffering and the Politics of Denial* (London: Politico's Publishing, 2008)

Sponeck, H.C. von, *A Different Kind of War: The UN Sanctions Regime in Iraq* (New York: Berghahn Books, 2006)

Stewart, Rory, *Occupational Hazards: My Time Governing in Iraq* (London: Picador, 2006)

Verini, James, *They Will Have to Die Now: Mosul and the Fall of the Caliphate* (London: Oneworld, 2019)

White, Andrew, *The Vicar of Baghdad: Fighting for Peace in the Middle East* (Oxford: Monarch Books, 2009)

Woodward, Bob, *The War Within: A Secret White House History 2006–2008* (London: Simon and Schuster, 2008)

Israel and Palestine

Achcar, Gilbert, *The Arabs and the Holocaust: The Arab–Israeli War of Narratives* (London: Saqi, 2009)

——*Eichmann au Caire et autres essais* (transl. Jean-Claude Pons), (Paris: Institute of Palestine Studies and Actes Sud, 2012)

Al-Ali, Naji (cartoons), *A Child in Palestine* (London: Verso, 2009)

Ateek, Naim Stifan, *A Palestinian Christian Cry for Reconciliation* (New York: Orbis Books, 2008)

Atwan, Abdul Bari, *A Country of Words: A Palestinian Journey from the Refugee Camp to the Front Page* (London: Saqi, 2008)

Backmann, Rene, *Un Mur En Palestine* (Paris: Fayard, 2006)

Barsamian, David, *The Pen and the Sword: Conversations with Edward Said* (Chicago: Haymarket Books, 2010)

Bird, Kai, *Crossing the Mandelbaum Gate: Coming of Age Between the Arabs and Israelis, 1956–78* (London: Simon and Schuster, 2010)

Carter, Jimmy, *Palestine: Peace Not Apartheid* (London: Simon and Schuster, 2006)

Chehab, Zaki, *Inside Hamas: The Untold Story of Militants, Martyrs and Spies* (London: I.B. Tauris, 2004)

Chomsky, Noam, *The Fateful Triangle: The United States, Israel and the Palestinians* (London: Pluto Press, 1983)

Corrie, Rachel, *My Name is Rachel Corrie* (taken from the writings of Rachel Corrie, Alan Rickman and Katharine Viner, eds) (London: Royal Court, 2005)

Cronin, David, *Europe's Alliance with Israel: Aiding the Occupation* (London: Pluto Press, 2011)

Dershowitz, Alan, *The Case for Israel* (New York: Wiley, 2003)

Durrell, Lawrence, *Judith: A Novel* (Kerkyra, Greece: Durrell School of Corfu, 2012)

Enderlin, Charles, *Par le feu et par le sang: Le combat pour l'indépendance d'Israel 1936–1948* (Paris: Albin Michel, 2008)

——*Le Grand Aveuglement: Israel et l'irrésistible ascension de l'islam radical* (Paris: Albin Michel, 2009)

Filiu, Jean-Pierre (trans. John King), *Gaza: A History* (London: Hurst Co., 2014)

Finkelstein, Norman G., *Beyond Chutzpah: On the Misuse of Anti-Semitism and the Abuse of History* (London: Verso, 2005)

——'This Time We Went Too Far': Truth and Consequences of the Gaza Invasion (New York: OR Books, 2010)

——*Knowing Too Much: Why the American Jewish Romance with Israel is Coming to an End* (New York: OR Books, 2012)

Furlonge, Geoffrey, *Palestine is My Country: The Story of Musa Alami* (London: John Murray, 1969)

Ghandour, Zeina B., *A Discourse in Domination: Imperialism, Property and Insurgency* (Abingdon, UK: Routledge 2010)

Gilbert, Mads, and Erik Fosse, *Eyes in Gaza* (London: Quartet, 2010)

Al-Hout, Shafiq, *My Life in the PLO: The Inside Story of the Palestinian Struggle* (London: Pluto Press, 2011)

Kattan, Victor, *From Coexistence to Conquest: International Law and the Origins of the Arab-Israeli Conflict, 1891–1949* (London: Pluto Press, 2009)

Khalidi, Walid (ed.), *All That Remains: The Palestine Villages Occupied and Depopulated by Israel in 1948* (Washington DC: Institute for Palestine Studies, 1992)

Kimmerling, Baruch, *Politicide: The Real Legacy of Ariel Sharon* (London: Verso, 2003)

Laor, Yitzhak, *The Myths of Liberal Zionism* (London: Verso, 2009)

LeBor, Adam, *City of Oranges: Arabs and Jews in Jaffa* (London: Bloomsbury, 2006)

Loewenstein, Antony, *My Israel Question* (Carlton, Australia: Melbourne University Press, 2006)

Macintyre, Donald, *Gaza: Preparing for Dawn* (London: Oneworld, 2017)

Martin, Robin H., *Palestine Betrayed: A British Palestine Policeman's Memoirs (1936–1948)* (Ringwood, UK: Seglawi Press, 2007)

McCarthy, John, *You Can't Hide the Sun: A Journey Through Israel and Palestine* (London: Bantam Press, 2012)

Mearsheimer, John J. and Stephen M. Walt, *The Israel Lobby and US Foreign Policy* (London: Allen Lane, 2007)

Milo, Max, *Il n'y aura pas d'État palestinien: Journal d'un négociateur en Palestine* (Paris: Editions Max Milo, 2010)

Morris, Benny, *The Birth of the Palestine Refugee Problem 1947–1949* (Cambridge: CUP, 1987)

Murphy, Dervla, *Between River and Sea: Encounters in Israel and Palestine* (London: Eland Books, 2015)

Myer, Arno J., *Plowshares into Swords: From Zionism to Israel* (London: Verso, 2008)

Pappé, Ilan, *Britain and the Arab-Israeli Conflict 1948–1951* (London: St Antony's College / Macmillan, 1988)

——*The Making of the Arab–Israeli Conflict 1947–1951* (London: I.B. Tauris, 1992)

——*The Ethnic Cleansing of Palestine* (London: Oneworld, 2006)

——*The Rise and Fall of a Palestinian Dynasty: The Husaynis 1700–1948* (Berkeley Los Angeles: University of California Press, 2010)

Rabkin, Yakov M., *A Threat from Within: A Century of Jewish Opposition to Zionism* (Winnipeg: Fernwood Publishing, 2006)

Reinhart, Tanya, *The Road Map to Nowhere: Israel/Palestine Since 2003* (London: Verso, 2006)

Rodger, Peter, *Herzl's Nightmare: One Land, Two Peoples* (London: Constable, 2004)

Russell Tribunal on Palestine: *Responsibility of the European Union: Its Member States and Corporations in the Ongoing Occupation of Palestinian Territories. Providing Illegal Assistance to Israel?* (Brussels: Russell Tribunal on Palestine, 2011)

Salibi, Kemal, *The Historicity of Biblical Israel: Studies in 1 & 2 Samuel* (Beirut: Dar Nelson, 2009)

Sand, Shlomo, *The Invention of the Jewish People* (London, Verso, 2009)

——*On the Nation and the 'Jewish People'*, with two essays by Ernest Renan (London: Verso, 2010)

——*The Invention of the Land of Israel: From Holy Land to Homeland* (London: Verso, 2012)

Schneer, Jonathan, *The Balfour Declaration: The Origins of the Arab-Israeli Conflict* (London: Bloomsbury, 2010)

Shehadeh, Raja, *Occupation Diaries* (London: Profile Books, 2012)

Shlaim, Avi, *The Iron Wall: Israel and the Arab World* (London: Allen Lane (new edition), 2014)

——*Israel and Palestine: Reappraisals, Revisions, Refutations* (London: Verso, 2009)

Swisher, Clayton E., *The Truth about Camp David: The Untold Story about the Collapse of the Middle East Peace Process* (New York: Nation Books, 2004)

——(ed.) *The Palestine Papers: The End of the Road? Documents on the Israeli-Palestinian* (Israeli-Palestinian negotiation documents 1999–2010, full texts on Al Jazeera's Transparency Unit website www. transparency.aljazeera.net) (London: Hesperus Press, 2011)

Tamari, Salim, *Year of the Locust: A Soldier's Diary and the Erasure of Palestine's Ottoman Past* (Berkeley, USA: University of California Press, 2011)

Yizhar, S. (real name: Yizhar Smilansky), *Khirbet Khizeh* (London: Granta, 2011)

Syria and Lebanon

Ajami, Fouad *The Syrian Rebellion* (Stanford, California: Hoover Institution Press, Stanford University, 2012)

Bauer, Wolfgang, *Crossing the Sea: With Syrians on the Exodus to Europe* (High Wycombe, UK: And Other Stories, 2016)

Bouvier, Edith, *Chambre avec Vue sur la Guerre* (Paris: Flammarion, 2012)

Clonan, Tom, *Blood, Sweat and Tears: An Irish Soldier's Story of Love and Loss* (Dublin: Liberties Press, 2012)

Cortas, Wadad Makdisi, *A World I Loved: The Story of an Arab Woman* (New York: Nation Books, 2009)

Dagher, Sam, *Assad or We Burn the Country: How One Family's Lust for Power Destroyed Syria* (New York: Little, Brown, 2020)

De Wailly, Henri, *Invasion Syria 1941: Churchill and de Gaulle's Forgotten War* (London: I.B. Tauris, 2016)

Filiu, Jean-Pierre, *Je vous écrit d'Alep* (Paris: Denoel, 2013)

Fisk, Robert, *Pity the Nation: Lebanon at War* (London: Andre Deutsch, 1990, updated editions from Oxford University Press, 2003 and New York: Nation Books, 2003)

Glass, Charles, *Syria Burning: A Short History of Catastrophe* (London: Verso, 2016)

Al-Hout, Bayan Nuwayhed, *Sabra and Shatila: September 1982* (London: Pluto Press, 2004)

Kanafani-Zahar, Aida, *Liban: La guerre et la memoire* (Rennes, France: Presses Universitaires de Rennes, 2011)

Kassir, Samir, *Beirut* (Berkeley, USA: University of California Press, 2010)

Khalidi, Anbara Salam, *Memoirs of an Early Arab Feminist: The Life and Activism of Anbara Salam Khalidi* (London: Pluto Press, 2013)

Littell, Jonathan, *Syrian Notebooks: Inside the Homs Uprising* (London: Verso, 2015)

Maasri, Zeina, *Off the Wall: Political Posters of the Lebanese Civil War* (London: I.B. Tauris, 2009)

Makdisi, Ussama, *Artillery of Heaven: American Missionaries and the Failed Conversion of the Middle East* (Ithaca, New York: Cornell University Press, 2008)

Mardam Bey, Salma, *Syria's Quest for Independence 1939–1943* (Reading, UK: Ithaca Press, 1994)

McHugo, John, *Syria: From the Great War to Civil War* (London: Saqi, 2014)

Mobayed, Sami, *Under the Black Flag: At the Frontier of the New Jihad* (London: I.B. Tauris, 2015)

Rubin, Barry, *The Truth About Syria* (New York: Palgrave Macmillan, 2007)

Seale, Patrick, *The Struggle for Arab Independence: Riad el-Solh and the Makers of the Modern Middle East* (Cambridge: CUP, 2010)

Shaaban, Bouthaina, *Damascus Diary: An Inside Account of Hafez al-Assad's Peace Diplomacy, 1990–2000* (Boulder, Colorado: Lynne Rienner Publishers, 2013)

Starr, Stephen, *Revolt in Syria: Eye-witness to the Uprising* (London: C. Hurst & Co., 2012)

Thompson, Elizabeth, *Colonial Citizens: Republican Rights, Paternal Privilege, and Gender in French Syria and Lebanon* (New York: Colombia University Press, 2000)

Tveit, Odd Karsten, *Goodbye Lebanon: Israel's First Defeat* (London: Rimal, 2013)

Van Dam, Nikolaos, *The Struggle for Power in Syria: Politics and Society under Asad and the Ba'th Party* (London: I.B. Tauris, 1996)

——*Destroying a Nation: The Civil War in Syria* (London: I.B. Tauris, 2017)

Yazbek, Samar, *A Woman in the Crossfire: Diaries of the Syrian Revolution* (London: Haus Publishing, 2012)

Journalism

Bell, Martin, *The Truth That Sticks: New Labour's Breach of Trust* (London: Icon Books, 2008)

Bentley, Gareth (unpublished PhD thesis) *Journalistic Agency and the Subjective Turn in British Foreign Correspondent Discourse* (London: SOAS, 2011)

Caron, Sarah, *Le Pakistan à vif: Témoignage d'une photo-reporter* (Paris: Jean-Claude Gawsewitch, 2010)

Chomsky, Noam, *Media Control: The Spectacular Achievements of Propaganda* (New York: Seven Stories Press, 1997)

Crawford, Alex, *Colonel Gaddafi's Hat: The Real Story of the Libyan Uprising* (London: HarperCollins, 2012)

Fernández, Belén, *The Imperial Messenger: Thomas Friedman at Work* (London: Verso, 2011)

Friel, Howard, and Richard Falk, *Israel-Palestine On Record: How the New York Times Misreports Conflict in the Middle East* (London: Verso, 2007)

Goodman, Amy, and David Goodman, *Static: Government Liars, Media Cheerleaders, and the People Who Fight Back* (New York: Hyperion, 2006)

Huggler, Justin, *The Burden of the Desert* (a novel) (London: Short Books, 2014)

Hurndall, Tom, *The Only House Left Standing: The Middle East Journals of Tom Hurndall* (London: Trolley, 2012)

Labter, Lazhari, *Journalistes Algériens 1988–1998: Chronique des années d'espoir et de terreur* (Algiers: Chihab Editions, 2005)

Miles, Hugh, *Al-Jazeera: How Arab TV News Challenged the World* (London: Abacus, 2005)

Snow, John, *Shooting History: A Personal Journey* (London: HarperCollins, 2004)

Struk, Janina, *Private Pictures: Soldiers' Inside View of War* (London: I.B. Tauris, 2011)

Villiers, Frederic, *Pictures of Many Wars* (London: Cassell, 1902)

Wilson, Jean Moorcroft, and Cecil Woolf (eds), *Authors Take Sides on Iraq and the Gulf War* (London: Cecil Woolf Publishers, 2004)

Zinn, Howard (introduction), *Target Iraq: What the News Media Didn't Tell You* (New York: Context Books, 2003)

Select Documents

The Abbottabad Commission, 2013 Pakistan Government official inquiry into the death of Osama bin Laden on the night of 1–2 May 2011, by Justice Javed Iqbal (president), Abbas Khan, Ashraf Jehangir Qazi, Lt. Gen. (retired) and Nadeem Ahmed (members), document revealed by Al Jazeera, July 2013

Acts of Aggression: Policing 'Rogue' States, Chomsky, Noam, Ramsey Clark and Edward W. Said (New York: Seven Stories Press, 1999)

Ali, Tariq, 'President of Cant: Obama at War' in *New Left Review*, no. 61 (London: New Left Review, February 2010)

Amnesty International Report 2011: The State of the World's Human Rights (London: Amnesty, 2011)

Aruri, Naseer, 'United States Policy and Palestine: Oslo, the Intifada and Erasure' in *Race and Class: A Journal on Racism, Empire and Globalisation*, Vol. 52, January–March 2011 (London: Institute of Race Relations, 2011)

Barnett, Correlli, *Post-Conquest Civil Affairs: Comparing War's End in Iraq and in Germany* (London: Foreign Policy Centre, 2005)

Barrons, Genevieve, 'Suleiman: Mubarak Decided to Step Down Egypt Jan 25 OH MY GOD': Examining the Use of Social Media in the 2011 Egyptian Revolution, *Contemporary Arab Affairs*, Vol. 5. No. 1, January–March 2012

Beck, Peter, '"The Less Said about Suez the Better": British Governments and the Politics of Suez's History, 1956–67', see *English Historical Review*, Vol. CXXIV, No. 508, June 2009

Burke, Pat (Commander, Irish Naval Service) *In the Crosshairs: Targeted Killing in Contemporary Conflict* (Dublin: Defence Forces Review 2012, Óglaigh na hÉireann)

Carnegie Endowment for International Peace, *Iraq: A New Approach* (London: Carnegie Endowment, 2002)

Chomsky, Noam, *The Umbrella of US Power: The Universal Declaration of Human Rights and the Contradictions of US Policy* (New York: Seven Stories Press, 1999)

——*Power and Terror: Post 9/11 Talks and Interviews* (New York: Seven Stories Press, 2003)

——'Responsibility to Protest' in *The Spokesman* (Nottingham, UK: Bertrand Russell Peace Foundation, 2009)

——'"Exterminate All the Brutes": Gaza 2009' in *The Spokesman* (Nottingham, UK: Bertrand Russell Peace Foundation, 2009)

——'Exposing Western Leadership' (interview with Amy Goodman on Democracy Now!, 30 November 2010) reprinted in *The Spokesman*, No. 111 (Nottingham, UK: Bertrand Russell Peace Foundation, 2011)

Coury, Ralph M., 'A Syllabus of Errors: Pope Benedict XVI on Islam at Regensburg' in *Race and Class: A Journal on Racism, Empire and Globalisation*, January–March, 2009

Crow, Karim D., 'Distrust of Pluralism and Fear of Diversity Among Muslims' in *Islam and Civilisational Renewal* (Malaysia: International Institute of Advanced Islamic Studies, 2009)

Doyle, Colm, 'A Responsibility to Protect' in *Irish Studies in International Affairs*, Vol. 20 (Dublin: Royal Irish Academy, 2009)

Elworthy, Scilla, and Gabrielle Rifkind, *Making Terrorism History* (London: Rider, Random House, 2006)

Eqbal, Ahmad, (interview with David Barsamian) *Terrorism: Theirs and Ours* (New York: Seven Stories Press, 2001)

Esposito, John, 'Islam Studies, Foreign Policy and the Muslim World: From Bush to Obama' in *Delicate Debates on Islam* (Leiden, Netherlands: Leiden University Press, 2011)

Al-Hamid, Raed, 'The American Withdrawal from Iraq: Ways and Means for Remaining Behind', *Contemporary Arab Affairs*, Vol. 5, No. 2 (April 2012)

Haram al-Ein (Jerusalem: Centre for Jerusalem Studies, 2010)

Human Rights in Palestine and Other Occupied Arab Territories: Report of the United Nations Fact-Finding Mission on the Gaza Conflict (The Goldstone Report) (UN General Assembly, Human Rights Council, 25 September 2009)

Islam and the West (Ditchley Park, UK: Oxford Centre for Islamic Studies, 1994)

Islamic Art at the Musée du Louvre (ed. Sophie Makariou) (Paris: Hazan/ Musée du Louvre, 2012)

Karlsson, Ingmar, 'The Turk as a Threat and Europe's "Other"', *Istanbul Lectures 2003–2008* (Istanbul: Swedish Research Institute in Istanbul, 2008)

Kilo, Michel, 'Syria … the Road to Where?', *Contemporary Arab Affairs*, Vol. 4, No. 4 (October 2011)

Messages to the World: The Statements of Osama bin Laden (int. Bruce Lawrence, trans. James Howarth) (London: Verso, 2005)

Miller, Chris (ed.), 'War on Terror' (Oxford Amnesty Lectures) (Manchester: Manchester University Press 2009)

Newsinger, John, 'Liberal Imperialism and the Occupation of Egypt in 1882' in *Race and Class: A Journal on Racism, Empire and Globalisation*, Vol. 49 (January–March, 2008)

——'Taking Baghdad: Some US Marine Memoirs of the Invasion of Iraq' in *Race and Class: A Journal on Racism, Empire and Globalisation*, Vol. 52 (April–June 2011)

Omar Khadr, Oh Canada (ed. Janice Williamson) (Montreal: McGill-Queen's University Press, 2012)

Osama bin Laden and Al-Qaeda: Documents Captured at Abbottabad Compound, Original Arabic Transcriptions, English Translations and Annotations, available from BACM Research (www. PaperlessArchives.com), 264 South LaCienega Boulevard, no. 1142, Beverley Hills, CA 902

Owen, Roger, 'The Arab "Demonstration" Effect and the Revival of Arab Unity in the Arab Spring' (drawn from Owen, *The Rise and Fall of Arab Presidents for Life* (Boston: Harvard, 2012) (*Contemporary Arab Affairs*, Vol 5, No. 3, July–September 2012)

Piterberg, Gabriel, 'Zion's Rebel Daughter: Hannah Arendt on Palestine and Jewish Politics' in *New Left Review* (London: New Left Review No. 48, November–December 2007)

Rashed, Roshdi, 'Arabic Science and Reviewing the Historiography of Science' (translation from *Studies in the History of Arabic Sciences and Their Philosophy*, Ch. 2, Beirut: Centre for Arab Unity Studies, 2011) (*Contemporary Arab Affairs*, Vol. 5, No. 1, January–March 2012)

Al-Rasheed, Madawi, 'Saudi Arabia: Local and Regional Challenges', *Contemporary Arab Affairs*, Vol. 6, No. 1 (January 2013)

The Sabeel Survey on Palestinian Christians in the West Bank and Israel (Jerusalem: Sabeel, 2006)

Sawaf, Zina, 'Youth and the Revolution in Egypt: What Kinship Tells Us', *Contemporary Arab Affairs*, Vol. 6, No. 1 (January 2013)

Shah-Kazemi, Reza, *Crisis in Chechnya: Russian Imperialism, Chechen Nationalism, Militant Sufism* (London: Islamic World Report, 1995)

Siddiqui, Haroon, 'Anti-Muslim Bigotry Goes Official – Canada's Newest Dark Chapter', in *The Relevance of Islamic Identity in Canada: Culture, Politics, and Self* (ed. Nurjehan Aziz) (Toronto: Mawenzi House, 2015)

Strategic Foresight Group, *Cost of Middle East Conflict* (in cooperation with the AK Party, Turkey, Swiss Federal Department of Foreign Affairs, Norwegian Ministry of Foreign Affairs, Qatar Foundation) (Mumbai, India: Strategic Foresight Group, 2009)

A Time to Speak Out: Independent Jewish Voices on Israel, Zionism and Jewish Identity (London: Verso, 2008)

United Nations Mission to Investigate Allegations of the Use of Chemical Weapons in the Syrian Arab Republic: Report on the Alleged Use of Chemical Weapons in the Ghouta Area of Damascus on 21 August 2013

Voice of Hezbollah: The Statements of Sayyed Hassan Nasrallah (ed. Nicholas Noe) (London: Verso, 2007)

Wilber, Donald, 'Overthrow of Premier Mossadeq of Iran, 1954', in *Regime Change in Iran: Overthrow of Premier Mossadeq of Iran November 1952–August 1953* (London: Spokesman Books, 2006)

Winter Soldier: Iraq and Afghanistan: Eyewitness Accounts of the Occupation (Iraq Veterans Against the War, and Aaron Glantz) (Chicago: Haymarket Books, 2008)

ACKNOWLEDGEMENTS

Many of those who helped and encouraged me to write this book are now old friends; they have been researching and digging out information for me for over 30 years, calling and writing to me with political disclosures and classified documents, memories and revelations of unknown historical events. They include Arabs and Israelis and 'Westerners' – an unsatisfactory distinction that readers will have to work out for themselves. Others I would have to call 'contacts', rather than friends: they include militiamen, soldiers, intelligence officers, politicians, imams, bankers, diplomats, cops and, I fear, at least one suicide bomber and his family and several murderers. But without a multitude of others – the poor, the wounded and the oppressed of the Muslim world, from Pakistan to 'Palestine', Lebanon and Egypt – this book could never have been completed. Most still exist amid the terror and injustice in which they lived when I interviewed them. Several of them, alas, have died violent and painful deaths. For clarity, I have sometimes noted their roles, or the nature of their assistance to me.

Amal Abdulhadi; Jawad Adra and Alicia Jammal of Information International (Beirut); Mme Khour Afifa; Paddy Agnew in Rome; Dr Samira Alaani; Akik al-Aloussi of the pathology department at the Kindi hospital in Baghdad; George W. Appenzeller, Vietnam war-era veteran whose understanding of the US military was essential to my coverage of Iraq; Faik Amin Bakr of the Baghdad City mortuary; Dr Frazani Bari; Professor Peter Beck for his research and paper on the political aftermath of the 1956 Suez invasion; Robin Brooke-Smith, former principal of Edwards College in Peshawar; Dr Chris Busby for his reports and comments on child cancers and birth anomalies in Iraq;

ex-US Marine Corps Major Benjamin Busch for permission to quote from his eloquent letters home as a US Marine officer in Iraq; Charley Campbell of Ontario for his work *Reading Arabia: An Expatriate View*; Lamri Chirouf of Amnesty; the late Ken Coates of the Bertrand Russell Peace Foundation; Ed Cody of the *Washington Post*; my friend and colleague Patrick Cockburn of the *Independent*; Italian diplomat Pietro Cordone; Dr. Douglas Cox; Nadim Elissa for his information on the 1921 Cairo conference; Mohamed Fahmy; Joanne Farchakh for her guided tour of the broken cities of Sumaria; Ayman Gaballah, deputy chief editor of *Al Jazeera*; Tom Geddes for his correspondence with the UK Ministry of Defence; Zeinab al-Ghoneimi; Stella Gourney; Adrian Hamilton for his diligence in searching my own files at the *Independent*; rape victim 'Hanan'; Dr. Khair El-Din Haseeb of the Centre for Arab Unity Studies in Beirut; Nadhem Shokr al Hadidi of Fallujah General Hospital; the late Margaret Hassan of CARE; John Hellegers; Geoffrey Holland of Sussex University for his Iraqi 2004 chemical weapons report to the UK Parliament; Philip Hurst of the Ashurst Seminar; Alan and David Hurst-Brown for permission to quote from their great-grand-father's 1880 letters to his wife from Kandahar; Jack B. Hyde; my friend Lebanese economist Marwan Iskandar; Lahore lawyer Hina Jalani; Eva Jasiewicz for her help in Basra on oil trade unions; Dr Saleem Jahangeer; journalist Rania Kadri; Wadah Kanfar of *Al Jazeera*; Dutch photographer Geert van Kesteren; Missak Kelechian for his research into the Armenian 'death' orphanage at Aintoura (Lebanon) and his unfailing enquiries into the genocide; my friend and Islamic scholar Tarif Khalidi; my Iraqi driver Mohamed al-Khazraji; Jordanian lawyer and ex-minister Asma Khodr; Eric Kueffner; Armine Carapetian Koundakjian; Jennifer Lowenstein for her continued help in research; Ahmed Mansour of *Al Jazeera*; Maria al-Masani, Peter Metcalfe of the T.E. Lawrence Society; colleague and friend Donald Macintyre; Irish Army officer Comdt Kevin McDonald; Tewfiq and Philippa Mishlawi for their inexhaustible archives; Greg Muttitt, for his wisdom on Iraqi oil; women's activist Lima Nabil; lawyer Ahmed Najdawi; Dr Lubna Naji; Dr Kypros Nicolaides of King's College Hospital, London; Jonathan Pickering; Othmar Ploeckinger for his knowledge of Hitler's *Mein Kampf*; Mario Portanova of the Milan magazine *Diario*; Naima al-Rawagh of the Palestinian Women's Empowerment Programme; Rocío Da Riva for his research on Germany's Middle East spy in the

1914–18 war, Leo Frobenius; Benji Rogers; Prof Hugh Roberts of Tufts University; ex Flight Lieutenant Martin Rubenstein of the RAF; Haider al-Safi, for his wisdom and courage amid the bloodshed of Iraq; Imad and Leena Saidi; the late Kamal Salibi; Neil Sammonds of Amnesty; Manouchehr Sanadjian; Nadia Shamroukh of the Jordanian Women's Union; Israeli historian Avi Shlaim; Amira el-Solh; Huw Spanner, Egyptian activist Azza Sulieman; my friend Odd Karsten Tveit; Swedish Radio Middle East correspondent Cecilia Uddén and Agneta Ramberg; Rob Yellowhammer.

It has now become almost a ritual for me to thank my editors at the *Independent* without whose generosity and courage and forbearance neither *Night of Power* nor my previous work on the Middle East, *The Great War for Civilisation*, could have been undertaken. My thanks to former editors Andreas Whittam Smith, Simon Kelner, Chris Blackhurst, Amol Rajan, and to my present boss Christian Broughton. In an age when it is fashionable to berate editors for their gutlessness in the face of political orthodoxy, and when 'statesmen' try to suborn them with favours in return for supporting their wars, it is an infinite pleasure to record that my editors never changed a word I wrote, and always urged me to attack the 'bad guys', whatever the cost.

I must also pay homage to my editor at HarperCollins, Louise Haines, whose faith in my promise to produce this manuscript on time was, as usual, cruelly misplaced – journalists always meet their newspaper deadlines, never their publisher's delivery dates – but whose only reaction was to ask from year to year, very gently, if I had the faintest idea when I might complete this book. Louise has a nice line of flattery with her authors; she laughs with delight when she enjoys a passage of prose. But when she is bored or impatient at some supposed digression, she will tap her pencil rhythmically on the page with the irritation of an executioner's drum. Thank God she's not in journalism.

Finally, all my love and all my thanks go to my brilliant young wife, Nelofer, who always spoke of this book with affection because she knew it represented part of my life and hoped that its completion might mark the end of the many dangers which I have endured. In truth, we now share those perils in the most dangerous lands on earth. That, I think, is part of our destiny together.

* * *

Since Robert's death, a number of people have helped to make the publication of this book possible. Thanks to Louise Haines's unwavering support; Mia Colleran; Nick Humphrey's thoughtful approach to editing; Iain Hunt for his diligence and hard work. Thanks to Anthony Arnove; Noam Chomsky; Patrick Cockburn for the foreword and the *Independent* for the use of material; Amira Hass, Neil Jordan, Antony Loewenstein, Mouin Rabbani, Trita Parsi, Norman Stockwell, Islamic scholar Alexander Hainy-Khaleeli; Conor McCabe for his photograph of Robert; friends Oliver Byrne, Mark and Olga Hearns, Jennifer Lowenstein and Sian Smyth.

Robert was going to update the acknowledgements; I apologise to anyone who should have been included but are missing from this list. My heartfelt thanks goes to all of you.

INDEX